59th VOLUME
1991-92

HIGLEY COMMENTARY

International Uniform
Sunday School Lessons

Editor: William L. Wharton

Writers: Dr. Gordon Talbot
         Wesley C. Reagan

Illustrator: Leslie W. Smith

THE HIGLEY DIFFERENCE

TOP MANUFACTURED QUALITY:
    High rated paper opacity eliminates "see through"
    Durable stitched binding "Perfect Bound"
    Long lasting water-proof Kivar cover
    Genuine embossed Gold lettering
    Easy focus bold type highlights

FEATURES:
    Lesson Introduction
    Teacher's Target Objective
    teaching Outline
    Daily Bible Readings
    Verse by Verse exposition
    The Evangelistic Emphasis
    Memory Selection
    Daily Applications
    Superintendent's Sermonette
    Seed Thoughts (Questions & Answers)

The most affordable comprehensive Sunday School Commentary available

---

Higley Publishing Corporation
Post Office Box 5398
Jacksonville, FL 32247-5398

FOREWORD

The benefits of studying the Bible are cumulative. On any given Sunday a student might not feel a great sense of progress or growth. However, consistent Bible study over a year will make an observable difference in a person's understanding and insights. When such study is pursued over a number of years it has a significant life-changing effect.

The Higley Sunday School Commentary, now in its fifty-ninth year, is intended to encourage such study. It is offered for the benefit of both teachers and students who seriously desire to have a clearer and deeper knowledge of the Word of God.

Our prayer is that The Commentary will serve you faithfully and well and that God will bless your study and your teaching.

Lessons and/or Readings based on International Sunday School Lessons. The International Bible Lessons for Christian Training, copyright © 1988 by the Committee on the Uniform Series.

Copyright © 1991

Higley Publishing Corporation
ISBN 0-9614116-1-9 (Hardcover)
ISBN 0-9614116-0-0 (Paperback)

PREFACE

Sometimes we tend to consider the things that meet physical needs as practical and the things that meet spiritual or aesthetic needs as peripheral, if not optional. To do so is to restrict ourselves to a one-dimensional life, a life that is little above the animal level.

Because we are made in the image of God, there is in us that which yearns for beauty as well as that which hungers for food. We have a need for music and art as well as for clothes and shelter. We need a clearer understanding of Divine Truth as much as we need a regular exercise program. We need the refreshment of worship fully as much as we need the refreshment of sleep.

Unless we see the practicality of that which nourishes the spirit, our lives will become seriously unbalanced. If, for example, one can sit for three hours in front of a television set but cannot sit through Sunday School and Church, he may need to examine this point. If he never misses a meal but allows conflicts to interfere with communion, he may need to examine his priorities.

We are not field mules. We are children of God. Our lives need to include something more elevating than work, food, and rest. Our souls were made to soar. Let us take care of our bodies because they are temples of the Holy Spirit, but let us not neglect the soul because it was breathed into us by God and partakes of His nature.

Wesley C. Reagan

How To Use Seed Thoughts

The Seed Thoughts feature, with its ten questions at the end of each lesson, is designed to stimulate class participation. Use the questions where they best apply in the course of developing the lesson. The suggested answers are really just starters and can be enlarged upon as needed.

The duplicate questions on the outside portion of the page can be cut out and given to selected students the week before. The names of the students to whom questions have been assigned can be written on the teacher's half of the Seed Thoughts page.

HIGLEY Publishing Corporation
Reader Information Card

FREE GIFT! Help us improve our Higley Commentary and receive our keepsake pocket **Cross 'n Card** free! Just complete the brief questions and mail to the address below. You'll receive your gift from us in 3 to 4 weeks.

ARE YOU?
___ Pastor/Preacher
___ Teacher
___ Superintendent
___ Student

LESSON CONTENT
___ Meets Spiritual Need
___ Too Deep
___ Too Shallow
___ Easily Understood

USED BY?
___ Pastor(s)
___ Teacher Only
___ Teacher & Students
___ All of Above

PRINT STYLE/SIZE?
___ About Right
___ Too Small
___ Easy to Read
___ Hard to Read

CLASS SIZE
___ 1-10
___ 10-20
___ 20-30
___ 30 or more

AGE GROUP
___ Under 25
___ 25 - 40
___ 40 - 55
___ 55-plus

WOULD LIKE?
___ Student Edition
___ Notebook Organizer
___ Audio/Visual Aids
___ Loose-Leaf Format (3 ring)

CONSIDER YOURSELF
___ Evangelical
___ Fundamental
___ Conservative
___ Liberal

Do you use the Higley Commentary for? Sunday School ___ Sermon ___ Supplementary Self Study ___ All ___
What features do you like best about our commentary? _____
What features would you discontinue in our commentary? _____
What translation of the Bible do you use? _____ What parallel translation would you like added to the KJV text? _____

Name _____ Tel. _____ Mail to: Higley Publishing Corporation
Address _____
                                                                          P.O. 5398
City _____ Zip _____   Jacksonville, FL 32247

FALL QUARTER

Chosen by God (Lessons 1-2)
Emerging Leader (Lessons 3-5)
Traveling Preacher (Lessons 6-9)
Destination: Rome (Lessons 10-13)

September 1	A Chosen Instrument of God Acts 9:1-16
September 8	Barnabas and Saul Acts 9:26-30, 11:19-26
September 15	A Sermon at Antioch of Pisidia Acts 13:26-39
September 22	A Healing in Lystra Acts 14:8-18
September 29	A Conference in Jerusalem Acts 15:1-12
October 6	A Call from Macedonia Acts 16:9-12,16-23
October 13	A Song at Midnight Acts 16:19b-34
October 20	A Proclamation in Athens Acts 17:22-34
October 27	Disciples in Ephesus Acts 18:24-19:6
November 3	A Sad Farewell Acts 20:17-31
November 10	Arrested and Accused Acts 21:26-33, 37-39a
November 17	Before Agrippa Acts 26:1-8,22-23,27-29
November 24	Paul in Rome Acts 28:21-31

WINTER QUARTER

Songs from Ancient Israel (Lessons 1-4)
Songs from Festive Occasions (Lessons 5-9)
Songs and Prayers of the Church (Lessons 10-13)

December 1	Song of Moses Exodus 15:1-10,13
December 8	Song of Deborah and Barak Judges 5:1-11
December 15	David's Lament for Saul and Jonathan 2 Samuel 1:17-27
December 22	Songs of Hannah and Mary I Samuel 2:1-5; Luke 1:46-55
December 29	A Hymn to the Creator Psalm 8
January 5	A Song for Temple Visitors Psalm 84
January 12	A Hymn to the Redeemer Psalm 103:1-17
January 19	Lyrics of Love Song of Solomon 2:8-17
January 26	Song of the Vineyard Isaiah 5:1-7
February 2	The Model Prayer Matthew 6:7-15
February 9	Jesus' High Priestly Prayer John 17:1-11, 20-21
February 16	Praise for Christ, God's Servant Philippians 2:1-11
February 23	The Hallelujah Chorus Revelation 15:2-4; 19:4-8

SPRING QUARTER

Mission and Message (Lessons 1-4)
Confession and Crucifixion (Lessons 5-8)
God's People in the World (Lessons 9-14)

March 1	Identification and Testing Mark 1:1-15	
March 8	The Clash of Ideas Mark 2:23-3:6	
March 15	Without Honor in His Own Country Mark 6:1-13	
March 22	Restoration to Wholeness Mark 7:24-37	
March 29	The Messiah and Suffering Mark 8:27-9:1	
April 5	Love Says it All Mark 12:28-37	
April 12	The Crucified Son of God Mark 15:22-39	
April 19	An Empty Tomb Mark 15:42-16:8	
April 26	The Gift of Living Hope I Peter 1:3-9,13-21	
May 3	Called to be God's People I Peter 2:1-10	
May 10	Witness in the Midst of Suffering I Peter 3:13-18; 4:1-2,7-11	
May 17	Humble, Steadfast, Vigilant I Peter 5:1-11	
May 24	Growing in Grace 2 Peter 1:1-14	
May 31	Focused on the Future 2 Peter 3:3-14	

SUMMER QUARTER

Warnings and Promises from God (Lessons 1-5)
A Remnant is Saved (Lessons 6-7)
Guidelines for Leading (Lessons 8-10)
Guidelines for Serving (Lessons 11-13)

June 7	The Lord Will Restore Judah	Obadiah 1-4,10-11,15,17,21
June 14	Fleeing from God	Jonah 1:1-9,15-17
June 21	Jonah Sulks, and God Saves	Jonah 3:1-5,10;4:1-4,10-11
June 28	Judgment and Salvation	Nahum 1:2-3,6-9,12-13,15
July 5	A Question and an Answer	Habakkuk 1:1-7;2:1-4
July 12	Threatened Destruction of Humankind	Zephaniah 1:1-3,7,12;2:1-3
July 19	God Will Restore Israel	Zephaniah 3:12,14-20
July 26	Understand What You Teach	I Timothy 1:3-11,18-20
August 2	Train Yourself in Godliness	I Timothy 4
August 9	Set Your Priorities	I Timothy 6:6-14,17-21
August 16	Handle God's Word Rightly	2 Timothy 2:1-15
August 23	Fulfill Your Ministry Faithfully	2 Timothy 3:10-4:5
August 30	Be a Model in Deeds and Word	Titus 2:7-8,11-14;3:1-8

A Chosen Instrument Of God

Acts 9:1. And Saul, yet breathing out threatenings and slaughter against the disciples of the Lord, went unto the high priest,
2. And desired of him letters to Damascus to the synagogues, that if he found any of this way, whether they were men or women, he might bring them bound unto Jerusalem.
3. And as he journeyed, he came near Damascus: and suddenly there shined round about him a light from heaven.
4. And he fell to the earth, and heard a voice saying unto him, Saul, Saul, why persecutest thou me?
5. And he said who art thou, Lord? And the Lord said, I am Jesus whom thou persecutest: it is hard for thee to kick against the pricks.
6. And he trembling and astonished said, Lord, what wilt thou have me to do? And the Lord said unto him, Arise, and go into the city, and it shall be told thee what thou must do.
7. And the men which journeyed with him stood speechless, hearing a voice, but seeing no man.
8. And Saul arose from the earth; and when his eyes were opened, he saw no man: but they led him by the hand, and brought him into Damascus.
9. And he was three days without sight, and neither did eat nor drink.
10. And there was a certain disciple at Damascus, named Ananias; and to him said the Lord in a vision, Ananias. And he said, Behold, I am here, Lord.
11. And the Lord said unto him, Arise, and go into the street which is called Straight, and enquire in the house of Judas for one called Saul, of Tarsus: for, behold, he prayeth,
12. And hath seen in a vision a man named Ananias coming in, and putting his hand on him, that he might receive his sight.
13. Then Ananias answered, Lord, I have heard by many of this man, how much evil he hath done to thy saints at Jerusalem:
14. And here he hath authority from the chief priests to bind all that call on thy name.
15. But the Lord said unto him, Go thy way: for he is a chosen vessel unto me, to bear my name before the Gentiles, and kings, and the children of Israel:
16. For I will show him how great things he must suffer for my name's sake.

MEMORY SELECTION
Acts 9:15
DEVOTIONAL READING
Acts 22:3-16

BACKGROUND SCRIPTURE
Acts 7:54-8:3; 9:1-22
PRINTED SCRIPTURE
Acts 9:1-16

Teacher's Target

Conversion means to turn around, and there was much turning around required to change Saul the Pharisee into Paul the apostle. In this first lesson of "A Portrait of Paul," we learn how that process was begun. It all started with a crisis experience on the road from Jerusalem to Damascus. Saul met Jesus Christ there, and nothing would ever be the same in his life again.

Help your students to realize that every convert to Christ has to have a crisis experience in order to switch from the broad road leading to destruction to the narrow road leading to life everlasting. This may be a fairly mild crisis, or it may be a wrenching, terrifying one. Whatever the case, it begins the long journey toward Christlikeness. The first step is the most important, because it sets the pace for all the steps that follow.

Lesson Introduction

Saul summed up his early life when he wrote, " [I was] circumcised the eighth day, of the stock of Israel, of the tribe of Benjamin, an Hebrew of the Hebrews; as touching the law, a Pharisee; concerning zeal, persecuting the church; touching the [self-]righteousness which is in the law, blameless" (Phil. 3:5-6). It was while engaged in persecuting followers of the way of Christ that Saul made his trip to Damascus. His Jewish pedigree would be shattered, and he would spend the rest of his life promoting Christ and His church.

It probably took only three minutes for Jesus to hold a conversation with Saul after he was struck to the earth by a great light on the road to Damascus. It took three days in that city for Saul to learn what had happened to him and what God planned to do with him. He was lifted from physical and spiritual blindness and set on a new path.

Teaching Outline

I. Intention: Acts 9:1-2
   A. Dislike: 1
   B. Desire: 2

II. Interference: Acts 9:3-8
   A. Crisis: 3-4a
   B. Contact: 4b-6
   C. Confusion: 7-8

III. Insight: Acts 9:9-16
   A. Deprivation: 9
   B. DiscipLe: 10-12
   C. Distress: 13-14
   D. Designation 15-16

Daily Bible Readings

Mon. The Stoning of Stephen
Acts 7:54-8:3
Tue. Simon the Sorcerer
Acts 8:4-13
Wed. Simon Sins and Repents
Acts 8:14-25
Thu. Philip Teaches
an Ethiopian
Acts 8:26-33
Fri. The Ethiopian Baptized
Acts 8:34-40
Sat. The Road to Damascus
Acts 9:1-9
Sun. The Conversion of Saul
Acts 9:10-22

Verse By Verse

I. Intention: Acts 9:1-2

A. Dislike: 1
1. And Saul, yet breathing out threatenings and slaughter against the disciples of the Lord, went unto the high priest,
The rabid Jews who had illegally stoned Stephen to death had laid their robes for safekeeping at the feet of a young Pharisee named Saul (Acts 7:58). Who was this young man who rated highly in their estimation? He had grown up in Tarsus of Cilicia, a province in southeastern Asia Minor (Turkey) (Acts 21:39). He had studied at the feet of a scholar named Gamaliel in Jerusalem (Acts 5:34; 22:3). He had become enraged at the followers of Jesus and had scattered them out to foreign lands (Acts 26:11). Now he wanted to go up to Damascus in Syria and persecute them, but he needed permission from the high priest in Jerusalem.

B. Desire: 2
2. And desired of him letters to Damascus to the synagogues, that if he found any of this way, whether they were men or women, he might bring them bound unto Jerusalem.
We might wonder how Caiaphas, the high priest, had any authority over Jews living as far away as Damascus The fact was that the Romans never really understood the Jews, and they were willing to turn religious matters regarding them over to Jewish leaders. Thus it was that Rome sanctioned the high priest's action in granting letters authorizing Saul to deal with Jews considered wayward in the city of Damascus,
Christians were first called by that name in Antioch, Syria at a later time (Acts 11: 26). Up to that time, they were simply referred to as "people of the way" of Christ. Saul made no difference in his thinking regarding men and women. He planned to bind them both and bring them back to Jerusalem for judgment, probably by the Sanhedrin (Jewish Council). He gathered a group of supporters and headed northward.

II. Interference: Acts 9:3-8

A. Crisis: 3-4a
3. And as he journeyed, he came near Damascus: and suddenly there shined round about him a light from heaven:
4a. And he fell to the earth,...
Damascus was about a hundred and twenty five miles from Jerusalem. It was a long journey by old-fashioned means of transportation, As it came near its end, Saul was suddenly struck down to the ground by an overpowering blast of great light. He was also blinded by it (vs. 8). Here was a man accustomed to being in charge of things, but now he was overwhelmed by something outside of his control. It was an unnerving experience. It was the beginning of his transformation from persecutor of believers to protector of them. Some might assume that he merely had a bad case of sun-stroke, but it was obviously more than that.

B. Contact: 4b-6
4b. ...and heard a voice saying unto him, Saul, Saul, why persecutest thou me?

11

It was about noontime that Saul was struck down (Acts 22:6; 26:13). Both he and his companions had fallen, but he alone appeared to understand what was being said (Acts 9:7; 22:9). The heavenly voice accused Saul of persecuting Him by asking why he did it. This must have been unsettling to Saul, for he had not intended to offend deity.

5. And he said, Who art thou, Lord? And the Lord said, I am Jesus whom thou persecutest: it is hard for thee to kick against the pricks.

It was with shock and alarm that Saul discovered it was Jesus talking to him. He had considered Jesus an impostor, claiming to be the divine Son of God, but now he had to admit that it was true. Saul had not personally persecuted Jesus, but he had persecuted the followers of Jesus. The unity between Jesus and His followers is seen here.

The remark by Jesus regarding Saul finding it hard to kick against the pricks was an analogy drawn from treatment of oxen hitched to wagons. Slow and cumbersome, their drivers goaded them along with sharply-pointed sticks. It was hard on the oxen to kick back and be hurt by these. Jesus was telling Saul that his mistreatment of believers was hard on him. It went against his conscience, that built-in ability to distinguish right from wrong. Being a persecutor had not really made Saul happy or content.

6. And he trembling and astonished said, Lord, what wilt thou have me to do? And the Lord said unto him, Arise, and go into the city, and it shall be told thee what thou must do.

Stung by the divine rebuke, Saul trembled and asked in astonishment what he ought to do. Jesus told him to get up and go into the city of Damascus. In due time he would be told what he must do. He had no idea that his instructions would be delayed three days.

C. Confusion: 7-8

7. And the men which journeyed with him stood speechless, hearing a voice, but seeing no man.

By this time, the men traveling with Saul had evidently risen to their feet. They were amazed at what had happened and did not know what to say. They had heard a voice speaking, but they had seen no man. The message spoken by Jesus was apparently understood only by Saul, The implication was that Saul had seen Jesus at this time, and that is supported by what Paul wrote in I Corinthians 15:8.

8. And Saul arose from the earth; and when his eyes were opened, he saw no man: but they led him by the hand, and brought him into Damascus,

Saul may have seen Jesus with his spiritual eyes, but his physical eyes were blinded. He was helped up from the ground and led into Damascus by the hand. It must have been a frightening and humiliating experience for this proud young man. He was taken to the house of a man named Judas on Straight Street (vs. 11).

III. Insight: Acts 9:9-16

A. Deprivation: 9

9. And he was three days without sight, and neither did eat nor drink.

It would appear that Saul deprived himself of food and drink during this time. Unable to read, he seems to have spent the time in prayer and meditation (vs. 11). We can well imagine that he was trying to straighten out his thoughts and feelings in light of the crisis experience he had had on the road leading into Damascus.

B. Disciple: 10-12

10. And there was a certain disciple at Damascus, named Ananias and to him said the Lord in a vision, Ananias. And he said, Behold, I am here, Lord.

This Ananias was a follower of Jesus, Who came to him in a vision and called his name. We know that the Lord Jesus was meant here, because Ananias later described Him as the One coming to him in the vision (vs. 17), Ananias quickly responded to Jesus' call.

11. And the Lord said unto him, Arise, and go into the street which is called Straight', and enquire in the house of Judas for

one called Saul, of Tarsus: for, behold, he prayeth,
12. And hath seen in a vision a man named Ananias coming in, and putting his hand on him, that he might receive his sight.

We know that Ananias was "a devout man according to the [Jewish] law, having a good report of all the Jews which dwelt there [Damascus]" (Acts 22:12). Now he was being told to go and find Saul at the house of Judas on Straight Street. Saul had been praying, and he had received a vision of a man name Ananias coming to restore his sight.

C. Distress: 13-14
13. Then Ananias answered, Lord, I have heard by many of this man, how much evil he hath done to thy saints at Jerusalem:
14. And here he hath authority from the chief priests to bind all that call on thy name,

Ananias appeared reluctant to become involved with Saul. Word had spread around among believers in Damascus that Saul had done much evil to the saints in Jerusalem. He had come to Damascus with authority from the chief priests to arrest and bind all who placed their faith in Christ. It was even possible that Ananias was afraid that Saul would take <u>him</u> back to Jerusalem.

D. Designation: 15-16
15. But the Lord said unto him, Go thy way: for he is a chosen vessel unto me, to bear my name before the Gentiles, and kings, and the children of Israel:

The Lord Jesus did not allow Ananias to indulge his fear of Saul. He declared that things had changed. Saul was a chosen vessel (instrument) to be used to take the name of Christ to Gentiles, kings, and Jews. He who had formerly persecuted the church would now protect and promote it.
16. For I will shew him how great things he must suffer for my name's sake.

There was a sobering side to the prediction made by Jesus concerning Saul. During the course of his efforts to propagate the gospel, he would suffer many things. An extensive list of these may be found in II Corinthians 11:23-28. Jesus intended to prepare Saul to face these difficulties.

Ananias obeyed Jesus and went to see Saul. He helped Saul receive both his physical and spiritual sight. Scales fell from his eyes. He rose up and was baptized in the name of Christ. He ate and was strengthened. He spent certain days with followers of Christ in Damascus (Acts 9:17-19).

Jews in the synagogues were amazed at the facility with which Saul argued that Jesus was the Christ, the divine Son of God. After a while, however, some of them became so angry with him that they plotted to kill him. Friends helped him escape by letting him down over the wall of the city in a large basket (Acts 9:20-25).

The next stage in Saul's life is vague. Some scholars think that Galatians 1:17-18 describes what happened next. The suggestion is that Saul went into the wilderness of Arabia for three years to study and meditate on what had happened to him and how he wanted to proceed from that point onward.

In our next lesson, we will see how Saul made contact with the believers in Jerusalem. They did not readily receive him as a fellow believer until Barnabas befriended him and spoke on his behalf.

Evangelistic Emphasis

This passage brims with good news. It begins with the fact that God seeks and calls. He does not leave us groping in darkness hoping to stumble on the direction and purpose of our lives. He seeks us, finds us, and calls us to the life he has planned for us. Even though Saul was doggedly going in another direction, God found him and helped him to turn around.

The passage also promises the possibility of major change. We do not have to be content with minor adjustments. Neither do we need to feel discouraged if we feel that we are a long way from being what God wants us to be. The God who was capable of turning Saul the Persecutor into Paul the Apostle can certainly handle whatever changes need to be made in our lives.

We also have good news in the form of the emphasis that is given to the support role of Ananias in this story. We think of Saul as being the primary character that God is using, but a necessary part of activating Saul was the work of Ananias.

One problem that we sometimes have is an inability to see major significance in what we do. This story reminds us that fulfilling a support role that helps to complete some larger task is important too. Ananias contributed to the evangelism of the Gentiles, the broad missionary thrust of Paul's work, and the writing of several books of the New Testament. Paul, historically, has had good deal of spotlight because of his work. Ananias has had little by comparison, yet he was an essential link to what Paul did.

Memory Selection

He is a chosen vessel unto me, to bear my name before the Gentiles, and kings, and the children of Israel."
Acts 9:15.

The choice of Saul was deliberate, not an accident. He had the character and the endurance to be faithful in persecution, discouragement, anxiety, and betrayal. His activity of persecuting Christians did not make him look like a good candidate to become a missionary. Yet God knew what he was doing when he chose Saul.

It is important to remember that God works with us as individuals. The fact that he called Saul in a dramatic experience on the road to Damascus does not mean that he will necessarily call us in the same way. Neither does it mean that we will be called to do the same things Saul was called to do.

Nevertheless, the God who called Saul also calls us. The God who had plans for Saul's life also has plans for our lives. Saul had nations of people to evangelize and heads of state to preach to. Most of us will not teach the gospel on such a grand scale. Yet we are able to teach the same glorious gospel. We are able to teach it to souls that are just as precious in the sight of God.

Weekday Problems

John is pastor of a huge church. He is well known and very influential. He is a devout man who has done a great deal of good in his life.

Recently, however, whether because of weariness or discouragement, he has developed a negative attitude. He is critical of others, uncharacteristically sharp in his comments to them, and seems cynical about the possibility of doing much good. It has been a gradual change. He is only vaguely aware of it and people who are not with him regularly have not noticed it.

His secretary, however, has observed the change and wants desperately to help him. She knows what a force for good he has been in the past and is saddened to see that force weakened. She is afraid that if she brings the problem to the surface, John, in his present mood, will not have a positive reaction. she admires and appreciates him. She does not want to lose his friendship. She is in no position to jeopardize her job which is essential to her livelihood.

* All of us know that some risk is inevitable in life, but how do we decide what degree of risk it is advisable to take?
* Is it possible to risk too much for too small a concern?

Superintendent's Sermonette

How does God produce a spiritual giant? In some cases that person may be born to Christian parents and grow up in the fear and admonition of the Lord. In other cases that person may be headed in the wrong direction and have to be persuaded to make a one-hundred-and-eighty-degree turnaround. A third type may be a person who has a form of godliness but needs a course correction. It would appear that Saul (later Paul) was of the third type. He was a misguided Pharisee until he met Jesus on the road to Damascus.

In subsequent testimonies, Paul always referred back to that crisis experience. Every individual who comes to God through Christ has to have a similar experience, although it may not be as dramatic as the one Paul had. Nobody just grows into being a Christian. A new birth must take place. Only then is it possible for that person to begin the long, steady growth and development which leads to maturity in Christ. An acorn grows into a mighty oak. A babe in Christ grows into a spiritual giant over a long period of time.

This Lesson in <u>Your</u> Life

The story of Saul throbs with a sense of humanity that makes it easy for us to identify with him. He was a man of energy and passion. We have reason to believe that he was a man of considerable ego and that he was strong-minded. His guileless integrity enabled him to make surprising changes in an amazingly short period of time. Let us see what we can learn for our own lives from his Damascus Road experience.

First, we need to remain attentive to the Lord's guidance throughout life. Saul's life direction seemed to be well set. His education and training as a young Rabbi had been pursued vigorously. His faith in God and the Law were thoroughly entrenched. The last thing in his mind was the possibility of a basic change on such a fundamental matter.

Saul reminds me of the story of the stubborn man's prayer, "Lord, start me off right, because you know how hard I am to change once I get started."

All of us would no doubt admit that we are not at the zenith of Christlikeness. There are some changes that would be beneficial in our lives. We may be aware of some of those changes that need to be made, but some of them are blind spots. We go confidently on, as Saul was doing, not seeing the need to reconsider views or practices that are deeply held. We will be more effective servants of the Lord if we will watch for signs that our lives can be brought more fully into harmony with the Lord's will.

Second, we will be blessed if we take note of the fact that Saul had the courage and honesty to make radical changes when they were necessary. Although he was confident that what he was doing was right, he instantly gave it up when he was convinced of his mistake. Pride sometimes causes us to pursue a course even after we have learned it is mistaken. It may make us defend a mistake rather than change a bad practice.

Third, we know a lot about the ministry of Saul's life and not much about Ananias. We should remember that Ananias shares in all the good that was done by Saul. Ananias is partially responsible for every sermon that Saul preached, every missionary visit that he made, every word of Scripture that he wrote, and every Christian minister that he inspired. Ananias was behind the scenes, but he was very vital to one of the most important ministries the world has ever known. This knowledge will help to sustain the work of every quiet, unknown, and unheralded servant of the Lord in the world.

Fourth, there is a note of warning in this text. It has to do with misguided zeal. However sincere Saul was, his persecution of the church was painful and destructive. We should be solemnly aware of the need to be extremely cautious when we oppose others or are in conflict with them.

Fifth, this story reminds us that sometimes following Christ involves risk and danger. Ananias must have had his heart in his throat when he went to see the man who was noted for the viciousness of his opposition to Christianity. It is not always easy to be a minister of Christ, but great things happen when we are faithful to our task.

Seed Thoughts

1. What motivates someone to persecute followers of Christ?
He may feel that his own beliefs are threatened by Christians. He is motivated by Satan, who is against Christ.

2. How did Saul seek authority from the wrong source?
Instead of going to God for direction, Saul sought letters from the high priest to arrest believers in Damascus.

3. Why will critics try to give what happened to Saul on the road to Damascus a natural explanation?
The possibility of a sun-stroke appeals more to them than a personal appearance by the risen Christ to Saul.

4. What part does humiliation play in the crisis of conversion?
Even as Saul was struck to the ground, so it is that all who come to Christ must be humbled before Him.

5. What does it mean to "kick against the pricks" (Acts 9:5)?
A person's conscience usually makes him feel uncomfortable when he is doing what is wrong.

(Please Turn Page)

---

1. What motivates someone to persecute followers of Christ?

2. How did Saul seek authority from the wrong source?

3. Why will critics try to give what happened to Saul on the road to Damascus a natural explanation?

4. What part does humiliation play in the crisis of conversion?

5. What does it mean to "kick against the pricks" (Acts 9:5)?

6. What good is a period of contemplation after suffering trauma?

7. How may the right state of mind be cultivated for God to speak?

8. How does God make contact with a person He has chosen for His work?

9. Why should we not question divine instructions, as Ananias did?

10. What does it mean to be "a chosen vessel unto God" (Acts 9:15)?

Seed Thoughts - Continued

He may feel that his own beliefs are threatened by Christians. He is motivated by Satan, who is against Christ.

Instead of going to God for direction, Saul sought letters from the high priest to arrest believers in Damascus.

The possibility of a sun-stroke appeals more to them than a personal appearance by the risen Christ to Saul.

Even as Saul was struck to the ground, so it is that all who come to Christ must be humbled before Him.

A person's conscience usually makes him feel uncomfortable when he is doing what is wrong.

It helps a person to gain a proper perspective on what happened to him.

Saul fasted and prayed for three days, and then God spoke to him in a vision.

God speaks to us through His word. He may use another believer to speak to us by teaching us our responsibility. He may do both, plus using other means.

God will not give us a task to do but what He will also give us ability to do it with the desired result.

Paul was a unique situation. He had been chosen by God to speak His word to even Kings and rulers. Paul (Saul), though chosen still had the responsibility to submit and obey the voice of God.

6. What good is a period of contemplation after suffering trauma?
It helps a person to gain a proper perspective on what happened to him.

7. How may the right state of mind be cultivated for God to speak?
Saul fasted and prayed for three days, and then God spoke to him in a vision.

8. How does God make contact with a person He has chosen for His work?
God speaks to us through His word. He may use another believer to speak to us by teaching us our responsibility. He may do both, plus using other means.

9. Why should we not question divine instructions, as Ananias did?
God will not give us a task to do but what He will also give us ability to do it with the desired result.

10. What does it mean to be "a chosen vessel unto God" (Acts 9:15)?
Paul was a unique situation. He had been chosen by God to speak His word to even Kings and rulers. Paul (Saul), though chosen still had the responsibility to submit and obey the voice of God.

Barnabas And Saul

Acts 9:26. And when Saul was come to Jerusalem, he assayed to join himself to the disciples: but they were all afraid of him, and believed not that he was a disciple.
27. But Barnabas took him, and brought him to the apostles, and declared unto them how he had seen the Lord in the way, and that he had spoken to him, and how he had preached boldly at Damascus in the name of Jesus.
28. And he was with them coming in and going out at Jerusalem.
29. And he spake boldly in the name of the Lord Jesus, and disputed against the Grecians: but they went about to slay him.
30. Which when the brethren knew, they brought him down to Caesarea, and sent him forth to Tarsus.
Acts 11:19. Now they which were scattered abroad upon the persecution that arose about Stephen travelled as far as Phenice, and Cyprus, and Antioch, preaching the word to none but unto the Jews only.
20. And some of them were men of Cyprus and Cyrene, which, when they were come to Antioch, spake unto the Grecians, preaching the Lord Jesus.
21. And the hand of the Lord was with them: and a great number believed, and turned unto the Lord.
22. Then tidings of these things came unto the ears of the church which was in Jerusalem: and they sent forth Barnabas, that he should go as far as Antioch.
23. Who, when he came, and had seen the grace of God, was glad, and exhorted them all, that with purpose of heart they would cleave unto the Lord.
24. For he was a good man, and full of the Holy Ghost and of faith: and much people was added unto the Lord.
25. Then departed Barnabas to Tarsus, for to seek Saul:
26. And when he had found him, he brought him unto Antioch. And it came to pass, that a whole year they assembled themselves with the church, and taught much people. And the disciples were called Christians first in Antioch.

MEMORY SELECTION
Acts 11:25-26
DEVOTIONAL READING
Acts 12:25-13:3
BACKGROUND SCRIPTURE
Acts 9:26-30; 11:19-30;12:25
PRINTED SCRIPTURE
Acts 9:26-30, 11:19-26

Teacher's Target

It seems sometimes as if news is too good to be true. That may have been the case when Saul, persecutor of the church, ceased his activity and offered to help the followers of Christ. Church leaders in Jerusalem were wary of him and could not seem to believe at first that he was now a disciple. It took the sympathetic mediation of Barnabas to convince them that Saul was now a believer.

View converts, not for what they have been, but for what they have become through the grace of God. should accept the testimonies of believers, unless there are reasons to discount them. need to realize that some of the rough edges on new converts will take time to be smoothed down Mediators have their role to play in developing good relationships among old and new believers.

Lesson Introduction

As mentioned before, Saul was thought to have spent three years in Arabia meditating on the ministry into which God was leading him (Gal. 1:15-18). The same drive which he had put into persecuting the church was now directed into building it up, but he felt that he had to make contact with the church leaders in Jerusalem. Imagine his disappointment when he received a cool reception by them. However, he found a friend in Barnabas.

Barnabas was a Levite from the island of Cyprus, who sold his land and contributed the proceeds to the apostles in Jerusalem (Acts 4:36-37). He was held in high regard by the early church leaders, who sent him to organize a new church in Antioch, Syria. He was a good man, filled with the Holy Spirit. He brought Saul from Tarsus to become his assistant in the work at Antioch (Acts 11:22-26).

Teaching Outline

I. Apprehension: Acts 9:26-30
   A. Fear: 26
   B. Fellowship: 27-28
   C. Feud: 29-30

II. Antioch: Acts ll:19-26
   A. Expansion I: 19-21
   B. Expansion II: 22-24
   C. Expansion III: 25-26

III. Assistance: Acts 11:29-30
   A. Principle: 29
   B. Participants: 30

Daily Bible Readings

Mon. Aeneas and Tabitha
Acts 9:26-43
Tue. Devout Cornelius
Acts 10:1-8
Wed. Peter's Vision
Acts 10:9-18
Thu. Peter Meets Cornelius
Acts 10:19-29
Fri. Peter's Sermon
Acts 10:30-43
Sat. Peter's Defense
Acts 11:1-18
Sun. The Spread of the Church
Acts 11:19-30

Verse By Verse

I. Apprehension: Acts 9:26-30

A. Fear: 26
26. And when Saul was come to Jerusalem, he assayed to join himself to the disciples: but they were all afraid of him, and believed not that he was a disciple.

Ananias had formerly been afraid of Saul in Damascus (Acts 9:13-14). Believers in Jerusalem were also afraid of him. In both cases, those affected did not exercise spiritual discernment regarding the matter. They could have asked God what to think about Saul. They could have examined him carefully to determine whether or not he was a genuine follower of Christ. They chose, instead, to let fear govern their reactions to him. Here is the record of a mistake which we ought not to repeat in our evaluation of converts.

B. Fellowship: 27-28
27. But Barnabas took him, and brought him to the apostles, and declared unto them how he had seen the Lord in the way, and that he had spoken to him, and how he had preached boldly at Damascus in the name of Jesus.

The Lord had an ally for Saul positioned among the apostles at Jerusalem. His name was Barnabas, meaning "son of consolation" (Acts 4:36). He defended Saul by telling the apostles what had happened to him on the road to Damascus and how he had witnessed for Christ in that city three years before.

This was the beginning of a partnership between Barnabas and Saul which was to last from that time up through the first missionary journey they shared together (Acts 15: 36-41). However, they were to be separated for a period of time when Saul had to leave Jerusalem and before they came together again at Antioch, Syria (Acts 9:30; 11:25-26).

28. And he was with them coming in and going out at Jerusalem.

Saul managed to gain the confidence of the apostles at Jerusalem, and he moved in fellowship with them in their ministry in the province of Judaea. It appears that his contacts were limited (Gal. 1:22-24).

C. Feud:-29-30
29. And he spake boldly in the name of the Lord Jesus, and disputed against the Grecians: but they went about to slay him.

Saul seemed to be most effective when debating with the Grecians (Hellenists, Greek-oriented Jews). He boldly declared the Lord Jesus to be the divine Son of God and Savior of men. This provoked a reaction so negative that his opponents tried to kill him. This was the second attempt to take his life, for it had been tried at Damascus (Acts 9: 23-24). There were to be many more similar attempts in the future.

30. Which when the brethren knew, they brought him down to Caesarea, and sent him forth to Tarsus.

Believers in Jerusalem feared for Saul's life, and they persuaded him that he should leave the area. They took him down to the Mediterranean seaport of Caesarea and put him aboard a ship heading northward to Tarsus, his hometown in the province of Cilicia (southeastern Turkey). He later wrote, "I came into the regions of Syria and Cilicia" (Gal. 1:21). We assume that he continued to witness for Christ in that area, but he seemed to drop out of sight.

II. Antioch: Acts 11:19-26

A. Expansion I: 19-21
19. Now they which were scattered abroad upon the persecution that arose about Stephen travelled as far as Phenice, and Cyprus, and Antioch, preaching the word to none but unto the Jews only.

Just before He ascended to heaven, Jesus had told His followers, "Ye shall receive power, after that the Holy Ghost is come upon you: and ye shall be witnesses unto me both in Jerusalem, and in all Judaea, and in Samaria, and unto the uttermost part of the earth" (Acts 1:8). However, they remained in and around Jerusalem until they were scattered out following the persecution which arose at the stoning of Stephen. Expansion of the church really began at this point. "They that were scattered abroad went every where preaching the word" (Acts 8:4).

Some traveled to Phenice, which may have been a town of that name on the island of Cyprus, but which more likely was Phoenicia (Lebanon). Some went to the island of Cyprus to the west. Some went to Antioch in Syria. They confined their witnessing to Jews.

20. And some of them were men of Cyprus and Cyrene, which, when they were come to Antioch, spake unto the Grecians, preaching the Lord Jesus.

This tells us that the main witnesses for Christ came from the island of Cyprus and from Cyrene (Libya) in northern Africa. It was their custom to speak to the Grecians (Hellenists, Greek-oriented Jews) about the Lord Jesus. They wanted to convince them that Jesus was the promised Messiah.

21. And the hand of the Lord was with them: and a great number believed, and turned unto the Lord.

The act of witnessing was a combination of divine and human effort. It was God Who moved in the hearts of the listeners as believers told them about Christ. A large number turned to the Lord in believing faith and committed themselves to Jesus as Savior.

B. Expansion II: 22-24
22. Then tidings of these things came unto the ears of the church which was in Jerusalem: and they sent forth Barnabas, that he should go as far as Antioch,

The wording here suggests that church leaders in Jerusalem expected Barnabas to speak to believers at various points along the way to Antioch, Syria, but his main work was to be done at Antioch itself. They felt there was a need for organization and teaching of the new converts there, and they saw Barnabas as the man equipped to provide this kind of leadership in building up the local church. The gains of evangelization had to be secured by the work of education.

23. Who, when he came, and had seen the grace of God, was glad, and exhorted them all, that with purpose of heart they would cleave unto the Lord.

Barnabas arrived on the scene and rejoiced at evidence that the grace of God was working in the hearts and lives of people. He gathered them together and strongly urged them to embrace the Lord with all of their strength. Their conversion had been but the first step on a long road to Christlikeness, and there was much ground to be taken.

24. For he was a good man, and full of the Holy Ghost and of faith: and much people was added unto the Lord.

Barnabas was well-suited to his task in Antioch. As a Levite from Cyprus, he understood both Jews and Gentiles. He was a righteous man, and he was filled with the power of the Holy Spirit and of faith to believe in the promises of God. Under his ministry, many converts to Christ were made and added to the body of believers. All that Barnabas had learned under the tutelage of the apostles in Jerusalem he was able to apply in this situation,- and the Lord blessed his efforts with spiritual fruit.

C. Expansion III: 25-26
25. Then departed Barnabas to Tarsus, for to seek Saul:
26a. And when he had found him, he brought him unto Antioch.

As the work in the church at Antioch grew, Barnabas knew that he could not bear the burden of pastoral leadership all by himself. He decided to go over to Tarsus, which was not far away, and see if he could find Saul and persuade him to come back to Antioch to assist him. He was able to accomplish this. Now the stage was set for great expansion.

26b. And it came to pass, that a whole year they assembled themselves with the church, and taught much people. And the disciples were called Christians first in Antioch.

It must have been wonderful to be in the Antioch church for the year which followed. Under the combined ministries of Barnabas and Saul, the believers laid hold of truths from God's Word and applied them to their lives. Pagans among whom they moved realized that these people were really different, and they attributed this to their adherence to the principles of Christ. Thus it was that "people of the way" were first called Christians in Antioch. It is a label which has attached itself to them ever since that time.

At the end of that year, prophets came from Jerusalem to Antioch and predicted that there was going to be a drought affecting food supplies in Judaea (Acts 11:27-28).

III. Assistance: Acts 11:29-30

A. Principle: 29

29. Then the disciples, every man according to his ability, determined to send relief unto the brethren which dwelt in Judaea:

This incident was significant, because it came between two important events. When the church was first launched in Jerusalem, believers had come together to share their material resources for the common good of all (Acts 4:44-45). Christians in Antioch now decided to follow this example. Each of them determined to send relief to needy brothers in Judaea according to his ability to give. Later on, it was the church at Antioch which launched Barnabas and Saul on their first missionary journey to take the gospel to needy people in foreign lands (Acts 13:1-3).

It has been the spirit of sacrificial giving and faithful support exemplified by the believers in Antioch which has set the pace for Christian outreach ever since that time.

B. Participants: 30
30. Which also they did, and sent it to the elders by the hands of Barnabas and Saul.

Believers in Antioch not only talked about sending relief to Judaea, but they did it. Barnabas and Saul were chosen to carry their contributions southward to elders of the church in Jerusalem. This gave the two men opportunity to renew contacts with the apostles and other church leaders there. We assume that Agabus and the other prophets from Jerusalem accompanied them on the journey. Acts 12 shifts emphasis from Saul (Paul) back to Peter and his trouble with Jewish leaders. Acts 13 will bring us back to Barnabas and Saul and their experience in a synagogue in Antioch of Pisidia.

Evangelistic Emphasis

Sometimes news seems too good to be true. Saul wanted to join himself to the disciples at Jerusalem and they were afraid to accept him. Can you imagine a situation in which he who was to become the Apostle Paul would be rejected for participation in church activities?

When we consider evangelism we need to be alert for unlikely-looking candidates for receiving the gospel. Saul certainly did not appear to be one who could be led to Christ, but he was.

Do you know someone who is too involved in sin to be interested in the gospel? Is there someone who is too wealthy to have any interest in spiritual things? Is there someone who is too powerful to take time for being involved in church? Perhaps you know someone whose beliefs are so in conflict with Christianity that he would not possibly be interested?

There are two reasons we should not give up on any of the above people. One is that we may be wrong in our assessment of how interested any of these people would be. The second reason is that anybody can change. Even if a person is not interested now, he may become interested.

Memory Selection

"Then departed Barnabas to Tarsus, for to seek Saul: And when he had found him, he brought him unto Antioch. And it came to pass, that a whole year they assembled themselves with the church, and taught much people."
Acts 11:25,26.

When we do something good for someone it is like sowing seeds. Later some unexpected ones may come up and provide surprising blessings. Such was the case with Barnabas in our text today.

Barnabas went out on a limb to stand up for Saul at Jerusalem. Saul's reputation as a persecutor of Christians was well known at Jerusalem. The church there was afraid to accept Saul. Barnabas placed his own reputation on the line when he recommended Saul to the Jerusalem fellowship.

At a later date Barnabas needed Saul to help preach at Antioch. You can be sure that the request was well received. Saul may well have recalled, "Barnabas is the one who defended me when all others were standing against me. Anything I can do to help him, I will."

A most significant church, containing both Jews and Greeks, resulted from this work.

Weekday Problems

Jeremy has a great love for the church. He has been active in its work all of his life and his parents were active before him. It is dear to his heart and he would do anything for it. These affectionate feelings cause him to feel protective toward it.

Recently, a local politician who has an unsavory reputation has started attending Sunday services. He sits toward the back and has done nothing to call undue attention to himself. He participates in the various acts of worship and shows careful attention to the preaching.

Jeremy knows that the gospel is for all men, but he is surprisingly uncomfortable at the thought that this man might request church membership. "What will people think?" Jeremy wonders. "Will they think that the church identifies with the wrong this man has done in his past?" "I would like to help him, but I am afraid for him to be identified with our church?" Jeremy feels guilty about feeling this way but he can not deny his concerns.

* How does the church protect itself against those who would exploit and abuse the privileges of membership?
* Does the reputation of the church depend on the reputation of its individual members?

Superintendent's Sermonette

Most good relationships are formed between family members and individuals who become friends through various circumstances. Life can hardly be considered full or complete if we lack these relationships. Fellowship with God, Christ, and the Holy Spirit is also available to believers, and that adds a whole new dimension to this life and the life to come.

Saul and Barnabas formed their friendship at the time that the former persecutor of the church came to Jerusalem. It was interrupted when persecution forced Saul to go home to Tarsus, but it was renewed when Barnabas went to Tarsus, took Saul back with him to Antioch, and made him assistant pastor of the church.

Unfortunately, Saul and Barnabas later disagreed over John Mark and severed their relationship (Acts 15:36-41). However, during the time they served God together, they knew the blessing of a good human relationship. We need to guard our Christian friendships and do all that we can to enhance them. The Lord works through individuals and through partners, as well.

This Lesson in Your Life

Let us examine this story from the standpoint of the Jerusalem Christians. It was natural for them to be afraid. Saul was the man who had been breathing "threatenings and slaughters" against the church. Some at Jerusalem might have had friends of relatives imprisoned, driven out of town, or even killed. Even some of them may have personally felt the brunt of Saul's persecution. Fear and suspicion were natural reactions when Saul showed up wanting to take a part.

Then look at the situation from Saul's point of view. Rejection is always painful. No one like to be excluded. A weaker person could have been permanently lost to the cause of Christ. No one knows how many people have been lost because they did not feel warmly received or totally accepted.

Barnabas also had a point of view. He knew about Saul's conversion but he also knew about the deep feelings of the Jerusalem church toward Saul's aggressive persecution. He did not know how his commendation of Saul would be received. What if the Jerusalem church deduced that it was Barnabas who had reverted to Judaism rather than Saul who had converted to Christianity? It took a great deal of courage for Barnabas to step up and be counted on Saul's behalf.

There is a beautiful change in attitude on the part of the Jerusalem brethren. They changed from suspicious to protective. They who had been afraid to allow Saul to help with their work became his guardians when his safety was threatened. They slipped him out of the city to the coastal town of Caesarea where they saw him safely off to the security of his home town, Tarsus.

Today's text has two examples of love being returned. The first is that of Saul returning the love of Barnabas. After Barnabas stood up for Saul against opposition, Saul responded to Barnabas' request to go to Antioch. The second example is that of the brethren at Antioch who showed their appreciation of the gospel by sending relief to the brethren in Jerusalem at a time of famine. It would have been easy for a church with Gentiles in it to think, "We have received a lot of persecution at the hands of Jews. Why should we send relief to Jerusalem?"

Here are some important lessons we can learn from this story:

(1) We should avoid shunning people. No one who is made in the image of God should be shunned. Besides, in shunning another, we might be missing a blessing that would benefit ourselves as well as him.

(2) We should stand up for those who deserve it even when it is unpopular to do so. It may be a case of entertaining angels unaware. Whether that is the case or not, it maintains our own integrity when we do what is right even when it is uncomfortable.

(3) We should share freely what we have, whether physical or spiritual. When we do this we will find others returning to us blessings that we would not otherwise have.

Seed Thoughts

1. Why might believers be afraid of another believer?
They might not trust his testimony. They might be afraid that he will lure them into a trap by means of deceit.

2. What could believers in Jerusalem have done to check out Saul?
They could have asked God about him. They could have closely examined his testimony of faith in Christ.

3. Did Barnabas take a chance when he befriended Saul?
Filled with the Holy Ghost (Acts 11:24), Barnabas was led of God and was under no threat in befriending Saul.

4. What can mature believers do in order to encourage new converts?
They can give them opportunities to witness to others regarding their faith.

5. Should a Christian ever retreat from a dangerous situation?
As in all conflicts there are times to advance and times to retreat, so is it true in spiritual battles.

(Please Turn Page)

---

1. Why might believers be afraid of another believer?

2. What could believers in Jerusalem have done to check out Saul?

3. Did Barnabas take a chance when he befriended Saul?

4. What can mature believers do in order to encourage new converts?

5. Should a Christian ever retreat from a dangerous situation?

6. How was Acts 1:8 implemented by persecution?

7. Do clergymen or laymen get involved in establishing churches?

8. What equipped Barnabas to lead the church at Antioch?

9. How can a minister show confidence in fellow believers?

10. How much should believers be involved in one another's problems?

Seed Thoughts - Continued

They might not trust his testimony. They might be afraid that he will lure them into a trap by means of deceit.

They could have asked God about him. They could have closely examined his testimony of faith in Christ.

Filled with the Holy Ghost (Acts 11: 24), Barnabas was led of God and was under no threat in befriending Saul.

They can give them opportunities to witness to others regarding their faith.

As in all conflicts there are times to advance and times to retreat, so is it true in spiritual battles.

Believers were scattered out from Jerusalem to places mentioned in that verse.

Both get involved, sometimes separately and sometimes together. Full development requires participation by both.

Positive personal qualities, plus firsthand experience with church leaders in Jerusalem, prepared him for this work.

He can go to them and invite them to take part with him in his ministry, even as Barnabas did with Saul.

They should discover and seek solutions for the spiritual, material, physical, emotional, and social problems faced by all members of their fellowship.

6. How was Acts 1:8 implemented by persecution?
Believers were scattered out from Jerusalem to places mentioned in that verse.

7. Do clergymen or laymen get involved in establishing churches?
Both get involved, sometimes separately and sometimes together. Full development requires participation by both.

8. What equipped Barnabas to lead the church at Antioch?
Positive personal qualities, plus firsthand experience with church leaders in Jerusalem, prepared him for this work.

9. How can a minister show confidence in fellow believers?
He can go to them and invite them to take part with him in his ministry, even as Barnabas did with Saul.

10. How much should believers be involved in one another's problems?
They should discover and seek solutions for the spiritual, material, physical, emotional, and social problems faced by all members of their fellowship.

A Sermon At Antioch Of Pisidia

Acts 13:26. Men and brethren, children of the stock of Abraham, and whosoever among you feareth God, to you is the word of this salvation sent.
27. For they that dwell at Jerusalem, and their rulers, because they knew him not, nor yet the voices of the prophets which are read every Sabbath day, they have fulfilled them in condemning him.
28. And though they found no cause of death in him, yet desired they Pilate that he should be slain.
29. And when they had fulfilled all that was written of him, they took him down from the tree, and laid him in a sepulcher.
30. But God raised him from the dead:
31. And he was seen many days of them which came up with him from Galilee to Jerusalem, who are his witnesses unto the people.
32. And we declare unto you glad tidings, how that the promise which was made unto the fathers,
33. God hath fulfilled the same unto us their children, in that he hath raised up Jesus again; as it is also written in the second psalm, Thou art my Son, this day have I begotten thee.
34. And as concerning that he raised him up from the dead, now no more to return to corruption, he said on this wise, I will give you the sure mercies of David.
35. Wherefore he saith also in another psalm, Thou shalt not suffer thine Holy One to see corruption.
36. For David, after he had served his own generation by the will of God, fell on sleep, and was laid unto his fathers, and saw corruption:
37. But he, whom God raised again, saw no corruption.
38. Be it known unto you therefore, men and brethren, that through this man is preached unto you the forgiveness of sins:
39. And by him all that believe are justified from all things, from which ye could not be justified by the law of Moses.

MEMORY SELECTION
Acts 13:38
DEVOTIONAL READING
Galatians 3:1-3, 21-29

BACKGROUND SCRIPTURE
Acts 13:1-3, 13-52
PRINTED SCRIPTURE
Acts 13:26-39

Teacher's Target

Church leaders in Antioch, Syria were fasting and praying one day when the Holy Spirit said, "Separate me Barnabas and Saul for the work whereunto I have called them" (Acts 13:2). This was done, and the two men soon set sail for the island of Cyprus. John Mark was with them, but he left them at Perga in Pamphylia (south central Turkey) and went back to Jerusalem. Saul's name changed to Paul at this point. He and Barnabas continued inland to Antioch, Pisidia and went into the synagogue on the Sabbath Day (Acts 13:3-14).

Help your students to see that the sermon preached by Paul at that synagogue was designed to prove that Jesus was the long-awaited Messiah and Savior. The sermon's theme was justification by faith, and that is still a basic theme for preaching today. What appears foolishness to men becomes the power of God to believers (I Cor. 1:18).

Lesson Introduction

People often wonder how a preacher creates a sermon. He usually has a basic procedure in mind, involving an introduction, development, and conclusion. He may do a Bible-book study, a theme-study, or a topical study, and he usually requires several hours for preparation, When Paul stood up in the synagogue at Antioch, Pisidia, he had to speak in an impromptu fashion. He was so saturated with the gospel message that he was able to talk freely about justification by faith.

The whole sermon is recorded in Acts 13:16-41. Our lesson text covers only verses 26-39, but you would do well to read all of it. Paul began by reviewing the history of Israel from bondage in Egypt up to the time of Jesus. He concluded by warning his hearers not to remain unbelievers . Some Jews and religious proselytes believed, and the Gentiles wanted to hear more the next Sabbath (Acts 13: 41-43).

Teaching Outline

I. Rejection: Acts 13:26-29
   A. Recipients: 26
   B. Rejecters: 27-28
   C. Retrieval: 29

II. Resurrection: Acts 13:30-37
   A. Raising: 30-33a
   B. References: 33b-37

III. Redeemer: Acts 13:38-39
   A. Liberty: 38-39a
   B. Law: 39b

Daily Bible Readings

Mon. Barnabas and Saul Sent Out
Acts 13:1-3
Tue. Conversion of Sergius Paulus
Acts 13:4-13
Wed. Sermon at Antioch
Acts 13:14-24
Thu. Sermon Continued
Acts 13:25-31
Fri. Sermon Continued
Acts 13:32-37
Sat. Sermon Concluded
Acts 13:38-43
Sun. Many Gentiles Converted
Acts 13:44-52

Verse By Verse

I. Rejection: Acts 13:26-29

A. Recipients: 26
26. Men and brethren, children of the stock of Abraham, and whosoever among you feareth God, to you is the word of this salvation sent.

Paul had begun his sermon by referring to the Exodus of the Israelites from bondage in Egypt He told of the forty years of wandering in the wilderness, the destruction of pagans in Canaan, and the division of the Land among the tribes of Israel. He talked about the judges who served until Samuel came and Saul, son of Kish, was made king. He mentioned David and the fact that Jesus was his descendant. He described the ministry of John the Baptist (Acts 13:16-25).

Now Paul was ready to challenge his audience, composed of Jews, proselytes to Judaism, and some Gentiles (Acts 13:42-43). His remarks were directed primarily to Jews and proselytes. Jews were called "children of the stock of Abraham," the first Hebrew. Proselytes were called "whosoever among you feareth God,'" meaning Gentiles who had attached themselves to Judaism. Note the universality of the gospel proposed by Paul when he said that the word of salvation was sent to both kinds of people.

B. Rejecters: 27-28
27. For they that dwell at Jerusalem, and their rulers, because they knew him not, nor yet the voices of the prophets which are read every sabbath day, they have fulfilled them in condemning him

Paul proceeded to lay a strong charge against both Jews and Romans for their mistreatment of Jesus in Jerusalem. Rulers here referred to Jewish religious leaders. Neither they nor their people recognized Jesus as the Messiah when He appeared among them. They did not see Him described in the voices (writings) of their own prophets read every Sabbath Day in the synagogues. Indeed, they fulfilled the predictions made by the prophets that Jesus would be condemned by His Own people. It was by extension that Paul considered the Jews in Antioch, Pisidia guilty as well.

28. And though they found no cause of death in him, yet desired they Pilate that he should be slain.

John 18:28-32 and 19:1-16 give the details of what happened when the Jews brought Jesus to judgment before the Roman governor, Pilate. They had no real case against Him. They had no right to execute Him. They intended to persuade Pilate by the pressure of numbers and noise that he should condemn Jesus to death, and they succeeded in their goal. Here were the people chosen by God to provide the pagans with a moral and ethical standard to imitate, and they failed miserably.

C. Retrieval: 29
29. And when they had fulfilled all that was written of him, they took him down from the tree, and laid him in a sepulchre.

There were two kinds of Jews in mind here. The first "they" refers to the unbelieving Jews who demanded that Jesus be crucified, even as the prophets had predicted. The second "they" refers to Nicodemus and Joseph of Arimathaea, secret believers who persuaded Pilate to let them have the body of Jesus for burial. Details of this are given in Matthew 27:57-60 and John 19:38-42. The sepulchre used was a new one, hewn out of solid rock, belonging to Joseph. However, it was scheduled for only temporary use.

II. Resurrection: Acts 13:30-37

A. Raising: 30-33a
30. But God raised him from the dead. . .
In this short statement, the Activator and the miracle of the resurrection of Jesus are central. It was God Himself Who raised Jesus from the dead, despite the various efforts of the Jews to thwart it. God would not allow His precious Son to remain in the grave and experience corruption (Acts 13:35).
31. And he was seen many days of them which Came up with him from Galilee to Jerusalem, who are his witnesses unto the people.
Jesus was seen by many people during the forty days separating His resurrection from His ascension to heaven. Helpful references on this may be found in Acts 1:3; 7:55; 9:3-6; I Corinthians 15:4-8 and Revelation 1:9-18. Many witnesses to these appearances were still alive in Paul's time. The term "people" used at the end of Acts 13:31 probably referred to the Jews.
32. And we declare unto you glad tidings, how that the promise which was made unto the fathers, 33a. God hath fulfilled the same unto us their children, in that he hath raised up Jesus again . . .
Declaration of the resurrection of Jesus was central to propagation of the gospel (good tidings) by first-century preachers. They were proclaiming the existence of a living Savior, not a dead and buried one. The promise made through the Old Testament prophets had been made a reality by God to descendants of the ancient Jews. The greatest miracle of the New Testament was the raising of Jesus from the dead.

It was because of the resurrection that believers had hope for the future (I Cor. 15:19-23).

B. References: 33b-37
33b. . . .as it is also written in the second psalm, Thou art my Son, this day have I begotten thee.
Having already referred to Jewish prophets, whom the Jews in Antioch, Pisidia claimed to believe, Paul began to quote from prophetic writings. He mentioned Psalm 2:7—"The Lord hath said unto me, Thou art my Son; this day have I begotten thee." We know that Jesus was eternal and never begotten in the same sense that we are born. The meaning here was probably that God presented His Son to the world as the Messiah when He raised Him up from the dead. It was a very important event in God's master plan of redemption.
Note that the word "corruption" occurs four times in Acts 13:34-37, showing that it is vital to understanding the upcoming passage.
34. And as concerning that he raised him up from the dead, now no more to return to corruption, he said on this wise, I will give you the sure mercies of David.
In Isaiah 55:3 we hear God saying, "Incline your ear, and come unto me: hear, and your soul shall live and I will make an everlasting covenant with you, even the sure mercies of David " By quoting that now, Paul evidently meant that the sure mercies promised to David and Old Testament believers also belonged to New Testament believers. This would be possible only through identification by faith with Jesus Christ, the Savior descending from David's line.
35. Wherefore he saith also in another psalm, Thou shalt not suffer thine Holy One to see corruption.
Psalm 16:10 reads, "Thou wilt not leave my soul in hell [Hades]; neither wilt thou suffer thine Holy One to see corruption." This must have been the Messiah speaking, for He is called the "Holy One," God could not allow Him to remain in the state of death and the corruption associated with it.

36. For David, after he had served his own generation by the will of God, fell on sleep, and was laid unto his fathers, and saw corruption:
37. But he, whom God raised again, saw no corruption,

Paul simply made it clear that the references did not apply to David. After he had lived his life according to the span God willed for him, David had died (fallen asleep) and been buried (laid unto his ancestors). His body decomposed and experienced the normal corruption common to all men. On the other hand, Jesus was raised from the dead in order that His body might not decay.

III. Redeemers Acts 13:38-39

A. Liberty: 38-39a
38. Be it known unto you therefore, men and brethren, that through this man is preached unto you the forgiveness of sins:
39a. And by him all that believe are justified from all things, . . .

Here was the obvious climax of Paul's sermon, He challenged those listening to him in the synagogue to realize that it was by means of Christ's death, burial, and resurrection that preaching about the forgiveness of sins had been made possible. The great theme of justification by faith in Christ was now presented. All who placed their trust in Him could be declared righteous and delivered from their sins. Paul offered the Jews in Antioch of Pisidia liberty (freedom, release) from the burden of their sins. He did this by calling for them to place their faith in Jesus Christ.

Justification, the act of being declared righteous, had to come by means of allegiance to a Person and not through works performed by individuals on the human level. It had to involve the Son of God raising men up so that they could benefit from divine power and pardon. This seemed to be a foreign concept to most Jews, for they had been conditioned by the law of Moses and by Jewish traditions which had grown up around it.

B. Law: 39b
39b. . . .from which ye could not be justified by the law of Moses.

What Paul said was a shock to many of his Jewish listeners. They had spent their lifetime seeking to adhere to the numerous stipulations of the law and of tradition, thinking that this would justify them and make them righteous. None of them had been perfectly successful in this endeavor, but they felt that atoning sacrifices had restored them to divine favor time and again. Paul wanted them to realize that the law was not supposed to be an end in itself. It was designed to be a schoolmaster to lead men to Christ, the true Savior (Gal. 3:24-26).

Paul concluded his sermon by quoting from Habakkuk 1:5. This warned people not to miss God's great work being performed in their midst, referring to the preaching of the gospel in Christ's name (Acts 13:40-41).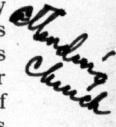

As disgruntled Jews were leaving the synagogue, Gentile listeners stayed behind to ask Paul to preach these words to them again on the next Sabbath Day. They were naturally interested in the concept that justification came apart from strict adherence to the Mosaic law. Many Jews and religious proselytes followed Paul and Barnabas afterward, and they took further time to do their best to persuade them to continue in the saving grace of God. The next Saturday, almost the whole city's population came together to hear the Word of God preached. This enraged the envious Jews, and they sought to contradict what Paul said (Acts 13:42-45).

Evangelistic Emphasis

In the first epistle to the Corinthian church Paul wrote, "I determined not to know anything among you, save Jesus Christ, and him crucified." (I Corinthians 2:2). The sermon in our text is a good example of the way he fulfilled that commitment.

The sermon was adapted to his audience. He took into consideration their background and their faith. He quoted from their Scriptures. Yet he related each of these needs to the central message of Jesus Christ, crucified and resurrected.

Paul's sermon addressed the problems of the people. It was relevant to their need. He talked about their sin and guilt. He gave them the promise of forgiveness and provided a basis for them to hope. Yet, once again, this good news came directly out of the story of Jesus.

We have important evangelistic guidance here. Each sermon or evangelistic conversation should take into consideration the background and faith of the hearers. It should also consider their needs and tell them how those needs can be met in Christ. It should be focused entirely on Jesus as the answer to every need and the fulfillment of every promise.

Every evangelistic effort should be understandable, relevant, and, most of all, it must carry true evangelistic power. When those three criteria are met, evangelism will be effective even as it was in Antioch of Pisidia where there "came almost the whole city together to hear the word of God."

Memory Selection

"Be it known unto you therefore, men and brethren, that through this man is preached unto you the forgiveness of sins."
Acts 13:38.

In Paul's preaching he made strong accusations. He indicted his hearers for their failure to recognize Jesus as being sent from God. He accused them of rejecting the Messiah that God sent. He even implicated them in the death of Jesus.

With those accusations, however, came promise and hope. Even though the sins had been serious, the situation was not hopeless. Through the very man who had been rejected the forgiveness of sins was now offered.

Forgiveness is a strong concept. It does not minimize sin or its consequences. It does not justify it. It takes full account of sin and the damage that it does. It provides for the payment of the full price of sin. It gives thorough relief from sin.

Herein we have hope. It is not hopeful to rationalize our sin away or deny the significance of our sin. To take it into full consideration and receive forgiveness gives true hope.

Weekday Problems

Stuart is a recent convert to Christianity. He has the exuberance of one who has made a glorious discovery. He wants to tell everyone about his faith. His spirit is contagious. He has attracted dozens of others into the little church he attends.

At first, the influx of new people was exciting and welcome, but it soon became apparent that different backgrounds and attitudes were being reflected in the church. Some of the people who have worshiped there for years are nervous and uncomfortable with the new atmosphere.

Stuart is confused because he cannot understand why all are not thrilled that the gospel is being so well received. He has not been acquainted with the church for a long period of time, so he has no adjustments to make because of the changes that are taking place.

* What can church leaders do to help their followers relate better to change?
* What can the church do to become more flexible in receiving new and different kinds of people?
* What is likely to happen to Stuart's enthusiasm for bringing new people to church?

Superintendent's Sermonette

Some people look forward to a sermon as the central part of a worship service. Others think of it as boring and the low part of a service. Much depends, of course, on the ability of the speaker to make the sermon interesting to the listeners. He must grab hold of their attention, give them an idea of where he intends to go, lead them into the Scriptures for information, apply biblical principles to real-life situations, and then challenge the people to make changes posed by the dynamic Word of God.

One thing every pastor, evangelist, missionary, or conference speaker has to learn is that response to his message is going to be mixed. Some will believe divine truths and let their lives be affected by it. Others will be passive or indifferent to it. Some may even ridicule it. The job of the sower is to sow the seeds of truth and be ready for varied results (Matt. 13:1-8, 18-23). This is what Paul did in Antioch of Pisidia, and today's lesson explains what happened as a result.

This Lesson in <u>Your</u> Life

With this lesson we have reached the place in the text where Saul begins to be referred to as Paul. We see in some of his early activities the characteristics that made him the exceptional Christian leader that he was.

One reason he was so strong is that he had a distinct call by the Holy Spirit. Nothing causes a message to have a stronger ring of truth than for the preacher to have a clear and unwavering conviction that he is from God and that he is preaching the message of God.

Paul not only knew that he was called to be a Christian but he also knew that he was set apart for the work that God planned for him. This certitude about his own mission was backed up by the fasting, prayer, and laying on of hands of the brethren. He was called by God and that call was recognized by the church.

Another characteristic of leadership is the courage to take the message directly to the people even when it is likely to arouse opposition. Paul did not timidly think he should avoid the Jewish leaders because they did not agree with his belief in Jesus as the Messiah. He went directly to the synagogue. He did that on the Sabbath day when the greatest collection of hearers could be expected. He faced candidly the objections both the Jews and the Greeks might have had to his message.

Another thing about a leader that was true of Paul is that he did not vary from the center of his message. Those who have the greatest impact on others are those who issue a clear call. Paul only preached Jesus Christ. Almost like a broken record he continuously said that Jesus was from God, He lived a good life, He was unjustly killed, He was raised from the dead, and He is the source of forgiveness of sins.

Still another characteristic of a good leader is the use of the type of reasoning that will be convincing to the hearers. Paul appealed to the Jews by using the Jewish Scriptures and by offering what the Law of Moses could not offer.

What can we learn from these leadership characteristics for our own lives? First, it is important that we have a clear sense of call. If we are uncertain about whether we are doing the work of God, we will not be convincing to anyone else.

Second, we must have the courage to speak out where there is a need that the message be heard. We are not intended merely to come to church, close the doors, and speak the message only to other believers. Let us rather go to the points of human need and tell people about the one who came from God, was unjustly killed, was raised from the dead, and who forgives sins.

Third, we can experience the joy of carrying good news. Most of us are so excited about having good news that we would almost burst if we could not tell it. Let us treat the gospel that way. It is the best news of all.

Fourth, from this text we can learn the blessing of forgiveness, both for ourselves and others. Man is in a tragic predicament apart from the forgiveness of God. Let us be thankful for that great gift and let us take it to others.

Seed Thoughts

1. Why did Paul and Barnabas go to the synagogue in Antioch, Pisidia?
They followed the pattern of giving the gospel "to the Jew first, and also to the Greek [Gentile] " (Rom. 1:16).

2. How were religious proselytes to Judaism described?
Paul referred to these Gentile adherents as "whosoever among [the Jews] feareth [reverences] God" (Acts 13:26).

3. Are there proselytes to Judaism today?
A few Gentiles convert to it, but Jews do not readily seek this.

4. What has happened to make Gentiles avoid conversion to Judaism?
Anti-Semitism may affect this. Gentiles realize that Jews do not have exclusive rights to truth anymore (Eph, 2:11-18).

5. What defeated the worst that men could do to Jesus?
The Jews persuaded Pilate to crucify Jesus, but "God raised him from the dead" (Acts 13:30).

(Please Turn Page)

---

1. Why did Paul and Barnabas go to the synagogue in Antioch, Pisidia?

2. How were religious proselytes to Judaism described?

3. Are there proselytes to Judaism today?

4. What has happened to make Gentiles avoid conversion to Judaism?

5. What defeated the worst that men could do to Jesus?

6. Is Christ's resurrection vital to the gospel message?

7. Why did Paul mention witnesses to appearances by Jesus after His resurrection?

8. Why couldn't David be the fulfillment of prophecies regarding the Holy One?

9. What is justification, and how may it be obtained?

10. What did the Mosaic law do?

Seed Thoughts - Continued

They followed the pattern of giving the gospel "to the Jew first, and also to the Greek [Gentile] " (Rom. 1:16).

Paul referred to these Gentile adherents as "whosoever among [the Jews] feareth [reverences] God" (Acts 13:26).

A few Gentiles convert to it, but Jews do not readily seek this.

Anti-Semitism may affect this. Gentiles realize that Jews do not have exclusive rights to truth anymore (Eph. 2:11-18).

The Jews persuaded Pilate to crucify Jesus, but "God raised him from the dead" (Acts 13:30).

Yes, for a living gospel demands a living Savior (I Cor. 15:19-23).

Many were still living at that time and could serve as proofs of the truth of the resurrection.

David suffered bodily corruption (decay after death), but the Holy One was Jesus resurrected from the dead.

It is a divine declaration that sinners are made righteous in Christ. It comes only by faith in Him, not by works.

It showed people their sins and their need for a Savior from heaven. It led them to faith in Christ (Gal. 3:24-26).

6. Is Christ's resurrection vital to the gospel message?
Yes, for a living gospel demands a living Savior (I Cor. 15:19-23).

7. Why did Paul mention witnesses to appearances by Jesus after His resurrection?
Many were still living at that time and could serve as proofs of the truth of the resurrection.

8. Why couldn't David be the fulfillment of prophecies regarding the Holy One?
David suffered bodily corruption (decay after death), but the Holy One was Jesus resurrected from the dead.

9. What is justification, and how may it be obtained?
It is a divine declaration that sinners are made righteous in Christ. It comes only by faith in Him, not by works.

10. What did the Mosaic law do?
It showed people their sins and their need for a Savior from heaven. It led them to faith in Christ (Gal. 3:24-26).

A Healing In Lystra

Acts 14:8. And there sat a certain man at Lystra, impotent in his feet, being a cripple from his mother's womb, who never had walked:
9. The same heard Paul speak: who steadfastly beholding him, and perceiving that he had faith to be healed,
10. Said with a loud voice, Stand upright on thy feet. And he leaped and walked.
11. And when the people saw what Paul had done, they lifted up their voices, saying in the speech of Lycaonia, The gods are come down to us in the likeness of men.
12. And they called Barnabas, Jupiter; and Paul, Mercurius, because he was the chief speaker.
13. Then the priest of Jupiter, which was before their city, brought oxen and garlands unto the gates, and would have done sacrifice with the people.
14. Which when the apostles, Barnabas and Paul, heard of, they rent their clothes and ran in among the people, crying out,
15. And saying, Sirs, why do ye these things? We also are men of like passions with you, and preach unto you that ye should turn from these vanities unto the living God, which made heaven, and earth, and the sea, and all things that are therein:
16. Who in times past suffered all nations to walk in their own ways.
17. Nevertheless he left not himself without witness, in that he did good, and gave us rain from heaven, and fruitful seasons, filling our hearts with food and gladness.
18. And with these sayings scarce restrained they the people, that they had not done sacrifice unto them.

MEMORY SELECTION
Acts 14:9-10
DEVOTIONAL READING
Romans 5:1-11

BACKGROUND SCRIPTURE
Acts 14
PRINTED SCRIPTURE
Acts 14:8-18

Teacher's Target

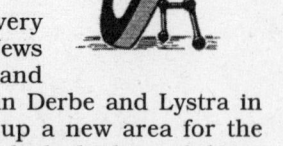

Not every defeat is a disaster, and not every victory is a blessing. Opposed by the hostile Jews at Antioch of Pisidia and at Iconium, Paul and Barnabas moved on to make new converts in Derbe and Lystra in central Asia Minor (Turkey), thus opening up a new area for the gospel. However, at Lystra something happened which alarmed them. The people were so receptive following a healing miracle that they wanted to worship the missionaries as if they were gods.

~~Help your students to~~ Beware of sudden popularity in doing God's work. Satan can take a positive situation and turn it into a negative one. Easy acceptance by the world can lead to perversion and corruption, unless believers are on guard and are willing to fight against self-aggrandizement. God's work must always go forward on humility, and He must receive the glory for all accomplishments.

Lesson Introduction

Jesus had told Ananias in Antioch, Syria that He would show Saul (Paul) "how great things he must suffer for my name's sake" (Acts 9:16). Persecution became a regular part of Paul's life as he sought to fulfill his great commission. Dissident Jews stirred up the leading men and women of Antioch, Pisidia, and Paul and Barnabas were expelled (Acts 13:50). Jews and Gentiles in Iconium tried to stone them (Acts 14:5).

It was because of persecution that the missionaries came to Lystra. By one miracle of healing, they were propelled into tremendous popularity which led to a desire to deify them as the Roman gods Jupiter and Mercury. After this movement was stopped, Jews from Antioch and Iconium persuaded the people of Lystra to stone Paul (Acts 14:19). Thus it was that man's glory passed quickly. We may expect such situations as this to pass quickly today as well.

Teaching Outline

I. Action: Acts 14:8-10
   A. Cripple: 8
   B. Challenge: 9-10a
   C. Compliance: 10b

II. Acclaim: Acts 14:11-13
   A. Perception: 11-12
   B. Plan: 13

III. Alarm: Acts 14:14-18
   A. Exasperation: 14-15a
   B. Explanation: 15b-17
   C. Execution: 18

Daily Bible Readings

Mon. Preaching in Iconium
Acts 14:1-3
Tue. Conflict
Acts 14:4-7
Wed. Healing of a Lame Man
Acts 14:8-10
Thu. Mistaken for gods
Acts 14:11-14
Fri. Correcting the Error
Acts 14:15-18
Sat. The Stoning of Paul
Acts 14:19-23
Sun. More Mission Work
Acts 14:24-28

Verse By Verse

I. Actions Acts 14:8-10

A. Cripple: 8
8. And there sat a certain man at Lystra, impotent in his feet, being a cripple from his mother's womb, who never had walked:

Miracles of divine power were common in the ministry of the missionaries. For example, in Iconium the Lord "gave testimony unto the word of his grace, and granted signs and wonders to be done by their hands" (Acts 14:3). When they arrived at Lystra, they saw a man crippled from birth. He was probably getting along by the humiliation of begging. He had no strength in his feet, and the muscles used for walking had not been developed.

B. Challenge: 9-10a
9a. The same heard Paul speak: ...

There evidently was nothing wrong with the crippled man's hearing. Either he happened to be where he could hear Paul, or he was carried to the place where Paul spoke. It was obvious that this man's faith was stirred as he listened to the missionary.

9b. ... who steadfastly beholding him, and perceiving that he had faith to be healed,
10a. Said with a loud voice, Stand upright on thy feet.

Paul had spiritual discernment and realized that faith was at work in the crippled man's heart. This was important, because there had to be faith in order for divine power to operate. In cases where a person was too ill to exercise faith or had already died, it was faith by family members or friends which was able to meet this need. Paul felt confident in ordering the man to stand up on his feet. Paul acted with apostolic authority as he called on the man to act on his faith. It was a challenge which brought good results.

C. Compliance: 10b
10b. And he leaped and walked.

Consider the magnitude of this miracle. The crippled man had lacked the power to stand on his own feet. He had lacked the muscular coordination and balance necessary for walking. In a moment he leaped to his feet and was able to walk in a normal way. People who observed this incident could not help but be amazed at the change which had taken place.

Before we look more closely at that aspect of the account, let us consider not only the physical but the emotional impact of the healing on the man who had been crippled from birth, Rather than depending on others for movement and support, he now had to get around on his own and find work to sustain himself. Think about the various ramifications of this in his life and in the lives of others who have benefited from God's miracles, By complying with Paul's order, this man was ushered into a whole new world of challenges.

II. Acclaim: Acts 14:11-13

A. Perception: 11-12
11. And when the people saw what Paul had done, they lifted up their voices, saying in the speech of Lycaonia, The gods are come down to us in the likeness of men.

No doubt Paul had intended the miracle to lead the people of Lystra to listen to the gospel and perhaps place their faith in Jesus Christ. However, something unusual took place at that time. Seeing only the missionaries, and not the invisible God at work, the pagans perceived this as a visitation to them of two of their mythological gods. They reverted from the normal Greek language in use to their own dialect of Lycaonia. There were already legends of such incidents in this area, and they were thrilled to think that they were in the middle of another one. This was not a situation suitable for preaching the gospel of Christ.

12. And they called Barnabas, Jupiter; and Paul, Mercurius, because he was the chief speaker.

The people quickly assumed that Barnabas must be Jupiter and that Paul must be Mercury. They thought of Barnabas as Zeus and Paul as Hermes, since he was the main speaker. It is unlikely that the missionaries understood the local dialect, but they must have known the names of gods which the people were ascribing to them, and this kind of acclaim could only lead to alarm on their part. The missionaries had no intention of taking credit for the miracle of healing.

B. Plan: 13
13. Then the priest of Jupiter, which was before their city, brought oxen and garlands unto the gates, and would have done sacrifice with the people.

The fervor of the pagans motivated them to put their adoration of Paul and Barnabas into some concrete action. The priest of Jupiter was only too willing to take advantage of the situation and play the central role in a great celebration. From his place on the city's outskirts he brought oxen for sacrifice and garlands of flowers to bestow on Paul and Barnabas. The matter was really getting out of hand, and the missionaries determined to try to stop it.

Although there is no hint in the scriptural record of Paul and Barnabas being tempted by the move to deify them, consider that fact that some in history have succumbed to some form of acclaim and popularity while pursuing God's work. They have shamed themselves and the Lord by allowing men to venerate them and enrich them for this reason. We can think of modern examples of individuals who have allowed their celebrity status in the Christian world to turn them away from their original mission. In some cases, they have sunk into a variety of sins and have even had to face the justice systems of men.

III. Alarm: Acts 14:14-18

A. Exasperation: 14-15a
14. Which when the apostles, Barnabas and Paul, heard of, they rent their clothes, and ran in among the people, crying out,
15a. And saying, Sirs, why do ye these things?

This verse makes it clear that Barnabas and Paul were considered apostles in the early church. Living close to the Lord, they knew that deification of them by the pagans at Lystra was absolutely wrong and must be stopped, if possible. They finally discovered what was being said and planned, and they immediately tore their clothing as a sign of displeasure and mourning. They ran into the crowd and excitedly asked why the people were doing these things.

B. Explanation: 15b-17
15b. We also are men of like passions with you, and preach unto you that ye should turn from these vanities unto the living God, which made heaven, and earth, and the sea, and all things that are therein:

In doing what they felt they had to do, the missionaries put themselves into a dangerous position. The people did not like to have their self-made heroes be unwilling to accept their adoration. They were irritated when the missionaries said that they were not gods come down in the likeness of men. They did not appreciate having their religious beliefs and practices referred to as useless vanities. They were not ready to cut themselves off from their mythological gods and accept the one true God, Whom the missionaries described as the Creator of the heavens, the earth, and all things contained in it.

16. Who in times past suffered all nations to walk in their own ways.

This is an interesting statement, and it finds support in Acts 17:30—"The times of this ignorance God winked at (overlooked)." This means that God allowed men to walk in sinful idolatry without judging and destroying them immediately. There is no implication here that God condoned these things. With the coming of the gospel, all men were called on to forsake idolatry and the false gods connected with them.

17. Nevertheless he left not himself without witness, in that he did good, and gave us rain from heaven, and fruitful seasons, filling our hearts with food and gladness.

This finds support in Psalm 104:13-14—"He watereth the hills from his chambers: the earth is satisfied with the fruit of thy works. He causeth the grass to grow for the cattle, and herb for the service of man: that he may bring forth food out of the earth." Matthew 5:45 agrees—"He maketh his sun to rise on the evil and on the good, and sendeth rain on the just and on the unjust." This refers to the providential grace of God, which is available to sinners and saints alike. Saving faith is operable only in believers.

C. Execution: 18

18. And with these sayings scarce restrained they the people, that they had not done sacrifice unto them.

The hastily-contrived plan of the missionaries to stop the people from sacrificing the oxen unto them was executed, but it almost came short of its goal. Paul and Barnabas must have breathed a sign of relief as the crowd of pagans dispersed. Now they had to face the animosity generated when the people had not been allowed to have their own way. A great celebration had been aborted, and the people were in a sour and vulnerable mood.

Hostile Jews from Antioch and Iconium appeared on the scene and took advantage of the people's black mood. They found it rather easy to convince the pagans that Paul ought to be stoned. This was done, and he was thrown out of the city, supposedly dead. However, as the believers stood around him to mourn, he rose up and went back with them into the city of Lystra (Acts 14:19-20).

We cannot be sure if Paul was actually alive but assumed to be dead or if God raised him from the dead at this time. It scarcely affects the miraculous nature of his quick recovery, for it was the power of God which allowed him to get up and move back into Lystra. This would not normally have been possible under the circumstances.

Paul and Barnabas were apparently hidden from the pagans during the night, The next day they went on to Derbe and preached the gospel in spite of the previous day's setback. They then had the audacity and courage to go back to Lystra, Iconium, and Antioch of Pisidia to confirm the souls of those who had become disciples of Christ. They exhorted them to continue in the faith. They warned them that they would have to endure much tribulation to enter the kingdom of God (Acts 14: 20-22).

Although their converts were new to the faith, Paul and Barnabas boldly ordained elders in every church. They passed down through Pisidia and Pamphylia and sailed back to Antioch, Syria (Acts 14:23-26).

Evangelistic Emphasis

Life has its occasions of good news. Babies are born, students are graduated, lovers are married, workers are promoted, and Christmases finally come. In the story of our text a man receives an incredible piece of good news. He had been born lame and had never walked in his life. God, through Paul, gave him the ability to leap and walk.

Although that seems like almost unbelievably good news, there is even better news than that. It is the news that we can be one with God in spite of our sin. This news transcends all other good news because it is more basic and is eternal.

One who is lame has other avenues to experience joy. He is likely to be able to see, speak, hear, and love. He regrets his lameness but the disaster is not total. One, however, who has lost his relationship with God through sin, is cut off from his source of life. That affects, not just one area of his life, but every part of his life. It affects, not just the present, but the future. It affects, not just time, but eternity.

Good news in regard to one's relationship with God is beyond comparison with all other good news. It is more important than births, graduations, weddings, promotions, or even having physical wholeness restored.

Memory Selection

"The same heard Paul speak: who steadfastly beholding him, and perceiving that he had faith to be healed, said with a loud voice, Stand upright on thy feet. And he leaped and walked."
Acts 14:9, 10.

Troubled people cherish hope as the rest of us do. The existence of a problem, even a serious one, does not dull the need to hope. There is no real indication that this man hoped for the healing of his lameness, but it is obvious that he hoped for some sort of blessing from hearing Paul preach. A person who has a defect or a deformity does not consider his whole life to revolve around that problem. He has other interests and needs. We should listen for them and respond to them as we can.

It is notable that the faith of this man helped. Paul was able to see that he had faith. It is important for us to remember that faith makes it possible for good things to happen. Cynicism and unbelief do not make things better. Faith does.

It is also important to let one's faith be seen. It was because Paul could perceive this man's faith that healing occurred. Had the faith been hidden, we cannot know that his legs would have been healed.

Weekday Problems

Leslie is terminally ill with cancer. He has already passed the stage where therapy is indicated. Now his family and his physicians talk only in terms of pain control.

Leslie is a devout and mature Christian man. He is wise in both the ways of God and the ways of people. He knows well his condition and has made what preparation he can for his own death. Papers are in order. Instructions have been given to his wife and son. Relationships have been renewed and enhanced. Words of love and encouragement have been pronounced. He has talked soberly with his family and his pastor about matters that are important to him.

He has no expectation of ever leaving his bed. Nor does he expect again to be able to enjoy a normal meal. Nor does he anticipate a restful night's sleep. His life is an existence confined to the bed while awaiting death. There are moments of affection, prayer, and even of laughter, but generally the specter of impending death rules the day.

* What can be said to Leslie that will be meaningful to him in this extreme situation?
* What can be done that will not seem frivolous and shallow?

Superintendent's Sermonette

We live in a society where democratic principles are at work. Basic to this is the concept that power flows upward from the common people. We often assume that the majority is right on any issue. However, this is not always the case. There are times when the majority of people are wrong, and the minority are right. Our standard for truth and what is right or wrong must be the inspired Word of God, not the opinions of men. "Broad is the way that leadeth to destruction,...and narrow is the way which leadeth unto life" (Matt. 7:13-14).

Paul and Barnabas arrived in Lystra, healed a crippled man in the name of Jesus, and were immediately assumed by the majority of pagans to be the gods named Jupiter and Mercury. It was only by strenuous objection that they finally persuaded the people to stop venerating them in this way. The people did not like their heroes disclaiming their status, and persecution followed. May God help us to refrain from being man-made celebrities but to work for His glory alone!

This Lesson in <u>Your</u> Life

It is significant that the man in our text, though crippled since birth, was looking for a way to improve his life. There seems to be a tendency among many to focus on their areas of pain to the exclusion of areas of possibility in their lives. If their back hurts or their head aches, that is the only thing they can think about. As a result their whole lives are centered around problems.

This man was not that way. Though he had never been able to walk, he did not concentrate on that lameness but rather went to hear Paul preach. Being crippled does not make one deaf to good news.

All of us who share the human condition have some ache, pain, or defect. We can concentrate on that and build our lives around a negative. Or, we can follow the example of the man in this text and seek the blessings that are available to us.

This man also radiated faith. We usually do not think of faith as visible. When a person really believes, there usually are signs that can be observed by one who is perceptive. Do people notice your faith? If not, is it because you do not have enough of it for it to show? Or, is it because it is so hidden that no one can uncover it? Remember that faith became the occasion of a great blessing in the case in our text. Let your faith be visible so that it also can attract blessings.

Paul called on the man to stand. This must have been a frightening command to one who had never been able to walk. Sometimes we, too, are called on to do things that are frightening to us. God inevitably expects us to act on the basis of our faith. This is true to the point that if we do not act the very existence of faith is suspect. Faith is not a collector's item to be held in safekeeping. It is a commitment to be acted upon.

This man dared to respond. Though, no doubt, frightened, he leaped to his feet and began to walk. We do not get the picture that he took a few cautious, limping steps. Rather we conceive of a bold and joyous leaping walk.

The observers of this event knew they had seen a miracle but they misinterpreted the significance of it. They wanted to worship Barnabas and Paul as the gods, Jupiter and Mercury. Of course Paul and Barnabas did not allow such a misperception to go unchallenged, but we are here warned to be certain that we not only understand an event but also the significance of it.

Men have always tended to misunderstand miracles. We tend to want to trust the phenomenon rather than the God who caused it to happen. Paul told these people to turn to the living God who made heaven, and earth, and the sea, and all things therein.

God is the only ultimate solution to life's needs. It is our relationship with him that enables us to be secure in grace, grow in love, and abound in hope. A miracle might make the blind see or the lame walk, but only faith in God causes the lost to be saved and eternity to be secure.

Seed Thoughts

1. Why are some individuals born with handicaps?
The man in Jerusalem was born blind "that the works of God should be made manifest in him" (John 9:3). This may have been true of the cripple in Lystra.

2. What is there in people which must combine with divine power in order for a miracle to occur?
Man's faith and God's power are required for a miracle to take place, as shown in Acts 14:9-10.

3. How does faith come to a person?
"Faith cometh by hearing, and hearing by the word of God" (Rom. 10:17).

4. What did the crippled man hear which brought him faith?
He heard Paul preaching the gospel. Paul perceived (discerned spiritually) that the man had faith to be healed.

5. Why was what happened a double miracle?
The crippled man received strength to rise up and balance for walking and leaping without previous experience.

(Please Turn Page)

---

1. Why are some individuals born with handicaps?

2. What is there in people which must combine with divine power in order for a miracle to occur?

3. How does faith come to a person?

4. What did the crippled man hear which brought him faith?

5. Why was what happened a double miracle?

6. How did imagination affect the pagans of Lystra?

7. Don't non-Christians have the right to their own beliefs?

8. Are Christian leaders today tempted by attempts to deify them?

9. What is the antidote for personal aggrandizement?

10. How should Christians divert attention from themselves?

Seed Thoughts - Continued

The man in Jerusalem was born blind "that the works of God should be made manifest in him" (John 9:3). This may have been true of the cripple in Lystra.

Man's faith and God's power are required for a miracle to take place, as shown in Acts 14:9-10.

"Faith cometh by hearing, and hearing by the word of God" (Rom. 10:17).

He heard Paul preaching the gospel. Paul perceived (discerned spiritually) that the man had faith to be healed.

The crippled man received strength to rise up and balance for walking and leaping without previous experience.

They imagined Paul and Barnabas to be imaginary gods come to them in the flesh.

They have the right to be wrong, but their eternal destiny rests on learning divine truth and acting upon it.

Some accept veneration which can be dangerous as it builds to celebrity status and personal power.

Christians should keep their focus on God and Christ, asking the Holy Spirit to keep them humble as servants.

They should urge people to concentrate their attention on God and His Word, for that is where all power originates.

6. How did imagination affect the pagans of Lystra?
They imagined Paul and Barnabas to be imaginary gods come to them in the flesh.

7. Don't non-Christians have the right to their own beliefs?
They have the right to be wrong, but their eternal destiny rests on learning divine truth and acting upon it.

8. Are Christian leaders today tempted by attempts to deify them?
Some accept veneration which can be dangerous as it builds to celebrity status and personal power.

9. What is the antidote for personal aggrandizement?
Christians should keep their focus on God and Christ, asking the Holy Spirit to keep them humble as servants.

10. How should Christians divert attention from themselves?
They should urge people to concentrate their attention on God and His Word, for that is where all power originates.

A Conference In Jerusalem

Acts 15:1. And certain men which came down from Judea taught the brethren, and said, Except ye be circumcised after the manner of Moses, ye cannot be saved.
2. When therefore Paul and Barnabas had no small dissension and disputation with them, they determined that Paul and Barnabas, and certain other of them should go up to Jerusalem unto the apostles and elders about this question.
3. And being brought on their way by the church, they passed through Phenice and Samaria, declaring the conversion of the Gentiles: and they caused great joy unto all the brethren.
4. And when they were come to Jerusalem, they were received of the church, and of the apostles and elders, and they declared all things that God had done with them.
5. But there rose up certain of the sect of the Pharisees which believed, saying, That it was needful to circumcise them, and to command them to keep the law of Moses.
6. And the apostles and elders came together for to consider of this matter.
7. And when there had been much disputing, Peter rose up, and said unto them, Men and brethren, ye know how that a good while ago God made choice among us, that the Gentiles by my mouth should hear the word of the gospel, and believe.
8. And God, which knoweth the hearts, bare them witness, giving them the Holy Ghost, even as he did unto us;
9. And put no difference between us and them, purifying their hearts by faith.
10. Now therefore why tempt ye God, to put a yoke upon the neck of the disciples, which neither our fathers nor we were able to bear?
11. But we believe that through the grace of the Lord Jesus Christ we shall be saved, even as they.
12. Then all the multitude kept silence and gave audience to Barnabas and Paul, declaring what miracles and wonders God had wrought among the Gentiles by them.

MEMORY SELECTION
Acts 15:11
DEVOTIONAL READING
Galatians 5:25-6:10

BACKGROUND SCRIPTURE
Acts 15:1-35
PRINTED SCRIPTURE
Acts 15:1-12

Teacher's Target

Most Christians in the world today are Gentiles, but that was not true in the early days of the church. Most believers at that time were Jews who had been convinced that Jesus was their long-awaited Messiah and Savior. It was through the ministry of such men as Paul, Barnabas, and others that Gentile converts began to outnumber Jewish converts. Controversy was bound to occur, and it would take a decision by the church leaders in Jerusalem to resolve it. We can appreciate the feelings of the Judaizers who demanded that law and grace be merged for salvation, but that faith in Christ can free men from their sins. Bold Peter deserved much credit for his insistence that it could only be through "the grace of the Lord Jesus Christ [that] we [all] shall be saved" (Acts 15:11).

Lesson Introduction

Peter had seen the grace of God fall upon Gentile believers when he went to minister at the home of Cornelius, the Roman centurion in Caesarea. He did not demand that they keep the Mosaic law, and this had generated opposition from Judaizers in Jerusalem (Acts 10:1-18). Paul and Barnabas had seen the grace of God fall upon Gentile believers when they ministered in many lands during their first missionary journey (Acts 13:42-43, 48; 14:23).

The Judaizers who came up from Jerusalem to harass Gentile believers in Antioch, Syria threatened to split the church there. A delegation composed of Paul, Barnabas, and others was chosen to go to Jerusalem to get a ruling from the apostles and elders on this matter. The church council which resulted produced a clear decision favoring salvation by faith alone, apart from works of the law. Gentiles have benefited from it ever since that time.

Teaching Outline

I. Decision: Acts 15:1-4
   A. Men: 1
   B. Method: 2
   C. Messages: 3-4

II. Demand: Acts 15:5-6
   A. Demands: 5
   B. Deliberation: 6

III. Declaration: Acts 15:7-12
   A. Choice: 7
   B. Comparison: 8-9
   C. Conversion: 10-12

Daily Bible Readings

Mon. Dispute about Circumcision
Acts 15:1-5
Tue. Peter Speaks
Acts 15:6-11
Wed. Paul, Barnabas, and James Speak
Acts 15:12-17
Thu. James Reasons
Acts 15:18-21
Fri. Letter of Encouragement
Acts 15:22-26
Sat. Words of Encouragement
Acts 15:27-29
Sun. Work in Antioch
Acts 15:30-35

Verse By Verse

I. Decision: Acts 15:1-4

A. Men: 1

1. **And certain men which came down from Judaea taught the brethren, and said, Except ye be circumcised after the manner of Moses, ye cannot be saved.**

When we travel, we think of going up north or down south, but when Luke wrote in the first century he considered the trip from Jerusalem to Antioch as going down and the trip from Antioch to Jerusalem as going up (Acts 15:1-2). The Jews who came to Antioch from Jerusalem have since been labeled as Judaizers, meaning that they expected even Gentile believers to be governed by Judaism.

They taught that physical circumcision after the Jewish manner and the Mosaic code was required in order that men might be saved from their sins. This was an attempt to mix law and grace, works and faith. Their counterparts may still be found in the world today, and we need to be on guard against them. God alone has the power to save us from our sins. There is nothing we can do to merit salvation. It comes only as a free gift of grace to those who have faith in Christ and the redemption He purchased for us at Calvary. "For by grace are ye saved through faith; and that not of yourselves: it is the gift of God: not of works, lest any man should boast" (Eph. 2:8-9). Beware of any other so-called "gospel."

B Method: 2

2. **When therefore Paul and Barnabas had no small dissension and disputation with them, they determined that Paul and Barnabas, and certain other of them, should go up to Jerusalem unto the apostles and elders about this question.**

We are not told the specific things said as Paul and Barnabas argued with the Judaizers from Jerusalem. Perhaps Paul expressed his support of Jewish monotheism and denunciation of idolatry (I Cor. 8:5-6). Perhaps he called for circumcision of the heart in place of physical circumcision (Rom. 2:29; I Cor. 7:18-19). Perhaps he said that Gentile believers should not be bound by Jewish holy days, including the Sabbath Day (Rom. 14:5-6; Col. 2:16-17). The Apostle John later counted Sunday as the Christian "Lord's day" (Rev. 1:10).

After heated discussions reached an impasse, it was decided in Antioch that an appeal should be made to a higher authority for resolution of the problem. That authority was composed of apostles and elders in the mother church at Jerusalem. Paul, Barnabas, and other church leaders were chosen to go to Jerusalem. We assume that the visiting Judaizers agreed to this and probably left to go home by themselves.

Consider briefly the fact that many quarrels today are settled by compromise. That may work well in secondary matters, but it cannot be used in doctrinal matters. We dare not compromise on divine truth. Our goal should be to determine God's will and then abide by it on every issue.

C. Messages: 3-4

3. **And being brought on their way**

by the church, they passed through Phenice and Samaria, declaring the conversion of the Gentiles: and they caused great joy unto all the brethren

Galatians 2:1 suggests that Titus went with the delegation from Antioch to Jerusalem. It appears that members of the Antioch church escorted the delegation during the first part of its trip toward Jerusalem. Paul and the others then continued southward through Phenice (Phoenicia) and Samaria, stopping to meet with Christian groups along the way and reporting to them how Gentiles were being saved where they had ministered. This brought great joy to those who heard it. It was by means such as this that scattered believers were being stitched together as a unified church.

4. And when they were come to Jerusalem, they were received of the church, and of the apostles and elders, and they declared all things that God had done with them.

Messages given on the trip southward were but preludes to the message given by the delegation from Antioch after it reached Jerusalem. Apostles, elders, and ordinary members of the church welcomed the delegation and listened to the good news about conversions God had wrought through His faithful servants. Details regarding miracles and wonders among the Gentiles would come later (Acts 15:12).

II. Demand: Acts 15:5-6

A. Demands: 5

5. But there rose up certain of the sect of the Pharisees which believed, saying, That it was needful to circumcise them, and to command them to keep the law of Moses.

It is interesting that there were some super-conservative Pharisees in Judaism who came to believe that Jesus was the Messiah. However, they were so entrenched in Judaism that they could not leave it behind and embrace Christianity by itself. They sought to mix law and grace, works and faith. They demanded that even Gentile believers be circumcised and keep all of the regulations laid down in the Mosaic code. The moral principles contained in the law were required of Christians, but the ceremonial principles fulfilled in Christ were no longer binding on them. The Judaizers refused to accept this, and the battle lines were fixed.

B. Deliberation: 6

6. And the apostles and elders came together for to consider of this matter.

Church leaders heard the demands of the Judaizers and the reports of the missionaries, and they decided to hold a church council to resolve the matter. The outcome was crucial to the continued expansion of the gospel, particularly into the Gentile world. If the Judaizers had their way, missionary work could be hampered or curtailed. Christian liberty would be at stake throughout the church. It was time to give solemn deliberation and to seek the mind of the Spirit (Acts 15:28).

III. Declaration: Acts 15:7-12

A. Choice: 7

7. And when there had been much disputing, Peter rose up, and said unto them, Men and brethren, ye know how that a good while ago God made choice among us, that the Gentiles by my mouth should hear the word of the gospel, and believe.

We are not told if the apostles and elders met in private or in public for this council. There were evidently differences of opinion among them, for much arguing took place on the issue at hand. Peter stood up and reviewed the fact that God had chosen him to go to the Gentiles at Caesarea and give them the gospel so that they might believe and be converted to Christ. Details regarding this incident may be found in Acts 10:1-11:18. It had already been agreed by the church that God had opened the door of salvation to the Gentiles by faith apart from the Mosaic law. This should have pointed out the direction for the current council to take.

B. Comparison: 8-9
8. And God, which knoweth the hearts, bare them witness, giving them the Holy Ghost, even as he did unto us;

Peter reminded them of the fact that God knows the hearts of all men, Jew and Gentile alike. God had born witness to the reality of Gentiles receiving the gift of salvation through the ministry of the Holy Spirit, and it had paralleled the experience of the Jewish believers.

9. And put no difference between us and them, purifying their hearts by faith.

Here was the basic principle toward which Peter was pushing the council. God had saved Gentiles at Caesarea by purifying their hearts through faith. Salvation for them was the same as salvation for believing Jews. It naturally followed that the works of the Mosaic law had nothing to do with salvation. Paul would later put the law in proper perspective by calling it a schoolmaster to lead the Jews to faith in Christ (Gal. 3:24-26). Peter wanted the council to accept the conversion of other Gentiles in other lands on the same basis as those saved in Caesarea.

C. Conversion: 10-12
10. Now therefore why tempt ye God, to put a yoke upon the neck of the disciples, which neither our fathers nor we were able to bear?

Peter said that it was wrong to tempt (test) God by trying to put a yoke (requirement) on the necks of Gentiles believers which neither current nor past Jews had been able to bear. This referred to the Mosaic law and its ceremonial regulations in particular, things which had been types fulfilled in Jesus Christ.

11. But we believe that through the grace of the Lord Jesus Christ we shall be saved, even as they.

Peter obviously directed this comment toward his fellow Jewish believers. They had to realize that faith alone saved them, too, apart from works of the law.

12. Then all the multitude kept silence, and gave audience to Barnabas and Paul, declaring what miracles and wonders God had wrought among the Gentiles by them.

The crisis appeared to be past now, although some secondary matters had to be discussed by the council. In the meantime, Barnabas and Paul were given opportunity to tell about their adventures on their first missionary journey. They told about the miraculous things God had done through them as they had ministered among the Gentiles.

It would appear that the apostles and elders had further discussion and then had James, the half-brother of Jesus, announce the results. The council had decided that Gentiles should not be required to keep the law of Moses. However, in order to avoid offending pious Jews among whom they lived in various lands, they were to abstain from idols, fornication, strangled animals, and consumption of blood (Acts 15:13-21).

Letters were drawn up to the Gentile churches by the apostles and elders to send by the hands of such men as Paul, Barnabas, Judas Barsabas, and Silas. These would give official notice from the church council that the Judaizers were to be resisted and that salvation was by faith in Christ alone, apart from requirements of the law (Acts 13:22-29).

The enlarged delegation made it back to Antioch and reported the council's decisions to a multitude of believers. Judas and Silas shared in the ministry there, and Silas stayed behind when Judas returned to Jerusalem (Acts 15:30-34).

Evangelistic Emphasis

When we sift through the agitation of the controversy in this text, a glorious fact emerges. Huge numbers of Gentiles were being brought to faith. Those who kept their eye on this were filled with joy. Those who were distracted by the noise of the controversy were distraught.

There is a lesson here for us. When people work together closely, differences always will occur. If the people focus on the differences they will be discouraged and upset. If, however, they concentrate on their mission, the differences fade in significance.

The most important thing to all of us is that Christ died for our sins. That message can be preached. Souls can be saved. In comparison to that, our differences of opinion, though strong, are of minor importance.

This does not imply that we have to stifle our perception of the Christian message. We can affirm our views strongly and can oppose views that we think incorrect. We do this always, however, in the context of the knowledge that Christ can be preached even when opinions on lesser matters do not agree. It is more important to win a soul than to win an argument.

Memory Selection

"We believe that through the grace of the Lord Jesus Christ we shall be saved, even as they (the Gentiles)."
Acts 15:11.

The salvation of the Gentiles was by grace. They had a background of paganism. They had been involved in idolatry. Fornication was often a part of their worship. It was not unusual for the fertility cults to have temple prostitutes. The eating of things that had been offered to an idol was a type of communion with the idol. These sacrifices, naturally, were not in harmony with Jewish dietary laws. It took a lot of grace to bring people with such backgrounds into relationship with the one true God. The Gentiles were saved by grace.

However, Peter reminds the Jews that they, too, had been saved by grace. Their problems had been different, but they nonetheless required the grace of God to bring them the benefits of the death of Christ. They had not kept the law. Peter reminds them that "neither our fathers nor we were able to bear" the yoke that some were wanting to impose on the Gentiles. In spite of the fact that the Jews had had special teachers and blessings they still were in violation.

Peter urged them to recognize that all were in the same boat and were dependent on grace for salvation.

Weekday Problems

A group of young adults became involved in home Bible studies and devotions. A strong spirit of new life grew among them. The periods of fellowship, spontaneous prayer, testifying, and long sessions of introspection brought them to a state of excitement and joy. They had never felt so understood or so in touch with God. They had never felt that their faith was so relevant to the daily activities of their lives.

These young people had an urgent desire to share their new found joy with the rest of the church. They were members of a sedate church. Some of the members had been there for forty or more years. The older members were comfortable with familiarity. The spontaneity of the young people made them nervous. They did not like not knowing what to expect in a worship service and did not know where such practices would lead.

* How can these two groups worship together in a way that honors their needs and convictions?
* Sort out the things that you would consider essential to the Christian faith in the views of both the young and the old.
* What are the areas where mutual consideration can be shown?

Superintendent's Sermonette

In making individuals different from one another God provides opportunity for conflicting opinions to appear. This may not necessarily lead to conflict, but it can sometimes. People on opposite sides of an issue may be sincere in how they think and feel about it, but some way must be found to resolve the situation or they will separate. Compromise works in many secondary matters regarding personal preferences, but it must not be allowed to dominate doctrinal beliefs. Once God's truth is determined, it should be firmly held.

Our lesson today describes tension which developed between Judaizers and Christians in the first century. Judaizers demanded that all believers adhere to the law of Moses, including circumcision. Paul, Barnabas, and Peter argued that believers were saved by faith in Christ alone, apart from the law. It took a church council to decide in favor of justification by faith alone. Be wary of any person or group which demands man-made works in addition to faith in Christ. Defend Christian liberty which is based on grace alone

This Lesson in **Your** Life

These Jews had a problem that is common to all of us. They were more comfortable with others who shared their point of view. They were willing to bend enough to allow Gentiles to come into the church, but they wanted the Gentiles to become more like them first. That would make it possible for the Gentiles to be received without making it necessary for the Jews to make such a large adjustment in their views.

We also tend to be more comfortable with people who will become more like us before they come into our fellowship. I was quite unaware of this characteristic in myself until I moved out of the country for a period of time. I found myself in an area where some of my regional biases were not shared. Things were done in a different way. It was not wrong, but it was disconcerting because it was different. At a later date I had occasion to be with a church that reflected a much more basic cultural difference. I could admire the work they did, but could not have been comfortable as a permanent member of that church. We need to be patient with these Jewish Christians because they are not that different from us.

Another lesson we need to learn from this passage is that there can be vigorous differences of opinion and they can be strongly expressed without destroying the fellowship of the body of Christ. Here there was a spirited debate. However, mutual respect was maintained and good leadership was exercised and the unity of the body was protected. When dissenting opinions can be freely expressed it maintains the integrity of the body. It also facilitates learning because points of view are sharply challenged and contrary views are clearly affirmed. Another value is that it makes those with minority views feel included.

Strong opinions are not to be discouraged in the church. They should be expressed with consideration but the church is not to be a collection of timid people who do not think and who do not speak out.

The church at Jerusalem is an example to us in the way differences should be handled. They did not panic but called for calm consideration. They were clear on the fact that the admission of the Gentiles was not a debatable matter. It was a matter of the revelation of God and could not be debated. However, what should be expected of the new converts was a matter of legitimate difference of opinion and could be strongly argued.

Essentially, the outcome was that the Jews were asked to accept the Gentiles and the Gentiles were asked to honor Jewish sensibilities. They were to avoid the sins of paganism and not flaunt their freedom by doing that which was offensive to the Jews.

Even severe controversies can often be settled without alienation. Some principles that will help with this are

1) Areas of agreement should be carefully sorted out. Both Jew and Gentile in this passage could rejoice at the advancement of the gospel.

2) A determination should be made of what differences can be tolerated without violating basic faith. There are some things that all of us can tolerate in others that we would not do ourselves.

3) All possible concessions should be made to another's opinion in a spirit of Christian charity. We must all go beyond what we see the requirements to be to allow others an area of grace.

Seed Thoughts

1. Is being sincere all that ought to be required of people?
No, because it is possible to be sincerely wrong about things. Judaizers who came to Antioch were wrong.

2. What kind of circumcision is important to Christians?
It is not the physical circumcision demanded by the law of Moses but spiritual circumcision of the heart (Rom. 2:29).

3. How may converts be defended against doctrinal marauders?
God will provide mature believers to come to their aid. Paul and Barnabas did this for Gentiles in Antioch.

4. What should local church leaders do if a situation is deadlocked?
They should appeal to a higher authority for resolution of the problem. Discuss what this is for your church.

5. How can a trip for one purpose also serve another purpose?
The delegation from Antioch testified of God's blessings enroute to Jerusalem.

(Please Turn Page)

---

1. Is being sincere all that ought to be required of people?

2. What kind of circumcision is important to Christians?

3. How may converts be defended against doctrinal marauders?

4. What should local church leaders do if a situation is deadlocked?

5. How can a trip for one purpose also serve another purpose?

6. What helps tie separated believers together as a whole?

7. How should troublemakers be handled by the church?

8. What role can history play in resolving conflicts?

9. Who is the great Comforter and Facilitator in the church?

10. What should be the relationship of works and faith?

Seed Thoughts - Continued

No, because it is possible to be sincerely wrong about things. Judaizers who came to Antioch were wrong.

It is not the physical circumcision demanded by the law of Moses but spiritual circumcision of the heart (Rom. 2:29).

God will provide mature believers to come to their aid. Paul and Barnabas did this for Gentiles in Antioch.

They should appeal to a higher authority for resolution of the problem. Discuss what this is for your church.

The delegation from Antioch testified of God's blessings enroute to Jerusalem.

Believers should visit other groups in other places and reveal what God is doing in their lives.

They may be tolerated, cautioned, and even expelled, if necessary, but whatever is done should be done in love.

Experiences of the past may be reviewed to see if parallel situations existed which can shed light on current problems.

This has to be the Holy Spirit (John 14:16-17; Acts 15:8, 28). He was given to promote harmony among believers.

Works should grow out of saving faith. This is aptly described in Ephesians 2:8-10. Read and meditate on it.

6. What helps tie separated believers together as a whole?
Believers should visit other groups in other places and reveal what God is doing in their lives.

7. How should troublemakers be handled by the church?
They may be tolerated, cautioned, and even expelled, if necessary, but whatever is done should be done in love.

8. What role can history play in resolving conflicts?
Experiences of the past may be reviewed to see if parallel situations existed which can shed light on current problems.

9. Who is the great Comforter and Facilitator in the church?
This has to be the Holy Spirit (John 14:16-17; Acts 15:8, 28). He was given to promote harmony among believers.

10. What should be the relationship of works and faith?
Works should grow out of saving faith. This is aptly described in Ephesians 2:8-10. Read and meditate on it.

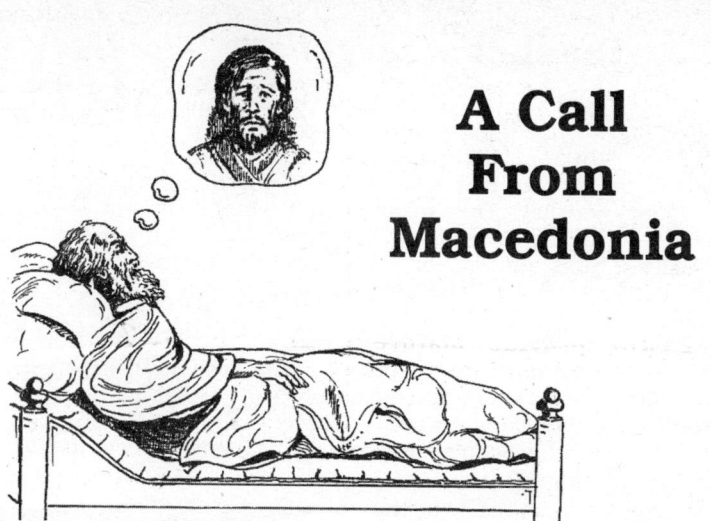

A Call From Macedonia

Acts 16:9. And a vision appeared to Paul in the night; There stood a man of Macedonia, and prayed him, saying, Come over into Macedonia, and help us.
10. And after he had seen the vision, immediately we endeavored to go into Macedonia, assuredly gathering that the Lord had called us for to preach the gospel unto them.
11. Therefore loosing from Troas, we came with a straight course to Samothracia, and the next day to Neapolis;
12. And from thence to Philippi, which is the chief city of that part of Macedonia, and a colony: and we were in that city abiding certain days. Acts 16:16. And it came to pass, as we went to prayer, a certain damsel possessed with a spirit of divination met us, which brought her masters much gain by soothsaying:
17. The same followed Paul and us, and cried, saying, These men are the servants of the most high God, which show unto us the way of salvation.
18. And this did she many days. But Paul being grieved, turned and said to the spirit, I command thee in the name of Jesus Christ to come out of her. And he came out the same hour.
19. And when her masters saw that the hope of their gains was gone they caught Paul and Silas, and drew them into the marketplace unto the rulers,
20. And brought them to the magistrates, saying, These men, being Jews, do exceedingly trouble our city,
21. And teach customs, which are not lawful for us to receive, neither to observe, being Romans.
22. And the multitude rose up together against them: and the magistrates rent off their clothes, and commanded to beat them.
23. And when they had laid many stripes upon them, they cast them into prison, charging the jailer to keep them safely.

MEMORY SELECTION
Acts 16:9-10
DEVOTIONAL READING
Colossians 1:3-14

BACKGROUND SCRIPTURE
Acts 15:36-16:23
PRINTED SCRIPTURE
Acts 16:9-12, 17-23

Teacher's Target

The decision by the council at Jerusalem cleared the way for expansion of the gospel to the Gentiles. Not long after Paul and Barnabas returned to Antioch, they agreed that it was time to make a second missionary journey. They disagreed on whether or not John Mark should accompany them. Barnabas chose Mark and left for Cyprus. Paul chose Silas and left for Syria and Cilicia. Moving on to Derbe and Lystra, Paul met Timothy and added him to his team (Acts 15:36—16:5).

Help your students to see in this lesson's text that the Holy Spirit directs believers into specific places of ministry, even if persecution awaits them there. God wanted Europe evangelized, for He knew that it was believers in Europe who would eventually take the gospel to the world. Paul and his team were God's instruments to begin that work.

Lesson Introduction

God's timing is important in His master plan of redemption. Paul wanted to evangelize the provinces of Asia and Bithynia in western and northern Asia Minor (Turkey), but he was forbidden to do this by the Holy Spirit (Acts 16:6-7). He later preached the gospel at Ephesus (Acts 19:1-20:1), but we have no record of his preaching in Bithynia. God used others to evangelize it, because Governor Pliny wrote of there being many believers there by the end of the first century.

Our text today tells how God moved Paul and his team into position in Macedonia (northern Greece) on the European side of the Aegean Sea. It was in Europe that tremendous events were scheduled to take place. Explorers, tradesmen, and missionaries would go out from that continent to change the map of the globe. Christianity came mainly from Europe before it came mainly from North America.

Teaching Outline

I. Call: Acts 16:9-12
   A. Direction: 9-10
   B. Departure: 11-12

II. Command: Acts 16:16-18
   A. Damsel: 16-17
   B. Deliverance: 18

III. Charge: Acts 16:19-21
   A. Detractors: 19
   B. Denunciation: 20-21

Daily Bible Readings

Mon. Paul and Barnabas Differ
Acts 15:36-41
Tue. Timothy Recruited
Acts 16:1-3
Wed. A Closed Door
Acts 16:4-8
Thu. A Divine Call
Acts 16:9-10
Fri. Conversion of Lydia
Acts 16:11-15
Sat. A spirit Cast Out
Acts 16:16-18
Sun. Opposition and Prison
Acts 16:19-23

Verse By Verse

I. Call: Acts 16:9-12

A. Direction: 9-10

9. And a vision appeared to Paul in the night; there stood a man of Macedonia, and prayed him, saying, Come over into Macedonia, and help us.

Passing by or through Mysia, Paul came to the Aegean seaport of Troas, site of the famous Trojan War in the twelfth century B.C. God gave him a vision that night. In it he saw a man of Macedonia stand and beg him to come over to his country and help him and others there. He was not named or identified and probably served as a general representative of his people.

10. And after he had seen the vision, immediately we endeavored to go into Macedonia, assuredly gathering that the Lord had called us for to preach the gospel unto them.

The "we" in this verse may indicate that Luke, the physician, joined Paul's team here. He authored the gospel bearing his name and the book of Acts (Luke 1:1-4; Acts 1:1-2). Luke made it clear that the vision was accepted by the missionaries as a directive from the Lord to move on from the continent of Asia to the continent of Europe. Direction had been given by the Spirit forbidding them to minister in the provinces of Asia (western Turkey) and Bithynia (south of the Black Sea) and by the vision beckoning them to Macedonia. We see in this the value of what appear to be both negative and positive influences on our lives.

B. Departure: 11-12

11. Therefore loosing from Troas, we came with a straight course to Samothracia, and the next day to Neapolis;

12a. And from thence to Philippi, which is the chief city of that part of Macedonia, and a colony: . . .

Embarking at Troas, the team went straight across the Aegean Sea, stopping at the island of Samothracia overnight, and continuing on to the seaport of Neapolis on the mainland the following day. From there they moved inland to the city of Philippi some ten miles away. Philippi was the main city in one of the four districts of Macedonia. It held the status of a Roman colony, allowing it to govern itself, be free from imperial taxes, and have the same citizenship rights as held by people living in Italy itself. It appears that no mention was made of Paul and Silas holding Roman citizenship at this time, but it would become a crucial factor at a later time (Acts 16:37-38).

12b. . . . and we were in that city abiding certain days.

We do not know the significance of this statement, but we assume that they spent the time familiarizing themselves with the community and perhaps waiting for the Sabbath Day to come, as implied by verse 13. The stage was being set for the launching of the gospel in the continent of Europe, and it was to have a modest beginning.

On Saturday the missionaries went to the riverside beyond the city where it was customary for prayers to be offered. They sat down and spoke to the group of women gathered there. God touched the heart of a woman named Lydia, a seller of purple fabric who had come from Thyatira. She worshiped God, evidently as a proselyte of Judaism or an enlightened pagan. She and the other members of her household were converted to Christ and baptized. She persuaded the missionaries to stay at her house (Acts 16:13-15).

II. Command: Acts 16:16-18

A. Damsel: 16-17
16. And it came to pass, as we went to prayer, a certain damsel possessed with a spirit of divination met us, which brought her masters much gain by soothsaying:

Satan did not like the missionaries making headway in Philippi, and he placed an obstacle in their path one day. While going to prayer, they were confronted by a taunting young woman who was demon-possessed. Claiming that she had the power to foresee the future, her masters made money from her services. She was a victim of both Satanic and human bondage with no prospect of deliverance apart from divine power. There are modern counterparts for her today, because Satan and unscrupulous men still enslave and exploit those who give themselves over to them.

17. The same followed Paul and us, and cried, saying, These men are the servants of the most high God, which shew unto us the way of salvation.

The irony of what the damsel said about the missionaries is that it was true but was apparently said in a satirical manner implying that it really was <u>not</u> true. It was a nuisance which the missionaries tolerated for their own unspecified reasons, but they must have been annoyed by it and wished that it would stop. It finally became unbearable.

B. Deliverance: 18
18. And this did she many days. But Paul, being grieved, turned and said to the spirit, I command thee in the name of Jesus Christ to come out of her. And he came out the same hour.

After enduring the damsel's taunting for many days, Paul's patience came to an end. He realized that the young woman was being controlled by a spirit (demon) within her and he commanded the demon to come out of her in the name of Jesus Christ. Within the hour the exorcism was accomplished, and the damsel was delivered from her bondage on the spiritual level. We are not told if she managed to be delivered from bondage to her human masters, but they may have lost interest in her once her supposed power disappeared.

Paul and his friends had just had a victory over the power of darkness, but they were to pay dearly for it when confronted by the delivered damsel's masters.

III. Charge: Acts 16:19-21

A. Detractors: 19
19. And when her masters saw that the hope of their gains was gone, they caught Paul and Silas, and drew them into the marketplace unto the rulers,

Having been defeated on one front, Satan now shifted his attention to another front. The young woman's masters were alarmed that they could no longer use her to earn money for them by fortunetelling. They had no joy in learning that she had been delivered from an evil power. They were concerned only that their income had been cut off. Their malice focused on the missionaries and on Paul and Silas in particular. They grabbed them and hauled them into the marketplace to face the local rulers. It has been suggested that Paul and Silas may have been dragged by their feet, thus suffering scrapes and bruises to other parts of their bodies. It seems obvious that the city leaders positioned themselves in the marketplace in order to see what was happening and be readily available to perform whatever functions they had.

We might wonder why Paul and Silas did not mention their rights as Roman citizens and be spared the indignities to which they were subjected. Perhaps they had no opportunity to do this in the noisy and riotous environment surrounding them. Perhaps they wanted to see how far this thing would go when they were considered to be only foreign Jews supposedly causing trouble in Philippi.

B Denunciation: 20-21
20a. And brought them to the magistrates, . . .
We are not told if these magistrates were different from the rulers mentioned in verse 19 or the same men. Whatever the case, they evidently had the power to decide what should or should not be done with those charged with any crime.
20b. . . .saying, These men, being Jews, do exceedingly trouble our city.
This remark, certainly implied the presence of anti-Semitism, hatred of Jews which has persisted from ancient to modern times. The fact that Paul and Silas were Jews seemed to automatically make them suspect as trouble makers in Philippi. This is true in our world today. Despite the many contributions made to humanity by professional and business Jews, they are despised by many. Christian Gentiles should search their own hearts to see if they are prejudiced toward Jews and then ask God to forgive them and help them to love His chosen people.
21. And teach customs, which are not lawful for us to receive, neither to observe, being Romans.
Along with being anti-Semitic, the detractors of Paul and Silas were also nationalistic in the wrong sense. They played upon similar feelings in other citizens of Philippi by denouncing the missionaries for teaching customs which they labeled unlawful to receive (accept) and observe (practice), seeing that they were Romans. Little did they realize at this time that Paul and Silas were also Roman citizens.

We cannot help but wonder what was going through the minds of Paul, Silas, and the other missionaries and converts at this sudden turn of events for the worse. The situation was obviously ominous and could turn into a life-threatening episode. Things had been going well up to this point, but now the prospects seemed very grim. Some may have even questioned the goodness of God in allowing trouble to come.

The outcome of this matter will be given in our next lesson text. Let it be sufficient to say here that God was working in the shadows as well as in the light, in the negative situation as well as in the positive situation. When things appear to be the darkest for us, we need to lift up our eyes and see the Lord's glory shining above the troubles facing us. These are character-building experiences which He allows to come into our lives to make us stronger.

Evangelistic Emphasis

Occasionally we read in the newspaper a story about someone who is robbed or beaten in plain view of other citizens who do not raise a hand to protect the victim. The fear of personal injury or involvement is greater than the desire to help a fellow human in trouble. There are circumstances which are so frightening that any of us would have serious reservations about becoming involved.

The best examples of human character, however, are those of people who are willing to accept personal risk in order to respond to another's need. Such was the example of Paul in our text today. His heart would not allow him to ignore the plight of this woman who was being exploited. Paul had every reason to expect that he would get into trouble if he interfered. Heedless of this danger, he cast out the demon and freed the woman.

Teaching the gospel to others is a loving and generous thing to do. Yet those who have done much of it know that it is a vulnerable thing to do. They expose their tender feelings of faith and concern to the risk of rejection or perhaps ridicule. Sometimes they encounter hostility. Often they are criticized for interfering in another's life or trying to influence another's religious convictions.

This text teaches that we cannot withhold the good news because of fear of repercussions to ourselves. We must summon enough strength and courage to accept the rejection, ridicule, hostility, and criticism that come on behalf of those souls that depend on us for their knowledge of the gospel. Remember that you may fail or be hurt if you do teach the gospel. Another might live and die without knowing Christ if you do not.

Memory Selection

"A vision appeared to Paul in the night... And after he had seen the vision, immediately we endeavored to go into Macedonia, assuredly gathering that the Lord had called us for to preach the gospel unto them."
Acts 16:9,10

In this passage we have an example of the Lord guiding his servant into the particular work that the Lord wanted him to do. It is true that the Lord does not always lead people in the same way. We will never have a vision such as the one Paul had. Nevertheless we are not aimless drifters, working but not knowing whether we are doing what the Lord wants us to be doing. We are part of a coordinated effort that is being guided by God to accomplish his mission in the world. That makes our spirited participation even more significant.

Neither can we conclude that because the Lord has not appeared to us in a dramatic vision we have no certain direction that we should be following. It is mandatory that Christians respond to the call of God. When we come to a clear vision of his plan for us, it is our responsibility to follow that plan. It becomes, not an option, but an ultimatum. It is not a "may" but a "must."

Weekday Problems

For as long as he can remember, Tim was groomed to take over the family business when his father retired. He did so twenty years ago and has operated it successfully and profitably since that time. He is conscientious and dedicated, both about his business and his faith.

Recently it has been discovered that the major food product that Tim's company sells is a cause of cancer. To withdraw it from the market would mean a serious setback, if not a collapse, of the company.

To continue to sell it seems unthinkable. This is the only business that Tim knows. He has no alternative way of making a suitable living for his family.

When he looks at his family he sees his parents who are living off of a retirement income that comes from the company. Tim's sons are depending on his income for their education and eventual livelihood. Tim and his wife have substantial financial obligations. The employees of the company rely on their jobs for their living.

* On what basis should Tim make a decision about what to do?
* What order of priority does he give to the concerns of public health, his family, his employees, his future?

Superintendent's Sermonette

It is important for us as Christians to see God's perspective on events in our lives. He sees the whole picture from beginning to end when we see only small parts of it. He knows how everything fits together for good to those who love Him (Rom. 8 28). By His Spirit, He directed Paul and his team to go to Macedonia and thus shift the expansion of the gospel from Asia to Europe When they arrived, they first had success with Lydia and her household but then ran into trouble with the masters of a demon-possessed girl.

One of the signs of spiritual maturity is that we learn to leave things in God's hands and not be dominated or depressed by events which seem to be against us. Seen from God's perspective, these events may be placing us into positions of divine blessing It is at this point that we need to develop complete trust in the Lord and allow Him to work out all things for His glory and our good. Are you willing to let faith guide you? Paul wrote, "We walk by faith, not by sight." (II Cor. 5:7).

This Lesson in <u>Your</u> Life

Paul saw a vision that gave him a clear sense of direction about doing the Lord's will. A confidence about what one needs to be doing is a necessary first step for a purposeful life. Paul could set sail for Macedonia without the ambiguity of wondering whether he had made the right decision or not.

We do not always have that luxury. We may ponder, "Should I go to seminary?" "Should I take a certain job?" "Should I marry a certain person?" "Should I move to an area where I can be more of a missionary?" "Would God want me to use my abilities primarily in helping the needy or in preaching the gospel to the lost?"

We have observed that those who flounder around, trying first one thing and then another, uncertain about what they really ought to be doing, cannot accomplish much. Paul knew where he needed to go and what he needed to do when he got there.

What if we do not receive as dramatic a vision? God has given us some guidelines that will help. A serious study of the Scriptures helps us to perceive God's priorities and relate them to our own gifts and talents. Prayer provides the option of stating our concerns and confusions to God and having him respond with guidance in his own way. Conscience often nudges us in certain directions. The counsel of Christian friends is an important source of insights and correction. A combination of these resources can give us a clarity that brings certainty about God's intent for our lives.

It is noteworthy that when Paul saw his duty he immediately set out to do it. Perception without action is to no avail. It takes courage to make the changes that are often required to follow the Lord's guidance. Sometimes people are asked to change locations, as Paul was. They may be asked to change their activity, their associates, and perhaps risk their reputation. Only those who are willing to act on the guidance of God will be successful in doing his will.

This passage also illustrates the fact that good deeds do not always bring the most desired result. Paul acted out of the goodness of his heart to heal the possessed woman. It was a blessing to her, but it was harshly responded to by those who had been profiting from her soothsaying ability.

It is normal for people to respond to goodness with goodness. Sometimes, however, as in this case, incongruous factors get into the way. When people are controlled by pride, jealousy, or a threat to their vested interests, they do not react naturally to good deeds. The people that used this woman's abilities for their profit were not able to rejoice with her at being free from the spirit of divination. They could see only the loss of their own income and they lashed out viciously at Paul.

We note also that accusations do not necessarily resemble the facts. Paul had only acted to relieve the burden of an innocent woman. He was accused of troubling the city and teaching illegal customs. Because he was perceived to be a threat to the power structure, those accusations were easily accepted and he was beaten and cast into prison.

Seed Thoughts

1. Does God speak to men through visions today?
He routinely speaks to men through His word, but He has the power to speak to them in anyway He chooses.

2. What was significant about Paul's vision of the Macedonian?
He saw it as a directive to take the gospel to Europe, This began God's plan for worldwide propagation of the gospel.

3. How did Paul's trip to Macedonia set an example for us?
He went immediately, and he went in a direct line. God expects us to implement His will quickly and directly.

4. How important is a point of contact when evangelizing?
You must begin with what you have. Paul met with women who prayed, and he made converts by the riverside.

5. How do Satan and his hosts affect people on the earth?
They seek to oppress, obsess, or possess people and control them.

---

1. Does God speak to men through visions today?

2. What was significant about Paul's vision of the Macedonian?

3. How did Paul's trip to Macedonia set an example for us?

4. How important is a point of contact when evangelizing?

5. How do Satan and his hosts affect people on the earth?

6. Can fortune tellers really see into the future?

7. How should Christians react to those claiming psychic powers?

8. How may a compliment seem to result in derision?

9. Why did God allow Paul and Silas to be unjustly accused?

(Please Turn Page)

He routinely speaks to men through His word, but He has the power to speak to them in anyway He chooses.

He saw it as a directive to take the gospel to Europe, This began God's plan for worldwide propagation of the gospel.

He went immediately, and he went in a direct line. God expects us to implement His will quickly and directly.

You must begin with what you have. Paul met with women who prayed, and he made converts by the riverside.

They seek to oppress, obsess, or possess people and control them.

No, but they may give some people the appearance of doing it.

They may count some as trickster and some as having unexplainable insights. (I Cor. 10:20).

Something good said about a person may be said satirically or derisively. A demon spoke the truth about Paul and the other missionaries in this way.

This was done in order to move them into position for spreading the gospel in an unusual place and way.

Seed Thoughts - Continued

6. Can fortune tellers really see into the future?
No, but they may give some people the appearance of doing it.

7. How should Christians react to those claiming psychic powers?
They may count some as trickster and some as having unexplainable insights. (I Cor. 10:20).

8. How may a compliment seem to result in derision?
Something good said about a person may be said satirically or derisively. A demon spoke the truth about Paul and the other missionaries in this way.

9. Why did God allow Paul and Silas to be unjustly accused?
This was done in order to move them into position for spreading the gospel in an unusual place and way.

A Song At Midnight

Acts 16:19b. They caught Paul and Silas, and drew them into the marketplace unto the rulers,
20. And brought them to the magistrates, saying, These men, being Jews, do exceedingly trouble our city,
21. And teach customs, which are not lawful for us to receive, neither to observe, being Romans.
22. And the multitude rose up together against them: and the magistrates rent off their clothes, and commanded to beat them.
23. And when they had laid many stripes upon them, they cast them into prison, charging the jailer to keep them safely:
24. Who, having received such a charge, thrust them into the inner prison, and made their feet fast in the stocks.
25. And at midnight Paul and Silas prayed, and sang praises unto God: and the prisoners heard them.
26. And suddenly there was a great earthquake, so that the foundations of the prison were shaken: and immediately all the doors were opened, and every one's bands were loosed.
27. And the keeper of the prison awakening out of his sleep, and seeing the prison doors open, he drew out his sword, and would have killed himself, supposing that the prisoners had been fled.
28. But Paul cried with a loud voice, saying, Do thyself no harm; for we are all here.
29. Then he called for a light, and sprang in, and came trembling, and fell down before Paul and Silas,
30. And brought them out, and said, Sirs, what must I do to be saved?
31. And they said, Believe on the Lord Jesus Christ, and thou shalt be saved, and thy house.
32. And they spake unto him the word of the Lord, and to all that were in his house.
33. And he took them the same hour of the night, and washed their stripes; and was baptized, he and all his, straightway.
34. And when he had brought them into his house, he set meat before them, and rejoiced, believing in God with all his house.

MEMORY SELECTION
Acts 16:30,31
DEVOTIONAL READING
Philippians 1:1-11
BACKGROUND SCRIPTURE
Acts 16:16-40
PRINTED SCRIPTURE
Acts 16:19b-34

Teacher's Target

Caught up in what amounted to a sanctioned riot in Philippi, Paul and Silas were subjected to beating and imprisonment because of the charge laid against them by the masters of the delivered fortuneteller. It was a disappointing development in the launching of the gospel in the continent of Europe, but it turned out well in the end. The jailer and his household were converted to Christ.

Help your students to look for the silver lining in each cloud which comes their way. God can take a bad situation and make something beautiful out of it. Some opportunities for witnessing come only through persecution. From the ashes of seeming defeat can come the phoenix of victory. Adversity turns to blessing in God's hands, and then it is only natural that He should receive all of the praise for what happens. The world cannot help but be impressed.

Lesson Introduction

It is the duty of authorized magistrates to dispense justice for citizens and foreigners alike. However, some of them buckle under pressure from an aroused populace, whether the rioters are right or wrong. This is what happened to the magistrates in Philippi when the multitude rose up against Paul and Silas. A public whipping and consignment to prison of the missionaries followed. The other believers must have despaired, thinking that this was the end, but God had other plans.

It is interesting to note the attitude of Paul and Silas. Although mistreated and bound fast in the stocks of the inner prison, they sang praises to God at midnight. Regardless of their present situation or what might happen later, they trusted God to use the circumstances in carrying out His will. Their expectation was fulfilled in a dramatic and fruitful way, and God was glorified.

Teaching Outline

I. Imprisonments Acts 16:22-24
   A. Severity: 22-23
   B. Security: 24

II. Impression: Acts 16:25-29
   A. Singing: 25
   B. Shaking: 26
   C. Seeing: 27
   D. Sparing: 28-29

III. Improvement: Acts 16:30-34
   A. Conviction: 30
   B. Conversion: 31-32
   C. Compassion: 33-34

Daily Bible Readings

Mon. Singing at Midnight
Acts 16:24-25
Tue. Released!
Acts 16:26-27
Wed. Mercy to the Jailor
Acts 16:28-29
Thu. The Ultimate Question
Acts 16:30-31
Fri. Celebration
Acts 16:32-34
Sat. Charges Dropped
Acts 16:35-36
Sun. Vindicated
Acts 16:37-40

Verse By Verse

I. Imprisonment: Acts 16:22-24

A. Severity: 22-23
22a. And the multitude rose up together against them: . . .

There were many parties arrayed against Paul and Silas. Satan was against them, because Paul had cast one of his demons out of the young woman who used to tell fortunes. The young woman's masters were against them, because the missionaries had deprived them of income. The multitude, aroused by what the girl's masters said, were against them. Severe repercussions followed.

22b. . . .and the magistrates rent off their clothes, and commanded to beat them,

The magistrates, pressured by the crowd, ordered their officers to rip off the robes of Paul and Silas and beat them, probably with rods. This was an illegal act. The missionaries had not been given a trial involving recourse to defense procedures. At a later time, Paul insisted that he be given just treatment as a Roman citizen. Bound, and about to be beaten in Jerusalem, Paul claimed his rights as a Roman and was not harmed (Acts 22:25-29) In Philippi, however, the situation was apparently not appropriate for this action.

23. And when they had laid many stripes on them, they cast them into prison, charging the jailer to keep them safely: . . .

In some cases, beating and banishment from the city might have sufficed, but the magistrates wanted more. Paul and Silas, bruised and bleeding from their wounds, were taken to prison. The jailer was told to keep them safely, giving them no means of escaping.

B. Security: 24
24. Who, having received such a charge, thrust them into the inner prison, and made their feet fast in the stocks.

The jailer was well aware of the punishment which he could receive if he allowed these prisoners to get away. It could lead to his own death. Therefore, he took them into the inner chamber and placed their feet in wooden stocks. This added indignity prevented the missionaries from moving about or tending to their personal wounds. Everyone assumed that the need for complete security had been met, but God had a surprise coming.

II. Impression: Acts 16:25-29

A. Singing: 25
25. And at midnight Paul and Silas prayed, and sang praises unto God: and the prisoners heard them.

Paul and Silas probably lay rather still during the daylight and evening hours, trying to recover somewhat from their beating. As midnight came around, they were feeling well enough to pray and sing praises to the Lord. The other prisoners heard them and must have wondered at their ability to act that way.

It is likely that Paul and Silas sang Hebrew psalms. They may have thought of Psalm 42:8—"The Lord will command his loving kindness in the daytime, and in the night his song shall be with me." By praying and singing, the missionaries were witnessing to others and making an impression on them. Prison became a place of opportunity to testify.

B. Shaking: 26
26. And suddenly there was a great earthquake, so that the foundations of the prison were shaken: and immediately all the doors were opened, and every one's bands were loosed.

This was such a localized and unusual phenomenon that it could not have been coincidental. God sent the earthquake to shake the foundations of the prison, open its doors, and loose the bands (shackles) from all of the prisoners. The fact that none of them was harmed during the shaking showed that this was a divine act for a specific purpose. Another amazing fact was that no one tried to escape, despite open doors and loss of shackles, and we assume that God held all there in the prison.

C. Seeing: 27
27. And the keeper of the prison awaking out of his sleep, and seeing the prison doors open, he drew out his sword, and would have killed himself, supposing that the prisoners had been fled.

The jailer had been sleeping in his residential quarters nearby. Awakened by the sound of the earthquake, he was appalled to see that the prison doors stood ajar. He decided that open doors meant escaped prisoners, including Paul and Silas, and he knew this could lead to his own execution. Preferring to commit suicide rather than face a cruel Roman death, he drew out his sword and was ready to thrust it into himself. One incident of prison guards being slain for allowing a prisoner to escape may be found in Acts 12:1-19.

D. Sparing: 28-29
28. But Paul cried with a loud voice, saying, Do thyself no harm: for we are all here.

Many prisoners might have been pleased to see the jailer take his own life, but Paul was concerned about it. He called out in a loud voice to advise the jailer to do himself no harm. It was unnecessary, because all of the prisoners were still on hand, perhaps held there by the restrictive power of God. The Lord did not want criminals turned loose on society. He simply wanted Paul and Silas to be free. The jailer's life was spared in order that he and his household might be changed.

29. Then he called for a light, and sprang in, and came trembling, and fell down before Paul and Silas, . . .

As the jailer came fully awake and noticed the unusual situation, it is quite possible that his superstitious beliefs prompted him to think of Paul and Silas as gods come down to earth in human forms, much as the people of Lystra had thought (Acts 14:11-12). Calling for a light (lamp, torch), he came into the inner chamber of the prison and prostrated himself before the missionaries. His action may have caused them some alarm, and they probably told him to stand up and count them as being fellow human beings.

III. Improvement: Acts 16:30-34

A. Conviction: 30
30. And brought them out, and said, Sirs, what must I do to be saved?

It is unlikely that the jailer was concerned about the salvation of his soul at this time, unless the missionaries had turned his attention to it before their arrest or while in his custody. The jailer may have wondered how he could save his life, but Paul and Silas gave him a theological answer to his question. They must have realized that the man was under conviction and was ready for the gospel.

B. Conversion: 31-32
31. And they said, Believe on the Lord Jesus Christ, and thou shalt be saved, and thy house.

This was the general statement capsulizing what the jailer and his household must do in order to find spiritual salvation. It required faith in the Lord Jesus Christ on their part. Perhaps the jailer had heard something about the gospel which the missionaries had been preaching in Philippi in previous days. Whether he had or not, here was the truth he needed to embrace.

32. And they spake unto him the

word of the Lord, and to all that were in his house.

This verse is very important. It tells us that Paul and Silas took time to explain the gospel to the jailer and members of his household, probably composed of family and servants. The general principle of how to be saved had to be supported by further details of what it meant and how to act on it. Saving faith comes through hearing the Word of God.

C. Compassion: 33-34
33a. And he took them the same hour of the night, and washed their stripes; . . .

The compassion of the jailer should be seen as an outgrowth of his conviction. Once he knew God's saving power, he was anxious to help Paul and Silas get cleaned up from the dirt and blood caused by their rough arrest and public whipping.

33b. . . .and was baptized, he and all his, straightway.

Christian baptism followed directly after conversion in the early church, and that was what happened to the jailer and his household. We are not told where or how this was done, but we assume that it was on the premises. There evidently was enough water to use for this purpose in that location.

34. And when he had brought them into his house, he set meat before them, and rejoiced, believing in God with all his house.

Following their baptism, the jailer and members of his household set meat (food) before Paul and Silas. They rejoiced about their newly-found faith in God through His Son, their Savior. As in Lydia's case, the conversion of the head of the household had led to conversion of everyone in it. It seems safe to assume that these individuals became regular members of the church which developed in Philippi.

The lesson text does not complete the account of what happened to Paul and Silas in Philippi. In the remainder of chapter 16, we see that the next day the magistrates send the officers to order the missionaries released. The jailer informed Paul and Silas and urged them to go on their way in peace. Paul refused, stating that the magistrates had ordered them beaten and cast into prison while they were uncondemned in a normal court proceeding, even though they held Roman citizenship. He demanded that the magistrates come themselves and fetch them out of the prison.

When the officers reported this to the magistrates, they were afraid of being punished for what they had done. They came and pled with Paul and Silas to leave the city. The missionaries complied, although they took time to visit the house of Lydia and comfort the believers before going. This incident helps to point out the fact that Christians have the right to demand their legal rights under human law whenever that is possible.

Traveling westward through Amphipolis and Apollonia, the missionaries came to Thessalonica for three weeks. Some Jews and Greeks accepted Christ as Savior there, but Jewish opposition drove them out. Paul and Silas went by night to Berea, where they found a better reception by sincere students of the Word of God. Jews from Thessalonica came to Berea and caused trouble. Paul left for Athens, with Silas and Timothy planning to join him there later (Acts 17:1-15). We find Paul at Athens in our next lesson.

Evangelistic Emphasis

Our text today overflows with good news. It begins by telling of a gospel that can bring singing out of pain. Every life has a significant amount of pain in it. There is no way to avoid that pain entirely. What the gospel does is give enough transcending joy to make it possible to rejoice even during times of pain.

We also have here a story which gives people a reason to live when they are trying to die. The jailer was so upset by the freeing of the prisoners that he wanted to take his own life. The message of Paul gave him not only permission but the incentive to continue to live.

Here is a story of a gospel that offers salvation to sinners. It is not simply a message of the salvation of the good or the salvation of those who have deserved it. It is a story of salvation of those who do not and cannot deserve it. That is why it is such good news to all of us.

Here also is a story of a gospel that allows us to give the most precious of gifts to those we love the most. Not only did the jailer benefit from the good news Paul and Silas taught him, but he also passed the benefit of that message on to his household.

What greater incentive could we have for evangelistic fervor than a gospel that can bring singing out of pain, one which gives people a reason to live when they are trying to die, one which offers salvation even to the worst of sinners, and one which allows the most desirable of all gifts to be passed on to those we love the most.

Memory Selection

"(The jailer) brought them out, and said, Sirs, what must I do to be saved? And they said, Believe on the Lord Jesus Christ, and thou shalt be saved, and thy house."
Acts 16:30,31.

Why did the jailer ask Paul and Silas what to do to be saved? A guard would not ordinarily ask such information from prisoners. What had they done that had convinced the jailer that they had this important information?

Perhaps he had noticed that they rejoiced in the midst of a depressing situation. It is doubtful that he ever before had had prisoners who sang and prayed at midnight. Their unusual serenity and joy while in jail must have impressed the jailer.

No doubt he was impressed with the fact that they declined to escape when the opportunity was afforded them. It is unlikely that this jailer had ever before had prisoners who would not flee when they could.

He may have been touched by the fact that they cared for his welfare. Most people in prison are worried about themselves, not about their captors.

The jailer may have noticed that Paul and Silas demonstrated their faith without embarrassment or ostentation.

We do not know all the details of his thinking, but we do know that this jailer was impressed enough that he asked for help from his wards.

Weekday Problems

Elizabeth has had a series of discouraging things happen in her life. Her mother was seriously ill and in a nursing home for months. At the last she did not recognize Elizabeth and was not able to communicate with her. Several months after her mother's death, Elizabeth lost a brother who was dear to her. Not long after that, one of her children had serious marriage problems and appeared to be headed for the divorce court.

When it seemed that a lot of things in her life were turning sour, Elizabeth had some discouragements at church. People seemed critical and unappreciative of her efforts.

Then a young neighbor told her, "I have watched you go through these struggles and have been inspired by your faith. You have caused me to resolve to be a better person." It seemed to Elizabeth that out of the ashes of despair had risen a cause for rejoicing.

* How can we learn to rejoice even in the midst of a discouraging situation?
* Can you tell of an experience when you were very discouraged and something happened to make you rejoice?

Superintendent's Sermonette

Christians should remain God's faithful servants, no matter where they go. Most of us may never be beaten and imprisoned for Christ's sake, but the possibility of it happening cannot be ruled out, We may attempt to fortify ourselves for coping with this, but we shall have to depend on the leading of the Holy Spirit if and when the experience comes. Jesus promised, "Lo, I am with you always, even unto the end of the world [age]" (Matt, 28:20). Paul later wrote, "Though our outward man [body] perish [or is perishing], yet the inward man [spirit] is renewed day by day" (II Cor. 4:16).

Our lesson text today describes how Christ by His Spirit was with Paul and Silas during their beating and imprisonment in Philippi. It reveals how their spirits were renewed in spite of the physical persecution they suffered. They were no different from other believers who have lived and suffered since the first century. If God sustained them, He can and will sustain us as we put our trust in Him. Let us continue to pray and praise the Lord in every harsh circumstance.

This Lesson in <u>Your</u> Life

A primary practical lesson in this text is that we should not let the circumstances of our lives determine the kind of person we are to be. Paul and Silas had been falsely accused, cruelly beaten, and unjustly imprisoned. If they had allowed those circumstances to determine how they would live, it would have been a dreary existence. They would have been consumed with discouragement and self-pity. They would have felt that they lived under a cloud of injustice. They would have responded to life with a whimper or a moan.

Instead, the darkness of that painful night was brightened by the sound of singing and praying. In spite of their surface troubles, Paul and Silas had much to rejoice about. Their relationship with God was intact. Their faith was firmly grounded. The cause in which they labored would prevail. Their sins were forgiven. They were bound for heaven. Those were enough reasons to sing.

All of us have enough troubles and pains that we could be demoralized by them if we would allow it. No life is so sheltered that it is happy because of external circumstances. Anyone who decides to concentrate on his problems will be able to convince himself that his life is made up of problems.

All of us also have enough blessings and joys that we have reason to sing and pray. This is not because of an unrealistic attitude which denies the difficulties of life. It is simply a result of a decision not to allow those difficulties to dominate our lives. Whether or not to rejoice is a matter of choice, not of context. Some who are much blessed spend their lives in complaining. Some who have much adversity find the ability to do a great deal of rejoicing. It is a matter of whether we choose to focus on blessings and be thankful or on problems and feel picked on.

One observation we should make from this story is that destructive decisions come out of fear. The jailer feared that the prisoner had escaped. Based on that fear he decided to kill himself. He made two serious mistakes. The first was that his fear was not based on facts. Fear is often not based on facts. The nature of it is that it deals in emotion and feelings. It is not objective. Therefore it can rarely be reasoned with and it often leads to devastating consequences.

A second mistake the jailer made is that even if his fears had been soundly based, suicide would not have been a good solution to his problem. We will be benefited if we will examine our fears to see whether they are legitimate. If we find that they are, we will be further benefited if we will examine our proposed solution to see whether it is healthy and constructive. Admittedly, it is difficult to do this while in the throes of high emotion. Yet the stakes are so high that it is vital that we attempt to do so.

To his credit, when the jailer learned the prisoners had not escaped, he turned toward a more promising decision. "What must I do to be saved?" he asked. This change of direction led to a whole new set of circumstances. Instead of becoming a suicide, he became a Christian. Further, he led his whole household in that direction.

Seed Thoughts

1. How might mob psychology affect believers in Christ?
Non-Christians may unjustly accuse Christians and turn a crowd against them, using techniques of mass persuasion,

2. What weakness may be found in secular magistrates?
They may allow injustice to prevail because of personal reasons or pressure from large numbers of people.

3. What is the responsibility of a person in a jail or prison system?
A staff member should be firm but fair in enforcing regulations for inmates.

4. What kind of attitude allows Christians to sing in the night?
It is an attitude of trust in God, knowing that His will can be done in the midst of the harshest circumstances.

5. Does immobilization shut down a believer's ability to witness?
It may restrict it but not shut it down completely. Prisoners, sick people, and shut-ins can find opportunities.

(Please Turn Page)

---

1. How might mob psychology affect believers in Christ?

2. What weakness may be found in secular magistrates?

3. What is the responsibility of a person in a jail or prison system?

4. What kind of attitude allows Christians to sing in the night?

5. Does immobilization shut down a believer's ability to witness?

6. What acts by Christians might impress unbelievers?

7. How might God change difficult circumstances for believers?

8. How should believers feel toward pagans who persecute them?

9. Are people saved as individuals or as groups?

10. What activities normally follow conversion to Christ?

Seed Thoughts - Continued

Non-Christians may unjustly accuse Christians and turn a crowd against them, using techniques of mass persuasion,

They may allow injustice to prevail because of personal reasons or pressure from large numbers of people.

A staff member should be firm but fair in enforcing regulations for inmates.

It is an attitude of trust in God, knowing that His will can be done in the midst of the harshest circumstances.

It may restrict it but not shut it down completely. Prisoners, sick people, and shut-ins can find opportunities.

Hearing them pray and sing sincerely in hard times will impress many.

He may change them quickly or gradually. He may use a dramatic method (earthquake) or something very simple (word of encouragement from a fellow believer).

They should pity their sinful condition and work toward their salvation. Changed hearts produce changed behavior.

Individuals must accept Christ for themselves, but households and even whole tribes have done it together.

In the early church, baptism and acts of compassion typically followed it. We would do well to have them today, too.

6. What acts by Christians might impress unbelievers?
Hearing them pray and sing sincerely in hard times will impress many.

7. How might God change difficult circumstances for believers?
He may change them quickly or gradually. He may use a dramatic method (earthquake) or something very simple (word of encouragement from a fellow believer).

8. How should believers feel toward pagans who persecute them?
They should pity their sinful condition and work toward their salvation. Changed hearts produce changed behavior.

9. Are people saved as individuals or as groups?
Individuals must accept Christ for themselves, but households and even whole tribes have done it together.

10. What activities normally follow conversion to Christ?
In the early church, baptism and acts of compassion typically followed it. We would do well to have them today, too.

A Proclamation In Athens

Acts 17:22. Then Paul stood in the midst of Mars' hill, and said, Ye men of Athens, I perceive that in all things ye are too superstitious.
23. For as I passed by, and beheld your devotions, I found an altar with this inscription, TO THE UNKNOWN GOD. Whom therefore ye ignorantly worship, him declare I unto you.
24. God that made the world and all things therein, seeing that he is Lord of Heaven and earth, dwelleth not in temples made with hands;
25. Neither is worshiped with men's hands, as though he needed anything, seeing he giveth to all life, and breath, and all things;
26. And hath made of one blood all nations of men for to dwell on all the face of the earth, and hath determined the times before appointed and the bounds of their habitation;
27. That they should seek the Lord, if haply they might feel after him, and find him, though he be not far from every one of us:
28. For in him we live, and move, and have our being; as certain also of your own poets have said, For we are also his offspring.
29. Forasmuch then as we are the offspring of God, we ought not to think that the Godhead is like unto gold, or silver, or stone, graven by art and man's device.
30. And the times of this ignorance God winked at; but now commandeth all men every where to repent:
31. Because he hath appointed a day in the which he will judge the world in righteousness by that man whom he hath ordained; whereof he hath given assurance unto all men, in that he hath raised him from the dead.
32. And when they heard of the resurrection of the dead, some mocked: and others said, We will hear thee again of this matter.
33. So Paul departed from among them.
34. Howbeit certain men clave unto him, and believed: among the which was Dionysius the Areopagite, and a woman named Damaris, and others with them.

MEMORY SELECTION
Acts 17:24-25
DEVOTIONAL READING
I Corinthians 15:51-58

BACKGROUND SCRIPTURE
Acts 17
PRINTED SCRIPTURE
Acts 17:22-34

Teacher's Target

Paul's righteous spirit was stirred within him as he waited for Silas and Timothy to join him in Athens. He saw that the city was wholly given over to idolatry. He began to reason with Jews and Gentile proselytes to Judaism in the synagogue. He did the same with any who would listen to him daily in the marketplace. Epicurean and Stoic philosophers took him to the Areopagus (Mars' hill) and asked him about his new doctrine (teaching) (Acts 17:16-21).

Help your students to analyze Paul's brief sermon on Mars' hill to see how the gospel was presented to pagans. Note his approach, his statement of truth, and the reactions it produced. Our witness to the unsaved is similar in many ways. We meet them where they are, give them the truth, and deal with their reactions. Confronted with the gospel, people always have varied responses.

Lesson Introduction

Did Paul say the right things in his sermon on Mars' hill? We find no record in the New Testament of a church being formed in Athens, although Paul left converts behind when he left there. Some assume that he took the wrong approach to the philosophers by referring to their own poets. They point to his remarks to the Corinthians afterward—"I . . . came not with excellency of speech or of [human] wisdom, . . . for I determined not to know any thing among you, save Jesus Christ, and him crucified" (I Cor. 2:1-2)—as being the right approach.

Paul was no more infallible than any other human being who preached the gospel from that time until now, but he did let the Holy Spirit lead him. He said what God wanted him to say at Mars' hill. The truth of the gospel is never affected by men's responses to it, even if they are primarily negative.

Teaching Outline

I. Approach: Acts 17:22-23
   A. Description: 22-23a
   B. Declaration: 23b

II. Appointment: Acts 17:24-31
   A. Description: 24-26
   B. Discovery: 27-28
   C. Difference: 29
   D. Destiny: 30-31

III. Appraisals: Acts 17:32-34
   A. Appraisal I: 32a
   B. Appraisal II: 32b-33
   C. Appraisal III: 34

Daily Bible Readings

Mon. Conversions at Thessalonica
Acts 17:1-4
Tue. Opposition
Acts 17:5-9
Wed. Noble Bereans
Acts 17:10-15
Thu. Idolatry in Athens
Acts 17:16-21
Fri. The Unknown God
Acts 17:22-25
Sat. The True God
Acts 17:26-30
Sun. The Resurrection
Acts 17:31-34

Verse By Verse

I. Approach Acts 17:22-23

A. Description: 22-23a

**22. Then Paul stood in the midst of Mars' hill, and said, Ye men of Athens, I perceive that in all things ye are too superstitious.
23a. For as I passed by, and beheld your devotions, I found an altar with this inscription, TO THE UNKNOWN GOD.**

We all know that ancient Athens was a center of learning. This is supported by Acts 17:21—"All the Athenians and strangers [outsiders] which were there spent their time in nothing else, but either to tell, or to hear some new thing." This had led to a massive accumulation of idols, for "the city was wholly given to idolatry" (Acts 17:16). In other words, Athens had become a focus for all kinds of pagan religions.

In his approach to the philosophers on Mars' hill, Paul remarked that he found them to be too superstitious (religious). To illustrate this, he said that in his moving about the city he had come across an altar inscribed TO THE UNKNOWN GOD. This implied that the Athenians wanted to cover themselves by being devoted to even an unknown deity. He might exist, and he might not, but they wanted to make sure that he was not offended. This was religion carried to the extreme. However, Paul saw in this an opportunity to present the true God to his audience.

B Declaration: 23b

23b. Whom therefore ye ignorantly worship, him declare I unto you.

Paul had the attention of his listeners now, for he offered to tell them about a deity they knew not. Their curiosity made them anxious for him to continue. He did not mention God's Son at this time nor that the Son had been raised from the dead, but he knew this would have to be done later.

II. Appointment: Acts 17:24-31

A. Description: 24-26

24a. God that made the world and all things therein, . . .

When witnessing to Jews, Paul began with references to the Jewish Scriptures (Old Testament) in order to establish a point of contact with them before leading them on to see Jesus as the Messiah and Savior. In Athens, speaking to the pagan philosophers, he began with references to the Creator of the universe, something they could comprehend.

24b, ... seeing that he is Lord of heaven and earth, dwelleth not in temples made with hands;

Paul compared the true God with the pagans' mythological gods which had been given literal representation in idols made of metal, wood, or stone. He claimed that the Lord of the universe could not dwell in temples (shrines) made by men's hands. Implied was the thought that He existed long before the stars, planets, and earth itself were made.

25. Neither is worshiped with men's hands, as though he needed any thing, seeing he giveth to all life, and breath, and all things;

Whether pagans would admit it or not, they were the ones who had formed the gods whom they worshiped, using idols to represent the gods they could not see. It was an entirely different thing with the true God. He existed before men existed. He did not need them, but he created them and gave them life, breath, and all things to sustain them.

26. And hath made of one blood all nations of men for to dwell on all the face of the earth, and hath determined the times before appointed, and the bounds of their habitation;

Epicurean and Stoic philosophers taught that the lives of men were governed by fate or chance. Paul claimed that it was the true God who controlled what happened to men. He made all nations of men dwelling on the face of the earth. He decided <u>when</u> they would live and <u>where</u> they would live, no doubt including various migrations from one place to another. It was because of God's sovereign control that men were appointed to follow a divine master plan.

B. Discovery: 27-28

27. That they should seek the Lord, if haply they might feel after him, and find him, though he be not far from every one of us:

God expected men to seek after Him as the first Cause of all that they saw in nature. We now refer to this as the ontological argument for His existence. He expected men to see design in nature and count Him to be the great Designer. We call this the teleological argument for the existence of God. Paul said that God was not far from any of the people He had created. Although He inhabited the highest heaven, He was also here on the earth among His creatures and could be contacted by them. Paul was not teaching the pantheistic idea that God indwells everything, but rather that He by His Spirit is omnipresent (everywhere present) in the universe.

28. For in him we live, and move, and have our being; as certain also of your own poets have said, For we are also his offspring.

Paul stated that all men live, move, and have life through the power of God. He said that certain pagan poets had described men as the offspring of God. He may have been referring to Cleanthes, Epimenides of Crete, and Aratus of Cilicia, where he grew up. Paul mentioned ideas of other philosophers elsewhere. His quote in I Corinthians 15:33 may have come from Menander, who may have borrowed it from Euripides. His reference to Cretans in Titus 1:12 may have come from Epimenides. Those who would criticize Paul for quoting from pagan philosophers should realize that truth is truth, no matter where it is found.

C. Difference: 29

29. Forasmuch then as we are the offspring of God, we ought not to think that the Godhead is like unto gold, or silver, or stone, graven by art and man's device.

Paul returned here to an attack on the prevailing idolatry found in ancient Athens. It was not logical to say that God existed and created men and then turn around and say that men made God, represented by images of gold, silver, or stone engraved by men's artistry. There was a vast difference in these concepts.

D. Destiny: 30-31

30a. And the times of this ignorance God winked at; . . .

Handle this statement very carefully. Paul did not mean to imply that there was a time in the past when God condoned the ignorance of idolatry. It means, instead, that there was a time when He allowed it to exist and overlooked it to the extent that He did not immediately judge and destroy idolaters.

30b. . . . but now commandeth all men every where to repent:

Now that the light of revelation was shining on the world, Paul said that God demanded men to repent of their sin of idolatry. This was universal, affecting all nations as the gospel expanded around the world.

31a. Because he hath appointed a day, in the which he will judge the world in righteousness by that man whom he hath ordained: . . .

Men of all nations face a judgment day set by God. On that day they will be judged by Him and will be counted righteous only if they are identified by faith with that special Man Whom He has ordained to be Savior. Details are given in the description of the great white throne judgment scheduled for the end times (Rev. 20:11-15).

31b. ... whereof he hath given assurance unto all men, in that he hath raised him from the dead.

Here was the explosive point Paul had to make in his sermon. He must have known that the Greek philosophers did not believe in bodily resurrection, and yet the raising of Christ from the dead was a crucial part of the gospel message and had to be presented. Whoever did not meet Christ in mercy and faith would have to meet Him in judgment and condemnation. The hope and assurance of eternal life was keyed to Christ's resurrection as Savior and Judge. The destiny of every person was and is in His hands.

III. Appraisals: Acts 17:32-34

A. Appraisal I: 32a

32a. And when they heard of the resurrection of the dead, some mocked; ...

The reaction to mention of bodily resurrection was immediate on the part of some of the philosophers, probably the greater part of them. They began to jeer Paul for saying it. Since there is no description of them arguing with him about it, we assume that they began to move out of the meeting place and go on their way. It was an ignominious way for the session to end.

B. Appraisal II: 32b-33

32b. ... and others said, We will hear thee again of this matter.

There were those who were still interested in Paul and what he had to say, but they had had enough for that day and wanted to postpone hearing what he had [said]. At least polite to have open minds.

33. So Paul departed them.

Having lost the major audience, there was little Paul could do but leave the Areopagus and elsewhere, He may have thought best to relocate in case detractors returned to make trouble for him as others had done in other cities.

C. Appraisal III: 34

34. Howbeit certain men clave unto him, and believed: among the which was Dionysius the Areopagite, and a woman named Damaris, and others with them,

There were a few individuals who embraced what Paul taught, and this led to belief in Jesus Christ as the Savior. Dionysius was a member of the Areopagus. We are told nothing more about a woman named Damaris and other individuals who became believers. We assume that they met together for mutual instruction, worship, fellowship, and service, but we have no references to them elsewhere.

Paul next went to the city of Corinth, a strategically-located city at the connecting point between Macedonia (northern Greece) and Achaia (southern Greece). He was there for a year and a half, teaching the Word of God and making converts to Christ. Following trouble there, Paul went back to Jerusalem and Antioch, Syria before embarking on his third missionary journey (Acts 18:1-23).

Next time we will study about Apollos at Ephesus and Achaia and Paul at Ephesus and learn how they were used of God to spread the gospel in these places.

Evangelistic Emphasis

Paul's sermon in Athens is a model of effective evangelistic techniques. They include the following:

1) Begin by recognizing the good. Paul noted the religious nature of the people of Athens and complimented them on their yearning to worship.

2) Identify with points of agreement. Instead of criticizing them for worshiping false gods, Paul told them that the god who to them was unknown is the God who made the world and all things therein.

3) Build on existing knowledge to expand understanding. It is axiomatic that everyone must start where he is. Paul started with their current state of awareness and led them beyond it to understand that God is not properly represented by things made by men's hands.

4) Connect the message of the gospel with the person. The doctrine of God is not a religious abstraction. God made us all. In him we live, move, and have being.

5) When the proper foundation has been laid, make the necessary connections. Paul pointed out that the God in whose image we are made cannot be conceived of in terms of stone, silver, or gold.

6) Call for a commitment. Gospel preaching is not for the sake of satisfying intellectual curiosity. It is an appeal for a verdict. Paul told the Athenians that God requires repentance and that the day is coming on which we will face him in judgment.

When you evangelize, follow these principles and you will be more effective. Give special emphasis to the step of calling for a commitment. It is the vital close which is so often omitted.

Memory Selection

"God that made the world and all things therein, . . . dwelleth not in temples made with hands; neither is worshiped with men's hands, as though he needed any thing, seeing he giveth to all life, and breath, and all things." *Acts 17:24,25.*

History seems to indicate that man has always had a problem separating the aids to worship from the object of worship. The tabernacle in the Old Testament, though portable, was an ornate and elaborate house of worship. Yet it was not divine, but a place for meeting God.

The temple built by Solomon was a splendid edifice made of the finest stone and wood. It glittered with gold and tapestries. It was a sanctuary for worship, not an object of worship.

In Athens there were spectacular temples built as gifts and expressions of reverence to various gods. Paul was teaching that these magnificent structures could not put men in touch with God.

Perhaps we still, in a more subtle way, sometimes blur the distinction between those objects which help us worship and the God who alone is to be worshiped. Let us honor structures and other tools for the contribution they make to worship, but let us be clear that only God is to be worshiped.

Weekday Problems

The debate reached a fever pitch in the church building committee. "We must build the most elegant and beautiful sanctuary we can because it reflects the value that we put on the worship of God," Stanley insisted. "If we build a house of worship the same way we build a school, warehouse, or shopping center, it will show that we value our faith in God only on the level of other interests in our lives."

"Nonsense," Earl rejoined. "God can be worshiped under a tree or on a battlefield. A church structure is a convenience to man, not a shrine to God. It should be inexpensive and utilitarian so people will focus on God, not on the church building."

"Besides," he continued, "those who would be induced to attend church because of an impressive building are coming for the wrong purpose anyway. It cheapens our faith to think it can be shored up with an ostentatious building."

Each of these points of view had a substantial following in the church. Feelings got so high that there was a danger that the church would split over the issue.

* Mention all the reasons you can think of for having an attractive and impressive church building.
* Mention all the reasons you can think of for having a simple, inexpensive building.

Superintendent's Sermonette

Witnessing for Christ may seem easy for some people and difficult for others, The fact is that it demands much from everyone who does it. Satan will try to prevent us from witnessing by making us lazy, unconcerned, or afraid. We will have to ask the Lord to energize us by His Spirit and open up opportunities for us to tell others the gospel message. We will have to depend on Him to help us say what we ought to say and do what we ought to do. If anything good is accomplished, we must give Him the glory and praise for it.

Paul was all alone in Athens while waiting for Silas and Timothy to come from Berea and join him. The need for the truth in that spiritual vacuum constrained Paul to get involved in witnessing for Christ. He was welcomed at first and invited to speak to Greek philosophers at Mars' hill. This honor soon turned to rejection and mockery when the resurrection of Christ was mentioned. However Paul made a few converts by his effort. We should witness even in difficult places and even if the results are limited.

This Lesson in <u>Your</u> Life

There are many ways in which God is unknown to all of us. We need always to be learning more. Some subjects we may be able to master, but God, never. The Athenians knew some things but not nearly enough. Further, they had some erroneous concepts that needed to be corrected. In many ways, we who are Christians know a great deal more about God than did these idolaters. However, it would be a mistake to suppose that we do not yet have areas of ignorance and erroneous concepts that need to be corrected.

Therefore we ought to approach every educational opportunity with a mind that is receptive to growth. That is not to suggest that we ought to spend a great deal of time listening to idle theories or philosophies. However, when we are in the presence of one who has done serious study, shown unusual devotion, or experienced noticeable spiritual growth, we ought to listen and observe carefully.

Paul's sermon in Athens emphasizes that there is a connection between God and all else. God made the world and everything in it. He made all of us. Therefore all of the created world reflects something of the nature of God.

Everything made shows something about the nature of its maker. A watch demonstrates something about the mind, the skills, the precision, and the logic of its maker. A house shows something of the care, talent, and experience of its builder. A garden or park is, in some ways, a picture of the person who planned and planted it. So, also, it is logical to perceive that the creation of God reflects the nature of the creator.

Paul says that God made of one blood all nations of men. At the time he said that, there were those who believed that there were superior and inferior races of people. Unfortunately, there are yet those who believe that. Some who do not assert that belief openly still hold it covertly. In the worship of God there is no room for racial prejudice. Every person alive is made in the image of God. When we scorn or abuse any one of those persons, for whatever reason, we are rejecting that which reflects the nature of God.

The sermon in Athens has a lot of basic theology in it. Paul emphasizes the sovereignty of God. God has not only created the world, but he has determined its seasons and boundaries. He does, as the song says, "have the whole world in his hands."

As awesome as the doctrine of sovereignty is, Paul says God is also near to us. In him we live, move, and have being. The God who sets seasons and boundaries is also the God who hears the prayers of children, the whispers of the weak, the crying of the lonely, and the appeal of the sinful. He understands and responds to these appeals.

Yet, although God is merciful and understanding, he is not weak or irresponsible. He requires accountability. He does not wink at ignorance, but requires repentance and has scheduled a time when he will judge the world in righteousness.

When we hear this message we are required to respond. Some of Paul's hearers mocked. Others delayed. However, some believed. It makes a critical difference how we respond.

Seed Thoughts

1. What is a good way to open a gospel message to people?
Begin by mentioning something familiar to them. Paul talked about the idolatrous shrines in the city of Athens.

2. Will people be offended if you tell them they are too religious?
As in Paul's case, this may simply motivate them to want to hear more of what you have to say. Many people today do not want to be called religious at all.

3. What did a shrine to the unknown God in Athens imply?
It implied that the pagans sought supernatural help from even a deity they did not know, thus covering all bases.

4. How did Paul utilize the concept of the unknown God?
He said that he knew Him and would describe him to the pagans in Athens.

5. How did Paul begin his description of the one true God?
He referred to Him as the Creator of the universe and everything in it. We may have to start this way with some.

(Please Turn Page)

---

1. What is a good way to open a gospel message to people?

2. Will people be offended if you tell them they are too religious?

3. What did a shrine to the unknown God in Athens imply?

4. How did Paul utilize the concept of the unknown God?

5. How did Paul begin his description of the one true God?

6. What argument did Paul use to show God to be greater than idols?

7. How can we oppose the secular idea that men are governed by chance?

8. Is God located in a distant place, or is He nearby?

9. Did God ever condone idolatry?

10. How may men react to the gospel of the resurrected Christ?

Seed Thoughts - Continued

Begin by mentioning something familiar to them. Paul talked about the idolatrous shrines in the city of Athens.

As in Paul's case, this may simply motivate them to want to hear more of what you have to say. Many people today do not want to be called religious at all.

It implied that the pagans sought supernatural help from even a deity they did not know, thus covering all bases.

He said that he knew Him and would describe him to the pagans in Athens.

He referred to Him as the Creator of the universe and everything in it. We may have to start this way with some.

He suggested that it was ridiculous for men to make gods and idols to represent them when God made all men.

We can teach the biblical truth that God exerts sovereign control over men.

Paul made it clear that God, by His Spirit, is omnipresent (everywhere present) in His universe. We may reach out and touch Him by faith.

No, but in ancient times He overlooked it in the sense that He allowed men to practice it without immediate judgment. He now demands that they repent of it.

Some may mock it, some postpone hearing it, and some embrace it and be saved.

6. What argument did Paul use to show God to be greater than idols?
He suggested that it was ridiculous for men to make gods and idols to represent them when God made all men.

7 How can we oppose the secular idea that men are governed by chance?
We can teach the biblical truth that God exerts sovereign control over men.

8. Is God located in a distant place, or is He nearby?
Paul made it clear that God, by His Spirit, is omnipresent (everywhere present) in His universe. We may reach out and touch Him by faith.

9. Did God ever condone idolatry?
No, but in ancient times He overlooked it in the sense that He allowed men to practice it without immediate judgment. He now demands that they repent of it.

10. How may men react to the gospel of the resurrected Christ?
Some may mock it, some postpone hearing it, and some embrace it and be saved.

Disciples In Ephesus

Acts 18:24. And a certain Jew named Apollos, born at Alexandria, an eloquent man, and mighty in the scriptures, came to Ephesus.
25. This man was instructed in the way of the Lord; and being fervent in the spirit, he spake and taught diligently the things of the Lord, knowing only the baptism of John.
26. And he began to speak boldly in the synagogue: whom when Aquila and Priscilla had heard, they took him unto them, and expounded unto him the way of God more perfectly.
27. And when he was disposed to pass into Achaia, the brethren wrote, exhorting the disciples to receive him: who, when he was come, helped them much which had believed through grace:
28. For he mightily convinced the Jews, and that publicly, showing by the scriptures that Jesus was the Christ.
Acts 19:1. And it came to pass, that, while Apollos was at Corinth, Paul having passed through the upper coasts came to Ephesus: and finding certain disciples,
2. He said unto them, Have ye received the Holy Ghost since ye believed? And they said unto him, We have not so much as heard whether there be any Holy Ghost.
3. And he said unto them, Unto what then were ye baptized? And they said, Unto John's baptism.
4. Then said Paul, John verily baptized with the baptism of repentance, saying unto the people, that they should believe on him which should come after him, that is, on Christ Jesus.
5. When they heard this, they were baptized in the name of the Lord Jesus.
6. And when Paul had laid his hands upon them, the Holy Ghost came on them; and they spake with tongues, and prophesied.

MEMORY SELECTION
Acts 19:6
DEVOTIONAL READING
Ephesians 6:10-20

BACKGROUND SCRIPTURE
Acts 18:1-19:20
PRINTED SCRIPTURE
Acts 18:24-19:6

Teacher's Target

Partnerships were formed in the spread of the gospel in the first century. Paul went from Athens to Corinth, worked with a couple named Aquila and Priscilla in tentmaking, and witnessed in the synagogue each Sabbath Day (Acts 18:1-5). Apollos went from Alexandria, Egypt to Ephesus, where he met Aquila and Priscilla and was taken beyond knowledge of John the Baptist to that of Jesus Christ (Acts 18:24-26). They smoothed the way for Apollos to minister in Achaia (Acts 18:27-28).

Help your students to see the need for cooperation in evangelism. Individual believers must assist one another through providing information, encouragement, and perhaps even employment. It is easier and more productive to move together as a team than to work in isolation. God blesses believers who love one another and work together in harmony. Individualism must sometimes be sacrificed for the sake of harmony

Lesson Introduction

This lesson features two servants of God at work in the first century. Both needed to be involved in expanded knowledge. Apollos came from Alexandria with a solid record of scholarship and eloquence, but his zeal for God was limited to a knowledge of John the Baptist. Aquila and Priscilla enlarged his understanding by teaching him about Christ and the Holy Spirit. He then became even more useful in God's service.

While Apollos was ministering at Corinth, Paul came to Ephesus and found disciples of John the Baptist. He enlarged their understanding by teaching them about Christ and the Holy Spirit, and they were baptized in Christ's name. Changes of heart must always be based on knowledge of truth. As in the cases of Apollos and Paul, we need to be involved in learning and teaching divine truth. Both we and those we teach will be influenced by it.

Teaching Outline

I. Restriction: Acts 18:24-25
   A. Dynamism: 24-25a
   B. Deficiency: 25b

II. Reformation: Acts 18:26-28
   A. Information: 26
   B. Influence: 27-28

III. Revelation: Acts 19:1-6
   A. Discovery: 1
   B. Deficiency: 2-3
   C. Details: 4
   D. Development: 5-6

Daily Bible Readings

Mon. Paul in Corinth
Acts 18:1-11
Tue. Paul Charged and Beaten
Acts 18:12-17
Wed. Paul in Ephesus
Acts 18:18-23
Thu. Apollos
Acts 18:24-28
Fri. Baptized in the name of the Lord
Acts 19:1-7
Sat. Preaching in Ephesus
Acts 19:8-12
Sun. Mighty Works
Acts 19:13-20

Verse By Verse

I. Restriction: Acts 18:24-25

A. Dynamism: 24-25a
24. And a certain Jew named Apollos, born at Alexandria, an eloquent man, and mighty in the scriptures, came to Ephesus.

The ancient city of Alexandria, Egypt had an excellent reputation as an educational, cultural, and business center. It was founded in 332 B.C. by Alexander the Great of Macedonia. It was the capital of lower (northern) Egypt and the chief port for shipment of grain to Rome. Mathematics, medicine, astronomy, art, and literature were taught there. It boasted a library of almost a million books and scrolls. Egyptians, Greeks, and Jews coexisted in it.

A man named Apollos had been born and raised in Alexandria, benefiting from its advantages. As a Jew, he had naturally been trained in the Jewish Scriptures and traditions. He was an outstanding public speaker. He made his way to Ephesus, located on the west coast of Asia Minor (Turkey).

25a. This man was instructed in the way of the Lord and being fervent in the spirit, he spake and taught diligently the things of the Lord, . . .

Apollos was a dynamic person. His fervency (zeal) motivated him to teach diligently what he knew about the Old Testament. He did what he did well, but he lacked important truth.

B. Deficiency: 25b

25b. . . . knowing only the baptism of John.

Jews from Egypt had evidently visited Judaea and had learned about the ministry of John the Baptist in the wilderness there. They may have even heard him speak and observed him baptizing people as a purification rite signifying a desire for the Messiah to come. Apollos had embraced this teaching but was restricted to it and knew nothing of the coming of Christ and the Holy Spirit.

II. Reformation: Acts 18:26-28
A. Information: 26
26a. And he began to speak boldly in the synagogue: . . .

After Paul had left Corinth, taking Aquila and Priscilla with him, he came to Ephesus and left them there while he went on to Jerusalem and Antioch, Syria. They were still in Ephesus when he began his third missionary journey (Acts 18:18-23). It was in Ephesus that they heard Apollos speak boldly in the Jewish synagogue there.

26b. . . .whom when Aquila and Priscilla had heard, they took him unto them, and expounded unto him the way of God more perfectly.

Aquila and Priscilla were impressed by the knowledge and eloquence of Apollos, but they realized that his understanding was limited. He could trace God's dealings from Adam up to John the Baptist, but he stopped there. He needed to be brought up to date and learn about the way of God more perfectly (completely). They took him aside and explained to him facts concerning the ministry of Christ and of the Holy Spirit. They helped him tie all of this together with the Old Testament and the ministry of John the Baptist following four centuries of prophetic silence.

Aquila and Priscilla had an

important task of informing Apollos about the development of the Christian church and its spread into the Mediterranean world. He must have caught a vision of the great work to be done, because he soon expressed a desire to move on to Achaia (southern Greece).

B. Influence: 27-28
27a. And when he was disposed to pass into Achaia, the brethren wrote, exhorting the disciples to receive him: . . .
Christians in Ephesus honored the desire of Apollos to move on by giving him a letter of introduction to take to believers in Achaia, recommending that they welcome him and use him in their ministry there. This must have been reassuring to Apollos as he contemplated meeting those who were strangers. The same type of thing is sometimes used today.
27b. . . .who, when he was come, helped them much which had believed through grace:
This observation by Luke, who was a Gentile himself, showed his satisfaction that Apollos was appreciated by Gentile converts to Christ in Achaia. They had been saved through grace, free from the works of the Mosaic law, and Apollos helped them to see that this was right and proper for them,
28. For he mightily convinced the Jews, and that publicly, shewing by the scriptures that Jesus was Christ.
Paul had been stiffly opposed by Jews when he tried to minister to them in Corinth (Acts 18:5-6). Apollos apparently was more successful with them than Paul had been, for he convinced many in public debates that the Jewish Scriptures proved that Jesus was the Christ. Both men had their followers in Corinth, something which caused Paul considerable apprehension when he wrote to the church there at a later time (I Cor. 3:1-8). He explained that he planted and Apollos watered, but it was God Who gave the increase to the gospel. We do not hear much more about Apollos, although he was mentioned in I Corinthians 16:12 and in Titus 3:13. He was one of God's chosen servants in the first century.

III. Revelation: Acts 19:1-6

A. Discovery: 1
1. And it came to pass, that, while Apollos was at Corinth, Paul having passed through the upper coasts came to Ephesus: and finding certain disciples,
While Apollos was at Corinth, Paul had been traveling on his third missionary journey by visiting and strengthening believers formerly won to Christ in the provinces of Galatia and Phrygia in central Asia Minor (Turkey) (Acts 18:23). In Acts 19:1 these were referred to as "upper coasts," meaning inland districts. Paul came down to the Aegean seaport of Ephesus, and there he found disciples (followers) of the Lord. We are not told if they were Jews or Gentiles.

B. Deficiency: 2-3
2. He said unto them, Have ye received the Holy Ghost since ye believed? And they said unto him, We have not so much as heard whether there be any Holy Ghost.
Paul wanted to know if these disciples had received the Holy Spirit at the time they had become believers. Their ignorance of the existence of the Holy Spirit makes us wonder if they were Gentiles, for there were many references to the Holy Spirit in the Old Testament. However, Paul's question might have referred to a specific anointing by the Holy Spirit such as other believers had experienced on the Day of Pentecost, and these people, even if they were Jews, had not yet heard about that.
3. And he said unto them, Unto what then were ye baptized? And they said, Unto John's baptism.
We find here the same deficiency in these people that we had found in Apollos. Both had been taught only up to the point where John the Baptist preached about the coming of the Messiah and urged people to be baptized as a sign of purification in preparation for the Messiah. They were not aware of the actual coming of Christ and the Holy Spirit nor of the establishment of the church.

C. Details: 4

4. Then said Paul, John verily baptized with the baptism of repentance, saying unto the people, that they should believe on him which should come after him, that is, on Christ Jesus.

The disciples in Ephesus must have been delighted to have Paul explain details about Jesus Christ to them. He did not denigrate the ministry of John the Baptist, for he showed that John baptized people unto repentance in preparation for the coming of the Messiah. Paul also made it clear that Jesus Christ was the true Messiah who fulfilled the predictions made by John. Although it is not recorded here, it is likely that Paul spent considerable time teaching these people much more about Christ, the Holy Spirit, and the church so that they might be ready to submit themselves to Christian baptism.

D. Development: 5-6

5. When they heard this, they were baptized in the name of the Lord Jesus.

Now that they were enlightened, the disciples in Ephesus were baptized in the name of Jesus. This was not merely unto repentance but unto regeneration, for they were to have new life in Christ.

6a. And when Paul had laid his hands upon them, the Holy Ghost came on them; . . .

There were similar events recorded in the New Testament. Peter saw the Holy Ghost come down upon Gentile believers in Caesarea, even before they were baptized with water (Acts 10:44-48). The apostles had bestowed the Spirit on converts by the laying on of hands. Peter and John had done it in Samaria (Acts 8:17), Paul, as an apostle, did it here in Ephesus. These would all appear to be extensions of the baptism of the Holy Spirit on believers in Jerusalem on the Day of Pentecost (Acts 2:1-4).

6b. . . . and they spake with tongues, and prophesied.

These signs accompanying the baptism of the Holy Spirit were mentioned in Acts 2:4 and 10:46, referred to above, and were typical in the first-century church. Some evangelicals feel that these gifts are still manifested in the church, while others feel that they ceased with the deaths of the apostles. ~~See what your church teaches on this subject~~. There were about twelve men involved in this account of disciples in Ephesus (Acts 19:7). We are not told if there were women and children in addition to the men.

Paul spent the next three months disputing with Jews in the synagogue there in Ephesus, When they strongly opposed him, he left and continued teaching in the school run by a man called Tyrannus. He kept at it for two years (Acts 19:8-10), although he claimed to have spent about three years altogether in Ephesus (Acts 20:31).

Miracles wrought by Paul in the name of Jesus caused many people in Ephesus to become believers, but this led to a riot by the silversmiths who made images. Paul decided to leave to visit Macedonia and Greece. On his way back to Jerusalem, he stopped at Miletus and sent for the elders of the church at Ephesus to bid them farewell (Acts 19:11 — 20:17).

Evangelistic Emphasis

There are a lot of evangelistic references in this text but let us spotlight the work of Aquila and Priscilla. They apparently were not gifted to the extraordinary degree that Apollos was. Yet they found a way to extend the gospel far beyond their personal ability to take it. It may be that the most important contribution they ever made to evangelism was their instruction to Apollos.

It is obvious that not everyone has the ability to be an Apollos. He was brilliant, eloquent, and had a charismatic dimension to his leadership. He had the power to convince and persuade multitudes of people.

He was made stronger and better informed by the work that Aquila and Priscilla did. The information that they possessed, when placed in the hands of Apollos, became a dynamic force for good.

You may have the potential to be the kind of leader that Apollos was. If so, your life can be extremely exciting and rewarding. Congratulations! The church needs you and will praise God for your gifts and accomplishments.

Many of the rest of us, however, will be aware that our role will have to be different. We may be equally dedicated and equally concerned, but we just do not have the same gifts. If that is the case, our task is to see if we can find an Apollos to encourage and support. Through our efforts we can make his (or her) work more effective. Through his (or her) achievements, our supportive ministry becomes more meaningful.

Memory Selection

"When Paul had laid his hands upon them (the disciples), the Holy Ghost came on them; and they spake with tongues, and prophesied."
Acts 19:6.

The doctrine of the indwelling of the Holy Spirit is strongly emphasized in the Scriptures and has been often neglected by the church. The Holy Spirit is to our spiritual lives what the soul is to the body. Without the Spirit we are dead.

With the Spirit, we are not only alive but are equipped for the work we have to do. We have God's internal guidance system in our lives. With the Spirit we have absolute security because the indwelling Spirit is the earnest (guarantee) of God's promise. With the Spirit we know that even our groans which cannot be put into words are understood by the one who knows the mind of the Spirit. With the Spirit we are empowered to do the work of God in ways in which we might otherwise be too weak.

Therefore, not to be aware of or not to appropriate the blessings of the indwelling Spirit would be a devastating omission to the Christian. Paul, in our text, is initiating new Christians into the glory of this blessing.

Weekday Problems

Jim is a bright young man who has recently been led to faith in Jesus by one of his friends. Jim's life has not been a model of Christian behavior. Illicit sex, drugs, alcohol, and serious brushes with the law are all a part of his background.

Jim has discovered that telling about these experiences lends an air of excitement to the story of his conversion. His eyes sparkle and his voice becomes animated as he talks about them. This has a dynamic effect on his hearers. This has created a great demand for Jim to speak and testify at various churches and youth groups.

Unfortunately, Jim does not know much about the Scriptures at this point. He does not seem very interested in learning. He enjoys the excitement of telling his story and the notoriety that goes with it, but he is not inclined to the hours of study that would strengthen his overall knowledge of the Christian message.

* You are Jim's friend. How can you help him to see the need for a more balanced approach to evangelism?
* What is the place of testimony and this type of excitement in spreading the message of Christ?

Superintendent's Sermonette

A person in the world who refuses to learn is going to find himseLf severely limited in what he can do, where he can go, and what he can earn. Education is probably the most extensive activity we have today. Spiritual knowledge is also important. We cannot make correct decisions or have proper emotions if we lack truths to guide us in what we think and feel. Most people favor education in worldly things, but only a comparative few are concerned about spiritual information.

In today's text we find two examples of deficiency in spiritual knowledge. Apollos from Alexandria was an intelligent and talented man, but he lacked knowledge of Christ, the Holy Spirit, and the church. The same was true of a group of twelve men whom Paul discovered in Ephesus. In both cases, informed believers were able to remove spiritual deficiency and lead sincere people into greater knowledge of God's way. Let us be teachable, and let us teach others, so that God may bless us and them. He seeks to increase our knowledge every day.

This Lesson in <u>Your</u> Life

Apollos had a lot of qualities we would do well to emulate. We might not be able to cultivate his eloquence, but we can become knowledgeable in the Scriptures as he was. Anyone who takes the study of the Scriptures seriously over a period of time can learn a great deal.

Some become discouraged because they do not see an instant result when they begin to study. That is an experience that is common to any type of education. In school we did not feel noticeably smarter at the end of any given day than we did at the beginning of that day. Yet as the days accumulated, so also did knowledge. After a year a difference could be seen. When we graduated from high school we knew a lot more than we did when we started first grade.

So also Bible knowledge accumulates, almost imperceptibly, but surely. I work regularly in a class of adults. Over a period of about four years they have completed a detailed study of Luke, Romans, I Corinthians, Job, Genesis, a New Testament Survey course, and an Old Testament History course. Anyone who dropped in for a single class would not think it would make that much difference. Those who have participated regularly know that it has made a substantial difference in their knowledge of the Scriptures.

Apollos was not only well informed, but he also was fervent in spirit. My favorite kind of people are those who have some enthusiasm. I once heard someone say that the one unpardonable sin of the pulpit is dullness. Preaching might be able to survive split infinitives, poor organization, and a rasping voice. It cannot, however, survive if it tells the remarkable story of God's love in a dull and droning fashion. We have to admire Apollos' exuberance.

He is also to be credited with teaching diligently the Word of the Lord. He treated the Word like a treasure to be handled with great care. He did not take liberties with it. He was a reliable teacher.

One important thing about Apollos is that, though a teacher, he was willing to be taught. He did not become defensive when Aquila and Priscilla took him aside to expand his knowledge. Truth is never in competition with other truth. The more we learn, the better off we will be. With his additional knowledge, Apollos became an even greater power.

This passage emphasizes the importance of receiving the Holy Spirit. Those who had known only the baptism of John knew about repentance and commitment, but they had not been introduced to the important source of strength, guidance, and identity that is available to Christians. They had been blessed by the Christian teaching they had received, but there were significant additional blessings that were available to them.

We see here the importance of staying open to the teachings and blessings of God even when we do not realize that we are missing any. These people at Ephesus did not know the Spirit because they did not know of his existence. We may already be much blessed, but there are no doubt still other blessings available to us as time passes. Let us stay receptive to them.

Seed Thoughts

1. How important is an education?
God expects believers to be well-informed, and He wants them to know divine truth and be governed by it.

2. What might have made Apollos eloquent?
Besides having natural talent, his training was probably largely oral due to lack of abundant paper at that time.

3. What did it mean to be "mighty in the scriptures" (Acts 18:24)?
The phrase implied intelligent and experiential knowledge of God's Word.

4. What was it to be "instructed in the way of the Lord" (Acts 18:25)?
It meant having a knowledge of God's dealings with men up to a point, even though further knowledge was available.

5. How was the baptism of John different from Christian baptism?
John's baptism was unto repentance in view of Christ's coming. Christian baptism was unto regeneration in view of Christ's sacrifice at Calvary.

(Please Turn Page)

---

1. How important is an education?

2. What might have made Apollos eloquent?

3. What did it mean to be "mighty in the scriptures" (Acts 18:24)?

4. What was it to be "instructed in the way of the Lord" (Acts 18:25)?

5. How was the baptism of John different from Christian baptism?

6. How did Aquila and Priscilla dare to teach the learned Apollos?

7. What should we teach others?

8. Was it right for Apollos to leave Ephesus and go to Achaia?

9. How important is the Holy Spirit in accepting Jesus as Lord?

10. What does the Holy Spirit do when He comes on believers?

Seed Thoughts - Continued

God expects believers to be well-informed, and He wants them to know divine truth and be governed by it.

Besides having natural talent, his training was probably largely oral due to lack of abundant paper at that time.

The phrase implied intelligent and experiential knowledge of God's Word.

It meant having a knowledge of God's dealings with men up to a point, even though further knowledge was available.

John's baptism was unto repentance in view of Christ's coming. Christian baptism was unto regeneration in view of Christ's sacrifice at Calvary.

They had information he needed and found him to be teachable.

We should share with them whatever we know in order to fill any lack in their knowledge of spiritual things.

Points suggesting the rightness of his decision were that he felt led of the Lord to go, other believers agreed, and he was successful in ministry there.

Paul wrote, "No man can say that Jesus is the Lord, but by the Holy Ghost" (I Cor. 12:3). See also Romans 8:9b and Galatians 4:6.

He convicts of sin, cleanses from sin, seals with God's ownership, sanctifies, comforts, energizes, and restrains them.

6. How did Aquila and Priscilla dare to teach the learned Apollos?
They had information he needed and found him to be teachable.

7. What should we teach others?
We should share with them whatever we know in order to fill any lack in their knowledge of spiritual things.

8. Was it right for Apollos to leave Ephesus and go to Achaia?
Points suggesting the rightness of his decision were that he felt led of the Lord to go, other believers agreed, and he was successful in ministry there.

9. How important is the Holy Spirit in accepting Jesus as Lord?
Paul wrote, "No man can say that Jesus is the Lord, but by the Holy Ghost" (I Cor. 12:3). See also Romans 8:9b and Galatians 4:6.

10. What does the Holy Spirit do when He comes on believers?
He convicts of sin, cleanses from sin, seals with God's ownership, sanctifies, comforts, energizes, and restrains them.

A Sad Farewell

Acts 20:17. And from Miletus he sent to Ephesus, and called the elders of the church.
18. And when they were come to him, he said unto them, Ye know, from the first day that I came into Asia, after what manner I have been with you at all seasons,
19. Serving the Lord with all humility of mind, and with many tears, and temptations, which befell me by the lying in wait of the Jews:
20. And how I kept back nothing that was profitable unto you, but have showed you, and have taught you publicly, and from house to house,
21. Testifying both to the Jews, and also to the Greeks, repentance toward God, and faith toward our Lord Jesus Christ.
22. And now, behold, I go bound in the spirit unto Jerusalem, not knowing the things that shall befall me there:
23. Save that the Holy Ghost witnesseth in every city, saying that bonds and afflictions abide me.
24. But none of these things move me, neither count I my life dear unto myself, so that I might finish my course with joy, and the ministry, which I have received of the Lord Jesus, to testify the gospel of the grace of God.
25. And now, behold, I know that ye all, among whom I have gone preaching the kingdom of God, shall see my face no more.
26. Wherefore I take you to record this day, that I am pure from the blood of all men.
27. For I have not shunned to declare unto you all the counsel of God.
28. Take heed therefore unto yourselves, and to all the flock, over the which the Holy Ghost hath made you overseers, to feed the church of God, which he hath purchased with his own blood.
29. For I know this, that after my departing shall grievous wolves enter in among you not sparing the flock.
30. Also of your own selves shall men arise, speaking perverse things, to draw away disciples after them.
31. Therefore watch, and remember, that by the space of three years I ceased not to warn everyone night and day with tears.

MEMORY SELECTION
Acts 20:37-38
DEVOTIONAL READING
2 Timothy 4:1-8

BACKGROUND SCRIPTURE
Acts 20
PRINTED SCRIPTURE
Acts 20:17-31

Teacher's Target

Drawing his third missionary journey to a close, Paul moved toward Jerusalem from Macedonia and Achaia. He bypassed Ephesus and landed at Miletus about forty miles to the south. He called for the elders of the church at Ephesus to meet him there. Our lesson text records about three-fourths of his remarks to them. This farewell address included a review, a disturbing prediction, a statement of determination, and a challenge.

Help your students to see into the heart of the great apostle and come away with an understanding and appreciation of what it meant for him to be a loyal servant of God. Remind them that intervening centuries have not altered the basic requirements of service from what they were in Paul's time. May they line up with what he wrote to the Corinthian church about service—"The love of Christ constraineth us" (II Cor. 5:14).

Lesson Introduction

Paul had been told soon after his conversion that he would have to suffer many things for the sake of Christ (Acts 9:16). As his life of service unfolded, he was persecuted often (II Cor. 11:23-28). All of these experiences seemed to prepare him to face the suffering he must endure as his ministry moved toward its end. Prophetic messages from the Holy Spirit were given to him in every city to let him know that trouble awaited him in Jerusalem (Acts 20:22-23).

The key to his fortitude may be found in I Corinthians 15:9-10: "I persecuted the church of God. But by the grace of God I am what I am: and his grace which was bestowed upon me was not in vain but I labored more abundantly that they all [apostles]: yet not I, but the grace of God which was with me." He counted God's sustaining grace as equal to whatever he had to suffer.

Teaching Outline

I. Past: Acts 20:17-21
   A. Summons: 17
   B. Summary: 18-21

II. Present: Acts 20:22-27
   A. Expectation: 22-23
   B. Examination: 24
   C. Exoneration: 25-27

III. Prospect: Acts 20:28-31
   A. Warning: 28
   B. Wolves: 29-30
   C. Watching: 31

Daily Bible Readings

Mon. Travel and Preaching
Acts 20:1-6
Tue. A Long Sermon
Acts 20:7-12
Wed. En Route to Jerusalem
Acts 20:13-16
Thu. Review of Paul's Work
Acts 20:17-21
Fri. What Paul Faced
Acts 20:22-27
Sat. Take Care of the Flock
Acts 20:28-31
Sun. A Sad Farewell
Acts 20:32-38

Verse By Verse

I. Past: Acts 20:17-21

A. Summons: 17
17. And from Miletus he sent to Ephesus, and called the elders of the church.

We are not told why Paul chose to stop at Miletus and call on the elders of the church in Ephesus to make an eighty-mile round trip to see him Perhaps he wanted to avoid a repeat of the kind of trouble he had had when last in Ephesus when the silversmith riot had occurred (Acts 19:23-41).

B. Summary: 18-21
18. And when they were come to him, he said unto them, Ye know, from the first day that I came into Asia, after what manner I have been with you at all seasons.

Verses 18-21 record a defense by Paul of his work in Ephesus, a theme to which he returned in verses 26-27 and 31-35. He claimed that from the first day among them in Asia (western Turkey) he had served them well at all seasons (during the whole time there). We do not know why Paul felt it necessary to defend himself as much as he did, but perhaps someone had reported criticisms to him and he wanted to set the record straight.

19. Serving the Lord with all humility of mind, and with many tears, and temptations, which befell me by the lying in wait of the Jews:

Paul said that he had served the Lord in humility. He had shed many tears and gone through many temptations (trials) because of plots by Jews opposed to him. We can well imagine that there were sympathetic nods on this from members of his audience who knew that he spoke the truth.

20. And how I kept back nothing that was profitable unto you, but have shewed you, and have taught you publicly, and from house to house,

Paul said that he had maintained an open ministry in Ephesus, He had kept nothing important back from them in his preaching and teaching. He had taught them in public and in private (from house to house). No one could justifiably accuse him of manipulating people by withholding secret information as the teachers of mystery religions did. Whatever he knew he had passed on to others as soon as they were ready to receive it.

21. Testifying both to the Jews, and also to the Greeks, repentance toward God, and faith toward our Lord Jesus Christ.

Paul claimed that his messages had been given to both Jews and Gentiles. He had emphasized the doctrines of repentance for sin when facing God and faith to believe on the Lord Jesus Christ when seeking salvation. Paul had told Timothy how to go about this work when he wrote, "Preach the word; be instant in season, out of season reprove, rebuke, exhort with all longsuffering [patience] and doctrine" (II Tim. 4:2).

II. Present: Acts 20:22-27

A. Expectation: 22-23
**22. And now, behold, I go bound in the spirit unto Jerusalem, not knowing the things that shall befall me there:
23. Save that the Holy Ghost**

witnesseth in every city, saying that bonds and afflictions abide me.

We are not sure exactly what Paul meant by saying that he was going to Jerusalem "bound in the spirit." He may have referred to his own inner compulsion of spirit, or he may have referred to a binding by the Holy Spirit which required him to keep moving toward Jerusalem. The cause of his apprehension was not clear as far as details go, for he had not been told specifically what would happen to him. All he had to go on were general predictions given by the Holy Spirit through various individuals in every city where he went. We find examples of this in Acts 21:4 and 10-11. Agabus distinctly told Paul that he would be bound and delivered over to the Gentiles, no doubt referring to the Romans.

B. Examination: 24
24a. But none of these things move me, neither count I my life dear unto myself, . . .

In spite of warnings of impending calamity, Paul declared that he was unmoved by them. He did not count his life to be more valuable than any ministry he might have in Jerusalem or wherever his enemies might take him. No doubt some of his friends considered him foolish and stubborn, while others may have admired his devotion and determination,

24b. . . . so that I might finish my course with joy, and the ministry, which I have received of the Lord Jesus, to testify the gospel of the grace of God,

It was clear from these comments that Paul saw his life as planned by God. He was on the racecourse of life, and he would persevere to the end. These sentiments were also expressed by him in Philippians 3:10-14, and you would do well to turn to this passage and read it to your students. The same concept is found in Hebrews 12:1-2, and some scholars think that Paul wrote that letter. He was determined to keep on the track laid out for him and to finish it with joy by ministering as the Lord Jesus intended him to do. He felt that he could testify to the gospel of the grace of God in all places and situations. He had examined his prospects, and he was undeterred from his plan of action.

C. Exoneration: 25-27
25. And now, behold, I know that ye all, among whom I have gone preaching the kingdom of God, shall see my face no more,

We assume that Paul spoke these words in a wistful tone, for he had come to love these leaders of the Ephesian church. He was referring to earthly contact, of course. He knew that he would see them all when he and they went on to their heavenly reward. It was this hope that allowed him to leave them at this time without being devastated.

26. Wherefore I take you to record this day, that I am pure from the blood of all men.

Paul adopted the defensive attitude he had displayed according to verses 18-21 and to which he would return according to verses 31-35. He wanted to make absolutely sure that no one would accuse him of doing less than he should have done during his time of ministry in Ephesus. In saying that he was "pure from the blood of all men" he may have been thinking of Ezekiel 3:16-21, a solemn warning to God's servants and well worth reading at this point.

27. For I have not shunned to declare unto you all the counsel of God.

The reason Paul considered himself to be free from responsibility for others was that he had faithfully declared to them the whole counsel (purpose, plan, message) of God. He could only go so far, and they had to make their own decision as to whether or not they would act on the truths he had given them. It was in this sense that he felt exonerated.

III. Prospect: Acts 20:28-31

A. Warning: 28
28a. Take heed therefore unto yourselves, and to all the flock, over which the Holy Ghost hath made you overseers, . . .

Having declared his own faithfulness in service, Paul now

challenged the Ephesian elders to imitate him. He urged them to grow spiritually themselves so that they would be able to oversee the flock of believers entrusted to them by the Holy Spirit.

28b. . . . to feed the church of God, . . .

The duties of a shepherd were many, for they included finding adequate pasture where the sheep could eat, protection from human and animal marauders, treatment of the injured, finding of the lost, and supervision of the lambing process. Paul wanted the elders at Ephesus to provide spiritual nourishment to those under their care in the church. This was their primary function as overseers.

28c. . . . which he hath purchased with his own blood.

This was an obvious reference to Jesus Christ. God the Father and God the Spirit are also mentioned in this verse. Thus we see reference to the Trinity here. It was by shedding His blood at Calvary that Jesus redeemed (purchased, bought back from Satan) all those who place their faith in Him.

B. Wolves: 29-30

29. For I know this, that after my departing shall grievous wolves enter in among you, not sparing the flock.

Paul now shifted his emphasis to the role of elders serving as shepherds protecting the flock of believers from marauders. He referred to false teachers as "grievous wolves" and said that they would invade the flock to cause havoc if they were allowed to do it. They would have to be confronted and dealt with by use of spiritual weapons. The chief weapon would be "the sword of the Spirit, which is the word of God" (Eph. 6:17).

30. Also of your own selves shall men arise, speaking perverse things, to draw away disciples after them.

Paul said that some enemies of the flock would develop within the church itself. Perhaps he had heretics such as the Gnostics in mind here. Their perverse (distorted, corrupt, false) teachings would tend to draw believers away after them, but they would have to be resisted and probably expelled.

C. Watching: 31

31. Therefore watch, and remember, that by the space of three years I ceased not to warn every one night and day with tears.

Returning to his defensive mood, Paul told the Ephesian elders to watch over the flock, remembering how he had done this faithfully for up to three years while he was among them. He had been very intense about this, shedding tears night and day to protect them from error.

In his closing remarks, found in Acts 20:32-35, Paul commended the elders into God's care and to the word of His grace, which was able to build them up in their faith and give them an inheritance (set of blessings) available to all who were sanctified (set apart _from_ sin and set apart _to_ God). He reminded the elders that he had coveted no man's silver, gold, or clothing. He had worked to support himself while he had been with them. He praised manual labor, not only to take care of their own needs but for charity toward the weak and poor. He quoted the words of Jesus, "It is more blessed to give than to receive," a statement found only here.

Paul knelt down and prayed with the elders. They wept and embraced him, sorrowing that they would see him no more (Acts 20:36-38).

Evangelistic Emphasis

The Book of Acts is a gold mine of evangelistic instruction and example. Note how much we can learn from Paul's work at Ephesus.

We note first that he had humility of mind. What an endearing quality that is. Arrogance repels and humility attracts. If Paul, as brilliant and accomplished as he was, was humble, it certainly behooves us to be humble also. All of us are sinners, saved by the grace of God. Of all people we should be most sensitive to this attitude.

Then we see what great care and feeling Paul had for the people at Ephesus. His tears showed how deeply he felt. The gospel is a gift of love. It breaks the heart of the true evangelist when the gospel is ignored or rejected.

Paul also influenced people by his faithfulness. While it is true that faith needs to be in God, not man, one must be true to his values if he would be an effective evangelist.

We also admire Paul's candor. He said, "I kept back nothing that was profitable unto you." The evangelist sometimes has to correct error, rebuke sin, and repudiate prejudices. He cannot always say that which is popular.

Paul was also flexible. He taught publicly and from house to house. This reminds us that the Christian who speaks to a neighbor is an evangelist. One does not have to speak to thousands in mass meetings. He simply has to tell the evangel (gospel) to someone who needs it. Some will be reached through mass communication but some will be taught one by one.

Memory Selection

"They all wept sore, and fell on Paul's neck, and kissed him, sorrowing most of all for the words which he spake, that they should see his face no more."
Acts 20:37,38.

What great love is shown in this passage. It made parting painful, but it would enrich the lives of those involved from then on. Paul would be sustained by the knowledge of the love of the Ephesian elders. They would be inspired by the way he loved them.

The blessing of a loving relationship does not stop when circumstances sever it. The most painful experience of my life was the death of my grown son. The warmth of his love and the tenderness of his affection are still with me. He left treasures that will always be mine. I cannot imagine what it would be like not to have had him in my life.

So these Ephesian elders, though heartbroken, were rich from their close ties with one of the greatest men who ever lived. They were left with a beacon of inspiration, an example of godliness, the instruction of a master, and the love of a saint.

The tears which blurred their vision could not completely block out their knowledge of how blessed they were.

Weekday Problems

As I write this I think of a saint I know. He is eighty-six years old and dying. He is in pain twenty-four hours a day and has been for over a year. He cannot get comfortable in bed and has, no doubt, already experienced his last occasion to be out of bed. He is rarely able to enjoy the taste of food and is past the time for visitors save for family and pastor.

He has a remarkable wife who is a ninety-five pound giant. He has an accomplished son who walks a tightrope between being attentive and being patronizing. He also has a dutiful and perceptive daughter-in-law and two grown grandsons who adore and respect him.

As he has set an example in living, he is now setting an example in dying. He is encouraging and commending in his conversation. He must think the time for giving instructions is past because he does not say much to anyone about how they should live. He just supports. He shows both courage and pathos. He is neither a stoic nor a complainer.

* If you learned that you had only a short time to live, what would you want to tell your family? Your friends?
* If a loved one had only a short time, what would you want to tell him or her?

Superintendent's Sermonette

Some people find it very difficult to say goodbye. They may avoid it, if possible. They may linger for a long time before going. They may do it quickly and brusquely in order to hide their true feelings. Then there are those who take time to express farewell in a deliberate and thoughtful manner. It appears that Paul wanted to follow the last procedure in his farewell to the elders of the church at Ephesus, He chose to meet them down the coast some forty miles at Miletus, where they could be by themselves and free from disruption.

We will experience many farewells of various types during our lifetime. Some will be virtually painless, because our relationships will be brief and casual. Others will be difficult, because our relationships will be long and involved. Changes must come, and we will have to accept them. Family members and friends may move away, abandon us, or die. Christians, however, have a sure hope that no separation is forever. They know that they will meet other believers in heaven. Let us be comforted and rejoice in this truth.

This Lesson in <u>Your</u> Life

This passage is replete with lessons for our lives. Notice number one: Form strong relationships. Paul loved these brethren and they loved him. There were deep ties. This closeness made parting difficult, but it was a tribute to the greatness of love.

Close relationships require time, attention, and shared experiences. I know people who complain about not having friends. They are self-centered people. They do not go out of their way for others and do not have time for them. Others must conform to their schedules.

Paul had worked, prayed, sacrificed, and suffered with and for the Ephesian church. He loved it with an unselfish love. He had a special identity with its leaders. They had wept together, experienced persecution together, and worked together. They were bound together with a strong bond. We need not expect this quality of friendship without this depth of participation.

Lesson two is that love brings pain but also gratification. Had the Ephesians not been loving they would have not been brought to tears. Yet the richness of joy Paul had brought into their lives made it well worth the cost.

I have been with a lot of people at a time of the death of a loved one. I have seen great pain and sorrow. Never have I seen anyone who regretted the love because of the pain. Even in the throes of grief, people still know that love is worth the cost.

Lesson three is that where our investment is, our heart is. Paul had been exposed to danger and betrayal at Ephesus. He had preached publicly and taught the gospel from house to house. He had taught both Jews and Greeks. Because of all this investment of time, energy, sweat, and tears, Paul felt extremely close to the church at Ephesus. He wanted a farewell moment with its leaders before his fateful trip to Jerusalem.

The fourth lesson is that as we face life with courage we must also face death with courage. The Holy Spirit had revealed to Paul that bonds and afflictions awaited him. He knew that he was going to Jerusalem at the risk of his life. Though his death did not occur there, the events leading to it did. No one lives in this mortal body forever. The important thing is whether we fulfill our purpose while in it.

Lesson five is on the joy and peace of a clear conscience. Paul had faithfully done his job. He could say, "I am pure from the blood of all men." He did not face death looking back on a life of neglect and disobedience. Paul was the first to acknowledge that he was a sinner saved by grace. Yet he knew he had been true to his mission and took great comfort in that.

Lesson six has to do with the love and nurture of the church. The church as we experience it is not always easy to love. It can be frustrating and disappointing. Yet it is the Lord's church. He loved it and gave himself for it. If he can love it with all of its flaws and weaknesses, it behooves us to love it also. Paul urged the Ephesian elders to love and nurture the church.

Seed Thoughts

1. What authority did Paul have to summon elders from Ephesus?
He exercised his apostolic authority, but they probably would have come solely out of friendship with him.

2. Why might Miletus have been better than Ephesus for a farewell?
It was forty miles away and probably free from distractions. If it is feasible, Christians do well to come away from crowded places sometimes.

3. Why was Paul defensive about his ministry in Ephesus?
Perhaps he had been criticized for it. Perhaps he wanted to convince himself that he had done everything possible

4 What qualities of Christian leadership had Paul exhibited which we should exhibit, too?
Acts 20:18-21 refers to faithfulness, humility, intense concern, endurance under trial, openness, and doctrinal soundness or integrity.

5. Was Paul foolish to continue on to Jerusalem despite warnings?
Some thought that, but he was doing what his conscience told him to do.

(Please Turn Page)

---

1. What authority did Paul have to summon elders from Ephesus?

2. Why might Miletus have been better than Ephesus for a farewell?

3. Why was Paul defensive about his ministry in Ephesus?

4 What qualities of Christian leadership had Paul exhibited which we should exhibit, too?

5. Was Paul foolish to continue on to Jerusalem despite warnings?

6. Does the Holy Spirit still give prophesies through believers?

7. What gives Christians courage to face suffering for Christ's sake?

8. Can we really say that we will never see fellow believers again?

9. What kind of marauders must we guard against to protect the church?

10. How can be deal with those intent on destroying the flock?

Seed Thoughts - Continued

He exercised his apostolic authority, but they probably would have come solely out of friendship with him,

It was forty miles away and probably free from distractions. If it is feasible, Christians do well to come away from crowded places sometimes.

Perhaps he had been criticized for it. Perhaps he wanted to convince himself that he had done everything possible

Acts 20:18-21 refers to faithfulness, humility, intense concern, endurance under trial, openness, and doctrinal soundness or integrity.

Some thought that, but he was doing what his conscience told him to do.

Some evangelicals think they have ceased (I Cor. 13:8), while others think they continue to be given. Discuss.

They draw on God's grace to sustain them in times of trial.

We may not see them on this earth, but we know we will see them in heaven.

Some will be grievous wolves from outside the flock, and some will be inside.

We need to be aware of their presence, and then we must change them from their heretical ways or expel them.

6. Does the Holy Spirit still give prophesies through believers?
Some evangelicals think they have ceased (I Cor. 13:8), while others think they continue to be given. Discuss.

7. What gives Christians courage to face suffering for Christ's sake?
They draw on God's grace to sustain them in times of trial.

8. Can we really say that we will never see fellow believers again?
We may not see them on this earth, but we know we will see them in heaven.

9. What kind of marauders must we guard against to protect the church?
Some will be grievous wolves from outside the flock, and some will be inside.

10. How can be deal with those intent on destroying the flock?
We need to be aware of their presence, and then we must change them from their heretical ways or expel them.

Arrested And Accused

Acts 21:26. Then Paul took the men, and the next day purifying himself with them entered into the temple, to signify the accomplishment of the days of purification, until that an offering should be offered for every one of them.
27. And when the seven days were almost ended, the Jews which were of Asia, when they saw him in the temple, stirred up all the people, and laid hands on him,
28. Crying out, Men of Israel, help: This is the man, that teacheth all men every where against the people, and the law, and this place: and further brought Greeks also into the temple, and hath polluted this holy place.
29. (For they had seen before with him in the city Trophimus an Ephesian, whom they supposed that Paul had brought into the temple.)
30. And all the city was moved, and the people ran together: and they took Paul, and drew him out of the temple: and forthwith the doors were shut.
31. And as they went about to kill him, tidings came unto the chief captain of the band, that all Jerusalem was in an uproar.
32. Who immediately took soldiers and centurions, and ran down unto them: and when they saw the chief captain and the soldiers, they left beating of Paul.
33. Then the chief captain came near, and took him, and commanded him to be bound with two chains; and demanded who he was, and what he had done.
Acts 21:37. And as Paul was to be led into the castle, he said unto the chief captain, May I speak unto thee? Who said, Canst thou speak Greek?
38. Art not thou that Egyptian, which before these days madest an uproar, and leddest out into the wilderness four thousand men that were murderers?
39. But Paul said, I am a man which am a Jew of Tarsus, a city in Cilicia, a citizen of no mean city.

MEMORY SELECTION
Acts 23:11
DEVOTIONAL READING
2 Corinthians 6:1-10
BACKGROUND SCRIPTURE
Acts 21:17-40; 22:25-23:11
PRINTED SCRIPTURE
Acts 21:26-33, 37-39a

Teacher's Target

Although warned by the Holy Spirit that he would face arrest in Jerusalem, Paul continued moving in that direction. Leaving Miletus, he and his team sailed for Coos (Cos), the island of Rhodes, Patara on the mainland, and Tyre in Phoenicia. Having visited believers in Tyre and Ptolemais, they came to Caesarea and stayed with Philip the evangelist. They finally reached Jerusalem and were welcomed by the brethren, who persuaded Paul to join four men about to go through a Jewish purification. Before the week was up, however, Paul was arrested (Acts 21:1-27).

Help your students to analyze what happened to Paul in Jerusalem and decide whether or not his going there served any useful purpose. Keep in mind that fact that the results of both good and bad decisions can be part of an overall pattern laid down by the Lord He can take circumstances and work out His divine plan through them.

Lesson Introduction

Did apostles ever make mistakes? We do not normally like to think along this line, but it can be helpful if we do. There are those who feel that Paul was wrong to agree to join four Jews going through a purification which would end in an offering being made in the temple. Blood offerings were supposed to have ended at Christ's death as far as His followers were concerned. Paul went against this when he tried to please Jewish Christians (Acts 21:21-26).

Peter went to Antioch, Syria and ate with Gentile converts until Jewish believers came, and then he separated himself and persuaded Barnabas and others to do the same. Paul withstood him to his face for doing this (Gal. 2:11-21). Perhaps such incidents were recorded so that we as believers will realize that no one but Christ was or is perfect. We all need God's forgiving grace. We all need to experience spiritual growth.

Teaching Outline

I. Riot: Acts 21:26-29
   A. Purification: 26
   B. Pandemonium: 27-29

II. Rescue: Acts 21:30-33
   A. Intention: 30-31
   B. Interference: 32
   C. Indictment: 33

III. Request: Acts 21:37-39a
   A. Inquiries: 37-38
   B. Identification: 39a

Daily Bible Readings

Mon. Received Well at Jerusalem
Acts 21:17-20
Tue. Avoiding Offense
Acts 21:21-26
Wed. Opposition and Arrest
Acts 21:27-33
Thu. Paul a Jew
Acts 21:34-40
Fri. Paul a Roman
Acts 22:25-30
Sat. Paul a Defender
Acts 23:1-5
Sun. Paul a Pharisee
Acts 23:6-11

Verse By Verse

I. Riot: Acts 21:26-29

A. Purification: 26
26. Then Paul took the men, and the next day purifying himself with them entered into the temple, to signify the accomplishment of the days of purification, until that an offering should be offered for every one of them.

James and elders of the church in Jerusalem welcomed Paul and his team. They listened to reports of God at work through the missionaries among the Gentiles. However, they were afraid that Jewish believers would criticize Paul for not requiring Gentile converts to keep the law of Moses, circumcise their children, and keep Jewish customs. They thought that Paul should join himself to four Jewish men taking a Nazarite vow lasting thirty days (Num. 6:14-21 Acts 21:18-24).

The four men had evidently encountered some type of ceremonial uncleanness which demanded a seven-day purification ending in a sacrificial offering. Paul joined in this, even though he must have known that blood sacrifices in the Mosaic law were ended for Christians because Christ fulfilled them when He sacrificed Himself at Calvary. Paul entered with the men into the temple to announce when the days of purification were to end.

B. Pandemonium: 27-29
27. And when the seven days were almost ended, the Jews which were of Asia, when they saw him in the temple, stirred up all the people, and laid hands on him,

Things seemed to go along peacefully, but before the week was up pandemonium broke loose. Jews from Asia (western Turkey) came to the temple and saw Paul there. They deliberately stirred up the people and laid hands on Paul. They saw an opportunity to oppose him in the central, sacred shrine of Judaism. He would not get away from them as he had done back in the Gentile land where they lived.

28. Crying out, Men of Israel, help: This is the man, that teacheth all men every where against the people, and the law, and this place: and further brought Greeks also into the temple, and hath polluted this holy place.

The visiting Jews called on the men of Israel for help, as if Paul were a great danger to them. They said that here was the man who taught others to be against the people (Jews), against the law (of Moses), and against this place (the temple). They also accused Paul of bringing Greeks (Gentiles) into the temple and thus polluting the holy place of Judaism. There was a section called the court of the Gentiles, where proselytes were allowed to assemble, but they were not to go beyond that,

29. (For they had seen before with him in the city Trophimus an Ephesian, whom they supposed that Paul had brought into the temple.)

The trouble makers accused Paul of bringing Gentiles into the temple simply because they had seen Trophimus from Ephesus walking with him in the city of Jerusalem and had assumed that Paul had brought him into the temple. This illustrates how assumption and exaggeration can be produced by mean-spirited individuals who want to slander someone.

We have only a few references to Trophimus. He was with Paul during at least part of his third missionary journey (Acts 20:4). He may have been the unnamed person who traveled with Titus when he took offerings from Gentile churches to the poor saints in Jerusalem (II Cor. 8:18-22). Paul wrote Timothy that he left Trophimus sick at Miletum (Miletus), perhaps while going to Rome (II Tim. 4:20). We are not told what happened to him following Paul's arrest in Jerusalem, but he may have stayed in the area until Paul was later sent to Rome.

II. Rescue: Acts 21:30-33

A. Intention: 30-31

30. And all the city was moved, and the people ran together: and they took Paul, and drew him out of the temple: and forthwith the doors were shut.

News about the arrest of Paul by the mob spread rapidly throughout the city, and the people ran toward the temple. Before the temple could be profaned by their violence, the Jews hauled Paul out (or perhaps into the court of the Gentiles) and shut the doors. Their intention was deadly, and it was illegal, but they had managed to kill Stephen and apparently had gone unpunished by the Romans (Acts 7:54-60). They evidently had the same thing in mind for Paul.

31. And as they went about to kill him, tidings came unto the chief captain of the band, that all Jerusalem was in an uproar.

As the mob proceeded to kill Paul, someone had enough sense to run to the Romans and tell them about the riot taking place. The chief captain of the Roman band was a man named Claudius Lysias (Acts 23:26). As a captain (chiliarch, tribune) he had a thousand soldiers under his command with headquarters in the Tower of Antonia adjacent to the temple.

B Interference: 32

32a. Who immediately took soldiers and centurions, and ran down unto them: . . .

We should give Claudius credit for courage in facing an angry mob which probably could have overcome him and his men numerically. Without hesitation, he and his centurions (leaders of a hundred men) ran to the scene with their soldiers and attempted to restore order. Claudius would later claim that he had rescued Paul because he knew he was a Roman citizen, but this was not true (Acts 21:37-38; 23:27). However, he did rescue him from a horrible death.

32b. . . . **and when they saw the chief captain and the soldiers, they left beating of Paul,**

Although they were enraged and were in the process of beating Paul to death, the Jews were intimidated by the Romans and feared for their own safety. They decided to stop what they were doing. They may have figured that they could find some legal way to persuade the Romans to condemn Paul and execute him. They had earlier persuaded Pilate to do these things with Jesus.

C. Indictment: 33

33. Then the chief captain came near, and took him, and commanded him to be bound with two chains; and demanded who he was, and what he had done.

Under the stress of the moment, Claudius took drastic action against Paul. He ordered his men to bind him with two chains. He demanded that Paul identify himself and say what he had done to cause the tumult. He would later regret this highhanded way of handling the situation, but for the time being, he may have been doing what he thought best.

It appears that Paul had no opportunity to speak for himself. The crowd was hurling accusations at him, some people shouting one thing and some another thing. Claudius decided to have Paul taken to the castle (the barracks of the Tower of Antonia, named for Mark Antony). While going up the stairs, Paul was carried by the soldiers to protect him against the violence of the mob. The multitude followed, calling for Paul's death (Acts 21:34-36). It would appear that this might be the end for the apostle, but God had other plans for him.

III. Request: Acts 21:37-39a

A. Inquiries: 37-38
37a. And as Paul was to be led into the castle, he said unto the chief captain, May I speak unto thee?
Paul spoke to Claudius in Greek before they entered the barracks, asking if he could talk with him. This was apparently the first time that Paul could make himself heard.
37b. Who said, Canst thou speak Greek?
Claudius might have ignored Paul's request, but he was startled to hear himself addressed in Greek, and he made this known to Paul. It began to dawn on the captain that his prisoner might not be a criminal.
38. Art not thou that Egyptian, which before these days madest an uproar, and leddest out into the wilderness four thousand men that were murderers?
Claudius had assumed that Paul was an Egyptian Jew who had led a revolt to overthrow the Romans in Jerusalem. It had been put down by Felix, but the Egyptian had escaped. The man's followers had been called assassins, and that name has been used to describe murderers since that time.

B. Identification: 39a
39a. But Paul said, I am a man which am a Jew of Tarsus, a city in Cilicia, a citizen of no mean city: . . .
Claudius had originally told Paul to identify himself (vs. 33), but the crowd had been too noisy and Paul may have been hurt too much to respond. Now he identified himself as a Jew from Tarsus, a city in Cilicia, a province in southeastern Asia Minor (Turkey) Paul claimed that Tarsus was not a mean (insignificant, unimportant) city, and it was clear that he was proud to be a citizen of it. However, he did not mention his Roman citizenship at this time.

Claudius had originally told Paul to say what he had done to cause the tumult. Paul now wanted the opportunity to respond to it. He asked that he be allowed to address the crowd seething below him, and Claudius said that he could. Paul stood on the stairs, held up his hand in an appeal for silence, and began to speak in the Hebrew language (Acts 21:39-40).

Paul's defense of himself is recorded in Acts 22. He told the multitude that he was a Jew from Tarsus in Cilicia and that he had studied under the scholar named Gamaliel in Jerusalem. He told of persecuting the church until his life was changed by encountering Jesus on the road to Damascus and he had become His follower. He told about his mission to go to the Gentiles with the gospel. The Jews were not impressed by his testimony, and they repeated their demand that he be slain. Claudius ordered that Paul be brought into the barracks and "examined" by whipping. As the soldiers prepared to do this, Paul revealed his Roman citizenship, and the whipping was cancelled. It was decided that he should appear before the Sanhedrin.

This produced only a plot to kill Paul, and he was taken down to Caesarea. He appeared before Felix, was imprisoned for two years under Festus, and appeared before King Agrippa

Evangelistic Emphasis

The book of Acts is the foremost record of evangelism in the Scriptures. This passage illustrates some of the basic principles of effective evangelism.

1) This text shows the importance of honoring the background of those we are teaching the gospel to. Failure to do so is offensive and is virtually certain to result in evangelistic impotence. Paul purified himself and went to the temple to make offerings. He was honoring his own background and laying the basis for good communication with those who were still Jewish in their faith.

2) A second principle is that we must be prepared to be misunderstood and/or misrepresented. Evangelism must, on occasion, challenge vested interests and oppose biases. It cannot usually do this without arousing opposition. Those who feel threatened will fight back in some way, fair or unfair.

3) Third, when opposition does occur, it must be faced with courage. It will not serve the gospel for its advocates to melt in the face of resistance or run when they encounter those with contrary views.

4) A fourth principle is that reasonable precautions for self-preservation must be taken. While an evangelist should be willing to risk his life for the cause of Christ and for the salvation of souls, he should not expose himself to rash or foolish losses. It is good to be willing to be a martyr for Christ, but martyrdom in a small cause is an insufferable waste. Paul eventually died for the Lord, but he did not die prematurely or because he was unwilling to seek appropriate protection.

Memory Selection

"The night following the Lord stood by him, and said, Be of good cheer, Paul: for as thou hast testified of me in Jerusalem, so must thou bear witness also at Rome." Acts 23:11.

As a lot of people have found out the hard way, doing the Lord's work can get a person in serious trouble. Paul experienced imprisonment and the threat of death in our passage today. We may or may not experience the same dangers Paul did, but we should be aware that the preaching of the gospel can be hazardous to one's safety.

It is comforting to know, however, that when danger comes, the Lord will be close. The Lord stood by Paul and assured him that he would survive the crisis and live to take the gospel to Rome.

The good news that the Lord gave Paul was that there was a mission for him to fulfill. God had plans for Paul and would protect him so that he might fulfill those plans. Some people seem to be living just for the time that they will not have to work any more. Paul lived for the opportunity to do the will of Christ. He did not see idleness and ease as good news. To him, a challenging mission was good news.

Be glad that you are called to a great task. It will bring happiness as well as busyness.

Weekday Problems

Rhonda had a traumatic childhood. Her parents were killed in a car wreck when she was nine years old. She was placed in a foster home but did not respond well and had to be moved. After a series of such experiences, she became more adept at manipulation and deception. By the age of fourteen it was deemed necessary to place her in an institutional setting. She became a resident of a home for girls with behavioral problems.

The disciplines there were chafing to her. She resolved to find a way to be released. Her attempt to do so was in the form of a fabricated story she told on the director of the home. She said that he was physically abusive to her. She even injured herself so she could show bruises to substantiate her story.

The director was a highly motivated and competent man who had Rhonda's interests at heart. Nevertheless, the accusation and the attendant publicity raised a cloud of suspicion over his work.

* What protection against false accusation do people have who serve in caregiving, teaching, counselling, and other such vulnerable roles?
* How should we feel about a person who has been accused of abuse but is subsequently exonerated?

Superintendent's Sermonette

We have been told since childhood that we have to bear responsibility for our mistakes and take the consequences. Paul's friends felt that he was making a mistake to continue on to Jerusalem in spite of many warnings from the Holy Spirit that he would be persecuted there Some have felt Paul made a mistake in joining four Jewish men going through a purification which would end with a sacrifice, because Christians believed that Jesus fulfilled all blood sacrifices when He died at Calvary. The conclusion might be reached that Paul deserved what he got in Jerusalem.

There is a balancing factor in all of this, however, for God has His ways of taking circumstances and molding them to His Own purpose. It was because Paul went to Jerusalem that he was able to witness to Jews and Romans there, and he also did this in Caesarea, the island of Melita (Malta), and the capital of Rome. We are not perfect, and we will make mistakes, but God can use even these as opportunities to bring glory to His name, Let us take comfort in knowing His sovereign will prevails.

This Lesson in <u>Your</u> Life

Each of us is a part of a continuing stream of humanity. We are preceded by our ancestors and followed by our posterity. We did not come into a vacuum. We have not only the lateral relationships of peers but also relationships with predecessors and successors.

Some cultures put more emphasis on this than others. Among Jewish people, this type of relationship is extremely important. Therefore, although Paul was a devout convert to Christianity, he still had deep feelings and a strong commitment to his background in Judaism. He treated it with great respect, honoring its customs and practices.

In our lives, we sometimes find it necessary to break with the views and practices of the past. It may be that we learn things that our parents did not have the opportunity to know. It may be that we have to deal with conditions and problems that were nonexistent at an earlier day. It may be that our experiences help correct some biases from an earlier day.

When such is the case, we will do well to follow Paul's example. Let us make the changes that are necessary, but let us honor history, feelings, and relationships as we do. Let us take good care of our relationship with those who still hold views which we formerly held. That way, the human family can grow and make necessary changes without having destructive intergenerational civil war.

If Jesus was falsely accused and Paul was falsely accused, we should be aware that we also might be falsely accused if we preach the gospel. They said of Paul that he taught against the people, the law, and the temple. These accusations came even though he had used a great deal of care to show respect to Jewish institutions.

It is a comfort to us to know that Jesus anticipated this problem and spoke to us about it. "Blessed are ye, when men shall revile you, and persecute you, and shall say all manner of evil against you falsely, for my sake. Rejoice, and be exceeding glad: for great is your reward in heaven: for so persecuted they the prophets which were before you."

One lesson to be learned from this text is that religious controversy can arouse passionate emotions. There was even a danger that Paul would be killed. All of us have known people who refused to discuss religion and politics because of the heated nature these conversations sometimes develop.

To refuse to discuss religion is too extreme a remedy. It is necessary to be able to talk about things that are important to us. It is necessary also to be able to share that which is of value to us. It would be unthinkable to believe that our current blessedness and eternal welfare depended on our relationship with Jesus and not be able to communicate that fact to those we love.

While we do not refrain from discussing our faith, we should realize the need to discuss it with care. A conversation which generates deep feelings should be replete with courtesy, gentleness, and mutual respect.

A final note is that Christianity is not masochistic. Paul was willing to be a martyr for Christ, but was also willing to use information that would protect him from premature death. "I am . . . a Jew of Tarsus, a city in Cilicia, a citizen of no mean city," he said.

Seed Thoughts

1. Should Paul have yielded to pressure from church leaders?
He evidently thought their proposal to join the four men was reasonable in one sense, but he and they appeared to be on shaky doctrinal ground.

2. What should we do if we are pressured by church leaders?
We must demand biblical reasons from them, plus freedom of conscience, for whatever we are asked to do.

3. Should Christians look over their shoulders for enemies?
Paul might have avoided trouble if he had noted enemies from Asia (western Turkey) in the temple and left there.

4. What was unfair about the Jews' accusation of Paul?
They said he was against Jews, the Mosaic law, and the temple, and they assumed he brought Trophimus into it.

5. What makes a mob form?
It usually begins with a small group of agitators shouting an accusation, and excitement about it produces hysteria.

(Please Turn Page)

---

1. Should Paul have yielded to pressure from church leaders?

2. What should we do if we are pressured by church leaders?

3. Should Christians look over their shoulders for enemies?

4. What was unfair about the Jews' accusation of Paul?

5. What makes a mob form?

6. How did the Jews dare to attempt executing Paul themselves?

7. Should Christians depend on unsaved officers to rescue them?

8. Should Christians expect unsaved officers to be truthful?

9. Should Christians identify themselves with this world?

10. Did any good come out of the predicament Paul met in Jerusalem?

He evidently thought their proposal to join the four men was reasonable in one sense, but he and they appeared to be on shaky doctrinal ground.

We must demand biblical reasons from them, plus freedom of conscience, for whatever we are asked to do.

Paul might have avoided trouble if he had noted enemies from Asia (western Turkey) in the temple and left there.

They said he was against Jews, the Mosaic law, and the temple, and they assumed he brought Trophimus into it.

It usually begins with a small group of agitators shouting an accusation, and excitement about it produces hysteria.

They had been allowed to get away with their stoning of Stephen (Acts 7:54-60).

Sometimes it is feasible (Rom. 13:1-6) and they have rights under human law. At other times only God can rescue them.

Some unsaved officers will be careful to be truthful, but others may say what is self-serving, as Claudius Lysias did.

Christians have dual citizenship in heaven and on earth, and they should support both as needed,

God used the circumstances of Paul's arrest, rescue, and imprisonment to give him opportunities to witness for Christ.

Seed Thoughts - Continued

6. How did the Jews dare to attempt executing Paul themselves?
They had been allowed to get away with their stoning of Stephen (Acts 7:54-60).

7. Should Christians depend on unsaved officers to rescue them?
Sometimes it is feasible (Rom. 13:1-6) and they have rights under human law. At other times only God can rescue them.

8. Should Christians expect unsaved officers to be truthful?
Some unsaved officers will be careful to be truthful, but others may say what is self-serving, as Claudius Lysias did.

9. Should Christians identify themselves with this world?
Christians have dual citizenship in heaven and on earth, and they should support both as needed,

10. Did any good come out of the predicament Paul met in Jerusalem?
God used the circumstances of Paul's arrest, rescue, and imprisonment to give him opportunities to witness for Christ.

Before Agrippa

Acts 26:1. Then Agrippa said unto Paul, Thou art permitted to speak for thyself. Then Paul stretched forth the hand, and answered for himself:
2. I think myself happy, king Agrippa, because I shall answer for myself this day before thee touching all the things whereof I am accused of the Jews:
3. Especially because I know thee to be expert in all customs and questions which are among the Jews: wherefore I beseech thee to hear me patiently.
4. My manner of life from my youth, which was at the first among mine own nation at Jerusalem, know all the Jews;
5. Which knew me from the beginning, if they would testify, that after the most straitest sect of our religion I lived a Pharisee.
6. And now I stand and am judged for the hope of the promise made of God unto our fathers:
7. Unto which promise our twelve tribes, instantly serving God day and night, hope to come. For which hope's sake, king Agrippa, I am accused of the Jews.
8. Why should it be thought a thing incredible with you, that God should raise the dead?
Acts 26:22. Having therefore obtained help of God, I continue unto this day, witnessing both to small and great, saying none other things than those which the prophets and Moses did say should come:
23. That Christ should suffer, and that he should be the first that should rise from the dead, and should show light unto the people, and to the Gentiles.
Acts 26:27. King Agrippa, believest thou the prophets? I know that thou believest.
28. Then Agrippa said unto Paul, Almost thou persuadest me to be a Christian.
29. And Paul said, I would to God, that not only thou, but also all that hear me this day, were both almost, and altogether such as I am, except these bonds.

MEMORY SELECTION
Acts 26:22
DEVOTIONAL READING
Philippians 4:4-13

BACKGROUND SCRIPTURE
Acts 25:13-26:32
PRINTED SCRIPTURE
Acts 26:1-8,22-23,27-29

Teacher's Target

Jesus had told Ananias in Damascus that Paul would "bear my name before the Gentiles, and kings" (Acts 9:15). Following Paul's two appearances before Governor Felix and two years of imprisonment under Governor Festus, he had appealed to Caesar. Since Paul was a Roman citizen, this appeal had to be honored. In the meantime, King Agrippa came to Caesarea and expressed a desire to hear Paul himself. This gave Paul an opportunity to witness to a king.

Help your students to see that they need not be intimidated by secular authorities. If they depend on the Lord, He will give them words to speak when they have to defend themselves. Paul was even bold enough to give Agrippa an invitation to become a Christian. We never know what might impress someone to consider his soul's destiny, following a deposit of gospel truth in his heart.

Lesson Introduction

The two central characters in today's text were the Apostle Paul and King Agrippa. It might help to know something about Agrippa. His father was Herod Agrippa I (Acts 12:1), and his grandfather was Herod the Great (Matt. 2:1). Known as Herod Agrippa II, he served as president of the temple and its treasures. He appointed the high priest to his office. He maintained an incestuous relationship with his sister, Bernice, until she became the wife of King Ptolemy of Sicily. She returned to Agrippa and later became mistress to Vespasian and Titus, builder of the Colosseum in Rome.

In spite of his nominal connections with Judaism, it was obvious that Agrippa was a pagan bound for perdition. His brief contact with Paul was probably the closest he ever came to the kingdom of God, and he missed his opportunity to find salvation. In this case, the prisoner outranked the king.

Teaching Outline

I. Account: Acts 26:1-8
   A. Permission: 1-3
   B. Pharisee: 4-5
   C. Promise: 6-8

II. Actions: Acts 26:22-23
   A. Continuation: 22
   B. Christ: 23

III. Appeal: Acts 26:27-29
   A. Asking: 27
   B. Answering: 28
   C. Appealing: 29

Daily Bible Readings

Mon. Appeal to Caesar
Acts 25:13-21
Tue. Before Agrippa
Acts 25:22-27
Wed. Paul's Early Life
Acts 26:1-5
Thu. A Jewish Zealot
Acts 26:6-11
Fri. Called by Christ
Acts 26:12-18
Sat. Response to the Call
Acts 26:19-23
Sun. Agrippa's Reaction
Acts 26:24-32

Verse By Verse

I. Account: Acts 26:1-8

A. Permission: 1-3
1a. Then Agrippa said unto Paul, Thou art permitted to speak for thyself.
  Agrippa and Bernice had come to Caesarea for a visit. Governor Festus told the king about Paul and reviewed the case against him. Although Agrippa knew that Paul had appealed to Caesar and must be sent to Rome, he wanted to hear him. A hearing was set for the next day, and the king and his officials came to the hall with great pomp and ceremony. Festus spoke first, explaining that he wanted Paul to appear before Agrippa so that he might be examined and the governor would have something substantial to write to Caesar when he sent Paul to him (Acts 25:13-27). Agrippa then invited Paul to speak for himself.
1b. Then Paul stretched forth the hand, and answered for himself:
  Stretching forth his hand may have been meant as a salute to the king, but Paul may have done this to signal for silence (Acts 21:40). Whatever else he thought about this hearing Paul wanted to use it as an opportunity to witness for Christ.
2. I think myself happy, king Agrippa, because I shall answer for myself this day before thee touching all the things whereof I am accused of the Jews:
3a. Especially because I know thee to be expert in all customs and questions which are among the Jews: . . .
  Some might think that Paul indulged in unnecessary flattery here, Others would say that he was merely observing current customs of courtesy when addressing royalty. He considered himself fortunate to be speaking to an authority who at least knew Jewish customs and questions (controversies). This would help the king understand the accusations made by the Jews against Paul.
3b. . . .wherefore I beseech thee to hear me patiently.
  Since he had appealed to Caesar, Paul knew that his case could not be decided by King Agrippa. Therefore, Paul meant to use this occasion to explain the tremendous change in his life and to urge others to accept Christ as Savior themselves, beginning with Agrippa. If the king would hear him patiently, Paul could get gospel truth out to this audience, and he knew it would be reported elsewhere.

B. Pharisee: 4-5
4. My manner of life from my youth, which was at the first among mine own nation at Jerusalem, know all the Jews;
  Paul told Agrippa that the Jews had known about him from his childhood, first in his own nation (Tarsus of Cilicia) and later in Jerusalem (under Gamaliel).
5. Which knew me from the beginning, if they would testify, that after the most straitest sect of our religion I lived a Pharisee.
  Paul said that the Jews who had known him as he was growing up would have to admit, if they testified, that he had been brought up according to the straitest (strictest) sect in Judaism, namely that of the Pharisees. These archconservatives considered themselves to be "guardians of the law of Moses." Normally at odds

with the more liberal Sadducees and Herodians, they nevertheless had joined forces with them in opposing Jesus during His time of ministry among them. Paul (originally called Saul) had persecuted the followers of Jesus early in his life (Acts 26:9-11).

C. Promise: 6-8
6. And now I stand and am judged for the hope of the promise made of God unto our fathers:
7a. Unto which promise our twelve tribes, instantly serving God day and night, hope to come.

Paul wanted to give a theological reason for his faith, even before he went into the details of what had changed him dramatically. He claimed that he was being judged evil by the Jews for believing something which they themselves had been waiting to happen since ancient times. The "hope of the promise made of [or by] God unto our fathers [ancestors]" referred to the resurrection of Jesus from the dead.

Turn to Acts 13:32-33 and Psalm 2:7 to recall what Paul had said in his sermon in the synagogue of Antioch in Pisidia—"We declare unto you glad tidings, how that the promise which was made unto the fathers [ancestors], God hath fulfilled the same unto us their children [descendants], in that he hath raised up Jesus again; as it is also written in the second psalm, Thou art my Son, this day have I begotten [honored] thee."

7b. For which hope's sake, king Agrippa, I am accused of the Jews.

The hope-generating promise had been made by God to the Jews. It had been fulfilled in the resurrection of Jesus, and Paul had accepted that, but the Jews were accusing him of doing something wrong.

8. Why should it be thought a thing incredible with you, that God should raise the dead?

Addressing everyone in the hall, Paul asked why it seemed unbelievable that God could raise someone from the dead. Paul had earlier told the Sanhedrin (Jewish Council) in Jerusalem that the Sadducees did not believe in resurrection of the dead nor in angels, but that Pharisees believed in both. At that time, the Pharisees had come to Paul's defense (Acts 23:8-9). However, the Jews appeared to be united against Paul, and that did not seem reasonable or fair.

Paul next told Agrippa about his persecution of the church, his encounter with Jesus on the road to Damascus, and his obedient response to the heavenly vision. He said that his ministry had led to Jews arresting him in the temple and trying to murder him (Acts 26:9-21).

II. Actions: Acts 26:22-23

A. Continuation: 22
22a. Having therefore obtained help of God, I continue unto this day, witnessing both to small and great, . . .

Paul made an interesting point here by saying that it was with God's help that he continued his ministry to this day. In spite of wholesale opposition from the Jews, and in spite of detention by Roman authorities, he continued to witness the truth to anyone who would listen, whether small or great in this world's evaluation. In other words, God was preserving him, and that should count for something.

22b. . . . saying none other things than those which the prophets and Moses did say should come:

Paul took a stand on the Jewish Scriptures (Old Testament) here, claiming that he had taught nothing but what they contained. The honored prophets and Moses himself had foretold the coming of the Messiah, and Paul did accept Jesus as the fulfillment of their predictions.

B. Christ: 23
23. That Christ should suffer, and that he should be the first that should rise from the dead, and should shew light unto the people, and to the Gentiles.

The Jewish Scriptures had clearly prophesied that the Messiah would suffer and die. He would rise from the dead, He would show the light of truth to the people (of Israel) and to the Gentiles (pagans). Beginning with Genesis 3:15 and moving through the Old Testament, references could be found to the Messiah which had been fulfilled in Jesus, including His suffering, death, burial, and resurrection. The gospel had gone out through His followers to both Jews and Gentiles, fulfilling such references as Isaiah 42:6, 49:6, 60:3, and 66:15. Even the Romans could lay claim to the gospel, if they chose to do it.

At this point, Governor Festus became exasperated with Paul. He told him in a loud voice that he was mad (insane) due to much learning. Paul disagreed with him, and he claimed to speak the truth. Paul said that the king knew about these things, for they had not been done in a corner (secretly) (Acts 26:24-26),

III. Appeal: Acts 26:27-29

A. Asking: 27
27. King Agrippa, believest thou the prophets? I know that thou believest.

Turning directly to Agrippa, Paul bluntly asked the king if he believed what the Jewish prophets had written, implying that he believed what they had written about the Messiah. We do not know if Agrippa replied or not, but Paul answered it for him by saying he knew Agrippa believed the prophecies.

B. Answering: 28
28. Then Agrippa said unto Paul, Almost thou persuadest me to be a Christian,

Here is a case of a written account not telling us as much as an oral account might be able to do. Agrippa's response might have been meant to convey various meanings. He may have implied, "You almost persuade _me_ to become a Christian," and been sincere about it. On the other hand, he may have spoken sarcastically as if to say, "A little more of this and you will make _me_ out to be a Christian'" We would have to hear the tone in which he spoke that day.

C. Appealing: 29
29. And Paul said, I would to God, that not only thou, but also all that hear me this day, were both almost, and altogether such as I am, except these bonds.

Paul seemed to accept Agrippa's statement at face value. He then remarked that he wished all of the people in the hall could be Christians, the same as he was. Looking down at his bonds, Paul added that he would not wish anyone to have similar constraints.

The hearing ended, and the king, governor, Bernice, and others moved to one side of the hall to talk together about the case. They agreed that Paul had done nothing worthy of death. Agrippa told Festus that Paul could have been set at liberty, if he had not appealed to Caesar (Acts 26:30-32).

Paul was put aboard a ship bound for Lycia, and he was later transferred to one sailing from Alexandria, Egypt to Rome, A storm came up, and the ship was driven before it and eventually shipwrecked on the island of Melita (Malta). The primitives there treated the survivors kindly, and they went aboard another ship from Alexandria three months later, finally arriving in Rome (Acts 27:1—28:16). A new ministry was about to begin.

Evangelistic Emphasis

As we further study the master evangelist, we can observe additional principles of effective evangelism.

1) It is important to establish a bond. A person's religious faith is a most personal matter. Most do not like it to be intruded upon by someone who has not gained their trust. Paul spoke warmly and respectfully to Agrippa. He won a sympathetic hearing for his message.

2) One should connect the message of Christ to areas of one's hearers' experiences. Agrippa had knowledge of Jewish views and customs. Therefore Paul showed the way the message of Christ relates to those views. Others will have other areas of knowledge and experience. If you perceive grief, pain, guilt, concerns for poverty, or other indications of knowledge or interest, you can make your message more appealing. You can show that the gospel is relevant to those areas of life with which they are already acquainted.

3) Be careful that your life is consistent with your message. In effect, Paul said, "My life is an open book." Demonstrated faith lends strong support to one's credibility.

4) One should reason with his hearers, not rant at them. Paul is most reasonable when he says, "Why should it be thought a thing incredible with you, that God should raise the dead?" He did not rely on blustery pronouncements. He appealed to Agrippa on the basis of the reasonableness of the faith.

Memory Selection

"Having therefore obtained help of God, I continue unto this day, witnessing both to small and great, saying none other things than those which the prophets and Moses did say should come."
Acts 26:22.

It was also Paul who said, "I planted, Apollos watered, God gave the increase." The growth of the kingdom is the work of God. We could not do it if we would. It overwhelms us when we think about being responsible for it.

Paul was most conscious of this. He did his work "with the help of God." It was because God was with him that he was able to respond to the call of God.

He witnessed to both the small and great. There are two extremes that we need to avoid. One is to think the "nobodies" of the world are insignificant and therefore it is not important to witness to them. Every person is made in the image of God. Christ died for every one. The gospel is intended for every one. Therefore we ought to take the gospel to all, even those who are unknown and appear incapable.

A second danger is thinking the great are inaccessible and therefore not within reach of the gospel. Great people have guilts, fears, anxieties, and needs, just as other people do.

Weekday Problems

Harold is a recent convert to Christianity. His newfound faith has brought such joy and vitality to his life that he is eager to share it with everyone he knows. Because of his intensity, he dominates every conversation with discussion of it. Without realizing it, he talks too loud, stands too close, listens too little, and is too quick to criticize and correct the views of others.

His motives are good. He is most genuine in his concern, but very ineffective in his manner. He is losing friends. People do not invite him to participate in groups. No one wants to go anywhere with him, especially not to church. They fear that the slightest expression of interest on their part will make him more aggressive yet. Therefore they shun him.

A number of people in his church are critical of Harold, but few of them ever talk to others about Christ. He may do it awkwardly, and even offensively, but they do not do it at all.

* Point out as many differences between Harold's approach and Paul's address to King Agrippa as you can.
* What positive qualities does Harold have that all of us need more of?
* How can Harold's technique be improved without stifling his enthusiasm?

Superintendent's Sermonette

Most of us do not like to have to go to court, even for minor traffic violations under or beyond our control. We certainly like to avoid anything of a more serious nature. Christians should be the best citizens of a community, state (or province), and nation. However, situations may arise which require them to come before civil authorities, and they can prepare themselves to have the right kind of attitude on these occasions. They should demand their rights under the law. They should depend on God for words to speak. They should seek an opportunity to witness

Paul seemed ready, and perhaps even eager, to appear before King Agrippa in Caesarea. He felt that the king would be understanding and fair in his evaluation of his case. He treated him with courtesy and respect. He told him the truth about his life. He even challenged him to become a Christian. We can take Paul as an example in our approach to a similar situation. Let authorities know what we believe, and make it clear that we wish they could join us in those beliefs.

This Lesson in <u>Your</u> Life

There are lots of lessons to learn in this text. One of the more obvious ones is that we should take advantage of whatever situation we are in to express our faith. Paul was a prisoner. He could not travel at will, nor could he stand in the synagogue or marketplace to speak to crowds. His opportunities were limited. Yet he could speak to jailers, judges, and fellow prisoners.

Paul was no doubt concerned about his own fate. However, a greater concern was to communicate the gospel to Agrippa. If our priorities are in order, we will often find opportunities to give others a better knowledge of the Lord, even in circumstances that appear to be uninviting.

Some of the best times to talk with others about the gospel are when we are with them in a non-agenda situation. For example when we are riding in a car or on a plane, we could use some of our time to talk about Christ rather than sports, weather, or politics. People with fitness concerns could address spiritual concerns while walking, jogging, biking, or working out at the spa. An occasional coffee break at work could be turned toward the teaching of the gospel.

At times like these, people are relaxed, open, and comfortable. We should avoid theological jargon, smugness, and pompousness. As Paul did, we should speak simply and directly about our faith in a tone of conviction. It is important to say enough about our own faith and response so that those who hear us will know that we speak out of our own experience.

Another lesson is that we ought not to be afraid to acknowledge our own mistakes. Paul had opposed the faith, imprisoned Christians, voted for the death penalty for them, and followed them to distant cities to persecute them. The people that we speak with are not looking for a faith that cannot deal with mistakes and sins. They would not fit in. Such a faith would not offer them any help with their problems. When we acknowledge our mistakes, it gives them hope that they can, though sinners, have a secure and happy relationship with the Lord.

Not only should we admit our faults, but we should also share the story of our response to God's call. Many who would not go when another points the way, will follow if he leads the way instead of points to it. Most of us do not like to be given advice about what we ought to do. However, we are willing to follow leaders who themselves are committed to the way they are leading. Paul acknowledged that he had obeyed the heavenly vision. That laid the groundwork for Agrippa to follow his example.

We must also learn not to make following Christ sound too easy. Paul pointed out that he was commissioned to take the gospel to the Gentiles, that he was captured by the Jews and in danger of death. The appeal of the gospel is not ease, comfort, or prestige. It is truth, righteousness, and obedience.

We must remember to ask for a decision. The gospel is not to be lectured in order to satisfy academic curiosity. It is to be preached to save souls. It appeals for a verdict.

Finally, we must allow our hearers to make their own decision. Paul did not bring Agrippa to a decision. We will work with some people who do not respond. This is their choice. Let us not be discouraged.

Seed Thoughts

1. How could Paul appear before King Agrippa in a confident manner?
Paul was well-educated, sure of his innocence, and dependent on divine help.

2. Should Christians ever use flattery with civil authorities?
It may be distasteful and counterproductive. Authorities should be approached with courtesy and respect.

3. What advantage did Paul gain by complimenting Agrippa on his understanding of Jewish customs?
Paul provided himself with a basis for making a defense using an established set of beliefs.

4. Why did Paul mention that he had been a strict Pharisee?
He wanted to make it clear that his early life lined up properly with the teachings of Judaism.

5. Should Christians put much stress on the Old Testament?
Yes, for it provided the basis for addition of the New Testament, showing Jesus fulfilled its prophecies.

(Please Turn Page)

---

1. How could Paul appear before King Agrippa in a confident manner?

2. Should Christians ever use flattery with civil authorities?

3. What advantage did Paul gain by complimenting Agrippa on his understanding of Jewish customs?

4. Why did Paul mention that he had been a strict Pharisee?

5. Should Christians put much stress on the Old Testament?

6. How important is Jesus' resurrection to the gospel message?

7. How does God's protection validate a believer's testimony?

8. Did the Old Testament predict that the Messiah would have universal appeal to the whole world?

9. Who persuades a person to become a Christian?

10. Is a Christian always free?

Seed Thoughts - Continued

Paul was well-educated, sure of his innocence, and dependent on divine help.

It may be distasteful and counterproductive. Authorities should be approached with courtesy and respect.

Paul provided himself with a basis for making a defense using an established set of beliefs.

He wanted to make it clear that his early life lined up properly with the teachings of Judaism.

Yes, for it provided the basis for addition of the New Testament, showing Jesus fulfilled its prophecies.

It is all-important, for a living hope demands a living Savior.

If, in spite of persecution, a believer perseveres and remains a constant witness, the world must see God's hand in it.

Yes. Isaiah especially foretold that the light of God would shine to the Gentiles as well as to the Jews.

God works through divine means (the Holy Spirit) and human means (witnesses) to bring sinners to Christ.

He can be free in his spirit, even if he is physically bound. His condition is superior to all worldly conditions.

---

6. How important is Jesus' resurrection to the gospel message?
It is all-important, for a living hope demands a living Savior.

7. How does God's protection validate a believer's testimony?
If, in spite of persecution, a believer perseveres and remains a constant witness, the world must see God's hand in it.

8. Did the Old Testament predict that the Messiah would have universal appeal to the whole world?
Yes. Isaiah especially foretold that the light of God would shine to the Gentiles as well as to the Jews.

9. Who persuades a person to become a Christian?
God works through divine means (the Holy Spirit) and human means (witnesses) to bring sinners to Christ.

10. Is a Christian always free?
He can be free in his spirit, even if he is physically bound. His condition is superior to all worldly conditions.

Paul In Rome

Acts 28:21. And they said unto him, We neither received letters out of Judea concerning thee, neither any of the brethren that came showed or spake any harm of thee.

22. But we desire to hear of thee what thou thinkest: for as concerning this sect, we know that every where it is spoken against.

23. And when they had appointed him a day, there came many to him into his lodging; to whom he expounded and testified the kingdom of God, persuading them concerning Jesus, both out of the law of Moses, and out of the prophets, from morning till evening.

24. And some believed the things which were spoken, and some believed not.

25. And when they agreed not among themselves, they departed, after that Paul had spoken one word, Well spake the Holy Ghost by Esaias the prophet unto our fathers,

26. Saying, Go unto this people, and say, Hearing ye shall hear, and shall not understand; and seeing ye shall see, and not perceive:

27. For the heart of this people is waxed gross, and their ears are dull of hearing, and their eyes have they closed; lest they should see with their eyes, and hear with their ears, and understand with their heart, and should be converted, and I should heal them.

28. Be it known therefore unto you, that the salvation of God is sent unto the Gentiles, and that they will hear it.

29. And when he had said these words, the Jews departed, and had great reasoning among themselves.

30. And Paul dwelt two whole years in his own hired house, and received all that came in unto him,

31. Preaching the kingdom of God, and teaching those things which concern the Lord Jesus Christ, with all confidence, no man forbidding him.

MEMORY SELECTION
Acts 28:30-31
DEVOTIONAL READING
Romans 8:18-30

BACKGROUND SCRIPTURE
Acts 27-28
PRINTED SCRIPTURE
Acts 28:21-31

Teacher's Target

Paul had a longstanding desire to go to Rome, and he had expressed this at Ephesus while on his third missionary journey (Acts 19:21). After his arrest and appearance before the Sanhedrin (Jewish Council) in Jerusalem, God had told him, "Be of good cheer, Paul: for as thou hast testified of me in Jerusalem, so must thou bear witness also at Rome" (Acts 23:11). During the storm which ended in shipwreck, the angel of the Lord had said, "Fear not, Paul, thou must be brought before Caesar: and, lo, God hath given thee all them that sail with thee" (Acts 27:24).

Help your students to see that God can have a ministry for His servants regardless of location. He may have been under house arrest, but Paul penetrated Rome with the gospel by receiving visitors. He also wrote letters to believers elsewhere which became doctrinal guides to the church.

Lesson Introduction

The three months spent on the island of Melita (Malta) following the shipwreck had turned out to be a good period. The primitives there were kind to the survivors during a time of rain and cold weather. Their chief, Publius, received and lodged them courteously the first three days. Paul was able to heal Publius' sick father by the laying on of hands in Jesus' name. The chief gave the survivors supplies when they boarded another ship for Italy. Paul visited believers in Puteoli for seven days and was escorted onward to Rome by believers who had come out from the capital (Acts 28:1-15).

Rather than being put in prison, the Romans allowed Paul to rent a house where he was watched by rotating soldiers. After three days in Rome, Paul called for Jews in the city to come and visit him. This was the beginning of his amazing ministry there (Acts 28:16-20).

Teaching Outline

I. Testimony: Acts 28:21-24
    A. Apprehension: 21-22
    B. Appointment: 23
    C. Appraisals: 24

II. Transfer: Acts 28:25-29
    A. Departure: 25a
    B. Description: 25b-27
    C. Destination: 28
    D. Discussion: 29

III. Teaching: Acts 28:30-31
    A. Reception: 30
    B. Revelation: 31

Daily Bible Readings

Mon. En Route to Rome
Acts 27:1-11
Tue. The Storm
Acts 27:12-20
Wed. Paul's Words of Hope
Acts 27:21-37
Thu. Safety
Acts 27:38-44
Fri. Melita
Acts 28:1-10
Sat. Arrival at Rome
Acts 28:11-20
Sun. House Arrest
Acts 28:21-31

Verse By Verse

I. Testimony: Acts 28:21-24

A. Apprehension: 21-22
21. And they said unto him, We neither received letters out of Judaea concerning thee, neither any of the brethren that came shewed or spake any harm of thee.

After being in Rome three days, Paul had called the chief Jews together and explained to them why he was there. This fit into the pattern of his giving the gospel first to Jews and then to Gentiles (Rom. 1:16), although he continued to minister to <u>all</u> who came to see him (Acts 28:30).

Paul told the Jews in Rome that he had done nothing wrong, but that some Jews had strongly opposed him. He had felt the need to appeal to Caesar for justice, and that was why he was there (Acts 28:17-20).

The Jews replied by saying that they had received no warning letters about him from Judaea nor had they been told anything harmful about him from visiting Jews. However, they did have apprehension about Christianity.

22. But we desire to hear of thee what thou thinkest: for as concerning this sect, we know that every where it is spoken against.

Jews in Rome had a right to be apprehensive. Emperor Claudius had expelled them, and Emperor Nero had allowed them to return during the early part of his reign. The leaders who came to meet Paul thought of Christianity as an offshoot sect of Judaism, and they did not want trouble with the authorities over it. These men may not have known that Paul was a Christian himself, for he had not mentioned it in his introductory comments to them (Acts 28:17-20). They were interested in knowing what he thought of this new-sect, for it had been condemned among Jews in the reports they had received from various lands.

B. Appointment: 23
23a. And when they had appointed him a day, there came many to him into his lodging;...

The first meeting Paul held with the Jews was apparently brief. They set a time when they could return to visit him in his rented house and discuss things at more length. Paul probably appreciated the interlude, because it gave him time to decide how he should approach these men and show them that he believed the "hope of Israel" was Jesus Christ. They would have other Jews with them when they returned, thus broadening Paul's influence on the Jewish community in the capital.

23b. ...to whom he expounded and testified the kingdom of God, persuading them concerning Jesus, both out of the law of Moses, and out of the prophets, from morning till evening,

Once the enlarged group of Jews arrived at his house, Paul launched into a presentation of the gospel. He sought to prove that Jesus met the predictions laid down by Moses and the prophets of the Old Testament for the coming Messiah. It was an all-day affair.

C. Appraisals: 24
24. And some believed the things which were spoken, and some believed not.

Responses to Paul's presentation moved typically in two directions, with some believing what he said and others not believing it. Paul had tried hard to convince all of them, but past experience must have taught him that he would not succeed as far as some were concerned. We, too, must be aware that our task is to sow the seed of truth and be prepared for different responses to it (Matt. 13:1-9, 18-23).

II. Transfer: Acts 28:25-29

A. Departure: 25a
25a. And when they agreed not among themselves, they departed...

As the Jews argued among themselves, Paul became exasperated with them. References to their departure are found here and in verse 29, while what Paul said to them in his frustration is recorded in verses 25b-28.

B. Description: 25b-27
25b. ... after that Paul had spoken one word, Well spake the Holy Ghost by Esaias the prophet unto our fathers.

Paul turned to the book of Isaiah to describe the unbelieving Jews. We may find the quote he used in Isaiah 6:9-10. Differences in wording between the original and the quote may be attributed to the fact that the original was written in Hebrew while the quote was taken from the Septuagint written in Greek. The meanings are the same.

26. Saying, Go unto this people, and say, Hearing ye shall hear, and shall not understand and seeing ye shall see, and not perceive:

These were strong words to apply to his Jewish guests, but Paul was saying that they had physical hearing and sight but lacked spiritual hearing and sight.

27. For the heart of this people is waxed gross, and their ears are dull of hearing, and their eyes have they closed lest they should see with their eyes, and hear with their ears, and understand with their heart, and should be converted, and I should heal them.

With this quote, Paul was showing that the problem with the unbelieving Jews lay in their hearts. This affected their spiritual discernment and prevented them from being converted (turned around) and spiritually healed of their malady. Thus it was that words first given by God in the eighth century before Christ were applied to Jews in the first century of the Christian era.

C. Destination: 28
28. Be it known therefore unto you, that the salvation of God is sent unto the Gentiles, and that they will hear it.

Paul further vented his frustration at the unbelieving Jews by declaring that the gospel of salvation would be transferred from them to the Gentiles, who would hear it and receive it. This must have sounded radical to the Jews, because they thought of themselves as set apart from pagans as recipients of the ordinances of God. God has never taken His hand completely off of the Jews, but the gospel has found its greatest reception among the Gentiles around the world.

D. Discussion: 29
29. And when he had said these words, the Jews departed, and had great reasoning among themselves.

We are not told where the departing Jews went, but they had a long discussion regarding what Paul had said that day. Once again, the gospel had served to divide a group of people into two opposing factions, and this has continued to the present time. Divine truth always seems to have this effect. We dare not tone it down in an effort to have harmony through compromise, although this is what some people advocate. Nothing is gained by an effort to draw the teachings of all religions into one united belief. The Bible sets the standard for faith,- and we must align ourselves with it or drift off into error and spiritual darkness.

III. Teaching: Acts 28:30-31

A. Reception: 30
30a. And Paul dwelt two whole years in his own hired house, ...

Paul had spent two years imprisoned by Governor Festus in Caesarea (Acts 24:27). He now had it somewhat easier in Rome, because he was able to live in his own rented house for two years. It must have taken a long time for Paul's appeal to come up on Caesar's schedule. Some have even thought that Paul was released for a while to travel before returning to Rome for his appeal.

30b. . . .and received all that came in unto him.

This implies that Paul was unable to leave his hired house during the two-year period, but he was allowed to have all kinds of visitors come to see him there. Despite what he had said about the gospel being shifted from Jews to Gentiles (Acts 13:46; 18:6; 28:28), we assume that some of his visitors were Jews seeking the truth, as well as Gentiles who became interested in it.

B. Revelation: 31

31a. Preaching the kingdom of God, . . .

This phrase was also used in verse 23, and you might want to take time to define it for your students. This indicates to us that the kingdom of God is among men as they accept Him as King and live as His obedient subjects. The "kingdom of God" can be translated "the reign of God."

31b. . . .and teaching those things which concern the Lord Jesus Christ . . .

Paul spent two years providing details concerning the life, death, burial, resurrection, ascension, and ongoing ministry of Jesus in heaven during this age of grace.

31c. . . .with all confidence, no man forbidding him.

This was a period of freedom to proclaim the gospel, despite the fact that Paul was under house arrest. He was able to speak boldly about spiritual things. No one forbade him teaching the whole counsel of God. Although we may give the Romans credit for their tolerance, we may be sure that it was God Himself Who made this freedom possible. Paul wrote several epistles while he was a prisoner in Rome, thus extending his ministry outside of Rome, In his letter to the Philippians he wrote, "All the saints [here] salute [greet] you, chiefly they that are of Caesar's household" (Phil. 4:22). This shows that converts to Christ had been made even in the emperor's palace. This must have been a great source of satisfaction to Paul.

During this quarter we have traced the ministry of this outstanding missionary, pastor, evangelist, author, and Christian statesman. He who had once persecuted the church became its great champion. He endured much for the sake of the gospel and its propagation by relying on the sustaining grace of God. In the face of continual harassment and outright persecution, he became an example for all believers to follow.

If time permits, quickly review the career of Paul for your students. Ask them if they have anything to say about his impact on them personally. See if anyone has been impressed enough to dedicate his or her life to Christian service as a result. Pray that each one may seek to emulate this apostle.

Evangelistic Emphasis

Some people feel they cannot be evangelistic because they do not fit into the mold of the evangelistic stereotype. They may suppose that to be evangelistic one must be an extrovert, a fluent teacher, or a persuader of multitudes. They may feel that a college level of biblical and theological knowledge is necessary before one can teach others.

We need to break that mold. Some of our finest examples of evangelism are private conversations in a wide variety of circumstances. Some who have been most effective in communicating the gospel do not have a broad knowledge but have a deep conviction about the blessing Christ has been in their own lives.

Although Paul could be eloquent and was certainly well informed, in our text he teaches individuals and small groups which come to his home. The facts that he teaches them are simple and basic. They are known to virtually every Christian.

Can you put people at ease and make them feel comfortable with you? You might do this by baking a loaf of hot bread for them, taking in their paper when they are out of town, or making a pot of soup for them when they are sick.

What will you teach them? Teach them what you know and have experienced. If you know anything about God, Christ, the gospel, or the church that has been helpful and meaningful to you, teach them that.

What if they do not accept it? You will be in the company of such great evangelists as Paul. Some did not believe him. Yet, he continued to communicate the good news, and uncounted millions of us are the beneficiaries of his work.

Memory Selection

"Paul dwelt two whole years in his own hired house, . . . preaching the kingdom of God, and teaching those things which concern the Lord Jesus Christ, with all confidence, no man forbidding him."
Acts 28:30,31.

Sometimes opportunities are greater than we think. Paul probably had no anticipation that he would have two years to work in Rome. Yet he taught all who would come to him. Sometimes we think, "If I had only known I was going to be here this long I would have . . ." Paul, in contrast, thought, "I am here now and I will do what I can now. If I am here longer I will be able to expand what I can do."

Paul also made the best of the situation he was in. He was a prisoner but it could have been worse. In fact it had been. Paul had been confined to a prison cell at midnight. He had also made the best of that situation. Now he was under house arrest, but had the privilege of having guests. He taught whom he could, when he could, as long as he could.

It is notable that he taught openly and confidently. He was not embarrassed nor ashamed of his faith. He wanted to be identified with it. Though it was not a popular point of view, he taught openly and confidently.

Weekday Problems

Gerald had high aspirations for his life as a geologist. He dreamed of traveling the world, exploring ancient civilizations, and being involved in major discoveries. He was part scholar and part outdoorsman. The opportunity to be out of an office and participate in adventure was exciting to him. Then he would teach and lecture to others.

At an early age he experienced an episode of congestive heart failure. His heart was weak enough that it could not pump enough blood to supply his body with adequate oxygen. He was placed on a severely restricted activity schedule. He had to take oxygen several hours a day. His dreams seemed to go up in smoke.

In the light of these developments, he reevaluated his career objectives. Some things he could not do. Yet he could still teach if he would do so through the written word. His word processor became his door to a world of wider contacts. He wrote with animation and inspiration. Where he could not go, his readers went.

* Have you had any major event that blocked your plans and changed the course of your life?
* How can Gerald best deal with the disappointment and change in his life?

Superintendent's Sermonette

Some people see opportunities where other people see only obstacles. How would you feel if you were unjustly accused and made a prisoner? Suppose that you had to travel hundreds of miles away from home to make an appeal, only to have it delayed for two years or more. Could you look beyond the obstacles and see opportunities waiting for you to make the gospel known to others in spite of your adverse circumstances? Could you see a new chapter opening up in your lifelong effort to win others to Christ?

This was the situation facing the Apostle Paul as he was shipped off to Rome to appeal his case to Caesar. He was fortunate in being able to live under house arrest and to be able to have all the visitors he wanted. He took advantage of this set of circumstances and continued his ministry. Those who wanted to know the gospel found it there. He sent out letters to believers in other places. He somehow penetrated even Caesar's household with the truth and made converts there. Paul was fruitful because he was adaptable.

This Lesson in <u>Your</u> Life

Those who read biographies often get insights into the lives of outstanding people. Those insights often become guides to inspire the reader to deal better with the circumstances of his own life. In our text, Paul gives us some such insights.

He did not react to unfair treatment with abuse and bitterness. He acted conscientiously as a Jewish rabbi to affirm, defend, and protect the faith. It is doubtful that any other rabbi was more energetic or zealous than he. Yet when he learned about the Messiahship of Jesus on the road to Damascus, he began to work in the light of this new knowledge. He was severely persecuted by those he had previously been such a hero to. He could understandably have been angry and bitter.

Instead, Paul said, "I was constrained to appeal unto Caesar; not that I had aught to accuse my nation of." He could understand why the Jewish leaders felt threatened. He saw things from their point of view and interpreted their actions kindly. He was not consumed with bitterness and they did not feel the onslaught of his anger.

Most of us need to develop a better ability to see things from another's point of view. Even if that view is in conflict with our own, we will be better off to understand it. It helps communications and on occasion resolves differences completely. Even when differences are not resolved, this approach helps to avoid bitterness and recriminations.

Another lesson for daily life in this story is that we should avoid being guided by popular opinion. Christianity was known as a sect that was "everywhere spoken against." The prevailing opinion was against Paul and against the gospel. As we know, the prevailing opinion was in error, but it probably was hard to make that assessment at the time. It will help if we keep that in mind when we are tempted to be carried away by popular prejudice or by a lynch mob mentality. Let us do our own thinking and act on the basis of our own faith and values.

In this story Paul was a prisoner. Yet he did much good for the gospel and the spread of the kingdom. It reminds us that we must not wait to do anything good until conditions are ideal. It was over significant odds that Paul completed his mission to take the gospel to the Gentiles.

Most worthwhile things in the world are accomplished in spite of inconvenience, conflict, and adversity. We will never do much good if we do only what is convenient, what is not opposed, and what can be easily done. If it is worthwhile doing it, let us try to do it even if we are in jail and threatened with death.

Many "ordinary" Christians can learn from this passage the effectiveness of hospitality. Paul could not go, so he received. Some of us are not able (or comfortable) going to others with the gospel. If that is our case, let us consider receiving others into our homes. If we are more relaxed showing hospitality than receiving it, let us have others into our home for meals and visits so that we may tell them of our faith in a wonderful Lord.

Seed Thoughts

1. How should we feel if we are told we have no apparent detractors?
We should be thankful, but we should expect critics to appear on the scene sooner or later.

2. Can we talk about Christianity objectively without being involved with it subjectively?
We may be able to do it for a limited time, but we will soon have to take a personal stand regarding it.

3. How can we best defend the gospel and our loyalty to it?
We must back up the gospel by both precept and example so that others will be impressed by our allegiance to it.

4. How do we defend the gospel by precept?
We must find our guiding principles within the framework of God's holy and revealed Word.

5. How do we defend the gospel by example?
We must know, love, and live the principles of God's Word continually.

(Please Turn Page)

---

1. How should we feel if we are told we have no apparent detractors?

2. Can we talk about Christianity objectively without being involved with it subjectively?

3. How can we best defend the gospel and our loyalty to it?

4. How do we defend the gospel by precept?

5. How do we defend the gospel by example?

6. Why won't all hearers understand and accept the gospel?

7. How can a person hear but not hear or see but not see?

8. Has God pulled the gospel away from Jews and given it to Gentiles only?

9. What was remarkable about Paul's ministry while in Rome?

10. What is the kingdom of God?

Seed Thoughts - Continued

We should be thankful, but we should expect critics to appear on the scene sooner or later.

We may be able to do it for a limited time, but we will soon have to take a personal stand regarding it.

We must back up the gospel by both precept and example so that others will be impressed by our allegiance to it.

We must find our guiding principles within the framework of God's holy and revealed Word.

We must know, love, and live the principles of God's Word continually.

Experience teaches that some are always blinded by Satan (II Cor. 4:3-4).

Isaiah 6:9-10 and Acts 28:26-27 reveal that a person can lack spiritual discernment for understanding and believing truth,

Although Jews generally refuse the gospel, it is still available to them as well as to Gentiles.

He adapted to a limited situation and ministered to visitors at his house and to others by letters sent abroad.

It is the rule or reign of God in the hearts of men.

6. Why won't all hearers understand and accept the gospel?
Experience teaches that some are always blinded by Satan (II Cor. 4:3-4).

7. How can a person hear but not hear or see but not see?
Isaiah 6:9-10 and Acts 28:26-27 reveal that a person can lack spiritual discernment for understanding and believing truth,

8. Has God pulled the gospel away from Jews and given it to Gentiles only?
Although Jews generally refuse the gospel, it is still available to them as well as to Gentiles.

9. What was remarkable about Paul's ministry while in Rome?
He adapted to a limited situation and ministered to visitors at his house and to others by letters sent abroad.

10. What is the kingdom of God?
It is the rule or reign of God in the hearts of men.

Song Of Moses

Exodus 15:1. Then sang Moses and the children of Israel this song unto the Lord, and spake, saying, I will sing unto the Lord, for he hath triumphed gloriously: the horse and his rider hath he thrown into the sea.
2. The Lord is my strength and song, and he is become my salvation: he is my God, and I will prepare him an habitation; my father's God, and I will exalt him.
3. The Lord is a man of war: the Lord is his name.
4. Pharaoh's chariots and his host hath he cast into the sea: his chosen captains also are drowned in the Red sea.
5. The depths have covered them: they sank into the bottom as a stone.
6. Thy right hand, O Lord, is become glorious in power: thy right hand, O Lord, hath dashed in pieces the enemy.
7. And in the greatness of thine excellency thou hast overthrown them that rose up against thee: thou sentest forth thy wrath, which consumed them as stubble.
8. And with the blast of thy nostrils the waters were gathered together, the floods stood upright as an heap, and the depths were congealed in the heart of the sea.
9. The enemy said, I will pursue, I will overtake, I will divide the spoil; my lust shall be satisfied upon them; I will draw my sword, my hand shall destroy them
10. Thou didst blow with thy wind, the sea covered them: they sank as lead in the mighty waters.
Exodus 15:13. Thou in thy mercy hast led forth the people which thou hast redeemed: thou hast guided them in thy strength unto thy holy habitation.
14. The people shall hear, and be afraid: sorrow shall take hold on the inhabitants of Palestina.

MEMORY SELECTION
Exodus 15:2
DEVOTIONAL READING
Psalm 115:1-9

BACKGROUND SCRIPTURE
Exodus 14:19-15:21
PRINTED SCRIPTURE
Exodus 15:1-10, 13-14

Teacher's Target

Pursued by the Egyptians to the western shore of the Red Sea, the Israelites were in a desperate position. An estimated two to three million may have taken part in the exodus from bondage, and there was no way that they could outrun the enemy chariots by going north or south. Then God opened up the waters to allow the Israelites to go through on the seabed. He closed the waters to trap the pursuing Egyptians, and their bloated corpses floated up on the eastern shore. Now it was time for Israel to rejoice with singing.

Help your students to analyze the song sung by the Israelites to see how God cares for His own and destroys those who persecute them. The power of God still operates in the world today, although it may take different and more modest forms than opening up a sea. We need to see His hand in our lives day by day.

Lesson Introduction

The Israelites, residing in Egypt for four centuries, had multiplied to the point where they were feared and then made slaves. God had sent Moses to them with a message of hope for deliverance, and they were thrilled when freedom finally came. However, they still had a slave-type mentality. When pursued by the Egyptians, they accused Moses of bringing them out into the wilderness to die. He told them, "Fear ye not, stand still, and see the salvation of the Lord,...The Lord shall fight for you" (Exod, 14:13-14).

There are times when God's people should fight for themselves, but there are also times when they are helpless and must depend on Him to fight for them. After deliverance comes, they should praise Him, even as the Israelites did, and one of the best ways to do this is with singing. Let us uphold this tradition from the ancient past.

Teaching Outline

I. Praise: Exod. 15:1-8
   A. Song: 1a
   B. Strength: 1b-3
   C. Seas 4-5
   D. Sovereignty: 6-8

II. Pursuit: Exod. 15:9-10
   A. Intention: 9
   B. Intervention: 10

III. Prospect: Exod. 15:13
   A. Redemption: 13a
   B. Redirection: 13b

Daily Bible Readings

Mon. The Red Sea Parted
Exodus 14:19-22
Tue. Egyptians Troubled
Exodus 14:23-25
Wed. Egyptians Drowned
Exodus 14:26-28
Thu. Israel Protected
Exodus 14:29-31
Fri. The Victory Song
Exodus 15:1-10
Sat. Victory Song Continued
Exodus 15:11-19
Sun. Miriam's Victory Dance
Exodus 15:20-21

Verse By Verse
Praise: Exod. 15:1-8

A. Song: 1a.
1a. Then sang Moses and the children of Israel this song unto the Lord, and spake, saying, I will sing unto the Lord, . . .
Music has long been used to accompany soldiers going into battle, perhaps to give them courage under pressure Battle brings tremendous suffering, wounds, and death, but in its aftermath comes singing from the hearts and throats of the victors. The unique factor in Israel's victory over the Egyptian pursuers was that none of God's people suffered and all of their enemies were drowned through divine action. This was sureLy a time to sing the praises of Jehovah, and the words seemed to spring spontaneously from the lips of Moses and his people.

B. Strength: 1b-3
1b. .for he hath triumphed gloriously: the horse and his rider hath he thrown into the sea.
God had demonstrated His strength by sending ten devastating plagues on the Egyptians while sparing the Israelites. He had overcome the stubbornness of the Pharaoh and persuaded him to let the Israelites go from his land. He had caused the Egyptians to give goods to the Israelites, a sort of delayed payment for their years of slavery. He had brought the nation of Israel to the Red Sea and through it, using its waters to destroy those pursuers. It was the greatest miracle recorded in the Old Testament, and succeeding generations would mention it to the end of earthly time.

In this, as in all of His works, God had triumphed gloriously. Egypt was famous as a land of great horses. Her cavalry was known and feared by surrounding nations. Her hundreds of chariots were a threat to all of her enemies, but there was one exception. God threw both horse and chariot rider into the sea, and their carcasses littered the shoreline when the drowning was complete.

2a. The Lord is my strength and song, and he is become my salvation: . . .
Moses made God's power personal when he declared that the Lord was _his_ strength and the source of _his_ song of victory. He counted God to be _his_ salvation. We are so used to calling Jesus our Savior that we may neglect to call God our Savior, too. They are united in their redemptive work in our behalf.

2b. . . .he is my God, and I will prepare him an habitation; . . .
Most translations differ from the Authorized Version here, simply translating this as "He is my God, and I will praise him."

2c. . . .my father's God, and I will exalt him.
Moses here referred to the Lord as the God of his ancestors in general. One way to exalt Him was to sing in a way which would glorify Him. Music appears to have been an integral part of worship since early times, although we might wonder if some of the light, superficial music used by some believers today really glorifies the Lord.

3. The Lord is a man of war: the Lord is his name.
There was no intention of

presenting the Lord here as a mere man. Moses saw Him as a divine Warrior. The Pharaoh had once asked, "Who is the Lord, that I should obey his voice to let Israel go? I know not the Lord, neither will I let Israel go" (Exod 5:2). Since that statement, he had had ample opportunity to learn just Who Jehovah was.

C. Sea: 4-5
4. Pharaoh's chariots and his host hath he cast into the sea: his chosen captains also are drowned in the Red sea.
5 The depths have covered them: they sank into the bottom as a stone.

The narrative of this event is found in Exodus 14:21-28, and you would do well to read it or summarize it. Moses had stretched out his hand over the sea, and the Lord had sent a strong east wind to divide the waters during the night. The Israelites went forward on dry ground between the walls of water on either side of them. The Egyptians pursued them with their horses and chariots.

The next morning God troubled the Egyptians by taking off their chariot wheels. They tried to flee back to the shoreline, but God had Moses stretch out his hand over the sea so that the waters came together again over the Egyptians, killing every one of them.

Exodus 15:4-5 is a poetic recall of what had happened. Hebrew poetry often repeated items with perhaps slightly different wording or embellishment. Verse 4 stated that Pharaoh's chariots and soldiers were cast into the sea, including his best officers. Verse 5 repeats the fact of drowning and adds that the victims sank to the bottom like stones.

D. Sovereignty: 6-8
6. Thy right hand, O Lord, is become glorious in power: thy right hand, O Lord, hath dashed in pieces the enemy.

The Lord's right hand or His scepter has been a symbol of His sovereign power. God is, of course, a Spirit without body parts such as we have, but these terms are used as an accommodation to our way of thinking. His power is projected in divine ways, and men feel it. We cannot see electricity, but we know the reality of an electric shock. God's name or reputation is enhanced by every act of power performed by Him, and this has often included His dashing Israel's enemies into pieces.

7. And in the greatness of thine excellency thou hast overthrown them that rose up against thee: thou sentest forth thy wrath, which consumed them as stubble.

This verse points out the futility of men trying to go against God. The greatness of His excellency (majesty) overthrows (pulls down) those who dare rise up to fight Him. He sends forth His wrath (fury, anger, indignation), and it consumes them as fire consumes stubble (straw). It is interesting that this analogy is used here, because the main emphasis in the song is the destruction of the Egyptian hosts by water. God can use all the elements at His disposal to accomplish His sovereign purposes.

8. And with the blast of thy nostrils the waters were gathered together, the floods stood upright as an heap, and the depths were congealed in the heart of the sea.

This description of the parting of the Red Sea certainly is different from the descriptions of what happened put forth by those who refuse to believe in divine miracles. What happened was not some natural phenomenon. It was a divine act which set aside the normal movement of water. God made the waters divide to the right and the left by a blast from His nostrils (an accommodation to our way of thinking). The point is that His divine power divided the waters. They stood up as walls on either side. In their depths they congealed into solid masses.

II. Pursuit: Exod 15:9-10

A. Intention: 9
9a. The enemy said, I will pursue, I will overtake, I will divide the spoil; ...

The Israelites were not poor when they left Egypt, They carried some of the treasures of that land with them. They had been told to ask the Egyptians for gold, silver, and raiment (Exod 11:2-3; 12:35-36). The Egyptian soldiers wanted to take all of that back again by running down the Israelites and overcoming them.

9b. . . .my lust shall be satisfied upon them; . . .

This seems to have referred to a passion for material booty, but we know that some soldiers have sought to satisfy sexual passion by misusing their victims.

9c. . . .I will draw my sword, my hand shall destroy them.

Soldiers caught up in the emotion of battle often became crazed with blood-lust, slashing in all directions with their swords. This was what the Egyptians intended to do.

B. Intervention: 10
10. Thou didst blow with thy wind, the sea covered them: they sank as lead in the mighty waters.

Regardless of what the murderous Egyptians intended to do, God intervened and they themselves became the helpless victims of a power greater than their own God used His breath (the wind) to perform His will. The sea covered them. The metaphor changes here from a stone (vs. 5) to lead to describe how they sank to the bottom before becoming bloated and washing up on the seashore (Exod. 14:30).

III. Prospect: Exod 15:13

A. Redemption: 13a
13a. Thou in thy mercy hast led forth the people which thou hast redeemed: . . .

Moses praised the Lord for showing mercy to His chosen people, for redeeming them from their enemies, and for leading them onward. God had not brought the Israelites out of bondage in Egypt so that they might perish in the wilderness. They had a long journey ahead of them, but they were bound for a better place. Passing through the Red Sea has often been used as a type of redemption by the blood of Christ. Those who know Him as Savior are not to be haunted by past sins. They are to press on to new blessings.

B. Redirection: 13b
13b. ...thou hast guided them in thy strength unto thy holy habitation.

We are not told by Moses what the holy habitation was, but verse 14 implies that he was referring to the land of Palestine. It was the land God originally gave to Abraham and his descendants (Gen. 12:7). That made it a special, sacred place, and it would be natural for Moses to think of Palestine in those terms. The final habitation for believers will be heaven itself, and they shall dwell forever with the Lord there.

The remainder of the song of Moses is recorded in Exodus 15:14-19. It speaks of the dread which would take hold of the inhabitants of Palestine, Edom, and Moab as God's people came into their midst and settled down to stay. Verse 19 is a brief summary of the destruction of the pursuing Egyptians and the deliverance of the Israelites through the Red Sea.

Miriam, the prophetess and sister of Moses and Aaron, led the women of Israel in the use of timbrels and dances to celebrate the people's deliverance. She entered into an antiphonal chorus with the other women in order to praise the Lord (Exod 15:20-21).

Evangelistic Emphasis

What a wonderful blessing it is to have something to sing about. Sometimes we feel like life is a succession of blue Mondays. We think we are living demonstrations of Murphy's law, "Whatever can go wrong will go wrong." We are not inclined to laugh and sing, but rather to weep and moan.

When, on the other hand, we feel greatly blessed, there are happy emotions that need to be released. We need to sing, praise, and give thanks. We need to share our joy with others because most lives have too much dreariness and not enough ecstasy. When we have something to sing about let us sing with vigor and enthusiasm whether or not we can do so with musical talent.

In the case of our text, Moses and the children of Israel were celebrating the fact that the powerful right hand of the Lord had delivered them from their enemies. Those who had oppressed Israel could no longer do so. Those who had exploited Israel could no longer do so. Those who had threatened Israel were no longer any threat. How natural to break out in song over such a great victory.

Paul must have had similar feelings when he wrote, "In all these things we are more than conquerors through him that loved us. For I am persuaded, that neither death, nor life, nor angels, nor principalities, nor powers, nor things present, nor things to come, nor heights, nor depth, nor any other creature shall be able to separate us from the love of God, which is in Christ Jesus our Lord." (Romans 8:38,39). That sounds like a song too. Let it be our song!

Memory Selection

"The Lord is my strength and song, and he is become my salvation: he is my God, and I will prepare him an habitation; my father's God, and I will exalt him."
Exodus 15:2.

What good news it is that the Lord is our strength. All of us have enemies, either present or potential, that are larger and stronger than we can deal with. We may encounter doubt, despair, temptation, or heartache that would devastate us if we had to face them alone. However, none of them is large enough or powerful enough to gain victory over the Lord. He is able. He is there for us when we need him. He hears our prayers and responds to them. He is our strength. Further, he is our song. He is not only a protector, but also a cause for rejoicing. Our Christian faith need not be observed somberly. There is much about it that is so exciting and so filled with joy that we often will be inclined to express our rejoicing in song. The Lord is not only our strength and our song but also our salvation. As he saved Israel from the Egyptians he saves us from those forces which oppress us. They may be physical or spiritual enemies that threaten us in daily life.

Weekday Problems

As I write, I have just visited in the home of a man who is terminally ill. In one sense all of us are terminal cases, but this particular man's life expectancy is down to a matter of hours. He is in constant pain. His wife is frail. During this illness she has gradually lost weight as she nursed him until she is down to one hundred pounds. She is worried about him and worried about what life will be like without him. This man has been devout in his faith for decades. That faith has not wavered, but has grown stronger. Nevertheless, it is a sobering matter to contemplate one's approaching death. As the wife worries about her husband, he also worries about her. Can she see well enough to drive? Can she manage the chores, the errands, and the decisions necessary to cope with the needs of her life? How will she deal with the loneliness after being happily married for so many years?

* What can be said to a person who is not expected to recover from his illness?
* What statements have you heard made to a seriously ill person that did not help?
* What word of hope and support can you give to his wife?

Superintendent's Sermonette

Most people seem to like music, although their tastes may vary widely. God's people have long used music in worship, instruction, and fellowship. Our choice of lyrics and tunes should line up with standards which God can approve, but this is easier said than done. The words we use ought to be true, edifying, and suitable to sacred uses. The music we use ought to be the same. There is room for different opinions, but we should avoid that which is worldly and superficial.

We will be looking at several examples of biblical songs this quarter, beginning with today's lesson on the song of Moses which was sung by Israelites after the dividing of the Red Sea to let them escape and the closing of it to drown their pursuers. The song grew out of a real-life experience, and its purpose was obviously to praise Jehovah. We shouLd look for musical expressions to commemorate our experiences and use them to bring glory to God. We have rich resources for doing this, and God still gives creative abilities to produce new songs, as well.

This Lesson in <u>Your</u> Life

One important element that is lacking in many lives is that of celebration. Some seem to think it is frivolous and relatively unimportant. They may work hard and accomplish a great deal, but they do not take time to celebrate their blessings and their achievements.

Moses did not feel that way. He realized that there were times for celebration. They were not frivolous times, but had a most serious purpose. They ventilated the joyful and thankful feelings of his heart and they expressed appropriate praise to the God who had given great blessings.

Our lives will be richer and happier if we see occasions for celebration and acknowledge them. Celebrations do several things for us. One is that they acknowledge significance. When there is a birth, a graduation, a wedding, or some other happy occasion, it is good to elevate that above the normal activities of life. A celebration says, "This is not just routinely good, it is exceptionally good."

Times for celebration need not be limited to the usual ones. Why not celebrate the answer to prayer? Instead of doing so with a party, why not with a time of worship? Do you feel particularly loving toward your family or spouse? Is that not a reason for singing and being thankful? Has someone shown you affection and love in a particularly meaningful way? Did that not cause feelings to well up in your heart that could well be expressed in song or prayer?

Another purpose that celebration serves is that it allows emotional and spiritual expression. We know how to express many things verbally and physically. We also have emotions that long for expression and yearnings for worship that need to find outlet. These may best be expressed in music, poetry, or prayer.

Celebration is also important because it provides inspiration for the future. As the memory of the Exodus was an inspiration to Israel in later times, the celebration of our victories will offer us hope in future crises.

Pharaoh's army was one kind of enemy. We are likely to have different kinds. Our enemies may be temptation, provocation, or discouragement. They may not be clothed in military garb and may not carry physical weapons. They are, nonetheless, authentic enemies and victory over them is essential to our eternal well-being. Therefore a victory in that arena deserves celebration also.

Have you overcome a bad habit? It would be appropriate for you to sing and pray. You may even be inclined to leap and dance. Have you made a courageous decision that will be a blessing to your life and that of others? Have you reconciled with an enemy so that there is no longer animosity? Have you completed a project or a course of study that was long and difficult? Find positive and constructive outlets for the happy and thankful feelings in your breast. You will be better for it and others will also.

Further, celebration of a decisive victory, can, at times, make that victory more secure. If we celebrate bravely a victory over temptation or discouragement, we are less likely to be trapped by that same danger again.

Seed Thoughts

1. Should a song used by believers have a particular theme?
This seems natural and helpful. The song of Moses had the theme of deliverance by God from Israel's enemies.

2. Should believers sing about the power of God?
It is one of His attributes and is worthy of praise. Many hymns use this as their main theme.

3. Do we as human beings have the right to exalt God in song?
He is great without our efforts, but He is pleased when we glorify Him by singing about Him.

4. How does sacred music enhance God's name and reputation?
It helps even unbelievers to better appreciate Who God is and what He does.

5. Is it all right to use repetition in song lyrics?
Hebrew poetry used it, evidently to good advantage. We can say similar things in different ways.

(Please Turn Page)

---

1. Should a song used by believers have a particular theme?

2. Should believers sing about the power of God?

3. Do we as human beings have the right to exalt God in song?

4. How does sacred music enhance God's name and reputation?

5. Is it all right to use repetition in song lyrics?

6. Should we sing only of the love of God and not of His wrath?

7. Should we sing about God's body parts (hand, nostrils, etc.)?

8. Should we rejoice in the overthrow of our worldly enemies?

9. How does the dividing of the Red Sea for Israel serve as a type of our redemption?

10. Where is our holy habitation?

This seems natural and helpful. The song of Moses had the theme of deliverance by God from Israel's enemies.

It is one of His attributes and is worthy of praise. Many hymns use this as their main theme.

He is great without our efforts, but He is pleased when we glorify Him by singing about Him.

It helps even unbelievers to better appreciate Who God is and what He does.

Hebrew poetry used it, evidently to good advantage. We can say similar things in different ways.

Despite what some people say, God should be described in all of His ways. His love is matched by His judgment.

He is a Spirit (John 4:24), but we can use these terms, as the Bible does, to accommodate our human way of thinking.

Our first desire should be to see them experience God's saving grace, If they refuse, we commit them to His judgment.

Even as God delivered the Israelites from their enemies, so it is that God delivers us from our sins.

For Israel it was the promised land of Palestine. For all believers it is heaven, where God and Christ dwell.

Seed Thoughts - Continued

6. Should we sing only of the love of God and not of His wrath?
Despite what some people say, God should be described in all of His ways. His love is matched by His judgment.

7. Should we sing about God's body parts (hand, nostrils, etc.)?
He is a Spirit (John 4:24), but we can use these terms, as the Bible does, to accommodate our human way of thinking.

8. Should we rejoice in the overthrow of our worldly enemies?
Our first desire should be to see them experience God's saving grace, If they refuse, we commit them to His judgment.

9. How does the dividing of the Red Sea for Israel serve as a type of our redemption?
Even as God delivered the Israelites from their enemies, so it is that God delivers us from our sins.

10. Where is our holy habitation?
For Israel it was the promised land of Palestine. For all believers it is heaven, where God and Christ dwell.

Song Of Deborah And Barak

Judges 5:1. Then sang Deborah and Barak the son of Abinoam on that day, saying,
2. Praise ye the Lord for the avenging of Israel, when the people willingly offered themselves.
3. Hear, O ye kings; give ear, O ye princes; I, even I, will sing unto the Lord; I will sing praise to the Lord God of Israel.
4. Lord, when thou wentest out of Seir, when thou marchedst out of the field of Edom, the earth trembled, and the heavens dropped, the clouds also dropped water.
5. The mountains melted from before the Lord, even that Sinai from before the Lord God of Israel.
6. In the days of Shamgar the son of Anath, in the days of Jael, the highways were unoccupied, and the travellers walked through byways.
7. The inhabitants of the villages ceased, they ceased in Israel, until that I Deborah arose, that I arose a mother in Israel.
8. They chose new gods; then was war in the gates: was there a shield or spear seen among forty thousand in Israel?
9. My heart is towrd the governors of Israel, that offered themselves willingly among the people. Bless ye the Lord.
10. Speak, ye that ride on white asses, ye that sit in judgment, and walk by the way.
11. They that are delivered from the noise of archers in the places of drawing water, there shall they rehearse the righteous acts of the Lord, even the righteous acts toward the inhabitants of his villages in Israel: then shall the people of the Lord go down to the gates.

MEMORY SELECTION
Judges 5:3
DEVOTIONAL READING
Psalm 81

BACKGROUND SCRIPTURE
Judges 4:4-5:31
PRINTED SCRIPTURE
Judges 5:1-11

Teacher's Target

Our lesson text is Judges 5:1-11, but it must be studied in the context of all of chapter 4 and chapter 5. Chapter 4 gives the account of Deborah and Barak in prose, while chapter 5 gives it in poetry. Some of the facts in the narrative are not given until chapter 5. Deborah and Barak are taken together as one when counting the thirteen "judges" (military saviors) who operated between the theocratic (rule of God) and the monarchic (rule of kings) periods in Israel's history.

Help your students to study the song of Deborah and Barak to see how God avenges His people when they willingly offer themselves to do His will. It is this divine-human relationship which we should develop in our time, too. God wants to work with us and through us to do great things.

Lesson Introduction

The Bible makes it clear that God expects men to take places of leadership and women to support them in their own special ways. This is certainly true of husbands and wives (Eph 5:22-33; I Tim. 2:8-15). However, this does not rule out the fact that God also uses women in situations where men may fail to live up to divine expectations. God has the right to use whomever He chooses to carry out His sovereign will, and He exercises it.

The account of Deborah and Barak showed how God used a combination of a man and a woman, not related, who went forth to do what neither could do singly. A third person, a woman named Jael, also had a part to play in the elimination of the warrior named Sisera. The result of their various efforts was victory for Israel, and the song of Deborah and Barak celebrated that victory.

Teaching Outline

I. Rejoicing: Judg. 5:1-3
  A. Persons: 1
  B. Praise: 2
  C. Proposal: 3

II. Reviewing: Judg. 5:4-8
  A. Power: 4-5
  B. Persecution: 6-7
  C. Perversion: 8

III. Rehearsing: Judg. 5:9-11
  A. Sacrificing: 9
  B. Speaking: 10
  C. Singing: 11

Daily Bible Readings

Mon. Deborah and Barak
Judges 4:4-9
Tue. Sisera's Forces Defeated
Judges 4:10-17
Wed. Jael Slays Sisera
Judges 4:18-24
Thu. Deborah and Barak Sing
Judges 5:1-8
Fri. The Song Continued
Judges 5:9-15
Sat. The Song Continued
Judges 5:16-23
Sun. The Song Concluded
Judges 5:24-31

Verse By Verse

I. Rejoicing: Judg. 5:1-3

A. Persons: 1
1. **Then sang Deborah and Barak the son of Abinoam on that day, saying,**

What we know about Deborah and Barak is contained in Judges 4-5, although Barak is also mentioned in Hebrews 11:32. Deborah was a prophetess, married to a man named Lapidoth, and she was a judge in Israel in the sense that people came to her for advice on solving their problems. Her judgments were given under a palm tree located between Ramah and Bethel in the hill country of Ephraim. Deborah evidently possessed spiritual discernment, and this made it possible for her to be highly respected by other people. Barak, son of a man named Abinoam, must have had some leadership skills and experience, but he was afraid to operate on his own. He insisted that Deborah join with him in raising an army and taking it into battle (Judg. 4:4-8).

B. Praise: 2
2. **Praise ye the Lord for the avenging of Israel, when the people willingly offered themselves.**

Jabin, the Canaanite king of Hazor, had oppressed the people of Israel, and they had cried out for deliverance. God's people went through some thirteen cycles of this type during the period of the judges, who were really not magistrates as much as they were military saviors raised up by God to deliver Israel. The song of Deborah and Barak celebrated the avenging of Israel against her pagan enemies. Credit was given not only to God for what He had done but also to the people who had willingly volunteered themselves to fight. Deborah and Barak were the human instruments used by God to inspire the people to throw off their oppressors.

C. Proposal: 3
3. **Hear, O ye kings give ear, O ye princes; I, even I, will sing unto the Lord I will sing praise to the Lord God of Israel.**

This was a time when pagan nations thought that each country had its own god or gods. The person singing the song of Deborah and Barak called on Gentile kings and princes to hear praise given to Jehovah, God of Israel. This had tremendous significance, because Jehovah was considered as being weak or strong depending on how Israel fared among the nations. God's reputation was at stake in all of this. He was respected when Israel did well, and He was dishonored when she did poorly, even when He was disciplining her. In the time of Deborah and Barak, God's people rejoiced over God's power and pagans respected Him for using it on their behalf.

II. Reviewing: Judg. 5:4-8

A. Power: 4-5
4. **Lord, when thou wentest out of Seir, when thou marchedst out of the field of Edom, the earth trembled, and the heavens dropped, the clouds also dropped water.**

The gods of the pagan fertility cults were associated with Canaan itself. Jehovah was associated with the arid regions to the south, such as the Sinai Peninsula and the wilderness between there and Canaan. Seir was the old name for Edom, a mountainous, rocky land stretching between the Dead Sea and the Gulf of Aqaba. The God of Israel was seen as coming in power out of that region, announced by earthquakes and violent storms dropping down huge amounts of water.

5. The mountains melted from before the Lord, even that Sinai from before the Lord God of Israel.

This carried on the thought begun in verse 4. Mountains melted (flowed) down before the power of the Lord, probably referring to earthquake activity such as occurred at Mount Sinai. This is described in Exodus 19:18—"Mount Sinai was altogether on a smoke, because the Lord descended upon it in fire: and the smoke thereof ascended as the smoke of a furnace, and the whole mount quaked greatly." What happened there in the time of Moses evidently was repeated in the time of Elijah—"A great and strong wind rent the mountains, and brake in pieces the rocks before the Lord;...and after the wind an earthquake and after the earthquake a fire" (I Kings 19:11-12).

In spite of all the progress made in the fields of science and technology, modern men have to stand helpless before demonstrations of God's power in such natural phenomena as earthquakes, hurricanes, floods, and fires. The term "acts of God" is still in vogue, even among unbelievers. All men must recognize the fact that these forces of nature are outside of their control for the most part. Bible believers should emphasize their acceptance of God's role in these things and seek to get others to believe in divine power

B. Persecution: 6-7
6. In the days of Shamgar the son of Anath, in the days of Jael, the highways were unoccupied, and the travellers walked through byways.

In the days of the judges named Shamgar and Jael (actually Ehud), the Israelites had to avoid using the main roads. They moved about by following back paths in hope of not being seen and assaulted by their enemies. This naturally inhibited trade and freedom of movement, making life more difficult.

7. The inhabitants of the villages ceased, they ceased in Israel, until that I Deborah arose, that I arose a mother in Israel.

During the time of persecution, the communities of Israel shriveled in size. Rulers ceased to function as before. Judges 21:25 sums up the situation by saying, "In those days there was no king in Israel: every man did that which was right in his own eyes." However, God was faithful to His people, and the time came when He raised Deborah up to be a mother to Israel. She helped to fill the vacuum which existed at that time.

At various levels in society, from the family to the nation, God expects men to be leaders. However, when they fail to meet the challenge, God raises up women and even children to serve in places of leadership. There is no intention here of denigrating the abilities of women. They deserve to get credit due them for what they accomplish in positions of leadership where God places them.

C. Perversion: 8
8. They chose new gods; then was war in the gates: was there a shield or spear seen among forty thousand in Israel?

The Israelites were guilty of spiritual perversion. Having turned their backs on Jehovah, their one true God, they ran after the false gods of the pagans surrounding them. God could not tolerate this apostasy, and he used Israel's enemies to chastise her in an attempt to drive His people back to Himself. This resulted in Israel's enemies coming right to the gates of her cities. The Israelites were helpless to defend themselves. Their weapons were either hidden for fear of being taken away, or they actually were taken away by their enemies. A shield or spear could not be found among 40,000 men in Israel. This ratio apparently meant that only a handful of weapons could have been found in the whole nation.

III. Rehearsing: Judg. 5:9-11

A. Sacrificing: 9
9. My heart is toward the governors of Israel, that offered themselves willingly among the people. Bless ye the Lord.

The singer's heart went out in gratitude to the commanders in Israel who volunteered to go to war to set their people free. They had to go up against Sisera's army equipped with nine hundred iron chariots. The troops from the tribes of Naphtali and Zebulun were 10,000 strong. We do not know where they acquired weapons with which to fight. We do know that God discomfited the enemy by causing the chariot wheels to become mired in mud. All but Sisera were slain, and he was able to escape but was killed by a woman named Jael while he slept in her tent (Judg. 4:10-21). Note the use of the term "willingly offered themselves" (vs. 2) and "offered themselves willingly" (vs. 9). The spirit of sacrifice has always been required in times of war. Many have paid with their lives in order that others could be free. This, of course, is the whole idea behind the sacrifice of Christ for sinners at Calvary.

The singer called on people to "Bless ye the Lord." He had been faithful to Israel, and volunteers in Israel had been faithful to the rest of the nation.

B. Speaking: 10
10. Speak, ye that ride on white asses, ye that sit in judgment, and walk by the way.

The singer called on all levels of Israelite society to join in praise to Jehovah. White asses were rare and highly prized, and that meant that only the rich and famous were able to have them and ride on them. Those described as sitting in judgment may have referred to magistrates, although some translate this as those sitting on tapestries or carpets reserved for the rich. Those who walked on the roadways were the poorer class who could not afford animals to ride.

C. Singing: 11
11a. They that are delivered from the noise of archers in the places of drawing water, there shall they rehearse the righteous acts of the Lord, even the righteous acts toward the inhabitants of his villages in Israel: . . .

The meaning here is somewhat obscure. It may mean that those delivered from the noise of enemy archers could gather at community wells to rehearse the righteous acts of God in delivering them from their enemies. One suggestion is that Israelite archers joined with common people at the wells to rejoice over their victory against their enemies.

11b. . . .then shall the people of the Lord go down to the gates.

The areas around city gates were important public gathering places in ancient Israel. The people went there to learn what was new, to mingle with others, and to have judgments made in disputes before magistrates. Once the enemies were dispersed, the gates could resume their normal functions in public life. The song of Deborah and Barak continued on to the end of Judges 5, but we have seen enough of it to appreciate the victory that it celebrated. Once again, God had come to the aid of His repentant people and brought them out from under foreign oppression to a place of freedom and independence. This was a cycle repeated many times during the period of the judges.

Evangelistic Emphasis

Evangelism is telling good news. The best of all news is the story of Jesus and the shedding of his blood for the forgiveness of our sins. This ultimate good news is foreshadowed by many stories of the Lord delivering his people throughout history. One such story is that of Deborah and Barak giving Israel the victory over their oppressors.

Sometimes when we are trying to communicate the good news of Jesus to others, we can help them to accept it by reminding them of other times the Lord has rescued people. This may be by referring to stories in the Scriptures, but it may also be by referring to experiences in life. If a person can perceive that he has been in difficulty before and has been saved or sheltered by the goodness of God, that will prepare him to think in terms of being saved by the gospel.

Good news needs not only to be told, but also to be sung. When there is only talking and not singing, some of our emotional and spiritual feelings remain unexpressed. Sometimes those we are trying to teach have their hearts locked by locks which can only be opened by the keys of music.

Some people will never really hear the gospel until they hear it in song. Their minds might understand the facts but their hearts are yet unmoved by the grace and love. They will be taught but unconverted. It is for this reason that we need to participate in and/or support the music that fills the air waves with the sweet message of Jesus.

Memory Selection

"I, even I, will sing unto the Lord; I will sing praise to the Lord God of Israel."
Judges 5:3

This memory selection raises three questions for those of us who are Christians. The first is, "Do I sing?" It should be axiomatic that Christians sing. Our hearts are full of a kind of love and joy that can only be properly expressed in singing. Yet in most churches there are those who do not sing in the church service and one wonders whether they ever sing at all.

Notice that it is not a question of, "How well do I sing?" or "Do I sing in public?" or "Have I had training in music?" It is not a question of skill or training, but a question of whether there is enough gospel in our hearts that it cannot be contained. It must under some circumstances burst forth in song.

A second question is, "Is there a message in my heart that calls for singing?" If I do not find myself singing, I need to inventory the amount of Christian joy and thanksgiving that are in my heart. I will certainly find the need to build up that inventory until there are feelings that must be expressed in song.

A third and related question is, "Do I put enough emphasis on praise in my worship?" The praise dimension gives release to singing. I may have gotten off balance in my relationship with God, thinking too much about duty and not enough about praise.

Weekday Problems

Sam feels that he has been called to preach the gospel. Although he has had some opportunities to preach, he has had trouble being recognized by his church as a minister. He feels this is because others have not given enough attention to his needs and problems. He is quite bitter and does a great deal of complaining about his frustrations of feeling called and yet not being encouraged and used.

He has counseled with the minister of his own church. The minister wanted to tell him how to take the next step that would move him in the direction of his goal. Sam was not interested in that. He wanted to rehearse the alleged neglect that he had experienced. The minister kept saying, "Have you done this?" Sam kept replying, "They dropped the ball. They did not follow through. They are not interested in me."

Instead of doing what he can and singing of success, Sam does nothing and sings the blues about his failure.

* Explain why something needs to be done first and singing about the victory needs to be done later.
* How can we be sure there will be a victory?
* Explain why complaining not only blames others but ultimately blames God.

Superintendent's Sermonette

We have heard people say, "It is darkest before dawn." We have heard them say, "To every cloud there is a silver lining." How should we, as believers in God, think and feel about hard times? The Bible contains numerous examples which illustrate the fact that God does take harsh circumstances and turn them around for His people. Sometimes it was the times of oppression themselves which He used in order to draw people back to Himself after they had apostasized.

We may expect the Lord to deal with us as believers today in the same manner. Rather than accusing Him of abandoning us, let us search our hearts to see if we have detoured away from Him and need to be brought back on track again. God may also allow us to go through hard experiences in order to test our faith and strengthen our character. We need to trust Him for deliverance, and we need to praise Him when it comes. As did Deborah and Barak of old, let us raise our voices in song so that we may honor and glorify the One Who gives us all good things.

This Lesson in Your Life

There are two things I would like for us to learn from this lesson. The first is that there is a decisive power in confident leadership. The second is that when God gives us a victory it is worth singing about.

First, notice how vital the leadership of Deborah was. Without it, the battle would not only not have been won, it would not even have been engaged. Barak refused to go unless Deborah would go with him. Barak was a competent soldier, but he lacked the will and the nerve that were necessary in this case. Deborah had to supply them. When she did so, Barak was able to lead Israel successfully into battle.

Deborah's leadership changed Barak. He who said, "If thou wilt not go with me, then I will not go," not only went, but led Israelite armies to a great victory. We need to remember that when our faith and confidence are strongly expressed, we not only improve our own situation but we give strength to others. They are able to do more because of our supply of the faith they lack.

It is interesting that Deborah knew that her manifestation of faith would not be lost on the people. She said, "The Lord shall sell Sisera into the hand of a woman." Whatever the politicians say, the people usually know who is deserving of honor.

It was ultimately Deborah's leadership that claimed the day. The victory came because Deborah could say to Barak, "This is the day in which the Lord hath delivered Sisera into thine hand." Of course it was God who gave the victory but he used the leadership of Deborah to give it.

It is important for us to do all that we can and then to thank the Lord for the successful results. Deborah and Barak and their forces did not remain idle hoping for the salvation of the Lord. They took the risks of leadership. They attacked and pursued. When they were victorious they praised the Lord.

The victory song was a rehearsal of what God had done for Israel. He had made the earth to tremble and the mountain to melt. He had raised up Deborah, a mother of Israel. Therefore, the victory song said, "Let everyone from the rich and the powerful to the poor and unknown praise him."

As it was good for Deborah to rehearse God's gifts in song, so it is also good for us to do so. We can rehearse what God did in creation, in the development of his people, in the giving of His Son, in the providing of the Scriptures, in the formation of the church, and in the confident hope of heaven.

There are songs that will allow us to rehearse the blessings of our own personal lives. We can be thankful for life, for love, for grace, for hope, for loving relationships, for healing, and for a multitude of other blessings.

Some among us have musical and poetic ability. We can compose songs and poems of praise about what the Lord has done for us personally and corporately. We have much to praise him for. Let the songs of victory ring out through the church.

Seed Thoughts

1. Should we seek revenge on our enemies?
The biblical principle has been to let God function in this role, if necessary, and for us to love them (Matt. 5:44; Rom. 12:17-21).

2. Does God ever use believers to carry out His judgments?
The Bible gives many illustrations that God does use believers to do this.

3. Why is it better to volunteer for God's service than to be drafted into it?
God appreciates those who willingly offer themselves to do His will, although He may sometimes force them to do it.

4. Why should we ask unbelievers to hear us praise our God?
This is a form of witness, for by our songs of praise we show our love for God and suggest others love Him, too.

5. How should we present God to a pagan world?
We should show Him to be all-powerful and ready to judge sin but also merciful and ready to forgive sinners.

(Please Turn Page)

---

1. Should we seek revenge on our enemies?

2. Does God ever use believers to carry out His judgments?

3. Why is it better to volunteer for God's service than to be drafted into it?

4. Why should we ask unbelievers to hear us praise our God?

5. How should we present God to a pagan world?

6. Why does God allow people to be oppressed by their enemies?

7. Where should believers seek help when oppressed?

8. Are people today guilty of choosing new gods?

9. To what levels of society should Christians witness?

10. Should believers be involved in public life?

Seed Thoughts - Continued

6. Why does God allow people to be oppressed by their enemies?
He may discipline them for their sins and seek to restore them to Himself,

7. Where should believers seek help when oppressed?
If they trust in the Lord, He will raise up deliverers in His Own time and in His Own way.

8. Are people today guilty of choosing new gods?
Literal idolatry may not be practiced by many advanced cultures, but they may be guilty of devoting themselves to unworthy people or things instead of God.

9. To what levels of society should Christians witness?
All levels should be included, Upper levels are sometimes neglected.

10. Should believers be involved in public life?
This is the only way that they can have a complete testimony to others.

David's Lament For Saul And Jonathan

2 Samuel 1:17. And David lamented with this lamentation over Saul and over Jonathan his son:
18. (And he bade them teach the children of Judah the use of the bow: behold, it is written in the book of Jasher.)
19. The beauty of Israel is slain upon thy high places: how are the mighty fallen!
20. Tell it not in Gath, publish it not in the streets of Askelon; lest the daughters of the Philistines rejoice, lest the daughters of the uncir-cumcised triumph.
21. Ye mountains of Gilboa, let there be no dew, neither let there be rain, upon you, nor fields of offerings: for there the shield of the mighty is vilely cast away, the shield of Saul, as though he had not been anointed with oil.
22. From the blood of the slain, from the fat of the mighty, the bow of Jonathan turned not back, and the sword of Saul returned not empty.
23. Saul and Jonathan were lovely and pleasant in their lives, and in their death they were not divided: they were swifter than eagles, they were stronger than lions.
24. Ye daughters of Israel, weep over Saul, who clothed you in scarlet, with other delights, who put on ornaments of gold upon your apparel.
25. How are the mighty fallen in the midst of the battle! O Jonathan, thou wast slain in thine high places.
26. I am distressed for thee, my brother Jonathan: very pleasant hast thou been unto me: thy love to me was wonderful, passing the love of women.
27. How are the mighty fallen, and the weapons of war perished.

MEMORY SELECTION
2 Samuel 1:23
DEVOTIONAL READING
Psalm 61

BACKGROUND SCRIPTURE
2 Samuel 1
PRINTED SCRIPTURE
2 Samuel 1:17-27

Teacher's Target

Saul had started out well as Israel's first king, but he had gone against God's will and become the victim of divine judgment. David had served Saul well, and he had formed a strong attachment to Jonathan, Saul's son. After Saul turned against David, the friendship with Jonathan had continued. David accepted the anointing of Saul as king by Samuel as permanent, and he was deeply distressed when he heard that he had died in battle. He was naturally also distressed to hear of the death of Jonathan at the same time.

Help your students to realize that A person can think well of others, whether or not they treated him fairly when they were alive. This is possible if those individuals are seen from God's perspective. The psalmist quoted God as saying, "Touch not mine annoited, and do my prophets no harm" (Ps. 105:15). David applied this to King Saul and mourned his passing.

Lesson Introduction

Details regarding David's lament over Saul and Jonathan are found in I Samuel 31:1-II Samuel 1:16. In a battle with the Philistines, Saul's three sons, Jonathan, Abinadab, and Melchi-shua were slain at Mount Gilboa. Saul was sorely wounded by an enemy archer and fell upon his sword to commit suicide. The Philistines beheaded Saul, took his body to Beth-shan, and fastened it as a spectacle to the wall there. Valiant Israelites came at night, recovered his body and those of his sons, and buried them at Jabesh.

Meanwhile, David returned from battle with the Amalekites and rested at Ziklag. A young man showed up in camp with the message that Saul and Jonathan had died at Mount Gilboa. This man claimed to have actually slain Saul at the king's urgent request. David had the Amalekite slain because he had dared to touch the Lord's anointed one.

Teaching Outline

I. Esteem: II Sam. 1:17-19
   A. Ballad:17-18
   B. Beauty: 19

II. Entreaties: II Sam. 1:20-21
   A. Request I: 20
   B. Request II: 21

III. Eulogiess II Sam. 1:22-27
   A. Distresss 22-23
   B. Description I: 24
   C. Description II: 25-27

Daily Bible Readings

Mon. The Bad News
2 Samuel 1:1-4
Tue. An Eye Witness
2 Samuel 1:5-8
Wed. "I Slew Him"
2 Samuel 1:9-11
Thu. Mourning
2 Samuel 1:12-13
Fri. Accountability
2 Samuel 1:14-16
Sat. The Lament
2 Samuel 1:17-22
Sun. The Mighty are Fallen
2 Samuel 1:23-27

Verse By Verse

I. Esteem: II Sam. 1:17-19

A. Ballad: 17-18
17. And David lamented with this lamentation over Saul and over Jonathan his son:

Mourning was serious business in ancient Israel, and David paused to express his feelings regarding King Saul and Prince Jonathan. Saul had been guilty of trying to kill David with a javelin and of hounding him into the wilderness repeatedly, but David still held him in esteem as God's anointed one. His lamentation included Jonathan, as well, for he had a deep love for this prince. David's ability to create poetry is demonstrated here as surely as it is demonstrated in the many psalms which he wrote.

18. (Also he bade them teach the children of Judah the use of the bow: behold, it is written in the book of Jasher.)

The lamentation by David became known by its title, "The Bow," and he insisted that it be taught to all of the children of Judah. This title was probably taken from mention of the bow in verse 22. The song was evidently employed in a training program to increase the skill of archery among the young people in Judah. It was recorded in the book of Jasher (Heroic Ballads). References to this book may be found in Joshua 10:13 and the Septuagint Version of I Kings 8:53. It celebrated wars in Israel's history.

B. Beauty: 19
19. The beauty of Israel is slain upon thy high places: how are the mighty fallen!

David saw in Saul and his sons the beauty (honor, glory) of Israel personified or symbolized. They were slain in high places or in the hills. David saw them as the mighty (heroes) who had fallen in battle. Perhaps this was tied to the thought that sacrificing their lives in defense of the nation gave their deaths a special meaning.

II. Entreaties: II Sam. 1:20-21

A. Request I: 20
20. Tell it not in Gath, publish it not in the streets of Askelon; lest the daughters of the Philistines rejoice, lest the daughters of the uncircumcised triumph.

Israelite women were used in celebrating Israel's victories in war, as shown in I Samuel 18:6-7—"And it came to pass as they came, when David was returned from the slaughter of the Philistine [Goliath], that the women came out of all cities of Israel, singing and dancing, to meet king Saul, with tabrets, with joy, and with instruments of musick. And the women answered [antiphonally] one another as they played, and said, Saul hath slain his thousands, and David his ten thousands." David was afraid that news of the deaths of Saul and his sons would become a cause for rejoicing on the part of the Philistines in their chief cities, such as Gath and Askelon (Ashkelon). He could not prevent this, but he expressed his desire that it not be done as a form of protest on his part. He knew that such a celebration would enhance people's view of Philistine gods and take away from their view of Jehovah.

B. Request II: 21
21. Ye mountains of Gilboa, let

there be no dew, neither let there be rain, upon you, nor fields of offerings: for there the shield of the mighty is vilely cast away, the shield of Saul, as though he had not been anointed with oil.

The mountains (or hills) of Gilboa were located on the eastern side of the Plain of Esdraelon and averaged about 1600 feet in height. David expressed the desire that they be devoid of moisture (dew and rain) and that their hillside fields be barren. He lamented the fact that it was here that Saul cast away his shield as if he had not been anointed with oil to become Israel's first king. One view sees this verse describing the shield itself as being unpolished with oil after it had been discarded in battle.

III. Eulogies: II Sam, 1:22-27

A. Distress: 22-23
22. From the blood of the slain, from the fat of the mighty, the bow of Jonathan turned not back, and the sword of Saul returned not empty.

Deuteronomy 32:42 has a gruesome description of the effect of weapons upon enemies—"I will make mine arrows drunk with blood, and my sword shall devour flesh." The same thought is reflected in David's references to the weapons used by Jonathan and Saul. Jonathan's arrows consumed the blood and fat (flesh) of his enemies. The sword of Saul was filled with the flesh of his enemies. David attributed this ferocity to the courage and skill of these two men.

23a. Saul and Jonathan were lovely and pleasant in their lives, and in their death they were not divided: . . .

David declared that Saul and Jonathan had been lovely and pleasant while alive. We can understand how he used such terms to describe Jonathan, but we wonder at his use of them for Saul. He must have viewed the king as displaying good points, and it was these which he had in mind in this description.

David declared that Saul and Jonathan had been together at the time of their deaths. This must have seemed fitting and proper as far as David was concerned, perhaps because it meant that they finished their earthly course together in a common purpose.

23b. . . .they were swifter than eagles, they were stronger than lions.

Warlike characteristics were much in vogue in ancient times. Borrowing from the world of animals, David compared Saul and Jonathan to swift eagles and strong lions, declaring them both to excel these creatures. This was hyperbole, of course, using exaggeration for poetic effect.

B. Description I: 24
24. Ye daughters of Israel, weep over Saul, who clothed you in scarlet, with other delights, who put on ornaments of gold upon your apparel.

Even as the women of Israel had celebrated Saul's victories with singing and dancing, so now David urged them to mourn his death. David's description of Saul was very favorable. He gave the king credit for clothing the women with fine scarlet clothes and with other delightful things. He said that it was Saul who gave them gold ornaments to wear on their garments. Here, again, David was remembering and emphasizing the good things Saul had done for his nation. His dark moods and violent actions were set aside for this time of mourning.

C. Description II: 25-27
25a. How are the mighty fallen in the midst of the battle!

David's agony of heart burst forth in this phrase again, as it had before (vs. 19). It seemed difficult for him to accept the fact that Saul and Jonathan were really gone.

25b. O Jonathan, thou wast slain in thine high places.

David's description of Jonathan was one of deep, almost unconsolable regret. This repeat of what was said before (vs. 19) may have helped David to come to grips with the reality of his close friend's death.

26a. I am distressed for thee, my brother Jonathan: . . .

David grieved for Jonathan as if

he had been his own blood brother. Although David stood to gain position because of Jonathan's death, it seems clear that he would have preferred that Jonathan had lived and assumed the throne left vacant by his father.

26b. . . .very pleasant hast thou been unto me: . . .

David seemed to remember only good things from his long association with Jonathan when he was alive. He remembered the kindnesses shown to him by the prince. This is perhaps the best legacy which can be left by one who passes from this world into the next. Good memories of kindnesses shown remain and may generate repetition among those left behind.

26c. . . .thy love to me was wonderful, passing the love of women.

We live in an age when this kind of wording may cause some students to wonder if David was describing a homosexual connection between himself and Jonathan. A study of Jonathan's life would imply that he was of the highest moral character and one who would not be involved in this kind of sexual perversion. We need to also consider the fact that two males can have a deep relationship which has nothing to do with sexual activity. Women in ancient cultures had their roles to play in establishing relationships with men, but it was equally true that men might become strongly attached to one another out of mutual respect and admiration. The companionship of David and Jonathan was evidently a prime example of this kind of partnership.

On a one-to-one basis, David declared that his love for Jonathan had been even greater than that he had felt for various women. As strange as it may seem to anyone in a western culture, men may still be seen walking hand in hand down a street in the Middle East, and it does not have the same connotation as this type of scene would have elsewhere.

27a. How are the mighty fallen,...

This is the third and final time that David's lament mentions this thought. As in verses 19 and 25, it again seems to burst forth from his inner spirit to express his tremendous grief over the loss of the king and the prince who fought for their homeland.

27b. . . .and the weapons of war perished!

David was probably referring to the specific weapons carried by Saul and Jonathan and not to weapons of war in general. We have a strong peace movement in the world today which advocates eliminating all manner of weapons from men's arsenals. This was not the case with David, for he used his weapons many times following the deaths of Saul and Jonathan.

As every Bible student knows, David went on to become king over Judah first and then over Israel afterward, thus uniting the two kingdoms of God's people again and passing on the united kingdom to his son, Solomon, in due time. He stockpiled materials when God prevented him from building the first temple, reserving this for Solomon.

David's lament over Saul and Jonathan helps to point up an important matter. We may not approve of all that a national leader does, but we should respect the office which he holds. Our leaders may not come into office after being anointed with oil by a prophet of God, but they may well fit the category of being "the powers that . . . are ordained of God" (Rom. 13:1). Let us pray for them and cooperate with them.

Evangelistic Emphasis

Our story today tells the story of David's faithfulness to Saul and his love for Jonathan. He also, of course, loved Saul and was faithful to Jonathan, but he related to them in different ways. He was true to both in spite of the fact that Saul was often not true to him.

In teaching the gospel we will find that different people relate to the Lord in different ways. All need to feel both love and duty, but they will not feel them in precisely the same proportions. Therefore one motivation will work better with one person and another

Some have a highly-developed sense of duty. They can be called to responsibility. They will respond to being needed in a great cause. They are not likely to pass up an opportunity to do significant good in the world. They want their lives to be meaningful, to count. They can be drawn to Christ because it is right, it will accomplish good, and it is the responsible thing to do.

Others will be most attracted to the message of selfless love in the gospel. Their hearts will melt. They will fall in love with Jesus and will follow him out of sheer personal devotion. They can be drawn to Christ because they find his love irresistible.

The original disciples show some such differences. John related to Jesus in a different way than Peter did. We will be more effective in evangelism if we give due consideration to the type of motivation a person would be most receptive to.

Memory Selection

"Saul and Jonathan were lovely and pleasant in their lives, and in their death they were not divided: they were swifter than eagles, they were stronger than lions."
2 Samuel 1:23.

Whenever anyone dies there is good to be remembered and bad to be remembered. David remembered the good about both Saul and Jonathan. I have known some that would have considered that hypocritical. To have praised Saul as being lovely and pleasant would have been more than they could stand. They would have felt constrained to recall his cruelty, his violence, and his jealousy. David felt no such constraint.

Perhaps it would be helpful if we gave thought to the fact that all of us need our lives interpreted in a kind manner.

That does not mean that we must deny the existence of faults. The Scriptures are clear on the character deterioration of Saul. Nobody was more aware of this than David. He had seen Saul's blackest moods. He had been the king's harpist when Saul was morosely mad. He had been the object of Saul's intense jealousy and had often been in danger of his life because of Saul.

Yet David loved Saul and felt like singing a song of love and sorrow. He was able to say Saul was swifter than an eagle and stronger than a lion.

Weekday Problems

Bennie was a cruel and selfish man. No doubt there were reasons for it, but his behavior made his wife's life a torment. He was abusive in his speech. He made money but did not share any of it for the support of his wife or children. In fact, he took money from her nursing salary for financing his own pleasures and extravagances. He was abusive to the children. It was hard to find a redeeming quality.

Bennie was not in good health and refused to take proper care of himself. It was not a total surprise when he dropped dead at a relatively early age. Neighbors and friends of the family thought Bennie's death would bring nothing but relief. It would stop the abuse and eliminate the financial drain. No longer would there be worry about a midnight phone call saying he was in jail, in a fight, or in a car wreck.

To everyone's surprise, Bennie's wife was grief-stricken. She wept as though an important part of her life was gone. She had lost one of her reasons for living. She did not see it as a relief but as a loss.

* What losses would Bennie's wife have experienced?
* What needs in her life may have been met by her relationship with Bennie?

Superintendent's Sermonette

We live in a world which has been seething with the demand for freedom. This gained impetus as the various world powers divested themselves of their colonial holdings following World War II. It gained new impetus as the Communist bloc began to crack apart in recent years. One of the dangers which developed, however, was that anarchy would take hold in the absence of leaders who were experienced and competent for governing according to democratic principles. Examples of this have become apparent, and the conclusion has emerged that even bad government is better than no government at all.

David truly mourned the deaths of King Saul and Prince Jonathan. He missed Saul because he counted him to be the anointed one sent by God to lead the nation of Israel. He missed Jonathan because he loved him deeply as a good and loyal friend. Let us learn from his attitude, and let us give our leaders our respect and our prayers. This is what we would like to receive if and when God calls us to places of leadership, and He may do that in due time. He did it with David.

This Lesson in <u>Your</u> Life

Grief is neither predictable nor logical. Saul had experienced periods of smoldering melancholy about David. He was consumed with jealousy. He was frightened of David's popularity. The women of Israel had taunted him with a song, "Saul has slain his thousands; David has slain his ten thousands." Saul had tried repeatedly to kill David. Most would have expected the news of Saul's death to be an occasion of joy for David.

It was not so. David, who had himself spared the life of Saul on more than one occasion, did not rejoice over Saul's death. He saw Saul as the anointed one of God. Because he respected God, he respected Saul. However, there appears to be an added dimension of true affection. David appeared to have some empathy with Saul's problems and was not willing to rejoice over his death.

That reminds us that we have attachments, affections, and dependencies even on those who create problems and frustrations for us. It would be a mistake to assume that when a relationship is troubled, grief will not be strong. Many times our lives are partially defined by a relationship. Perhaps our sense of worth comes partly from the fact that we care for one who does not treat us well. We can experience true grief at the loss of a relationship even if it is an adversary one.

Grief does not smite the human heart at a consistent level. It comes in waves. In between those waves, we might suppose that we have solved our problem or at least made progress with it. Then another wave will hit with surprising force and we will realize that grief is still strongly in our heart. The waves of grief are often triggered by incidental or innocuous occurrences. We cannot anticipate them because we do not know what will cause us to have sorrow aroused.

There are yet many things we do not understand about grief. One thing, however, that we do understand is that grief needs to be appropriately expressed. Those who bottle up feelings without ventilating them are creating time bombs that can eventually be very destructive.

Appropriate expression does not mean a constant brooding over loss. Neither does it mean that we vomit our pain on everyone we are with. It means that honest emotions need to be expressed in honest ways to people who can be trusted with them. It may be that frustrations need to be talked out. Perhaps a deceased person hurt us in a way that we cannot let go until it is ventilated in wholesome discussion. Perhaps we hurt that person in a way that requires our guilt to be dealt with.

One way to express grief is through song. As music can touch the chords of joy, thanksgiving, patriotism, and worship, so it also can touch the chords of sorrow. The dirge, the lament, and the melancholy psalm can give a Christian outlet for grief that is too large to be contained.

This lesson also teaches that however large one's faults, there are positive things to be remembered. Saul had been cruel and corrupt. David remembered how mighty he had been and what he had done for Israel. Honesty does not require saying everything bad we know about everybody. Such unguarded candor is not a virtue but a folly.

Seed Thoughts

1. Is it worthwhile to have funerals with dirges and lamentations?
Funerals provide the only opportunities for some people to hear Bible truths presented in a constructive way.

2. Can ballads arising out of people's deaths be instructive?
David's lamentation became part of the Heroic Ballads book in training children. We might find modern counterparts to it.

3. Should the essence of a nation be personified in its heroes?
This is often the case, for people identify readily with others who have distinguished themselves in national life.

4. Should we care if enemies rejoice over the deaths of our national leaders?
Yes, we should care and be concerned with the implications, but our trust is in God, not in human leaders alone.

5. Should we curse the places where our leaders die?
No, we should not curse at all, and this applies to natural locations.

(Please Turn Page)

---

1. Is it worthwhile to have funerals with dirges and lamentations?

2. Can ballads arising out of people's deaths be instructive?

3. Should the essence of a nation be personified in its heroes?

4. Should we care if enemies rejoice over the deaths of our national leaders?

5. Should we curse the places where our leaders die?

6. What may displace the power to wage war in settling disputes today?

7. What is the best legacy a person can leave behind?

8. Should believers weep at the passing of others?

9. What should believers use to comfort one another when death comes?

10. How can believers overcome bereavement and move ahead?

Seed Thoughts - Continued

Funerals provide the only opportunities for some people to hear Bible truths presented in a constructive way.

David's lamentation became part of the Heroic Ballads book in training children. We might find modern counterparts to it.

This is often the case, for people identify readily with others who have distinguished themselves in national life.

Yes, we should care and be concerned with the implications, but our trust is in God, not in human leaders alone.

No, we should not curse at all, and this applies to natural locations.

As much as possible, we are to live at peace with all men (Rom. 12:18). Diplomacy and prayer are better than war.

The remembrance of a strong moral and spiritual character producing kindnesses to others is our best legacy.

The Bible commends weeping when appropriate. It has therapeutic value.

They should remind each other of the promise of I Thessalonians 4:13-18 regarding Christ's second coming.

They can do as David did by bringing their mourning to an end and pursuing God's will for the rest of their lives.

6. What may displace the power to wage war in settling disputes today?
As much as possible, we are to live at peace with all men (Rom. 12:18). Diplomacy and prayer are better than war.

7. What is the best legacy a person can leave behind?
The remembrance of a strong moral and spiritual character producing kindnesses to others is our best legacy.

8. Should believers weep at the passing of others?
The Bible commends weeping when appropriate. It has therapeutic value.

9. What should believers use to comfort one another when death comes?
They should remind each other of the promise of I Thessalonians 4:13-18 regarding Christ's second coming.

10. How can believers overcome bereavement and move ahead?
They can do as David did by bringing their mourning to an end and pursuing God's will for the rest of their lives.

Songs Of Hannah And Mary

I Samuel 2:1. And Hannah prayed, and said, My heart rejoiceth in the Lord, mine horn is exalted in the Lord: my mouth is enlarged over mine enemies; because I rejoice in thy salvation.
2. There is none holy as the Lord: for there is none beside thee: neither is there any rock like our God.
3. Talk no more so exceeding proudly; let not arrogancy come out of your mouth: for the Lord is a God of knowledge, and by him actions are weighed.
4. The bows of the mighty men are broken, and they that stumbled are girded with strength.
5. They that were full have hired out themselves for bread; and they that were hungry ceased: so that the barren hath born seven; and she that hath many children is waxed feeble.
Luke 1:46. And Mary said, My soul doth magnify the Lord,
47. And my spirit hath rejoiced in God my Savior.
48. For he hath regarded the low estate of his handmaiden: for, behold, from henceforth all generations shall call me blessed.
49. For he that is mighty hath done to me great things; and holy is his name.
50. And his mercy is on them that fear him from generation to generation.
51. He hath showed strength with his arm; he hath scattered the proud in the imagination of their hearts.
52. He hath put down the mighty from their seats, and exalted them of low degree.
53. He hath filled the hungry with good things; and the rich he hath sent empty away.
54. He hath holpen his servant Israel, in remembrance of his mercy;
55. As he spake to our fathers, to Abraham, and to his seed forever.

MEMORY SELECTION
Luke 1:46-47
DEVOTIONAL READING
Isaiah 9:2-7
BACKGROUND SCRIPTURE
I Samuel 2:1-10; Luke 1:26-56
PRINTED SCRIPTURE
I Samuel 2:1-5; Luke 1:46-55

Teacher's Target

Hannah and Mary were Jewish women living under the law of Moses. Hannah, living in the millennium before Christ, had to share her husband, Elkanah, with another wife named Peninnah. Mary, living at the end of the four hundred years of prophetic silence between the Old and New Testaments, was a virgin engaged to marry Joseph. Hannah wanted a child to end her barrenness. Mary was chaste and waited for marriage before expecting her first child. God had surprises in store for both of them, and these produced songs from each of them that were similar.

Help your students to study the songs of Hannah and Mary and to learn about God from both of them. The emphasis of these songs was on the power of God. Circumstances were very different in their lives, but they saw the Lord in an identical way.

Lesson Introduction

Hannah was ridiculed by Peninnah for her barrenness. During an annual visit to the tabernacle of God at Shiloh, Hannah prayed that God would give her a male child. The Lord answered her prayer, and Samuel was born. She dedicated him to the Lord's service and took him to live in Shiloh as soon as he was weaned (I Sam, 1:1-28).

The angel Gabriel went to Nazareth and told Mary that the Holy Spirit would overshadow her, that she would conceive, and that she would bear a son to be named Jesus, the Son of God (Luke 1:26-35).

Hannah's prayer of thanksgiving to God was offered up after Samuel went to Shiloh. Mary's prayer was offered up while she was visiting Elisabeth before Jesus was born. Both prayers praise God for His sovereign power and control in the affairs of men. Separated by time, place, and circumstances, their theme was the same.

Teaching Outline

I. Changes: I Sam. 2:1-5
   A. Contribution: 1-2
   B. Control: 3
   C. Contrasts: 4-5

II. Conclusions: Luke 1:46-55
   A. Adoration: 46-47
   B. Action: 48-50
   C. Arrangement: 51-53
   D. Abraham: 54-55

Daily Bible Readings

Mon. Hannah's Song
1 Samuel 2:1-5
Tue. Hannah's Song
1 Samuel 2:6-10
Wed. Gabriel's Announcement
Luke 1:26-33
Thu. Mary's Response
Luke 1:34-38
Fri. Visit to Elizabeth
Luke 1:39-45
Sat. Mary's Song
Luke 1:46-50
Sun. Mary's Song
Luke 1:51-56

Verse By Verse

I. Changes: I Sam. 2:1-5

A. Contribution: 1-2
1a. And Hannah prayed, and said, My heart rejoiceth in the Lord, mine horn is exalted in the Lord: . . .
Our text includes only the first half of Hannah's prayer. She began by stating that her heart rejoiced in Jehovah. She saw Him as the Source of her blessing in having the child named Samuel. The meaning of Samuel was "asked of God" (I Sam. 1:20). In saying that her horn was exalted in the Lord, we see the wild ox with its head held high in a show of strength and confidence. It was because of what God had done for her that Hannah could hold her head up within her family and in society, for her barrenness had been taken away by divine help.

1b. . . .my mouth is enlarged over mine enemies . . .
An open, gaping mouth was used in the Middle East to show derision and contempt for one's enemies. Rather than remaining silent, Hannah could now speak, and what she said was to give God credit for her changed condition.

1c. . . . because I rejoice in thy salvation
Summing up this verse, Hannah said that her heart rejoiced, her confidence was strong, and she could speak out against her enemies because she viewed God as her salvation (deliverance, help). His contribution of Samuel had been of immeasurable value to her.

2a. There is none holy as the Lord: for there is none beside thee: . . .
Hannah saw God as being unique. No one else was holy as He was. No one else could stand beside Him as an equal.

2b. . . .neither is there any rock like our God.
The term rock was used as a metaphor for the Lord because of His unmovable strength. He was like a rock fortress in which His children could stay for protection against their enemies. David wrote, "The Lord is my rock, and my fortress, and my deliverer my God, my strength, in whom I will trust" (Ps. 18:2). See also Psalm 91:2.

B. Control: 3
3a. Talk no more so exceeding proudly let not arrogancy come out of your mouth: . . .
Typical of Hebrew poetry, these statements say essentially the same thing. Hannah was probably thinking of Peninnah as her adversary here, remembering how she had ridiculed her when she was barren. "Her adversary also provoked her sore, for to make her fret, because the Lord had shut up her womb" (I Sam. 1:6). Peninnah had been fruitful in bearing children because God had given her this ability. Hannah would remind her that she should not speak proudly or arrogantly for something over which she had no control while at the same time denigrating Hannah for something over which she had no control.

3b. . . .for the Lord is a God of knowledge, and by him actions are weighed.
The insensitive person taunting another person should be aware that God knows all that goes on, and He weighs all actions in each person's life on His divine scale of evaluation. Evil actions result in

judgment. Righteous actions result in blessing.

C. Contrasts: 4-5

4a. The bows of the mighty men are broken, . . .

Hannah declared that bows for shooting arrows of even mighty men can be broken, leaving them defenseless against their enemies. This could refer to all kinds of arrogant people who lose their strength and confidence.

4b. . . .and they that stumbled are girded with strength.

In contrast to the mighty men who are humbled and made weak, there are those who stumbled from fatigue who are fed and rested so that they are renewed in strength.

5a. They that were full have hired out themselves for bread; and they that were hungry ceased: . . .

Proud, unthankful people who were once full now are so hungry that they hire themselves out to get some bread. Those who were once hungry now have stopped being hungry, for God has changed their circumstances.

5b. . . . so that the barren hath borne seven; and she that hath many children is waxed feeble.

Hannah here concentrated on feminine situations. One woman who was barren might bear seven children, whereas a fruitful mother of many children might become feeble.

In all of these contrasts in her prayer, Hannah's point was that it is God Who makes the difference in the lives of men and women. He is sovereign over His creation and His creatures. Going against Him and His laws brings only defeat, while aligning oneself with Him and His laws brings victory. Her son, Samuel, whom she loaned to the Lord, went on to become a spiritual giant and leader in Israel. He served as a transition person between the anarchy of the time of the judges and the establishment of the monarchy under Saul, which led to the golden age of Israel under David and Solomon.

II. Conclusions: Luke 1:46-55

A. Adoration: 46-47

46. And Mary said, My soul doth magnify the Lord,

47. And my spirit hath rejoiced in God my Saviour,

It was over a thousand years after Hannah's time that a peasant girl in Nazareth had a visit from the angel Gabriel and was told that she would bring the long-awaited Messiah into the world. Although she was still a virgin, this holy Child would be conceived within her by the overshadowing of the Holy Spirit. She went to visit a relative named Elisabeth in the hill country of Judah, and it was there that she was confirmed as the coming mother of the Lord Jesus (Luke 1:26-45).

In response to this, Mary broke into spontaneous prayer. She said that her soul magnified the Lord and her spirit rejoiced in God her Savior. This has become known in the church as the Magnificat. By her words, Mary brought praise and glory to the Lord, making Him great in her estimation. It may have been that Mary's knowledge of the Jewish Scriptures, even Hannah's prayer, helped her to put her feelings into words at this time.

B. Action: 48-50

48. For he hath regarded the low estate of his handmaiden: for, behold, from henceforth all generations shall call me blessed.

49a. For he that is mighty hath done to me great things;...

Prompted by the Holy Spirit, Elisabeth had said of Mary, "Blessed art thou among women, and blessed is the fruit of thy womb" (Luke 1:42). Mary accepted this as coming from the Lord, and she concluded that God had seen her low standing in society as a peasant maid but had exalted her to a unique position as the virgin mother of the Son of God. She was right in stating that all future generations would call her blessed. He Who was and is almighty had done great things for her.

49b. . . . and holy is his name.

50. And his mercy is on them that fear him from generation to generation.

Note carefully here that Mary ascribed divine attributes to the Lord but not to herself. She declared God to be holy and merciful to people from generation to generation, including herself. This is a good place to disavow those claims of some who hold Mary to be immaculately conceived, bodily ascended into heaven, the recipient of people's petitions, and even co-redemptrix with Jesus of the sinful human race. All of these fabrications are of human origin and are unworthy of evangelical consideration. Truth is truth, and error is error. We must take our stand on truth and not be moved from it in an attempt to keep from hurting others' feelings. We should take nothing away from Mary which belongs to her, but neither should we add anything.

C. Arrangement: 51-53
51. He hath shewed strength with his arm he hath scattered the proud in the imagination of their hearts.
52. He hath put down the mighty from their seats, and exalted them of low degree.

It is because He is in sovereign control that God makes suitable arrangements among people on the earth. He shows His great strength and scatters the proud whose evaluation of themselves is faulty. He takes the mighty (rulers) from their seats of prestige and human power and disposes of them. In their places he raises up those of low degree and gives them authority. He is the great Equalizer to honor the righteous and condemn the wicked.

53. He hath filled the hungry with good things; and the rich he hath sent empty away.

God's arrangements in human society also include filling the hungry with food but sending the selfish rich people away empty to teach them a lesson. If all of this is not apparent in this life, it certainly will be apparent in the life to come. This was illustrated in the account Jesus gave of the rich man and the beggar named Lazarus found in Luke 16:19-31.

D. Abraham: 54-55
54. He hath holpen his servant Israel, in remembrance of his mercy;
55. As he spake to our fathers, to Abraham, and to his seed for ever.

Mary looked backward to the time of Abraham and the establishment of God's covenant with him and his descendants. He was the first Hebrew (one who crossed over from Mesopotamia to Canaan), and he was the father of the Jewish race. The promises of God laid down as recorded in Genesis 12:1-3 and 7 made it certain that God would make of Abraham a great people and give to them the land of Canaan for their inheritance. Mary probably thought of the Messiah in the same terms as other Jews did in her time. He was supposed to come as King and give Israel back her freedom and independence.

The testimony of Mary to God's greatness is enhanced by the history of His dealings with men from her time to the present. God's Word and church history validate the truth of His power operating among men. We can join with Mary in ascribing praise to the Lord for His power and blessings.

Evangelistic Emphasis

What exciting good news is in our texts today! There is the good news that God is the keeper of promises. The God who fulfilled his promise to Hannah by giving a son to a woman previously barren, will also fulfill his promise to us. Sometimes promises are not fulfilled as soon as we would hope, but we can be confident that all of God's promises will be kept.

There is the good news that God is the giver of salvation. Our burdens of guilt and fear can be turned over to him and we can live in secure relationship with him. We need not be afraid of either the present or the future. There is the good news that he is the recognizer of the lowly. We may never have been noticed by anyone else but we are noticed by him. Not only does he notice the unknown but he gives them significant blessings and, on occasion, uses them in major ways in fulfilling his purpose in the world. It may be true that few people know our name and we live in what seems to be an obscure corner of the world, but God knows both our name and our address.

These passages tell of hope, forgiveness, and purpose. We could scarcely ask for anything more. The people that need to hear the gospel have yearning in their hearts for these three things. We can speak meaningfully to those hungers with the stories of Hannah and Mary.

Memory Selection

"My soul doth magnify the Lord, and my spirit hath rejoiced in God my Savior."
Luke 1:46,47.

The soul is seen as the center of our deepest emotions. It is what we are at the core. A response of the soul is not superficial. In saying she was magnifying the Lord in her soul, Mary was commenting on how deep and profound her sense of worship and praise was.

Sometimes there seems to be a tendency to allow worship to become routine and perfunctory. There are jokes and comments about people sleeping in church. Often there is criticism that a sermon is boring. This may be because there is no soul involvement.

There needs to be, first, soul involvement by those who lead in worship. Unless those who preach, pray, and sing publicly have devout feelings of worship, it will be impossible for them to stimulate those feelings in others. Secondly, of course, there must be soul involvement on the part of the worshiper. Worship is not something that is imposed on us from the outside. It must come from within.

What if we do not feel it? Let us pray harder, think more about God, and read the Scriptures more earnestly. Feelings will come.

Weekday Problems

Hilda is a quiet, home loving, and unpretentious person. She is not widely known. A few neighbors know her well and she has some church friends. Those who know her think highly of her. She lives in a plain house and has a modest life style. To many observers, she would not seem to be a person of great significance.

She has reared three children. All are professionally accomplished, culturally sophisticated, and, most importantly, models of Christian candor and compassion. In spite of graduate degrees, world travel, and significant recognition, Hilda's grown children are humble people, interested in others to an unusual degree. Each has made significant contributions to his community and in his field of work.

Hilda's grandchildren are old enough now to be displaying the same kinds of values that she has projected so well through her children.

* By what criteria do you measure the significance of your life?
* Is it or is it not a success in terms of values that you consider important?
* What goals must you meet in order to feel that you have fulfilled your purpose in living?
* Is Hilda's life one of great significance? Why or why not?

Superintendent's Sermonette

An analysis of prayer reveals that it is composed of various elements, including adoration, thanksgiving, confession, plea for forgiveness, requests for one's own needs (petition), requests for the needs of others (intercession), and closing in Christ's name It is interesting to note that the two prayers studied in this lesson are composed primarily of praise to God for his power, mercy, and kindness. We have to admit that much of our prayers are concerned primarily with requests.

One of the encouraging developments regarding prayer among Bible-believing Christians in recent years has been an increased emphasis on praise. This can be noted in prayer and in singing. God must be pleased to hear the praises of His people, for He made them in order that they might bring glory to Him.

We would do well to follow the example given by both Hannah and Mary by composing prayers which deal mainly with praise. It would give us good experience for seeing the value of praise in prayer, although we need not neglect our usual petitions.

This Lesson in **Your** Life

The songs of Hannah and Mary have a number of things in common. We can learn from both of them how to better express praise and gratitude.

Both songs were songs of praise. Both Hannah and Mary rejoiced. Both were thankful. Both attributed their blessings to God. These are dimensions of worship that are too often neglected. Is it possible that we have heard the news of the Lord's salvation so much that we are no longer excited by it? Do we take it for granted?

Are there no exuberant feelings to be expressed? Have we become so dignified and sedate that we do not want to express those feelings? Have we forgotten how to express them?

It would be good for us to retrace some of our steps from time to time. If we can go back in our memory to the time when we first caught a glimpse of the glory of the gospel and seek to awaken those feelings, it will help us to praise better. If we think of the joy that we felt when we personally experienced the salvation of God, perhaps we can feel that joy again.

Both Hannah and Mary felt that God had acted to reverse the fortunes of men. Hannah spoke of the mighty falling and the stumblers being made strong. Mary spoke of the mighty being brought down and those of low degree exalted.

We need to be reminded from time to time that God is sovereign. He can handle all of our problems. We need not worry about evil people being in positions of power. God can bring them down. Neither do we need to worry about good people going unnoticed. God can exalt them.

This also reminds us that we ought not to take anyone for granted. He or she may be a key to the fulfillment of God's purpose for our day. God uses unlikely-looking people. When we take notice of lowly people we may be becoming acquainted with one of God's significant saints.

Mary would not have been considered a very important person when she received the promise that Jesus would be born to her. Little did her neighbors realize that in association with her they were getting to know the mother of the Lord. The whole world would have flocked to her doorstep in the light of later knowledge. Practically everybody ignored her at the time. Let us pay attention to the lowly, for their sakes, and possibly for our great blessings.

Both Hannah and Mary saw their blessings as a part of the fulfillment of God's plan. They were not given sons merely for their own honor and pleasure. They were a part of the unfolding will of God.

Both women also knew that their blessing was an indication that God keeps his promises. The birth of Samuel and the birth of Jesus give hope for the future to all who believe in the promises of God. He has unlimited power. As Hannah said, "The barren will bear seven." If God could bring Samuel into the world via a woman who had been barren all her life and Jesus into the world via a woman who was yet a virgin, can he not also do whatever we need?

Seed Thoughts

1. What will help keep us from becoming proud and overly confident when God answers our prayers?
We can concentrate on giving Him all of the praise for His blessings.

2. How does our estimate of God affect our praying?
If we see Him as being holy, powerful, and concerned about us, we will be able to trust Him more fully.

3. How can we know the divine attributes of God?
We can study them and their application in His Word, in the records of church history, and in experience.

4. What should our attitude be toward prevailing human injustice?
We must keep our focus on the Lord and believe that He weighs all things and will judge or bless as needed

5. Why was Hannah an optimist?
She knew that a sovereign God raised up the righteous and put down the evil.

(Please Turn Page)

---

1. What will help keep us from becoming proud and overly confident when God answers our prayers?

2. How does our estimate of God affect our praying?

3. How can we know the divine attributes of God?

4. What should our attitude be toward prevailing human injustice?

5. Why was Hannah an optimist?

6. What does it mean to magnify the Lord in our souls and spirits?

7. What does it mean for God to regard the low estate of His servant?

8. How did Mary evaluate God?

9. Why might God be called the great Arranger of men's lives?

10. Can Christians today claim covenant promises given to Abraham?

Seed Thoughts - Continued

We can concentrate on giving Him all of the praise for His blessings.

If we see Him as being holy, powerful, and concerned about us, we will be able to trust Him more fully.

We can study them and their application in His Word, in the records of church history, and in experience.

We must keep our focus on the Lord and believe that He weighs all things and will judge or bless as needed

She knew that a sovereign God raised up the righteous and put down the evil.

It means to make Him great in our estimation by praising Him for blessings. We can do this in prayer, in music, in witnessing, and in various other ways.

It means that He sees and appreciates humility and makes plans to exalt His servant in some way.

She saw Him as being holy, merciful, and all-powerful. These are primary attributes of God which we should accept and propagate to others.

As both Hannah and Mary pointed out, God puts down the mighty and exalts those of low degree.

Galatians 3:6-9 and I Peter 2:9-10 appear to say that even Gentile believers are spiritual inheritors of the covenant.

6. What does it mean to magnify the Lord in our souls and spirits?
It means to make Him great in our estimation by praising Him for blessings. We can do this in prayer, in music, in witnessing, and in various other ways.

7. What does it mean for God to regard the low estate of His servant?
It means that He sees and appreciates humility and makes plans to exalt His servant in some way.

8. How did Mary evaluate God?
She saw Him as being holy, merciful, and all-powerful. These are primary attributes of God which we should accept and propagate to others.

9. Why might God be called the great Arranger of men's lives?
As both Hannah and Mary pointed out, God puts down the mighty and exalts those of low degree.

10. Can Christians today claim covenant promises given to Abraham?
Galatians 3:6-9 and I Peter 2:9-10 appear to say that even Gentile believers are spiritual inheritors of the covenant.

A Hymn To The Creator

Psalm 8:1.
O Lord, our Lord, how excellent is thy name in all the earth! who hast set thy glory above the heavens.

2. Out of the mouth of babes and sucklings hast thou ordained strength because of thine enemies, that thou mightest still the enemy and the avenger.

3. When I consider the heavens, the work of thy fingers, the moon and the stars, which thou hast ordained;

4. What is man, that thou art mindful of him? and the son of man, that thou visitest him?

5. For thou hast made him a little lower than the angels, and hast crowned him with glory and honor.

6. Thou madest him to have dominion over the works of thy hands; thou hast put all things under his feet:

7. All sheep and oxen, yea, and the beasts of the field;

8. The fowl of the air, and the fish of the sea, and whatsoever passeth through the paths of the seas.

9. O Lord our Lord, how excellent is thy name in all the earth!

MEMORY SELECTION
Psalm 8:9
DEVOTIONAL READING
John 1:1-18

BACKGROUND SCRIPTURE
Psalm: 8
PRINTED SCRIPTURE
Psalm 8

Teacher's Target

It is unfortunate that the speculative views of many scientists have become pervasive in our world, because they are in conflict with the revealed Word of God. The origin of the universe and its created beings and things is explained in the Bible, but unbelievers refuse to accept it. They have produced various theories on the subject and then been upset if everyone does not accept them as factual.

We need to see in Psalm 8 a description of creation and man's place in it. The opening chapters of the book of Genesis give the factual details, and Psalm 8 gives a poetic response to them. Human beings did not evolve to what they now are by accident or an evolutionary process. They are essentially the same as when God created Adam and Eve, and their functions remain unchanged, although those functions may have new forms.

Lesson Introduction

Belief in the evolutionary hypothesis of the origin and development of plant, animal, and human life has led to an astounding conclusion in the space age. It is that there must be intelligent life elsewhere in the universe besides on the planet Earth, and that it is probably more advanced than our own. All evidence thus far to the contrary, it is assumed that conditions on some planet which are identical or similar to what we find on earth would cause life to originate and evolve. Public and private funds are spent in attempts to make contact with intelligent beings somewhere out there.

God's Word makes it clear that He created the universe and furnished the earth with all forms of mineral, vegetable, animal, and human elements. The earth is special, and man is special as its overseer. This is where God wants us to focus our attention to do His will and carry out His program.

Teaching Outline

I. Heavens: Ps. 8:1-3
   A. Excellence: 1
   B. Example I: 2
   C. Example II: 3

II. Humans: Ps. 8:4-9
   A. Purpose: 4
   B. Position: 5
   C. Power: 6-8
   D. Praise: 9

Daily Bible Readings

Mon. Praise
Psalm 8:1
Tue. God's Wisdom
Psalm 8:2
Wed.- God's Creation
Psalm 8:3-4
Thu. Man
Psalm 8:5
Fri. Dominion
Psalm 8:6
Sat. Animals and Birds
Psalm 8:7-8
Sun. Praise
Psalm 8:9

Verse By Verse

I. Heavens: Ps. 8:1-3

A. Excellence: 1
1a. O Lord our Lord, how excellent is thy name in all the earth! . . .

Note that this psalm begins and ends with an identical expression of praise to the excellence of God's name. This is called a doxology, and it was spoken by David. This sets the tone for the entire psalm, for it is all praise and has no petition in it. David viewed Jehovah as being excellent (magnificent, majestic, perfect). When God's name was mentioned, His glorious attributes came to mind in the hearts of believers.

We live in an age in which God's name is often taken in vain and thus profaned. We may not feel that we can try to stop all of this, but we can speak and act in ways which will let others know that we hold God's name in reverence and do not appreciate hearing it profaned repeatedly. Some people in the world will respect our position and begin to tone down their profanity in our presence.

1b. . . .who hast set thy glory above the heavens.

Ancient mythological gods, which were actually figments of men's imaginations (or perhaps demons masquerading as gods—I Cor. 10:20), were described as inhabiting the earth, its atmosphere, or its netherworld. David described God and His glory as high and lifted up above the heavens, as if the earth itself could not even contain it. The fact was, of course, that God by His Holy Spirit, was omnipresent in all of the universe, but the highest heaven was His natural dwelling place. It was from here that Jesus descended to the earth at Bethlehem, and it was to here that He ascended from the Mount of Olives. It was here that Stephen and John saw Him at His Father's right hand (Acts 7:55-56 Rev. 1:10-18).

B. Example I: 2
2. Out of the mouth of babes and sucklings hast thou ordained strength because of thine enemies, that thou mightest still the enemy and the avenger.

The word "babes" apparently refers to little children, and the term "sucklings" refers to unweaned ones. Since they sometimes nursed until two or three years of age in Bible times, they could be talking and singing even as sucklings, thus joining older children in praising God. Jesus referred to this psalm one day in the temple at Jerusalem—"When the chief priests and scribes saw the wonderful things that he did, and the children crying in the temple, and saying, Hosanna to the son of David; they were sore displeased, and said unto him, Hearest thou what these say? And Jesus saith unto them, Yea; have ye never read, Out of the mouth of babes and sucklings thou has perfected praise?" (Matt. 21:15-16).

The enemies of God include Satan and all of his fallen angels, plus all evil people who loudly declare their animosity toward God. Satan is the great avenger and adversary, and he influences many to follow his example. Little children provide an example of innocence which God wants the pure in heart to emulate in their lives. Childlike faith takes God at His Word and acts upon it.

C. Example II: 3
3. When I consider thy heavens, the work of thy fingers, the moon and the stars, which thou hast ordained . . .

This is the declarative part of a statement which ends in a question in verse 4, and we will look at it by itself. David had many opportunities in his life to look up at the heavens while he was a shepherd, fugitive, and soldier. He gazed upward and saw what God had created there. Being a Spirit, God had no literal fingers, but it was by His power that the heavenly bodies, such as the moon's earth and the myriads of stars, had been flung into space. The term "ordained," as it was used here, might be translated as "established" or "made" to move in their various orbits. No one who has done as David did, can look up at the firmament without being strongly impressed by its magnificence. Those who have faith to believe, and who know God's Word, will accept Him as the Creator of all that is presented there. Here, then, is another example of the greatness and goodness of the Lord.

II. Humans: Ps. 8:4-9

A. Purpose: 4
4. What is man, that thou art mindful of him? and the son of man, that thou visitest him?

What David had said about the heavens served as a backdrop for what he wanted to say about mankind. The two parts of this verse say essentially the same thing, "Who is man that you are concerned about him or the son of man that you pay attention to him?" Some have thought that this referred to the coming Messiah, but it more likely referred to mankind in general. David was awed by the fact that the God Who had created the universe would focus in on mere man on the earth and give him many blessings. Psalm 8:4-6 is mentioned in Hebrews 2:6-8. It is not until Hebrews 2:9-10 that Jesus is mentioned as the One Who became human in order to brings many sons to glory. This seems to support the opinion that Psalm 8 was referring to mankind in general.

David was searching for the purpose or meaning of God's action in visiting mankind with blessings.

B. Position: 5
5. For thou hast made him a little lower than the angels, and hast crowned him with glory and honour.

David was impressed with the position God had given to mankind. Angels excelled in wisdom and strength (Ps. 103:20), but God placed men next in order below them and made them superior to animals. He crowned them with glory and honor by bestowing human dignity upon them, making them in His Own image (likeness) (Gen. 1:26). Sin often tears down human dignity and leaves people in deplorable states, but that does not take away from God's conferral of dignity upon them. Whenever the providential or saving grace of God is applied to men, they can produce many wonderful things to benefit themselves, other men, the animals, and the environment.

C. Power: 6-3
6. Thou madest him to have dominion over the works of thy hands; thou hast put all things under his feet.

Beginning with Adam and Eve, God placed mankind in control of the earth (Gen. 1:26). He was fewer in numbers and inferior in physical strength to many of the animals, but he was endowed with superior intelligence, the power of speech and language, and various skills which gave him dominance over the rest of the world's creatures. He was able to mine minerals and make useful things from them. He was able to plant crops and harvest them for immediate use and storage. He was able to domesticate some animals for his own use. He was able to extract food from the streams, lakes, and oceans. The list goes on and on, and it has reached new heights in the sciences and technologies of the twentieth century. He has even traveled to the moon and sent unmanned probes into outer space to learn its secrets.

7a. All sheep and oxen, . . .

These animals represented those

whom man had been able to domesticate for his own use. Various other domesticated animals might have been mentioned here as being under the dominion of human beings, such as goats, horses, donkeys, dogs, and cats.

7b. ... yea, and the beasts of the field.

This referred to wild animals still running free. These had to be hunted and downed with weapons or trapped in order to be used.

8a. The fowl of the air, ...

It would appear that these, too, were wild for the most part and had to be hunted or trapped in order to be used.

8b. ... and the fish of the sea, and whatsoever passeth through the paths of the seas.

The wording here is interesting, for not all creatures in the seas were fish. Some, such as whales, were mammals, and some were creatures unrelated to fish (lobsters, clams, crabs, and other types).

We have heard increasing reports from environmentalists and conservationists in recent years about the need for men to stop polluting the earth and to allow the natural balance of nature to operate. There would seem to be merit in much of what they propose. On the other hand, God has given men resources which they have the right to use for their survival and betterment, and they ought not to be denied the use of them.

God's conferral on men of the power to dominate the earth ought to be interpreted as ruling out harmful exploitation and as advocating careful development. Some things, such as oil, cannot be replaced in our generation or for many generations to come. Other things, such as forests, can be replaced and serve future generations well,

Exploitation finds its source in greed and a lack of concern for others. This can be dealt with somewhat by governmental and nongovernmental pressures, but its basic solution is a moral and spiritual one. That is the point at which Bible believers can have a marked impact, explaining that God wants men to use His resources but to do so in a wise and prudent manner.

D. Praise: 9

9. O Lord our Lord, how excellent is thy name in all the earth!

The psalm ends with the same doxology with which it began. Praise is expressed to the Lord for His excellent name and all that it means. David was happy that Jehovah was his Lord and the Lord of Israel. Gentiles can join in this doxology and let God know that He is their God, too.

Even as the emphasis of Psalm 8 was on God as Creator and mankind as recipients of divine blessings, so it is that many of our hymns and other songs have concentrated on this theme. It is good to go through a hymnal and see these objective type musical compositions. They should be used in a balanced way with the subjective numbers which express how we feel about salvation, sanctification, and future events. God is great, and we ought to sing about it often.

Evangelistic Emphasis

One of the common problems in the world is the feeling of insignificance and unworthiness. Some of it, no doubt, is due to a sense of guilt because we identify with sinful things that we have done. Some of it is due to conditioning. A person who has excessive criticism, particularly in early years, and is deprived of adequate positive reinforcement will have inferiority feelings. Some of it may be due to life experiences that cause us to feel defeated and incompetent.

However we came by these feelings of low self-esteem, most of us seem to be troubled by them. They cause problems within ourselves. We experience anxiety, stress, and depression as a result. These feelings also cause relationship problems. We cannot be successful in loving our neighbors as ourselves if we do not love ourselves. The security of self-acceptance is necessary to the ability to participate successfully in relationships.

Even some who appear arrogant are victims of a negative self-image. Their pseudo arrogance is a defensive mask intended to hide the inferiority that they feel is characteristic of them.

This widespread problem can be cured only by experiencing love. Only God can, in our sinful and self-rejecting state, love us enough to help us begin to love ourselves. That is why it is important to understand that although we are minuscule in comparison to the vastness of God's creation, he has crowned us with glory and honor.

Memory Selection

"O Lord our Lord, how excellent is thy name in all the earth!"
Psalm 8:9.

When we consider, as did the Psalmist, the majesty of God's creation, we are moved to praise him. Think, for example about the wisdom that conceived of and created the complexly interconnected world that we live in. Think of the ways that life is propagated and sustained. Think of the circulation of waters vaporized in the atmosphere, distributed in drops of rain, and moved to the seas through a network of rivers and streams. Consider plant life, the dispersal of seeds, the response to seasonal changes, and the oxygen that is given into the air.

Think about the sun, the moon, and the stars. Reflect on daytime and nighttime. Think about how food is supplied to all the different kinds of populations of the living world. Think most profoundly about the human family with its divine ability to love, to show mercy, and to act morally.

These ponderings, as monumental as they may become, are but a token of the intricacies of the world that God saw in his mind and then formed with his creative power. It is no wonder that his name is to be called excellent throughout the earth!

Weekday Problems

Ron is constantly belittling himself. He seems to have such a low opinion of himself that he expects to be rejected. He eases the pain of rejection by doing it to himself first.

He cannot receive a compliment. Because he thinks so negatively about himself, he cannot trust others when they say nice things about him. He suspects their motives and looks for some other explanation when they speak well of him.

Ron takes the most pessimistic view of any set of circumstances. One would think that his life had been one long series of bad experiences. When you look at his life, however, you note that his experiences have not been significantly worse or better than those of many other people. He has had enough pain and sorrow to document, in his own mind, his gloomy self-view. There are many others who have had an equal or greater number of problems yet are more self-accepting and more hopeful about life.

* How would you analyze the basis of Ron's problem?
* What can you do to help him with it?
* What can Ron do to help himself?

Superintendent's Sermonette

David thought that all creation praised the Creator. Creatures such as little children praised the Lord, and the stars and planets in the heavens praised Him (Ps. 8:2-3). Many centuries later, David's descendant named Jesus taught that creation praised His heavenly Father. During the triumphal entry into Jerusalem, the Pharisees told Jesus to rebuke His celebrating disciples, and Jesus said, "I tell you that, if these should hold their peace, the stones would immediately cry out" (Luke 19:40). That was an amazing statement.

Whether animate or inanimate, all that God created should bring glory to His name. This should be done by their remaining what He created them to be and by allowing His glory to be reflected in them. The stars and planets, including the earth, are testimonies to God's power and majesty. The inhabitants of this globe can choose to honor Him or dishonor Him. Let us be those who devote ourselves to honor Him and His name by what we think, say, and do. He is mindful of us; let us be mindful of Him in all things.

This Lesson in <u>Your</u> Life

The glory of creation testifies to the existence and nature of God. Its precision and complexity testify of the divine brilliance of the creative genius that caused it to be. The beauty of it witnesses to God's aesthetic nature. The very existence of the created universe makes us know of his power and authority.

The sunshine and rain, seed time and harvest time, provisions of food, fresh air and water, and people to provide comfort and companionship, all tell of the loving and relational nature of God. The rising of the sun each day speaks of the hope of a new day and reminds us of the promises of God.

We can learn a great deal about God just from reflecting on the world in which we live. The psalmist considered the heavens and meditated on the significance of man.

There are many things, of course, that are revealed to us in Scripture and in the person of Jesus Christ that cannot be deduced from reflecting on the created world. There is much that we would not know about sin and forgiveness, about grace and gospel, about the gentleness and mercy of God, and about the ethical and spiritual qualities that will bring us more into the likeness of God.

However, we are a part of a generation which may be better about reading than it is about reflecting. It appears that at least in some quarters there are more people who read their Bibles than there are that "consider the heavens." There is something about contemplation that brings one to a deeper and fuller knowledge of God. We need not merely to have an intellectual knowledge of the data that is supplied in Scripture. We need also the expansion of heart and soul that comes from letting his grandeur soak in during prolonged periods of thought.

Perhaps no one has ever been better at this than the Psalmist. By allowing his thoughts to linger in our minds and hearts, we can stimulate the flow of our own thoughts on the magnificence of God.

As we begin to catch a glimpse of his greatness, we are likely to feel a sense of our own relative insignificance. We may also ask, "What is man?" We may wonder as did the psalmist why God has taken such notice of man.

Even if we wonder why, we know that God has crowned us with glory and honor and has given us dominion over the world that he made. We can therefore seek to perceive ourselves though God's eyes. We can stand tall, feel worthwhile, and be responsible to the tasks he has given us to do.

One of those tasks that is suggested in our text is that of the care of the world and those animals, birds, and fish that occupy it with us. We have a stewardship, not only of our personal possessions, but also of the world we inhabit. The matter of proper care and use of the world and its resources is not just an environmentalist concern. It is a Christian concern also.

Seed Thoughts

1. What does it mean to say that God has an excellent name?
His name becomes a symbol for all that He is. It reminds us of His excellent (magnificent, majestic) attributes.

2. Where does God dwell?
He is, by His Holy Spirit, everywhere present in the universe, but He dwells in the highest heaven.

3. How can little children praise the Lord?
The innocence of little children pictures for us the goodness of God. As children learn to praise God, they testify of Him.

4. How should we be impressed when we look at the heavens?
We should rejoice at the greatness of God in creating and sustaining the universe and giving us a special planet.

5. Why is God mindful of men?
God created men, and He did this in order that they might praise Him for His blessings to them.

(Please Turn Page)

---

1. What does it mean to say that God has an excellent name?

2. Where does God dwell?

3. How can little children praise the Lord?

4. How should we be impressed when we look at the heavens?

5. Why is God mindful of men?

6. Where do men stand in God's order of creatures?

7. How has God crowned men with glory and honor?

8. How have some men misused God's gift of dominance over things He created?

9. How have men exercised control over animals?

10. Will God judge men for their use of resources He gives them?

Seed Thoughts - Continued

His name becomes a symbol for all that He is. It reminds us of His excellent (magnificent, majestic) attributes.

He is, by His Holy Spirit, everywhere present in the universe, but He dwells in the highest heaven.

The innocence of little children pictures for us the goodness of God. As children learn to praise God, they testify of Him.

We should rejoice at the greatness of God in creating and sustaining the universe and giving us a special planet.

God created men, and He did this in order that they might praise Him for His blessings to them.

Good angels are wiser and stronger, but men dominate over animals.

By providential and saving grace, God gives men human dignity and sustenance. They can love Him and reflect His glory.

They have polluted and wasted resources which cannot be replaced or which need massive amounts of remedial treatment.

They have domesticated some for their own use, and they have hunted or trapped others. In either case, good treatment should be the rule.

Every man's actions will be judged, including this type (I Cor. 3:13).

6. Where do men stand in God's order of creatures?
Good angels are wiser and stronger, but men dominate over animals.

7. How has God crowned men with glory and honor?
By providential and saving grace, God gives men human dignity and sustenance. They can love Him and reflect His glory.

8. How have some men misused God's gift of dominance over things He created?
They have polluted and wasted resources which cannot be replaced or which need massive amounts of remedial treatment.

9. How have men exercised control over animals?
They have domesticated some for their own use, and they have hunted or trapped others. In either case, good treatment should be the rule.

10. Will God judge men for their use of resources He gives them?
Every man's actions will be judged, including this type (I Cor. 3:13).

A Song For Temple Visitors

Psalm 84:1. How amiable are thy tabernacles, O Lord of hosts!
2. My soul longeth, yea, even fainteth for the courts of the Lord: my heart and my flesh crieth out for the living God.
3. Yea, the sparrow hath found an house, and the swallow a nest for herself, where she may lay her young, even thine altars, O Lord of hosts, my King, and my God.
4. Blessed are they that dwell in thy house: they will be still praising thee. Selah.
5. Blessed is the man whose strength is in thee; in whose heart are the ways of them.
6. Who passing through the valley of Baca make it a well; the rain also filleth the pools.
7. They go from strength to strength, every one of them in Zion appeareth before God.
8. O Lord God of hosts, hear my prayer: give ear, O God of Jacob. Selah.
9. Behold, O God our shield, and look upon the face of thine anointed.
10. For a day in thy courts is better than a thousand. I had rather be a doorkeeper in the house of my God, than to dwell in the tents of wickedness.
11. For the Lord God is a sun and shield: the Lord will give grace and glory: no good thing will he withhold from them that walk uprightly.
12. O Lord of hosts, blessed is the man that trusteth in thee.

MEMORY SELECTION
Psalm 84:2
DEVOTIONAL READING
Psalm 90

BACKGROUND SCRIPTURE
Psalm 84
PRINTED SCRIPTURE
Psalm 84

Teacher's Target

Psalm 84 was written for the sons of Korah, meaning descendants of a Levite by that name, who served in the tabernacle and later in the temple as doorkeepers and musicians. However, the psalm found wider use as one of the "songs of ascent" sung by Jewish pilgrims coming up the hill from the Kidron Valley to enter the holy city of Jerusalem for annual religious festivals. Even when they were backslidden, Jews continued to go through the motions of coming to the temple to worship Jehovah.

Help your students to see in Psalm 84 the importance attached to God's house in ancient times. This can serve as a foundation for discussing how reverence should be shown to God in His house (church) today. It is God's presence which makes His house have spiritual vitality. Let Him be recognized, respected, and revered in it.

Lesson Introduction

Old Testament patriarchs from Adam onward met God at crude stone altars where they sacrificed selected animals to worship God and atone for their sins. When the nation of Israel left bondage in Egypt, they set up a portable sanctuary called the tabernacle, and God was present there in a special way. After Israel settled in Canaan, the tabernacle was pitched in various places (Gilgal, Shechem, Shiloh, Nob, and Gibeon).

David stockpiled materials with which to build the first temple, but it was his son, Solomon, who actually had it built. After its destruction by the Babylonians in 586 B.C., the site was desolate for seventy years. Jews returned to the sacred hill and put up the restoration temple under Zerubbabel, and it was enlarged by Herod the Great. This was destroyed by the Romans in A.D. 70 and has not yet been replaced.

Teaching Outline

I. God's houses Ps. 84:1-4
   A. Delight: 1
   B. Desire: 2
   C. Dwellers: 3-4

II. God's blessing: Ps. 84:5-8
   A. Valley: 5-6
   B. Victory: 7-8

III. God's protection: Ps. 84:9-12
   A. Preference: 9-10
   B. Protectors 11-12

Daily Bible Readings

Mon. Yearning
Psalm 84:1-2
Tue. Safety
Psalm 84:3
Wed. Blessing
Psalm 84:4-5
Thu. A Haven
Psalm 84:6
Fri. Rely on the Lord
Psalm 84:7-8
Sat. Joy in the House of God
Psalm 84:9-10
Sun. Praise
Psalm 84:11-12

Verse By Verse

I. God's house: Ps. 84:1-4

A. Delight: 1
1. **How amiable are thy tabernacles, O Lord of hosts!**

The psalmist saw the tabernacle of the Lord as an amiable (friendly, lovely, beloved) place. The best materials gathered from the Egyptians by the Israelites prior to their exodus from bondage were used in its construction, furnishings, and vestments for priests and Levites ministering in it. The psalmist saw it as the special dwelling place of the Lord of hosts, a term meaning that He was the commanding General of the armies of heaven.

B. Desire: 2
2a. **My soul longeth, yea, even fainteth for the courts of the Lord:...**

The Israelites saw God's house as the center and core of their national life. The psalmist said that he had a deep yearning and was homesick for the tabernacle whenever he had to be away from it for a while.

2b. **. . . .my heart and my flesh crieth out for the living God.**

These terms show that the psalmist had an emotional and even a physical hunger to be in the house of the Lord. In the midst of a pagan world with its temples built for false gods, here was a structure which honored the one true and living God. It drew to itself like a magnet those who were truly spiritual and who wanted to approach God.

C. Dwellers: 3-4

3. **Yea, the sparrow hath found an house, and the swallow a nest for herself, where she may lay her young, even thine altars, O Lord of hosts, my King, and my God.**

This verse suggests that birds had found various niches within the tabernacle where they could build nests and lay their eggs to hatch. It is unlikely that they would have been allowed to build nests on the altars, but there were other places for this. The point is that they were located <u>near</u> the sacred altars without being disturbed. The psalmist may have been even envious of them. The three titles for Jehovah here reveal Him to be the Lord of hosts (commanding General), King, and personal God.

4. **Blessed are they that dwell in thy house: they will be still praising thee. Selah.**

The psalmist may have had not only the fortunate birds in mind but also the priests and Levites who lived in the tabernacle complex. Here again, the psalmist sounded almost envious of those who were able to remain there and sing the praises of the Lord. The term "Selah" meant to pause and think about what was said. You will note that it occurred in verses 4 and 8. It was used numerous times in the book of Psalms and in Habakkuk 3:3, 9, and 13.

II. God's blessing: Ps. 84:5-8

A. Valley: 5-6
5. **Blessed is the man whose strength is in thee; in whose heart are the ways of them.**

The psalmist felt that the man who trusted in Jehovah would be able to appropriate His strength by faith. The latter part of the verse is more difficult to understand. Note that the words "of them" are in italics in the Authorized Version, which means that they were not in the original text but were supplied by translators. Some versions would suggest that the ways referred to God's ways, while others think that highways to Zion were meant. Mount Zion in Jerusalem may have had a special significance in David's time, but the temple was not built there until Solomon's time, and it is likely that Psalm 84 was written by David or a contemporary. If highways were meant here, they probably led to God's tabernacle, wherever it was located.

6. Who passing through the valley of Baca make it a well; the rain also filleth the pools,

There seemed to be no literal Valley of Baca (Tears, Weeping). This probably referred to any arid, parched place where a well or abundant rainfall would be a welcome relief. The meaning seemed to be spiritual. Any child of God going through a difficult experience in his life could trust God to bring him out of it in His Own time and way. Even in walking through the valley of the shadow of death, he need fear no evil, for God would be with him (Ps. 23:4).

B. Victory: 7-8
7. They go from strength to strength, every one of them in Zion appeareth before God.

The Amplified Version renders the first part of this verse as "They go from strength to strength—increasing in victorious power." The meaning seems to be that children of God grow spiritually as they walk with Him. Zion was originally a hill on which stood a Jebusite fortress. David brought the ark of God here, thus making the place sacred. When Solomon transferred it to the temple on nearby Mount Moriah, Zion became the name used to designate the temple complex, and it even became synonymous with the name of the city of Jerusalem. Zion is used also as a synonym for heaven (Heb. 12:22; Rev. 14:1). Its use in Psalm 84:7 may have referred to appearing before God at His earthly dwelling place or ultimately in His heavenly sanctuary.

8. O Lord God of hosts, hear my prayer: give ear, O God of Jacob. Selah.

God was called "Lord of hosts" four times in Psalm 84 (vss. 1, 3, 8, and 12). The psalmist saw Him as Commander of the heavenly hosts of angels and thus the greatest Power in the universe. He called on God to hear his prayer for strength, perhaps to complete his pilgrimage to the house of God. In referring to God as the "God of Jacob," the psalmist was stating that he was a descendant of the patriarchs Abraham, Isaac, and Jacob and was therefore included in the covenant given by God to them. He wanted Jehovah to pause and think about what that implied.

III. God's protection: Ps. 84:9-12

A. Preference: 9-10
9. Behold, O God our shield, and look upon the face of thine anointed.

The psalmist called on God to provide him and others with a protective shield and to look with favor on His anointed. A shield was used by a warrior to deflect spears, swords, arrows, and darts launched against him by his enemies. In the spiritual realm, we are told to take "the shield of faith, wherewith ye shall be able to quench all the fiery darts of the wicked [one, meaning Satan]" (Eph. 6:16). Some think that the "shield" and the "anointed" in Psalm 84:9 both referred to the king in power at that time. "Behold our shield [the king as Your agent], O God, and look upon the face of Your anointed!" (Amplified Bible). One paraphrase says, "O God, our Defender and our Shield, have mercy on the one you have anointed as your king" (Living Bible).

10a. For a day in thy courts is better than a thousand.

We obviously have to supply the remainder of the thought presented here. The psalmist said that he would rather spend one day in God's house than a thousand days anywhere else. Being in God's presence was unique.

10b. I had rather be a doorkeeper in the house of my God, than to dwell in the tents of wickedness.

The psalmist said that he would rather be the lowest servant in God's house (doorkeeper, gatekeeper) than to live luxuriously in the tents of wickedness. We are not told what went on in these tents, but we can imagine that they were ancient counterparts of the nightclubs, gambling casinos, and brothels we hear about today. True happiness is found in spiritual things, not in gratification of sensual pleasures.

We must remind ourselves periodically that the world-system is opposed to Bible teaching about what constitutes the "good life." Ask any unbeliever to define it, and he will probably talk about having prestige, power, money, and material things. He is likely to sneer at righteousness being a worthy goal. About the farthest he may go is to admit that he should help somebody out once in a while and perhaps contribute something to charity. His view of life is different from that of the true child of God. We have to make sure that we avoid being pulled his way and that we do what we can to pull him our way. By precept and example, we have to demonstrate that spiritual life and righteousness are worthwhile and bring us joy and peace.

B. Protector: 11-12
lla. For the Lord God is a sun and shield: the Lord will give grace and glory: . . . .

The psalmist definitely referred to God here as being a Sun and a Shield. We have already considered God as a Shield in protecting His children (vs. 9). By calling Him a Sun, the psalmist probably thought of Him as the Source of all life on the planet earth. He may also have been thinking of God as the great Enlightener of men in spiritual truths. He certainly saw God as the Source of grace and glory for mankind,

11b. . . .no good thing will he withhold from them that walk uprightly.

This echoes what was written in Psalm 34: 9-10—"0 fear [reverence] the Lord, ye his saints: for there is no want to them that fear him. The young lions do lack, and suffer hunger: but they that seek the Lord shall not want any good thing." To walk uprightly is to walk righteously, meaning that a person walks according to God's commands.

Note that neither Psalm 34:10 nor Psalm 84:11 teaches that the Lord gives His child everything he may want. He knows that some things are not good for him. He has promised not to withhold any good thing from him. See also Matthew 7:11 and Philippians 4:19.

12. O Lord of hosts, blessed is the man that trusteth in thee.

The psalmist concluded by stating that God blessed any man who trusted Him. In other words, faith was the key by which to unlock the blessings of the Lord in a person's life. Coming into God's house regularly is one way to build up that trust and faith, because it is here that the Word of God is promoted. "Faith cometh by hearing, and hearing by the word of God" (Rom, 10:17).

If time allows, try to have a frank discussion with your students regarding the matter of reverence in God's house. What do students expect to find there? What is their attitude toward attendance? Are there things which annoy them and could be corrected? What may they contribute to a proper atmosphere in church services and activities?

We have to admit that many churches have improvements to make, and the best place to begin making them is in our own assembly.

Evangelistic Emphasis

What a blessing it is to be in the presence of God in worship. It is so highly desirable that even the sparrows and swallows that nest in the house of worship are blessed. There is a yearning in the heart of man to be in communion with his maker that is satisfied only by a worshipful relationship with God. This is not an optional extra in life. It is the essence of life itself.

Those who tune their lives to communion with God are living in harmony with their own most basic nature. They are made by God and made in his image. When they stay in relationship with him they are honoring their own roots and are living compatibly with their own nature.

Man was made to live with a spirit of love, justice, and humility. For him to do so gives a sense of fulfillment and reconciliation. To do otherwise is to bring that which is incongruous into life. It results in abrasions and conflict.

There is, deep within us, the hunger to be in communion with God. No earthly blessing is better. In fact, none can even compare. It is better to be a doorkeeper, that is, to occupy the most lowly place in the house of God, than to occupy the position of greatest exaltation elsewhere.

Memory Selection

"My soul longeth, yea, even fainteth for the courts of the Lord: my heart and my flesh crieth out for the living God."
Psalm 84:2.

In one sense, worship is the home of the soul. It is where our spirit experiences communion with our Father. The joy of worship is like the joy of homecoming after a long absence. Our spirit comes away from the world of conflict, separateness, and hostility to a God of peace, relationship, and reconciliation.

Worship, to those who best understand it, is not an unpleasant duty but a welcome feast. It meets needs and satisfies longings. A child might have to be reminded or even scolded to get him to clean his room or mow the lawn. He does not have to be chided, however, to get him to eat when he is hungry or to play a game he likes to play. He bounds eagerly to those activities because they satisfy hungers and longings.

So we, when we see worship in its proper light, do not have to be reminded or scolded to participate. It is like food to the hungry and is pleasurable to the soul. Instead of being driven to reluctant participation, we eagerly seek the opportunity and relish it when we find it.

Weekday Problems

Dwain was not reared in a Christian family. When he was seventeen years old he started attending church with a friend. It was a strange experience for him. Others seemed to experience emotions and satisfactions that evaded him. The songs spoke of themes that were strange to him, such as redemption and intercession. Prayer seemed to be speaking to one who was not present, or who at least was not discernible in any way Dwain could see. The sermons seemed irrelevant to his life and were usually boring.

Dwain was not sure whether there was something wrong with church or something wrong with him. He clearly was not feeling what one was expected to feel in worship. He asked his friend, but their backgrounds were so different that it was hard for either to understand the perspective of the other.

As time passed there were some points of worship that made meaningful contact with Dwain. He experienced a sense of guilt. The message of love and acceptance made him feel good. Belief in a God who was in control was comforting.

* What can we do to stimulate appropriate feelings in worship if we do not have them already?

* How can we be sure that our emotional and spiritual responses are not arbitrarily fabricated?

Superintendent's Sermonette

Bible believers today can profit from taking as high a view of God's house as the writer of Psalm 84 did thousands of years ago. We seldom call such a place a tabernacle or a temple today. We usually refer to it as a church. Some people like to avoid churches. They feel that they are outdated, irrelevant, and time-wasting. Some people want minimal connections with a church for such things as christenings, weddings, funerals and perhaps for special meetings at Christmas and Easter time.

Those who give their full support to a church should make sure that it provides four basic things for its people. They are instruction in the Word of God, worship at all age levels, fellowship among believers, and opportunities for service both inside and outside of the church. If this balanced program is faithfully funded and promoted by Spirit-led believers, the church will grow and be the kind of lighthouse God intended it to be. Let each of us ask the Lord what He would have us do in the church.

This Lesson in Your Life

This psalm is a song for temple visitors. From it we notice some things that will help us to worship more meaningfully. Let us notice first that the spirit of worship can often best be expressed in song. Some messages can be well communicated in ordinary speech. Such speech can communicate data, make inquiries, transact business, and exchange social pleasantries.

There are, however, some feelings in the human breast that cry out for expression beyond the expressive powers of ordinary speech. We have observed this phenomenon in other areas of our lives. For example, feelings of love and romance will feel the need for using the language of poetry and music because they are better vehicles for emotion.

Feelings of reverence and awe are like that also. Routine speech does not have the dimensions to express those feelings fully. Speech may be able to teach us about worship, but it is lacking in ability to express fully the emotion of worship. Therefore we need something beyond a written or spoken sermon. We need a way to burst forth in song with pent-up feelings for God.

This passage also illustrates the importance of coming to worship with a spirit of anticipation. It describes a yearning to go to the temple. Picture in your mind two families that are preparing to go to church on a Sunday morning. The first goes out of a sense of obligation rather than from desire. They are chafed by what they see to be an intrusion into their "day off." They are likely to be irritable with each other and will probably cast a longing glance at the Sunday paper as they go out the door.

The second family sees worship as a meeting place between their spirit and God. They are hungry to experience and express their praise and adoration. There are songs in their hearts that need to be sung, prayers that they are hungry to pray. They eagerly approach the house of worship, convinced they will be greatly blessed there.

It clearly makes all the difference in the world whether we are expectant of good things when we enter the place of worship. If we are we will see more good things, hear more good messages, receive answers to more prayers, and experience more of the emotions of joy and gratitude.

This psalm also reminds us of the significance of the place of worship. I have heard it said that the church is always a body and never a building, always a people and never a place. There is a truth in that statement, but it does not justify the conclusion that the place of worship is unimportant.

In the Old Testament when there was a significant event in the life of Israel, they would erect a pillar to commemorate the place where it occurred. The promised land was an important place. The holy city of Jerusalem was an important place. The temple was an important place. They were important because of their association with God, but nonetheless, they were important.

Our place of worship should be honored. It should be well cared for out of respect for the important thing that occurs there. It should be aesthetically supportive to the praise of God. This does not necessarily mean expensive or ornate, but it does mean that the place where worship occurs is to be honored.

Seed Thoughts

1. Why did the psalmist call God's tabernacles amiable?
He saw them as friendly, lovely, and beloved. Some people view churches differently today. Discuss.

2. What should be our attitude toward God's house?
We should love and reverence it, realizing that God's presence is there in a special way to bless us.

3. What significance is there in birds dwelling near God's altars?
Animals, living by instincts, seem to respect God more than some intelligent human beings. God watches over them.

4. Can we dwell in God's house?
We do not live there as ancient priests and Levites did, but we can attend often enough to feel we are a part of it.

5. What part should praise play in our church attendance?
Beyond obvious singing and testifying, everything we do can contribute to adoration for the Lord.

(Please Turn Page)

---

1. Why did the psalmist call God's tabernacles amiable?

2. What should be our attitude toward God's house?

3. What significance is there in birds dwelling near God's altars?

4. Can we dwell in God's house?

5. What part should praise play in our church attendance?

6. How does God help us go through the Valley of Baca (Tears, Weeping)?

7. What does it mean for a believer to go from strength to strength?

8. When will all believers ultimately appear in Zion?

9. Why is a day in God's house worth more than a thousand elsewhere?

10. What can we expect to receive from God as our Sun and Shield?

Seed Thoughts - Continued

He saw them as friendly, lovely, and beloved. Some people view churches differently today. Discuss.

We should love and reverence it, realizing that God's presence is there in a special way to bless us.

Animals, living by instincts, seem to respect God more than some intelligent human beings. God watches over them.

We do not live there as ancient priests and Levites did, but we can attend often enough to feel we are a part of it.

Beyond obvious singing and testifying, everything we do can contribute to adoration for the Lord.

His presence and the help of His people help us endure difficult experiences.

It means that he has spiritual victories as he walks with God. Each victory makes his faith in God stronger.

Coming to God's house in this life is but a prelude to arriving at His sanctuary in heaven (Heb. 12:22; Rev. 14:1).

The quality of what we receive when we are in God's presence outweighs whatever the world has to offer, Service for Him is better than gratification of self.

He will give us grace and glory by enlightening us. He will give protection and good things to bless us.

6. How does God help us go through the Valley of Baca (Tears, Weeping)?
His presence and the help of His people help us endure difficult experiences.

7. What does it mean for a believer to go from strength to strength?
It means that he has spiritual victories as he walks with God. Each victory makes his faith in God stronger.

8. When will all believers ultimately appear in Zion?
Coming to God's house in this life is but a prelude to arriving at His sanctuary in heaven (Heb. 12:22; Rev. 14:1).

9. Why is a day in God's house worth more than a thousand elsewhere?
The quality of what we receive when we are in God's presence outweighs whatever the world has to offer, Service for Him is better than gratification of self.

10. What can we expect to receive from God as our Sun and Shield?
He will give us grace and glory by enlightening us. He will give protection and good things to bless us.

A Hymn To The Redeemer

Psalm 103:1. Bless the Lord, O my soul: and all that is within me, bless his holy name.
2. Bless the Lord, O my soul, and forget not all his benefits:
3. Who forgiveth all thine iniquities; who healeth all thy diseases;
4. Who redeemeth thy life from destruction; who crowneth thee with lovingkindness and tender mercies;
5. Who satisfieth thy mouth with good things; so that thy youth is renewed like the eagle's.
6. The Lord executeth righteousness and judgment for all that are oppressed.
7. He made known his ways unto Moses, his acts unto the children of Israel.
8. The Lord is merciful and gracious, slow to anger, and plenteous in mercy.
9. He will not always chide: neither will he keep his anger for ever.
10. He hath not dealt with us after our sins; nor rewarded us according to our iniquities.
11. For as the heaven is high above the earth, so great is his mercy toward them that fear him.
12. As far as the east is from the west, so far hath he removed our transgressions from us.
13. Like as a father pitieth his children, so the Lord pitieth them that fear him.
14. For he knoweth our frame; he remembereth that we are dust.
15. As for man, his days are as grass: as a flower of the field, so he flourisheth.
16. For the wind passeth over it, and it is gone; and the place thereof shall know it no more.
17. But the mercy of the Lord is from everlasting to everlasting upon them that fear him, and his righteousness unto children's children.

MEMORY SELECTION
Psalm 103:8
DEVOTIONAL READING
Psalm 146

BACKGROUND SCRIPTURE
Psalm 103
PRINTED SCRIPTURE
Psalm 103:1-17

Teacher's Target

Some Old Testament passages sound almost New Testament in tone, and Psalm 103 is one of them. It speaks of God's forgiving and redeeming love. He is described as merciful and gracious. He removes our transgressions from us as far as the east is from the west. Emphasis on these themes helped people in ancient Israel to look forward to the coming of a Messiah from heaven. It was obvious that they could not meet God's holy standard without a delivering Savior.

Help your students to see in Psalm 103 how God's love flowed toward sinners and met the needs of those who were willing to put their trust in Him. David stood on the other side of Calvary and anticipated redeeming grace. We stand on this side of Calvary and thank God for what Christ did. Understanding both positions helps us to appreciate the significance of God's love in Christ.

Lesson Introduction

David had a promising start as a young man. While tending his father's sheep, he killed a marauding lion and a bear. He managed to slay the Philistine giant, Goliath, with his sling and stones. He rose quickly in the ranks of the Israelite army. He was a singer and harp player. He managed to escape several attempts on his life made by King Saul. He became king over Judah and Israel. He became famous over a wide area of the Middle East.

However, David was not perfect, and he knew it. He admitted that he sinned when he committed adultery with Bathsheba and had her husband slain in battle (II Sam. 12:13). He knew the reality of being pardoned by God. This is the background for his marvelous psalm which we study in this lesson.

Teaching Outline

I. Provision: Ps. 103:1-5
   A. Blessing: 1-2
   B. Benefits: 3-5

II. Pardon: Ps. 103:6-12
   A. Services 6-7
   B. Slowness: 8-9
   C. Salvations 10-12

III. Pity: Ps. 103:13-17
   A. Evaluation: 13-14
   B. Elimination: 15-16
   C. Endurance: 17

Daily Bible Readings

Mon. Bless the Lord
Psalm 103:1-3
Tue. The Lord is Good
Psalm 103:4-6
Wed. Plenteous in Mercy
Psalm 103:7-9
Thu. Great in Mercy
Psalm 103:10-12
Fri. Man is Weak
Psalm 103:13-15
Sat. God's Mercy is Everlasting
Psalm 103:16-18
Sun. Bless the Lord
Psalm 103:19-22

Verse By Verse

I. Provision: Ps. 103

A. Blessing: 1-2
1. Bless the Lord, O my soul: and all that is within me, bless his holy name.
David was right in assuming that praise to God should begin with himself. Starting with verse 6, he spoke of others being grateful to God. In verse 20 he called on angels to join the chorus. In verse 22 he suggested that God's works should bless the Lord. David wanted universal adoration of Jehovah. The starting point was to be the outpouring of his own soul and all that was within him.

2. Bless the Lord, O my soul, and forget not all his benefits:
David realized that praise to God can grow out of consideration of all of His benefits or blessings. The Lord's help is required in all aspects of one's life—material, physical, mental, emotional, social, and spiritual. Examination of these reveals what God has done for the individual, group, or nation.

B. Benefits: 3-5
3. Who forgiveth all thine iniquities who healeth all thy diseases, . . .
David began listing divine benefits here. He praised God for forgiving personal sins when they were confessed. He was thankful for the healing of diseases, perhaps those contracted from sinful activities or imposed by God as punishments for various sins. It may have been simply a reference to healing of the body due to its natural recuperative powers, which was very important in an age when medical care was much more primitive than it was in later centuries.

4. Who redeemeth thy life from destruction who crowneth thee with lovingkindness and tender mercies
Reference here seems to be to the pit of corruption known as hell. Only God could save a person from that. He also showed compassion with many acts of love and mercy. The Lord's double purpose toward men is to deliver them from what is evil and to deliver them unto what is good.

5. Who satisfieth thy mouth with good things so that thy youth is renewed like the eagle's.
Although the primary meaning here would be that God supplies the mouth of a person with good food, it may also refer to other kinds of blessings throughout life. The renewal of youth such as that known by the eagle is reflected in Isaiah 40:31—"They that wait upon the Lord shall renew their strength; they shall mount up with wings as eagles; they shall run, and not be weary; and they shall walk, and not faint."

II. Pardon: Ps. 103:6-12

A. Service: 6-7
6. The Lord executeth righteousness and judgment for all that are oppressed.
This was a general statement which described the Lord as One Who executes (administers, gives) fairness and justice to all who are oppressed. When we despair of human lack of justice, let us remember that the Judge in heaven will make sure that all oppressors who reject His mercy will eventually

be condemned and punished for their sins. This is a divine service on which we may depend, and it warns us not to be unjust toward others ourselves.

7. He made known his ways unto Moses, his acts unto the children of Israel.

Did any Israelite doubt what God had done in the nation's past? Let him study history and be reminded that the Lord made His merciful ways known to Moses and to the children of Israel. He brought them out of Egyptian bondage and destroyed their enemies in the Red Sea when they pursued them. He took them through the wilderness and preserved them for forty years. He brought the second generation, and a few of the first generation, into the promised land of Canaan. This was a divine service performed by God for His chosen people.

B. Slowness: 8-9
8. The Lord is merciful and gracious, slow to anger, and plenteous in mercy.

Sometimes men want the Lord to act quickly, and sometimes they want Him to act slowly. They want Him to be merciful and gracious quickly, but they want Him to be slow to get angry with them. They want Him to be filled with mercy but sparing in judgment in their cases.

9. He will not always chide: neither will he keep his anger for ever.

The thought here seems to be that something interposes between an angry God and sinful men. If they repent, God will not continue rebuking them, and He will not hold a grudge against them.

C. Salvation: 10-12
10. He hath not dealt with us after our sins nor rewarded us according to our iniquities.

We have been afflicted by sin, but God has not condemned us as we deserved nor rewarded (in this case punished) us because of our iniquities. His mercy has caused Him to withhold judgment, and His grace has given us unmerited favor. This refers to those who have sought His pardon. Judgment surely waits for those who have persisted in their sinful ways.

11. For as the heaven is high above the earth, so great is his mercy toward them that fear him.

The Psalmist searched for superlatives in order to describe the greatness of God's pardoning mercy. His first illustration was a vertical one, referring to the distance between heaven and earth. We know today that this could be billions of light years.

12. As far as the east is from the west, so far hath he removed our transgressions from us,

The Psalmist's second illustration was a horizontal one, referring to the distance between east and west. We know today that this is approximately twenty-five thousand miles. The point being made was that God separated repentant people from their sins so that they need not be haunted by them. This does not mean, of course, that the scars of past sins will not continue to bother us on the human level, but they are removed as far as God is concerned. Micah 7:19 described God as casting sins into the depths of the sea.

III. Pity: Ps. 103:13-17

A. Evaluation: 13-14
13. Like as a father pitieth his children, so the Lord pitieth them that fear him.

When David pitied his infant son, born to him and Bathsheba, he went into protracted prayer that the boy's life would be spared, but God allowed him to die. David's pity was unable to save the child. However, he knew that someday he could go to the child again in the other world (II Sam. 12:13-23). The Lord's pity was all-powerful, and He could save those who feared (reverenced) Him.

14. For he knoweth our frame he remembereth that we are dust.

No one need be afraid that God will make an incorrect evaluation of him. The Lord knows each person better than he knows himself. God knows how man is constructed. He knows that man is made of dust. He does not expect more of him than He should.

Having said that, however, we need to avoid the worldly

conclusion that human weakness allows us to give in to our baser passions. Satan likes to convince people that they are within their rights to give in to temptations. He tries to make righteousness look insipid and unrealistic. He even causes some people to boast of their wickedness as if it were something commendable. God sees us as weak and vulnerable, but He also sees us as having potential for what is best.

B. Elimination 15-16
15. As for man, his days are as grass: as a flower of the field, so he flourisheth.
16. For the wind passeth over it, and it is gone; and the place thereof shall know it no more.

God, Who created and sustains man, has no illusions about his temporary status on this earth. Man's days (or years) are limited. The Psalmist compared him to grass and wildflowers. They flourish with life for a period of time, but the searing wind passes over them and they die. Their place on the face of the earth vanishes as they shrivel, die, and perhaps are blown away.

The point made here by the Psalmist was that even God's providential care for man is transitory. There is no eternal hope for man apart from God's saving grace. Caught within Satan's tenacious grasp, man must be redeemed (bought back) by divine grace, or he faces judgment and eternal punishment.

C. Endurance: 17
17. But the mercy of the Lord is from everlasting to everlasting upon them that fear him, and his righteousness unto children's children;

The deciding factor in man's destiny is the everlasting mercy of the Lord. If it is rejected, there is no hope for the sinner. If it is accepted, it brings forgiveness and pardon. The sign of acceptance on man's part is demonstration of fear (reverence) for God. No one gains favor with the Lord if he lacks true humility and sorrow for sin. A man who is proud, arrogant, and self-righteous will doom himself. A man who confesses his sin and sincerely seeks deliverance from it will find God merciful. His righteousness is available to a man and to his descendants.

Note carefully, however, that God's mercy and righteousness are offered only to those who "keep his covenant, and to those who remember his commandments to do them" (Ps. 103:18). In the Psalmist's time, the covenant in force was the law of God as given to Moses. Its requirements had to be obeyed if righteousness was to be known and promoted in Israel. Since Calvary, we have lived under the covenant of grace. We are not bound by ceremonial laws which were fulfilled in Christ, but we are obligated to continue to keep the moral commandments of God, The closing verses of Psalm 103 are not in our printed text for this lesson, but you would do well to look at them. The psalmist pictures God as sitting on His throne in heaven and ruling over all the universe. The psalmist called on the angelic hosts of heaven to bless (praise) the Lord. He also called on all of God's works to praise Him. The psalmist closed in the same way he had opened the psalm by saying, "Bless the Lord, O my soul" (Ps. 103:1, 22). Having followed his thoughts throughout this psalm, we can add our praise to the Lord, as well.

Evangelistic Emphasis

This psalm is a hymn to the Redeemer. It affirms that God has not dealt with us according to our sins. He could have convicted us, but chose not to do so. Were he to reward us according to what we have earned, he would treat us severely. However, he treats us graciously, better than we deserve.

Some conceive of God as keeping a list of our wrongs so he can prosecute us at judgment. It is almost as though they believe God takes pleasure in not letting us get away with anything. This psalm pictures a much more generous and solicitous attitude than that. God is full of grace and mercy. He finds ways to help us in spite of our sins.

His mercy is as high at the heavens. It is without limit. Instead of being afraid we are going to be judged by God, we should be thankful that we are going to be judged by him. He is so much more generous and gracious than men are. He understands us better and loves us more.

He has moved our transgressions as far away from us as the east is the from the west. The intent is to say that we are at one extremity and our sins are at the other. While our sins are at the other side of the world, we are securely in the loving embrace of God. Our salvation is not a close call but a sure thing.

Memory Selection

"The Lord is merciful and gracious, slow to anger, and plenteous in mercy."
Psalm 103:8.

Early in life we discover that some things are in limited supply. Many people have limited amount of food. Some get an inadequate supply of a mother's love. Some are cold because there are not enough clothes or enough heating oil. Many feel that there is not enough money to go around. Perhaps others do not get enough rest. In every life there seems to be some shortage somewhere, and in some lives shortages seem to be the primary experience.

In the matter of the Lord's mercy there is no shortage. He has an abundant supply. It is not parceled out in meager amounts as if in short supply. It is drawn from the ever-bountiful source, the heart of God.

As you could not dip all the water out of the Pacific Ocean, so you cannot exhaust the supply of the graciousness of God. It is like trying to fill a cup under Niagara Falls or finding a breath of fresh air in the state of Montana.

Though God is bounteous in mercy, he is not to be presumed on.

Weekday Problems

Jack had a cruel and oppressive father. The father was erratic in his behavior. He would often not come home for weeks at a time. When he did come home, he was a bully of intimidation and on occasion was even physically abusive. He showed more gentleness to the girls in the family, which gave Jack a further feeling that fathers are unfair. Never did Jack's father show him any affection or approval.

Over the years, Jack was driven so deeply into his shell that he dreaded to see his father come home. He was not only afraid of his father but came to distrust others, particularly men. He supposed that all were out to hurt him. He reacted negatively to teachers in school and especially to coaches, who were more like father-figures to him. After graduation he went into military service. The authoritarianism of that system rekindled the deep feelings of resentment he had toward his father. He did not do well and was eventually discharged. When out of the service, he was not able to relate to people in authority, so he had trouble holding a job.

* What complications would there be for Jack to hear that God is his father?
* Would it be better to abandon this terminology or attempt to re-educate it?

Superintendent's Sermonette

Some sinners who have been invited to accept Christ as Savior have felt that they were too sinful to be redeemed. They somehow thought that they would have to make themselves better before they could present themselves to Him. There are believers who feel that they are not good enough to witness to others. They somehow think that they must perfect themselves before they can make contact with sinners. Satan uses these attitudes to keep people from experiencing the saving and developing grace of God.

King David knew that he was a sinner and an imperfect believer. He must have agonized over his weaknesses, as illustrated in Psalm 51, but he knew the answer to his problem. He threw himself on the mercy of God and requested a new heart and the righteous attitude which went with it. Nothing has basically changed since his time when it comes to dealing with our own weaknesses. Let us praise God for His blessings, and let us take full advantage of His redeeming grace. He knows what we are and what we can become.

This Lesson in Your Life

The Psalmist calls on himself to praise God with his whole being. "Bless the Lord, O my soul: and all that is within me, bless his holy name." It is an interesting concept for a person to call himself to his best effort. We are accustomed to being called by others to harder work, longer hours, or better performance. This person called himself to praise God with every fiber of his being.

All of us know that the self-motivated person will accomplish more and do better than the person who relies on external motivation. There are several reasons for this. A self-chosen goal is not reached with resentment. Internal motivation works when no one is watching or checking. Self-motivation usually lasts longer than that which comes from other sources.

It makes sense, then, for us as Christians to do all we can to motivate ourselves. It is not unwise to seek other sources of motivation, but they are not adequate . We also must reach down to find the springs of motivation that are within ourselves.

This psalm is talking about what motivation has to do with intensity of worship. By its nature, almost all of this motivation has to be internal. A small percentage of it might come from inspiration or examples given by others, but most of it must come from inside

Christianity is not a "do-it-yourself" religion. Yet it does call for the active participation of the Christian in the process of his own eternal redemption. We are not saved by our works, but neither are we mindless automatons who are just worked on from the outside.

With this spirit of calling for the best from ourselves, we need to set out to inventory his blessings. We will be able to praise better and therefore worship with more intensity when we reflect on what he has done for us. We can begin by putting our whole hearts into remembering how he has forgiven our iniquities. Then we can dwell on who makes us well when we are sick. Then we can remember the source of our protection and meditate on who shows us mercy and kindness.

Some time and energy should then go into reflecting on who provides our food. Some thankful thinking should be done on God's revelation of himself to us. God's patience is a matter that deserves a good deal of thought. The thoroughness of his mercy and forgiveness is a cause for much considered rejoicing.

A culminating contemplation might be the eternal nature of God's care. We are like grass that appears in the spring but is gone in the winter. His mercy is from everlasting to everlasting.

After we have spent a good amount of time concentrating on this list of blessings that we have from God, we should be able to praise him with much intensity. "Bless the Lord, O my soul: and all that is within me, bless his holy name."

Seed Thoughts

1. Whom did David invite to praise the Lord in Psalm 103?
He called on his own soul, other men, angels, and the works of God to do this.

2. What benefits given by God warranted men's praise?
Forgiveness of iniquities, healing of diseases, redemption from destruction, crowning with love and mercies, satisfaction of hunger, and renewal of youth are mentioned in Psalm 103:3-5.

3. What comfort can be given to victims of human injustice?
"The Lord executeth righteousness and judgment for all that are oppressed" (Ps. 103:6). Consider the implications.

4. How can history help people to understand how God works?
Even as God made His ways known to Moses and the Israelites, so it is that He can work on people's behalf today.

5. Is it reasonable that God be slow to anger when evil persists?
Patience is one of God's attributes. We want it when we are evil.

(Please Turn Page)

---

1. Whom did David invite to praise the Lord in Psalm 103?

2. What benefits given by God warranted men's praise?

3. What comfort can be given to victims of human injustice?

4. How can history help people to understand how God works?

5. Is it reasonable that God be slow to anger when evil persists?

6. When does God stop chiding us for our sins?

7. What vertical and horizontal illustrations describe how far God removes our sins from us?

8. Does God's understanding of our weak human frame cause Him to condone or overlook our sins?

9. Does God pass righteousness on to succeeding generations?

10. What covenant should we keep?

Seed Thoughts - Continued

He called on his own soul, other men, angels, and the works of God to do this.

Forgiveness of iniquities, healing of diseases, redemption from destruction, crowning with love and mercies, satisfaction of hunger, and renewal of youth are mentioned in Psalm 103:3-5.

"The Lord executeth righteousness and judgment for all that are oppressed" (Ps. 103:6). Consider the implications.

Even as God made His ways known to Moses and the Israelites, so it is that He can work on people's behalf today.

Patience is one of God's attributes. We want it when we are evil.

The moment we confess our sin and ask His forgiveness, God stops chiding us.

He takes them away as far as heaven is above the earth and east is from west.

No, for God is holy and must deal with human sins, but He offers everlasting mercy and pardon to those who sin and seek His forgiveness.

Each generation is dealt with individually, but righteousness in one generation promotes it in another generation.

Christians are to keep the Law of Christ, the New Covenant.

6. When does God stop chiding us for our sins?
The moment we confess our sin and ask His forgiveness, God stops chiding us.

7. What vertical and horizontal illustrations describe how far God removes our sins from us?
He takes them away as far as heaven is above the earth and east is from west.

8. Does God's understanding of our weak human frame cause Him to condone or overlook our sins?
No, for God is holy and must deal with human sins, but He offers everlasting mercy and pardon to those who sin and seek His forgiveness.

9. Does God pass righteousness on to succeeding generations?
Each generation is dealt with individually, but righteousness in one generation promotes it in another generation.

10. What covenant should we keep?
Christians are to keep the Law of Christ, the New Covenant.

Lyrics Of Love

Song of Solomon 2:8. The voice of my beloved! behold, he cometh leaping upon the mountains, skipping upon the hills.
9. My beloved is like a roe or a young hart: Behold, he standeth behind our wall, he looketh forth at the windows, showing himself through the lattice.
10. My beloved spake, and said unto me, Rise up, my love, my fair one, and come away.
11. For, lo, the winter is past, the rain is over and gone;
12. The flowers appear on the earth; the time of the singing of birds is come, and the voice of the turtle is heard in our land;
13. The fig tree putteth forth her green figs, and the vines with the tender grape give a good smell. Arise, my love, my fair one, and come away.
14. O my dove, that art in the clefts of the rock, in the secret places of the stains, let me see thy countenance, let me hear thy voice; for sweet is thy voice, and thy countenance is comely.
15. Take us the foxes, the little foxes, that spoil the vines: for our vines have tender grapes.
16. My beloved is mine, and I am his: he feedeth among the lilies.
17. Until the day break, and the shadows flee away, turn, my beloved, and be thou like a roe or a young hart upon the mountains of Bether.

MEMORY SELECTION
Song of Solomon 8:7
DEVOTIONAL READING
I Corinthians 13

BACKGROUND SCRIPTURE
Song of Solomon 2:8-17
PRINTED SCRIPTURE
Song of Solomon 2:8-17

Teacher's Target

The Song of Solomon may be, in some ways, the most mysterious book in the Bible. We know that it was Solomon's (vs. 1), but we are unsure whether it was written by him, about him, or both. It was obviously a poem of love, but it may have had a natural meaning, allegorical meaning, or both. Some see it simply as a description of married bliss, some as a description of Christ (Bridegroom) and the church (bride), or both.

Help your students to study the language of the text to discover the depth of feeling existing between the loving man and woman. Guide them into transposing this into the deep relationship existing between Christ and His church. If the relationship suffers, it is due to our failure, not to His. Joy is possible only if true fellowship is present.

Lesson Introduction

We live in an age when lust is often substituted for love in our literature, broadcasts, and even fine arts. Although the language used in the Song of Solomon is quite frank, it is intended to be pure and honorable, rather than bordering on the lewd and licentious. We should see in the descriptions presented the personal love and respect held by Solomon and the Shulamite woman for one another. We should see the high view of marriage which is portrayed.

Our lesson text deals with a lapse in the relationship and a restoration, we look beyond to chapter three, verses one through five. Whether a separation occurs on the natural or spiritual level, reconciliation is the best answer for solving the problem. God stands ready to help in either case, and we need to appropriate that help.

Teaching Outline

I. Skipping: Song of Sol. 2:8-9
  A. Speed: 8-9a
  B. Stance: 9b

II. Speaking: Song of Sol. 2:10-13
  A. Invitation I: 10
  B. Indicators: 11-13b
  C. Invitation II: 13c

III. Savoring: Song of Sol. 2:14-17
  A. The dove: 14
  B. The foxes: 15
  C. The deer: 16-17

Daily Bible Readings

Mon. The Voice of My Beloved
Song of Solomon 2:8
Tue. The Beauty of My Beloved
Song of Solomon 2:9
Wed. The Yearning of Love
Song of Solomon 2:10
Thu. The Urgency of Love
Song of Solomon 2:11-12
Fri. Time is Fleeting
Isaiah 2:13
Sat. Sweet is Thy Voice
Isaiah 2:14-15
Sun. He is Mine; I am His
Isaiah 2:16-17

Verse By Verse

I. Skipping: Song of Sol. 2:8-9

A. Speed: 8-9a
**8. The voice of my beloved! behold, he cometh leaping upon the mountains, skipping upon the hills.
9a. My beloved is like a roe or a young hart: . . .**

The first part of the book described the sweet communion which existed between Solomon and his bride. A separation evidently came about, and our text describes how restoration began. The conclusion is found in 3:1-5.

The bride was delighted to hear the voice of her beloved again. He came leaping upon the mountains, skipping upon the hills. His action was compared to that of the fleetfooted roe (gazelle) or the young hart (deer). Gazelles were small antelopes capable of running at speeds up to forty-five miles per hour for six to seven miles. Deer described here were males weighing up to three hundred pounds and carrying six-pronged antlers. Females were called hinds. The swiftness of the gazelle and the deer may speak of the quickness of the loving husband to return to his bride. It may, by extension, refer to the willingness of Christ to be reconciled to members of His church if they stray from Him, provided they seek His pardon.

B. Stance: 9b
9b. . . .behold, he standeth behind our wall, he looketh forth at the windows, shewing himself through the lattice.

The husband did not push boldly into the courtyard but stood respectfully outside the wall. He looked through (not forth or out from) the windows. He showed himself discreetly through the latticework. Lattices were used to cover openings for privacy and decoration while allowing cool breezes to come through. The husband's stance here reminds us of Christ, Who said, "Behold, I stand at the door [of a person's heart]: if any man [or woman] hear my voice, and open the door, I will come in to him [or her], and will sup [eat] with him [or her], and he [or she] with me" (Rev. 3:20). He comes not by intrusion but by invitation.

II. Speaking: Song of Sol. 2:10-13

A. Invitation I: 10
10. My beloved spake, and said unto me, Rise up, my love, my fair one, and come away.

It was time for a change, and the husband invited his bride to rise up and come away with him. In reassuring words, he let her know that she was still his beloved, and he still thought of her as fair (beautiful). Too often husbands get past the honeymoon stage and stop telling their wives that they love them and find them attractive. This is unfortunate, because women find security in being reminded of these things. Sensitive husbands will find ways to express their feelings in overt and in subtle ways. We know that the day will come when Christ will call away His bride, the church, and take her to her heavenly home. In the meantime, He gives many assurances of His love for her in this troublesome world.

B. Indicators 11-13b

11. For, lo, the winter is past, the rain is over and gone;

The first indicator that change was taking place was that winter was over and the rains following it had stopped. Winter in Palestine ended about April, and it was followed by showers until May. With the return of warm weather, things could grow again.

12a. The flowers appear on the earth; . . .

This probably referred to wildflowers that sprang up everywhere. Jesus referred to the "lilies of the field" as examples (Matt. 6: 28). They were heralds of spring.

12b. . . .the time of the singing of birds is come, and the voice of the turtle is heard in our land;

All those who wait for springtime watch for the arrival of migrating birds, and they rejoice when they hear their songs. Other versions translate "turtle" as "turtledove."

13a. The fig tree putteth forth her green figs, . . .

The thought here is that the fig trees put forth their green figs and ripen them.

13b. . . .and the vines with the tender grape give a good smell.

This refers to vines in flower. The blossoms were sometimes dried and used to flavor new wine because of their sweetness.

C. Invitation II: 13c

13c. Arise, my love, my fair one, and come away.

The original invitation, as given before (vs. 10), is repeated here, thus adding urgency to the call. We are reminded of the fact that the second coming of Christ will be preceded by signs of His coming. A list of these may be found in Luke 21:8-28. In James 5:7-8 we find a parallel passage—"Behold, the husbandman waiteth for the precious fruit of the earth, and hath long patience for it, until he receive the early and the latter rain. Be ye also patient; stablish your hearts: for the coming of the Lord [Jesus Christ] draweth nigh."

III. Savoring: Song of Sol. 2:14-17

A. The dove: 14

14. O my dove, that art in the clefts of the rock, in the secret places of the stairs, let me see thy countenance, let me hear thy voice: for sweet is thy voice, and thy countenance is comely.

The Amplified Bible has an interesting way of presenting this verse—" [So I went with him, and when we were climbing the rocky steps up the hillside, my beloved shepherd said to me] O my dove, [while you are there] in the seclusion of the clefts in the solid rock, in the sheltered and secret place of the cliff, let me see your face, let me hear your voice, for your voice is sweet and your face is lovely." If this rendering is correct, the husband's invitation had been accepted by the bride and acted upon.

Some would see a parallel here between Christ and His church. Those who have put their trust in Him feel secure, much as a dove would feel secure while protected from a storm in a cleft in the rock. The fellowship experienced by the husband and wife would be a type of the fellowship enjoyed by Christ and believers. As used in the Bible, dove is a term of endearment, and it apparently can be applied to a believer in Jesus Christ.

B. The foxes: 15

15. Take us the foxes, the little foxes, that spoil the vines: for our vines have tender grapes.

This was a warning to prevent the little foxes from ruining the vineyards. Verse 13 already made it clear that the vines were in blossom. They had to be protected against marauding foxes (and perhaps jackals) which ate grapes but not blossoms. We are not told what or whom these foxes represented. It has been suggested that they might have referred to rival lovers. Perhaps they represented anyone or anything which sought to destroy fellowship between husband and wife.

We know that sometimes it is not so much the big things which endanger our spiritual development as it is the little things. We are harassed by Satan through small, subtle temptations. If we give in to them, they rob us of our fellowship with God and with other believers.

Numbered among these might be such things as pride, envy, and gossip.

C. The deer: 16-17
16. My beloved is mine, and I am his: he feedeth among the lilies.

The bride declares that she and her husband are devoted to one another. The latter part of the verse suggests that he was a shepherd who had to be away from her in the meadows where wildflowers grew. She looked upon this as merely a temporary separation and waited for him to return to her.

We see a parallel here to Christ, the great and good Shepherd, Who through the ages has been calling out a flock to Himself. When the age of grace ends, He will surely return to gather that flock and take it to heaven (I Thess. 4:13-18).

17. Until the day break, and the shadows flee away, turn, my beloved, and be thou like a roe or a young hart upon the mountains of Bether.

Returning to the imagery of the bridegroom as a roe (gazelle) or young hart (deer), we hear the bride calling to him in his absence and plaintively urging him to return quickly to her as soon as dawn came and the shadows of night fled away. She wanted him to come bounding over the mountains of Bether (rugged mountains, craggy mountains) which separated them. In allegorical terms, these mountains might represent the obstacles and difficulties which face believers as they wait for Christ to return.

In order to finish this section of the Song of Solomon, we should look at 3:1-5. The bride was in bed at night searching for her beloved, but she could not find him. She rose up, either literally or in a dream, and went out into the city streets to look for him. The night watchmen who patrolled the city found her, and she asked them if they had seen her beloved. They evidently said that they had not. As she walked on, she found him herself. She grasped him and would not let him go until she had taken him to her mother's house and into a special room. She cautioned the daughters of Jerusalem not to disturb her husband and to let him sleep as long as he desired.

The theme of separation and reunion put forth in Song of Solomon 2:8—3:5 involved a loving couple in Solomon's time. Scholars during the past three thousand years have sought to unravel its meaning. Jewish scholars have wanted to know if it described their relationship to Jehovah. Christian scholars have tried to see if it described their relationship to Christ, seeing that He referred to Himself as the Bridegroom and the church as His bride. We are the inheritors of this latter view and need to decide if it is plausible or should be discarded.

No illustration is completely identical to the real thing. For example, in the Song of Solomon we see the bride chasing after the bridegroom, whereas in our experience we know that it was God in Christ Who sought for us until He found us and made us His Own.

The most conservative thing we might say about the Song of Solomon is that it describes a natural romance between a husband and wife and that it serves as a type of Christ and His bride, the church. If we see abundant parallels there, we assume that we are free to use them in describing our relationship to our great Shepherd and Savior. In spite of temporary separation, we will dwell with Him in love and bliss for all eternity.

Evangelistic Emphasis

The stamp of God's approval on human love is wonderful news. While all of us clearly require the love of God, it is also true that we need the love of other people. We need to be touched and embraced. We need to be approved and admired. We need to be forgiven and accepted. We need to be special to somebody. We also need to make somebody feel special to us.

These needs go all the way back to creation. God made us to live in relationship, not in isolation. Being made in the image of God means having the capacity to give and to receive love. This, of course, includes a broader concept of love than romantic love, but let it be noted that it does include romantic love.

It is in romantic love that commitment and intimacy find their fullest expression. Our Christian faith is not in conflict with that expression. It nurtures and protects it so that we can be whole and mature persons in all ways.

There are some who would hesitate to become Christians because they associate a kind of ethereal piety with the practice of religion. We can assure them that a robust and passionate marriage relationship is fully compatible with the kind of piety and spirituality that was taught by Christ.

Memory Selection

"Many waters cannot quench love, neither can the floods drown it."
Song of Solomon 8:7.

This passage is talking about a permanent kind of love. In any love relationship that lasts over a significant period of time, there will be some problems and tensions. Marriages do not survive forty, fifty, or sixty years because they are sheltered from difficulties. They last that long because the people who are involved in them are so committed to each other that even serious difficulties cannot destroy their love.

The fact that there is a commitment to a permanent love does not imply that the relationship does not need to be nurtured. The contrary is true. The relationship is considered to be of such value that it is cared for with great attention.

Those partners to the relationship need to speak to and of each other with support and respect. It is always encouraging to hear a wife speak warmly and admiringly of her husband or to hear a husband speak protectively and tenderly of his wife. It makes us uncomfortable for marriage partners to make snide and disparaging remarks about their mates. In a permanent love relationship there must be absolute faithfulness and loyalty.

Weekday Problems

Norman and Thelma have been married for more than twenty years. Both are honorable and conscientious Christian people. They have reared two exemplary children. They have dutifully fulfilled their vocational and homemaking roles. They have been active in the life of the church. They have shown respect and consideration to each other.

In fact, all of the external criteria of a good marriage are clearly in place. Not only that, but they love each other. Neither is interested in anyone else or desirous of a marriage other than the one they are in.

Yet, in both Norman and Thelma, there is a vague awareness that something is missing. They feel that there should be greater intimacy, more romance, and a bit more excitement in their relationship. Neither would be critical of the other. Neither has a good feel for how to change things. Patterns of relating have been long established and would be difficult to change.

* Discuss the problem of feelings that are hard to put into words.
* How can a relationship be made more romantic without requiring people to do that which seems uncomfortable and unnatural to them?

Superintendent's Sermonette

Proverbs 30:19 mentions four things too wonderful for Agur to understand—"the way of an eagle in the air; the way of a serpent upon a rock; the way of a ship in the midst of the sea; and the way of a man with a maid." It is this last wondrous thing, the way of a man with a maid, which is highlighted in this lesson's text and in the whole book called the Song of Solomon. The relationship between the bride and the bridegroom had its ups and downs, but the love which held them together prevailed.

This biblical description of intimate romantic love serves as a basis for development of husband-wife relationships today. It also is used to serve as a type of Christ, the Bridegroom, and His church, the bride. The Old Testament provides the characters and the setting, while the New Testament provides the fulfilling of the type. During the age of grace, Christ is calling out His bride from among men of all generations. Let us look forward with anticipation to our coming marriage with the Lamb (Rev. 19:7-8).

This Lesson in <u>Your</u> Life

Solomon's song is a celebration of the love between a man and a woman. It reminds us of the fact that the attraction between the sexes is a part of the creation of God. God made our sexuality: "God created man in his own image, in the image of God created he him; male and female created he them." Genesis 1:27.

Furthermore, it was God who planted sexual yearnings in our hearts. Jesus said, "Have you not read, that he which made them at the beginning made them male and female, and said, For this cause shall a man leave father and mother, and shall cleave to his wife: and they twain shall be one flesh." Matthew 19:4,5.

Sometimes we have not felt free to celebrate the beauty and joy of romantic love. This may be the result of ill-advised teaching or of hangovers of confusion and guilt from our period of puberty. It will help if we understand that the yearning for physical intimacy did not come from any baseness within ourselves or from the devil. Those yearnings came from God. Romantic love is of divine origin.

That is not to suggest, of course, any concept of sexual permissiveness that does not honor the structures and safeguards with which God has protected this treasure. Overt sexual relationships, in the Scriptures, are to be enjoyed within the commitment of marriage. These relationships touch our lives at such a profound level that they require extraordinary care, tenderness, and integrity.

When those qualifications are met it is appropriate that there be a warm and tender sexual intimacy that calls forth the language of romantic love. The passage of our text is an example of both the purity and passion of such love.

Many married people would do well to learn from the example in this text. Love which exists in their hearts may never find expression from their lips. They are too much like the man who told his wife, "I told you I loved you when we married. If I change my mind I'll let you know."

How much better to exclaim about the excitement of hearing the voice of one's beloved! How many marriages would be benefitted by the spouses speaking of each other with admiration and enthusiasm? How many marriages would be revived by the return of romance to the relationship?

The bringing of flowers, even the simplest ones that have been gathered by hand, would work wonders in many cases. An evening walk to listen to the singing of the birds would restore a sense of closeness to some. The doing of some chore so that one's spouse could get a bit of extra rest would greatly enhance some relationships. An unexpected arrangement to share some time away from worries, chores, and routines would mean a great deal to many. A simple empathetic appreciation of the work and effort of a spouse who feels taken for granted would work wonders sometimes.

Try to find a way to bring romance into your marriage. It will be good for your spouse, and that will be good for you.

Seed Thoughts

1. What might the leaping and skipping in Song of Solomon 2:8 signify in spiritual terms?
The energetic bridegroom may serve as a type of Christ, the Source of all life according to John 1:3-4.

2. How did the reserve of the bridegroom set an example for a husband to follow today?
A husband should approach his wife in loving and gentle ways rather than demanding his marital rights.

3. Why is timing important in a marriage relationship?
Various indicators will reveal the right time for a couple to share life's experiences together.

4. Should a wife move about where her husband finds work?
Although this may be debated, it has generally been found best for her to be with him and encourage him in this way.

5. How may a woman find her "cleft of the rock"?
God expects her to find security within her husband's loving care.

(Please Turn Page)

---

1. What might the leaping and skipping in Song of Solomon 2:8 signify in spiritual terms?

2. How did the reserve of the bridegroom set an example for a husband to follow today?

3. Why is timing important in a marriage relationship?

4. Should a wife move about where her husband finds work?

5. How may a woman find her "cleft of the rock"?

6. What may be "little foxes that spoil the vines" in marriage?

7. How should a married couple handle unavoidable separations?

8. How should Christian couples deal with pressures exerted by the modern feminist movement?

9. Should reconciliation be implemented by the man or the woman?

10. When will Christ and His bride, the church, be wed?

Seed Thoughts - Continued

The energetic bridegroom may serve as a type of Christ, the Source of all life according to John 1:3-4.

A husband should approach his wife in loving and gentle ways rather than demanding his marital rights.

Various indicators will reveal the right time for a couple to share life's experiences together.

Although this may be debated, it has generally been found best for her to be with him and encourage him in this way.

God expects her to find security within her husband's loving care.

These may include pride, envy, gossip, insensitivity, and other negative traits.

Their love can remain strong, and they can make contacts in person, by phone calls, and by written correspondence.

They should subject all proposals to biblical principles and accept only those which line up with the Scriptures.

Either or both of them may get things moving in the right direction.

United in love now, they will be wed at the end of the age of grace.

6. What may be "little foxes that spoil the vines" in marriage?
These may include pride, envy, gossip, insensitivity, and other negative traits.

7. How should a married couple handle unavoidable separations?
Their love can remain strong, and they can make contacts in person, by phone calls, and by written correspondence.

8. How should Christian couples deal with pressures exerted by the modern feminist movement?
They should subject all proposals to biblical principles and accept only those which line up with the Scriptures.

9. Should reconciliation be implemented by the man or the woman?
Either or both of them may get things moving in the right direction.

10. When will Christ and His bride, the church, be wed?
United in love now, they will be wed at the end of the age of grace.

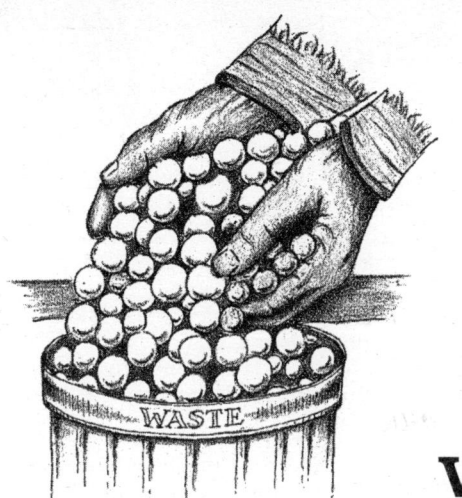

Song Of The Vineyard

Isaiah 5:1. Now will I sing to my well beloved a song of my beloved touching his vineyard. My well beloved hath a vineyard in a very fruitful hill:
2. And he fenced it, and gathered out the stones thereof, and planted it with the choicest vine, and built a tower in the midst of it, and also made a winepress therein: and he looked that it should bring forth grapes, and it brought forth wild grapes.
3. And now, O inhabitants of Jerusalem, and men of Judah, judge, I pray you, betwixt me and my vineyard.
4. What could have been done more to my vineyard, that I have not done in it? wherefore, when I looked that it should bring forth grapes, brought it forth wild grapes?
5. And now go to; I will tell you what I will do to my vineyard: I will take away the hedge thereof, and it shall be eaten up; and break down the wall thereof, and it shall be trodden down:
6. And I will lay it waste: it shall not be pruned, nor digged; but there shall come up briers and thorns: I will also command the clouds that they rain no rain upon it.
7. For the vineyard of the Lord of hosts is the house of Israel, and the men of Judah his pleasant plant: and he looked for judgment, but behold oppression; for righteousness, but behold a cry.

MEMORY SELECTION
Isaiah 5:7
DEVOTIONAL READING
Psalm 51

BACKGROUND SCRIPTURE
Isaiah 5:1-7
PRINTED SCRIPTURE
Isaiah 5:1-7

Teacher's Target

Divine disappointment is the theme of the sad song in this lesson's text. God had singled out the nation of Israel to be a spiritual beacon for Him in a pagan world, but she had failed to produce the fruit He wanted. This, then, is a dirge, a song expressing sorrow regarding unfilfilled expectation. It is set in a vineyard, meaning Israel, for it was there that God planted His truths to take root, flower, and produce good results. Instead, He got only wild grapes unfit for use. This parable of Jehovah's vineyard is a type of the disappointment God suffers when believers today fail to bear the spiritual fruit expected of them. It is by studying something as negative as this that they can turn toward the positive hope of giving God what He wants in their lives.

Lesson Introduction

Jesus often quoted from or made references to the Jewish Scriptures (Old Testament) during His ministry on the earth. He may have been thinking of Isaiah 5:1-7 when He told the parable of the householder who turned his vineyard over to others, went away to a far country, and then demanded fruit from it. The householder sent two sets of servants, and finally his son, for this purpose, but they were beaten or killed. On his return home, he had these wicked stewards slain and let his vineyard out to those who would produce fruit (Matt. 21:33-41).

Jesus may also have been thinking of Isaiah 5:1-7 when He told the parable of the vine and the branches, He counted Himself to be the Vine, and believers were the branches. They had to remain connected to Him in order to receive spiritual life and produce spiritual fruit (John 15:1-14).

Teaching Outline

I. Examination: Isa. 5:1-2
   A. Resolution: 1a
   B. Remembrance: 1b-2a
   C. Result: 2b

II. Expiration: Isa. 5:3-6
   A. Invitation: 3
   B. Inquiries: 4
   C. Indictment: 5-6

III. Explanations Isa. 5:7
   A. Identification: 7a
   B. Indignation: 7b

Daily Bible Readings

Mon. A Song to My Beloved
Isaiah 5:1
Tue. Wild Grapes
Isaiah 5:2
Wed. You be the Judge
Isaiah 5:3
Thu. What More Could Have Been Done?
Isaiah 5:4
Fri. The Vineyard Will be Destroyed
Isaiah 5:5
Sat. It Will be Laid Waste
Isaiah 5:6
Sun. The Vineyard is Isarel
Isaiah 5:7

Verse By Verse

I. Examination: Isa. 5:1-2

A. Resolution: 1a
1a. Now will I sing to my well beloved a song of my beloved touching his vineyard.

Isaiah was a prince among prophets, and his literary skills were ably displayed in the long book which he wrote bearing his name. He chose to express how God felt about Israel by composing the sad song which forms our text. He no doubt hoped that this song would become part of his people's musical repertoire and thus be perpetuated in succeeding generations. It was a song designed to show where the people of Israel went wrong in their relationship to Jehovah and to move them in the direction of finding a remedy for spiritual laxity. The literary vehicle selected by Isaiah was a parable of a vineyard planted by God, Whom the prophet loved. It is likely that Isaiah composed both the lyrics and the melody for the song which was sung.

B. Remembrance: 1b-2a
1b. My wellbeloved hath a vineyard in a very fruitful hill:

Isaiah made the point that God gave Israel every advantage when He planted her in the world. It is possible that the fruitful hill mentioned here was the land of Canaan, well known as a land of milk and honey. The soil was fertile in those days and produced good crops of grains and fruits. The spiritual meaning was that God planted Israel in a setting which featured His divine ordinances as contained in the law of Moses. These were far superior to anything revealed through nature or conscience to the pagans around them.

2a. And he fenced it, and gathered out the stones thereof, and planted it with the choicest vine, and built a tower in the midst of it, and also made a winepress therein: . . .

God did five things to make sure that His vineyard got off to a good start. In saying that He fenced it, Isaiah may have been referring to the soil being plowed or spaded. During this process, stones were turned up out of the soil, and these were collected to be taken off to the sides. Perhaps they were used to build fences or other structures.

God went out to purchase the best vine stocks available and brought them home to plant them in straight rows in His vineyard. He put up a watchtower in the middle of the vineyard so that watchers might see and drive away either human or animal marauders. He chose the site for a winepress. It was probably a ledge with a shallow depression where the grapes might be trod upon, with the juice flowing down into a collection vat below. It could then be stored in earthen jars or wineskins for future use.

Spiritually speaking, God prepared Israel to be a beacon light in a dark pagan world. He gave her His law, His prophets, and His priests. He gave her protection from her enemies. He gave her the means to make His will known among the surrounding nations. The things which Isaiah remembered about God and His dealings with Israel should have been thought of by every Israelite.

C. Result: 2b

2b. . . .and he looked that it should bring forth grapes, and it brought forth wild grapes.

God expected His vineyard to produce large clusters of luscious, tasty grapes, but all that grew were wild grapes. God bemoaned the appearance of these sour grapes when He said, "I had planted thee a noble vine, wholly a right seed: how then art thou turned into the degenerate plant of a strange vine unto me?" (Jer. 2:21).

How had Israel failed God in a spiritual way? From the leaders down to the common people, they had become stereotyped in their worship of Jehovah, going through the motions but lacking in sincerity. They had a form of godliness but no true power (II Tim. 3:5). Pagans were not favorably impressed by what they saw and heard, especially when the Israelites forsook Jehovah and ran after strange gods and the idols representing them. What they produced had no resemblance to real spirituality as defined by the Lord.

II. Expiration: Isa. 5:3-6

A. Invitation: 3

3. And now, O inhabitants of Jerusalem, and men of Judah, judge, I pray you, betwixt me and my vineyard.

It seems obvious that verses 3-6 featured the Lord Himself speaking. He addressed the people of the city of Jerusalem and the nation of Judah, calling on them to evaluate the situation facing Him and His vineyard. The prophet had made his evaluation, and now God wanted the people to make theirs. He knew that it would mean more to them if they put it into their own words although we have no record that they did this except in the case of the true prophets. What God did here was to challenge the people; their silence would condemn them, for they had no defense for their failure.

B. Inquiries: 4

4a. What could have been done more to my vineyard, that I have not done in it?

God gave men the opportunity to speak up and say what they thought He could have done in addition to what He had done to make His vineyard fruitful. Isaiah had already summarized what God had done to prepare the ground, plant the best vinestocks, protect it, and provide a winepress. All that was left was for His stewards to cultivate the vines and wait for the harvest, but something had gone drastically wrong in their part of the whole process.

4b. . . .wherefore, when I looked that it should bring forth grapes, brought it forth wild grapes?

Here was an amazing situation. Nature cannot alter its basic functions, with good vinestocks producing bitter grapes. As in all illustrations, the analogy breaks down. We have to switch to the spiritual interpretation here. God gave Israel good truths, but Satan was allowed to pervert them to serve his own ends. The Israelites followed his lead in this kind of perversion, and the results were heretical and strange. Man-made traditions put God's pure truths into the kind of religious straightjackets which altered their original meanings and applications to life experiences. This is aptly described in Isaiah 5:8-23, which lists six woes pronounced upon sinful people.

Perhaps the best description of spiritual perversion is found in Isaiah 5:20—"Woe unto them that call evil good, and good evil; that put darkness for light, and light for darkness that put bitter for sweet, and sweet for bitter!" We find this type of thing happening today, and it causes tremendous confusion among people seeking for the truth.

C. Indictment: 5-6

5. And now go to; I will tell you what I will do to my vineyard: I will take away the hedge thereof, and it shall be eaten up; and break down the wall thereof, and it shall be trodden down:

In saying, "Now go to," God was demanding that His people listen to Him. Future prospects were ominous, for God's patience had come to an end, and He was ready to punish Israel for her sins. By declaring that He would take away her hedge and break down her wall, He was forecasting national calamity brought about by invading enemies. With His protection withdrawn, Israel would become an easy mark for foreign domination.

6. And I will lay it waste: it shall not be pruned, nor digged but there shall come up briers and thorns: I will also command the clouds that they rain no rain upon it.

In addition to foreign invaders, God said that He would turn nature itself against His wayward people and their land. It would become a desolate wilderness, not pruned nor digged (cultivated). It would revert to wild briars and thornbushes. He said that He would command the clouds to withhold rain from it. History has proved that Palestine suffered this kind of desolation when the Jews were forced out of it by famines or by deportations to other lands.

It has been interesting to note the physical progress which has been made since the formation of the modern nation of Israel in 1948. This tiny country has irrigated desert areas with amazing results, so that Israel even exports citrus fruits to other countries. Perhaps this is a foretaste of what will happen during the kingdom age—"The wilderness and the solitary place shall be glad for them; and the desert shall rejoice, and blossom as the rose" (Isa. 35:1).

III. Explanation: Isa. 5:7

A. Identification: 7a

7a. For the vineyard of the Lord of hosts is the house of Israel, and the men of Judah his pleasant plant: . . .

This was probably Isaiah speaking again. He identified the vineyard of Jehovah as being the "house of Israel" and the "men of Judah," referring to the Jews in both the northern and southern kingdoms. He had planted them under pleasant circumstances, as described in verses 1-2.

B. Indignation: 7b

7b. . . .and he looked for judgment, but behold oppression for righteousness, but behold a cry.

Isaiah could feel the indignation of Jehovah toward His people. The Lord had looked for judgment (justice) among them, but He had seen oppression take place. He had sought for righteousness, but He had heard the cry of oppressed victims come up to Him.

What foreign instruments did God use in order to punish His people and seek to drive them back to Himself? We know that Assyria swept down from the north and overran the northern kingdom of Israel in 722 B.C. We know that Babylon came against Judah in 586 B.C. and destroyed Jerusalem, the pride of the nation. We know that deportations took place under both the Assyrians and the Babylonians, so that Jews were largely resettled in eastern lands and only a remnant remained in Palestine. Following the seventy-year Babylonian captivity, comparatively few returned, and the vast majority remained in their new homes in the east.

What happened in Old Testament times was repeated in A.D. 70, when the Romans destroyed Jerusalem and Jews were scattered abroad to many lands. They still remain mostly in foreign countries, although some three million live in modern Israel. God has promised to regather them in the end times. In the meantime, they remain for the most part outside of redeeming grace through faith in Jesus Christ.

Evangelistic Emphasis

Only a small portion of this lesson is about judgment. The major part of it is about God's provisions and preparation. It is a lesson about God's dreams for his people and the heartbreak of having those dreams shattered.

God has provided and prepared for us also. He has dreams for us and longs to see those dreams fulfilled. Our lives are gifted with skills and abilities. We have some degree of health and energy. We have some training and education. We know some people and have some opportunities. We have resources that can be drawn on to accomplish our goals.

Therefore it can be expected that our lives will produce some attractive and useful fruit. There should be more kindness, integrity, and love in the world because of our lives. There should be less hunger, neglect, and pain because of our lives. The lost should be taught the gospel and the despairing should be cheered. The sorrowful should be comforted.

If these dreams are not fulfilled, it will be a tragedy because God has given us the ability and the opportunity to live this kind of life. It is important to know that judgment is a part of a gospel of grace. The goodness, kindness, and mercy of God are not to be taken as invitations to rejection and abuse. They are doors of opportunity, but opportunities not taken bring the consequences of rejection.

Memory Selection

"The vineyard of the Lord of hosts is the house of Israel, . . . and he looked for judgment, but behold oppression; for righteousness, but behold a cry."
Isaiah 5:7.

The Lord expects an appropriate response to his goodness. His mercy is not an invitation to anarchy. The fact that he forgives sins does not mean that sin is of no consequence to him. The fact that he continues to give blessings to people living in disobedience does not mean that he respects or rewards disobedience.

God acts according to his nature, not according to how people act toward him. He will be good to them even when they reject Him. When they misinterpret this as an indication that they can sin with impunity, they violate his tender generosity and will suffer the pain of that violation. That is not because God is vindictive, but because the alternative to his mercy is pain. When we reject mercy, we choose pain.

God expects us to respond to his goodness with justice and righteousness. The day of judgment will hold terror for us if we expect to say, "I knew you were merciful, so I thought I could get away with insubordination and disobedience."

Weekday Problems

Lois and Erma were daughters of a widow who reared them in difficult financial circumstances. Erma was the older by six years and was more aware of the precariousness of the situation. Whether by nature or because of circumstances, she developed a suspicious and defensive attitude toward life. She has a highly-developed sense of responsibility and is always an exceptional achiever, but has continually had trouble with personal relationships. She always feels this is because others have let her down or have been irresponsible.

Lois, on the other hand, is a softer, warmer, and more secure person. She relates to people generously and easily. She has many friends and enjoys happy family relationships. However, she has never been able to have a happy relationship with Erma.

Lois has tried repeatedly to cultivate a better relationship, but she never gets far before she feels the sting of Erma's rejection. Nevertheless, she is always hopeful that things will be different next time.

* What should Lois do? Should she continue trying or give up on Erma and find a sisterly relationship with someone else?
* What can be done to help Erma? What if she does not acknowledge any need for help?

Superintendent's Sermonette

Gift-givers are sometimes baffled by the question, "How do you give someone something who already has everything?" They may give such a person as this a bizarre gift or something very expensive in an attempt to make it a novel gift. Thinking along this same line, we might wonder how we could give a self-existing and self-sufficient God anything of value to Him. However, the Bible makes it clear that the Lord wants to receive the praise of His people. That ought to be all the stimulation we need to give it to Him.

One way to praise the Lord is to express our love for Him. Another way is to fulfill whatever expectations of us He may have. It is in this second way that we find significance in this lesson's text. God gave ancient Israel material and spiritual blessings, and He looked for good results but was disappointed. Let us determine that the same thing will not happen in our case. We should strive to be all that God wants us to be, and that will bring praise and honor to His name. We can begin to give Him this gift today.

This Lesson in <u>Your</u> Life

The basic story here is about God's unrequited love from Israel. God's love is compared to a vineyard owner who lavished extraordinary care on an unresponsive vineyard. With work and expense he fenced, gathered stones, planted, and built a wine press. He spared no effort to make it a beautiful and fruitful vineyard.

This pictures the way God had taken care of Israel. Through Joseph he spared them from being destroyed by a famine. Through Moses he delivered them from bondage and gave them the law, the sacrifice system, and the priesthood. In the wilderness he fed and led them. Through Joshua he settled them in the promised land. Through judges, kings, and prophets he responded to them again and again. They had every opportunity to demonstrate that they were a people of destiny.

The vineyard owner of our story, after all his trouble, found that his vineyard produced only wild grapes. So God saw Israel spurn his love and care time after time. Instead of the beautiful fruits he was hoping for, he saw idolatry, immorality, and cruelty.

As the vineyard owner withdrew his care and allowed the vineyard to be trodden down and laid in waste, so God would exhaust his patience with Israel. The God of such great love cannot be rejected repeatedly without his people being held accountable.

One application we can make of this story to our own lives is to consider how we have responded to the goodness of God. He has filled our lives with blessings, both physical and spiritual. From the air that we breathe to the forgiveness of our sins we are literally dependent on him for every blessing. We are the vineyard that has been built, dressed, and planted.

What kind of fruit have we returned? Has it been of exemplary quality and in bountiful amounts? Or, have we returned small and bitter grapes? Do we do too little for God? Do we serve him with a sour and grudging attitude?

Are we aware of the fact that accountability is built into our relationship with God? We cannot continually respond to his goodness with rebellion and disobedience without facing the consequences of that rejection.

A second application that might throw some light on our lives is that occasionally love that we give is not returned. If even God's love is sometimes rejected, we should not be surprised that ours is rejected sometimes also.

Parents sometimes have their hearts broken by their children. Love can be mocked. Tenderness can be scorned. Parents who would do anything to make relationships right find that there is nothing that they can do. They learn the bitter truth that it takes two to make a relationship. As God could not singlehandedly forge a healthy relationship with Israel, so parents cannot with their children.

Unrequited love can also characterize a marriage or a friendship. We should always try to follow God's example to show love even to those who do not return it, but we may be comforted by remembering that even the love of God is at times rejected.

Seed Thoughts

1. Does God have emotions?
Yes, the Bible reveals that He can be happy or sad, loving or angry, in His relationships with angels and people.

2. What emotion might be attached to the parable of Jehovah's vineyard?
God was disappointed with Israel, which is a form of sadness. He was angry enough to promise destruction of sinners.

3. What did God do for Israel in a physical way?
God provided Israel with a land of promise and protection in Canaan after delivering her from Egyptian bondage.

4. What did God do for Israel in a spiritual way?
God gave Israel His law and ordinances to lift her above the pagan nations surrounding her.

5. Instead of good grapes, what did Israel produce in God's vineyard?
Israel produced "wild grapes," referring to perversions of spiritual things, such as the practice of idolatry.

(Please Turn Page)

---

1. Does God have emotions?

2. What emotion might be attached to the parable of Jehovah's vineyard?

3. What did God do for Israel in a physical way?

4. What did God do for Israel in a spiritual way?

5. Instead of good grapes, what did Israel produce in God's vineyard?

6. Why might God ask His people to judge Him and His performance?

7. Are God's blessings on men permanent or conditional?

8. What might God do to show His disappointment with sinners?

9. What seem to be the main means by which God disciplines His people?

10. What does God look for, and what does He sometimes find?

Seed Thoughts - Continued

Yes, the Bible reveals that He can be happy or sad, loving or angry, in His relationships with angels and people.

God was disappointed with Israel, which is a form of sadness. He was angry enough to promise destruction of sinners.

God provided Israel with a land of promise and protection in Canaan after delivering her from Egyptian bondage.

God gave Israel His law and ordinances to lift her above the pagan nations surrounding her.

Israel produced "wild grapes," referring to perversions of spiritual things, such as the practice of idolatry.

This helps them to understand His perfection and their own imperfection.

The Bible and history have shown that He blesses those who remain loyal, but He withdraws blessings from the disloyal.

He might withdraw His material support and protection from them until they repent and seek His forgiveness.

Experience has shown that He may allow enemies to overcome them for a time. He may turn negative forces of nature against them (drought, flood, fire, etc.).

According to Isaiah 5:7, He looks for judgment (justice) and righteousness, but He finds oppression and victims' cries.

6. Why might God ask His people to judge Him and His performance?
This helps them to understand His perfection and their own imperfection.

7. Are God's blessings on men permanent or conditional?
The Bible and history have shown that He blesses those who remain loyal, but He withdraws blessings from the disloyal.

8. What might God do to show His disappointment with sinners?
He might withdraw His material support and protection from them until they repent and seek His forgiveness.

9. What seem to be the main means by which God disciplines His people?
Experience has shown that He may allow enemies to overcome them for a time. He may turn negative forces of nature against them (drought, flood, fire, etc.).

10. What does God look for, and what does He sometimes find?
According to Isaiah 5:7, He looks for judgment (justice) and righteousness, but He finds oppression and victims' cries.

The Model Prayer

Matthew 6:7.

But when ye pray, use not vain repetitions, as the heathen do: for they think that they shall be heard for their much speaking.

8. Be not ye therefore like unto them: for your Father knoweth what things ye have need of, before ye ask him.

9. After this manner therefore pray ye: Our Father which art in heaven, Hallowed be thy name.

10. Thy kingdom come. Thy will be done in earth, as it is in heaven.

11. Give us this day our daily bread.

12. And forgive us our debts, as we forgive our debtors.

13. And lead us not into temptation, but deliver us from evil: For thine is the kingdom, and the power, and the glory, for ever. Amen.

14. For if ye forgive men their trespasses, your heavenly Father will also forgive you:

15. But if ye forgive not men their trespasses, neither will your Father forgive your trespasses.

MEMORY SELECTION
I Chronicles 29:13
DEVOTIONAL READING
Psalm 143

BACKGROUND SCRIPTURE
I Chronicles 29:10-13
PRINTED SCRIPTURE
Matthew 6:7-15

Teacher's Target

Jesus' sermon on the mount is recorded in Matthew 5-7. It covered many subjects and is probably His best known discourse. One of those subjects was prayer, and it is found in the middle of the sermon (Matt. 6:5-15). You will also find it helpful to look at Luke 13 to see what Jesus said when His disciples asked Him to teach them to pray even as John the Baptist had taught his disciples to pray. Christians have been traditionally taught to memorize Jesus' model prayer (Matt. 6:9-13 Luke 11:2-4).

Help your students to learn what Jesus taught about private prayer, avoiding vain repetition, and practicing forgiveness. If the model prayer has become stereotyped by frequent use, here is an opportunity to give it fresh meaning by analyzing its various parts and relating them to life today. It gives a starting point for creative prayer.

Lesson Introduction

In His teaching on prayer, Jesus presented four topics. The first one warned believers against praying in public for the sake of impressing others with outward piety. Jesus said that it was better for them to pray in private. The Lord would then reward them openly (Matt. 6:5-6). The second topic warned believers against vain repetition in prayer such as that practiced by the heathen. Jesus said that God already knew their needs before they voiced them (Matt. 6:7-8).

The third topic was the model prayer Jesus gave to His disciples. It featured an approach to God, hope for the kingdom, petitions (for bread, forgiveness, and deliverance from evil), and another kingdom reference (Matt. 6:9-13) The fourth topic warned against failure to forgive others (Matt. 6: 14-15). Topics two through four are covered in this lesson's exposition.

Teaching Outline

I. Prohibition: Matt. 6:7-8
   A. Repetition: 7
   B. Recognition: 8

II. Prayers Matt. 6:9-13
   A . Reverence: 9
   B. Requests: 10-13

III. Predictions: Matt. 6:14-15
   A . Response I: 14
   B. Response II: 15

Daily Bible Readings

Mon. David Blessed the Lord
I Chronicles 29:10-11
Tue. David Thanked the Lord
I Chronicles 29:12-13
Wed. Not Heard for Much Speaking
Matthew 6:7-8
Thu. Thy Will be Done
Matthew 6:9-10
Fri. Forgive us
Matthew 6:11-12
Sat. Deliver Us from Evil
Matthew 6:13
Sun. If you Forgive
Matthew 6:14-15

Verse By Verse

I. Prohibition: Matt 6:7-8

A. Repetition: 7
7. But when ye pray, use not vain repetitions, as the heathen do: for they think that they shall be heard for their much speaking.

Jesus warned His followers to avoid babbling speech when they prayed to the Lord. He referred to the pagan custom of useless repetitions of prayers which were designed to get and hold the attention of the gods. A study of false religions reveals the tendency for their adherents to memorize and endlessly repeat prayers as chants. Christians sometimes can be guilty of this when they repeat form prayers which have become so stereotyped that they have lost their meaning. They have been used as forms of penance for those who confess their sins and seek to make amends, but this has undercut their use as means by which to express their personal feelings.

One extreme example of pagan repetition of prayers is the use of a prayer wheel. Prayers are written out and attached to cylinders which blow around in the wind to build up merit. This mute form of repetition may seem good to the devotee, but the futility of it is obvious to us. True prayer demands the personal involvement of those who pray.

B. Recognition: 8
8. Be not ye therefore like unto them: for your Father knoweth what things ye have need of, before ye ask him.

Jesus did not object to long prayers, for He could pray all night (Luke 6:12). He did not object to repeated petitions, for He made the same request three times in the garden of Gethsemane (Matt. 26:44). What He did not want was for believers to engage in meaningless repetition for the purpose of trying to wear God down and make Him answer their petitions. Therefore, He said that the heavenly Father already knew what their needs were before they voiced them. Vain repetition would involve insulting God, as if He did not know or care what His children wanted.

Out of this teaching by Jesus grows the principle of commitment in prayer. Believers can get great comfort from committing their problems to the Lord and trusting Him to provide solutions for them. Once the burdens are shifted to Him, they can sincerely remind Him of their needs and call on Him to resolve them in His Own way and time. His sustaining grace is available to them while they patiently wait for Him to help them.

II. Prayer: Matt. 6:9-13

A. Reverence: 9
9a. After this manner therefore pray ye: . . .

The model prayer taught by Jesus is interesting in the fact that it gives an example of how to pray, and it is a prayer to be prayed, as well. We should study its structure, and we should use it in making contact with the Lord.

9b. Our Father which art in heaven, Hallowed be thy name.

The first part of this invocation shows familiarity with the Lord. Believers can refer to Him as "our Father" because of their loving relationship to Him. The latter part of the invocation shows the great distance separating men on earth from God in His highest heaven. There is also a great difference between men in their sins and God in His holiness. Thus, it is quite appropriate to address Him as being hallowed (reverenced) and His name as being hallowed, God's name represents all that He is in His many perfections and unique attributes.

Some might count the last phrase in verse 9 as being the first petition in the model prayer, We have used it, instead, as the approach to God. There is no doubt that petitions are found in verses 10-13.

B. Requests: 10-13
10a. Thy kingdom come.

This might be stated as the petition, "Let thy kingdom come." Jesus was referring to the arrival of the Messianic kingdom here. His disciples expected Him to set it up in a literal fashion at His first coming, but He suggested that it was to come in the future. "They asked of him saying, Lord, wilt thou at this time restore again the kingdom to Israel? And he said unto them, It is not for you to know the times or the seasons, which the Father hath put in his own power" (Acts 1:6-7).

The kingdom of God operates today among those who accept and live according to the rule of God their King.

10b. Thy will be done in earth, as it is in heaven.

We know that God's sovereign will is going to prevail throughout the universe in due time. This petition expresses the believer's sure hope that this will be done. Those who seek to know and do God's will on the earth can have an influence for good in the midst of degraded human society. Their prayer should be that the Lord will work through them for that high and noble purpose.

11. Give us this day our daily bread.

The emphasis now shifts from the spiritual to the temporal. This petition deals with a request for help from God in meeting daily needs. Luke 11:3 says, "Give us day by day [or for the day] our daily bread." Some may want to interpret this as asking for spiritual nourishment, but the literal meaning is probably what was intended here. This was not a new concept. Many centuries before, David had written, "I have been young, and now am old yet have I not seen the righteous forsaken, nor his seed [children] begging bread" (Ps. 37:25). Later in His sermon on the mount, Jesus said, "Seek ye first the kingdom of God, and his righteousness, and all these things [food, drink, clothing] shall be added [by God] unto you" (Matt. 6:33) Paul later wrote, "My God shall supply all your need according to his riches in glory by Christ Jesus" (Phil. 4:19).

12. And forgive us our debts, as we forgive our debtors.

This request is definitely a spiritual one. God is asked to forgive believers their sins, even as they forgive others for sins perpetrated against them. More will be said about this when we get to verses 14-15.

13a. And lead us not into temptation, but deliver us from evil: . . .

We have to be careful here that we do not blame God for men being tempted to sin. A helpful reference is James 1:13-14—"Let no man say when he is tempted, I am tempted of [or by] God: for God cannot be tempted with evil, neither tempteth he any man: but every man is tempted, when he is drawn away of his own lust [desire, passion], and enticed [by Satan]." Believers live in a sinful world, and they will be tempted to sin, but Jesus Himself said to His heavenly Father, "I pray not that thou shouldest take them out of the world, but that thou shouldest keep them from the evil [one, meaning Satan]" (John 17:15). If they do fall into sin, they should ask God to deliver them from it by His pardoning grace. Paul wrote, "Let him that thinketh he standeth take heed lest he fall. There hath no temptation taken you but such as is common to man: but God is faithful, who will not suffer [allow] you to be tempted above that ye are able; but will with the temptation also make a way to escape, that ye may be able to bear it" (I Cor. 10:12-13).

13b. . . . For thine is the kingdom, and the power, and the glory, for ever. Amen.

David had earlier stated this kind of doxology when he wrote, "Thine, O Lord, is the greatness, and the power, and the glory, and the victory, and the majesty: for all that is in the heaven and in the earth is thine; thine is the kingdom, O Lord, and thou art exalted as head above all" (I Chron. 29:11). Some versions leave this part of Matthew 6:13 out or put it in italics or in parentheses, because it did not appear in the oldest manuscripts. They apparently felt that it was inserted by scholars, perhaps as an interpolation from I Chronicles 29:11. Compilers of the Authorized King James Version decided to include it as regular text.

III. Predictions: Matt. 6:14-1

A. Response I: 14

14. For if ye forgive men their trespasses, your heavenly Father will also forgive you:

Let us remember that Jesus addressed these remarks to believers. They were told to have a forgiving spirit toward offenders, in order that God might forgive them for their offenses. In another place, Jesus said to His disciples, "If thy brother trespass against thee, rebuke him and if he repent, forgive him" (Luke 17:3). The time was coming when they would claim forgiveness of sins through the atoning work of Christ at Calvary.

Paul would later write on this subject. "Brethren, if a man be overtaken in a fault, ye which are spiritual, restore such an one in the spirit of meekness considering thyself, lest thou also be tempted [and fall]" (Gal. 6:1). "Be ye kind one to another, tenderhearted, forgiving one another, even as God for Christ's sake hath forgiven you" (Eph. 4:32). These still apply to us today.

B. Response II: 15

15. But if ye forgive not men their trespasses, neither will your Father forgive your trespasses.

What was stated in the positive in verse 14 was now stated in the negative. Jesus later told a parable about an unmerciful man whose large debt to his king had been forgiven but who refused to cancel a much smaller debt owed to him by someone else. When this was reported to the king, he called his servant before him and delivered him to the tormentors (jailors) until he paid all that he owed (Matt. 18:23-35).

Christ's model prayer, usually called the Lord's prayer, has been used down through the centuries by believers as a form prayer and also as a standard by which to compose prayers. As a form prayer, it is used in public services and in private devotions. As a standard, it is used to show the various elements of prayer, such as approach to God, petitions, and doxology.

Although form prayers are useful, they should be joined with creative prayers in both public and private situations. By using a combination, believers can express longstanding sentiments, and they can compose prayers designed to deal with current needs. Whichever kinds of prayers are used, let them come from sincere hearts.

Evangelistic Emphasis

In the world we live in, it is hard to get an audience with someone who is extremely important or powerful. For example, most of us would not be able to get an appointment to talk with the President of our country. There are so many demands on his time and attention that he necessarily has to limit the number of people he can see.

As I write this, I have a friend who is in flight to a distant city where he will meet with a medical "super specialist" about a health problem. That doctor is so much in demand that it is difficult to get an appointment with him. When one became available, my friend dropped everything on the briefest of notice and boarded a plane to fly twenty-three hundred miles. What a value my friend places on the opportunity to have an audience with an exceptional doctor.

Another young friend recently exclaimed that the head of a major, multi-national corporation took time to sit down and visit with him. The executive showed no signs of being rushed or impatient. The young man felt significantly blessed that he was considered of such importance that he could occupy the time of a powerful man.

These things impress us, but how much more impressive to have the ear of God as often as we want, for as long as we want? We know that he will hear us with patience, understanding, and care. We further know that he will respond to our needs and requests with sensitivity and generosity. The assurance of a ready audience with God is an impressive evangelistic tool.

Memory Selection

"Now therefore, our God, we thank thee, and praise thy glorious name."
I Chronicles 29:13.

Most of the Bible consists of God's words to man. Some parts of it, however, consist of man's words to God. This is particularly true in the areas of praise and thanksgiving.

I believe that one reason for this is we often find that our feelings are bigger than we have the words for. We may be able to express our needs and wants, but we feel handicapped in trying to express our praise and gratitude. We need help. Our words seem too small and too shallow of meaning.

Therefore, there are a number of places in the Bible where we are given words of praise that can serve as vehicles to communicate the praise that is in our hearts. Here is one. It is a simple but regal statement of praise.

When the feeling of praise is in our heart, and the words to express it do not seem to be there, we can appropriate phrases like these to say what we want to to God. We are not all poets or musicians, but we all have access to the poetry and song that have been written by others. Let us use it to express our larger feelings.

Weekday Problems

Norman is his own worst enemy. He has developed the habit of speaking of his faith in a pompous way. When he talks to others about the Lord, his language is so full of religious jargon that he sounds pretentious and insincere. When he leads public prayer his language drips with sanctimonious phrasing. Those who would be interested in having a real conversation with him are put off by his pseudo pious manner of speaking.

The problem is not with his heart but with his way of expressing himself. Norman is a gentle and sincere believer. He wants nothing more than to help others to come to a knowledge of the Lord who has meant so much to him. Somehow he has gotten the impression that "sounding religious" will be a help.

Norman does not see the problem in himself and cannot understand why he is not able to get through to others. He wants so badly to share the gospel and is so obviously ineffective that he is frustrated.

* How can we evaluate our own speech to see if we have picked up mannerisms or vocabularies that interfere with communication?
* Are there religious idioms or speech patterns that irritate you? If so, what are they?
* How can we help Norman to become more simple and real in his language?

Superintendent's Sermonette

We hear about answered and unanswered prayer, but is there such a thing as unanswered prayer? Psalm 66:18 says, "If I regard [see, discover] iniquity in my heart, the Lord will not hear me." First John 5:14 says, "If we ask any thing according to his [God's] will, he heareth us," implying that if we ask something out of His will He will not hear us. If He does not hear us, He cannot answer us. Our hearts must be aligned with Him and His will if we want our prayers to be answered.

It is good for us to remind ourselves that God answers prayer in three ways. Sometimes He will grant what we ask. Sometimes He will refuse to give what we ask, perhaps because He knows it would not be good for us to have. Sometimes He may require us to wait for what we ask, because timing is important.

We can always pray the model prayer that Jesus taught to His disciples, because it includes a plea for forgiveness of sin and petitions which are always in God's will. Let us be ready to accept His answers.

This Lesson in <u>Your</u> Life

Perhaps the most famous speech ever delivered in this country is the Gettysburg Address. Lincoln said, "The world will little note, nor long remember, what we say here." That was over one hundred twenty-five years ago. The words were of such singular humility, such simple clarity, and such earnest power that they are unforgettable. The world has forgotten millions of speeches, but not this one. It can be read aloud in ninety seconds. It, along with the Lord's prayer, is an example of the fact that we do not find repetitious rambling memorable.

It is easy to forget the ornate, the pompous, and the self-serving. There is something about simple, honest humility that makes it stick. Apparently the Lord shares with us this preference because after warning that God is not impressed by "much speaking," Jesus said, "Pray like this ..." Then he gave us the brief, simple, easy-to-understand prayer.

From this prayer we can learn to begin our prayer with praise and recognition. This restores to us a sense of the fact that God is creator, we are creature. He does not exist to please us but we exist to please him. This is the starting point and ought to deal with any shred of pompousness that might be lingering in our thoughts.

Then Jesus goes to the heart of all prayer, "Thy will be done." The primary purpose of prayer is not to change God's will, but to bring ourselves into harmony with it. God's will is flawlessly loving, merciful, generous, and kind. It cannot be improved on. Our basic purpose in prayer is to learn to yield to the will of God, to be molded by it, to become one with it.

The request for daily bread is an acknowledgement of our dependence on God. That is an essential part of bringing our lives into harmony with his will. We eat God's food every day. We breathe His air. We drink His water. Our only security is with Him. When we feel independent of that we will go off on destructive tangents. When we acknowledge that dependence, we will be nurtured to fuller growth.

Then there is a request for forgiveness tied to a responsibility to be forgiving. Receiving and giving forgiveness is like inhaling and exhaling. We cannot do one without the other. One cannot continue to take air into his lungs without eventually expelling the air that is there. To stop one part of the breathing process is to stop the process entirely. So it is with the receiving of God's forgiveness and the giving of forgiveness to those who have offended us.

The request for guidance and strength reminds us that there are forces in the world that are so great we cannot deal with them by ourselves. We would be crushed by them. The only reason that we are not guilty of some sins is that we have been spared the temptation. Some temptations can be overcome and some need to be entirely avoided.

This prayer begins and ends with an acknowledgement of the greatness of God. It is simple, humble, and honest. If it guides our prayer life, we will be greatly blessed.

Seed Thoughts

1. What are vain repetitions in prayer?
They are futile babblings supposedly used by the heathen to wear down their gods and force them to bless them.

2. Why is it unnecessary for believers to use vain repetitions?
God already knows their needs before they petition Him, and He simply wants them to commit those needs to Him.

3. Why did Jesus give His disciples a model prayer to use?
He responded to their request that He teach them to pray, even as John the Baptist taught his disciples (Luke 11:1).

4. How does the opening of the model prayer show closeness and distance between believers and God?
Closeness is shown in calling God "Our Father." Distance is shown by saying He is in His highest heaven.

5. What is the kingdom for which believers should pray?
It is the rule of God in the hearts of men. Let us pray that all will accept it.

(Please Turn Page)

---

1. What are vain repetitions in prayer?

2. Why is it unnecessary for believers to use vain repetitions?

3. Why did Jesus give His disciples a model prayer to use?

4. How does the opening of the model prayer show closeness and distance between believers and God?

5. What is the kingdom for which believers should pray?

6. How can believers help God's will to be done on the earth?

7. What does asking God for daily bread represent?

8. In what way is forgiveness of our sins conditional?

9. Does God ever lead a believer into temptation?

10. How should Jesus' model prayer be used by believers?

Seed Thoughts - Continued

They are futile babblings supposedly used by the heathen to wear down their gods and force them to bless them.

God already knows their needs before they petition Him, and He simply wants them to commit those needs to Him.

He responded to their request that He teach them to pray, even as John the Baptist taught his disciples (Luke 11:1).

Closeness is shown in calling God "Our Father." Distance is shown by saying He is in His highest heaven.

It is the rule of God in the hearts of men. Let us pray that all will accept it.

They can know and propagate His holy Word by both precept and example.

This refers to dependence on God for all of our temporal needs,

We must forgive others their offenses against us, if we expect God to forgive us our offenses (Matt. 6:12, 14-15).

James 1:13-14 categorically states that God does not tempt men, and we should ask Him to deliver us from Satan who does.

It should be used as a form prayer to be repeated and as a standard by which to understand the elements of creative prayer.

6. How can believers help God's will to be done on the earth?
They can know and propagate His holy Word by both precept and example.

7. What does asking God for daily bread represent?
This refers to dependence on God for all of our temporal needs,

8. In what way is forgiveness of our sins conditional?
We must forgive others their offenses against us, if we expect God to forgive us our offenses (Matt. 6:12, 14-15).

9. Does God ever lead a believer into temptation?
James 1:13-14 categorically states that God does not tempt men, and we should ask Him to deliver us from Satan who does.

10. How should Jesus' model prayer be used by believers?
It should be used as a form prayer to be repeated and as a standard by which to understand the elements of creative prayer.

Jesus' High Priestly Prayer

John 17:1. These words spake Jesus, and lifted up his eyes to heaven, and said, Father, the hour is come; glorify thy Son, that thy Son also may glorify thee:
2. As thou hast given him power over all flesh, that he should give eternal life to as many as thou hast given him.
3. And this is life eternal, that they might know thee the only true God, and Jesus Christ, whom thou hast sent.
4. I have glorified thee on the earth: I have finished the work which thou gavest me to do.
5. And now, O Father, glorify thou me with thine own self with the glory which I had with thee before the world was.
6. I have manifested thy name unto the men which thou gavest me out of the world: thine they were, and thou gavest them me; and they have kept thy word.
7. Now they have known that all things whatsoever thou hast given me are of thee.
8. For I have given unto them the words which thou gavest me; and they have received them, and have known surely that I came out from thee, and they have believed that thou didst send me.
9. I pray for them: I pray not for the world, but for them which thou hast given me; for they are thine.
10. And all mine are thine, and thine are mine; and I am glorified in them:
11. And now I am no more in the world, but these are in the world, and I come to thee. Holy Father, keep through thine own name those whom thou hast given me, that they may be one, as we are.
John 17:20, Neither pray I for these alone, but for them also which shall believe on me through their word;
21. That they all may be one; as thou, Father, art in me, and I in thee, that they also may be one in us: that the world may believe that thou hast sent me.

MEMORY SELECTION
John 17:20-21
DEVOTIONAL READING
Ephesians 1:11-22

BACKGROUND SCRIPTURE
John 17
PRINTED SCRIPTURE
John 17:1-11, 20-21

Teacher's Target

In the last lesson, we studied one of the New Testament's shortest prayers, the model prayer taught by Jesus to His disciples (Matt. 6:9-13). In this lesson, we study perhaps the longest recorded prayer in the New Testament, the high priestly prayer offered up by Jesus (John 17:1-26). We can deal only with two portions of the chapter (vss. 1-10, 20-21), but these will give us enough to appreciate the whole prayer.

Help your students ~~we look~~ to find in the high priestly prayer of Jesus the concerns which He had for unity between Himself and His heavenly Father and between believers and their heavenly Father. If these concerns were important to Him, they should also be important to us. Jesus is now united with His Father in heaven, and we are heading in that same direction. Let us follow the lead set by our Master.

Lesson Introduction

The high priestly prayer of Jesus was composed of alternating petitions and reports concerning believers, Our lesson centers on the first, second, third, and sixth petitions. Here are the whole seven petitions: (1) Glorify thy Son (John 17:1-4), (2) Glorify thou me (John 17:2-10), (3) Keep. . .those whom thou has given me (John 17:11-14), (4) Keep them from the evil (John 17:15-16), (5) Sanctify them through thy truth (John 17:17-19), (6) [Grant] that they all may be one (John 17: 20-23), and (7) I will that they. . . be with me (John 17:24-26).

The first and second petitions may seem identical, but differences will be shown. The fourth, fifth, and seventh petitions will be mentioned, even though the others are the subjects of our analysis. Keep this question in mind, "Would God refuse to answer any petition made by His holy and beloved Son?"

Teaching Outline

I. Request I: John 17:1-4
   A. Enhancement: 1
   B. Eternal life: 2-3
   C. Entirety: 4
II. Request II: John 17:5-10
   A. Restoration: 5
   B. Revelation: 6-7
   C. Reception: 8
   D. Relationship:9-10
III. Request III: John 17:11
   A. Ascension: 11a
   B. Assurance: 11b
IV. Request VI: John 17:20-21
   A. Projection: 20
   B. Participation: 21

Daily Bible Readings

Mon. This is Life Eternal
John 17:1-3
Tue. I Have Finished
John 17:4-6
Wed. I Pray for Them
John 17:7-9
Thu. Take Care of My Disciples
John 17:10-12
Fri. They are not of the World
John 17:13-16
Sat. Thy Word is Truth
John 17:17-20
Sun. That They All May Be One
John 17:21-26

Verse By Verse

I. Request I: John 17:1-4

A. Enhancement: 1

1. These words spake Jesus, and lifted up his eyes to heaven, and said, Father, the hour is come; glorify thy Son, that thy Son also may glorify thee:

Jesus had celebrated the Passover supper and the first Lord's supper in the upper room of a house in Jerusalem. After the betrayer, Judas Iscariot, had left there, Jesus had said, "Now is the Son of man glorified, and God is glorified in him. If God be glorified in him, God shall also glorify him in himself, and shall straightway glorify him" (John 13:31-32). These statements were evidently preparatory for what Jesus was to say in His high priestly prayer as recorded in John 17. The hour (time) had come for the great act of redemption to be implemented as planned before the foundation of the world, and it involved the slaying of the Lamb of God (Rev. 13:8). More glory would accrue to the Son and the Father through this. It was for this enhancement of divine glory that Jesus prayed.

B. Eternal life: 2-3

2. As thou hast given him power over all flesh, that he should give eternal life to as many as thou hast given him.

Jesus reminded His heavenly Father that He had given Him power (right, authority) over all flesh (people). This was the power to give eternal life to as many as God had given to Him. This was supported by John 3:35-36—"The Father loveth the Son, and hath given all things into his hand. He that believeth on the Son hath everlasting life: and he that believeth not the Son shall not see life; but the wrath of God abideth on him." The phrase "those given to Jesus" referred to believers throughout His high priestly prayer. There could be no eternal life apart from faith in Christ.

3. And this is life eternal, that they might know thee the only true God, and Jesus Christ, whom thou hast sent.

Here is a rare definition of eternal life. It is the experiential knowledge of the one true God and of Jesus Christ, the One sent by God to atone for the sins of the world. It implies a relationship with God and His Son which is possible only through identification with His life, death, and resurrection, "Whosoever believeth in him should not perish, but have everlasting life" (John 3:16). This is the gospel in concise form. "Truly our fellowship is with the Father, and with his Son Jesus Christ" (I John 153)

C. Entirety: 4

4. I have glorified thee on the earth: I have finished the work which thou gavest me to do.

Jesus was so determined to follow through in the divine plan of redemption that He spoke here as if it were already accomplished. He had glorified the Lord by His ministry of preaching, teaching, healing, exorcising, and performing miracles. That work was now drawing to a close. From now on He would suffer, die, be buried, and rise again. All of this was to happen in a few days. Except for the forty days of post-resurrection appearances prior to His ascension to heaven, the earthly ministry of Jesus would be finished.

II. Request II: John 17:5-10

A. Restoration: 5
5. And now, O Father, glorify thou me with thine own self with the glory which I had with thee before the world was.

God and His Son had lived in heavenly glory before the creation of the world. Now that the time for glorifying God on the earth was coming to a close, Jesus yearned to return to His heavenly glory. He wanted to go to His rightful place at God's right hand, and it was there that Stephen later saw Him as he was about to be martyred (Acts 7:55-56). Jesus prayed for the restoration of glory, and we know that he received it.

B. Revelation: 6-7
6. I have manifested thy name unto the men which thou gavest me out of the world: thine they were, and thou gavest them me; and they have kept thy word.

Verses 6-10 provide a report by Jesus regarding believers. It was because of their response to the word of God that Jesus felt ready to go back up to His original glory in heaven. He had manifested (revealed) God's name to them, meaning that He had taught them about God, His attributes, and His dealings with men. Belonging to God, they had been given by Him to Jesus.

7. Now they have known that all things whatsoever thou hast given me are of thee.

The eleven remaining disciples of Jesus may have been particularly in mind here. They had exercised faith to believe that whatever Jesus taught had come from His heavenly Father.

C. Reception: 8
8. For I have given unto them the words which thou gavest me; and they have received them, and have known surely that I came out from thee, and they have believed that thou didst send me.

The followers of Jesus had been convinced that His words had been authorized by Jehovah, They were sure that Jesus was the promised Messiah, the Christ (anointed One) sent to them from heaven. They were soon to receive the great commission to evangelize the whole world (Matt. 28:19-20). Their brief missions during the time of Christ's ministry on the earth were soon to be expanded to lifetime vocations. As God had sent Christ, so it was that Christ was sending them to take the gospel to all men, Reception of truth had obligated them to propagate truth.

D. Relationship: 9-10
9 I pray for them: I pray not for the world, but for them which thou hast given me; for they are thine.
10. And all mine are thine, and thine are mine; and I am glorified in them.

Jesus was concerned about sinners, but He was praying specifically for believers at this time. Both the Father and the Son had proprietary rights over these people, and it would be through their actions that God and Christ would be further glorified. It was a divine-human relationship which operated to bring praise to the Almighty.

III. Request III: John 17:11

A. Ascension: 11a
11a. And now I am no more in the world, but these are in the world, and I come to thee.

Jesus was so sure of His ascension to heaven that He could speak of it here as if it had already happened, He was leaving His followers behind, and He was concerned about their spiritual welfare.

B. Assurance: 11b
11b. Holy Father, keep through thine own name those whom thou hast given me, that they may be one, as we are.

Jesus sought assurance from His holy Father that believers would be kept (protected, preserved, safeguarded) from error and betrayal so that they would be worthy of God's name and all that it implied. Jesus wanted believers to be unified, even as He and His Father were united.

Jesus went on to say that He had kept the loyalty of those God had given Him, except for "the son of perdition" (Judas Iscariot), and his defection was the fulfillment of a scriptural prediction. As He was coming to God, Jesus wanted His followers to have joy, in spite of the fact that the evil world system hated them (John 17:12-14).

In His fourth petition, Jesus asked not that God should take believers out of the world but that He would keep them from the evil one, meaning Satan (John 17:15-16).

In His fifth petition, Jesus asked God to sanctify believers through the truth of His word. By separating them <u>from</u> sin and <u>unto</u> righteousness, they would be prepared to be sent into the world to evangelize the lost (John 17:17-19).

IV. Request VI: John 17:20-21

A. Projection: 20
20. Neither pray I for these alone, but for them also which shall believe on me through their word;

This is what might be termed an open-ended verse. Jesus prayed not only for believers who were then alive. He prayed for those who would become believers in the future through their faithful ministry of the Word of God. By extension, we may project this part of Jesus' prayer to include us today, as well as others who will become believers in the future. The long parade of witnesses may have expanded and shriveled over the intervening centuries, but there has been an unbroken line of them.

We know that Jesus continues to pray for believers while He is in heaven waiting to come back to earth again. "He ever liveth to make intercession for them" (Heb, 7:25). The Holy Spirit also prays for believers. "The Spirit itself [or himself] maketh intercession for us with groanings [or sighings] which cannot be uttered" (Rom. 8:26).

B. Participation: 21
21a. That they all may be one; as thou, Father, art in me, and I in thee, that they also may be one in us: . .

Jesus prayed that all believers present and future might be united to one another as He and His Father were united. This was similar to the third petition (vs. 11), but the scope included believers yet to be born.

21b. . . .that the world may believe that thou has sent me.

The unity of believers was desired as a good testimony to the unbelieving world (cf. vss. 22-23). In His seventh petition, Jesus asked God to let believers be with Him where He was, referring to heaven as if He were already there. He wanted believers to share His glory following His ascension (John 17:24).

The final two verses appear to be a summary of what Jesus had included in His whole high priestly prayer (John 17:25-26). Did God grant the requests made by His beloved Son in this special prayer? We may be sure that God granted them, is granting them, or will grant them at the appropriate time in the future, This prayer should be a comfort and encour-agement to believers of all generations, for it shows them how to pray according to God's will (I John 5:14 -15).

Evangelistic Emphasis

We are the beneficiaries of Christ's willingness to come into the world and do the Father's redemptive will. He was with God before the world was. He was not responsible for any sin and was not deserving of any suffering or punishment. It was purely out of love that He was willing to assume the vulnerability of humanity so He could absorb the pain and shame of our sins.

He came so that we might know God and have eternal life. In coming, He accepted the commitment to complete the Father's will. This meant that He would have to be tempted in all points like we are. He would have to experience the pain, the sense of estrangement, the betrayal, the grief, and the cruelty that are a part of the human experience. He could not do what God sent Him to do if He insulated himself against the hurt which humanity experiences.

Therefore, He went to the extremity of human experience. He went to the extent of feeling forsaken even by God. His physical trauma took Him to death itself. He did not take any shortcut or claim any special privilege as a result of His divinity.

God has given Him the victory through the resurrection and has brought Him to God's own right hand where He now reigns as King of kings and Lord of lords. All mankind will one day acknowledge Him as every knee will bow and every tongue confess His name. The blessed ones are those who respond with gratitude to His remarkable love and confess Him voluntarily while still in this life.

Memory Selection

"Neither pray I for these alone, but for them also which shall believe on me through their word; that they all may be one."
John 17:20, 21.

The message of the gospel is one of reconciliation. That which has been torn apart by sin is brought back together by the reconciling life and death of Jesus. It is a travesty for those who are a part of the community of reconciliation to be split into hostile and competing camps. The major scandal of Christianity is that schisms, persecutions, and wars have been fostered in the name of Christ.

The Scriptures do not require that all be just alike. They recognize that there will be levels of immaturity, ignorance, and error. Therefore, some will understand things others do not. Some will believe doctrines that others have not reached or have grown beyond. As the writer of Hebrews says, it is important that we gently bear with the ignorant and the erring.

The fact is that we, ourselves, have been ignorant and erring. We have survived in the church because others have been patient with us. It takes but a little thought to realize that we are doubtless still ignorant and erring in some points. We require the patience of others and they require ours so that we may be one in Christ.

Weekday Problems

As the Sunday School class studied the practice of fasting, Bill became convinced that it was a seriously neglected Christian discipline. Bill was extremely conscientious and wanted to do everything exactly right. He also was worried about the apparent lack of life and effectiveness in the church. He concluded that these problems might be due to the fact that fasting was not practiced.

He proposed that the church begin fasting as a group on designated days that would be set aside for prayer and spiritual self-examination. Many were impressed with his intent and his earnestness, but most thought that the fasting regimen should be voluntary and not required by a group decision.

Convinced that he was doing what would revitalize the church, Bill became adamant in support of the plan. He believed that those who opposed it were opposing the will of God for the church. The reaction of the church was increased resistance. There were severe strains and a visible danger of splitting the church.

* What are the essential doctrines of the Christian faith on which no varying opinions can be countenanced?
* What protection does the church have against divisions caused by sincere people?

Superintendent's Sermonette

Jesus should be our great Example in all things, and that includes prayer. By studying His high priestly prayer, as recorded in John 17, we can better understand how to pray. Jesus wanted His heavenly Father to be with Him in His earthly ministry of redemption so that His Father would be glorified. We can pray that prayer. Jesus wanted to go up to heaven and be restored to His original glory. We can pray to go to heaven to experience its glory. Jesus prayed that believers would be united. We can pray for that. Jesus prayed that believers would be delivered from Satan, the evil one. We need to pray for that. Jesus prayed that believers would be sanctified, separated from sin and separated unto righteousness. We can pray for that. Jesus prayed that believers would have a good testimony to the world. We can pray for that. Jesus prayed that believers would join Him in heaven. We can pray for that. Let us follow in the footsteps of the Master in prayer, for we know that He prayed according to God's will, and we can, too.

This Lesson in Your Life

We find an example here of something that we sometimes do not think to mention, the importance of praying for one's self. We often hear about the importance of praying for others. Jesus did that as well, but he began by praying for himself. "Glorify thy Son, That thy Son also may glorify Thee," He prayed.

This points out to us that it is right to ask for blessings for ourselves. We need to esteem ourselves as worthy of blessings. The only way we can properly glorify the Father is because we have been glorified by Him.

Is this not contradictory to Christian humility? To the contrary, it is essential to it. Only those who have adequate self-esteem have the ability to focus loving attention on others. Those who do not feel loved and approved by God will be so painfully self-aware that they will not be able either to love others or glorify God.

A second lesson of this text is on the importance of acknowledging our gifts. Jesus recognized the authority that God had given him and that made it possible for him to use His gift as a good steward. It is not a proper Christian response to deny the existence of God-given gifts and abilities. If you have musical ability or teaching ability, do not deny those gifts but affirm them thankfully and use them productively in the kingdom of God. If you have the knack of encouraging others or expressing sympathy, thank God for it and use it. You are a conduit for the blessings of God. If you deny your gifts you will deprive others of needed benefits.

This text also points out that eternal life is knowing God. Eternal life does not begin at death but is ours now. It involves peace, security, joy, and love. Those are the ingredients of life and relationship and they are ours to enjoy even while on earth. No doubt there will be an enhanced enjoyment of them in heaven, but let us not wait until then for what we already have.

One useful message here is on the satisfaction of completing one's mission. Jesus said, "I have finished the work which thou gavest me to do." Our tasks, like his, are sometimes hard. We have to go through periods of discouragement. What joy it is to complete a major task and be able to look back over our accomplishment with thanksgiving!

In prayer, Jesus reflected on the fact that he had been with the Father before the world was. This important sense of identity helped him to face the agony of his suffering and death. We do not have the same identity as Jesus does, but we do have a God-given identity. Reflecting on who we are, who made us, and the purpose of our being will also help us to be sturdy in the face of difficulty and opposition.

Jesus not only prayed for his disciples, but also for those who would subsequently believe through their word. That means He prayed for us! What great strength and confidence it should give us to know that we have been prayed for by Jesus Himself!

Seed Thoughts

1. Should we always close our eyes when we pray?
Most people do this to shut out distractions. Jesus lifted up His eyes to heaven.

2. Why did Jesus want to be glorified during His redemptive mission?
He wanted to be glorified in order that His heavenly Father might be glorified. Any praise we get should be given to God.

3. What power does Jesus have in regard to believers?
He has the power to declare them sons of God through faith in His name (John 1:12; 17:2).

4. What is the scriptural definition of eternal life?
John 17:3 defines it as experiential knowledge of the one true God and of Jesus Christ sent by God. Identification by faith with them produces eternal life.

5. How does John 17:5 show the eternality of Christ?
It agrees with John 1:1-2, Colossians 1:16-17, and Hebrews 1:2 that Jesus existed with God in eternity past.

(Please Turn Page)

---

1. Should we always close our eyes when we pray?

2. Why did Jesus want to be glorified during His redemptive mission?

3. What power does Jesus have in regard to believers?

4. What is the scriptural definition of eternal life?

5. How does John 17:5 show the eternality of Christ?

6. How may believers be kept by God's name?

7. Did Jesus ever pray for us as believers in this century?

8. Why is it important for believers to remain united?

9. Can believers have a sure hope that they will one day be in heaven with Jesus?

10. Did God grant Jesus' requests?

Seed Thoughts - Continued

Most people do this to shut out distractions. Jesus lifted up His eyes to heaven.

He wanted to be glorified in order that His heavenly Father might be glorified. Any praise we get should be given to God.

He has the power to declare them sons of God through faith in His name (John 1:12; 17:2).

John 17:3 defines it as experiential knowledge of the one true God and of Jesus Christ sent by God. Identification by faith with them produces eternal life.

It agrees with John 1:1-2, Colossians 1:16-17, and Hebrews 1:2 that Jesus existed with God in eternity past.

They can remain faithful to His name and all the truths it implies.

According to John 17:20-21, He did. According to Hebrews 7:25, He still does. The Holy Spirit does (Rom. 8:26).

It makes for a good relationship among themselves, and it provides a good testimony to the unbelieving world.

That is where their citizenship is (Phil, 3:20). That is where they are going when Christ comes (I Thess. 4:13-18).

We may be sure that God did grant them, is granting them, or will grant them, for Jesus prayed in His will (I John 5:14-15).

---

6 How may believers be kept by God's name?
They can remain faithful to His name and all the truths it implies.

7 Did Jesus ever pray for us as believers in this century?
According to John 17:20-21, He did. According to Hebrews 7:25, He still does. The Holy Spirit does (Rom. 8:26).

8. Why is it important for believers to remain united?
It makes for a good relationship among themselves, and it provides a good testimony to the unbelieving world.

9 Can believers have a sure hope that they will one day be in heaven with Jesus?
That is where their citizenship is (Phil, 3:20). That is where they are going when Christ comes (I Thess. 4:13-18).

10. Did God grant Jesus' requests?
We may be sure that God did grant them, is granting them, or will grant them, for Jesus prayed in His will (I John 5:14-15).

Praise For Christ, God's Servant

Philippians 2:1. If there be therefore any consolation in Christ, if any comfort of love, if any fellowship of the Spirit, if any bowels and mercies,

2. Fulfil ye my joy, that ye be likeminded, having the same love, being of one accord, of one mind.

3. Let nothing be done through strife or vain glory; but in lowliness of mind let each esteem other better than themselves.

4. Look not every man on his own things, but every man also on the things of others.

5. Let this mind be in you, which was also in Christ Jesus:

6. Who, being in the form of God, thought it not robbery to be equal with God:

7. But made himself of no reputation, and took upon him the form of a servant, and was made in the likeness of men:

8. And being found in fashion as a man, he humbled himself, and became obedient unto death, even the death of the cross.

9. Wherefore God also hath highly exalted him, and given him a name which is above every name:

10. That at the name of Jesus every knee should bow, of things in heaven, and things in earth, and things under the earth;

11. And that every tongue should confess that Jesus Christ is Lord, to the glory of God the Father.

MEMORY SELECTION
Philippians 2:5
DEVOTIONAL READING
John 13:1-17

BACKGROUND SCRIPTURE
Philippians 2:1-11
PRINTED SCRIPTURE
Philippians 2:1-11

Teacher's Target

Current thinking features the development of selfishness and personal promotion. Cultic teaching urges people to look within themselves for the powers of the universe and turn them to their advantage. Celebrities are idolized and emulated, even when they provide poor role models. Abrasive treatment of others is often tolerated and perhaps praised as being therapeutic. Society is in danger of degenerating into self-centeredness and rudeness as everyone looks out for himself.

WE NEED to take a look in the other direction by considering the virtues of humility, sacrifice, and unity. Christ provides the great example to Follow, and nowhere in the Bible is this better described than in this lesson's text. He humbled Himself that He might be exalted. We need to identify with Him in death to self in order that we might rise with Him to eternal life.

Lesson Introduction

Every person is born with a compulsion for survival. That is helpful in avoiding problems which could be dangerous and life-threatening. However, it can be perverted into developing an inflated concept of one's own importance. It can lead to the use of strategies designed to gain and hold places of preferment and privilege. A person devoted to this way of life may reject the idea that the way up is often first the way down.

Joseph learned differently. As Jacob's favorite son, he was envied by his halfbrothers and sold into Egyptian slavery. However, God raised him up to become the Pharaoh's prime minister and thus save the Messianic line from extinction.

Jesus, God's beloved Son, humbled Himself to become a man in order to atone for men's sins. God raised Him from the dead, restored Him to His heavenly glory, and will one day make Him ruler over all the universe.

Teaching Outline

I. Expectation: Phil. 2:1-4
   A. Be unified: 1-2
   B. Be humble: 3
   C. Be concerned: 4

II. Example: Phil. 2:5-8
   A. Attitude: 5
   B. Actions: 6-8

III. Exultation: Phil, 2:9-11
   A. Position: 9
   B. Participation: 10-11

Daily Bible Readings

Mon. If There is Any Comfort
Philippians 2:1
Tue. Be of One Accord
Philippians 2:2
Wed. Esteem the Other Better
Philippians 2:3
Thu. Care for Each Other
Philippians 2:4
Fri. Have the Mind of Christ
Philippians 2:5
Sat. Christ Humbled Himself
Philippians 2:6-8
Sun. God Exalted Him
Philippians 2:9-11

Verse By Verse

I. Expectation: Phil. 2:1-4

A. Be unified: 1-2
1. **If there be therefore any consolation in Christ, if any comfort of love, if any fellowship of the Spirit, if any bowels and mercies,**

Paul had already urged believers in Philippi to let their heavenly citizenship enhance the gospel of Christ. He had told them not to be terrified by their adversaries but to accept the fact that they were to suffer for Christ's sake (Phil. 1:27-30).

Therefore, he stated four conditions for appealing to them to be unified. The word "if" here might be translated as "since," because Paul evidently felt that these conditions were present among believers in Philippi. They shared mutual blessings by having come by faith into the body of Christ, finding the comfort of love there, experiencing fellowship in the Spirit, and knowing the meaning of Christian compassion.

2. **Fulfill ye my joy, that ye be likeminded, having the same love, being of one accord, of one mind.**

Encouraged by the belief that the believers in Philippi had the virtues mentioned in verse 1, Paul urged them to fill up his joy by being likeminded, loving, and unified. Paul knew that Satan had many subtle tactics to use in trying to defeat Christians (II Cor 2:ll). One of these was to turn believers against one another. This could be as devastating as a frontal attack by unbelievers against the church. Dissension has torn many churches apart and thus destroyed their testimony for Christ. Paul's advice to cultivate unity is relevant today.

B. Be humble: 3
3a. **Let nothing be done through strife or vainglory; . . .**

In this negative part of the verse, Paul warned believers to avoid doing things for the sake of selfish ambition or vain conceit. These character traits can and do develop in believers who would condemn other sins. The desire to excel is not wrong, unless it is directed toward self-aggrandizement or pride. Sometimes even a strong Christian testimony can mask an attempt at self-promotion.

3b. **. . .but in lowliness of mind let each esteem other better than themselves.**

In this positive part of the verse, Paul urged believers to defer to one another in humility. Realistically speaking, a Christian might consider himself to be superior to another Christian in some physical, mental, emotional, social, or spiritual way, but he should not allow this to develop into sinful pride. He should thank God for whatever gifts He has bestowed on him and never consider himself the source of them.

C. Be concerned: 4
4a. **Look not every man on his own things, . . .**

In this negative part of the verse, Paul warned believers to avoid being consumed by concern for their own affairs. Those who did this would turn in upon themselves and lack the outward look which God demands.

4b. **. . .but every man also on the things of others**

In this positive part of the verse,

Paul urged believers to show concern for the welfare of others. In another place he expressed it this way—"As we have therefore opportunity, let us do good unto all men, especially unto them who are of the household of faith" (Gal. 6:10). James went so far as to state that a faith which produced no good works was a dead (spurious, false) faith (Jas. 2:14-26).

II. Example: Phil. 2:5-8

A. Attitude: 5
5. Let this mind be in you, which was also in Christ Jesus:

Note that Paul had already used such terms as "likeminded," "one mind," and "lowliness of mind" in verses 2 and 3. He now used the term "mind" again in the sense of attitude. He wanted believers in Philippi to have the same attitude as Jesus had. Thus began the great kenosis (emptying) passage of Philippians 2:5-8. It told how Jesus emptied Himself of His heavenly prerogatives in order to come down to earth and die for men's sins. In this, as in all things, Jesus serves as the great Example to follow. A humble attitude is not something we can manufacture for ourselves. It must be imparted to us by the ministry of the Holy Spirit. It is the meekness mentioned in Galatians 5:23.

B. Actions: 6-8
6. Who, being in the form of God, thought it not robbery to be equal with God:

Jesus was in eternity past with God the Father and the Holy Spirit, and He was a full Member of the Trinity. "In the beginning [eternity past] was the Word [Logos, Communicator], and the Word was with God, and the Word was God" (John 1:1). The latter part of the verse might better be translated as saying that Jesus did not think that equality with God was something to be grasped and held or retained. He never relinquished His divinity by coming to the earth, but He did give up some of His divine prerogatives. He took on certain limitations for the time He ministered here below.

7a. But made himself of no reputation, . . .

This says that Jesus stripped Himself of His heavenly majesty and glory. He left His place of power and privilege at His Father's right hand. He came down into the body which God had prepared for Him within the virgin's womb (Heb, 10:5). He was born to peasant parentage in the little town of Bethlehem, heralded by angels and welcomed by shepherds (Luke 2:1-20). It was a humble beginning by men's standards.

7b. . . .and took upon him the form of a servant, . . .

This "form of a servant" corresponds with "his form of God" found in verse 6. Jesus left His glorious divine appearance behind and took upon Himself the appearance of a servant. He Who should have been served in all things became a Servant to others through His preaching, teaching, exorcising, and performing of miracles.

7c. . . .and was made in the likeness of men:

Only in Jesus did divinity and humanity meet and compose one Person. He was fully divine, and He was fully human. He became like other men in that He was hungry, thirsty, tired, joyful, sad, and subject to suffering and death.

8. And being found in fashion as a man, he humbled himself, and became obedient unto death, even the death of the cross.

Paul wanted believers to realize the depth of Christ's humility. He was the Lord of glory, and yet He became a man, was willing to die as a man, and even accepted crucifixion on a cross as His means of death. Crucifixion, ordered by Pilate, was carried out by Roman soldiers who were hardened to this cruel form of execution. It was a most shameful way to die, and Jesus was held up between heaven and earth between two common thieves crucified with Him. The agony that He endured before He was nailed to the cross and while He was suspended there is almost too much to contemplate. In addition to the physical suffering, He was bearing the sins of all men of all generations upon His pure and sinless soul. We can hardly know what this meant to Him, for it is outside of anything we have experienced. By the act of atonement, Jesus redeemed all who believe on Him as their Savior from sin.

This is a good place to pause and think about your students, seeking to determine who is truly born again and who is not. You might want to extend an invitation to all who are unsure and would like to know how to be saved. Suggest that they contact you after class, during the week, or any time. If they would feel more comfortable discussing the matter with the pastor or some other person in the church, let them do that. You could help them set up an appointment.

III. Exultation: Phil. 2:9-11

A. Position: 9
9. Wherefore God also hath highly exalted him, and given him a name which is above every name:

In direct contrast to the shameful death of Jesus mentioned in verse 8, we now read that God highly exalted Him by first raising Him up from the grave and then raising Him up to heaven forty days after His resurrection, Jesus assumed the same position at His Father's right hand which He had held before He came to the earth.

We may wonder what the name is which God has given to Jesus, Who already had a proper name. This may refer to His title as Savior. He was called "the captain of...salvation" in Hebrews 2:10. He was called our "high priest" in Hebrews 10:21. He was called "the author and finisher of our faith" in Hebrews 12:2. All of these describe His saving ministry, made possible by the shedding of His blood to cleanse us from our sins.

However, Philippians 2:10-11 implies that the name given by God to Jesus is going to involve not only salvation but rulership, and all will have to participate in honoring Him as Lord of the universe.

B. Participation: 10-11
10. That at the name of Jesus every knee should bow, of things in heaven, and things in earth, and things under the earth;

The time is coming when all rational beings in the universe will have to humble themselves before Jesus. Every knee of every being in heaven in or on the earth, and under the earth must bend before Him. Nothing is mentioned here about intelligent beings being located in any place in the universe but heaven and earth.

11. And that every tongue should confess that Jesus Christ is Lord, to the glory of God the Father.

The title of Lord implies rulership and the right to judge. This agrees with John 5:22—"The Father judgeth no man, but hath committed all judgment unto the Son" (John 5:22). Honor thus given to Christ will add to God's glory, because it is His will that all rational beings confess that Jesus is Lord.

You may wonder why this quarter's series of lessons on "Songs and Prayers of the Bible" includes this text. Some see it as a hymn of praise to Christ, God's Servant. After Jesus has reigned over all, there is one more step to take. "When all things shall be subdued unto him, then shall the Son also himself be subject unto him that put all things under him, that God may be all in all" (I Cor. 15:28). This describes in a beautiful way the unity existing in the holy Godhead.

Evangelistic Emphasis

Jesus said, "And I, if I be lifted up from the earth, will draw all men unto me." (John 12:32) John specifies that Jesus was referring to the manner in which He was to die. The attracting power of the gospel is the sacrificial death on the cross.

There are many things about Jesus that greatly impress us. We are awed by His miracles, informed by His teaching, and inspired by His exemplary life. Yet that which has the strongest drawing power is the love that caused Him to die for us. That is the irresistible magnet that compels us to follow Him.

Since this is true, today's text is one of the most effective evangelistic passages in the Scriptures. If a person's heart can be touched at all, it should be touched by the message that Jesus left heaven, came to earth, became a man, made himself of no reputation, took the form of a servant, and became obedient to death. The death was not an ordinary one but was the painful, humiliating death of a criminal, that of the cross.

This story would be dramatically gripping if it had nothing to do with us. When, however, we realize that we are at the very center of it, it does not merely grip us, but propels us. We are the object of this incredibly loving sacrifice. Who could fail to be touched by having such a great sacrifice made for him by the Son of God Himself? It should melt the hardest heart, command the attention of the one who is most distracted, and compel the interest of the one who is most jaded.

Memory Selection

"Let this mind be in you, which was also in Christ Jesus.
Philippians 2:5.

The Scriptures consistently teach that happiness is not in self-centeredness but in loving, serving, and giving. They are nowhere more eloquent than here where we are exhorted to have in us the mind of Christ.

The passage then details what it means to have the mind of Christ. It is to put others' needs ahead of our own, to sacrifice for the benefit of others, to be unconcerned about our own status and prestige, and to be willing even to die for the benefit of others.

That might appear to some to be a defeatist philosophy that does not represent a proper amount of self-respect. Such is not the case. It is not low self-esteem, but trust in God, that motivates this view. It is the belief that in God's wisdom, He has revealed to us that self-centeredness results in pain and broken relationships. Self-giving love brings peace, joy and love. It heals and invigorates relationships.

Because God is sovereign and is the final judge of all, it is guaranteed that those who emulate the sacrificial example of his Son, will be eternally blessed for it.

Weekday Problems

Albert is an elderly gentleman who has a lifetime habit of giving first consideration to others. In his work as a school teacher, he gave unsparingly of himself to help and encourage his students. When he became an administrator he was the best friend and the greatest support the teachers had.

It was not that he was weak or had low self-esteem or did not expect to be treated with respect. He was strong, confident, and projected such an image of professional integrity that respect was never in question. He simply believed in giving of himself to others.

He is now nearing the end of his life. A terminal illness grips his frail body. It is an effort for him to talk. Yet, true to his well-established pattern, he still is a giver of encouragement and support to family, friends, nurses, and doctors. He is in much pain but he radiates an inner joy that cannot be questioned.

* How long has Albert been preparing for the saintly way he is facing major trauma?
* Will people take advantage of you if you follow his example? If so, does that negate the importance of his kind of life?

Superintendent's Sermonette

Two things exert a great influence on every child born into the world. One is his genetic make-up, derived from his parents and other ancestors. The other is his environment, along with everything and everybody involved in it as he grows and develops. The natural tendency is for him to reach out and increasingly take whatever he can get in order to move toward whatever goals he sets for himself. Sometimes this puts him in conflict with others who are looking out for their own interests, and the results can be disastrous.

The Bible teaches believers to follow a different life plan. They are told to empty themselves of selfish aspirations in order that God might fill them with His will. The world looks on and cannot understand how happiness can be found in doing this. We must look to Christ to comprehend it. He emptied Himself of heavenly prerogatives when He became a man and died to atone for men's sins, but God raised Him up to joy and glory. Let us empty out ourselves so that God might fill us with Himself. This is the way to true joy.

This Lesson in <u>Your</u> Life

Our relationship with one another is based on our relationship with Christ. If you have received consolation from Him, you are obliged to give such consolation to others. If you have received comfort, fellowship, and compassion from Him, you are expected to show those same attitudes toward others.

This is an extraordinarily helpful guideline for daily living. When we ponder what our responsibility to another is, we are enlightened by thinking how Christ has treated us. If He has shown us patience, we should show patience to the other. If Christ has been merciful instead of vengeful to us, we should be merciful to the other. If Christ has been generous beyond our ability to deserve, then we should be as generous to the other.

When we live in the atmosphere of Christ's goodness, it does not become us to be stingy and hateful to those who look to us for understanding and encouragement. If we have been blessed, let us bless others.

Paul reminds us here that good relationships not only bless those involved in them, but they also bring joy to others. "Fulfill my joy," he said, ". . . having the same love, being of one accord, of one mind." Most of us know from our personal experience that such is the case.

Are there parents anywhere who do not get pleasure out of seeing their children relate well to each other? My brother, sister, and I are all old enough to be grandparents, but our parents still enjoy seeing us together. They get pleasure out of laughter and expressions of affection that are exchanged.

This is not a one-way street. Children also enjoy seeing their parents relate well to each other. How painful for children to see parents fight and argue. How pleasant to see expressions of kindness and love!

All of us love to see a church where members relate to each other in harmony and love. We like to work in an atmosphere where there is mutual consideration and respect. Remember that you not only bring blessings into your own life when you relate well to others, but you radiate blessings to those who surround you as well.

We should be considerate of others, not merely because it is right, but also because it makes us happier. When we esteem others highly and care for their needs it creates an atmosphere of openness, warmth, and approval. When we selfishly seek our own ends we stimulate an atmosphere of suspicion, harshness, and defensiveness.

Consider the example of Christ. He was not under compulsion to humble himself but did so as an act of choice. In his divine wisdom, He knows this is the better way to be. It was the ultimate act of humility for divinity to become humanity. He voluntarily chose it. So we also should voluntarily humble ourselves.

Humility is not an act of self-abasement. Because all things are in the hands of God, there is an inevitable reward for being truly concerned about others. It is built into the fabric of the world God made. We cannot miss it if we follow the example of Christ. All men will one day see that and will acknowledge it on their knees. The blessed ones are those who see it now and shape their lives to it.

Seed Thoughts

1. What conditions did Paul think made Philippian believers unified?
They had mutual faith in Christ, the comfort of love, fellowship in the Spirit, and Christian compassion.

2. What did Paul say would fill up his joy concerning believers?
This would come if believers were likeminded, loving, and unified.

3. What does it mean to do something through strife or vainglory?
It means to do something for the sake of selfish ambition or vain conceit. This leads to self-aggrandizement.

4 How can a Christian keep from feeling himself superior to others?
He can realize that whatever he has comes from God and should not be allowed to lead him into sinful pride.

5. Shouldn't a person be concerned about his own affairs?
Yes, for he is responsible for himself, but he ought not to be consumed by selfish desires and thus neglect others.

(Please Turn Page)

---

1. What conditions did Paul think made Philippian believers unified?

2. What did Paul say would fill up his joy concerning believers?

3. What does it mean to do something through strife or vainglory?

4 How can a Christian keep from feeling himself superior to others?

5. Shouldn't a person be concerned about his own affairs?

6. What kind of mind, which was in Christ, should also be in us?

7. How did Jesus feel about being equal with God the Father?

8. Did Jesus give up His divinity by coming to the earth as a man?

9. What was the ultimate humiliation experienced by Jesus?

10. How has God exalted Jesus and given Him a unique name?

Seed Thoughts - Continued

6. What kind of mind, which was in Christ, should also be in us?
It is a mind-set or attitude of humility, love, and sacrifice.

7. How did Jesus feel about being equal with God the Father?
He did not feel it was something to be grasped and held onto when He had a mission on the earth to perform

8. Did Jesus give up His divinity by coming to the earth as a man?
No, He remained fully divine but became also fully human. This was the only such combination existing in one Person. It was needed for atonement to be made.

9. What was the ultimate humiliation experienced by Jesus?
He humbled Himself unto death, even the shameful death of crucifixion. He bore upon His pure soul the sins of all.

10. How has God exalted Jesus and given Him a unique name?
God raised Him from the dead and received Him back into heaven. His name is Lord, and all shall acknowledge Him.

They had mutual faith in Christ, the comfort of love, fellowship in the Spirit, and Christian compassion.

This would come if believers were likeminded, loving, and unified.

It means to do something for the sake of selfish ambition or vain conceit. This leads to self-aggrandizement.

He can realize that whatever he has comes from God and should not be allowed to lead him into sinful pride.

Yes, for he is responsible for himself, but he ought not to be consumed by selfish desires and thus neglect others.

It is a mind-set or attitude of humility, love, and sacrifice.

He did not feel it was something to be grasped and held onto when He had a mission on the earth to perform

No, He remained fully divine but became also fully human. This was the only such combination existing in one Person. It was needed for atonement to be made.

He humbled Himself unto death, even the shameful death of crucifixion. He bore upon His pure soul the sins of all.

God raised Him from the dead and received Him back into heaven. His name is Lord, and all shall acknowledge Him.

The Hallelujah Chorus

Revelation 15:2. And I saw as it wer a sea of glass mingled with fire: and them that had gotten the victory over the beast, and over his image, and over his mark, and over the number of his name, stand on the sea of glass, having the harps of God.
3. And they sing the song of Moses the servant of God, and the song of the Lamb, saying, Great and marvellous are thy works, Lord God Almighty; just and true are thy ways, thou King of saints.
4. Who shall not fear thee, O Lord, and glorify thy name? for thou only art holy: for all nations shall come and worship before thee; for thy judgments are made manifest.
Revelation 19:4. And the four and twenty elders and the four beasts fell down and worshipped God that sat on the throne, saying, Amen; Alleluia.
5. And a voice came out of the throne, saying, Praise our God, all ye his servants, and ye that fear him, both small and great.
6. And I heard as it were the voice of a great multitude, and as the voice of many waters, and as the voice of mighty thunderings, saying Alleluia: for the Lord God omnipotent reigneth.
7. Let us be glad and rejoice, and give honor to him for the marriage of the Lamb is come, and his wife hath made herself ready.
8. And to her was granted that she should be arrayed in fine linen, clean and white: for the fine linen is the righteousness of saints.

MEMORY SELECTION
Revelation 19:6-7
DEVOTIONAL READING
Colossians 1:9-20

BACKGROUND SCRIPTURE
Revelation 15:2-4; 19:1-8
PRINTED SCRIPTURE
Revelation 15:2-4; 19:4-8

Teacher's Target

We have all been stirred in our hearts when we have heard singing of the "Hallelujah Chorus." Audiences customarily rise to their feet to honor it. This is but a foretaste of what we shall hear when we get to heaven and hear the angels and redeemed people sing praise to God and to the Lamb. We are going to look briefly at two such choruses in this lesson. ~~Help your students~~ We should try to grasp and develop the concept of praise directed toward God the Father and God the Son. Angels and men were created to bring praise to them, and that should begin here on the earth now. It will be their main activity in eternity to come. Therefore, it is worthy of study and practice. It is appropriate that we end this quarter's series of lessons on "Songs and Prayers of the Bible" in this way.

Lesson Introduction

The heavenly setting for our first text is found in Revelation 15:1— "I saw another sign in heaven, great and marvellous, seven angels having the seven last plagues; for in them is filled up the wrath of God." Before these are poured out, as described in chapter 16, there appears a great host of voices singing praise to God and the Lamb, Thus it is that praise will precede judgment, for God and the Lamb are both glorious and just.

The heavenly setting for our second text is found in ReveLation 19:1-3, which describes many people ascribing salvation, glory, honor, and power to the Lord and stating that His judgments are true and righteous. In our text, the twenty-four elders and four beasts (creatures) fall down in worship of God on His throne, and a great multitude sings praise to the Lord.

Teaching Outline

I. Chorus I: Rev. 15:2-4
   A. Scene: 2
   B. Song: 3-4

II. Chorus II: Rev. 19:4-8
   A. Twenty eight: 4
   B. The voice: 5
   C. The multitude: 6
   D. The announcement: 7
   E. The raiment: 8

Daily Bible Readings

Mon. Heaven Praises God
Revelation 15:2-4
Tue. Glory to God
Revelation 19:1
Wed. God is Righteous
Revelation 19:2-3
Thu. God is Worshipped
Revelation 19:4
Fri. Great and Small Praise God
Revelation 19:5
Sat. The Lord Reigns
Revelation 19:6
Sun. The Marriage of the Lamb
Revelation 19:7-8

Verse By Verse

I. Chorus I: Rev. 15:2-4

A. Scene: 2
2a. And I saw as it were a sea of glass mingLed with fire: . . .

The Apostle John saw a scene in heaven wondrous to behold, There was a glassy sea on which water seemed mixed with fire. The sea is often a symbol of people in prophetic scriptures, and that may be the meaning here. The fire may refer to persecution of believers as described in I Peter 1:7.

2b. . . .and them that had gotten the victory over the beast, and over his image, and over his mark, and over the number of his name, . . .

John saw believers who had triumphed over the beast. A description of this beast may be found in Revelation 13:11-18. An image of him will be built and given life. All who refuse to worship it will be slain. Those who serve the Antichrist will be required to receive a mark in their right hands or foreheads in order to buy and sell. His name or number will identify them as belonging to him. His number will be 666.

2c. . . .stand on the sea of glass, having the harps of God.

It seems obvious that these believers will be in a place of safety under God's protection and care. They will hold in their hands harps given to them by God as instruments of praise accompanying their singing.

B Song: 3-4

3a. And they sing the song of Moses the servant of God, and the song of the Lamb, . . .

The song of Moses was composed and sung following God's deliverance of Israel from pursuing Egyptians at the Red Sea (Exod. 15:119), You might also look at Deuteronomy 32. The song of the Lamb will honor Jesus Christ, and it will probably describe the deliverance He made possible for sinners by atoning for their sins at Calvary. These deliverances will apparently precede the song of praise given to God as recorded in verses 3b-4.

3b . . .saying, Great and marvellous are thy works, Lord God Almighty just and true are thy ways, thou King of saints.

The heavenly chorus will praise God for His use of power in performing great and marvelous works on their behalf. They will praise Him for the justice and truth of His ways in dealing with men. The word "saints" is not in the early manuscripts, and some translate this as "King of the nations" or "King of the ages." The word "nations" is used in verse 4 as describing those who will come to worship the Lord.

4a. Who shall not fear thee, O Lord, and glorify thy name? for thou only art holy: . . .

This is a rhetorical question and could be presented in declarative form—"All must fear [reverence] thee, O Lord, and glorify thy name, for you alone are holy." Redeemed and glorified believers will thus declare that God is worthy of glory from all men and angels as the only Being perfect in holiness.

4b. ...for all nations shall come and worship before thee; for thy judgments are made manifest

The reason for which the nations

of the earth will come to worship the Lord will be that His judgments (righteous deeds or sentences, just actions) will be revealed to all. People will have to admit that God did the right thing in every case of dealing with the nations. John wrote that, following the song of the heavenly chorus, he saw the tabernacle opened in heaven and seven angels coming out. They were dressed in pure linen and carried seven plagues. One of the four beasts (creatures) gave them seven golden vials full of the wrath of God (Rev. 15:5-8). Revelation 16 describes the seven vials of divine wrath which will be poured out onto the earth.

II. Chorus II: Rev. 19:4-8

A. Twenty eight: 4
4. And the four and twenty elders and the four beasts fell down and worshipped God that sat on the throne, saying, Amen; Alleluia.

The twenty-four elders are sometimes called "the heavenly Sanhedrin." The four beasts are referred to as "living creatures" or "living beings." The elders may have represented a heavenly priesthood of the church under Jesus as the great High Priest. We know not their names nor the names of the four living creatures, but all twenty-eight are mentioned often in the book of Revelation. These all fell down before the Lord sitting upon His throne and worshiped Him by saying "Amen," meaning "So be it," and "Alleluia," coming from <u>hallel</u> (praise) and <u>iah</u> (a shortened name for God). These appeared to set an example for others to follow.

B The voice: 5
5. And a voice came out of the throne, saying, Praise our God, all ye his servants, and ye that fear him, both small and great.

The person to whom this voice belonged is not identified. We are not told the significance of the fact that the command came from out of the throne of God. All who had reverence for the Lord were told to praise Him, referring to His servants whether they were of small or great importance. The next verse shows the response to the command.

C. The multitude: 6
6a And I heard as it were the voice of a great multitude, and as the voice of many waters, and as the voice of mighty thunderings, . . .

This part of the verse describes the powerful sounds heard by the Apostle John in response to the command to praise God. Three descriptions are mentioned—voice of a great multitude, voice of many waters, and voice of mighty thunderings. This causes us to think of the roar of a crowd, the roar of a waterfall, and the roar of a rain storm. It seems as if all beings in heaven joined in this chorus of praise to the Lord

6b ...saying, Alleluja: for the Lord God omnipotent reigneth.

The chorus of praise mentioned in Revelation 19:1-3 referred to God overcoming the great whore of Babylon described in chapter 18, The chorus of praise in Revelation 19:6 referred to God's plan to marry the Lamb (Jesus Christ) to his wife (the church). It was because God reigned that the marriage could take place. With the forces of evil held in abeyance, the rightous saints could merge with their glorious Savior.

D The announcement: 7
7. Let us be glad and rejoice, and give honour to him: for the marriage of the Lamb is come, and his wife hath made herself ready.

The announcement of the impending wedding banquet refers to an event yet in the future. It will occur in heaven following the judgment of believers.

In stating that the Lamb's wife made herself ready, it is implied that certain things have to be done before the act of eternal union is performed. Perhaps this refers to the long process by which God calls out a people for Himself from among all of the generations of the earth (I Pet. 2:9-10). Perhaps it refers to the need for all believers to appear before the judgment seat of Christ and give account of themselves (Rom. 14:10-12 I Cor. 3:12-15; 4:5 II Cor. 5:10).

E The raiment: 3
8a. And to her was granted that she should be arrayed in fine linen, clean and white: . . .

Although the bride does what she is supposed to do to prepare herself for the wedding, it is what God does for her that is vitally important. He grants her the right to be clothed in fine linen, clean and white.

8b. ...for the fine linen is the righteousness of saints.

We know that no one can be righteous in his or her own wisdom or strength. "All our righteousnesses are as filthy rags" (Isa. 64:6). We know that whatever righteousness we have comes from God for Christ's sake. "For he hath made him to be sin [a sin-offering] for us, who knew no [personal] sin; that we might be made the righteousness of God in him" (II Cor. 5:21).

After our initial cleansing from sin by the atoning blood of Christ, we also have to be cleansed from errors by giving attention to the Word of God. "Christ...loved the church, and gave himself for it; that he might sanctify and cleanse it with the washing of water by the word, that he might present it to himself a glorious church, not having spot, or wrinkle, or any such thing; but that it should be holy and without blemish" (Eph, 5:25-27).

Revelation 19:9 is not in our printed text for this lesson, but it serves as a kind of postscript—"The angel dictated this sentence to me [Apostle John]: 'Blessed are those who are invited to the wedding feast of the Lamb.' And he added, 'God himself has stated this.'" (Living Bible). It will be a time of blessing, not of judgment.

Concluding this study, if time permits, you might turn with your students to Revelation 21:9-10, where the bride is defined in terms of the new Jerusalem, dwelling place of the redeemed—"There came unto me one of the seven angels which had the seven vials full of the seven last plagues [described in Rev. 15:5—16:21], and talked with me, saying, Come hither, I will shew thee the bride, the Lamb's wife. And he carried me away in the spirit to a great and high mountain, and shewed me that great city, the holy Jerusalem, descending out of heaven from God."

From Revelation 21:11 through 22:5 a detailed description of the glories awaiting believers is presented, including a wall, twelve gates, twelve foundations, a street of pure gold, a pure river, and the tree of life. Most important of all, of course, will be the presence of God Almighty and the Lamb. Their glory will dispel night forever, and all who belong to them by faith will live in eternal light. This is the Christian's sure hope, and this is why he can have a song to sing in the darkest night.

Evangelistic Emphasis

Not everybody wants to go to church, but everybody wants to go to heaven. Sometimes people have been offended by church members, neglected by a minister, bored by a dull sermon, or overlooked in a crowd. They may have become cynical because of sexual or financial scandals involving ministers or churches. These people may not have the least interest in attending a religious meeting regardless of how interesting, informative, or inspirational it might be.

Yet they all have a concern about the afterlife. This is a universal yearning. A person who would be turned off by talking about the church on the corner would be eager to be able to approach death with confidence of heaven.

Of course, at some point there must be some reconciliation between our celestial dreams and our terrestrial environment. As Jesus had to live in the real world and was often disappointed and opposed, so also must we. We must sustain our faith even when it is not easy to do so. We must be involved in the church even though there will be periods in which this is difficult for us.

When you are involved in evangelizing others, be sure that you do not spend all your time working on the problems of church membership. Give adequate emphasis to the final victory in heaven. This is what people want. If it is properly emphasized they will have a great incentive to work through the interim problems.

Memory Selection

"For the Lord God omnipotent reigneth. Let us be glad and rejoice, and give honor to him."
Revelation 19:6,7.

God is mightier than anything that could trouble us in this life. Our security is not in avoiding the troubles of earthly life, but in knowing that we serve a God who is greater. He will bless us while we are living this life and, most importantly, He has transcending blessings awaiting us that will make any earthly trouble irrelevant.

Are we worried about sickness and pain? Are we troubled about aging and the failure of our physical abilities? Are we anxious about crime and war? Do we dread to learn more about polluted air and water? Does it seem that far too many public officials are corrupt and dishonest? Do we fear that we live in the shadow of a depression, hunger, and homelessness?

These and a thousand other specters of darkness are exposed as the frauds they are in the light of the omnipotence of God. These problems and ills have no ultimate power over us. They can vex us sorely for a period of time, but they cannot interfere with our relationship with God, our security in His love, and our confidence in heaven when we die.

God is in control and is fully capable of handling all of our needs. Let us therefore sing His praises and let us be grateful in the blessedness of having Him care for us.

Weekday Problems

LaNell is a worrier. She has a good heart and lives a good life. Nobody is quicker than she is to prepare food, clean house, or do laundry for someone who is sick. Her purse is instantly opened when she learns of someone who is in need of money. The church doors are never open without her being there to participate and help where she can. She is scrupulously honest and truthful.

Yet she is never content. She worries about the corruption that she hears about in politics. She feels that crime is getting worse and is threatening the safety of people in all parts of the city. She never hears about a new disease that she does not worry about getting it. She is stung by the slightest criticism and worries about people not liking her. Someone said that if she did not have anything to worry about, she would worry about that.

* What does the doctrine of the omnipotence (all powerfulness) of God have to say about the things that trouble us daily?
* How does the hope of heaven help us to deal with the fear of cancer?
* While it is easy to say, "Don't worry," what can a worrier actually do to attain a more calm and peaceful attitude?

Superintendent's Sermonette

Job 38:7 says that "the morning stars sang together" in the past. David was called "the sweet psalmist of Israel" (II Sam. 23:1). He dedicated instrumentalists and singers to the work of the Lord (I Chron. 25:1-7), and Solomon later used them in the first Jewish temple. Paul and Silas sang praises to God at midnight in the Philippian jail (Acts 16:25). No music mentioned in the Bible, however, could compare with the heavenly choruses about which we study in this lesson.

We need to recognize the importance of music in human society today. At perhaps no time in history have there been more types available. These range anywhere from sublime classics and hymns at one end to demonic acid rock-and-roll at the other end. Live concerts draw huge audiences. Reproductions seem infinite through radio and television broadcasts, records, tapes, and compact discs.

We must learn to be as selective as possible of both lyrics and music so that we use what pleases God and leads us to love the music we will enjoy in heaven forever.

This Lesson in <u>Your</u> Life

With this lesson we are ending a quarter on the poetry and songs of God's people. We have been studying the language of the heart. Some feelings are not adequately expressed in ordinary prose. The language of poetry and music is called for to free these emotions. They may be emotions of penitence, sorrow, confusion, and despair. They throb with the beat of the human heart. They are the language of the soul. Their climactic moment comes with the "Hallelujah Chorus" in the book of Revelation. It is an outburst of joyous celebration, a song of victory.

It is a song of victory over the power of evil. One of our great frustrations in life is that we often feel impotent in the face of destructive forces that are larger than we are. We see things that destroy the body and spirit, wreaking unchecked havoc. We sometimes feel that we can do nothing but lament the pain and fear.

I know good people who have sickness, hunger, and poverty. I can respond to some of them with limited help, but the magnitude of the problem worldwide inclines me to sing a dirge rather than a song of victory.

What a wonderful day it will be when the will of God shows itself triumphant over all the forces of evil in the world! There will be no unbelief because every knee will bow and every tongue will confess that Jesus is Lord. There will be no oppression or exploitation because God will be making a final judgment on the deeds of men. There will be no cruelty or abuse because God will be protecting the weak and the helpless. There will be no grief or sorrow among God's people because God will be wiping away every tear from their eyes.

All wrongs will be righted. All inequities will be corrected. All distortions will be cleared up. All falseness will be exposed. All goodness will be vindicated. All truth will be affirmed. All love will be freely expressed.

That will be a time for the most magnificent of celebrations. The world will not contain it but it will require the expanse of heaven. Men and angels will join their voices in the praises of God. Joys that are too large to be contained in the human breast will burst forth in song. It will be so powerful that it will sound like the surge of the sea or the voice of mighty thunder.

This joyous praise will be based on what God has done for his people during this life. It will be clear that even while we were in a struggle which appeared to have an unsure outcome, God was in control and the certainty of the final victory was in his hand.

The celebration will last forever. On earth, our celebrations may be somewhat stifled because we know that they cannot last. Vacation pleasure may be dimmed a bit because we know it will be only for a short time. A bonus at work has the edge taken off when we realize it will be soon spent. The heavenly chorus, however, will never be over.

"When we've been there ten thousand years
Bright shining as the sun,
We've no less days to sing God's praise
Than when we'd first begun."
— John Newton

Seed Thoughts

1. When will believers stand on water and fire?
The Apostle John saw the time coming when they will stand on the sea of glass and fire to sing a victory song.

2. Over whom will the victory song be sung?
Saints will celebrate victory over the beast (Antichrist), his image, his mark, and his name or number,

3. What will be similar in the song of Moses and song of the Lamb?
Deliverance from foes was featured in the song of Moses, and deliverance from evil will no doubt be featured in the song of the Lamb

4. Why will the saints praise the Lord God Almighty?
They will thank Him for his works and His ways as their King.

5. Why should men give reverence to the Lord?
His name should be glorified, because He is unique in His holy perfections.

(Please Turn Page)

---

1. When will believers stand on water and fire?

2. Over whom will the victory song be sung?

3. What will be similar in the song of Moses and song of the Lamb?

4. Why will the saints praise the Lord God Almighty?

5. Why should men give reverence to the Lord?

6. Why will all nations come to worship the Lord?

7 What does hallelujah (or alleluia) mean?

8 What role will the twenty elders and four creatures play?

9 Prior to what great event will the great heavenly multitude sing?

10. What does fine, clean, white linen clothing represent?

Seed Thoughts - Continued

The Apostle John saw the time coming when they will stand on the sea of glass and fire to sing a victory song.

Saints will celebrate victory over the beast (Antichrist), his image, his mark, and his name or number,

Deliverance from foes was featured in the song of Moses, and deliverance from evil will no doubt be featured in the song of the Lamb

They will thank Him for his works and His ways as their King.

They will see that His judgments (just actions) have been revealed. This will happen

His name should be glorified, because He is unique in His holy perfections.

It comes from hallel (praise) and iah (a shortened form of God's name), and it means "Praise the Lord."

These heavenly beings set an example of praise for others to follow in their worship of God and the Lamb

They will sing as the marriage of the Lamb (Christ) and His bride (church) is announced at the end of time.

In the Bible it represents the righteousness of the saints, imputed to them by God because of their faith in Christ.

6. Why will all nations come to worship the Lord?
They will see that His judgments (just actions) have been revealed. This will happen when Christ comes to reign.

7 What does hallelujah (or alleluia) mean?
It comes from hallel (praise) and iah (a shortened form of God's name), and it means "Praise the Lord."

8 What role will the twenty elders and four creatures play?
These heavenly beings set an example of praise for others to follow in their worship of God and the Lamb

9 Prior to what great event will the great heavenly multitude sing?
They will sing as the marriage of the Lamb (Christ) and His bride (church) is announced at the end of time.

10. What does fine, clean, white linen clothing represent?
In the Bible it represents the righteousness of the saints, imputed to them by God because of their faith in Christ.

Identification And Testing

Mark 1:1. The beginning of the gospel of Jesus Christ, the Son of God;
2. As it is written in the prophets, Behold, I send my messenger before thy face, which shall prepare thy way before thee.
3. The voice of one crying in the wilderness, Prepare ye the way of the Lord, make his paths straight.
4. John did baptize in the wilderness, and preach the baptism of repentance for the remission of sins.
5. And there went out unto him all the land of Judea, and they of Jerusalem, and were all baptized of him in the river of Jordan, confessing their sins.
6. And John was clothed with camel's hair, and with a girdle of a skin about his loins; and he did eat locusts and wild honey;
7. And preached, saying, There cometh one mightier than I after me, the latchet of whose shoes I am not worthy to stoop down and unloose.
8. I indeed have baptized you with water: but he shall baptize you with the Holy Ghost.
9. And it came to pass in those days, that Jesus came from Nazareth of Galilee, and was baptized of John in Jordan.
10. And straightway coming up out of the water, he saw the heavens opened, and the Spirit like a dove descending upon him:
11. And there came a voice from heaven, saying, Thou art my beloved Son, in whom I am well pleased.
12. And immediately the spirit driveth him into the wilderness.
13. And he was there in the wilderness forty days, tempted of Satan; and was with the wild beasts; and the angels ministered unto him.
14. Now after that John was put in prison, Jesus came into Galilee, preaching the gospel of the kingdom of God.
15. And saying, The time is fulfilled, and the kingdom of God is at hand: repent ye, and believe the gospel.

MEMORY SELECTION
Mark 1:11
DEVOTIONAL READING
Hebrews 12:1-6
BACKGROUND SCRIPTURE
Mark 1:1-15
PRINTED SCRIPTURE
Mark 1:1-15

Identification & Testing

Teacher's Target

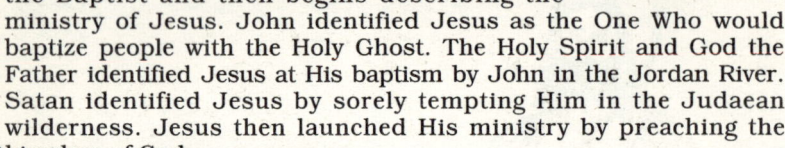

Mark, the briefest of the four gospels, moves directly into a summary of the ministry of John the Baptist and then begins describing the ministry of Jesus. John identified Jesus as the One Who would baptize people with the Holy Ghost. The Holy Spirit and God the Father identified Jesus at His baptism by John in the Jordan River. Satan identified Jesus by sorely tempting Him in the Judaean wilderness. Jesus then launched His ministry by preaching the kingdom of God.

There is a necessity of identifying Jesus as the divine Son of God and Savior of the world. Historical records, such as the gospel of Mark, help to do this. However, acceptance of Jesus Christ as being the One He claimed to be is basically a matter of faith. He must be first accepted by faith, and then we can grow in Him.

Lesson Introduction

The gospel of Mark provides the selected texts on which the first eight lessons of this quarter are based. This Gospel was written by John Mark, son of one of the Marys mentioned in the New Testament, and nephew of Barnabas. He joined Saul (Paul) and Barnabas on their first missionary journey from Antioch in Syria but left them at Perga in Pamphylia (south central Turkey). Paul refused to take him on the second journey, resulting in Barnabas taking Mark with him and Paul taking Silas with him.

Paul mentioned Mark in various writings, and the bad feeling between them was evidently modified as the years went by. Mark's Gospel may have been the first one written. It presented Jesus as the Servant of God, and it emphasized His deeds. The key verse is Mark 10:45—"The Son of man came not to be ministered unto, but to minister, and to give his life a ransom for many."

Teaching Outline

I. Appearance I: Mark 1:1-8
   A. John's arrival: 1-3
   B. John's baptism: 4-5
   C. John's clothing: 6
   D. John's message: 7-8
II. Approval: Mark 1:9-11
   A. Godhead I: 9
   B. Godhead II: 10
   C. Godhead III: 11
III. Appointment: Mark 1:12-13
   A. Pressure: 12
   B. Performance: 13
IV. Appearance II: Mark 1:14-15
   A. Galilee: 14a
   B. Gospel: 14b-15

Daily Bible Readings

Mon. Isaiah Foretells the Baptist
Mark 1:1-2
Tue. John's Work
Mark 1:3-4
Wed. John's Lifestyle
Mark 1:5-6
Thu. John's Message
Mark 1:7-8
Fri. The Baptism of Jesus
Mark 1:9-11
Sat. The Temptations of Jesus
Mark 1:12-13
Sun. Jesus Begins Preaching
Mark 1:14-15

Verse By Verse

I. Appearance I: Mark 1:1-8

A. John's arrival: 1-3
1. The beginning of the gospel of Jesus Christ, the Son of God;

Mark began his gospel by testifying that he believed Jesus to be the Son of God and here was the gospel (good news) that He brought to mankind. He sought to establish the divinity of Christ before describing His humanity throughout his gospel.

2. As it is written in the prophets, Behold, I send my messenger before thy face, which shall prepare thy way before thee.

This was an obvious reference to Malachi 3:1—"Behold, I will send my messenger, and he shall prepare the way before me: . . ." and it described the coming Messiah. The messenger, of course, was John the Baptist, the Old Testament-type prophet who ended the four centuries of prophetic silence which prevailed between the Old and New Testaments. He was a herald to announce the coming of the long-awaited Messiah.

3. The voice of one crying in the wilderness, Prepare ye the way of the Lord, make his paths straight.

This comes from Isaiah 40:3—"The voice of him that crieth in the wilderness, Prepare the way of the Lord, make straight in the desert a highway for our God." Although John literally ministered in the Judaean wilderness, this probably refers to the spiritual wilderness (or desert) which existed among the Jews of the first century of the Christian era. John came to point men to the Messiah from heaven, Who would lead all sincere believers on a straight path.

B. John's baptism: 4-5
4. John did baptize in the wilderness, and preach the baptism of repentance for the remission of sins.

Matthew 3:1 states that John preached in the wilderness of Judaea. John 1:28 states that John baptized in Bethabara beyond Jordan, which would have placed it in the province of Peraea. However, the exact location of Bethabara (or Bethany beyond Jordan) is uncertain, and the general area was known as the wilderness of Judaea. John's location was probably somewhere near the point where the Jordan River emptied into the Dead Sea.

John's message was a simple one. He said that people ought to repent of their sins and seek to have them remitted (sent away) from them. His baptism was actually a Jewish purification rite. It was not the same as Christian baptism which came later. The baptism of John represented repentance. The baptism in Christ's name represented repentance and regeneration by the Holy Spirit. John was merely preparing the way for the coming of the Messiah Who would baptize people with the Holy Ghost (vs. 8)

5. And there went out unto him all the land of Judaea, and they of Jerusalem, and were all baptized of him in the river of Jordan, confessing their sins.

People from all parts of the province of Judaea, including the city of Jerusalem, went out to listen to John. Some repented of their sins and were baptized by him in the Jordan River. Matthew 3:5 tells

Matt: 3:4-5 tells us

us that people from "all the region round about Jordan" came to John This must have included people from the province of Peraea east of the Jordan River. Nothing is said about people coming to him from the provinces of Galilee or Samaria. However, the route traveled from Galilee to Jerusalem came down the east side of the Jordan River to avoid Samaria, and people from Galilee likely did hear John and submit to his baptism

C. John's clothing: 6
6. And John was clothed with camel's hair, and with a girdle of a skin about his loins; and he did eat locusts and wild honey;

John's clothing reflected his rugged individuality. He seemed to pattern himself after another rugged prophet, Elijah, who also had worn a leather belt around his waist (II Kings 1:8). Jesus called John another "Elijah" (Matt. 17:12-13). John's robe of camel's hair was simple. His diet was simple, too, for he subsisted on such food as locusts and wild honey. Locusts, beetles, and grasshoppers had been approved by God as food (Lev. 11:22). Honey was often mentioned in the Old Testament as a delicacy.

D. John's message: 7-8
7. And preached, saying, There cometh one mightier than I after me, the latchet of whose shoes I am not worthy to stoop down and unloose.

John may have been rugged and individualistic, but he was a humble man. When comparing himself to the Messiah Who was to come, he said that He would be much more powerful. John said that he was not worthy to stoop down and untie the thong of His sandal. The humility of John was stated concisely in John 3:30—"He [Messiah] must increase [in reputation], but I must decrease."

8. I indeed have baptized you with water: but he shall baptize you with the Holy Ghost.

In a comparison of his ministry with that of the coming Messiah, John said that his baptism was with water, whereas that brought by the Messiah would be with the Holy Ghost. Following the death, burial, resurrection, and ascension of Jesus, He sent the Holy Spirit to guide His disciple into all truth. (Jn. 16:13) These disciples then baptized believers into Christ, in the name of the Father and of the Son, and of the Holy Ghost (Mt. 28:19). Christian baptism with water was the culmination of the regeneration of heart which took place in each believer. Those who had experienced only the baptism of John needed to go beyond it. They became born-again believers in Christ (Acts 18:24-26; 19:1-7).

II. Approval: Mark 1:9-11

A. God the Son: 9
9. And it came to pass in those days, that Jesus came from Nazareth of Galilee, and was baptized of John in Jordan.

Jesus was thirty years of age when he came down from his home province of Galilee and asked John to baptize Him. John objected at first, but Jesus convinced him that He wanted to identify Himself with sinful humanity and go through the ritual cleansing represented by John's baptism, and John consented (Matt. 3:13-15). Jesus, central Figure in this case, was the second Member of the Godhead.

B. God the Spirit: 10
10. And straightway coming up out of the water, he saw the heavens opened, and the Spirit like a dove descending upon him:

Coming up out of the Jordan River following His baptism by John, Jesus saw the sky opened up and the Holy Spirit coming down to rest upon Him in the form of a dove. Here was the third Member of the Godhead showing His approval of the second Member.

C. Godhead III: 11
11. And there came a voice from heaven, saying, Thou art my beloved Son, in whom I am well pleased.

A powerful voice from heaven declared that Jesus was the beloved Son of God the Father, and it stated that He was well pleased with Him, Here was the first Member of the

Godhead showing His approval of the second Member.

Thus it was that the literal Jesus was approved by the invisible Spirit (in the form of a dove) and by the voice of God the Father, Who is also a Spirit (John 4:24).

III. Appointment: Mark 1:12-13

A. Pressure: 12
12. And immediately the spirit driveth him into the wilderness.

Longer accounts of the temptation of Jesus may be found in Matthew 4:1-11 and Luke 4:1-13. Those gospels say that the Spirit led Jesus into the wilderness, while Mark's gospel says that He was driven. It is likely that Jesus shrank back from forty days of contact with Satan, but the Spirit persuaded Him to go through with this testing.

B. Performance: 13
13. And he was there in the wilderness forty days tempted of Satan; and was with the wild beasts; and the angels ministered unto him.

Combining this with other gospel accounts, we know that Jesus fasted during the forty days He was tempted. We are not told if the presence of wild beasts bothered Him or comforted Him. After being tempted by Satan in the physical, mental, and spiritual realms, Jesus was cared for by angels. Hebrews 4:15 tells us that He "was in all points tempted like as we are, yet without sin." Now He was ready to go out and deal with all kinds of sinful people.

IV. Appearance II: Mark 1:14-15

A. Galilee: 14a
14a. Now after that John was put in prison, Jesus came into Galilee,...

The synoptic gospel writers (Matthew, Mark, and Luke) move Jesus directly from His temptation to His Galilean ministry. John, who wrote his gospel toward the end of the first century, added other details, such as changing water to wine at Cana, cleansing the temple at Jerusalem, talking with Nicodemus at night, touring Judaea, and ministering to Samaritans at Sychar (John 2:1—4:45).

It appears that Jesus went up to Galilee from Judaea in order to get away from Herod for awhile. Herod had imprisoned John the Baptist in the fortress of Machaerus east of the Dead Sea, and he subsequently had him beheaded there (Mark 6:17-29)

B. Gospel: 14b-15

14b. ... preaching the gospel of the kingdom of God,

Some manuscripts omit "the kingdom" here, although it is included in the next verse. Preaching of the gospel involved submission to the rule of God as King, and in this spiritual sense Jesus offered the kingdom.

15. And saying, The time is fulfilled, and the kingdom of God is at hand: repent ye, and believe the Gospel.

Jesus was apparently referring to the fact that the time of preparation for the coming of God's kingdom was now past, meaning the Old Testament period. Jesus came as His Father's Representative to call men to repentance and belief in the good news of salvation. There was a sense in which Jesus personified the kingdom, and He was at hand. Entrance into the kingdom of God would come through placing faith in Him after He died at Calvary to atone for sin.

Evangelistic Emphasis

God prepared for centuries to bring Christ into the world. He revealed through the prophet Isaiah what some of his plans were. In advance of the coming of Jesus he had John do a special mission of preparation. When Jesus was ready to begin his ministry, it could at last be said, "The time is fulfilled."

All this preparation and forethought makes me wonder if our evangelistic efforts do not deserve better planning and preparation than we usually give them. It seems incongruous that God should make so much careful preparation and we should expect to make converts out of people with almost no thought about how to approach them, teach them, and motivate them.

Would we not be wise to spend time in bonding with a person that we want to teach the gospel? Learning about his background, his interests, his family, his problems, his joys, and his life experiences would help us to be able to work with him in a sensitive way. Most of us realize that significant life changes are usually not wrought by those with whom we have only superficial contact.

Should we not spend a great deal of time in study so that we can teach in an adept and informed manner? How many people would be willing to accept spiritual guidance from one who clearly did not know much about what he was talking about?

As we teach people, could we not be patient in working with any obstacles they might have? Such an important task should not be defeated because we are in too much of a hurry to work carefully with problems.

If God thought it was important for him to prepare in order to save the souls of men, surely we need to be equally concerned about our own preparation.

Memory Selection

"There came a voice from heaven, saying, Thou art my beloved Son, in whom I am well pleased."   Mark 1:11.

In this passage we have all three persons in the Godhead affirming the identity and mission of Jesus. Jesus was getting ready to enter a difficult period. He was to be in the wilderness for forty days of fasting. He would be tempted of Satan and in danger from wild beasts. His identity would be challenged and he would be enticed to abandon his mission. He needed the special encouragement and support that he was here given.

Sometimes we do not think to encourage the strong and the competent. They have done so well so consistently that it may not occur to us that they go through periods when they need encouragement. They may experience some identity confusion or lose sight of the clear sense of mission that they once had. Even though they are strong and true people, they may need the pat on the back, the special prayer, or the word of encouragement that we can provide.

At different times we see indications that Jesus struggled to maintain a clear sense of identity and be true to his purpose. No doubt the affirmation of the Father and Holy Spirit at his baptism helped.

Weekday Problems

Franklin graduated from college with a degree in hospital administration. He accepted a job as administrator of a hospital in a small town. The hospital had few beds, few doctors, and a small nursing staff. Yet, Franklin was involved in all the important decisions about running the hospital. He had a high profile in the community and felt important.

He did his work well and after two years was offered a job as an administrative assistant in a large medical center in a nearby city. Visions of a large facility with many patients, doctors, and nurses seemed exciting to him. At that center they were doing sophisticated research, advanced surgical procedures, and they were surrounded by state of the art equipment. It sounded so exhilarating that he did not hesitate to accept the job.

Once at work on the new job he discovered that he was no longer at the center of things. Nobody consulted him on hospital decisions. His work was primarily clerical and often consisted of running errands for the senior staff of the hospital.

* Is it possible that the same person would be in a leadership role during one stage of his life and in a supportive role in another?
* What personal qualities would be necessary to handle that kind of change?
* Should Franklin try to change his attitude or change his job?

Superintendent's Sermonette

One of the great obligations of a believer is that he know Christ and make Him known to others. Salvation is dependent on having a Savior and committing oneself to Him by faith. Only one Person in the whole universe could qualify to atone for the sins of all men, and His name must be proclaimed to those who need His help. The proclamation of that name and the plan of salvation through faith in that name constitutes the gospel (good news) which God wants people to hear.

In today's text, we find four who testified about Jesus Christ as Savior. Two of them are human, and two are divine. John Mark, author of the gospel bearing his name, began by calling Jesus Christ the Son of God. John the Baptist came to prepare the way for the coming of the Lord Jesus, Who would baptize believers with the Holy (Spirit). The Holy Spirit descended on Jesus at His baptism in the form of a dove. The voice of God the Father was heard at that time saying that Jesus was His beloved Son and pleased Him. Let us add our testimony to these through our words and our lives.

This Lesson in <u>Your</u> Life

One lesson for daily living we can learn from this text is the importance of a supportive role. John the Baptist was not Christ, but he made a significant contribution to the ministry of Christ. Most of us will never be dynamic public leaders. We will not sway the masses with our eloquence, dazzle the populace with our wisdom, or snatch away the breath of an electorate with our courage. Most of us are more ordinary people.

It may be that the most important role we can play is one which enhances and assists another who is more in the spotlight. If the other has great ability and we make it possible for him to use it better and with fewer distractions, we have done a great thing.

Fulfilling this kind of role requires a willingness to serve in the background. As a stage play has a relatively small cast of characters on stage, but a large group backstage, so it often is in the Lord's work. The people who are in the spotlight and who get most of the attention and most of the credit are in the minority. For their work to be effective, there must be a staff of humble and selfless people who are willing to work hard with little commendation or gratitude. It is true that someone must do the public presentations, but for every one who does that, there must be several behind the scenes.

God considered the work of John so important that he planned it centuries in advance. It was prophesied through Isaiah. Let us be sure that when we are planning works of ministry we give adequate attention to the support staff as well as the public performers. Without the support staff, the public performers are not likely to be effective.

Also, in this text as well as the Gospel of Mark in general, we see the value of being plainspoken. Not everyone responds to the same type of presentation. John the Baptist would be too blunt for some hearers. There are many, however, who desire a no-nonsense, no-frills approach to the gospel. When they are converted they are usually strong and courageous disciples.

Note also that John was clear about the demands of the gospel. He did not sugarcoat his message or make it sound easy. True conversions do not result from convincing people of the value of an air-conditioned church building, an entertaining preacher, or a comfortable pilgrimage. John told people of the greatness of Jesus and the highness of his expectations. Undoubtedly there were some who did not respond to such a stern-sounding message. However, there were many who did respond. Those who did were sturdy converts that were of great value to the cause of Christ.

We also can infer from this passage that people are more likely to be motivated by faith than by the appearance of greed and indulgence. John wore a garment of coarse camel's hair and ate the simple wilderness food of locusts and wild honey. It was clear that he was not in the ministry for the money. That gave his message extra power.

Jesus was, in some ways, more like John than we usually think. He was not indulgent. He could endure forty days of fasting and temptation in the wilderness. He talked straight about the necessity of repentance. His personality was different from that of John, but they worked together well in the same glorious mission.

Seed Thoughts

1. What makes Mark's gospel unique?
It is the shortest and perhaps the first of the four gospels written. It presents Jesus as Servant and emphasizes His deeds.

2. How did Mark begin his gospel with a testimony to Christ?
Mark referred to Jesus Christ as the Son of God and Proclaimer of the gospel, meaning the good news of salvation.

3. How did Mark help tie the Old and New Testaments together?
He quoted from Malachi 3:1 and from Isaiah 40:3 in describing John the Baptist (Mark 1:2-3).

4. What was the baptism of John?
It was a Jewish purification rite performed on those who repented of their sins and prepared to welcome the Messiah.

5. What made Christian baptism different from John's baptism?
John's baptism was in anticipation of Christ's coming. The baptism of Christ involves not only repentance for sin but also regeneration in Christ.

(Please Turn Page)

---

1. What makes Mark's gospel unique?

2. How did Mark begin his gospel with a testimony to Christ?

3. How did Mark help tie the Old and New Testaments together?

4. What was the baptism of John?

5. What made Christian baptism different from John's baptism?

6. How was the baptism of Jesus a revealer of the Holy Trinity?

7. If Jesus had no sin, why did He request baptism by John?

8. Why did the Holy Spirit have to persuade Jesus to be tempted?

9. How did Jesus profit from being tempted by Satan?

10. Why must men repent and believe the gospel in order to enter the kingdom of God?

Seed Thoughts - Continued

It is the shortest and perhaps the first of the four gospels written. It presents Jesus as Servant and emphasizes His deeds.

Mark referred to Jesus Christ as the Son of God and Proclaimer of the gospel, meaning the good news of salvation.

He quoted from Malachi 3:1 and from Isaiah 40:3 in describing John the Baptist (Mark 1:2-3).

It was a Jewish purification rite performed on those who repented of their sins and prepared to welcome the Messiah,

John's baptism was in anticipation of Christ's coming. The baptism of Christ involves not only repentance for sin but also regeneration in Christ.

All three Persons in the Godhead (Father, Son, and Spirit) were involved in the event.

Jesus chose to identify Himself as an obedient Son; and at the same time relate himself to sinful humanity in this way (Matthew 3:15).

There must have been a natural abhorrence on Jesus' part to meet Satan, for Jesus was holy.

Jesus was tempted in all points (physical, mental, spiritual) as all persons are so that He might experience their plight.

Entrance depends on cleansing through faith in Christ's atonement at Calvary.

6. How was the baptism of Jesus a revealer of the Holy Trinity?
All three Persons in the Godhead (Father, Son, and Spirit) were involved in the event.

7. If Jesus had no sin, why did He request baptism by John?
Jesus chose to identify Himself as an obedient Son; and at the same time relate himself to sinful humanity in this way (Matthew 3:15).

8. Why did the Holy Spirit have to persuade Jesus to be tempted?
There must have been a natural abhorrence on Jesus' part to meet Satan, for Jesus was holy.

9. How did Jesus profit from being tempted by Satan?
Jesus was tempted in all points (physical, mental, spiritual) as all persons are so that He might experience their plight.

10. Why must men repent and believe the gospel in order to enter the kingdom of God?
Entrance depends on cleansing through faith in Christ's atonement at Calvary.

The Clash Of Ideas

Mark 2:23. And it came to pass, that he went through the corn fields on the sabbath day; and his disciples began, as they went, to pluck the ears of corn.
24. And the Pharisees said unto him, Behold, why do they on the sabbath that which is not lawful?
25. And he said unto them, Have ye never read what David did, when he had need, and was an hungred, he, and they that were with him?
26. How he went into the house of God in the days of Abiathar the high priest, and did eat the showbread, which is not lawful to eat but for the priests, and gave also to them which were with him?
27. And he said unto them, The sabbath was made for man, and not man for the sabbath:
28. Therefore the Son of man is Lord also of the sabbath.
Mark 3:1. And he entered again into the synagogue; and there was a man there which had a withered hand.
2. And they watched him, whether he would heal him on the sabbath day; that they might accuse him.
3. And he saith unto the man which had the withered hand, Stand forth.
4. And he saith unto them, Is it lawful to do good on the sabbath day, or to do evil? to save life, or to kill? But they held their peace.
5. And when he had looked round about on them with anger,
being grieved for the hardness of their hearts, he saith unto the man, Stretch forth thine hand. And he stretched it out: and his hand was restored whole as the other.

And the Pharisees went forth, and straightway took counsel with the Herodians against him, how they might destroy him.

MEMORY SELECTION
Mark 2:27-28
DEVOTIONAL READING
Psalm 18:20-30

BACKGROUND SCRIPTURE
Mark 2:23-3:6
PRINTED SCRIPTURE
Mark 2:23-3:6

Teacher's Target

Pharisees, Sadducees, and Herodians joined together in opposing Jesus, because they realized that He threatened their positions of privilege and their power over common people. These hypocrites were concerned about their own interest, not the welfare of those under their influence. "The common people heard Him [Jesus] gladly" (Mark 12:37), for they knew that He loved them in spite of their weaknesses and sins.

We should study the ways in which Jesus handled His critics. He refused to be intimidated by them when it came to Sabbath Day activities. He allowed His disciples to "harvest" kernels of grain, and He "worked" to heal a man with a withered hand. Declaring Himself to be "Lord of the sabbath," Jesus put the welfare of common people ahead of the restrictions proposed by religious legalists of His time.

Lesson Introduction

One of Christ's great attributes was that of compassion. It bothered Him when people were hungry or handicapped, and He took steps to help them whether it was on a Sabbath Day or some other day of the week. He was annoyed by religious legalists in Judaism who made human traditions more important than divine intentions. This became apparent in His dealing with Pharisees who condemned His disciples for plucking kernels of grain to satisfy their hunger and who stood ready to condemn Him if He healed a man on the Sabbath.

Jesus used reference to the Jewish Scriptures in dealing with the first problem. He used compassionate reason in dealing with the second problem. When He was through, the Pharisees sought out the Herodians and plotted with them to destroy Him. Thus it was that the antagonism which normally existed between the Pharisees and the Herodians was set aside in the face of a common enemy.

Teaching Outline

I. Hungers Mark 2:23-28
 A. Criticism: 23-24
 B. Comparison: 25-26
 C. Conclusion: 27-28

II. Healing: Mark 3:1-5
 A. Intention: 1-2
 B. Inquiry: 3-4
 C. Implementation: 5

III. Herodians: Mark 3:6
 A. Participants: 6a
 B. Plot: 6b

Daily Bible Readings

Mon. Picking Grain on the Sabbath
Mark 2:23
Tue. The Pharisee's Question
Mark 2:24
Wed. The Example of David
Mark 2:25-26
Thu. The Purpose of the Sabbath
Mark 2:27
Fri. The Lord of the Sabbath
Mark 2:28
Sat. The Man With the Withered Hand
Mark 3:1-3
Sun. Healing on the Sabbath
Mark 3:4-6

If people don't do the things that we expect from our experiences, we criticize. ↑

Verse By Verse

I. Hunger: Mark 2:23-28

A. Criticism: 23-24
23. And it came to pass, that he went through the corn fields on the sabbath day; and his disciples began, as they went, to pluck the ears of corn.

Jesus and His disciples were coming up from Jerusalem to Galilee and were probably approaching the city of Capernaum. As they walked along between the grain fields, they began to "harvest" grain to have something to eat, even though it was a Sabbath Day. Corn (maize) as we know it was not grown in Palestine at that time, and we should not think of the disciples as picking ears of corn. The grain was probably wheat or barley, and they were rubbing the kernels in their hands to separate the chaff from them.

24. And the Pharisees said unto him, Behold, why do they on the sabbath day that which is not lawful?

Rather than speaking directly to the disciples, the Pharisees spoke to Jesus. They did not criticize the disciples for taking the kernels of grain. They knew that this was permitted by the Mosiac law, provided those who helped themselves did not move a sickle into the grain fields (Deut. 23:25). What they complained about was the "work" involved in "threshing" the grain by rubbing the chaff off the kernels between the disciples' hands. They considered this to be an act of breaking the law by working on the Sabbath Day. They were not concerned about the hunger of the disciples. They were concerned about upholding their self-assumed role as guardians of the Mosaic law and the hundreds of interpretations and traditions which had grown up around it over the centuries.

B. Comparison: 25-26
25. And he said unto them, Have ye never read what David did, when he had need, and was an hungred, he, and them which were with him?

The historical account to which Jesus referred may be found in I Samuel 21:1-6. Jesus sarcasticaLly asked the Pharisees if they had read about this incident in David's life, He knew that they prided themselves on being scholars in studying the Jewish Scriptures, but He implied that they had missed something relevant to this case. David and his men had been hungry and in need of food, the same as Jesus' disciples were now hungry and in need of food.

26. How he went into the house of God in the days of Abiathar the high priest, and did eat the shewbread, which is not lawful to eat but for the priests, and gave also to them which were with him?

David actually had his dealings with Ahimelech, the father of Abiathar the high priest, and what Jesus meant here was that the incident happened in the <u>time</u> of Abiathar, who soon succeeded his father. David came to the house of God (tabernacle) and asked for five loaves of bread. All the priest had was hallowed bread which had been replaced by new bread after one week, He gave this to David and his men to eat.

Jesus agreed that the priest had

over

done the right thing in giving David the bread. It was clear that Jesus placed human need over religious regulation in David's case. The implication was that the "work" done by His disciples in husking the grain between their hands was permissible because it met a human need which took precedence over the law to avoid working on the Sabbath Day.

C. Conclusions 27-28
27. And he said unto them, The sabbath was made for man, and not man for the sabbath:

Jesus next went beyond the particular incident involving David and his men and the incident involving His disciples. He stated a general principle for the Pharisees to consider. It was that God created the Sabbath for man's benefit, not the other way around. The Sabbath was to serve men, not men serve the Sabbath. The Pharisees would have trouble with this concept, for they liked to use Sabbath regulations to condemn men who offended their sense of what was right or wrong to do on that day. Jesus suggested that the Sabbath law could be bent to accommodate human need, whereas the Pharisees wanted it rigidly enforced according to their own interpretation of it.

28. Therefore the Son of man is Lord also of the sabbath.

What Jesus said now must have infuriated the Pharisees. Using the Messianic title of "the Son of man," Jesus declared Himself to be "Lord of the sabbath." In other words, He claimed the right to decide what He could do on the Sabbath Day. We know that Jesus did not come to destroy the law, but to fulfill it (Matt. 5:17). His critics may have thought that He desecrated the Sabbath Day, but He did not agree with their assessment.

He saw nothing wrong in helping people or animals on the Sabbath Day, if they were in need, and He would not let the Pharisees keep Him from carrying on His ministry. If you would like further details regarding Jesus' reasoning, see Matthew 12:5-7.

II. Healing: Mark 3:1-5

A. Intention: 1-2
1. And he entered again into the synagogue; and there was a man there which had a withered hand.

It was on another Sabbath Day that Jesus entered the synagogue to teach and saw scribes and Pharisees there. Luke, the physician, took note of the fact that it was the right hand of a man there which was withered (Luke 6:6-7). Mark 3:7 suggests that the synagogue may have been the one in Capernaum. Although it was Jesus' intention to teach, we suspect that His critics were present to see if something else would happen. We might even wonder if they made sure that the man with a withered hand was there that day.

2. And they watched him, whether he would heal him on the sabbath day; that they might accuse him.

Matthew said that these men asked Jesus if He considered it lawful to heal on the Sabbath Day (Matt. 12:10). Here, again, they interpreted healing as "work" and therefore something contrary to the Mosaic law regarding the Sabbath Day. They obviously thought that they had Jesus on the horns of a dilemma. If He healed the man, they could accuse Him. If He did not heal the man, He would appear to be lacking in compassion.

The spiritual bankruptcy characterizing the scribes and Pharisees was seen in their burning desire to condemn Jesus for performing an act of mercy. They would rather do this than rejoice that a crippled man could be made whole. They were looking out for their own selfish interests, for Jesus presented a growing threat to them.

B. Inquiry: 3-4
3. And he said unto the man which had the withered hand, Stand forth.

Jesus knew what His critics were thinking. He told the man with the withered hand to stand up, and the man complied (Luke 6:8).

Jesus had some comments to make to His critics which are recorded only in Matthew 12: 11-12—"And he said unto them, What man shall there be among you, that shall have one sheep, and if it fall into a pit on the sabbath day, will he not lay hold on it, and lift it out? How much then is a man better than a sheep?"

4. And he saith unto them, Is it lawful to do good on the sabbath days, or to do evil? to save life, or to kill? But they held their peace.

Luke 6:10 says that Jesus looked around on all of them, but they made no response to His questions. Their silence could only make people wonder if they really did think it was more important to uphold their Sabbath Day regulations than it was to do good or save life on that day. No doubt most people thought that the scribes and Pharisees would do good and save life on the Sabbath Day, if their own interests were involved. They knew how selfish these proud men were.

C. Implementation: 5
5a. And when he had looked round about on them with anger, being grieved for the hardness of their hearts, he saith unto the man, Stretch forth thine hand,

Knowing what their real thoughts were, Jesus stared at them in anger for their lack of compassion. They had nothing to offer the crippled man, but Jesus commanded him to stretch forth his hand for a miracle. Note that it was grief which caused Jesus to become angry with His critics. It was love which caused Him to heal the crippled man.

5b. And he stretched it out: and his hand was restored whole as the other,

As in the performance of other miracles, Jesus' love and power operated when there was a show of faith on the part of the one needing help. It was by rising when told to rise, and by stretching forth his arm when told to do that, that the man with the withered hand was healed. Now his right hand matched his left hand.

Luke 6:11 tells us that the scribes and Pharisees were filled with madness or foolishness after this incident. They talked among themselves and tried to decide what they could do about Jesus. They were determined to gain support in their effort to do away with Him,

III. Herodians: Mark 3:6

A. Participants: 6a
6a. And the Pharisees went forth, and straightway took counsel with the Herodians against him, . . .

It was in the face of a common enemy that the Pharisees and Herodians joined forces. This was not a normal coupling, because the Pharisees prided themselves on being superpatriots to the Jewish nation, while the Herodians were followers of the collaborators with Rome led by Herod the Great.

B. Plot: 6b
6b. . . . how they might destroy him.

Here was the beginning of a plan to catch Jesus in His talk and find something for which to condemn Him to death. Supporters of this plot would increase until the time came when the general population in Jerusalem would call for His crucifixion.

Jesus described such people when He said, "Beware of false prophets which come to you in sheep's clothing, but inwardly they are ravening wolves" (Matt. 7:15). Paul referred to them when talking to the Ephesian elders—"I know this, that after my departing shall grievous wolves enter in among you, not sparing the flock" (Acts 20:29). We would do well to guard against religious legalists who intend to rip us apart.

Evangelistic Emphasis

It is extremely good news that the teachings of Jesus are people-centered rather than rule-centered. Jesus was not a rebel for rebellion's sake. In an amazingly high percentage of the stories we have about him, he was a keeper of the law, a respecter of customs, and a conformer to tradition.

Neither did he advocate an overthrow of the religion of his day. He said, "Think not that I am come to destroy the law, or the prophets: I am not come to destroy, but to fulfill." (Matthew 5:17) Those who had destructive attitudes toward Judaism did not find a spokesman in Jesus.

When, however, there was a conflict between what was lawful and what was loving, Jesus placed the higher value on what was loving. He did not hurt people in the name of legality.

This view is not to be interpreted as a disrespect for the Sabbath. It is a superior respect for meeting human need. It would be wrong for us to use this text as an excuse to be careless or indifferent about any commandment of God. All of those should be carefully obeyed in a spirit of reverence and humility.

On occasion there is likely to be a situation in which a regulation is in conflict with that which is the loving thing to do. If the conflict is unavoidable and we cannot honor both, this passage teaches that we should give preference to that which best serves people. Because this is the teaching of Christ, we can know that he will put our needs ahead of any legal technicalities.

Memory Selection

"He said unto them, The sabbath was made for man, and not man for the sabbath: therefore the Son of man is Lord also of the sabbath."
Mark 2:27,28.

There are two principles here. The first is that people are more important than rules. Laws were made to serve human needs. They were given to us for our help and guidance. They were intended to be our friends and in most cases they are. They show us the right way. They inform our values. They remind us when we go astray.

Yet they are not gods to be worshiped. They are of lesser value than the people they were given to serve. When there is a conflict between a legal guideline and a human need, the human need must take precedence.

The second principle is that Jesus has authority even over the rules. He is Lord of the sabbath. We serve a Lord, not a law. A law or a rule can sometimes help us to serve the Lord better, but we should not be confused about who our Master is. Our spiritual life is to be guided by our allegiance to Jesus, not by our conformity to a set of laws.

Many will find Christianity makes more sense than they realized when they understand this principle.

Weekday Problems

Jerry was driving on a mountainous road when he came to the crest of a long steep hill that led into a town below. To his terror he realized that his brakes had gone out. His speed accelerated as he started down the hill.

In the stress of the moment he could think of only two alternatives. One was to speed into the town striking whatever pedestrians or vehicles happened to be in his path. The other was to deliberately run into the back of the car ahead of him. It would endanger that driver but it was his best hope of avoiding more extensive damage.

Jerry had no course of action that was really safe for himself, but he calculated that his risks were smaller if he hit another vehicle traveling in the same direction he was going. He believed there was a possibility of the brakes of the leading vehicle being able to bring both cars to a stop.

* What should Jerry do?
* Have you had to make decisions that seemed to be a choice between wrongs rather than between right and wrong?
* Is purposely hitting another car ever the "right" thing to do?

Superintendent's Sermonette

It has been said that God is restless if His creatures suffer. This means that God moves to help those in need. The coming of Jesus Christ to the earth showed divine concern in action. Satan had long been active in oppressing men with various problems, and Jesus withstood him in various ways. Victories were won in spite of Satan's emissaries who, in some cases, wore the robes of religious hypocrites. The scribes and Pharisees of Jesus' time were turned back time and again by His wisdom and power.

This lesson features Jesus taking charge of the Sabbath Day which He had created for man in the first place. He defended His disciples when they used a simple method to feed themselves when hungry. He boldly restored a crippled man's hand when challenged to do so by His critics. He would not back down from entrenched religious legalism because He, too, was restless when His creatures suffered. Let us take our stand by His side, refusing to let man-made obstacles keep us from doing God's work.

This Lesson in <u>Your</u> Life

Sometimes life forces us to make practical decisions where the guidelines are not completely clear. It may be, as in our text, two guidelines are in conflict with one another. Generally the right and good thing to do was to respect the sabbath. It also is usually the right and good thing to allow those who are hungry to eat. When one right thing is in conflict with another right thing, a choice between them has to be made.

Sometimes there are positives and negatives on both sides of a decision. Suppose that a man decides that in order to be the best possible steward of his life and ability it is necessary that he go back to school and further his education. In order to do that he would have to deprive his family, not only of needed income, but also of the time and affection they need at this stage of their lives. Either choice that he makes, he will have to sacrifice something good that he believes in and wants to protect.

Sometimes there is confusion about which guideline applies to a particular set of circumstances. Suppose you are transporting a person who has a critical and urgent need for oxygen. You are convinced that it is a matter of life or death that you reach a hospital as fast as possible. In order to do that you must drive in a way that poses some dangers to yourself and to others on the road. Do you honor the principle of safe driving for the protection of life or the principle of responding to a critical human need?

Perhaps you face a situation in which there is uncertainty about the outcome when you make a decision. Suppose you require surgery to prevent the loss of your sight over a period of a few years. To have the surgery poses a small but real risk of losing your sight instantly. There is no third alternative. If you could know the outcome in advance, the decision would be easy. What should you do?

In order to make decisions like these, one must have a sense of value priorities. He must know that the great and first commandment is love. He must know that mercy is better than sacrifice. He must know that human need is more important than ceremony.

Then he must apply what he knows and believes with common sense. Jesus simply asked, "Is it lawful to do good on the sabbath day, or to do evil? to save life, or to kill?" There are some common sense rules of thumb that are clear in the Scriptures. We should be loving. We should be kind. We should be merciful. We should be forgiving. We should be generous. We do not have to have an intellectual rationale to decide to act in these ways.

The most important thing is that our hearts be right. Jesus was grieved, not because the Pharisees were making an erroneous decision, but because of the hardness of their hearts. They were more concerned about the Lord's conformity to doctrine than they were about the plight of the man with the withered hand.

A final lesson from this text is that we ought to do what is good regardless of whether onlookers are approving or not. Jesus argued with the Pharisees. He failed to convince them. He went ahead and did what was right whether they approved or not.

Seed Thoughts

1. Were the disciples of Jesus guilty of stealing kernels of grain?
No, for the Mosaic law allowed people to take a few grains to satisfy hunger in this manner (Deut. 23:25).

2. Why were the Pharisees upset at what Jesus' disciples did?
The Pharisees decided that the disciples of Jesus were "working" on the Sabbath Day by husking the grain.

3. Why is a religious legalist dangerous to other people?
He determines a course of action and then demands that all others follow it. He claims divine sanction for this.

4. Why did Jesus refer to an incident in the life of David?
He sought to show that a Jewish hero put human need ahead of ritual dogma in obtaining food for himself and his men.

5. In what way did God make the Sabbath for man, not vice versa?
God made the Sabbath to give man time for rest and worship, not to oppress him with troublesome regulations.

(Please Turn Page)

---

1. Were the disciples of Jesus guilty of stealing kernels of grain?

2. Why were the Pharisees upset at what Jesus' disciples did?

3. Why is a religious legalist dangerous to other people?

4. Why did Jesus refer to an incident in the life of David?

5. In what way did God make the Sabbath for man, not vice versa?

6. Who is Lord of the Sabbath?

7. Why was Jesus a match for the hypocrites who watched to see if He would heal the crippled man?

8. What made Jesus angry?

9. Did Jesus make enemies for the crippled man by healing him?

10. Why did the normally antagonistic Pharisees and Herodians join together to plot against Jesus?

No, for the Mosaic law allowed people to take a few grains to satisfy hunger in this manner (Deut. 23:25).

The Pharisees decided that the disciples of Jesus were "working" on the Sabbath Day by husking the grain.

He determines a course of action and then demands that all others follow it. He claims divine sanction for this.

He sought to show that a Jewish hero put human need ahead of ritual dogma in obtaining food for himself and his men.

God made the Sabbath to give man time for rest and worship, not to oppress him with troublesome regulations.

Jesus declared Himself, as the Son of man (Messiah), to be this, thus claiming to be the divine Son of God.

He knew what they were thinking. He was wiser than they were. He had the strength of moral power on His side.

The anger of Jesus grew out of the grief He felt when His critics had no compassion for the crippled man.

This man probably was targeted by the Pharisees for scorn, but he was now whole and had a new spiritual Leader.

Opposites tend to merge when faced by someone they consider a common foe.

Seed Thoughts - Continued

6. Who is Lord of the Sabbath?
Jesus declared Himself, as the Son of man (Messiah), to be this, thus claiming to be the divine Son of God.

7. Why was Jesus a match for the hypocrites who watched to see if He would heal the crippled man?
He knew what they were thinking. He was wiser than they were. He had the strength of moral power on His side.

8. What made Jesus angry?
The anger of Jesus grew out of the grief He felt when His critics had no compassion for the crippled man.

9. Did Jesus make enemies for the crippled man by healing him?
This man probably was targeted by the Pharisees for scorn, but he was now whole and had a new spiritual Leader.

10. Why did the normally antagonistic Pharisees and Herodians join together to plot against Jesus?
Opposites tend to merge when faced by someone they consider a common foe.

Without Honor In His Own Country

Mark 6:1. And he went out from thence, and came into his own country; and his disciples follow him.
2. And when the sabbath day was come, he began to teach in the synagogue: and many hearing him were astonished, saying, From whence hath this man these things? and what wisdom is this which is given unto him, that even such mighty works are wrought by his hands?
3. Is not this the carpenter, the son of Mary, the brother of James, and Joses, and of Juda, and Simon? and are not his sisters here with us? And they were offended at him.
4. But Jesus said unto them, A prophet is not without honor, but in his own country, and among his own kin, and in his own house.
5. And he could there do no mighty work, save that he laid his hands upon a few sick folk, and healed them.
6. And he marvelled because of their unbelief. And he went round about the villages, teaching.
7. And he called unto him the twelve, and began to send them forth by two and two; and gave them power over unclean spirits;
8. And commanded them that they should take nothing for their journey, save a staff only; no scrip, no bread, no money in their purse:
9. But be shod with sandals; and not put on two coats.
10. And he said unto them, In what place soever ye enter into an house, there abide till ye depart from that place.
11. And whosoever shall not receive you, nor hear you, when ye depart thence, shake off the dust under your feet for a testimony against them. Verily I say unto you, It shall be more tolerable for Sodom and Gomorrha in the day of judgment, than for that city.
12. And they went out, and preached that men should repent.
13. And they cast out many devils, and anointed with oil many that were sick, and healed them.

MEMORY SELECTION
Mark 6:4
DEVOTIONAL READING
Psalm 119:137-152
BACKGROUND SCRIPTURE
Mark 6:1-13
PRINTED SCRIPTURE
Mark 6:1-13

Teacher's Target

We have heard that familiarity sometimes breeds contempt. People cannot understand or accept the fact that someone may arise out of their group and be greater than they are. In this lesson's texts we note that Jesus was without honor in His Own hometown of Nazareth, but His disciples went out to other locations and had good results there. Help your students to realize that their declaration of Christ may be hardest among their own family members and friends. This does not mean that they should refrain from teaching them, but they will have to be ready to face resistance from them. They will also discover that their testimony may be more easily accepted away from their original surroundings. No matter where they are, they must depend on the Lord to make their teaching appealing, effective, and convincing.

Lesson Introduction

Jesus had the greatest gift to offer which any person could possibly receive. It was the truth of the gospel, the knowledge of how to be redeemed through identification with Him by faith. The end result would be everlasting life. He supported His message by judicious use of divine power in performing miracles. In spite of the wisdom by which He spoke, plus His mighty works, the people of Nazareth found it difficult to accept Him as the Messiah. They thought of Him as originating with them, rather than in heaven.

When Jesus sent His disciples out to preach, heal, and exorcise, He told them to go with a minimum of equipment, an accommodating attitude toward opposers, and a dependence on God for the wisdom and ability to minister to the needs of others. They followed His instructions, and they were successful. We need to follow their example as we go out.

Teaching Outline

I. Misunderstanding: Mark 6:1-6
  A. Rejection: 1-3
  B. Remark: 4
  C. Reaction: 5-6

II. Mission: Mark 6:7-13
  A. Commands: 7-11
  B. Compliance: 12-13

Daily Bible Readings

Mon. Teaching in the Synagogue
Mark 6:1-2
Tue. A Prophet at Home
Mark 6:3-4
Wed. Limited by Unbelief
Mark 6:5-6
Thu. Sending Out the Twelve
Mark 6:7
Fri. Take No Provisions
Mark 6:8-9
Sat. Stay Where Received
Mark 6:10-11
Sun. Preaching and Miracles
Mark 6:12-13

Verse By Verse

I. Misunderstanding: Mark 6:1-6

A. Rejection: 1-3
1. And he went out from thence, and came into his own country; and his disciples follow him.

Jesus had been ministering down on the coasts of the Sea of Galilee. It was probably from Capernaum that He and His disciples journeyed westward to His hometown of Nazareth. Born in Bethlehem of Judaea, and exiled for a time in Egypt, Jesus had spent most of His first thirty years growing up in Nazareth. He had visited there early in His public ministry and had escaped from an attempt by the people to kill him there (Luke 4:16-30). Our text evidently describes a second visit.

2a. And when the sabbath day was come, he began to teach in the synagogue: . . .

It was the custom of Jesus to enter the synagogue each Saturday (Luke 4:16). As a traveling Teacher of some repute, He was offered an opportunity to read from the Jewish Scriptures and make comments.

2b. . . . and many hearing him were astonished, saying, From whence hath this man these things? and what wisdom is this which is given unto him, that even such mighty works are wrought by his hands?

People in Nazareth were amazed at the wisdom taught by Jesus and at the miraculous works performed by His hands. They wondered what the source of His wisdom and power was. Subsequent verses make it clear that they could not accept Jesus as being greater than His supposed humble origins in their town. They were not ready to believe that He was the Messiah, the divine Son of God. The most that they might grudgingly admit was that He might be a prophet given special powers by Jehovah.

3a. Is not this the carpenter, the son of Mary, the brother of James, and Joses, and of Juda, and Simon? and are not his sisters here with us?

It was common for members of the peasant class to follow their fathers in their vocations, and Jesus evidently became a carpenter (house builder) as his legal father, Joseph, had been. The fact that Joseph is not mentioned here suggests that he had died. The people of Nazareth identified Jesus as the son of Mary, the brother (actually halfbrother) of James, Joses, Juda, and Simon, and the brother of unnamed sisters (actually half-sisters). Jesus had been given to Mary when she conceived Him as a virgin, and Joseph had not had sexual relations with her until after Jesus had been born (Luke 1:35 Matt. 1:20-25). The other children had come along after that. The half-brothers of Jesus did not believe in Him as being the Messiah during His ministry (John 7:5). James later became leader of the Jerusalem church (Acts 15.13). Juda (Jude) wrote the little book bearing his name in the New Testament.

3b. And they were offended at him.

The Amplified Bible states, "And they took offense at Him—[that is], they were repelled and hindered from acknowledging His authority and caused to stumble." They felt too close to Him to accept Him for Who He was, and, as a result, they separated themselves from Him by their unbelief.

B. Remark: 4

4. But Jesus said unto them, A prophet is not without honour, but in his own country, and among his own kin, and in his own house.

Stated positively, this would have said, "A prophet is honored in places other than his own community or among his own relatives and family." Joseph and Mary had apparently raised Jesus in such a way that the people of Nazareth did not see Him as being very special. Jesus Himself must have masked His divine power in such a way that those who saw him from day to day did not realize how special He was. It was unfortunate that this became a stumbling block to them when the time came for Him to reveal His true identity as the Christ sent from God. People in other areas were more ready to see Him for Who He really was.

C. Reaction: 5-6

5a. And he could there do no mighty work, ...

There is an important lesson to be learned from this simple statement. Jesus had all the power required for performing miracles in Nazareth, but He refused to use it for many mighty acts because of a lack of faith on the part of most of the people there. The power and love of Jesus generally had to be combined with faith for miracles to happen,

5b. ... save that he laid his hands upon a few sick folk, and healed them.

The consistency of Jesus is shown in the fact that He still healed sick people when they expressed faith in Him. These were few in number in Nazareth.

6a. And he marvelled because of their unbelief.

This should not be interpreted to mean that Jesus lacked knowledge of what the people in Nazareth were thinking when He went there, for He knew what was in all men (John 2:24-25). It probably means that, in His humanity, He was amazed at the people's unbelief, or it may have been that He found it difficult to accept their unbelief.

6b. And he went round about the villages, teaching.

Matthew 9:35 tells us, "And Jesus went about all the cities and villages, teaching in their synagogues, and preaching the gospel of the kingdom, and healing every sickness and every disease among the people." This was in marked contrast to the kind of reception He had found in His hometown,

II. Mission: Mark 6:7-13

A. Commands: 7-11

7. And he called unto him the twelve, and began to send them forth by two and two; and gave them power over unclean spirits;

Jesus had chosen twelve disciples and ordained them to do three main things—preach the gospel, heal the sick, and cast out demons. (Mark 3:14-15). Now the time had come for them to go out two by two and carry on ministries apart from Jesus for a limited period of time. This was good training for them, because the time was coming when Jesus would leave them to go up to heaven, and they would have to minister on their own. He gave them power (authority) over unclean spirits (devils, demons).

8. And commanded them that they should take nothing for their journey, save a staff only; no scrip, no bread, no money in their purse:

9. But be shod with sandals; and not put on two coats.

You might want to study Matthew 10 in connection with this text, for it records many more details regarding what Jesus told His disciples before they went out. By comparing Matthew 10:9-10, Mark 6:8-9, and Luke 9:3, we compile what the disciples were told to take and not take with them. Each one was to have a walking stick, a pair of sandals, and the clothes on his back. They were not to have provision bags, bread, money in their belts, extra shoes, or even extra tunics worn next to the skin.

The reason for traveling lightly was that Jesus expected the disciples to be given what they needed by people who benefited from their ministry. He said, "The workman is worthy of his meat [food]" (Luke 10:10). Paul later wrote, "Let him that is taught in the word [of God] communicate unto [share with] him that teacheth in all good things" (Gal, 6:6).

10. And he said unto them, In what place soever ye enter into an house, there abide till ye depart from that place.

According to Matthew 10:11-13, Jesus told His disciples to enter a community, ask who would be congenial hosts, go to greet them warmly, and bless them if they offered to lodge them. If this was not possible, they were to seek other lodging. They were to remain in the homes offered as long as they were in town.

11. And whosoever shall not receive you, nor hear you, when ye depart thence, shake off the dust under your feet for a testimony against them. Verily I say unto you, It shall be more tolerable for Sodom and Gomorrha in the day of judgement, than for that city.

Any community which refused to welcome or hear the gospel message from Jesus' representatives was to be left. The act of shaking off the dust from under their feet was to be a symbol of God's judgment as a testimony against the community. The statement about Sodom and Gomorrha in the latter part of the verse did not appear in the earliest Greek manuscripts. The Authorized Version includes it, while other versions leave it out or put it in italics or parentheses.

B. Compliance: 12-13

12. And they went out, and preached that men should repent.

Luke 9:6 says that they went throughout the villages, preaching the gospel and healing everywhere. Matthew 11:1 says that Jesus went out to teach and preach in surrounding cities, apparently on His Own. In this way, a larger number of communities heard the gospel message and the requirement for repenting of sins in order to enter the kingdom of God,

13. And they cast out many devils, and anointed with oil many that were sick, and healed them,

Two of the actions used to support the propagation of the gospel were exorcisms and physical healings. These were both done in the name of Jesus.

Healings by the disciples involved the use of anointing oil (probably olive oil). We find support for this in James 5:14—"Is any sick among you? let him call for the elders of the church; and let them pray over him, anointing him with oil in the name of the Lord." There are many groups which still practice this anointing.

Thus it was that Jesus, largely rejected in His hometown of Nazareth, continued His ministry by Himself and through the itineraries of His twelve disciples, for God blessed their efforts in other places.

Evangelistic Emphasis

We should seek also.

God does not wait passively for people to come to him. He seeks. He teaches. He encourages. He loves. He takes the initiative.

We may be like a sheep that wanders away from the flock. We are separated by our mistake, not the shepherd's. We may be hungry and thirsty, but if we had stayed with the flock we would have been provided with food and water. We may be in danger of attack by wolves, but if we had stayed with the flock we would have been protected from them. We may be matted with brambles and thorns, but if we had stayed with the flock we would have avoided them.

The shepherd does not say, "It is his own fault. He should have stayed with the flock." Rather he says, "Where is my sheep? I will go and find him." The shepherd's objective is not the placing of blame but the care of the sheep. Even if the sheep is separated by his own actions, the shepherd will go out of his way to correct the problem.

When God finds us it is for a redemptive purpose. He does not look for us to criticize or condemn, but to help and save. He sent Jesus into the world to communicate his love and lead us into a relationship with him. It was a relationship that we had broken by our sin, but he took the initiative to restore it.

Memory Selection

"A prophet is not without honor, but in his own country, and among his own kin, and in his own house."
Mark 6:4.

Everyone has to be somewhere. Everyone has a home town. The brightest and most talented people are somebody's neighbors. If Jesus were going to live in the world, he had to be a part of some community somewhere.

Realizing that we should take a more careful look at those who surround us, we are likely to find skills and goodness in our own house. Spouses, children, or parents who have exceptional insight, kindness, or artistic or musical ability are living in somebody's home. Somewhere there is the finest father in the world, and his children may not know it. The most exemplary wife may be so taken for granted that her goodness is not recognized.

Our neighborhood, our city, and our church are filled with people that we tend to take for granted. In doing so, we may be overlooking outstanding gifts to humanity.

A friend of mine recently traveled over two thousand miles to see a special doctor. I wonder if that doctor's next door neighbor knows how exceptional he is. I wonder if we have a nearby doctor who is as exceptional but we have not realized it.

Weekday Problems

Dr. Wallace practices medicine in the small town where he was reared. As a youngster he was a lively, mischievous boy. He was never in very serious trouble but often skirted the edge. He was quite unregimentable at school and had frequent minor scrapes with the law.

He had a good mind, and after he settled some, he was a good student. He did well enough in college that he was able to get into medical school. He became a good physician. He was attentive and kind.

Many of the local people remember his youth and have trouble accepting him as their doctor. As the little town has dwindled in population, the number of doctors has dropped until Dr . Wallace is the only one left .

His competence and kindness have won many over, but some still are not able to accept him. They drive over one hundred miles to the nearest city of any size to see a doctor.

* Was Dr. Wallace wise in returning to his home town ?
* If he had been the best doctor in the world, would that have changed people's attitudes much ?
* What obligation does the community have to him for staying when all other doctors left?

Superintendent's Sermonette

Christians ought to refrain from applying earthly criteria to service performed by themselves and other believers. Paul wrote, "Who art thou that judgest another man's servant? to his own master he standeth or falleth" (Rom. 14:4). Paul also wrote, "We shall all stand before the judgment seat of Christ" (Rom, 14:10). Our first lesson text shows how Jesus did His Father's will in His hometown of Nazareth, with limited results because of a lack of faith on the people's part. Our second lesson text shows how Jesus' disciples went out to do His will two by two, facing the possibility of acceptance or rejection.

Every believer should consider the value of pairing up with another believer and going out to bear witness for Christ. They, like Jesus, may find it difficult to spread the gospel close to home. They, like Jesus' disciples, may find it difficult to persuade people to accept the gospel farther from home. Success should not be measured by numbers won but by faithfulness in doing the work to which God has called us.

This Lesson in Your Life

There are probably several reasons why gifts and talents are often overlooked in one's home territory. One is that growth is gradual and appears natural rather than dramatic. A person who is unusually bright or skilled develops gradually and the community never sees any dramatic change at a given time. They adjust bit by bit to the exceptional gifts. They do not tend to be as impressed as they would be if someone entered the community with the same level of giftedness fully developed the first time they saw it.

Another reason we are little impressed with home town people is that we tend to take the familiar for granted. It is the new and different that captures our imagination. A teacher, a doctor, a minister, or a carpenter who has been doing something well over a long period of time is not a cause for much conversation. An equally talented person from a distant city might receive rave notices.

We also overlook the exceptional among us because of our tendency to stereotype. "He's just the carpenter," was what the people of Nazareth said about Jesus. The implication is that he could not be the source of remarkable insight and revelation because carpenters are not like that.

Being aware that nearby talents are often overlooked should make us pay more attention to those about us. There are blessings in our home town that we are missing because we do not expect to find them. The people that we so admire are home town people to somebody else. Perhaps some of our home town people are admired by others who live at a distance. What a shame it would be to miss seeing their true talents because they are familiar to us.

Limitations are imposed by not seeing the potential in a person or situation. Jesus was limited in what he could do by what the people were prepared to receive. Some of the mighty works that he had done in other locations could not be done in Nazareth because of the attitude of the people.

This reminds us that the Christian ministry is a two-way street. Teaching requires both a teacher and a learner. Both must be active in the process. Love requires two persons. Unless both participate, a true relationship cannot develop.

Jesus sent out the disciples two by two. Wise leaders project themselves through others. No doubt Jesus could have done better in any given locality than the disciples who represented him. Yet he could not go to all the places that they could go. He would have limited the amount of good done if he had not been able to delegate.

Finally, we learn that a teacher is not ultimately responsible for the response of his hearers. The teacher should do his best. That includes giving attention to motivation. However, even when he has taught and motivated well, his hearers still have the privilege of choice. A hearer can say "no" even to the finest of teachers. Some rejected Jesus and we can be sure that some will reject us. This cannot keep us from fulfilling our responsibility to teach and we should try to avoid allowing it to dampen our enthusiasm for teaching.

Seed Thoughts

1. How did Jesus dare go to Nazareth after being mistreated there before (Luke 4:16-30)?
Danger did not dictate His itinerary. He knew what would happen there and that His ministry would not end there.

2. Why did the people of Nazareth evaluate Jesus incorrectly?
He had grown up among them, and they could not accept Him as being greater than themselves.

3. What hindrance do we face in witnessing to people in our hometowns?
They may know so much about us that they fail to take us seriously when we invite them to change for the better.

4. Why may we find it easier to witness away from home?
People who do not know us as well as those at home may accept our witness on a more objective basis.

5. What limits the power of even God and Christ in a given situation?
God and Christ do not work where there is a lack of faith on people's part.

(Please Turn Page)

---

1. How did Jesus dare go to Nazareth after being mistreated there before (Luke 4:16-30)?

2. Why did the people of Nazareth evaluate Jesus incorrectly?

3. What hindrance do we face in witnessing to people in our hometowns?

4. Why may we find it easier to witness away from home?

5. What limits the power of even God and Christ in a given situation?

6. Why did Jesus send His disciples out two by two?

7. Why did Jesus send the disciples out with meager equipment?

8. Why did Jesus want the disciples to lodge in one house during their stay in a community?

9. Should we endure mistreatment by hostile communities as we witness?

10. What supports the gospel?

Seed Thoughts - Continued

Danger did not dictate His itinerary. He knew what would happen there and that His ministry would not end there.

He had grown up among them, and they could not accept Him as being greater than themselves.

They may know so much about us that they fail to take us seriously when we invite them to change for the better.

People who do not know us as well as those at home may accept our witness on a more objective basis.

God and Christ do not work where there is a lack of faith on people's part.

Jesus realized that individual personalities complement one another and lend mutual support to one another.

He believed that God's servants ought to be supported by those to whom they minister (Matt. 10:10).

This helped give them a sense of stability and reduced possibilities of jealousies developing among hosts.

This may be required sometimes, but casting pearls before swine has its limits (Matt. 7:6).

Good deeds, miraculous or natural, help convince people to repent.

6. Why did Jesus send His disciples out two by two?
Jesus realized that individual personalities complement one another and lend mutual support to one another.

7. Why did Jesus send the disciples out with meager equipment?
He believed that God's servants ought to be supported by those to whom they minister (Matt. 10:10).

8. Why did Jesus want the disciples to lodge in one house during their stay in a community?
This helped give them a sense of stability and reduced possibilities of jealousies developing among hosts.

9. Should we endure mistreatment by hostile communities as we witness?
This may be required sometimes, but casting pearls before swine has its limits (Matt. 7:6).

10. What supports the gospel?
Good deeds, miraculous or natural, help convince people to repent.

Restoration To Wholeness

HEALING FOR BODY & SOUL TODAY

Mark 7:24. And from thence he arose, and went into the borders of Tyre and Sidon, and entered into an house, and would have no man know it: but he could not be hid.
25. For a certain woman, whose young daughter had an unclean spirit, heard of him, and came and fell at his feet:
26. The woman was a Greek, a Syrophenician by nation; and she besought him that he would cast forth the devil out of her daughter.
27. But Jesus said unto her, Let the children first be filled: for it is not meet to take the children's bread, and to cast it unto the dogs.
28. And she answered and said unto him, Yes, Lord: yet the dogs under the table eat of the children's crumbs.
29. And he said unto her, For this saying go thy way; the devil is gone out of thy daughter.
30. And when she was come to her house, she found the devil gone out, and her daughter laid upon the bed.
31. And again, departing from the coasts of Tyre and Sidon, he came unto the sea of Galilee, through the midst of the coasts of Decapolis.
32. And they bring unto him one that was deaf, and had an impediment in his speech; and they beseech him to put his hand upon him.
33. And he took him aside from the multitude, and put his fingers into his ears, and he spit, and touched his tongue;
34. And looking up to heaven, he sighed, and saith unto him, Ephphatha, that is, Be opened.
35. And straightway his ears were opened and the string of his tongue was loosed, and he spake plain.
36. And he charged them that they should tell no man: but the more he charged them, so much the more a great deal they published it;
37. And were beyond measure astonished, saying, He hath done all things well: he maketh both the deaf to hear, and the dumb to speak.

MEMORY SELECTION
Mark 7:37
DEVOTIONAL READING
Amos 5:4-15

BACKGROUND SCRIPTURE
Mark 7:24-37
PRINTED SCRIPTURE
Mark 7:24-37

Teacher's Target

Jesus had left the borders of His home country to go to Phoenicia, perhaps to spend time teaching His close disciples. Word got out that He was there, and a Gentile woman came seeking help for her daughter. Jesus next went to the Decapolis, a region east of the Jordan River containing a league of ten Gentile cities which had some measure of autonomy under the Romans. Here, again, the word got out, and a deaf and dumb man was brought to Him for help.

Help your students us see in these two incidents the willingness of Jesus to deliver individuals from problems and restore them to wholeness, even though they were not Jews. His means were miraculous and dramatic. Our means for helping others may be more normal and subdued, but we should follow His example of concern for those needing restoration.

Lesson Introduction

The miracles performed by Jesus featured three basic ingredients—love, power, and faith. It was His love and power which had to operate, and it was the faith of victims or those close to them which caused His love and power to operate on their behalf. The Syrophoenician woman provided the faith required for the exorcism of her daughter. She also displayed deep humility in her effort to get Jesus to help.

The deaf and dumb man in the Decapolis could not hear Jesus speak, but others brought him to Jesus. The Master evidently discerned faith in this man, and He proceeded to heal him of both his hearing and speech impediments. Let us trust Christ to release His love and power in us as we put our trust in Him. Let us seek to bring others to Him so that He might do the same for them.

Teaching Outline

I. Deliverance I: Mark 7:24-30
   A. Situation: 24
   B. Syrophoenician: 25-28
   C. Solution: 29-30

II. Deliverance II: Mark 7:31-37
   A. Situation: 31-32
   B. Solution: 33-35
   C. Surprise: 36-37

Daily Bible Readings

Mon. No Privacy
Mark 7:24
Tue. A Possessed Girl
Mark 7:25-26
Wed. Even Dogs Get Crumbs
Mark 7:27-28
Thu. The Demon Cast Out
Mark 7:29-30
Fri. A Deaf Man Brought
Mark 7:31-32
Sat. Healing
Mark 7:33-35
Sun. Astonishment
Mark 7:36-37

Verse By Verse

I. Deliverance I: Mark 7:24-30

A. Situations 24
24. And from thence he arose, and went into the borders of Tyre and Sidon, and entered into an house, and would have no man know it, but he could not be hid.

Pharisees from Jerusalem had come up to Capernaum and argued with Jesus (Mark 7:1-23). He may have left there in order to get away from them. Going to a Gentile location was not difficult, for He had only to go over to neighboring Phoenicia with its two seaports of Tyre and Sidon. He entered into a house and apparently wanted to remain unnoticed there, perhaps for the purpose of teaching His disciples in quiet, but news of His arrival spread out to the area.

B. Syrophoenician: 25-28
25. For a certain woman, whose young daughter had an unclean spirit, heard of him, and came and fell at his feet:

This unnamed woman had a young daughter who was demon-possessed. She must have heard that Jesus had been able to cast demons out, and she came to Him, perhaps as a last resort. Her daughter was not with her when she came to Jesus and fell humbly at His feet in an act of supplication. The faith required in this situation had to come from her.

26. The woman was a Greek, a Syrophenician by nation; and she besought him that he would cast forth the devil out of her daughter.

Saying that the woman was a Greek meant that she was a Gentile. Born a Syrian, she lived in Phoenicia. While humbled before Jesus, she begged Him to cast the demon out of her daughter at home. She reminds us of all parents who will do anything to get the help that their children need. Desperation prompts them to humbly seek that help.

Use of the imperfect tense here reveals that the woman kept up her pleading. Matthew 15:23-25 tells us that Jesus did not answer her one word. Irritated by her persistence, Jesus' disciples asked Him to send her away. They must have wanted Him to grant her request in order to get rid of her, but He said that He had not been sent to anyone but those of the lost sheep of Israel. She kept coming to Him, however, worshiping Him and asking Him to help her.

27. But Jesus said unto her, Let the children first be filled: for it is not meet to take the children's bread, and to cast it unto the dogs.

Jesus evidently was referring to the Jews when He said that the children should first be fed. He told the woman that it was not right to take the children's bread and give it to the dogs (<u>kunarion</u>, young dogs, puppies). Jews were accustomed to calling Gentiles "dogs," meaning the tough types found in the streets, but Jesus used the diminutive to soften His remark. He was testing the Gentile woman's faith and patience.

28. And she answered and said unto him, Yes, Lord: yet the dogs under the table eat of the children's crumbs.

The woman found hope in the reference made by Jesus to the young dogs, for she realized that even they could claim crumbs dropped by clumsy children under the table. She did not see Gentiles excluded from divine blessings but next in line for them. Jesus commended her for having great faith (Matt. 15:28). Now the way was open for a positive response to her request.

C. Solution: 29-30
29. And he said unto her, For this saying go thy way; the devil is gone out of thy daughter.

Jesus appreciated the insight expressed by the woman. He told her that it was because of what she said that she could go on her way rejoicing that the demon had gone out of her daughter. Matthew 15:28 states that the girl was healed that same hour. Note that Jesus did this healing by long distance, for He had no personal contact with the girl. The mother had to keep her faith active as she left Jesus and made her way home.

30. And when she was come to her house, she found the devil gone out, and her daughter laid upon the bed.

We assume that the girl, while demon possessed, had been highly agitated and perhaps self-destructive. When her mother came home, she found her daughter in a peaceful state, resting quietly on her pallet. The demon which had tormented her was gone. Jesus had entered Satan's territory and been victorious.

This scriptural account may raise the question as to whether or not Jesus was racially prejudiced toward Gentiles. He did say that His mission was to Jews before Gentiles, but the implication was that Gentiles would also be spiritually blessed in due time. He did help the woman's daughter, and He maintained a ministry to both Jews and Gentiles who came to Him while He was on the earth, such as the Samaritans at Sychar (John 4:1-43).

II. Deliverance II: Mark 7:31-37

A. Situation: 31-32
31. And again, departing from the coasts of Tyre and Sidon, he came unto the sea of Galilee, through the midst of the coasts of Decapolis.

Jesus left the region of Tyre and went northward to the region about Sidon before He came down on the eastern side of the Sea of Galilee to the Decapolis (deka, meaning ten, and polis, meaning city). He apparently was avoiding territory ruled by Herod Antipas and going to a region inhabited by Gentiles. The Romans allowed people in the Decapolis to mint their own coins, set up their own courts, and raise their own army. Ruins reveal that the Decapolis had temples, theaters, and other buildings indicative of a high degree of foreign culture. The Decapolis was located south and east of the Sea of Galilee and on both sides of the Jordan River. It was part of an area ruled by Philip the tetrarch, who seemed hospitable toward Jesus and His disciples. **32. And they bring unto him one that was deaf, and had an impediment in his speech; and they beseech him to put his hand upon him.**

Jesus had previously cast demons out of the maniac of Gadara in the Decapolis. "And he departed, and began to publish in Decapolis how great things Jesus had done for him: and all men did marvel" (Mark 5:20). Therefore, the people of the region were ready to expect miracles from Jesus again. They brought to Him a man who was deaf, and, because of his deafness, had not learned how to speak properly. They wanted Jesus to lay His hand upon this man to heal him. They had evidently heard that this was what He did in a case of this type. It was not necessary, as we saw in the exorcism of the Syrophoenician's daughter earlier in this lesson, but Jesus complied with the people's request.

B. Solution: 33-35
33. And he took him aside from the multitude, and put his fingers into his ears, and he spit, and touched his tongue;

Seeking relief from the pressure of the surrounding multitude, Jesus drew the deaf and dumb man aside to deal with him. Since the man could not hear what He said, Jesus used visual motions to convey to him that He was going to do something about his hearing and speech. This involved putting His fingers in the man's ears and touching the man's tongue with His saliva-laden finger. These motions were probably made to develop the man's faith in Him.

34. And looking up to heaven, he sighed, and saith unto him, Ephphatha, that is, Be opened.

Jesus looked up to heaven to indicate that what He was about to do was sanctioned by His heavenly Father. He sighed, perhaps showing that He was grieved with the effects of the curse of sin on mankind, including physical handicaps. Mark had used Aramaic before and then translated it into Greek when recording Jesus' raising of the daughter of Jairus (Mark 5:41). He did this again when recording what Jesus said in healing this man.

35. And straightway his ears were opened, and the string of his tongue was loosed, and he spake plain.

Mark said that the man's healing was done straightway, meaning instantaneously. His ears were opened in the sense that their inner parts worked as they should so that the man could hear. His tongue, which had sounded as if it were tied up with string, was now normal and capable of proper speech. This double miracle made it possible for the man to take up a normal life. He was delivered from the frustration and pity which he had experienced up to this point. The thoroughness of the miracles performed on him was seen in the fact that he needed no training period to hear and speak as he should.

C. Surprise: 36-37

36a. And he charged them that they should tell no man: . . .

Jesus requested the people who witnessed the healing of the deaf and dumb man to keep it to themselves. This was probably done because Jesus did not want the news to get out and bring down His opponents upon Him again.

36b. . . . but the more he charged them, so much the more a great deal they published it;

37. And were beyond measure astonished, saying, He hath done all things well: he maketh both the deaf to hear, and the dumb to speak.

The common people of the Decapolis were unable to keep quiet about what Jesus had done. They told everyone about it, giving Jesus credit for doing an amazing thing in His healing of the deaf and dumb man.

This produced a great influx of people who sought miraculous help from Jesus. "And great multitudes came unto him, having with them those that were lame, blind, dumb, maimed, and many others, and cast them down at Jesus' feet and he healed them: insomuch that the multitude wondered, when they saw the dumb to speak, the maimed to be whole, the lame to walk, and the blind to see: and they glorified the God of Israel" (Matt. 15:30-31).

The miracles were important, for they relieved much suffering, but the most important result was that people glorified the God of Israel for these things.

Evangelistic Emphasis

Sin generates guilt and guilt erodes one's sense of self worth. This is an important principle to understand if we would be successful in our evangelistic efforts. There are many in the world who could readily be forgiven by God but who cannot receive forgiveness or trust it because of their own sense of unworthiness. The problem is not convincing them of God's ability to give forgiveness, but convincing them of their ability to receive it.

This story can be a help when we are trying to teach the gospel to someone like that. The story does not deny a person's negative feelings toward himself, but identifies with them. If they are denied, the person will not feel understood, and even the good news will not help him because he will not feel that it relates to the person he really is.

If someone says, "I am just not worthy to be a Christian" or "I am just not good enough to be a Christian," we need to hear that carefully. It is a statement to be identified with, not argued with. If we respond, "Oh! Of course, you are good enough to be a Christian," the person is likely to feel not understood and be further alienated. To us it might seem clear that everyone is "good enough" to be a Christian because everyone has the worth of being made in the image of God and of being the object of God's love. However, the guilt-ridden, estranged soul may have great difficulty seeing that.

If, on the other hand, we say, "I know how you feel. This woman felt that way too. Yet she continued to struggle in search for a blessing until she eventually found one. Let me stay with you in your struggle until you can believe that God loves you."

Memory Selection

"(They) were beyond measure astonished, saying, He hath done all things well: he maketh both the deaf to hear, and the dumb to speak."
Mark 7:37.

These people were astonished by the goodness and power of Jesus. Sometimes we get into the habit of expecting bad things to happen. Murphy's Law says, "Anything that can go wrong will go wrong." I have a friend who has developed an addendum to Murphy's Law that says that Murphy was an optimist.

We may expect our parades to get rained on, our gardens to get frostbitten, our illnesses to be serious, and our cars to break down. We have probably had enough experience in those areas to be able to support our theory.

If that is our outlook on life, then we, too, will be astonished at the goodness and power of Jesus. However, he is the one who does all things well. If we believe in him and if we expect blessings, we can be sure they will come into our lives. Naturally, if we go through life looking for and expecting troubles, we will find more than our share of them.

Weekday Problems

Paula has not had an easy life. School was difficult for her. She had trouble making friends and often felt that her teachers discriminated against her. She did not relate well to her parents. They meant well and she did also, but they were never able to establish good communications. She felt that they did not understand her.

She left home at an early age and entered an unwise and ill-fated marriage. She quickly became pregnant and her husband, just as quickly, abandoned her to have and care for a child on her own. She did not have enough education to secure a good-paying job. Child care expenses ate up a major part of what she made.

Paula's child had some unusual health problems that required expensive surgery. Somehow she managed to get help with that. However, she is yet deeply entrenched in a negative view of life. She does not expect good things to happen.

* Paula's outlook is much like that of her parents and it is likely that her child will share those views. What can be done to break this chain of negativism?

* Can you give examples of blessings that have come into lives because of a positive attitude?

Superintendent's Sermonette

The curse of sin came upon the human race when Adam and Eve were tempted and fell from innocence in the garden of Eden. Implications of the curse have been extensive, producing such evils as disease, injury, handicap, mental illness, emotional trauma, social upheaval, immorality, and spiritual decline. Jesus came to deal with these things, as well as feeding the hungry, calming storms, and casting out demons. He did this through the power of His divine authority and with the goal of relieving suffering and increasing faith in the hearts of people.

The curse of sin is still very much with us today. We may have more sophisticated ways of dealing with physical, mental, emotion, social, and spiritual problems, but none of them can compare with divine help. We ought to bring people and their problems before the Lord and seek His deliverance. If human means are feasible, then we certainly should use them, too, but all praise for help received should go to God, the Source of all restoration to wholeness.

This Lesson in Your Life

For the sake of getting into the spirit of this passage, let us put ourselves in the place of this Syrophoenician woman. First, we note that she had a problem that was beyond the scope of her resources. Her daughter had an unclean spirit. This was not something that could be handled by a trip to a doctor or counselor. Neither could taking an extra job or saving up money make things better. She went to Jesus as a last resort, an only hope.

Sometimes in life we face problems like that. Seeing a doctor, a psychologist, or a lawyer will not help. No amount of money could bring about a solution. There is pain, anxiety, and perhaps despair. We feel very vulnerable and have no place to turn.

Second, this woman was a member of an outcast race. It was extraordinary that a Greek would solicit any kind of favor or blessing from a Jew. To fall at his feet and beg for help would have been, for most people, unthinkable.

Those of us who have struggled with feelings of inferiority and unworthiness can identify with this woman. Those who are members of minority races and have experienced overt discrimination have a special sense of identity with that. We have sometimes seemed to be shut out of the major blessings and gifts of life. To be bereft of resources and without status is a double burden

Third, this woman faced an apparently unsympathetic Jesus. His first response was, "It is not meet to take the children's bread, and to cast it unto the dogs." One would expect such a rebuff to send her reeling with rejection.

Some of us can also identify with the feeling of having our prayers fall on deaf ears. We may know in our minds that God hears and answers prayers with tenderness and sympathy. Nonetheless, during periods of despondency we may feel unheard and abandoned .

Fourth, this woman persisted when it was difficult . Instead of arguing with Jesus' characterization of her and her people, she reasoned, "...yet the dogs under the table eat of the children's crumbs. "

Fortunately, many of us have had this experience also. When the night seemed long and dark, when our troubles were great and our load heavy, when we were on the verge of despair, a gift of God's love has come into our lives to make things better. Jesus responded to this appeal by using his remarkable powers to cast out the demon.

For our own lives we can learn these lessons from this text:

(1) Even when no other resource can help with a problem, God can.

(2) Let us dare to ask even when we feel unworthy of receiving a blessing.

(3) Let us not give up when the answer does not come as quickly or decisively as we hoped.

(4) Let us claim the blessings that previously had seemed too good to be true because we felt we did not deserve them.

Seed Thoughts

1. What does the inability of Jesus to hide Himself say to us?
It says that His spiritual power and goodness could not be contained. We ought to have the same said about us.

2. What made Tyre and Sidon a dangerous place in which to live?
Pagans were in control. The demon possession of the girl was but one result. Satan still oppresses Lebanon.

3. What motivated the Syrophoenician woman to seek Jesus?
As with any loving parent, she was desperate to find help for her girl. We may find opportunities to witness for Christ in parents' extremities.

4. Why did Jesus tell the woman He sought to help Jews only?
Jesus tested the woman's humility and faith, as well as her patience.

5. What convinced Jesus to help the desperate woman?
Jesus appreciated her remark implying that Gentiles would also be helped.

(Please Turn Page)

---

1. What does the inability of Jesus to hide Himself say to us?

2. What made Tyre and Sidon a dangerous place in which to live?

3. What motivated the Syrophoenician woman to seek Jesus?

4. Why did Jesus tell the woman He sought to help Jews only?

5. What convinced Jesus to help the desperate woman?

6. What was unusual about Jesus' exorcising the woman's daughter?

7. Should we sometimes avoid contact with our enemies?

8. How was the cumulative effect of ministry shown in the Decapolis?

9. Why was the healing of the deaf and dumb man a triple miracle?

10. What two things resulted from Jesus' miracles in the Decapolis?

Seed Thoughts - Continued

It says that His spiritual power and goodness could not be contained. We ought to have the same said about us.

Pagans were in control. The demon possession of the girl was but one result. Satan still oppresses Lebanon.

As with any loving parent, she was desperate to find help for her girl. We may find opportunities to witness for Christ in parents' extremities.

Jesus tested the woman's humility and faith, as well as her patience.

Jesus appreciated her remark implying that Gentiles would also be helped.

He did it from a distance, rather than going to her personally. This tested the woman's faith en route home.

Jesus ministered in two Gentiles areas, Tyre/Sidon and the Decapolis, using a roundabout route to avoid His country.

Having helped the maniac of Gadara previously, Jesus gained a hearing with the people of the Decapolis at this later time.

Not only were his hearing and speech defects remedied, but he required no training period to hear and speak well.

People were relieved of suffering from physical maladies, and they glorified the God of Israel.

6. What was unusual about Jesus' exorcising the woman's daughter?
He did it from a distance, rather than going to her personally. This tested the woman's faith en route home.

7. Should we sometimes avoid contact with our enemies?
Jesus ministered in two Gentiles areas, Tyre/Sidon and the Decapolis, using a roundabout route to avoid His country.

8. How was the cumulative effect of ministry shown in the Decapolis?
Having helped the maniac of Gadara previously, Jesus gained a hearing with the people of the Decapolis at this later time.

9. Why was the healing of the deaf and dumb man a triple miracle?
Not only were his hearing and speech defects remedied, but he required no training period to hear and speak well.

10. What two things resulted from Jesus' miracles in the Decapolis?
People were relieved of suffering from physical maladies, and they glorified the God of Israel.

The Messiah And Suffering

Mark 8:27. And Jesus went out, and his disciples, into the towns of Caesarea Philippi: and by the way he asked his disciples, saying unto them, Whom do men say that I am?
28. And they answered, John the Baptist; but some say, Elias; and others, One of the prophets.
29. And he saith unto them, But whom say ye that I am? And Peter answereth and saith unto him, Thou art the Christ.
30. And he charged them that they should tell no man of him.
31. And he began to teach them, that the Son of man must suffer many things, and be rejected of the elders, and of the chief priests, and scribes, and be killed, and after three days rise again.
32. And he spake that saying openly. And Peter took him, and began to rebuke him.
33. But when he had turned about and looked on his disciples, he rebuked Peter, saying, Get thee behind me, Satan: for thou savorest not the things that be of God, but the things that be of men.
34. And when he had called the people unto him with his disciples also, he said unto them, Whosoever will come after me, let him deny himself, and take up his cross, and follow me.
35. For whosoever will save his life shall lose it; but whosoever shall lose his life for my sake and the gospel's, the same shall save it.
36. For what shall it profit a man, if he shall gain the whole world, and lose his own soul?
37. Or what shall a man give in exchange for his soul?
38. Whosoever therefore shall be ashamed of me and of my words in this adulterous and sinful generation; of him also shall the Son of man be ashamed, when he cometh in the glory of his Father with the holy angels.
Mark 9:1. And he said unto them, Verily I say unto you, That there be some of them that stand here, which shall not taste of death, till they have seen the kingdom of God come with power.

MEMORY SELECTION
Mark 8:34
DEVOTIONAL READING
Isaiah 55:1-13

BACKGROUND SCRIPTURE
Mark 8:27-9:13
PRINTED SCRIPTURE
Mark 8:27-9:1

Teacher's Target

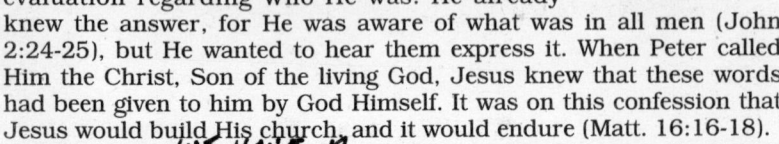

As Jesus' earthly ministry drew toward a close, He asked His disciples to give Him men's evaluation regarding Who He was. He already knew the answer, for He was aware of what was in all men (John 2:24-25), but He wanted to hear them express it. When Peter called Him the Christ, Son of the living God, Jesus knew that these words had been given to him by God Himself. It was on this confession that Jesus would build His church, and it would endure (Matt. 16:16-18).

Help your students to see their need to confess Jesus as the Son of God, to be willing to be His daily disciples, and to look forward to His second coming in glory to take them unto Himself. Peter, James, and John had a brief preview of the glorified Christ when they accompanied Him to the mount of transfiguration.

Lesson Introduction

Jesus had to suffer much in order to bring redemption to men. He mentioned this several times to His disciples, but they always sought to block it out of their thinking. Their main goal, even after His resurrection, was to see His kingdom come to earth, but God had other plans, an eternal kingdom (Acts 1:6-7 Rev. 22:5). In the meantime, during the age of grace, believers would also have to be willing to suffer for Christ's sake (Mark 8:34)

The Apostle Paul learned about this from firsthand experience (II Cor. 11:23-28). He summarized what the Christian must expect when he wrote "If we suffer [for Christ now] , we shall also reign with him [later]" (II Tim. 2:12). It is the sure hope of reigning with Christ that should help us to endure suffering in order that we might not be ashamed at His second coming (Luke 8:38).

Teaching Outline

I. Probe: Mark 8:27-30
   A. Search: 27
   B. Suggestions: 28
   C. Statement: 29-30
II. Prediction I: Mark 8:31-33
   A. Remarks: 31 -32a
   B. Rebukes: 32b-33
III. Prediction II: Mark 8:34-38
   A. Choice: 34-35
   B. Consideration: 36-37
   C. Contemplation: 38
IV. Prediction III: Mark 9:1
   A. Surviving: 1a
   B. Seeing: 1b

Daily Bible Readings

Mon. Who Do Men Think?
Mark 8:27-28
Tue. Who Do You Think?
Mark 8:29-30
Wed. Suffering Ahead
Mark 8:31-33
Thu. You Too Will Suffer
Mark 8:34-35
Fri. Faithfulness Will Be Rewarded
Mark 8:36-9:1
Sat. Transfigured
Mark 9:2-6
Sun. This is My Son
Mark 9:7-13

Verse By Verse

I. Probe: Mark 8:27-30

A. Search: 27
27a. And Jesus went out, and his disciples, into the towns of Caesarea Philippi:...

Jesus and His disciples went out from the community of Bethsaida, where He had healed a man of blindness in two stages (Mark 8:22-26). They were heading toward an area named Caesarea Philippi northeast of the Sea of Galilee. It had been named in honor of the emperor, Augustus Caesar, and of Philip, son of Herod the Great. Do not confuse this with the city of Caesarea, a Roman stronghold on the shore of the Great (Mediterranean) Sea.

27b. ...and by the way he asked his disciples, saying unto them, Whom do men say that I am?

It was evaluation time, and Jesus asked His disciples what people said about Him. He wanted to know how they identified Him.

B. Suggestions: 28
28. And they answered, John the Baptist: but some say, Elias; and others, One of the prophets.

The disciples replied that some thought Jesus was a resurrected John the Baptist, perhaps following the lead of Herod Antipas, who believed this (Matt. 14:1-2). Some thought Jesus was Elias (Elijah), who had gone to heaven without dying (II Kings 2:11) and who presumably had returned. Some thought Jesus was Jeremias (Jeremiah) (Matt. 16:14). The Apocrypha was thought by some to teach that Jeremiah would come back to restore the ark of the covenant hidden in a cave (II Maccabees 2:1-8). Some thought Jesus was one of several other prophets. These people did not identify Jesus as being Himself, nor did they think of Him as being the Son of God.

C. Statement: 29-30
29. And he saith unto them, But whom say ye that I am? And Peter answereth and saith unto him, Thou art the Christ.

Jesus was waiting for an accurate answer from His disciples. Whom did they think that He was? We do not know if Peter spoke impulsively here or as spokesman for the group after deliberate discussion, but he gave the right response. He said, "Thou art the Christ, the Son of the living God" (Matt. 16:16).

What Jesus said next was most interesting—"Blessed art thou, Simon Barjona: for flesh and blood hath not revealed it unto thee, but my Father which is in heaven. And I say also unto thee, That thou art Peter, and upon this rock I will build my church; and the gates of hell shall not prevail against it" (Matt. 16:17-18). This was a play on words. Jesus said that Peter (petros) was a little rock, and upon this rock (Petra), meaning confession of Christ as the divine Son of God, the church would be established. We ought not to think that this passage named Peter as the first pope. Remember that it was Peter who soon afterward was rebuked by Jesus as being motivated by Satan (Mark 8:33).

30. And he charged them that they should tell no man of him.

This echoes what Jesus had said following His healing of the blind man at Bethsaida—"He sent him away to his house, saying, Neither go into the town, nor tell it to any in the town" (Mark 8:26). Now Jesus told His Own disciples that they should not tell their opinion of Him to others. He evidently knew that people did not think of Him as the Messiah, the Christ, or the divine Son of God. To declare Him as such at this point would only bring unwanted trouble. There would be time later to make this truth known.

II. Prediction I: Mark 8:31-33

A. Remarks: 31-32a
31. And he began to teach them, that the Son of man must suffer many things, and be rejected of the elders, and of the chief priests, and scribes, and be killed, and after three days rise again.
32a. And he spake that saying openly.

Although the Old Testament prophecies described the coming Messiah as both suffering Servant and reigning King, the Jews got the idea that Israel was the suffering nation which would be rescued and restored to glory by the reigning Messiah. Jesus taught that He would indeed suffer, although He was the promised Messiah, before He became the reigning King. He would be rejected by the religious establishment of Judaism, composed of the elders, chief priests, and scribes (scholars). They would have Him killed, but after three days He would rise again. He talked about these things so much that Peter finally decided to take action.

B. Rebukes: 32b-33
32b. And Peter took him, and began to rebuke him.

Peter obviously did not like the negative statements Jesus was making. He loved Jesus and did not want Him to predict such dire things as suffering and death for Himself. He dared to rebuke the Master, perhaps in an attempt to show that he and the other disciples hoped to protect Jesus from these things.
33. But when he had turned about and looked on his disciples, he rebuked Peter, saying, Get thee behind me, Satan: for thou savourest not the things that be of God, but the things that be of men.

Surveying His disciples with a look which must have made them apprehensive, Jesus sternly rebuked Peter. He saw Peter at this time as the pawn of Satan. The one who had just recently spoken for God was now speaking for Satan. Peter was speaking from a human viewpoint, not from a heavenly viewpoint. Jesus could not condone this, for He came to do His Father's will regarding redemption, and that involved going all the way to the cross.

III. Prediction II: Mark 8:34-38

A. Choice: 34-35
34. And when he had called the people unto him with his disciples also, he said unto them, Whosoever will come after me, let him deny himself, and take up his cross, and follow me.

Jesus and His disciples finished their journey, and Jesus called for people to come and hear Him teach. His theme was discipleship in the broadest sense. He said that whoever wanted to follow Him must be willing to deny his own desires, take up the cross of shame and reproach associated with Him, and bear it continually.

Many people talk about having a cross to bear, but they may be speaking about some normal, human problem. The cross believers are to bear for Jesus is one of shame and reproach, as inferred by verse 38. It may have physical and emotional burdens similar to other human problems, but it is a special kind of cross to bear.

35. For whosoever will save his life shall lose it; but whosoever shall lose his life for my sake and the gospel's, the same shall save it.

The alternative to following Christ was to end up disillusioned. Anyone who sought to save his life (soul) by refusing to be associated with the despised and rejected Jesus would discover that he lost eternal life. On the other hand, anyone who was willing to lose his physical life for the sake of Christ and the gospel would discover that he had everlasting life, The choice was up to the individual.

B Consideration: 36-37
36. For what shall it profit a man, if he shall gain the whole world, and lose his own soul?
37. Or what shall a man give in exchange for his soul?

There is a shift here from the term "life" to the term "soul," that part of a person which continues on after physical life ends. Jesus asked rhetorical questions here, meaning that the answers could only be in the negative. Declarative statements would be, "A man would profit nothing from gaining the whole world and losing his own soul. There is nothing he can give in exchange for his soul." Jesus obviously meant to convey the fact that the soul is a person's most important part. It outlives this tabernacle of dust with its sensuous appetites and its tendency to crave material things. There can be no realistic exchange of material wealth for spiritual destiny. Everything an individual gains has to be left behind when he crosses over to the other side, except that "treasure" he has sent on ahead to be deposited to his account (Matt. 6: 19-21).

C. Contemplation: 38
38. Whosoever therefore shall be ashamed of me and of my words in this adulterous and sinful generation of him also shall the Son of man be ashamed, when he cometh in the glory of his Father with the holy angels.

Look at this first from the negative view. Jesus said that whoever is ashamed of Him, and who refuses to bear His cross of shame and reproach, yields to this spiritually adulterous and sinful generation. That person must expect the Son of man (Messiah) to be ashamed of him on the day that He descends in the glory of God the Father and the holy angels to take believers home to heaven.

Look at this next from the positive view. By implication, it is clear that anyone who does bear Christ's cross of shame and reproach, resists yielding to this spiritually adulterous and sinful generation. That person can expect Christ to be proud of him when He comes again for His Own.

IV. Prediction III: Mark 9:1

A. Surviving: 1a
1a. And he said unto them, Verily I say unto you, That there be some of them that stand here, which shall not taste of death, . . .

Verse 1 really belongs with chapter 8, for it concludes what was said there. Jesus said that some individuals standing with Him at that moment would by no means taste of death until something special happened to them.

B. Seeing: 1b
1b. . . . till they have seen the kingdom of God come with power.

Study this in its context. Subsequent verses describe Jesus taking Peter, James, and John up into a high mountain where He was transfigured before them. He and His clothing were suffused with heavenly radiance. We assume that this was a foretaste of the glory which will accompany Him when He comes again in the clouds.(Acts 1:11) His inner circle of disciples were allowed to see how Jesus would appear in His coming glory. They could look beyond His suffering and rejection to a brighter day.

Evangelistic Emphasis

In his book, <u>Excellence</u>, John Gardner wrote, "The best kept secret in America today is that men would rather work hard for what they really believe in than to enjoy a pampered idleness." In this day of instant gratification and easy payment plans, Gardner had an unusual insight into the attraction of being called to our best effort.

Gardner, however, was not the first to see this. Sages have long known that the deeper springs of motivation are appeals to noble efforts. We do better when called to truth, honor, courage, and love than when we are called to ease, comfort, idleness, and laziness.

Jesus always appealed for the greatest effort, not for the easiest path. John the Baptist did so also. People thronged around them to hear their words and accept their call. The religious teachers of their day who were promising an easier way did not attract such a following.

This is a basic principle of effective evangelism. It is a call to strong obedience, a willingness to suffer for Christ, and a commitment to be true to him at any cost. Such a call will not appeal to that which is lazy and indulgent in the hearts of men, but it will reach beneath it to touch deeper motivations to be good, to do right, and to serve God.

We actually do people an injustice when we assume that they would be Christians if it were easy and cheap, but would not be if it were difficult and demanding.

Memory Selection

"When he had called the people unto him with his disciples also, he said unto them, Whosoever will come after me, let him deny himself, and take up his cross, and follow me." Mark 8:34.

At the beginning of Jesus' ministry he was tempted to take the easy way out, and he was even quoted the Old Testament promise that God and his angels would not allow him to be hurt. He refused to yield to it then, determining to take the harder but truer path.

This type of temptation followed him through his ministry. Often it was his own disciples trying to protect him who counseled the easier way. Each time he insisted on being guided by the Father's will rather than his own comfort.

It was in the Garden of Gethsemane that the final resolution of this temptation came. He ardently desired to be spared the anguish and pain of the cross, but faithfully prayed, "Not my will but thine be done." To the last, he took the true path rather than the easy one.

Since he placed such a high value on this principle in his own life, it is not surprising that he called for it in his disciples. Let no one be surprised that in the following of Jesus, there will be difficult times when sacrifices must be made and burdens carried. Also no one should be surprised that those who are looking for the easy way will not follow Christ.

Weekday Problems

Dale and Henry both became Christians about the same time. Both experienced the flush of excitement about their new relationship with Christ and the sense of security it brought them.

Dale set out on a demanding regimen of prayer, study, worship, and ministry. He missed sleep, gave generous amounts of money to the church and to the poor, and worked hard on projects of Christian service.

Henry did not expect it to be that hard. He fell into a pattern of behaving like a nominal church member. He studied a little. He worshiped some but it was not a high priority. He rarely had time for Christian service because it interfered with rest and recreation.

Dale, in spite of the difficulty of his path (or perhaps because of it), had a growing sense of relationship with the Lord. His sense of inner peace and joy grew. He felt increasingly grateful to be a Christian.

Henry felt that his activities were empty and without meaning. He did not feel closer to the Lord and felt somewhat cheated because the benefits of Christianity he had expected did not materialize.

* Have you had periods both of sacrifice and of indulgence in your life? If so, how do you evaluate the spiritual blessings of each?
* Do you know people who feel cheated because they have not done enough for Christ? Do you know any who feel greatly blessed even though it has been hard for them to be Christians?

Superintendent's Sermonette

As every sincere believer knows, there is much more to salvation than being delivered from the consequences of sin and being placed on the road to heaven. There is a spiritual battle to be waged against the powers of darkness. "For we wrestle not against flesh and blood, but against principalities, against powers, against the rulers of the darkness of this world, against spiritual wickedness in high places" (Eph. 6:12), God and Christ expect a believer to be a committed disciple.

There has been a healthy development of discipleship in many evangelical churches in our time. Some larger churches even have ministers of discipleship. Converts are grounded in the Word of God and taken on to higher levels of Christian living. Mature believers are shown where their spiritual gifts lie and how to use them effectively. Each is urged to fortify himself to "endure hardness, as a good soldier of Jesus Christ" (II Tim. 2:3). Are you willing to grow into a serious, stable disciple of Jesus Christ regardless of the cost? Take up your cross, and follow Him.

This Lesson in <u>Your</u> Life

Popular opinion about Jesus was that he was an exceptional and godly teacher. People ranked him with the finest in their tradition. To be thought to be John the Baptist, Elijah, or one of the prophets was a high compliment. People recognized his goodness, his spiritual leadership, and to a great extent, the significance of his ministry. They did not compare him to ordinary rabbis or contemporary teachers. They knew he was something special.

Although they spoke highly of him, they had not perceived the fact that he was uniquely the Christ. He was the center of God's plan for the world. He was not only a teacher but was also the revelation of God and the source of an eternal relationship with God.

This situation is also a picture of the condition of many today. They speak well of Jesus. They are likely to consider themselves Christians. If asked, they would affirm a faith in him as the Christ.

The fact is, however, they respond to him as one of several commitments in their lives and not in a unique way. They are Christians in much the same way that they are business people, family members, and citizens of a certain community.

Therefore, Jesus does not have the formative influence over their lives that he needs to have. These people practice Christian behavior in the sense that they do not flagrantly violate principles of Christian conduct. Christ has about the same amount of influence over them that their job, their family and their community have. In a priority conflict or a value struggle, they evaluate their relationship with Christ along with several other values in their lives.

Many of these people feel that theirs is a high level of commitment to Christ. They take Christianity as seriously as they do their other significant commitments. They pay tribute to Christ as one of several major influences in their lives.

As this passage makes clear, the call to follow Jesus is a call to recognize him uniquely as the Christ. He has no peers, no rivals for our love and loyalty. Where others are to be treated with integrity, he is to be worshiped and adored.

To others we may fulfill responsibilities and pay debts. We may even feel love for them and be willing to make significant sacrifices on their behalf. For Jesus, however, we must be willing to deny ourselves, take up our cross and follow. We must be willing to give up all to be his disciple.

There is a singularity about Jesus that forbids that he be one of several, or even one of a few. He is the only begotten Son of God. His mission to us is unique. Our response to his call must also be unique.

When we give Jesus this kind of devotion, we enjoy a pleasant surprise. Instead of it being a problem, it is a blessing. It focuses all of our lives on that which is truly divine and allows us to fulfill our responsibilities to others in an even better way. Our families, our communities, and our jobs will benefit if our lives are ordered by a central, clear commitment to Christ.

Seed Thoughts

1. What might Caesarea Philippi represent to us today?
It was a place to get away from hostility and clamor. We may find our home, church, campground, or other place serves a similar purpose.

2. Does it matter what other people think of Jesus?
Yes, for their concept of Him determines their response to Him. Our task is to present Him truthfully.

3. What makes Jesus unique?
He was the one and only God-Man, having both divine and human natures in one Person. No other can compare to Him.

4. On what is the church built?
It is built on Christ Himself and the truth about Him being the divine Son of God, our Redeemer and King.

5. What caused Peter to commit the error of rebuking Jesus?
Peter's love for Jesus probably motivated Him to rebuke Him when He spoke of suffering and death.

(Please Turn Page)

---

1. What might Caesarea Philippi represent to us today?

2. Does it matter what other people think of Jesus?

3. What makes Jesus unique?

4. On what is the church built?

5. What caused Peter to commit the error of rebuking Jesus?

6. Does Satan exploit a believer's vulnerability?

7. Did any good come out of the suffering and rejection of Jesus?

8. What is the cross that Jesus expects believers to bear?

9. What will believers avoid by bearing Christ's cross?

10. How did Jesus' inner circle see God's kingdom come in power?

Seed Thoughts - Continued

It was a place to get away from hostility and clamor. We may find our home, church, campground, or other place serves a similar purpose.

Yes, for their concept of Him determines their response to Him. Our task is to present Him truthfully.

He was the one and only God-Man, having both divine and human natures in one Person. No other can compare to Him.

It is built on Christ Himself and the truth about Him being the divine Son of God, our Redeemer and King.

Peter's love for Jesus probably motivated Him to rebuke Him when He spoke of suffering and death.

As he did in Peter's case, Satan perverts a positive emotion and uses it for his own nefarious purpose.

It brought many sons to glory and made Him the captain of their salvation (Heb. 2:9-10).

It is a special cross of shame and reproach which believers are to bear for the sake of Christ and the gospel.

He will not be ashamed of them when He comes in glory to take them up to their heavenly reward.

His kingdom became a reality on earth When the power of the Spirit was unleashed on the day of Pentecost after the resurrection of Christ (Acts 2).

6. Does Satan exploit a believer's vulnerability?
As he did in Peter's case, Satan perverts a positive emotion and uses it for his own nefarious purpose.

7. Did any good come out of the suffering and rejection of Jesus?
It brought many sons to glory and made Him the captain of their salvation (Heb. 2:9-10).

8. What is the cross that Jesus expects believers to bear?
It is a special cross of shame and reproach which believers are to bear for the sake of Christ and the gospel.

9. What will believers avoid by bearing Christ's cross?
He will not be ashamed of them when He comes in glory to take them up to their heavenly reward.

10. How did Jesus' inner circle see God's kingdom come in power?
His kingdom became a reality on earth When the power of the Spirit was unleashed on the day of Pentecost after the resurrection of Christ (Acts 2).

Love Says It All

Mark 12:28. And one of the scribes came, and having heard them reasoning together, and perceiving that he had answered them well, asked him, Which is the first commandment of all?
29. And Jesus answered him, The first of all the commandments is, Hear, O Israel; The Lord our God is one Lord:
30. And thou shalt love the Lord thy God with all thy heart, and with all thy soul, and with all thy mind, and with all thy strength: this is the first commandment.
31. And the second is like, namely this, Thou shalt love thy neighbour as thyself. There is none other commandment greater than these.
32. And the scribe said unto him, Well, Master, thou hast said the truth: for there is one God; and there is none other but he:
33. And to love him with all the heart, and with all the understanding, and with all the soul, and with all the strength, and to love his neighbour as himself, is more than all whole burnt offerings and sacrifices.
34. And when Jesus saw that he answered discreetly, he said unto him, Thou art not far from the kingdom of God. And no man after durst ask him any question.
35. And Jesus answered and said, while he taught in the temple, How say the scribes that Christ is the son of David?
36. For David himself said by the Holy Ghost, The Lord said to my Lord, Sit thou on my right hand, till I make thine enemies thy footstool
37. David therefore himself calleth him Lord; and whence is he then his son? And the common people heard him gladly.

MEMORY SELECTION
Mark 12:30-31
DEVOTIONAL READING
John 15:9-17

BACKGROUND SCRIPTURE
Deuteronomy 6:4-9;
PRINTED SCRIPTURE
Mark 12:28-37

Teacher's Target

Asking and answering questions has long been a technique used by great teachers. Socrates (469-399 B.C.) raised this to a high art in ancient Athens. Jesus used it when He ministered upon the earth. Sometimes He was asked a question and gave an answer, and sometimes He asked a question and then gave the answer. We have an example of each in the lesson text today.

Help your students to be concerned about the question asked of Jesus by a scribe, "Which is the greatest commandment?" It is important that we realize its answer is to love God and men. Help them to be concerned about the question Jesus asked the Pharisees, even though it was rhetorical, for it resulted in Jesus declaring Himself to be Lord. Love to God includes love to the Lord Jesus Christ. It is imparted love which helps us to love other people.

Lesson Introduction

Inductive study of Mark 11:27—12:34 reveals that Jesus dealt with four questions. Chief priests, scribes, and elders asked by what authority He worked. He refused to tell them, probably because of their unbelief. Pharisees and Herodians asked Him about giving tribute to Caesar, and when He said to give Caesar what was his and God what was His, they marveled. Sadducees asked which of seven sisters married to a man in succession would be his wife after the resurrection. When He said none, they gave no response.

After Jesus answered the fourth question, the one asked by the scribe regarding the greatest commandment, "no man after that durst ask him any question" (Mark 12:34). Now He was ready to ask a question designed to show that David acknowledged Him as Lord. Jesus, being divine, had divine wisdom. It was no wonder that He could handle questions.

Teaching Outline

I. Commandments:
  Mark 12: 28-31
  A. Concern: 2 8
  B. Commandment I : 29-30
  C. Commandment II: 31

II. Closenesss Mark 12: 32-34
  A. Reaction: 32-33
  B. Responses: 34

III. Comment: Mark 12: 35-37
  A. Reference: 35-37a
  B. Response: 37b

Daily Bible Readings

Mon. Love God
Deuteronomy 6:4-5
Tue. Be Constantly Reminded
Deuteronomy 6:6-9
Wed. The First Commandment
Mark 12:28-30
Thu. The Second Commandment
Mark 12:31
Fri. Understanding
Mark 12:32-33
Sat. Not Far From the Kingdom
Mark 12:34
Sun. The Son of David
Mark 12:35-37

Verse By Verse

I. Commandments: Mark 12:28-31

A. Concern: 28
28. And one of the scribes came, and having heard them reasoning together, and perceiving that he had answered them well, asked him, Which is the first commandment of all?

This man may have been a Pharisee who appreciated the way that Jesus had handled the question asked by the Sadducees regarding the resurrection (Mark 12:18-27). Pharisees believed in resurrection, while Sadducees did not (Acts 23:6-8). It appeared that the scribe was sincere in asking Jesus what He considered to be the first (greatest) commandment of all. He really wanted to hear Jesus' answer, not just lure Him into saying something for which He could be condemned.

B. Commandment I: 29-30
29. And Jesus answered him, The first of all the commandments is, Hear, O Israel; The Lord our God is one Lord:
30. And thou shalt love the Lord thy God with all thy heart, and with all thy soul, and with all thy mind, and with all thy strength: this is the first commandment.

Jesus here referred to Deuteronomy 6:4-5 in the Septuagint Version (Greek translation of Hebrew Old Testament). The first part is a creed called the Shema, "Hear, O Israel; the Lord our God is one Lord." Devout Jews repeated this daily, supporting their belief that Jehovah was the one true God. Deuteronomy 6:5 said that men were to love God with all of their heart, soul, and might. Mark 12:30 added the mind, which was descriptive of the heart in Hebrew thought. The main thing in both passages was that God deserved to be loved with all of men's capacities.

Followers of Christ need to realize that God is an objective Person Who remains constant and unchanged, regardless of men's reactions to Him. Liberal thinkers would suggest that "God" is some subjective creation of men who learn how to be kind to one another. The fact is that men cannot love one another as they should until they love God first. It is their relationship to Him, or the lack of it, which determines their relationship toward other men. Human history has proved this over and over again.

C. Commandment II: 31
31a. And the second is like, namely this, Thou shalt love thy neighbour as thyself.

Jesus quoted this from Leviticus 19:18, and He gave it the force and importance of being the second greatest commandment. By tying the two together, He showed that a person cannot hope to have one without the other. The ultimate standard for brotherly love was that a person should love another even as he loved himself. Here was an indirect way of stating the golden rule that one should treat others as he himself would like to be treated.

31b. There is none other commandment greater than these.

When Jesus spoke of loving God and loving men, He summarized what was contained in the famous Ten Commandments given to Israel at Mount Sinai fifteen centuries before

before. They are contained in Exodus 20:1-17 and repeated in Deuteronomy 5:6-21. Note that the first four deal with one's relationship to God and the last six with one's relationship to men. Love is the binding force between us and God and between us and other men. If it is lacking, disaster results.

II. Closeness: Mark 12:32-34

A. Reaction: 32-33
32. And the scribe said unto him, Well, Master, thou hast said the truth: for there is one God; and there is none other but he:

The scribe was evidently sincere when he reacted to what Jesus had said. He agreed with the proclamation of the Shema that Jehovah is one God and He stands alone as the only true, unique Deity in a world where men claimed the existence of a multitude of gods. Belief in Him had to be the starting point.

33. And to love him with all the heart, and with all the understanding, and with all the soul, and with all the strength, and to love his neighbour as himself, is more than all whole burnt offerings and sacrifices.

Jesus had said that "on these two commandments hang [depend, rest] all [things taught in] the [writings of the] law and the prophets" (Matt. 22:40). The scribe agreed, and he personally seemed to want to measure up to this kind of standard. He felt that this was superior to the current practice of breaking God's law and then seeking to make up for it by offering up sacrifices for atonement.

B. Responses: 34
34a. And when Jesus saw that he answered discreetly, he said unto him, Thou art not far from the kingdom of God.

Jesus knew the condition of the inquiring scribe's heart, and He commended him for his understanding and attitude. To say that the man had answered Jesus discreetly meant that he had answered with spiritual understanding. Therefore, this man was heading in the right direction toward the kingdom of God and would eventually reach it, if he had faith to believe and act upon God's truth. We hear no more about him, but we hope that he made a commitment to Jesus as Messiah and Savior and did not allow the faithless Pharisees to draw him back into their hypocrisy.

34b. And no man after that durst ask him any question.

It was by His adroit use of divine wisdom that Jesus dealt with the four questions asked of Him by chief priests, scribes, elders, Pharisees, Herodians, and Sadducees, ending with the sincere scribe's question. From that point on, no one dared to test Him with further questions, for they had been reduced to wonder and silence.

We may not have the degree of wisdom that Jesus had, but we can face detractors of the truth by relying on a thorough knowledge of the completed revelation of God's Holy Word. The Holy Spirit stands ready to help us as we come in conflict with the powers of evil.

III. Comment: Mark 12:35-37

A. Reference: 35-37a
35. And Jesus answered and said, while he taught in the temple, How say the scribes that Christ is the son of David?

The Pharisees were gathered together when Jesus asked them what they thought of the Christ (anointed One, Messiah). He wanted to know whose Son they thought He would be.

They replied that He would be the Son (Descendant) of David (Matt. 22:41-42). It indicated their belief in Jesus being a descendent of David as God had promised.

36. For David himself said by the Holy Ghost, The Lord said to my Lord, Sit thou on my right hand, till I make thine enemies thy footstool.

Jesus said to them, "How then doth David in spirit call him Lord, saying, . . ." (Matt. 22:43). Mark's account puts this into the declarative, but the question is implied. Jesus was referring to the Messiah as described in Psalm 110:1. David, prompted by the Holy

Spirit, said of the Messiah, "The Lord [Jehovah] said unto my Lord [Messiah], Sit thou at my right hand [in heaven], until I make thine enemies thy footstool [subjects]." Other descriptions of the Christ (Son of man, Messiah) as victorious may be found in Matthew 26:64, Acts 2:34, I Corinthians 15:24-28, Colossians 3:1, and Hebrews 12:2.

37a. David therefore himself calleth him Lord; and whence is he then his son?

The paradox raised by Jesus was simply that the Messiah appeared to be inferior to David in being his Descendant, and yet David himself referred to Him as Lord, which implied superiority. The only way to resolve it was to admit that the Messiah was the divine Son of God. That is exactly what Paul declared when he wrote," [I send greeting] concerning his His [God's] Son Jesus Christ our Lord, which was made of the seed of David according to the flesh and declared to be the Son of God with power, according to the spirit [Holy Spirit] of holiness, by the resurrection from the dead" (Rom. 1:3-4).

Matthew 22:46 tells us, "And no man was able to answer him a word, neither durst any man from that day forth ask him any more questions." The latter part is identical to or similar to Mark 12:34, although it could have been said before and after this incident.

B. Response: 37b
37b. And the common people heard him gladly.

Mark was the only gospel writer to mention this, Another way to translate it is that the multitude of people delighted in hearing Jesus reason in this way. His approach was creative and authoritative. He stood before them as the personification of the Messianic description given by David in Psalm 110:1, and the people could decide for themselves.

In contrast to Him were the scribes of that time. Mark 12:38-40 is not in our printed text, but you would do well to refer to it in concluding this lesson. Jesus told His listeners, "Beware of the scribes which love to go in long clothing, and love salutations in the marketplaces, and the chief seats in the synagogues, and the uppermost rooms at feasts: which devour widows' houses, and for a pretence make long prayers: these shall receive greater damnation [condemnation]."

It was in this manner that Jesus contrasted the sincerity of the scribe who asked Him to declare the greatest of the commandments to scribes who lived lives of hypocrisy and selfish gratification. The first scribe wanted to know the truth, and Jesus said that he was not far from the kingdom of God because of his understanding and attitude. The hypocritical scribes made an ostentatious show of their rich clothing, marketplace greetings, and top positions in synagogues and at banquets. They were accustomed to making long prayers for others to admire. However, they were foreclosing on the properties of poor widows in order to enrich themselves.

Thus it was that the very religious leaders who should have been loving and caring for the needs of people under their authority were actually hating them and reducing them to desperation and perhaps death. Jesus came to demonstrate the love of His heavenly Father toward His creatures. That love was shown in teaching, preaching, and miracles of mercy. It would culminate in the act of atonement for sin on a cross at Calvary.

Evangelistic Emphasis

Some people have been taught a caricature of Christianity, suggesting that it is a maze of rituals and regulations. They may suppose that being a Christian is like trying to figure out a puzzle or solve a mystery. Those who are most clever will be rewarded and the more obtuse among us will be punished.

Thank God, such is not the case. The essence of Christianity is really quite simple. Love God and love your neighbor. In a given situation it might be difficult to know what the loving thing is. Sometimes people want things of us that we do not think would be good for them to have. The loving response may be "no" when they would have us believe it is "yes."

Sometimes there is ambiguity so that what appears to help in one way appears to hurt in another. Sometimes we feel the call of multiple expectations. We may have responsibilities to our family, our church, and our career that are in conflict with each other. If we give enough time and attention to one, it is at the expense of another.

We should not imply that it is easy always to do the loving thing. It is the hardest thing that could be asked of us. A clear set of rules would be far easier to conform to.

Yet, while the command to love is not easy to fulfill, it is simple to understand. My responsibility to God and to all men is always to do the loving thing.

Memory Selection

"Thou shalt love the Lord thy God with all thy heart, and with all thy soul, and with all thy mind, and with all thy strength. . . . And the second is like, namely this, Thou shalt love thy neighbor as thyself. There is none other commandment greater than these." Mark 12:30,31.

The expectations of Christian living are based squarely on the nature of God. "Every good gift and every perfect gift is from above." (James 1:17). He is the fountain of all good. He gives only good. We are to be like him.

Though others may be unloving to us, they are not our behavioral models. God is. How does he relate to those who are hateful or evil? It is with goodness and love.

"But I am nice to those who are nice to me," we argue. "So is everyone else," he replies. "I am asking more."

Our response must not be an intermittent or half-hearted effort. We are to love him with all our heart, soul, mind, and strength. We are to have the same concern for the welfare of our neighbor as we have for our own welfare.

When we obey these two simple commandments, we will have our attention fully occupied, our ability fully challenged, and our wisdom sorely tested.

Weekday Problems

"I just find Christianity too confusing," Joe said. "I want to be a Christian, but I hear people talking about religious doctrines in a way that I could never get straight. I have friends in different churches who keep trying to convince me of the correctness of their views on all manner of things. If my relationship with God depends on figuring out what is right on all of those details, I am sure I will never make it.

"It is not that I am looking for something easy. I would be willing to study with great care if I could just be sure that I would come up with the right answers. I am not lazy but would be willing to work hard to be a faithful Christian if I could just know what to do. I am looking for a faith to dedicate my life to, but I haven't been able to find that which makes me confident I am doing the right thing."

* What does today's text about the first and second commandments have to say to Joe?
* Can you give examples when doing the loving thing was hard to do and was not well received by another?

Superintendent's Sermonette

There are individuals today who claim to be mind-readers or have other extrasensory abilities, but their legitimacy is questionable. Jesus truly did know how to read the minds of men (John 2:24-25). He was able to separate a sincere scribe asking Him what the greatest commandment was from others who merely sought to trap Him by their questions. Jesus gave this man a simple answer when He told him that loving God was most important, and loving men was next to it.

Jesus later referred to scribes who thought one way and acted another. He was not fooled by the disparity of their hypocritical actions. We cannot expect to deceive Him by what we think, say, and do, for He knows our hearts.

We sometimes feel faced with a dilemma. How can we claim to love the unlovely when we have a natural revulsion toward them? The only answer is that we must ask the Lord to infuse us with love to meet this type of challenge. The Holy Spirit gives this divine love (agape) to believers who entrust their spiritual development to Him (Gal. 5:22-23).

This Lesson in <u>Your</u> Life

All of the commandments can be summed up in the single commandment to love. They can be divided into two sections: to love God and to love one's neighbor. They can further be divided into sections that spell out how that love can be expressed. Of the ten commandments, the first four deal with what it means to love God. It means a singular devotion to him: "Thou shalt have no other gods before me." It means not to be diverted from his true nature by worshiping material things: "Thou shalt not make unto thee any graven image." It means holding him in reverence: "Thou shalt not take the name of the Lord thy God in vain." It means honoring him in worship: "Remember the sabbath day, to keep it holy."

The latter six commandments deal with what it means to love one's neighbor. It means honoring one's parents, respecting life, protecting the sanctity of the marriage relationship, behaving honestly in regard to another's property, being scrupulously truthful, and being content with what one has rather than covetous of what his neighbor has.

Jesus further illuminated what it means to love by urging simplicity and humility in worship, discretion in giving, and modesty in fasting. He pointed out that neighbors are those who need us and they may be enemies as well as friends. Nonetheless, the commandment is love. We must relate to all people with love.

This is because God is our father and he relates to all people with love. He makes his sun to rise on both the evil and the good and sends his rain on both the just and the unjust. He loves because it is his nature to do so, not because the recipients are deserving of it. He does not steal because he is stolen from, lie because he is lied to, or hurt another because he has been hurt.

The love about which Jesus speaks is not a weak, indulgent, undemanding sentiment. It involves the heart, soul, mind, and strength. It does that which is for the true benefit of the beloved. Sometimes that is reproving, correcting, opposing, or setting limits. There is a great difference between being greatly blessed and being totally indulged.

A child who is totally indulged is destined for a life of misery, and will, at the same time, bring misery to others. Such a child will likely become selfcentered and will go through life feeling deprived of blessings he feels he should have. At the same, time he will miss the joy and exhilaration of giving, serving, and caring for the well-being of others.

The parent who wisely loves a child will show that love by teaching the child to love and to serve. That parent will not take the easy and irresponsible path of giving in to every whim of the child.

There is no better example of this than that of Jesus. He was beloved of God and yet he was expected to be the world's greatest giver and server. God was not depriving him of blessings, but leading him in the direction in which the greatest of blessings are found.

Seed Thoughts

1. What influenced the scribe to ask Jesus a question?
The scribe was impressed with the way Jesus reasoned with His critics. The multitude liked this, too (Mark 12:37).

2. Are not Christians supposed to be tied to faith rather than to reason?
Christians should base their reasoning on divine principles, including faith, as they deal with other people.

3. Why is it good to determine the greatest commandment first?
We should always work from the most important to the least important, giving priority to our concerns.

4. What gives the first and second commandments special quality?
Love needs to permeate all that believers think, say, and do, if they hope to please God in the way they live.

5. How are the first and second commandments interrelated?
We cannot love God without loving men and vice versa. Discuss ramifications.

(Please Turn Page)

---

1. What influenced the scribe to ask Jesus a question?

2. Are not Christians supposed to be tied to faith rather than to reason?

3. Why is it good to determine the greatest commandment first?

4. What gives the first and second commandments special quality?

5. How are the first and second commandments interrelated?

6. Why did the scribe consider love better than sacrifices?

7. How can we give discreet answers to perplexing questions?

8. How can we know if a person is close to the kingdom of God?

9. How could Jesus be considered both inferior and superior to King David?

10. Do common people still hear about Christ gladly?

Seed Thoughts - Continued

The scribe was impressed with the way Jesus reasoned with His critics. The multitude liked this, too (Mark 12:37).

Christians should base their reasoning on divine principles, including faith, as they deal with other people.

We should always work from the most important to the least important, giving priority to our concerns.

Love needs to permeate all that believers think, say, and do, if they hope to please God in the way they live.

We cannot love God without loving men and vice versa. Discuss ramifications.

Love could prevent evil situations, whereas sacrifices were remedial.

We must depend on the Holy Spirit to develop our spiritual discernment, and this takes time and experience.

We can evaluate his understanding and his attitude. If truth and sincerity are evident, we can be optimistic.

Jesus was inferior only in the sense of descending from David. He was superior in the fact that He was Lord.

Many do not, but most converts come from among the common people.

6. Why did the scribe consider love better than sacrifices?
Love could prevent evil situations, whereas sacrifices were remedial.

7. How can we give discreet answers to perplexing questions?
We must depend on the Holy Spirit to develop our spiritual discernment, and this takes time and experience.

8. How can we know if a person is close to the kingdom of God?
We can evaluate his understanding and his attitude. If truth and sincerity are evident, we can be optimistic.

9. How could Jesus be considered both inferior and superior to King David?
Jesus was inferior only in the sense of descending from David. He was superior in the fact that He was Lord.

10. Do common people still hear about Christ gladly?
Many do not, but most converts come from among the common people.

The Crucified Son Of God

Mark 15:22. And they bring him unto the place Golgotha, which is, being interpreted, The place of a skull.
23. And they gave him to drink wine mingled with myrrh: but he received it not.
24. And when they had crucified him, they parted his garments, casting lots upon them, what every man should take.
25. And it was the third hour, and they crucified him.
26. And the superscription of his accusation was written over, THE KING OF THE JEWS.
27. And with him they crucify two thieves; the one on his right hand, and the other on his left.
28. And the scripture was fulfilled, which saith, And he was numbered with the transgressors.
29. And they that passed by railed on him, wagging their heads and saying, Ah, thou that destroyest the temple, and buildest it in three days,
30. Save thyself, and come down from the cross.
31. Likewise also the chief priests mocking said among themselves with the scribes, He saved others; himself he cannot save.
32. Let Christ the King of Israel descend now from the cross, that we may see and believe. And they that were crucified with him reviled him.
33. And when the sixth hour was come, there was darkness over the whole land until the ninth hour.
34. And at the ninth hour Jesus cried with a loud voice, saying, Eloi, Eloi, lama sabachthani? which is, being interpreted, My God, my God, why hast thou forsaken me?
35. And some of them that stood by, when they heard it, said, Behold, he calleth Elias.
36. And one ran and filled a sponge full of vinegar, and put it on a reed, and gave him to drink, saying, Let alone; let us see whether Elias will come to take him down.
37. And Jesus cried with a loud voice, and gave up the ghost.
38. And the veil of the temple was rent in twain from the top to the bottom.
39. And when the centurion, which stood over against him, saw that he so cried out, and gave up the ghost, he said, Truly this man was the Son of God.

MEMORY SELECTION
Mark 15:39
DEVOTIONAL READING
Isaiah 53:1-12

BACKGROUND SCRIPTURE
Mark 15:1-41
PRINTED SCRIPTURE
Mark 15:22-39

Teacher's Target

During the week prior to Easter, it is appropriate for us to remember the crucifixion of the Lord Jesus Christ. This was the focal point of human history. Everything recorded in the Old Testament and the gospels led up to it, and everything recorded concerning the church since it took place looks back to it. The physical, mental, emotional, and spiritual suffering endured by Jesus on the cross cannot be fully understood or appreciated by us, but we should do our best to see it for what it was on our behalf.

Help your students to analyze details of the crucifixion (the offering of drink, the parting of garments, the sign over His head, the thieves on either side, the mocking, the cry of despair, and the conclusion of the centurion). Help them to see beyond these temporary things to the permanency of the redemption Jesus purchased for sinners there.

Lesson Introduction

We think of the horrors which led up to the crucifixion of Jesus, and we shudder to contemplate the effect that they had on His pure, holy, and sinless soul. There was the betrayal by Judas Iscariot. There was the arrest and binding which took place at night in the garden of Gethsemane following His agonizing prayers. There were the mock trials before the high priest, the Sanhedrin, and Pilate. There were the buffetings and scoffings by the Roman soldiers. There was the exhausting journey along the way of sorrows from Jerusalem to Calvary.

The crucifixion itself was one of the most shameful and terrible of pagan executions, involving the nails, the crown of thorns, and excruciating pain. Worse than all of these things, however, was the bearing of the sins of all men of all generations on Him there as He hung in a mediating position between heaven and earth. He did it to bring "many sons unto glory" (Heb. 2:10).

Teaching Outline

I. Crucifixion: Mark 15: 22-28
  A. Details: 22-26
  B. Degradation: 27-28

II. Contempt: Mark 15: 29-32
  A. Commoners: 29-30
  B. Chief priests: 31-32a
  C. Companions: 32b

III. Conclusion: Mark 15: 33-39
  A. Darkness: 33
  B. Development: 34-36
  C. Departure: 37
  D. Details: 38-39

Daily Bible Readings

Mon. The King of the Jews?
Mark 15:1-5
Tue. Which Shall I Release?
Mark 15:6-11
Wed. What About Jesus?
Mark 15:12-14
Thu. Cruelty and Crucifixion
Mark 15:15-25
Fri. Taunted on the Cross
Mark 15:26-32
Sat. Death
Mark 15:33-38
Sun. This was the Son of God
Mark 15:39-41

Verse By Verse

I. Crucifixion: Mark 15:22-28

A. Details: 22-26

22. And they bring him unto the place Golgotha, which is, being interpreted, The place of a skull.

Golgotha was the Aramaic name for a hill outside the walls of old Jerusalem. Calvary was its Latin name. We do not know if it was called the place of a skull because of many executions or because the hill had the configuration of a skull.

23. And they gave him to drink wine mingled with myrrh: but he received it not.

Jesus tasted the mixture but refused to drink it (Matt. 27:34). It appears that He did not want to feel drugged but chose to keep His senses alert for His ordeal.

24. And when they had crucified him, they parted his garments, casting lots upon them, what every man should take.

This was in fulfillment of Psalm 22:18, which predicted, "They part my garments among them, and cast lots upon my vesture." John 19:23-24 tells us that the soldiers divided Jesus' clothing into four parts. His robe was seamless, and they decided to gamble for it by casting lots and let the winner have it.

25. And it was the third hour, and they crucified him.

Mark was the only gospel writer who told us that Jesus was crucified on the cross at nine o'clock in the morning, meaning the third hour of the day by Jewish reckoning. He was to remain there for six hours. Darkness covered the land from noon (sixth hour) until three o'clock in the afternoon (ninth hour), when Jesus yielded up His spirit (Matt, 27:45-50).

26. And the superscription of his accusation was written over, THE KING OF THE JEWS.

John 19:19 states that Pilate wrote the title to go over Jesus' head on the cross, and it read in full "JESUS OF NAZARETH THE KING OF THE JEWS." Jewish opponents tried to get Pilate to add to it that "Jesus said, I am King of the Jews," but Pilate curtly replied, "What I have written I have written" (John 19:21-22).

B. Degradation: 27-28

27. And with him they crucify two thieves; the one on his right hand, and the other on his left.

Here was the great Teacher of Israel, the Messiah, the Christ, the divine Son of God, and He was crucified between two common criminals It was shame and degradation to treat Him in this way, and yet He submitted to it. The reason is given in the next verse.

28. And the scripture was fulfilled, which saith, And he was numbered with the transgressors.

This quotation from Isaiah 53:12 was omitted from some ancient manuscripts. Jesus did refer to it when talking to His disciples before His death (Luke 22:37). What happened here was a fulfillment of prophecy.

II. Contempt: Mark 15:29-32

A. Commoners: 29-30

29. And they that passed by railed on him, wagging their heads, and saying, Ah, thou that destroyest the temple, and buildest it in three days,

30. Save thyself, and come down from the cross.

This referred to what Jesus had said during the early part of His ministry when He cleansed the temple of money-changers and merchants. "Destroy this temple, and in three days I will raise it up. Then said the Jews, Forty and six years was this temple in building, and wilt thou rear it up in three days? But he spake of the temple of his body" (John 2:19-21). This meant that He planned to rise from the dead on the third day after His crucifixion. The common people who walked by the cross mocked Him by saying that He claimed to have power to build the temple in three days, but He could not bring Himself down from the cross. They were not aware of the deep love which held Jesus to that cross.

B. Chief priests: 31-32a
31. Likewise also the chief priests mocking said among themselves with the scribes, He saved others; himself he cannot save.

The sarcastic mockery begun by the common people spread to the chief priests, scribes (scholars), and elders (Matt. 27:41) These religious rulers "derided him, saying, He saved others [or so He claims to have done]; let him save himself, if he be Christ, the chosen of God" (Luke 23:35).

32a. Let Christ the King of Israel descend now from the cross, that we may see and believe.

This was a cruel and most insincere proposal flung at Jesus by the religious leaders. They did not believe Him to be the King of Israel. They did not believe that He was capable of coming down from the cross. They had no intention of believing on Him even if He did free Himself. They were worse than demons in their hypocrisy, for "devils . . . believe [In God, and no doubt in His Son], and tremble" (Jas. 2:19). These rulers of Judaism were smug in their opinion of Jesus, never realizing that some day they would have to face Him in judgment.

C. Companions: 32b
32b. And they that were crucified with him reviled him.

Both thieves scorned Jesus at first, but one of them changed. "One of the malefactors which were hanged railed on him, saying, If thou be Christ, save thyself and us. But the other answering rebuked him, saying, Dost not thou fear God, seeing thou art in the same condemnation? And we indeed justly; for we receive the due reward of our deeds: but this man hath done nothing amiss. And he said unto Jesus, Lord, remember me when thou comest into thy kingdom. And Jesus said unto him, Verily, I say unto thee, To day shalt thou be with me in paradise" (Luke 23:39-43). Here was the first example of the prediction made by Jesus in Jerusalem when He said, "I, if I be lifted up from the earth, will draw all men unto me" (John 12:32). This promise is still available to all who place their faith in Him.

III. Conclusion: Mark 15:33-39

A. Darkness: 33
33. And when the sixth hour was come, there was darkness over the whole land until the ninth hour.

The gloom which settled over the earth from noon until three o'clock in the afternoon was not a natural phenomenon occurring by coincidence. It was clearly a special manifestation of divine disapproval of what the enemies of Christ were doing at this time. Luke 23:45 tells us that "the sun was darkened [or its light failed]."

B. Development: 34-36
34. And at the ninth hour Jesus cried with a loud voice, saying, Eloi, Eloi, lama sabachthani? which is, being interpreted, My God, my God, why hast thou forsaken me?

Quoting from Psalm 22:1, Jesus cried out in despair when His heavenly Father abandoned Him temporarily. Jesus was carrying the accumulated load of sin for all men on Himself while on the cross, and God could not look upon it." [Jesus] his own self bare our sins in his own body on the tree [cross], that we, being dead to sins, should live unto righteousness" (I Pet. 2:24). It is because of what Jesus did there that we need never experience abandonment by God.

35. And some of them that stood by, when they heard it, said, Behold, he calleth Elias

People standing by the cross heard Jesus cry out. His speech was probably slurred because of His suffering, and they misunderstood what He said. They thought that He called out to Elijah This prophet had gone to heaven without dying (II Kings 2:11), and Malachi 4:5 seemed to predict that he would return to the earth. The onlookers assumed that Jesus was asking Elijah for help.

36. And one ran and filled a sponge full of vinegar, and put it on a reed, and gave him to drink, saying, Let alone; let us see whether Elias will come to take him down.

One of the bystanders filled a sponge with vinegar (sour wine), which was not a drug, and put it on the end of a reed to lift it up to Jesus to suck upon. Jesus may have accepted this in order to make what He had to say clear. The one who gave it to him suggested that the group might see Elijah come down from heaven and release Jesus. John 19:28 tells us that Jesus had said He was thirsty, prompting the man to give Him something to drink.

C. Departure: 37

37. And Jesus cried with a loud voice, and gave up the ghost.

At this time, Jesus said, "It is finished" (John 19:30). He also said, "Father, into thy hands I commend my spirit" (Luke 23:46), probably quoting from Psalm 31:5. It is important to note that Jesus died voluntarily. He had earlier said, "No man taketh it [my life] from me, but I lay it down of myself. I have power [authority] to lay it down, and I have power to take it again" (John 10:18).

D. Details: 38-39

38. And the veil of the temple was rent in twain from the top to the bottom.

The significance of the tearing of the heavy veil separating the holy place from the holy of holies in the temple is given to us in Hebrews 10:19-22—"Therefore, brethren, [we have] boldness to enter into the holiest [place, meaning the heavenly sanctuary] by the blood of Jesus, by a new and living way, which he hath consecrated for us, through the veil, that is to say, his flesh and, [we have in Him] an high priest over the house of God."

39. And when the centurion, which stood over against him, saw that he so cried out, and gave up the ghost, he said, Truly this man was the Son of God.

We should not read more into this than probably was meant The centurion, leader of a band of one hundred Roman soldiers, was in charge of the smaller detachment assigned to crucify Jesus and the two thieves. He had concluded that Jesus was a righteous (innocent) man (Luke 23:47). He and others, scared by the earthquake which took place, decided that Jesus must be "the [or a] Son of God" (Matt 27:54). This does not mean that they became committed followers of Christ, although we would hope that they did. This should be our hope for all sinners today. Let Calvary become the focal point for our lives.

Evangelistic Emphasis

It appears to me that more than any other single event, the crucifixion is the heart of the gospel. Other facts such as the virgin birth, the sinless life, the masterful teaching, the compassionate ministry, and the resurrection are all of enormous importance. Yet nothing is quite as central to evangelism as the cross.

Jesus said as much in John 12:32 "And I, if I be lifted up from the earth, will draw all men unto me." The magnetic power of the gospel is the vulnerable love of Christ. Those who could resist all doctrinal arguments will melt in the presence of the one who would lay down his life for them.

Paul also affirmed this point in I Corinthians 2:2, "I determined not to know anything among you, save Jesus Christ, and him crucified." It is neither cleverness nor oratory that wins the hearts of men. It is love.

Being loved this much is, to many, an irresistible attraction. It has an appeal both to the wise and to the simple, both to the sophisticated and to the naive, both to the famous and the unknown.

The story of the cross can be told in the simplest of terms by those who have sincere hearts but little education. Impressive vocabularies and eloquent sentence structures are not needed.

Memory Selection

"When the centurion, which stood over against him, saw that he so cried out, and gave up the ghost, he said, Truly this man was the Son of God."
Mark 15:39.

What impressed the Centurion with the divinity of Jesus was the nobility of his death. No doubt the soldier's attention had been captured by the courageous way the Lord faced death. He was calm and quiet before Pilate. He gave no answer to the false charges that were made about him. There was no whimpering at the cruel taunts and unjust accusations. He bore anguish without flinching. He was a marvel of discipline and control. He had qualities which are much admired by the military mind.

The more important factor, though, was not the bravery but the selflessness of the death. Though innocent, he died for the guilty. Though sinless, he died for the sinful. He could have come down from the cross and thereby saved himself. In doing so, however, he would not have saved others.

The willingness to give himself on behalf of others was what overwhelmed all resistance and convinced the centurion that Jesus truly was the Son of God.

Weekday Problems

Peggy and Darrell had a happy marriage. They had reared three children who are now admirable young adults with their own families. Darrell was successful in his work and highly respected by those who worked with him.

They had reached the stage of life where their income exceeded their basic requirements and were enjoying a more comfortable life style. There were travels, a nice home, a boat, and other creature comforts.

On a vacation trip to Yellowstone Park, Darrell became ill and had to be hospitalized. Though only in his mid-fifties, his condition worsened and he died while in the hospital.

Peggy, of course, was devastated. She had devoted her entire adult life to being a homemaker. Now there was no husband to make a home for and no children at home to care for. She felt forsaken and could not understand why Darrell was taken from her.

In her Bible reading she came to the crucifixion story. She read that even Jesus felt abandoned by God and cried, "My God, my God, why hast thou forsaken me?" This caused her to feel strangely comforted, knowing that Jesus could identify with her loneliness and confusion.

* Discuss why it helps us to know that Jesus reached such an extreme state of mind.
* What can Peggy do that will help her rebuild her life with Darrell gone?

Superintendent's Sermonette

Second Corinthians 5:21 sums up the crucifixion of Jesus and its effect on believers perhaps better than any other verse. Let us look at it a little at a time. "[God] hath made him [Jesus] to be sin for us." It was because God loved the world that He gave His Son to be the sin-offering which would atone for men's sins (John 3:16). "[Jesus] knew no sin." He was completely holy and without sin, and yet He identified Himself with sinful men in order to raise them to eternal life. Jesus died "that we might be made the righteousness of God in him." We have no rightteousness of our own. It has to be imparted to us by God after we have identified ourselves with Christ by faith.

This is the gospel in concise form. Have you acted upon it by giving your heart to Christ? No decision can be greater than this. If this study of the crucifixion of Christ motivates you to become a Christian, be sure to talk about it to your teacher, minister, or any other mature believer.

This Lesson in Your Life

One lesson that we can learn from this text is that it is impossible to reason with a mob. When Judas led the elders and chief priests to Jesus they were followed by a great crowd with swords and clubs. They did not go to the Garden of Gethsemane to have a conversation. It was a lynch mob. They had not bothered him while he had been teaching in the temple day after day. They found him at night, by torchlight, with the foaming frenzy of mad dogs dripping from their lips.

False charges were made, but Jesus remained silent. He knew there was no point in arguing with a mob. They spat on him and struck him. They wanted him to argue, to plead, to beg, to resist.

Another lesson we can learn from this passage is that it is impossible to avoid criticism. These people ridiculed the claims of Jesus. They accused him of saying he would destroy the temple. They taunted him to show that he was the Son of God by coming down from the cross. They accused him of promising to save others when he could not even save himself.

If one so wise and good as Jesus suffered such a barrage of criticism and judgment, why would we expect to be able to go through life unscathed? Sometimes we are so thin-skinned that we are devastated if everyone is not ecstatic about everything we say and do.

The appropriate response to criticism is to appraise it as realistically as possible, make the corrections that are indicated, and then forget it. It would be a mistake to live the rest of our lives with all the negative baggage we have collected in a lifetime.

A ~~third important~~ lesson here is that we cannot have a problem that is so great that Jesus cannot identify with it. After the taunting and ridicule came the crucifixion itself. It was a kind of death that was calculated to bring as much humiliation and pain as possible. It was a ventilation of the outrage of a barbarous society against its worst criminals. The combination of psychological assault, emotional exhaustion, and physical pain brought a man to a mental extremity that few have ever experienced.

At this point Jesus cried with despair, "My God, my God, why hast thou forsaken me?" He plunged to the absolute depth of human experience so that there will never be an occasion for you and me to take a step that he has not taken before. There will never be a pain, sorrow, fear, or anguish that he has not known.

Because he got to this point he understands when we feel despair. He understands when we are overwhelmed. He understands when we are at the end of our ropes. He understands when it seems like relief will never come. He knows our feelings though they be groanings which cannot even be put into words. We cannot go beyond the point of his understanding and care.

Seed Thoughts

1. What humbled Jesus more than any other thing?
"He became obedient unto death, even the death of the cross" (Phil 2:8).

2. How should Christians view Golgatha (Calvary)?
They should see it as the focal point of human history, with everything leading up to it and everything stemming from it.

3. How did the loss of Jesus' clothing suggest that we view the problem of materialism?
Jesus gave up all material things in order to bring spiritual blessing to all mankind. Our goal should be similar.

4. How did the title put over Jesus forecast His future title?
Pilate's designation of Him as King of the Jews has been upgraded to King of kings, and Lord of lords (Mat. 28:18; 19:16).

5. What did Jesus' crucifixion between two thieves signify?
In His death, He identified Himself with sinners, in order that He might offer them righteousness and eternal life.

(Please Turn Page)

---

1. What humbled Jesus more than any other thing?

2. How should Christians view Golgatha (Calvary)?

3. How did the loss of Jesus' clothing suggest that we view the problem of materialism?

4. How did the title put over Jesus forecast His future title?

5. What did Jesus' crucifixion between two thieves signify?

6. What did the general mockery of Jesus accomplish?

7. What would have happened if Jesus had come down from the cross as His enemies suggested in sarcasm?

8. What came out of the darkness which accompanied the crucifixion?

9. What was finished when Jesus yielded up His spirit?

10. What did the rending of the temple veil signify?

"He became obedient unto death, even the death of the cross" (Phil 2:8).

They should see it as the focal point of human history, with everything leading up to it and everything stemming from it.

Jesus gave up all material things in order to bring spiritual blessing to all mankind. Our goal should be similar.

Pilate's designation of Him as King of the Jews has been upgraded to King of kings, and Lord of lords (Mat. 28:18; 19:16).

In His death, He identified Himself with sinners, in order that He might offer them righteousness and eternal life.

It showed the depravity of all segments of society, showing that the majority can be wrong about something important.

Redemption would have been aborted, and all sinners would have been helpless and hopeless before a just God.

The light of salvation burst forth to a world lost in sin, and it still shines.

The greatest event in history was completed, Jesus' suffering and death broke the hold Satan had over sinful men.

It was a type of Christ opening up a way to God by sacrificing His flesh.

Seed Thoughts - Continued

6. What did the general mockery of Jesus accomplish?
It showed the depravity of all segments of society, showing that the majority can be wrong about something important.

7. What would have happened if Jesus had come down from the cross as His enemies suggested in sarcasm?
Redemption would have been aborted, and all sinners would have been helpless and hopeless before a just God.

8. What came out of the darkness which accompanied the crucifixion?
The light of salvation burst forth to a world lost in sin, and it still shines.

9. What was finished when Jesus yielded up His spirit?
The greatest event in history was completed, Jesus' suffering and death broke the hold Satan had over sinful men.

10. What did the rending of the temple veil signify?
It was a type of Christ opening up a way to God by sacrificing His flesh.

An Empty Tomb

Mark 15:42. And now when the even was come, because it was the preparation, that is, the day before the sabbath,

43. Joseph of Arimathea, an honorable counselor, which also waited for the kingdom of God, came, and went in boldly unto Pilate, and craved the body of Jesus.

44. And Pilate marvelled if he were already dead: and calling unto him the centurion, he asked him whether he had been any while dead.

45. And when he knew it of the centurion, he gave the body to Joseph.

46. And he bought fine linen, and took him down, and wrapped him in the linen, and laid him in a sepulchre which was hewn out of a rock, and rolled a stone unto the door of the sepulchre.

47. And Mary Magdalene and Mary the mother of Joses beheld where he was laid.

Mark 16:1. And when the sabbath was past, Mary Magdalene, and Mary the mother of James, and Salome, had bought sweet spices, that they might come and anoint him.

2. And very early in the morning the first day of the week, they came unto the sepulchre at the rising of the sun.

3. And they said among themselves, Who shall roll us away the stone from the door of the sepulchre?

4. And when they looked, they saw that the stone was rolled away: for it was very great.

5. And entering into the sepulchre, they saw a young man sitting on the right side, clothed in a long white garment; and they were affrighted.

6. And he saith unto them, Be not affrighted: Ye seek Jesus of Nazareth, which was crucified: he is risen; he is not here: behold the place where they laid him.

7. But go your way, tell his disciples and Peter that he goeth before you into Galilee: there shall ye see him, as he said unto you.

8. And they went out quickly, and fled from the sepulchre; for they trembled and were amazed: neither said they anything to any man; for they were afraid.

MEMORY SELECTION
Mark 16:6
DEVOTIONAL READING
Romans 6:1-11

BACKGROUND SCRIPTURE
Mark 15:42-16:8
PRINTED SCRIPTURE
Mark 15:42-16:8

Teacher's Target

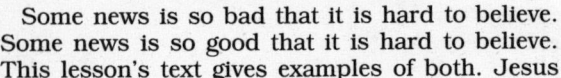

Some news is so bad that it is hard to believe. Some news is so good that it is hard to believe. This lesson's text gives examples of both. Jesus had died, and hope seemed to die with Him. John, who had been at the cross, apparently joined the other disciples in hiding. They feared for their own lives. Joseph of Arimathaea petitioned Pilate for the body of Jesus and received permission to prepare it for burial. He was joined in this by Nicodemus. Three days later, when the tomb was empty, visiting women became amazed, afraid, and silent.

Help your students to depend on God to help them cope with both bad news and good news. They need to face realities and deal with them properly, depending on God's help. Bad situations become opportunities for God's power to work. Good situations provide opportunities to praise God.

Lesson Introduction

The disciples of Jesus mourned His death and appeared to be in a state of shock. As they went into hiding, Joseph of Arimathaea and Nicodemus, secret believers, acquired the corpse and prepared it for burial in Joseph's rock-hewn sepulcher nearby. Guards were posted there. The Jewish Sabbath came and went, and on the first day of the new week women came to anoint the body. They discovered the tomb empty, and an angel announced that Jesus had risen as He promised.

Easter Sunday celebrates this great event. It was because Jesus died and rose again that we have hope of eternal life, As we look backward to that event, let us also look forward to taking the message of a living Savior to the whole world. The best way to celebrate Easter is to get people ready for His second coming!

Teaching Outline

I. Sepulcher: Mark 15:42-47
   A. Entreaty: 42-43
   B. Enquiry: 44-45
   C. Entombment: 46-47

II. Surprise: Mark 16:1-4
   A. Dawn: 1-2
   B. Discovery: 3-4

III. Statements: Mark 16:5-8
   A. Angel: 5
   B. Announcements: 6-7
   C. Amazement: 8

Daily Bible Readings

Mon. Joseph Asks for the Body
Mark 15:42-43
Tue. The Body Given to Joseph
Mark 15:44-45
Wed. Jesus Buried
Mark 15:46-47
Thu. An Early Morning Visit
Mark 16:1-2
Fri. The Stone Rolled Away
Mark 16:3-4
Sat. He is Risen
Mark 16:5-6
Sun. Go . . . Tell
Mark 16:7-8

Verse By Verse

I. Sepulcher: Mark 15:42-47

A. Entreaty: 42-43
42. And now when the even was come, because it was the preparation, that is, the day before the sabbath.
43. Joseph of Arimathaea, an honorable counselor, which also waited for the kingdom of God, came, and went in boldly unto Pilate, and craved the body of Jesus.

We know that Jesus yielded up His spirit about three o'clock in the afternoon (Mark 15:33-37). There were only a few hours before darkness, when the Jews would not allow any work to be done, for that was the beginning of the Sabbath Day. Joseph of Arimathaea was a rich and respected member of the Sanhedrin (Jewish Council), but he was also a secret believer in Jesus who waited for the coming of the kingdom of God (Matt. 27: 57; Luke 23:50-51; John 19:38). He went boldly to Pilate and asked that the body of Jesus be turned over to him for burial.

B. Enquiry: 44-45
44a. And Pilate marvelled if he were already dead: . . .

The Jews, unwilling to have their Sabbath Day desecrated by the lingering deaths of Jesus and the two thieves crucified with Him, asked Pilate to have their legs broken to hasten death. However, when the soldiers came to Jesus, they found that He had already expired and did not break His legs. In order to make sure that He was dead, one soldier pierced Jesus' side, releasing from it a mixture of blood and water (clear liquid). He unwittingly fulfilled the prophecy of Psalm 34:20 that not a bone of Him would be broken and of Zechariah 12:10 that they would look on Him Whom they had pierced (John 19:31-37). Pilate was surprised that Jesus had died as quickly as He had, not realizing that Jesus had the power to lay down His Own life (John 10:17-18).

44b. . . . and calling unto him the centurion, he asked him whether he had been any while dead.

Refusing to take the word of Joseph regarding the death of Jesus, Pilate summoned the centurion in charge of the crucifixion to confirm His death. Pilate wanted to make sure that Jesus had been dead awhile so that there would be no chance of Him appearing to be dead and then reviving.

45. And when he knew it of the centurion, he gave the body to Joseph.

We can only speculate on what motivated Pilate to let Joseph take the body of Jesus. We know that Pilate had been reluctant to condemn Jesus or order His execution. Perhaps what he did at this time was prompted by feelings of guilt and solicitude toward an innocent man.

C. Entombment: 46-47
46a. And he bought fine linen, and took him down, and wrapped him in the linen, . . .

At Jesus' birth in the stable at Bethlehem, Mary had wrapped Him in swaddling clothes (strips of cloth) (Luke 2:7). At His death, Joseph and Nicodemus wrapped Him in long strips of fine linen and a hundred-pound mixture of myrrh and aloes, according to the Jewish custom

(Luke 23:53; 24:12: John 19:39-40).

46b. . . . and laid him in a sepulchre which was hewn out of a rock, . . .

The sepulcher was in a garden near where Jesus had been crucified. No body had ever been laid in it up to this point (John 19:41). It had been newly hewn out of solid rock (Matt. 27:60). It seemed to be most secure.

46c. . . . and rolled a stone unto the door of the sepulchre.

This was probably a flat, circular slab of stone weighing hundreds of pounds and fitted into a trough along which it could be rolled to cover the opening into the rock. Joseph and Nicodemus may have had servants help them roll it, or they may have levered it over by use of a heavy bar of some kind.

47. And Mary Magdalene and Mary the mother of Joses beheld where he was laid.

There may have been more than the two Marys mentioned here who took note of where Jesus had been entombed. Luke 23:55-56 tells us that women who followed Jesus from Galilee did this. They returned to Jerusalem, fixed spices and ointments with which to anoint Him, and then rested over the Sabbath Day according to the fourth commandment.

Matthew 27:62-66 states that the chief priests and Pharisees thought that Jesus' disciples might attempt stealing His body in order to fulfill His prediction about rising from the dead on the third day. They asked Pilate to have the tomb sealed during that time to prevent this. He authorized the sealing and posting of guards at the sepulcher for this purpose.

II. Surprise: Mark 16:1-4

A. Dawns 1-2
1. And when the sabbath was past, Mary Magdalene, and Mary the mother of James, and Salome, had bought sweet spices, that they might come and anoint him.

Mary Magdalene (Mary from Magdala on the southwest shore of the Sea of Galilee) had been delivered of seven demons by Jesus (Luke 8:2). The second Mary mentioned here was apparently the mother of Joses and of James the Less (Mark 15:40, 47). Salome (feminine form of Solomon) was the mother of James and John and wife of Zebedee (Matt. 27:56). These women may have bought spiced ointments to use on Jesus' body before the Sabbath when they saw it entombed, or they may have bought them on Saturday evening after the Sabbath Day ended. Now they had come to anoint it.

2. And very early in the morning the first day of the week, they came unto the sepulchre at the rising of the sun.

The women came as dawn was breaking over the morbid scene. It was Sunday, the first day of the new week, and the day destined to become the Lord's Day for subsequent followers of Christ (Rev. 1:10).

B. Discovery: 3-4
3. And they said among themselves, Who shall roll us away the stone from the door of the sepulchre?

The fact that they were women may have caused them to feel safer than men, but they were concerned about being too weak to roll the big stone slab from the tomb opening. They need not have worried.

4. And when they looked, they saw that the stone was rolled away: for it was very great.

The women may have been walking with their heads bowed in sorrow, but when they looked up they saw that the heavy stone had already been rolled away in its trough, Matthew 28:2-4 tells us that this had been done by means of a great earthquake caused by an angel of the Lord who had come down from heaven. The guards at the tomb had been frightened into paralysis before they scurried away. Some of them reported to the chief priests in Jerusalem, who met with the elders and decided to bribe the soldiers into saying that the disciples of Jesus stole His body away while they slept (Matt. 28:11-15).

III. Statements: Mark 16:5-8

A. Angel: 5

5. And entering into the sepulchre, they saw a young man sitting on the right side, clothed in a long white garment; and they were affrighted.

Going inside the tomb, the women saw an angel on the right side who had taken on the appearance of a young man. The angel and his clothing had the shining radiance of heaven upon them (Matt. 28:3). Luke 24:4 recorded the presence of two angels. They may have spoken in unison, but it is more likely that one served as spokesman. They frightened (amazed) the women.

B. Announcements: 6-7
6. And he saith unto them, Be not affrighted: Ye seek Jesus of Nazareth, which was crucified: he is risen; he is not here: behold the place where they laid him.

The first thing to be done was to calm the women so that they might be able to absorb important messages about to be given to them. The first message had to do with the empty tomb.

The women were told that Jesus of Nazareth, who had been crucified, had risen from the dead and had left that location. The women were invited to inspect the place where they body had been laid by Joseph and Nicodemus. John 20:5-7 tells us that Peter and John, who later went to the tomb, saw the burial bands there and the napkin used to wrap the head laying folded in a place by itself.

The amazement of the women at the resurrection of Jesus could be attributed to the general practice of His followers to discount and forget His earlier predictions about rising again on the third day after His crucifixion. He had mentioned it several times (Mark 8:31; 9:31; 10:34), but they were slow to believe it.

7. But go your way, tell his disciples and Peter that he goeth before you into Galilee: there shall ye see him, as he said unto you.

The women were told to tell the eleven remaining disciples of Jesus, including the disloyal but repentant Peter, that they could see Him again by going to Galilee and meeting Him there. It was in Galilee that they and other followers would receive His great commission to evangelize the world (Matt. 28:16-20). Before that, however, Jesus would make various appearances to certain individuals and groups.

C. Amazement: 8
8. And they went out quickly, and fled from the sepulchre; for they trembled and were amazed: neither said they any thing to any man; for they were afraid.

The women fled from the tomb because they were afraid and amazed. They headed toward the disciples, not stopping to tell anyone about their tremendous discovery. Matthew 28:8 tells us that they had mixed feelings of fear and great joy as they ran.

Unfortunately, the disciples refused to believe the women's report at first and accused them of telling idle tales. Peter and John ran to the sepulcher to check it out for themselves (Luke 24:10-12; John 20: 2-10). They finally had to admit that what Jesus had predicted had come to pass.

Evangelistic Emphasis

Paul said, "If the Spirit of him that raised up Jesus from the dead dwell in you, he that raised up Christ from the dead shall also quicken your mortal bodies by his Spirit that dwelleth in you." (Romans 8:11). It is on the basis of the resurrection of Christ that our own resurrection rests. The God who spoke life into the dead body of Jesus in that Judean tomb can also speak life into our dead body in whatever final resting place it has.

That message should have a powerful evangelistic impact on anyone who has thought seriously about the prospect of his own death. Therefore, life experiences which cause people to contemplate dying become windows of opportunity for evangelism.

What life experiences bring about such awareness? No doubt, a variety of things trigger thinking about death, but some common ones can be mentioned. The death of a parent often causes people to realize that they are becoming the senior generation of the family. The death of a sibling or a friend of similar age sometimes makes people realize it could happen to them. The birth of one's own child can cause a person to realize that he who was once the baby is now the parent. He may realize in a new way the flow of ongoing generations. A particular birthday may bring an awareness of aging and the inexorable march toward death.

These are often not comfortable thoughts. The only thorough and convincing answer to them is the resurrection.

Memory Selection
"He saith unto them, Be not affrighted: Ye seek Jesus of Nazareth, which was crucified: he is risen; he is not here: behold the place where they laid him."
Mark 16:6.

The tangible evidence of the physical resurrection of Jesus is most impressive. If there were no bodily resurrection, there was no resurrection at all. The body is what is dead. The Bible is careful not to leave room for any spiritualized or rationalized explanation of the resurrection of Jesus. His physical body was brought back to life!

This was confirmed by the fact that many witnesses saw him, spoke with him, heard him speak, and ate with him. Many were those who knew him before his death and could be certain that it actually was he.

Thomas not only saw and heard, but he touched the resurrected body of Jesus. He was able to put his hand on the scarred hands of Jesus and to touch the Lord's side where it had been pierced with the sword.

In our text today, there is the testimony of the empty tomb. That which once housed a corpse became the launching pad for a victorious resurrected life. How great the news, "He is risen; he is not here."

Weekday Problems

Albert was on a fishing trip when he first noticed a sharp back pain that seemed out of proportion to anything he might have done to injure it. Tests and X-rays revealed the presence of a widespread malignancy in his body. He was a strong and candid man. That led his physician and his family to believe that he should be given full information about his condition.

When he was told that his life expectancy was no more than a few months, he began to face the prospect of his own death in a new light. Of course, he had always known he would one day die, but now there was more reality and concreteness to it.

After some serious thought and prayer, Albert began a period of putting his affairs in order and saying important things to family and friends. His words were loving and encouraging. He did more ministering to others than they did to him.

His faith of a lifetime had trusted that there would be life after death. This, too, took on a new note of meaning and reality. He lived bravely to the end, clinging to life in a positive and healthy way. When his eyes were finally closed, he was at peace and there was peace for his family.

* Discuss the connection between the resurrection of Jesus and our own resurrection.
* Is it appropriate for there to be weeping and sorrow when a Christian dies?

Superintendent's Sermonette

It is unfortunate that we sometimes wait until a person dies before we honor him. Joseph of Arimathaea and Nicodemus were secret believers in Jesus, but they maintained their positions in the religious establishment of their day. It was to their credit that they took charge of the burial of Jesus, but they should have shown allegiance to Him while He lived and ministered among them. We are not told what they did after His resurrection and after the church was established.

It is unfortunate that we sometimes wait until a divine prediction is fulfilled before we honor it and act upon it. The followers of Jesus were told by Psalm 16:10 and by Jesus Himself that He would rise from the dead. They either failed to comprehend this or chose to put it out of their heads. When He did rise from the dead, they were amazed to the point of incredulity until it was proved to them. May God help us to be open followers of Jesus and to accept and act on what He has said. The world may scorn us, but God will bless us.

This Lesson in <u>Your</u> Life

What a good man Joseph of Arimathea must have been. He was a respected member of the Sanhedrin Court. He was not a convert to Christianity but he must have known something about what a good man Jesus was. He also undoubtedly had a sense of the unfairness of the crucifixion of Jesus. Although opposition to Jesus was strong and heated among the Jewish leaders, Joseph stepped forward to ask for the body of Jesus and give it a respectful burial. This must have taken great integrity and courage. A lesser man might have lamented the injustice, but Joseph was willing to be publicly identified with it and do what he could to show honor for one who had been so shamefully treated.

In our own lives, we will do well to emulate Joseph's magnanimity. Let us stand tall for that which is right even when it is unpopular. Let us be strong for the needs of those who are weak even when it incurs the wrath of the powerful. Let us uphold the rights of minorities even in the face of clamoring majorities. Let us be like Joseph in making choices on the basis of truth and right rather than on the basis of personal safety and political expediency.

Not only did Joseph boldly claim the body but he furnished fine linen and a tomb. Many would have said, "What a shame, but it is not my responsibility." It was not particularly Joseph's responsibility either. He simply knew it was right and should be done. Therefore he did it.

The world's finest people are those who take their imperatives from the needs they see and the resources they have available. They do not wash their hands of a problem because it is not their responsibility. If they know about it and can do something about it, they feel that that creates a responsibility for them. They are not looking for an escape from the world's problems but for a way to help with them. This is the quality that got the Good Samaritan into the ditch and brought Jesus to earth and finally to the cross.

In our lives, let us respond to the needs that we see, with the resources that we have, at the time when we can. Let us not ask what we must do but what we can do that will help.

There is a sweetness to the sorrow of the three women who came to the tomb. They came with spices to anoint the body. Perhaps the anointing of a corpse with sweet smelling spices does not serve any practical purpose. Yet it shows love and honor.

Perhaps the lesson for our lives from this point is that sometimes gestures which seem to have no practical value become symbols of love, and do much good. When friends gather around bereaved families, they sometimes say and do things that do not seem to make much sense. Those things may still be valuable if through them come feelings of tenderness and compassion.

After the women left the tomb they trembled in amazement. So it is sometimes that even good news has sufficient impact to leave us stunned and insecure. That a dead one had been raised was enough to shake the foundations upon which one's life had been based. There must have been joy, but there also must have been some uneasy apprehension about what had happened and what it meant.

Seed Thoughts

1. Why were Joseph of Arimathaea and Nicodemus called secret disciples of Jesus?
They sought to be righteous and look for God's kingdom, but they kept their positions and did not openly testify that they belonged to Jesus.

2. Are there secret disciples of Jesus today?
Many Christians tend to hide their loyalty to Christ or maintain a very low profile in testifying for Him.

3. Why did Pilate marvel at the early demise of Jesus?
He did not realize that Jesus had power to lay down His Own life when He chose to do it.

4. Was the work done by Joseph of Arimathaea and Nicodemus wasted?
In one sense it was worthwhile, for it showed their love for Jesus. It also fulfilled Isaiah 53:9.

5. Why were the women who loved Jesus to be commended?
They mourned their loss by openly going to the tomb where Jesus lay.

(Please Turn Page)

---

1. Why were Joseph of Arimathaea and Nicodemus called secret disciples of Jesus?

2. Are there secret disciples of Jesus today?

3. Why did Pilate marvel at the early demise of Jesus?

4. Was the work done by Joseph of Arimathaea and Nicodemus wasted?

5. Why were the women who loved Jesus to be commended?

6. What happened when the women worried about a problem?

7. How does curiosity affect us?

8. Does God still send angels to help believers today?

9. Why is the resurrection of Jesus vital to redemption?

10. Why was it important for Jesus' followers to go to Galilee?

They sought to be righteous and look for God's kingdom, but they kept their positions and did not openly testify that they belonged to Jesus.

Many Christians tend to hide their loyalty to Christ or maintain a very low profile in testifying for Him.

He did not realize that Jesus had power to lay down His Own life when He chose to do it.

In one sense it was worthwhile, for it showed their love for Jesus. It also fulfilled Isaiah 53:9.

They mourned their loss by openly going to the tomb where Jesus lay.

The stone was rolled away before they arrived. God may solve our problems.

It may bring us grief, but it may lead to joyous discovery, as it did when the women found the sepulcher empty.

Some evangelical scholars believe that testimonies to this effect are valid, even if their appearances are more modest.

A living hope demands a living Savior. The death and resurrection of Jesus were essential to salvation.

He planned to meet with them there and give them His great commission. Jesus wants the world to know that He lives!

Seed Thoughts - Continued

6. What happened when the women worried about a problem?
The stone was rolled away before they arrived. God may solve our problems.

7. How does curiosity affect us?
It may bring us grief, but it may lead to joyous discovery, as it did when the women found the sepulcher empty.

8. Does God still send angels to help believers today?
Some evangelical scholars believe that testimonies to this effect are valid, even if their appearances are more modest.

9. Why is the resurrection of Jesus vital to redemption?
A living hope demands a living Savior. The death and resurrection of Jesus were essential to salvation.

10. Why was it important for Jesus' followers to go to Galilee?
He planned to meet with them there and give them His great commission. Jesus wants the world to know that He lives!

"BECAUSE I LIVE YOU SHALL LIVE FOREVER"

The Gift Of Living Hope

I Peter 1:3. Blessed be the God and Father of our Lord Jesus Christ, which according to his abundant mercy hath begotten us again unto a lively hope by the resurrection of Jesus Christ from the dead,

4. To an inheritance incorruptible, and undefiled, and that fadeth not away, reserved in heaven for you.

5. Who are kept by the power of God through faith unto salvation ready to be revealed in the last time.

6. Wherein ye greatly rejoice, though now for a season, if need be, ye are in heaviness through manifold temptations:

7. That the trial of your faith, being much more precious than of gold that perisheth, though it be tried with fire, might be found unto praise and honor and glory at the appearing of Jesus Christ:

8. Whom having not seen, ye love; in whom, though now ye see him not, yet believing, ye rejoice with joy unspeakable and full of glory:

9. Receiving the end of your faith, even the salvation of your souls.

I Peter 1:13. Wherefore gird up the loins of your mind, be sober, and hope to the end for the grace that is to be brought unto you at the revelation of Jesus Christ;

14. As obedient children, not fashioning yourselves according to the former lusts in your ignorance:

15. But as he which hath called you is holy, so be ye holy in all manner of conversation;

16. Because it is written, Be ye holy; for I am holy.

17. And if ye call on the Father, who without respect of persons judgeth according to every man's work, pass the time of your sojourning here in fear:

18. Forasmuch as ye know that ye were not redeemed with corruptible things, as silver and gold, from your vain conversation received by tradition from your fathers;

19. But with the precious blood of Christ, as of a lamb without blemish and without spot:

20. Who verily was foreordained before the foundation of the world, but was manifest in these last times for you,

21. Who by him do believe in God, that raised him up from the dead, and gave him glory; that your faith and hope might be in God.

MEMORY SELECTION
I Peter 1:3
DEVOTIONAL READING
Psalm 23:1-6

BACKGROUND SCRIPTURE
I Peter 1:1-25
PRINTED SCRIPTURE
I Peter 1:3-9, 13-21

Teacher's Target

The epistle of First Peter was written about A.D. 60-65. As the church grew, opposition to it increased. Christians expected to suffer, and reference to this is made some fifteen times in this letter. It was a ~~lively~~ (living) hope in the resurrected and returning Christ which sustained them in times of persecution. No matter what they had to endure, they knew that Jesus would ultimately come back to take them unto Himself.

Help your students to counteract the pessimism caused by worldly pressures with the optimism based on hope in Christ, their living Savior and Lord. As with beaten and jailed Paul and Silas in Philippi, believers can have a song in the night (Ps. 42:8; Acts 16:25). Suffering in a harsh situation may be used by God to open up an opportunity for believers to witness for Christ, thus becoming the means to a good end.

Lesson Introduction

We are not sure of the location of the "Babylon" from which Peter wrote his letter, but it was probably Rome, and Silvanus (Silas) and Marcus (Mark) were with him (I Pet. 5:12-13). We know that Christians in Rome suffered much persecution under Nero, Domitian, and Trajan (A.D. 54-117), and tradition states that Peter was martyred during Nero's reign.

Job, the ancient patriarch, knew the meaning of suffering and its purpose." [God] knoweth the way that I take when he hath tried me, I shall come forth as gold" (Job 23:10). Peter may have been thinking of this when he wrote, "The trial of your faith, being much more precious than of gold that perisheth, though it be tried [refined, purified] with fire, might be found unto praise and honour and glory at the [second] appearing of Jesus Christ" (I Pet. 1:7).

Teaching Outline

I. Review: I Pet. 1:3-9
   A. Resurrection: 3
   B. Reservation: 4-5
   C. Refining: 6-7
   D. Rejoicing: 8-9

II. Reminder: I Pet. 1:13-16
   A. Confidence: 13
   B. Conduct: 14-16

III. Redemption: I Pet. 1:17-21
   A. Reverence: 17
   B. Ransom: 18-19
   C. Resurrection: 20-21

Daily Bible Readings

Mon. A Living Hope
I Peter 1:3-5
Tue. Tried oy Fire
I Peter 1:6-7
Wed. Joy Unspeakable
I Peter 1:8-9
Thu. Gird Your Loins
I Peter 1:13-14
Fri. Be Ye Holy
I Peter 1:15-16
Sat. Redeemed With Blood
I Peter 1:17-19
Sun. The Foundation of Hope
I Peter 1:20,21

Verse By Verse

Review: I Pet. 1:3-9

A. Resurrection: 3
3. Blessed be the God and Father of our Lord Jesus Christ, which according to his abundant mercy hath begotten us again unto a lively hope by the resurrection of Jesus Christ from the dead, . . .

In the two opening verses, Peter greeted dispersed Jewish believers in the provinces of Pontus, Galatia, Cappadocia, Asia, and Bithynia in Asia Minor (Turkey). The elect ones mentioned in verse 2 must have included Gentile believers, as well, as noted in I Peter 2:9-10. He desired that grace and peace would be multiplied to them.

The doxology of praise which begins in verse 3 blesses God for Christ. It was the mercy of God which made it possible for sinners to be born again unto a lively (living) hope following the resurrection of Christ.

The sure hope of believers is based on the unalterable Word of God. They are raised up to heavenly places when they accept Christ as their Savior (Eph. 1:3; 2:6). Their bodies may go into graves at death, but their souls go upward to heaven (Phil. 1:21-23). Christ will raise the dead believers and unite them with their souls before translating them to heaven (I Cor. 15:51-53 I Thess. 4:13-18).

B. Reservations 4-5
4. To an inheritance incorruptible, and undefiled, and that fadeth not away, reserved in heaven for you,...

Receiving an earthly inheritance can lead to disappointment. What is gained may be squandered or taken by others. The inheritance reserved in heaven is not subject to corruption, defilement, or disappearance. Being in heaven with God, Jesus, angels, and the redeemed of all ages will be its own reward. Every abiding work by a believer is going to produce a reward at the judgment seat of Christ (Matt. 6:19-21; I Cor. 3:14).

5. Who are kept by the power of God through faith unto salvation ready to be revealed in the last time.

Peter said that believers are kept (guarded, shielded, protected) by the power of God as they exercise faith (trust) in Him until they inherit the final salvation which will be revealed in the end time. In the meantime, believers must depend on God's keeping power in order to withstand evil. Bible students note that this is an important theme throughout I and II Peter, I, II, and III John, and Jude. In fact, Jude ends with this doxology, "Now unto him that is able to keep you from falling, and to present you faultless before the presence of his glory with exceeding joy, to the only wise God our Saviour, be glory and majesty, dominion and power, both now and ever. Amen" (Jude 24-25).

C. Refinings 6-7
6. Wherein ye greatly rejoice, though now for a season, if need be, ye are in heaviness through manifold temptations:

Paul wrote, "Rejoice in the Lord always and again I say, Rejoice." He had learned the important lesson that believers may rejoice in the Lord despite circumstances which would normally make them grieve.

Peter was saying the same thing here when he said that believers could greatly rejoice, even though they had to endure temporary heaviness because of many trials. Both men knew that God stands above and beyond all harsh circumstances and exercises His sovereign power.

7. That the trial of your faith, being much more precious than of gold that perisheth, though it be tried with fire, might be found unto praise and honour and glory at the appearing of Jesus Christ: . . .

Here is the Christian philosophy for dealing with suffering for Christ's sake. It should be seen as a testing of faith, a refining process designed to enhance Christian character. Gold is melted so that any dross may be drawn off and the metal purified. So it is that believers placed under fire are purged of that which detracts from their testimony. Their lives become the kind which will bring praise, honor, and glory to Christ when He comes again.

D. Rejoicing: 8-9
8. Whom having not seen, ye love; in whom, though now ye see him not, yet believing, ye rejoice with joy unspeakable and full of glory:
9. Receiving the end of your faith, even the salvation of your souls.

The believer's joy centers in Jesus Christ. Unlike Peter, most of them had not yet seen Christ, and yet they loved Him. By placing their faith in Him for salvation, people today move into a life of faith and development which brings them unspeakable and glorious joy. The culmination of this life of faith is going to be the eternal salvation of their souls. In light of all of this, they should be ready to grapple with hard circumstances.

II. Reminder: I Pet. 1:13-16

A. Confidence: 13
13. Wherefore gird up the loins of your mind, be sober, and hope to the end for the grace that is to be brought unto you at the revelation of Jesus Christ;

Peter challenged believers to be courageous, braced for righteous action. He wanted them to be sober (disciplined, morally alert). He wanted them to be hopeful (optimistic) until sustaining grace will be replaced by culminating grace that will be brought by Jesus Christ when He comes again. He wanted them to be confident in Him.

B. Conduct: 14-16
14. As obedient children, not fashioning yourselves according to the former lusts in your ignorance:

Confidence in Christ needs to be matched by conduct in everyday life. Peter told believers to be obedient to their heavenly Father, They were to give up the passions which dominated them during their time of spiritual ignorance and sin.

15. But as he which hath called you is holy, so be ye holy in all manner of conversation:
16. Because it is written, Be ye holy for I am holy.

Teaching on holiness begins early in the Holy Bible. Look at Leviticus 11:44-45 and 19:2, which record the Lord saying that He is holy and expects His children to be holy. Satan would like to discourage believers and make them think that this is an unattainable goal. It is true that believers cannot be sinlessly perfect, but they can make progress toward that goal. All through their lives, they should seek to narrow the gap between their position in Christ and their practice of living a Christ-like life. In due time, they will become more and more spiritually mature. In the end, "we know that, when he [Christ] shall appear, we shall be like Him; for we shall see him as he is" (I John 3:2).

III. Redemption: I Pet. 1:17-21

A. Reverence: 17
17. And if ye call on the Father, who without respect of persons judgeth according to every man's work, pass the time of your sojourning here in fear:

Peter said that believers who pray to God should show Him proper fear (reverence), realizing that He judges all men impartially. His attributes of justice and holiness demand this. The psalmist wrote, "If I regard [see, discover] iniquity in my heart, the Lord will not hear me" (Ps. 66: 18). Holiness of heart and life should be seen as prerequisites to prayer.

B. Ransom: 18-19
18. Forasmuch as ye know that ye were not redeemed with corruptible things, as silver and gold, from your vain conversation received by tradition from your fathers;
19. But with the precious blood of Christ, as of a lamb without blemish and without spot:

Peter wanted believers to remember that they had not been redeemed (bought back from Satan's grasp) by material things such as silver and gold. They could not depend on the vain conversation (fruitless way of life) handed down to them by their ancestors. The only means for their salvation was the precious blood of Christ shed at Calvary to atone for their sins. He was the worthy Lamb of God free from blemish and defect of any kind. All of the animal sacrifices which preceded Him were but types, for He was the reality.

God required that a penalty be paid for sin. No man could ever acquire enough wealth to pay for his ransom from sin. Jesus was the only worthy sacrifice for sin, because He was divine and perfectly holy. It was by giving His life on the cross that a ransom for sin was provided. It was offered as a free gift to all who would place their faith in Him. Salvation is by grace : "By grace are ye saved through faith; and that not of yourselves: it is the gift of God not of works, lest any man should boast" (Eph, 2:8-9).

C. Resurrection: 20-21
20. Who verily was foreordained before the foundation of the world, but was manifest in these last times for you, . . .

Jesus was the Lamb of God scheduled to be slain since the foundation of the world (beginning of earthly time) (Rev. 13:8). He was reserved for this until the last times, meaning the age of grace between His first and second comings. He was revealed to people in the first century in person, and He has been revealed to others since that time by His faithful followers.

21. Who by him do believe in God, that raised him up from the dead, and gave him glory; that your faith and hope might be in God.

We began this lesson with reference to the resurrection of Christ (vs. 3), and we close with it. It is by showing faith in Christ that believers show their faith in God. We accept the fact that God raised Jesus up from the dead and gave Him glory in receiving Him back up into heaven. Our faith and hope for eternal life are in God and in Christ. Going back over the texts, note the great themes found in them—God, Christ, mercy, hope, resurrection, inheritance, power, faith, salvation (redemption), trial, grace, holiness, reverence, and glory. Be sure that you have a good understanding of each one.

Evangelistic Emphasis

The people with whom we come in contact are often battered into a state of hopelessness by the trials and tribulations of life. Their dreams have been shattered. Their ambitions have been left unrealized. They have watched their hopes evaporate. Their efforts seem often futile.

They may have worked at jobs for years only to be laid off by automation or company reorganization. They may have dreamed of a happy home only to experience hostility, aggression, passivity, or estrangement. They may have built up a business for years only to have a recession wipe out all their gains. They may have made bad investments that robbed them of their retirement money. They may have had a good marriage relationship which was broken by the death of a beloved spouse.

What message would they most like to hear and be able to believe? Is it not the news that there is a security and peace that transcends all earthly losses and dangers? Is it not the news that this great blessing is rooted in something as solid as the resurrection of Christ? Is it not the message that even when we suffer there is meaning to the suffering and there are good things that will come out of it?

One of the powerful evangelistic messages is that the bad news of life's troubles can be overcome decisively by the good news of salvation.

Memory Selection

"Blessed be the God and Father of our Lord Jesus Christ, which according to his abundant mercy hath begotten us again unto a lively hope by the resurrection of Jesus Christ from the dead."
I Peter 1:3.

The memory selection today has at least four key points. The first is that the good news comes from God. What we preach is not idle conversation or flimsy promises. It is a statement of what the Creator of the universe and the Father of Jesus Christ has promised to do. It is solid and reliable.

The second is that our promise is out of his abundant mercy. There is no question that we cannot possibly deserve the rich promises God has made us. He gives those promises out of his grace to the undeserving. To draw from His mercy is to draw from an abundant resource.

From God, according to the generosity of His mercy, we have received hope. The scriptural meaning of this term is "substantial expectation." Hope is not a wistful dream, but a confident trust based on the most dependable foundation.

That hope is founded on the resurrection of Jesus from the dead. We are not talking about an amorphous religious doctrine, but about a firm promise rooted in historical fact.

God, who is able, gives to the undeserving the substantial expectation of eternal life based on the resurrection of Jesus Christ. What an ironclad guarantee!

Weekday Problems

After thirty-five years with his company, George is out of a job. He is sixty years old, so most companies would not want to hire him, particularly at the level at which he has been working. His role is one which is usually filled from within by most companies, so his hope of a suitable job seems dim.

We might wonder why he does not just retire. The fact is that the company in which he has invested thirty-five years of his life has declared bankruptcy. Of course, a portion of the assets are protected, and George will receive a pittance of retirement pay. However, it is not enough for him and his wife to live comfortably on.

What about his own savings and investments? Again, there are some, but George, like many of us, intended to do better about money management than he did. Some of his investments were in real estate and they had to be sacrificed in a down market when George could no longer keep up the payments. Some were in poorly selected stocks which are now worth little or nothing.

* What encouragement or support does the Christian faith have for George in a practical problem like this?
* When a man is out of a job, how does it help to tell him he will go to heaven when he dies?
* What does God promise to do for us when we have problems like this?

Superintendent's Sermonette

Sometimes we have a tendency to view Bible characters as some kind of supersaints, but they were subject to the same feelings as we are (Jas. 5:17). They faced many dangers in a hostile, pagan world. At times this led them into persecution. Their desire for remaining healthy and surviving was the same as we have today. Christian leaders had to do what they could to console suffering believers and fortify them for additional suffering. This is what Peter sought to do in his two epistles, and the same was true of John and Jude in their epistles.

We live in an age when we like to demand what we call our rights to life, liberty, and the pursuit of happiness. We resent having to endure any kind of discrimination. We expect the government and anyone trying to be a good citizen to rush to our rescue if we are mistreated. We do enjoy many rights and freedoms, but we live in a hostile, pagan world just as our first-century brothers did. We need a ministry of consolation and of fortification for whatever trials God allows us.

This Lesson in <u>Your</u> Life

We do not experience any incorruptible inheritances on this earth. We are in a land where moth and rust consume and where thieves break through and steal. Even those who amass great wealth cannot protect themselves. Their control over their wealth can evaporate in an instant for any of a variety of causes. They could have a health problem that renders them incapable or even unconscious. There could be an economic reverse that leaves them overextended and poor. There could be a war that wipes out whole nations and leaves property owners without assets. There could be a world-wide food shortage that leaves even those with pockets full of money hungry and unable to do anything about it.

Whatever could happen to the wealthy could also happen to his heirs. They would be unable to find security in money, insurance, secret bank accounts, diversified investments, pure gold, precious gems, or any other asset. There is no investment so sound or bank vault so safe that there is absolute security. Nothing is secure against the possible encroachments of a corrosive world that consumes earthly treasures.

There is, however, an incorruptible inheritance that is absolutely secure because it is beyond the reach of moths, rust, and thieves. It is reserved in heaven. It is not in a Swiss bank but is guarded by the power of God.

This is a cause for great rejoicing. If we focus on the troubles of this life we will be driven to despondency if not to despair. The troubles are so large and the possibility of protecting against them is so small that we become a bundle of vulnerability. It is no wonder that so many people are bundles of anxiety and fear.

Those of us, however, who are secure in the salvation of God need not be captive to such negative emotions. While it is true that we may have to go through hard struggles for a season, the outcome is a positive and secure one.

In fact, we will experience additional benefits from even the trials we go through. Peter compares our struggle to the process of refining gold. When gold is tried by fire, the impurities are separated from it and it becomes purer and more valuable. When our faith is tested by suffering or persecution, it also will be purified and will shine forth with greater splendor at the coming of Christ.

How should we react to this good news that we will not only survive our problems but will be improved by them? We should be on the offense against the forces of evil. Instead of letting them assail us, we should gird up the loins of our minds and set forth bravely on the high path of Christian living. We should fear nothing and make no compromises in the area of holy living.

Seed Thoughts

1. What gives believers a lively (living) hope?
It is the resurrection of Christ from the dead. Because He rose, we, too, will rise from the dead (I Cor, 15:20-23).

2. What is a Christian's incorruptible inheritance?
It is the promise of going to heaven to dwell with God, Christ, the angels, and redeemed men of all ages.

3. What must believers do in order to remain faithful all their lives?
They must depend on the keeping power of God to carry them through all kinds of trials and temptations.

4. Is it not ridiculous to expect believers to rejoice during times of persecution?
The Bible teaches that believers can rejoice in the Lord despite circumstances.

5. What good purpose does trial by fire have for believers?
As in refining gold, it purges the dross and makes stronger character.

(Please Turn Page)

---

1. What gives believers a lively (living) hope?

2. What is a Christian's incorruptible inheritance?

3. What must believers do in order to remain faithful all their lives?

4. Is it not ridiculous to expect believers to rejoice during times of persecution?

5. What good purpose does trial by fire have for believers?

6. Why do believers love Jesus, Whom they have not seen?

7. What kind of attitude should believers have toward the world?

8. What connection does obedience have to holiness?

9. What connection does the sacrifice of Christ at Calvary have to our reverence for

10. When did Jesus die for the sins of the world?

Seed Thoughts - Continued

It is the resurrection of Christ from the dead. Because He rose, we, too, will rise from the dead (I Cor, 15:20-23).

It is the promise of going to heaven to dwell with God, Christ, the angels, and redeemed men of all ages.

They must depend on the keeping power of God to carry them through all kinds of trials and temptations.

The Bible teaches that believers can rejoice in the Lord despite circumstances.

As in refining gold, it purges the dross and makes stronger character.

They love Him because of the present salvation of their souls and the promised salvation of their bodies.

They should prepare mentally, morally, and spiritually to face a sinful world.

Christians need to obey the commandments of God in order to become as holy and Christ-like as possible.

Since Christ alone could save us by His shed blood, we need to reverence God Who gave His Son for our salvation.

It was determined before the creation of the world. It was implemented in the last times (age of grace).

6. Why do believers love Jesus, Whom they have not seen?
They love Him because of the present salvation of their souls and the promised salvation of their bodies.

7. What kind of attitude should believers have toward the world?
They should prepare mentally, morally, and spiritually to face a sinful world.

8. What connection does obedience have to holiness?
Christians need to obey the commandments of God in order to become as holy and Christ-like as possible.

9. What connection does the sacrifice of Christ at Calvary have to our reverence for God?
Since Christ alone could save us by His shed blood, we need to reverence God Who gave His Son for our salvation.

10. When did Jesus die for the sins of the world?
It was determined before the creation of the world. It was implemented in the last times (age of grace).

"GO AND SHARE GOD'S GIFT WITH OTHERS"

Called To Be God's People

I Peter 2:1. Wherefore laying aside all malice, and all guile, and hypocrisies, and envies, and all evil speakings,
2. As newborn babes, desire the sincere milk of the word, that ye may grow thereby:
3. If so be ye have tasted that the Lord is gracious.
4. To whom coming, as unto a living stone, disallowed indeed of men, but chosen of God, and precious,
5. Ye also, as lively stones, are built up a spiritual house, an holy priesthood, to offer up spiritual sacrifices, acceptable to God by Jesus Christ.
6. Wherefore also it is contained in the scripture, Behold, I lay in Sion a chief corner stone, elect, precious: and he that believeth on him shall not be confounded.
7. Unto you therefore which believe he is precious: but unto them which be disobedient, the stone which the builders disallowed, the same is made the head of the corner,
8. And a stone of stumbling, and a rock of offence, even to them which stumble at the word, being disobedient: whereunto also they were appointed.
9. But ye are a chosen generation, a royal priesthood, an holy nation, a peculiar people; that ye should show forth the praises of him who hath called you out of darkness into his marvellous light:
10. Which in time past were not a people, but are now the people of God: which had not obtained mercy, but now have obtained mercy.

MEMORY SELECTION
I Peter 2:9
DEVOTIONAL READING
Isaiah 62 1-12

BACKGROUND SCRIPTURE
I Peter 2:1-25
PRINTED SCRIPTURE
I Peter 2:1-10

Teacher's Target

Peter used various terms to describe true believers in Christ. He said that they were like newly-born babes desiring the milk of God's Word. They were like lively (living) stones which were being fitted into a building of which Jesus Christ was the chief Cornerstone. They were a chosen generation, a royal priesthood, a holy nation, a peculiar (special) people, and the people of God.

We should be aware of the transition which took place between a defunct Judaism and an emerging Christianity in the first century. God was turning away from apostate Israel and turning toward those Jews and Gentiles who placed their faith in His beloved Son. The grinding and polishing brought by persecution was shaping them to fit into the living temple where God dwelt. We must remind ourselves that this process is hard to endure, but it is necessary.

Lesson Introduction

It is possible that the religious freedom we enjoy in a democratic society has made us complacent and even arrogant. We do not know by experience how difficult it has been for other believers in other times and places. We need to realize that this freedom could be taken away from us or that we might be placed somewhere which deprives us of this freedom. If either of these things were to happen, we would appreciate more the teaching of I Peter with its emphasis on bearing up under persecution.

Next to personal experience itself, the best way for us to know how to handle persecution for Christ's sake is to study what has happened to other believers. The advice given to them can help fortify us to face harsh times if they come. This lesson's text shows us how to concentrate on Christ as central and make other concerns secondary. We can withstand pressure if we are in Him.

Teaching Outline

I. Choice I: I Pet. 2:1-3
   A. Malice: 1
   B. Milk: 2-3

II. Choice II: I Pet. 2: 4-8
   A. Stones: 4-5
   B. Stone: 6-7
   C. Stumbling: 8

III. Choice III: I Pet. 2: 9-10
   A. Chosen: 9
   B. Changed: 10

Daily Bible Readings

Mon. The Milk of the Word
I Peter 2:1-3
Tue. A Spiritual House
I Peter 2:4-6
Wed. A Royal Priesthood
I Peter 2:7-9
Thu. The People of God
I Peter 2:10-12
Fri. Good Citizens
I Peter 2:13-17
Sat. Suffering is Sometimes Unjust
I Peter 2:18-21
Sun. Follow His Example
I Peter 2:22-25

Verse By Verse

I. Choice I: I Pet. 2:1-3

A. Malice: 1
1. Wherefore laying aside all malice, and all guile, and hypocrisies, and envies, and all evil speakings,

Peter had urged believers to "love one another with a pure heart fervently" (I Pet. 1:22). Therefore, he suggested that they lay aside all malice (evil, vice, hatred, wickedness, depravity), guile (deceit, lying, dishonesty), hypocrisies (pretenses, insincerities), envies (jealousies, grudges), and evil speakings (gossipings, slanders, insults). These were things which characterized sinners, but they could also afflict followers of Christ (Eph. 4:30—5:5). It was implied here that Satan wanted to use these things to divide the people of God. They had to make a conscious choice about this, and Peter wanted them to choose to love one another fervently.

B. Milk: 2-3
2. As newborn babes, desire the sincere milk of the word, that ye may grow thereby:
3. If so be ye have tasted that the Lord is gracious.

Peter had said that "the word of the Lord endureth for ever" (I Pet. 1:25). Now he urged believers to develop a voracious appetite for it as a means for counteracting the evils mentioned in verse 1. They had experienced its grace (blessing) in their lives already. Now they were encouraged to make it a daily practice in order that they might know spiritual growth and development. He wanted them to heed Psalm 34:8—"O taste and see that the Lord is good: blessed is the man that trusteth in him."

II. Choice II: I Pet. 2:4-8

A. Stones: 4-5
4. To whom coming, as unto a living stone, disallowed indeed of men, but chosen of God, and precious,

What Peter was saying here was that believers were coming to Christ, the living Stone Who had been disallowed (rejected) by men but Who was chosen by God and precious to Him. Jesus may have seemed worthless to unbelievers, but God highly valued Him as His beloved Son (Matt. 3:17). It has been true, from the first century onward, that people's views of God and Jesus have determined their relationships to Them, either for good or bad.

5. Ye also, as lively stones, are built up a spiritual house, an holy priesthood, to offer up spiritual sacrifices, acceptable to God by Jesus Christ.

Peter challenged believers to come to Christ and view themselves as lively (living) stones designed to become integral parts of a spiritual house and a holy priesthood. The Jewish temple in Jerusalem, built by Herod, seemed permanent, but it would come crashing down under Roman assault in A.D. 70. The priests would be scattered. Christians had felt increasingly unwelcome there as their beliefs became better known, They could not appreciate the animal sacrifices made there, knowing that Christ had come and fulfilled those types.

Peter invited believers to come to

the kind of house where God dwelt in the hearts of men. Believers' souls would be eternal, long after the stones of the literal temple had fallen in the dust. They would come to God through Christ, their High Priest, long after Jewish priests ceased to function, They would become living sacrifices, long after animal sacrifices ceased.

Paul agreed, for he had written, "I beseech you therefore, brethren, by the mercies of God, that ye present your bodies a living sacrifice, holy, acceptable unto God, which is your reasonable service" (Rom. 12:1). Paul had also written that the household of God was "built upon the foundation of the apostles and prophets, Jesus Christ himself being the chief corner stone in whom all the building [parts] fitly framed together groweth unto an holy temple in the Lord: in whom ye also are builded together for an habitation of God through the Spirit" (Eph. 2:20-22).

Peter now gave the scriptural basis for the building of this habitation of God featuring Jesus as the chief Cornerstone.

B. Stone: 6-7
6. Wherefore also it is contained in the scripture, Behold, I lay in Sion a chief corner stone, elect, precious: and he that believeth on him shall not be confounded.

This was based on Isaiah 28:16— "Therefore thus saith the Lord God, Behold, I lay in Zion for a foundation a stone, a tried stone, a precious corner stone, a sure foundation; he that believeth [on him] shall not make haste [be ashamed or panic-stricken] ." God was referring to the coming of His Son, the One appointed to redeem mankind and become the Foundation for the church which would develop in subsequent centuries. Those who accepted Christ and His atonement for sin would never be disappointed for placing their trust in Him.

7. Unto you therefore which believe he is precious: but unto them which be disobedient, the stone which the builders disallowed, the same is made the head of the corner, . . .

Jesus Christ is precious to God, His heavenly Father (vs. 6). He is also precious to those who believe in Him as their Savior and Lord. They, in turn, being in Christ, are precious to God. On the other hand, those who are disobedient to God in disallowing (rejecting) Christ, the Stone, will discover that God has accepted Him fully and made Him the chief Cornerstone of His house.

C. Stumbling: 8
8. And a stone of stumbling, and a rock of offense, even to them which stumble at the word, being disobedient: whereunto also they were appointed.

This is taken from Isaiah 8:14— "And he [the Lord of hosts] shall be for a sanctuary [for those who trust in Him]; but [he shall be] for a stone of stumbling and for a rock of offense to both the houses of Israel," Applying it to people in his time, Peter declared that Jesus had become the Stone of stumbling and Rock of offense to those who were disobedient to the revealed Word of God. Be careful in explaining the latter part of verse 8, for you do not want to imply that God arbitrarily appointed sinners to be evil.

Peter later wrote, "The Lord...is longsuffering to us-ward, not willing [desiring] that any should perish, but that all should come to repentance" (II Pet. 3s9). However, God does not force anyone to be saved from their sins. He gives them over to what they are and to the consequences of their evil, if they refuse to come to Him on His terms (Rom, 1:24-32). Such individuals are scheduled for perdition, unless they are converted to Christ and change their direction.

The reaction of most Jews to Jesus seems to be summed up in John 1:11— "He came unto his own, and his own received him not." What the comparative few who did accept Him got is summed up in John 1:12—"As many as received him, to them gave he power [authority, right] to become the sons of God, even to them that believe on his name [and all that implies]. It was the Gentiles who were later to come to Him in larger numbers, although they represented but a small percentage of pagans. The Jews stumbled over Him because they did not accept Him as their Messiah, perhaps because they found His earthly origin to be too humble to fit His heavenly origin. They made an eternally fatal mistake when they chose not to receive Him as Savior.

III. Choice III: I Pet. 2:9-10

A. Chosen: 9
9a. But ye are a chosen generation, a royal priesthood, an holy nation, a peculiar people; . . .

In contrast to the unbelievers who chose to remain in their sins, Peter referred to believers in glowing terms. He called them collectively a chosen generation. The Jews had been called God's chosen people from the time of the giving of the covenant of law at Mount Sinai (Exod. 19:5-6). Their response to the Son of God had generally been so negative that God had turned toward the Gentiles, who made up most of the church in the latter part of the first century. It was to both converted Jews and Gentiles that the term of chosen generation was now applied.

Peter called believers collectively a royal priesthood. They might not perform functions of a priest as was done in ancient Israel, but they stood as intermediaries between a holy God and pagan people.

Peter called believers collectively a holy nation. Even as Israel stood as a beacon to the pagan world in times past, so the church must stand as a beacon to pagans today.

Peter called believers collectively a peculiar people. This means that they were God's possession and (unique) precious to Him. As mentioned before in this lesson, believers are precious to God because they are in Christ, and God loves His Son.

9b. . . . that ye should shew forth the praises of him who hath called you out of darkness into his marvellous light:

The reason that God has conferred special blessings on believers is that they might show forth His praises (attributes, virtues, excellencies) to others. He wants to persuade others to come out of the darkness of sin and ignorance and to come into the place of righteousness and truth.

B. Changed: 10
10a. Which in time past were not a people, but are now the people of God: . . .

This may have been taken from Hosea 2:23 —"I [God] will say to them which were not my people, Thou art my people and they shall say, Thou art my God." The original reference was to spiritually adulterous Israel, but Peter seemed to enlarge it to include Gentiles. Both Jews and Gentiles in sin were alienated from God and without hope, but their condition could be changed by placing their faith in Jesus Christ,

10b. . . . which had not obtained mercy, but now have obtained mercy.

Mercy in this sense refers to the withholding of punishment. There was the time when sinners had no right to claim mercy from God. The change came when they put their faith in Christ, let Him bear their penalty for sin, and reached out to grasp the gospel of grace. Only then could they be redeemed from sin.

Evangelistic Emphasis

Evangelism is teaching good news. It is teaching news that brings joy to the hearts of men. For some perverse reason, some have thought they were evangelizing when they criticized, condemned, and put down their hearers. They have trafficked in guilt and condemnation. They have made people feel low and worthless.

To be fair, we would have to understand that they often have done this to try to get people to understand the nature of grace. They want us to know that salvation cannot be earned, but that it is purely a gift. That point is well taken, but the approach is vastly different from the one used by Peter in our text.

Peter teaches in this passage that salvation is by grace. He says the Lord is gracious. He has been rejected by men on our behalf. We have received his gift by faith. We were once not a people but are now the people of God. Peter is affirming, not questioning, salvation by grace.

The question under discussion is not the basis of salvation but the incentive to holy living. Peter uses the greatness of God's gift as the incentive to godly living. Because you have tasted the Lord's gift, because you are a holy priesthood, and because you are the people of God, you should lay aside every evil and make every attempt to do all the good you can. Your exalted status must be lived up to.

✓ Memory Selection

"Ye are a chosen generation, a royal priesthood, a holy nation, a peculiar people; that ye should shew forth the praises of him who hath called you out of darkness into his marvellous light."
I Peter 2:9.

Notice the adjectives in this passage. You are a "chosen" generation. You have been selected and honored by being chosen to be God's children. You are a part of his elect.

You are a "holy" nation. You have been saved by the love of Christ and are committed to become like God. You are living by the command always to be loving regardless of how you are treated by others. You pray for your persecutors and return good for evil. You are people of commitment to an exemplary moral and spiritual standard.

You are a "peculiar" people. This is a somewhat dated use of a possessive term. It means that you belong particularly to God. You are his own personal property. That means you have an extraordinary giftedness. You are a child of the king. You are in the world as a prince or princess.

Not only do you have an extraordinary giftedness, but you also have high things expected of you. You must live in such a way that you show evidence of whose child you are and what He has done for you.

Weekday Problems

Three fathers live on the same street. All are rearing sons. Father A believes that most young people in modern times are too indulged. They have it too easy and as a result do not develop deep strength. They are exposed to dangers and needs that they cannot deal with because they are weak. He is demanding of his son. He criticizes even the slightest fault and never seems to be satisfied with his son's efforts. He loves his son and is trying to make him strong.

Father B also expects a lot of his son. However, he criticizes little but continually holds up high aspirations for the boy. He reminds the boy that he is loved both by his parents and by God. He tries to keep a vision in the boy's mind of the brave, true, and loving person he has the potential to be. He, too, loves his son and is trying to make him strong.

Father C thinks that life is too hard already and is trying to make it easier for his son by being extra good to him. He allows the boy to do what he wants to do and does not expect hard work or demanding disciplines. The father is sometimes surprised that the boy seems resentful and lazy after all that has been done for him.

* Which of the above homes most resembles the home you grew up in?
* What are the strengths, weaknesses, and danger points in each approach?

Superintendent's Sermonette

Evaluation is a big thing in our world today. Our factories have quality-control depart-ments. Government agencies decide whether or not products should go onto the market. Educational institutions are examined by regional and professional accrediting agencies. Consumer-protection org-anizations pro-liferate. Doctors, dentists, and lawyers must pass stiff examinations and be licensed.

The crucial elements in evaluation are the tester and the criteria he uses. Everything down the line flows from excel-lence or the lack of it at the top.

Why, then, are people often reluctant to accept the only worthwhile test for salvation and growth in grace? It comes from God Himself. It states that sinners must accept Jesus Christ as their Savior from sin, and they must become more and more like Him in order to give evidence of spiritual growth. Some may reject Him, but that changes nothing as far as God is concerned. Let us thank God for salvation through Christ, and let us be the living stones making up His household.

This Lesson in <u>Your</u> Life

To be one of God's own people means expectation as well as privilege. This is not an optional but an essential part of significant relationship. To expect nothing of someone is a patronizing rejection. It implies that he is of no value and that he has nothing worthwhile to contribute to the relationship.

This is true in a friendship. If one only gives (though he is willing to give) and the other only takes, the friendship cannot survive. There may be an unhealthy dependence that survives, but not an authentic friendship. There is an implicit rejection involved in not allowing another to contribute to a relationship. It will ultimately kill the ability to relate to each other as friends.

This is also true in a marriage. Sometimes one spouse will suppose that he or she can be more loving by doing an inordinate amount for the other spouse. An affectionate husband might not want his wife to lift a finger in work, make a decision in finances, or worry about a problem. While attempting to set her on a pedestal he may erode her self-esteem and cause her to be psychologically crippled. A doting wife might believe that her husband is "king of the castle" and that she would do everything for him. The well-meaning attempt might provoke anger and hostility which neither person may fully understand.

This is also true of the parent-child relationship. A child who is pampered and spoiled is likely to be resentful instead of grateful. He is not being taught to feel that he is a person of worth who has something of worth to contribute to family and to life.

As this principle is true in other life relationships, it is also true in regard to our relationship with God. Beyond doubt we are children of privilege. We are a chosen generation, a royal priesthood, and a people for God's own possession. That does not suggest that we should be idle, unproductive, and generally worthless. To the contrary, we are people with highest expectations.

Being the people of God does not license us to be lazy. It calls us to be holy.

We, of all people, should live by the highest standards. We should lay aside all the evil that might be rationalized, justified, or excused by others. However strong and good our lives are, we should aspire to make them better.

This passage motivates us by giving us a high calling to live up to. It does not scold or criticize, but rather tells us how important we are to God and calls us to live up to that exalted honor. We are living stones, a spiritual house, a holy priesthood.

Therefore, we should be exemplary worshipers. We should live pure and holy lives. We should seek to learn and grow so that we can be better.

Seed Thoughts

1. Are the evils mentioned in Ephesians 4:31, 5:3-4, and I Peter 2:1 descriptive of Christians?
Paul and Peter were addressing Christians in these passages, and they must have had reason to do it.

2. What secondary problem do sins among believers produce?
They tend to put believers at odds with one another and destroy unity needed for withstanding persecution.

3. What kind of voracious appetite should believers develop?
Peter urged them to desire the sincere milk of the Word of God, even as newly-born babies desire literal milk.

4. What did Peter offer believers in place of the Jewish temple?
He turned their attention to the spiritual house that God was building for His habitation.

5. What role does Christ play in God's spiritual house?
He, and the truth about Him form the chief Cornerstone and foundation for it.

(Please Turn Page)

---

1. Are the evils mentioned in Ephesians 4:31, 5:3-4, and I Peter 2:1 descriptive of Christians?

2. What secondary problem do sins among believers produce?

3. What kind of voracious appetite should believers develop?

4. What did Peter offer believers in place of the Jewish temple?

5. What role does Christ play in God's spiritual house?

6. What role do Christians play in God's spiritual house?

7. What may be difficult about being fitted as a living stone?

8. Why did the Jews stumble over Jesus when He came to them?

9. What terms once applied to Israel now apply to Christians?

10. Why have God's people been called out of darkness?

Paul and Peter were addressing Christians in these passages, and they must have had reason to do it.

They tend to put believers at odds with one another and destroy unity needed for withstanding persecution.

Peter urged them to desire the sincere milk of the Word of God, even as newly-born babies desire literal milk.

He turned their attention to the spiritual house that God was building for His habitation.

He, and the truth about Him form the chief Cornerstone and foundation for it.

They are living stones placed into the superstructure during their generation.

It requires cutting, grinding, and polishing, and this may involve persecution or hardship of various kinds.

Many could not accept Him as their Messiah and Savior, perhaps because His earthly origin was too humble.

Comparing Exodus 19:5-6 with I Peter 2:9-10, we see that they are a chosen generation, a royal priesthood, a holy nation, and a peculiar (precious) people.

God's mercy saves them, and they shine as lights for Him in a darkened world.

Seed Thoughts - Continued

6. What role do Christians play in God's spiritual house?
They are living stones placed into the superstructure during their generation.

7. What may be difficult about being fitted as a living stone?
It requires cutting, grinding, and polishing, and this may involve persecution or hardship of various kinds.

8. Why did the Jews stumble over Jesus when He came to them?
Many could not accept Him as their Messiah and Savior, perhaps because His earthly origin was too humble.

9. What terms once applied to Israel now apply to Christians?
Comparing Exodus 19:5-6 with I Peter 2:9-10, we see that they are a chosen generation, a royal priesthood, a holy nation, and a peculiar (precious) people.

10. Why have God's people been called out of darkness?
God's mercy saves them, and they shine as lights for Him in a darkened world.

Witness In The Midst Of Suffering

I Peter 3:13. And who is he that will harm you, if ye be followers of that which is good?
14. But and if ye suffer for righteousness sake, happy are ye: and be not afraid of their terror, neither be troubled;
15. But sanctify the Lord God in your hearts and be ready always to give an answer to every man that asketh you a reason of the hope that is in you with meekness and fear:
16. Having a good conscience; that, whereas they speak evil of you, as of evildoers, they may be ashamed that falsely accuse your good conversation in Christ.
17. For it is better, if the will of God be so, that ye suffer for well doing, than for evil doing.
18. For Christ also hath once suffered for sins, the just for the unjust, that he might bring us to God, being put to death in the flesh, but quickened by the spirit.
I Peter 4:1. Forasmuch then as Christ hath suffered for us in the flesh, arm yourselves likewise with the same mind: for he that hath suffered in the flesh hath ceased from sin;
2. That he no longer should live the rest of his time in the flesh to the lusts of men, but to the will of God.
I Peter 4:7. But the end of all things is at hand: be ye therefore sober, and watch unto prayer.
8. And above all things have fervent charity among yourselves: for charity shall cover the multitude of sins.
9. Use hospitality one to another without grudging.
10. As every man hath received the gift, even so minister the same one to another, as good stewards of the manifold grace of God.
11. If any man speak, let him speak as the oracles of God; if any man minister, let him do it as of the ability which God giveth: that God in all things may he glorified through Jesus Christ, to whom be praise and dominion forever and ever. Amen.

MEMORY SELECTION
I Peter 3:17
DEVOTIONAL READING
Psalm 96:1-13

BACKGROUND SCRIPTURE
I Peter 3:13-4:11
PRINTED SCRIPTURE
I Peter 3:13-18; 4:1 2, 7-11

Teacher's Target

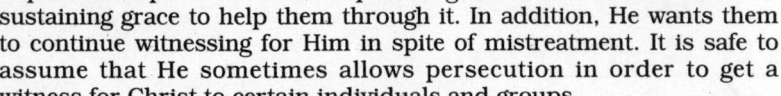

God demands a lot from those who claim to be devoted to Him. He may require them to experience persecution, depending on His sustaining grace to help them through it. In addition, He wants them to continue witnessing for Him in spite of mistreatment. It is safe to assume that He sometimes allows persecution in order to get a witness for Christ to certain individuals and groups.

Help your students to realize that Being Christians means involvement in the sufferings of Christ. Paul wrote that he rejoiced in filling up his quota of suffering for Christ's sake (Col. 1:24). He wrote that believers who suffer for Christ will one day reign with Him (II Tim, 2:12). Peter agreed with this and called on Christians to "arm yourselves likewise with the same mind" that Christ had (I Pet. 4:1).

Lesson Introduction

Persecution can take physical, mental, emotional, and spiritual forms. No one likes to be physically threatened, for it goes against his instinct for well being and survival No one likes to have his good intentions misunderstood and condemned, for it seems unfair. No one likes to be scorned by others, for it hurts personal pride. No one likes to have his good character called into question, for it strikes at his feeling of personal honor. How can anyone get beyond these feelings and suffer for Christ's sake?

New Testament writers viewed persecution for Christ as an honorable thing. It helped them to identify with Him, for He suffered much at the hands of men, and He did it for a noble purpose. It was through humiliation and suffering that Jesus implemented the divine master-plan of redemption. We need to view it in the same way and do our part to get the gospel message to a dying world.

Teaching Outline

I. Reason: I Pet. 3:13-18
   A. Comfort: 13-15
   B. Conscience: 16-17
   C. Christ: 18

II. Release: I Pet. 4:1-2
   A. Attitude: 1a
   B. Action: 1b-2

III. Requirements: I Pet. 4:7-11
   A. Sharing: 7-9
   B. Stewardship: 10
   C. Speaking: 11

Daily Bible Readings

Mon. Suffering for Righteousness
I Peter 3:13-15
Tue. A Clear Conscience
I Peter 3:16-18
Wed. The Long-suffering of God
I Peter 3:19-22
Thu. Christ Suffered for Us
I Peter 4:1-2
Fri. They Think it Strange
I Peter 4:3-5
Sat. Above All Things
I Peter 4:6-8
Sun. Minister Your Gift
I Peter 4:9-11

Verse By Verse

I. Reason: I Pet. 3:13-18

A. Comfort: 13-15
13. And who is he that will harm you, if ye be followers of that which is good?

Transposing this to a declarative statement would sound something like this—"No one will harm you, if you do what is good." This is the ideal, of course, and it is what one might expect for being righteous. As subsequent verses show, Peter realized that the ideal is not always present, but that did not detract from the common sense of asking the question posed here.

14a. But and if ye suffer for righteousness' sake, happy are ye: . . .

Persecution for Christ's sake puts believers into good company and serves as a promise of blessing to come in heaven. Consider what Jesus said on this subject in His sermon on the mount—"Blessed are ye, when men shall revile you, and persecute you, and shall say all manner of evil against you falsely, for my sake. Rejoice, and be exceeding glad: for great is your reward in heaven: for so persecuted they the prophets which were before you" (Matt. 5 :11- 12). A list of heroes of the faith is found in the eleventh chapter of the book of Hebrews.

14b. ...and be not afraid of their terror, neither be troubled;

Persecuted Christians need to remind themselves that they are on the winning side. God is sovereign, and He will right all wrongs in due time. He will give sustaining grace to help believers endure their trials. He will give courage and inner strength to deal with deprivation, humiliation, pain, and depraved mistreatment. This is the testimony of those who have experienced persecution.

15. But sanctify the Lord God in your hearts: and be ready always to give an answer to every man that asketh you a reason of the hope that is in you with meekness and fear:

Peter wanted believers to set Christ apart in their hearts as being holy and as being Lord of their lives. This being true, they were challenged to be ready at all times to explain to anyone who asked them the reason that they had hope in Christ. It did not matter if their hearers were receptive or enraged by their testimony. When believers spoke of this matter, they were to be meek and reverent.

B. Conscience: 16-17
16. Having a good conscience; that, whereas they speak evil of you, as of evildoers, they may be ashamed that falsely accuse your good conversation in Christ.

Peter urged believers to have a clear conscience before God and men. If others derided them, as if they were evil, those critics might be ashamed of themselves after noting the good conversation (conduct, behavior) of believers.

17. For it is better, if the will of God be so, that ye suffer for well doing, than for evil doing.

If God permits believers to suffer for Christ's sake, it is better that they suffer for doing what is right than for doing what is wrong, If their conscience is clear, they avoid the guilt associated with sinning, and they can concentrate on their ministry of suffering for the sake of Christ.

C. Christ: 18
18a. For Christ also hath once suffered for sins, the just for the unjust, . . .

Peter had earlier written, "[Christ] his own self bare our sins in his own body on the tree [cross], . . ." (I Pet. 2:24). This was the height of His persecution by His enemies, for he bore the terrible weight of the sins of all men on Himself at Calvary. His sacrifice was done once for all and need not be repeated. "Once in the end of the world hath he appeared to put away sin by the sacrifice of himself" (Heb, 9:26). Christ was perfectly holy and just, but He died for the unholy and unjust.

18b. ...that he might bring us to God, being put to death in the flesh, but quickened by the Spirit:

Christ was able to bring believers to God by dying and providing them with atonement for sin. His act of atonement was vindicated when God raised Him from the dead. "[Christ died] that we, being dead to sins, should live unto righteousness" (I Pet. 2:24). Paul knew the power of renewal through the Spirit when he wrote, "Though our outward man [physical body] perish [or is perishing], yet the inward man [spiritual self] is renewed day by day" (II Cor. 4:16).

II. Release: I Pet. 4:1-2

A. Attitude: 1a
1a. Forasmuch then as Christ hath suffered for us in the flesh, arm yourselves likewise with the same mind; . . .

This refers to the fact that Christ had a proper attitude toward suffering physically. He accepted it because of the goal He had in mind of redeeming mankind. Peter called on believers to arm (fortify) themselves with this same attitude in their minds. Suffering is not an end in itself. It is a means to a worthy end, and that is the salvation of all who call on Christ to save them.

B. Action: 1b-2
1b. . . . for he that hath suffered in the flesh hath ceased from sin;
2. That he no longer should live the rest of his time in the flesh to the lusts of men, but to the will of God.

Here is another way of putting this—"For whoever has suffered in the flesh [saving the mind of Christ] has done with [intentional] sin—has stopped pleasing himself and the world, and pleases God. So that he can no longer spend the rest of his natural life living by [his] human appetites and desires, but [he lives] for what God wills" (Amplified Bible). In other words, a believer who has died to self and been made alive in God is no longer motivated by sin but by the will of God. His action will reflect his attitude. He has been released from Satan's power in order to work in God's power, and his life will show it.

III. Requirements: I Pet. 4:7-11

A. Sharing: 7-9
7. But the end of all things is at hand: be ye therefore sober, and watch unto prayer.

Peter was typical of first-century Christians in believing that the second coming of Christ and the end times were close at hand.

The imminent return of Christ has been believed and taught since the church was formed and continues to this day. In light of such an event as this, Peter urged believers to be sober (disciplined, restrained, controlled) and thus thoughtful in what they said and did. Believers under persecution were urged to use the resource of prayer in developing boldness and receiving God's sustaining grace.

8. And above all things have fervent charity among yourselves: for charity shall cover the multitude of sins.

Peter advocated sharing of love among believers. This would be the antidote for any dissension sown among them by Satan. If they truly loved one another, they would give comfort, encouragement, and literal resources to others in times of need. Many minor offenses would be forgotten if love predominated.

9. Use hospitality one to another without grudging.

Regarding giving, Paul wrote, "Every man according as he

purposeth in his heart, so let him give; not grudgingly, or of necessity: for God loveth a cheerful giver" (II Cor. 9:7). The condition of a person's heart determines whether his hospitality toward others is approved by God or not.

Hebrews 13:1-2 says, "Let brotherly love continue, Be not forgetful to entertain strangers: for thereby some have entertained angels unawares," referring to Abraham's experience with angels (Gen. 18:1-8).

B. Stewardship: 10
10. As every man hath received the gift, even so minister the same one to another, as good stewards of the manifold grace of God.

Having touched on the sharing of literal resources, Peter seemed to move on to the sharing of spiritual gifts The gift mentioned here appears to have been spiritual ability given by the Holy Spirit.

This found expression in many kinds of particular gifts (I Cor 12). Peter wanted his readers to share their spiritual gifts with one another as good stewards of the manifold (varied diverse, different, many-faceted) grace of God.

C. Speaking: 11
11a. If any man speak, let him speak as the oracles of God; . . .

Paul would have called this the gift of prophecy (speaking forth) the truth of God, some of which might involve telling future events. The oracles of God mentioned here referred to His words, messages, or truths. Peter wanted believers to concentrate on God's Word more than on human opinions.

11b. . . .if any man minister, let him do it as of the ability which God giveth: . . .

In harmony with speaking God's words, Peter urged believers to perform deeds which reflected the special abilities God had bestowed on each one by His Spirit. It may have referred to helping others in general ways. Paul wrote, "As we have therefore opportunity, let us do good unto all men, especially unto them who are of the household of faith" (Gal. 6:10)

11c. ...that God in all things may be glorified through Jesus Christ, to whom be praise and dominion for ever and ever. Amen.

With this doxology, Peter brought this passage regarding ministering to others to an end, even though it is in the middle of the fourth chapter (as compiled by men). He wanted God to be glorified in all things done by believers as they showed their identification by faith with Jesus Christ. Peter ascribed praise and dominion (power) to Christ forever.

In the remainder of the chapter, Peter told believers not to think it strange when a fiery trial tested them. They were to rejoice at being partakers of Christ's sufferings, for when He appeared in glory they would be exceedingly glad to join Him He warned them not to suffer because of their own sins, but to suffer for Christ's sake, committing their souls to God.

Evangelistic Emphasis

The fact that earthly problems are not ultimate has an enormous amount of evangelistic appeal. We can be so inundated with problems that we cannot see beyond them. It can seem that our whole existence is bleak and troubled and that we have nowhere to turn.

I know one young mother whose life is such a collection of serious problems that she would be overwhelmed without faith in a reality beyond life. Her husband suffered from a mysterious and long-undiagnosed illness which ended in his early death. She has had multiple hospitalizations over the past year. Her symptoms are serious but the cause of them is obscure. She fears the same fate her husband met.

She has a teenage daughter who has experimented rather heavily with drugs and alcohol. The girl has problems in school and is seriously overweight. Also, this woman, as a result of the loss of her husband's income and her long hospitalizations, is destitute.

She is experiencing pain, anxiety, confusion, poverty, and despondency. She, no doubt, has made some unwise decisions along the way. Yet, for the most part, she is suffering for reasons beyond her control.

Christian friends can be helpful and empathetic with all these problems, but the only thing adequate to offer her real and lasting hope is belief in a God who transcends earthly problems and offers a future in which those problems cannot do harm. Knowing that she is in the hands of such a God will be a support and strength to this woman in the here and now, as well as in the afterlife.

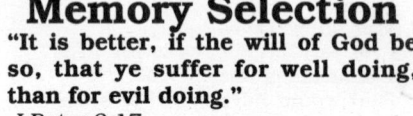

Memory Selection
"It is better, if the will of God be so, that ye suffer for well doing, than for evil doing."
I Peter 3:17.

Suffering, by definition, is not enjoyable. All of us avoid it when we can. Some of it can be avoided by making wise decisions, acting with care, living within the law, following good health habits, and nurturing good relationships. Those practices will protect us from suffering as a result of folly, rashness, criminality, avoidable sickness, and unnecessary conflict.

However, even when we have taken all the precautions possible, suffering still inevitably occurs. When it occurs through no fault of our own, or even as a result of a righteous action, it can be accepted more cheerfully. It is like a clean wound that is not complicated by the infections of guilt, remorse, and vindictiveness.

Since suffering is an unavoidable part of life, we should take care not to increase it by folly or sin. That which we cannot avoid and do not deserve should be accepted as a part of Christian living, without complaint.

When this is done, it is a witness to others to the authenticity of our faith. It will help them to see the possibility of avoiding unnecessary suffering, and of bearing with poise the suffering that cannot be avoided.

Weekday Problems

"Why would God let this happen to me?" Maria asked. She was a devout, God-fearing woman. She was always in church. She prayed often and with great sincerity. Her life was full of good deeds for the poor and the sick. She had worked hard at being a good wife and mother. Her children were grown now. She and her husband were settling comfortably into a more relaxed and comfortable period of their lives.

They were on a vacation trip when he became ill. He was taken from Disney World to the hospital. His condition steadily worsened and within a few short days he died. Although people die at all ages, he seemed young to die so unexpectedly at the age of fifty-five.

Maria meditated deeply and prayerfully about her loss and how she should respond to it. She wanted to do so with Christian faith, but the poignancy of her loss was so great and so intensely personal that she could not help asking, "Why?"

* How would you answer Maria's, "Why?"
* How would you suggest that she respond to the loss?
* Can you give examples of people who have suffered as a direct consequence of their Christian convictions?

Superintendent's Sermonette

Have you ever been pulled to the side of the road for a traffic violation? Have you had to appear in court, admit your guilt, and pay a fine? If you have, you know the shame of breaking man's law and paying the consequences for it. If the arresting officer and the judge were unbelievers, you knew that your Christian testimony could be hurt.

In this lesson, we are going to study about another kind of encounter with authorities. Peter and other first-century believers had to deal with persecution for Christ's sake. They were mistreated simply because they put their faith in Christ and witnessed for Him. They were urged to see themselves as partners with Christ in His suffering.

If we are called on to suffer unjustly for Christ's sake, we can look for comfort and encouragement in two directions. The first one is vertical, reaching up to God in prayer. The second is horizontal, reaching out to fellow believers in conversation. We need to remind ourselves that suffering is temporary, but our heavenly reward will be eternal.

This Lesson in <u>Your</u> Life

Sometimes when we suffer it is because we have brought it on ourselves. We may have done something that was foolish, intemperate, illegal, or provocative. Our actions may have triggered a reaction that is painful to us. The suffering is not pleasant, but we do not feel that we have much basis for complaint because we got what was coming to us.

Not all suffering, however, is self-induced. Christ had not acted sinfully or foolishly to cause him to suffer in the extreme ways that He did. He was suffering on behalf of others. He had a basis to complain but did not do so because he was suffering for a purpose. In his suffering we can learn some things about how we should respond to unjust suffering.

First, we should retain our perspective by remembering the cause in which we suffer. If we suffer because we have done right, we are making a significant investment in the work of Christ in the world. Therefore, we should rejoice in our suffering. This is not a morbidly martyrish attitude, but a willingness to experience pain for a cause we love. As we would be willing, even eager, to suffer in the protection of our families, we should also be willing to suffer for the work of the Lord.

Second, we should remember that there is no earthly foe that we should be afraid of. They can rant and rave. They can thunder their terrors at us. Yet those who trust in the Lord, in his resurrection, and in life eternal need not quaver. We do not enjoy pain nor do we wish to rush death. Yet we can stand pain in a good cause and death holds no permanent fear for us. Therefore, even in the midst of suffering we can enjoy peace.

Third, even during suffering we should remember our mission. Nothing authenticates a witness more than being willing to suffer rather than mute his testimony. Faith never stands out clearer or has a more winsome appeal than when it is voiced during a period of pain.

Fourth, although we may be abused by others, we must not become abusive. We must teach people about our hope with meekness and fear. Arrogance and brashness are not compatible with the Christian gospel. The message of God's love must be taught lovingly.

Fifth, it is not necessary to be defensive. If our lives are what they should be, they will speak for themselves. Those who make hateful accusations against us will find their own credibility in doubt.

Sixth, we should be certain that our testimony is a matter of how we live instead of merely what we say. We must not let the message of Christ come into disrepute because of scandal in our own lives.

In a court of law, when the objective behavior contradicts the oral testimony, it is inevitably the behavior that will be believed. When the behavior reinforces the testimony, it gives added weight to the testimony and encourages the court to believe other testimony that is not backed up by tangible evidence. Our oral testimony about Christ should be clear and true. Our lives should indicate that we are strong believers in that testimony ourselves.

Seed Thoughts

1. Will believers always escape harm if they do what is good?
This would be true, but there may be times when the ideal is not known. They may suffer for Christ's sake.

2. How should Christians feel if they suffer for righteousness' sake?
Peter told them to be happy and not to be intimidated by their adversaries. He felt they were in good company and that God's grace would sustain them in trial.

3. What should believers tell those who persecute them?
They should tell them the reason for the hope that they have in Christ, and it should be done with meekness and with reverence rather than with hostility.

4. What does a good conscience do for believers unjustly accused?
It frees them from guilt and makes it possible for their critics to be shamed.

5. Why did the holy Christ suffer?
God allowed Him to suffer in order that He might atone for men's sins. In this sense, good came out of evil.

(Please Turn Page)

---

1. Will believers always escape harm if they do what is good?

2. How should Christians feel if they suffer for righteousness' sake?

3. What should believers tell those who persecute them?

4. What does a good conscience do for believers unjustly accused?

5. Why did the holy Christ suffer?

6. Should Christians have the same attitude Jesus did?

7. Should believers feel that the end of all things is near?

8. What does charity do?

9. Who are good stewards?

10. How should believers speak and minister?

Seed Thoughts - Continued

This would be true, but there may be times when the ideal is not known. They may suffer for Christ's sake.

Peter told them to be happy and not to be intimidated by their adversaries. He felt they were in good company and that God's grace would sustain them in trial.

They should tell them the reason for the hope that they have in Christ, and it should be done with meekness and with reverence rather than with hostility.

It frees them from guilt and makes it possible for their critics to be shamed.

God allowed Him to suffer in order that He might atone for men's sins. In this sense, good came out of evil.

Yes, they should arm themselves with a willingness to die to self and to devote themselves to God's will,

The imminent return of Christ is to be taught and believed, producing sober believers who prayerfully watch for Him.

When love is practiced among believers, it covers a multitude of minor offenses.

They are those who use their physical and spiritual resources to help others in need, They should do this cheerfully and without grudging.

They should speak the words of God, and they should minister according to the gifts given to them by God's Spirit.

6. Should Christians have the same attitude Jesus did?
Yes, they should arm themselves with a willingness to die to self and to devote themselves to God's will,

7. Should believers feel that the end of all things is near?
The imminent return of Christ is to be taught and believed, producing sober believers who prayerfully watch for Him.

8. What does charity do?
When love is practiced among believers, it covers a multitude of minor offenses.

9. Who are good stewards?
They are those who use their physical and spiritual resources to help others in need, They should do this cheerfully and without grudging.

10. How should believers speak and minister?
They should speak the words of God, and they should minister according to the gifts given to them by God's Spirit.

Humble, Steadfast, Vigilant

PUBLICAN HUMILITY   PHARISEE PRIDE

I Peter 5:1. The elders which are among you I exhort, who am also an elder, and a witness of the sufferings of Christ, and also a partaker of the glory that shall be revealed:
2. Feed the flock of God which is among you, taking the oversight thereof, not by constraint, but willingly; not for filthy lucre, but of a ready mind;
3. Neither as being lords over God's heritage, but being examples to the flock.
4. And when the chief Shepherd shall appear, ye shall receive a crown of glory that fadeth not away.
5. Likewise, ye younger, submit yourselves unto the elder. Yea, all of you be subject one to another, and be clothed with humility: for God resisteth the proud, and giveth grace to the humble.
6. Humble yourselves therefore under the mighty hand of God, that he may exalt you in due time:
7. Casting all your care upon him; for he careth for you.
8. Be sober, be vigilant; because of your adversary the devil, as a roaring lion, walketh about, seeking whom he may devour:
9. Whom resist stedfast in the faith, knowing that the same afflictions are accomplished in your brethren that are in the world.
10. But the God of all grace, who hath called us unto his eternal glory by Christ Jesus, after that ye have suffered a while, make you perfect, stablish, strengthen, settle you.
11. To him be glory and dominion for ever and ever. Amen.

MEMORY SELECTION
I Peter 5:6-7
DEVOTIONAL READING
Philippians 3:1-21

BACKGROUND SCRIPTURE
I Peter 5 :1-11
PRINTED SCRIPTURE
I Peter 5:1-11

Teacher's Target

Peter knew that ignorance and dissension could tear believers apart. In his closing remarks to his first epistle, he sought to have his readers avoid these things. He exhorted the elders (leaders) to feed the flock with the truths of God. He urged younger believers to submit themselves to mature leaders and to be humble. He warned all believers to be on watch against Satan, whom he described as a voracious lion on the prowl. He pronounced a benediction on believers.

WE SHOULD identify ourselves with the believers of Peter's time and to take his advice. The apostle's suggestions came from his own experience over several decades of service and struggle. His practical remarks are relevant and applicable in our time. He had his sights set on the coming of Christ (I Pet. 5:1, 4, 6, and 10). We should do the same.

Lesson Introduction

Suffering for Christ's sake continues to be a main theme in this lesson's text, but it is counterbalanced by God's care in this life and by God's glory in the life to come. The Bible places no premium on self-inflicted asceticism and suffering, for this can lead to personal pride. It does,- however, commend believers who face up to suffering from worldly and devilish sources and do it in dependence on the Lord.

Peter looked back with remorse on the time he cracked under pressure and denied knowing Jesus when questioned by those involved in the Savior's arrest. He did not want others to make that kind of mistake. He kept before them the promise of glory and a crown which would never fade away. The path to glory was characterized by truth, faithfulness, humility, and steadfast resistance to Satan. These virtues built up personal character.

Teaching Outline

I. Concern: I Pet. 5:1-4
   A. Elders: 1
   B. Exhortation: 2
   C. Examples: 3
   D. Exaltation: 4
II. Care: I Pet. 5:5-7
   A. Humility: 5-6
   B. Help: 7
III. Conflict: I Pet. 5:8-9
   A. Roaring: 8
   B. Resisting: 9
IV. Call: I Pet. 5:10-11
   A. Perfecting: 10
   B. Praising: 11

Daily Bible Readings

Mon. Care for the Less Mature
I Peter 5:1-2
Tue. Leaders to be Humble
I Peter 5:3-4
Wed. All Should be Humble
I Peter 5:5-6
Thu. Free from Worry
I Peter 5:7
Fri. Be Vigilant
I Peter 5:8
Sat. Resist the Devil
I Peter 5:9
Sun. God Will Protect You
I Peter 5:10-11

Verse By Verse

I. Concern: I Pet. 1: 4

A. Elders: 1
1. The elders which are among you I exhort, who am also an elder, and a witness of the sufferings of Christ, and also a partaker of the glory that shall be revealed:

Laying aside his apostolic designation here, Peter appealed to spiritual leaders (elders, pastors, shepherds) as a fellow elder. He said that he had been a witness to the sufferings of Jesus. He evidently meant to imply that he himself had suffered for Christ's sake when he said that he was going to share in the glory which would later be revealed at His second coming. This would agree with II Timothy 2:12— "If we suffer for Christ], we shall also reign with him.

B. Exhortation: 2
2a. Feed the flock of God which is among you, taking the oversight thereof, . . .

In the epilogue to John's gospel, we find the section in which Jesus questioned Peter as to whether he loved Him. When Peter declared that he did, Jesus told him to feed His sheep, and this occurred three times for emphasis (John 21:15-17). Peter had endeavored to do this, and now he was concerned that other pastors do it, too. Even as natural shepherds watched over their flocks and made sure they received good pasturage, so it was that spiritual shepherds were to make sure that believers under their care received spiritual nourishment from God's Word.

2b. . . . not by constraint, but willingly; not for filthy lucre, but of a ready mind;

False teachers in the first century were often intent on gaining prestige, power, and money for themselves. Peter told true pastors to avoid these things. They were not to serve because they felt compelled to do it. They were not to seek wealth from it. They were to willingly work for the Lord and be cheerful in doing it.

C. Examples: 3
3. Neither as being lords over God's heritage, but being ensamples to the flock.

Peter was aware of the temptation for pastors to become tyrants, forcing their wills upon congregations. He wanted them to avoid this. He urged them to lead by examples of Christlikeness, He saw believers as God's inheritance, entrusted to the pastors until the time the great Shepherd appeared again.

D. Exaltation: 4
4. And when the chief Shepherd shall appear, ye shall receive a crown of glory that fadeth not away.

The chief Shepherd could be none other than the Lord Jesus Christ, Who will one day be revealed from heaven to gather His Own and take them to heaven (I Thess. 4:13-18). The promise of a crown for believers occurs at various places in the New Testament (see an exhaustive concordance). The laurel wreath given to the winner in a racing event was a foretype of the believer's heavenly crown of glory which would never fade away. This crown becomes the symbol of exaltation.

II. Care: I Pet. 5:5-7

A. Humility: 5-6
5a. Likewise, ye younger, submit yourselves unto the elder.

Peter cautioned younger believers to put themselves voluntarily under the care of mature believers. They were to temper their tendency to be independent and disregard the older generation.

5b. Yea, all of you be subject one to another, and be clothed with humility: . . .

Christ gave the best example when He humbled Himself to wash the feet of His disciples and then urged them to serve one another in like manner (John 13:1-17). This was the kind of humility which grew out of deep love. Believers were to wear it as a garment.

5c. . . . for God resisteth the proud, and giveth grace to the humble .

This must have come from Proverbs 3:34—"Surely he [God] scorneth the scorners: but he giveth grace unto the lowly" (cf. Prov. 18:12; Jas. 4:6). These references give the concept divine impetus.

6. Humble yourselves therefore under the mighty hand of God, that he may exalt you in due time: . . .

The word "exalt" hinted at in verses 1 and 4 is now actually used. Humility under the hand of God leads to exaltation by Him at the proper time, and we assume this refers to the time when Christ will come again. Works motivated by pride or any other earthly reason will be burned up in judgment of believers, but works motivated by humility will endure the test of fire and produce rewards for believers (I Cor. 3:12-15).

B. Help: 7
7. Casting all your care upon him; for he careth for you

Peter wanted believers to place their concerns on the Lord and not be anxious about them. Paul agreed, for he wrote, "Be careful [filled with care or anxiety] for nothing; but in everything by prayer and supplication with thanksgiving let your requests be made known unto God" (Phil. 4:6). It is important for believers to remember that God stands above their difficult circumstances and exercises His sovereign will on their behalf, They can trust Him.

III. Conflict: I Pet. 5:8-9

A. Roaring: 8
8. Be sober, be vigilant because your adversary the devil, as a roaring lion, walketh about, seeking whom he may devour:

Peter was no doubt referring to Satan here. Perhaps he had in mind also Emperor Nero and the gladitorial games in which condemned believers could be torn apart and consumed by literal lions. In the spiritual realm, Peter warned believers to be sober (calm, self controlled, composed, serious) and vigilant (watchful, alert, cautious, on guard). He named Satan as their adversary and pictured him as a prowling lion after its prey. We assume that the ones indicated by this terminology were false teachers working for Satan, but it may have also referred to outright persecutors of early Christians.

B. Resisting: 9
9a. Whom resist steadfast in the faith, . . .

This agrees with James 4: 7—"Resist the devil, and he will flee from you . " This implies that Satan, although powerful, can be pushed away from believers. It is obvious, of course, that they must be living close to the Lord in order to do this. James 4:8 states, "Draw nigh to God', and he will draw nigh to you," Standing firm in the faith is a prerequisite for battling with Satan.

9b. . . .knowing that the same afflictions are accomplished in your brethren that are in the world.

It should be of comfort and encouragement to believers in any one location to realize that there are other believers elsewhere in the world who suffer persecution, too, and their abiLity to cope with it comes from being firm in the faith. Their common experiences make them members of the brotherhood of redeemed believers who suffer for Christ.

IV. Call: I Pet. 5:10-11

A. Perfecting: 10
10a. But the God of all grace, who hath called us unto his eternal glory by Christ Jesus, ...

This closing benediction tells us that God is the Source of all grace (unmerited favor, blessing, kindness). Saving grace is offered to sinners who believe the gospel (I Pet. 1:10). Sustaining grace is offered to believers, if they are humble (I Pet. 5:5). Since people cannot work hard enough or pay enough to warrant God's favor, they must accept it as His free gift and appropriate it by faith. Therefore, He deserves their praise and adoration for whatever measure of grace they receive.

This closing benediction also tells us that God has called believers unto His eternal glory by Christ Jesus. He has set them on the road which eventually will bring them to their eternal home in heaven. Grace and peace belong to the "elect according to the foreknowledge of God the Father, through sanctification of the Spirit, unto obedience and sprinkling of the blood of Jesus Christ" (I Pet. 1:2). Note the Trinity shown here.

10b. ... after that ye have suffered a while, make you perfect, stablish, strengthen, settle you.

Believers were recipients of God's grace, and they had a glorious destiny ahead of them, but they were still suffering on this earth. Peter comforted them by saying that it was only temporary, and God's sustaining grace could help them deal with it. Suffering for Christ's sake would make them perfect, not in the sense of sinless perfection, but in the sense of maturity in Christ. There is in this the idea of being restored, completed, lifted up, and equipped. Suffering will stabilize a believer, setting him firmly in place. This testing will develop strength of character (Jas. 1:2-4). It will put him on a sure foundation for future growth and development.

B. Praising: 11
11. To him be glory and dominion for ever and ever. Amen.

Peter closed the instructive part of his letter with this brief doxology of praise to God, the One deserving of glory and dominion (power, authority, rule) forever. So be it. The remaining three verses of the letter are not in our printed text, but you might want to include them in this lesson.

Evangelistic Emphasis

Most people do not have to be convinced that the world is a frightening place in which to live. They have been thoroughly exposed to the evils and terrors that can devastate a life. If they could find a place of security and nurture, they would jump at the chance.

Our text today promises such a place. It is a fellowship whose leaders are committed to shepherding. They are not critics but servants and helpers. Above them there is the Chief Shepherd who allowed Himself to be a sacrifice for us all. Along with Him there is the Father who is committed to our care. Then, within this fellowship, we have each other. We try to help one another and be sensitive to each other.

Even the major things that would threaten us are under the control and sovereignty of God. We cannot avoid some problems and sufferings but we are being closely watched by the God of all grace who is committed to our entrance into His eternal kingdom.

This news of a sanctuary in the midst of a dangerous and destructive world will win the hearts of many who are troubled and afraid. They may have previously thought that the church was a place of criticism and judgment and that it would escalate the tensions in their lives. When they learn it is a refuge where sins are forgiven and tensions are eased, they will rush to find safety.

Memory Selection

"Humble yourselves therefore under the mighty hand of God, that he may exalt you in due time: casting all your care upon him; for he careth for you."
I Peter 5:6,7.

The opposite of worry is trust. We worry when we feel that our lives are out of control and we fear dire things are about to happen to us. We do not worry about things over which we have complete control. If we want them changed we change them. It is when we fear their consequences and have no power to change them that we worry.

For example, we may worry about an uncertain financial future. The real worry is, not about a predictable pay check for which we are willing to work. The real worry is that we might lose our job or have extraordinary expenses.

We might worry about health problems. This would not be so much about those that can be readily treated and cured as it would be about those that are untreatable, or those with an unpredictable outcome.

We might worry about the danger of war, natural disasters, fires, or car accidents. Whatever threatens us that we cannot guard against can be a cause of anxiety.

The alternative to such worry is to place it in the hands of the one who does have the ability to control it. God alone can see us through every contingency of life and bring us safely to His throne. Let us give Him all our cares for He cares for us.

Weekday Problems

Woody never has a happy day. The circumstances of his life cannot be good enough that he cannot find something to worry about. If the sun is shining he worries about his health. If he is feeling good he worries about high prices. If his finances are in good shape he worries about his children. If his children are doing well he worries about the weather.

His family and friends have tried to help by easing his mind about various problems. It does not help because as soon as they relax him on one matter his mind flits to another. They are dealing with symptoms. He is maintaining a behavior pattern.

Totally changing the environment of his life to a more pleasant and secure one would not help Woody. The only change that will help is an inner one. He has to come to a deep personal faith that God can and will take care of him.

* Telling people not to worry usually does not help with their problem. How can they learn to trust more and worry less?

* Discuss why the worrier lives in fear of many things that will never happen.

Superintendent's Sermonette

Men have been called incurable optimists. A thorough study of human history has much in it to support this. In spite of seemingly overwhelming problems, men have struggled to solve them, to survive, and to prosper. Literature is filled with the drama of their efforts, Human nature has remained basically the same, but tremendous developments in science and technology have brought great changes in the way men think, speak, and live. Can we really go back to the Bible of the first century and find relevant suggestions which will help us today?

The answer is "Yes," and our lesson text illustrates this fact. Peter advised church elders and younger believers on how to relate to each other through responsible teaching and humble service. He told them to be on guard against Satan and repel him if he attacks. He named God as the Source of all grace. He spoke of the second coming of Christ. These are all things we need to know if we would live successfully in our super-sophisticated but sinful world.

This Lesson in <u>Your</u> Life

Every organization needs leadership and the church is no exception. It is exceptional, however, in the model of leadership to which it aspires. It is a leadership, not of mastery, but of servanthood. The Lord set the example when He took the towel and basin of water and washed the disciples' feet. He reminded them that He came not to be served but to serve.

This was not an abdication of authority but a description of the kind of authority that is to be respected in the kingdom. He was not denying His status as the Messiah in the Messianic Age, the Christ in the Christian Age, the King of kings, and the Lord of lords. To the contrary, He affirmed that status. He said, "Ye call me Master and Lord: and ye say well; for so I am." (John 13:13).

The status was demonstrated, however, not in the customary symbols of power: wealth, privilege, and deference. It was demonstrated in an extraordinary dimension of serving. It called His disciples, not to conform to ultimatums , but to follow His example. "If I then, your Lord and Master, have washed your feet; ye also ought to wash one another's feet." (John 13:14).

Leadership in the kingdom is not to be selfserving. One must not do it for personal gain. He must serve out of a desire to be a blessing to others. Not only must his motivation not be financial (filthy lucre) but it must not be a lust for power. He must not seek a leadership role for the sake of lording it "over God's heritage."

As the shepherds follow the Chief Shepherd, so also the flock must follow the shepherds. Within the church there should not be covetousness for power and privilege. Rather, Christians should be seeking ways to be servants of each other. They should humbly desire the other's benefit rather than their own.

As leadership in the kingdom is different from the usual concept, so also is humility. Humility is not self-abasement or self-rejection. These are negative feelings toward self. Humility is a positive feeling toward others. It is a desire for the other's good, a willingness to serve the other.

Jesus was truly humble but He did not participate in repudiation of His worth or importance. He acknowledged that He was Master and Lord. He did not put Himself down. In this secure sense of His own identity and worth, He was able to get down on His knees and wash the disciples' feet.

All of us, whether shepherds or sheep in the flock, need to be aware of the dangers that threaten our safety as Christians. The power of the devil is real. It is aggressive and dangerous. It will mercilessly devour those who do not protect themselves against it.

Thank God, we have the power to resist it. We are not helpless pawns in a world controlled by others. We are children of God with the capability of making sound and good decisions that will make life safer and better.

Seed Thoughts

1. Who is a church elder?
He is a mature church Leader.

2. Was Peter only a witness of Christ's suffering and a partaker of His glory?
His statement implied that he had suffered for Christ's sake, too. See II Timothy 2:12 for the principle involved.

3. What is the basic responsibility of a pastor?
It is to feed the flock with spiritual nourishment from God's Word. Teaching should be backed up by good exampLe.

4. What will each believer receive when Christ comes again?
The chief Shepherd will give each believer a crown of unfading glory.

5. What form of love serves to hold members of a church together?
Peter emphasized the need for humility on each one's part. It is God who gives grace to the humble.

(Please Turn Page)

---

1. Who is a church elder?

2. Was Peter only a witness of Christ's suffering and a partaker of His glory?

3. What is the basic responsibility of a pastor?

4. What will each believer receive when Christ comes again?

5. What form of love serves to hold members of a church together?

6. What principle does I Peter 5:6 illustrate?

7. Is it ever right to cast your cares upon others?

8. Are we expected to believe that Satan really exists?

9. If Satan is more powerful than men, how can we resist him?

10. What good purpose can persecution have for believers?

Seed Thoughts - Continued

He is a mature church Leader.

His statement implied that he had suffered for Christ's sake, too. See II Timothy 2:12 for the principle involved.

It is to feed the flock with spiritual nourishment from God's Word. Teaching should be backed up by good exampLe.

The chief Shepherd will give each believer a crown of unfading glory.

Peter emphasized the need for humility on each one's part. It is God who gives grace to the humble.

The way up is first the way down. Exaltation must be preceded by humility.

God welcomes it, for it shows that you trust in Him to help you. Christians should share one another's burdens,

The Bible says that he does. Satanists believe it. Evidence of his existence is obvious everywhere.

We can resist Satan with God's help, He and His angels stand ready to aid us. Christians should unite to resist him, Rising occultism demands this.

It helps them become spiritually mature and strong in character, and it enhances their testimony for Christ.

6. What principle does I Peter 5:6 illustrate?
The way up is first the way down. Exaltation must be preceded by humility.

7. Is it ever right to cast your cares upon others?
God welcomes it, for it shows that you trust in Him to help you. Christians should share one another's burdens,

8. Are we expected to believe that Satan really exists?
The Bible says that he does. Satanists believe it. Evidence of his existence is obvious everywhere.

9. If Satan is more powerful than men, how can we resist him?
We can resist Satan with God's help, He and His angels stand ready to aid us. Christians should unite to resist him, Rising occultism demands this.

10. What good purpose can persecution have for believers?
It helps them become spiritually mature and strong in character, and it enhances their testimony for Christ.

20TH CENTURY CHURCH, OLD BUT FRUITFUL

Growing In Grace

2 Peter 1:1. Simon Peter, a servant and an apostle of Jesus Christ, to them that have obtained like precious faith with us through the righteousness of God and our Savior Jesus Christ:
2. Grace and peace be multiplied unto you through the knowledge of God, and of Jesus our Lord,
3. According as his divine power hath given unto us all things that pertain unto life and godliness, through the knowledge of him that hath called us to glory and virtue:
4. Whereby are given unto us exceeding great and precious promises: that by these ye might be partakers of the divine nature, having escaped the corruption that is in the world through lust.
5. And beside this, giving all diligence, add to your faith virtue; and to virtue knowledge;
6. And/ to knowledge temperance; and to temperance patience; and to patience godliness;
7. And to godliness brotherly kindness; and to brotherly kindness charity.
8. For if these things be in you, and abound, they make you that ye shall neither be barren nor unfruitful in the knowledge of our Lord Jesus Christ.
9. But he that lacketh these things is blind, and cannot see afar off, and hath forgotten that he was purged from his old sins.
10. Wherefore the rather, brethren, give diligence to make your calling and election sure: for if ye do these things, ye shall never fall:
11. For so an entrance shall be ministered unto you abundantly into the everlasting kingdom of our Lord and Savior Jesus Christ.
12. Wherefore I will not be negligent to put you always in remembrance of these things, though ye know them, and be established in the present truth.
13. Yea, I think it meet, as long as I am in this tabernacle to stir you up by putting you in remembrance.
14. Knowing that shortly I must put off this my tabernacle, even as our Lord Jesus hath showed me.

MEMORY SELECTION
2 Peter 1:3
DEVOTIONAL READING
I John 4:7-21

BACKGROUND SCRIPTURE
2 Peter 1:1-14
PRINTED SCRIPTURE
2 Peter 1:1-14

Teacher's Target

Both Paul and Peter knew when their lives were coming to a close. Paul wrote, "I am now ready to be offered, and the time of my departure is at hand" (II Tim. 4:6). Peter wrote, "Shortly I must put off this my tabernacle [body], even as our Lord Jesus Christ hath shewed me" (II Pet. 1:14). Both men foresaw the apostasy which would afflict the professing church and wanted to warn believers to resist it. Both were optimistic that Christ would come and prevail in the end.

Help your students to arm themselves with the characteristics advocated by Peter—virtue, knowledge, temperance, patience, godliness, brotherly kindness, and charity (II Pet. 1:5-7). These will equip them to face apostasy in our time, as well, and help to keep the church pure. The coming of Christ draws nearer with each passing day.

Lesson Introduction

Interwoven with the positive statements in our lesson text are negative ones which describe backsliding. Peter realized that Christians had to be continually growing in grace if they wanted to fend off apostasy. Having escaped corruption resulting from sinful passion, they had to develop holy characteristics or face the possibility of degenerating into a state of spiritual barrenness and blindness. Therefore, they had to diligently examine themselves to make sure of their calling and election unto salvation.

The danger of backsliding is present with all believers and should never be taken lightly. It generally comes creeping slowly upon us, rather than confronting us dramatically in some major experience. The best defense is a strong offense. By developing growth in grace on a daily basis, we assure ourselves that we will not fail God. We are thus prepared to face apostasy when we find it.

Teaching Outline

I. Contributions: II Pet. 1:1-4
   A. Greeting: 1
   B. Grace: 2
   C. Gifts: 3-4

II. Characteristics: II Pet. 1:5-9
   A. Improvements: 5-8
   B. Impairments: 9

III. Calling: II Pet. 1:10-14
   A. Resolution: 10-11
   B. Remembrance: 12-13
   C. Revelation: 14

Daily Bible Readings

Mon. Grace and Peace
2 Peter 1:1-2
Tue. Great and Precious Promises
2 Peter 1:3-4
Wed. Grow in Grace
2 Peter 1:5-7
Thu. You Will Be Fruitful
2 Peter 1:8
Fri. Make Your Calling Sure
2 Peter 1:9-10
Sat. An Abundant Entrance
2 Peter 1:11-12
Sun. This is a Reminder
2 Peter 1:13-14

Verse By Verse

I. Contributions: II Pet. 1:1-4

A. Greeting: 1
1. Simon Peter, a servant and an apostle of Jesus Christ, to them that have obtained like precious faith with us through the righteousness of God and our Saviour Jesus Christ:
Peter identified himself as the writer of this letter. He called himself a servant (slave) and an apostle (sent-one) of Jesus Christ. We need to supply the words "sends greeting" to those who had obtained (experienced) highly-prized faith through the righteousness of God and Christ. It was with a mixture of humility and authority that Peter approached other believers in this letter.

B. Grace: 2
2. Grace and peace be multiplied unto you through the knowledge of God, and of Jesus our Lord, . . .
Peter had written something similar in his first epistle—"Grace unto you, and peace, be multiplied" (I Pet. 1:2). In his second epistle, he added the thought that grace and peace come from the exact knowledge connected with God and the Lord Jesus. This indicates the existence of an accumulation of doctrine in the early church. Believers were to grow in it and use it to resist apostates.

C. Gifts: 3-4
3. According as his divine power hath given unto us all things that pertain unto life and godliness, through the knowledge of him that hath called us to glory and virtue:
Carrying his thought through, Peter said that it was due to divine power that God had given to believers all the things they needed in order to live lives of godliness. It was because they had received divine knowledge that they were called to glory and virtue (excellence).

4a. Whereby are given unto us exceeding great and precious promises: . . .
It was through the glory and excellence of God and Christ that believers were given exceedingly great and precious promises. It has been estimated that there are over three thousand promises in the Bible. Some refer to divine judgment coming on unrepentant sinners, but the best of them refer to blessings coming on true believers,

4b. . . . that by these ye might be partakers of the divine nature, having escaped the corruption that is in the world through lust.
It is believers' responsibility to put themselves in the way so that they become partakers of the divine nature. This does not mean that they can become like God in essence, but rather in holiness. It is by the imparted righteousness of God that believers escape from the corruption caused by worldly lust (passion). Growth in righteousness or holiness comes gradually as believers walk with God throughout life.

II. Characteristics: II Pet. 1:5-9

A. Improvements 5-8
5a. And beside this, giving all diligence, add to your faith virtue; . . .

Now begins a list of seven characteristics which Peter wanted believers to use for improving their basic faith in God. The first one was virtue, a term already used in verse 3 when referring to God's glory and excellence. Virtue in this sense is goodness, Christian energy, and resolution.

5b. . . . and to virtue knowledge;
This knowledge is the kind of intelligence gained from study and personal experience. What is learned by the head must be felt in the heart and worked out by the hands.

6a, And to knowledge temperance; . . .
This temperance is the discipline or self control required of believers and made available through the Holy Spirit (Gal. 5:23).

6b. . . . and to temperance patience; . . .
This patience is the steadfastness, endurance, and perseverance which is called longsuffering in Galatians 5:22.

6c. . . . and to patience godliness;
This godliness is the piety God expects believers to develop as they grow in grace.

7a. And to godliness brotherly kindness; . . .
This brotherly affection reaches out to comfort fellow believers and help them.

7b. . . . and to brotherly kindness charity.
This is Christian love reaching out, probably in a more widespread sense. Paul wrote, "As we have therefore opportunity, let us do good unto all men, especially unto them who are of the household of faith [fellow believers]" (Gal. 6:10).

8. For if these things be in you, and abound, they make you that ye shall neither be barren nor unfruitful in the knowledge of our Lord Jesus Christ.
Peter was convinced that believers who were growing in excellence, knowledge, self control, patience, piety, brotherly kindness, and Christian love would be neither spiritually barren nor unfruitful as they developed their experiential knowledge of Christ. The implication was that they could not consider these things optional or neglect them.

B. Impairments: 9
9a. But he that lacketh these things is blind, and cannot see afar off, . . .
A believer who lacks the seven characteristics listed in verses 5-7 is impaired by nearsightedness in spiritual things. He is unable to exercise spiritual discernment. He fails to move forward and possess the many blessings God has offered to him, His growth and development is stunted.

9b. . . . and hath forgotten that he was purged from his old sins.
A Christian suffering from arrested development may forget that he was freed from his old sins and sinful nature and allowed to grow in grace. Here is a reference to a believer who is so carnal that he becomes a failure in his own life, and he becomes a poor testimony for the whole body of believers. It is unfortunate that many hypocrites of this type exist within the church. They need to be reclaimed from backsliding.

III. Calling: II Pet. 1:10-14

A. Resolution: 10-11
10. Wherefore the rather, brethren, give diligence to make your calling and election sure: for if ye do these things, ye shall never fall:
Peter realized that growth in grace required effort on the part of believers, even though the gifts of grace were imparted by God's Spirit. Weak, carnal believers would be unsure of their standing with God. Strong, mature believers would be sure of where they stood, not questioning their call to salvation or their election (appointment) by God to it. Only those believers making spiritual progress could be confident that they would not fall. Peter wanted them to make a resolution to live close to God and then stick to it.

11. For so an entrance shall be ministered unto you abundantly into the everlasting kingdom of our Lord and Saviour Jesus Christ.
The end result of a progressive growth in grace will be for the believer to enter and be welcomed into the eternal kingdom of the Lord

Jesus Christ when it comes. It is this sure hope which helps him to endure deprivation and persecution along the way.

B. Remembrance: 12-13

12a. Wherefore I will not be negligent to put you always in remembrance of these things, . . .

Peter evidently felt that it was his apostolic responsibility to remind believers of their need to grow in grace and keep from backsliding. There is always a risk of offending people in an area as sensitive as their spiritual standing and profession, but it is the task of church leaders to take that risk as they seek to move believers ahead.

12b. . . . though ye know them, and be established in the present truth.

Peter softened his intention to keep on reminding believers of these things by stating that he did believe they were well-grounded in the truth at the present time. Implied was the thought that they had better stay that way or face his challenge in the future as long as he lived on this earth.

13. Yea, I think it meet, as long as I am in this tabernacle, to stir you up by putting you in remembrance;

It was obvious that Peter did not think that he had long to live at this time. It was in view of his coming death that he felt it especially important for him to remind believers of their Christian obligations.

C. Revelation: 14

14. Knowing that shortly I must put off this my tabernacle, even as our Lord Jesus Christ hath shewed me.

Peter said that his knowledge of coming death came as a revelation from the Lord Jesus Christ. Some think that John 21:18-19 showed that Peter would die as a martyr—"Verily, verily, I [Jesus] say unto thee, When thou [Peter] wast young, thou girdest thyself, and walkedst whither thou wouldest: but when thou shalt be old, thou shalt stretch forth thy hands, and another shall gird thee, and carry thee whither thou wouldest not. This spake he [Jesus], signifying by what death he [Peter] should glorify God."

Peter went on to write, "Moreover I will endeavour that ye may be able after my decease to have these things always in remembrance" (II Pet. 1:15). This probably referred to his two epistles.

In the remainder of the first chapter of II Peter, the apostle told his readers that he and others had not devised fables to teach but had been eyewitnesses of Christ's majesty and glory, He probably referred to James and John, who went with him and Jesus up the mount where Jesus was transfigured before them and where God gave vocal approval of His beloved Son (Matt, 16:28—17:5).

In the second chapter of II Peter, the apostle warned believers against apostate teachers who denied that redemption from sin came by the shed blood of Jesus. Many would follow them in their "damnable heresies,...and bring upon themselves swift destruction" (II Pet. 2:1).

As we come to our last lesson for this quarter (II Pet. 3:3-14), we will study descriptions of false teachers who will scorn the second coming of Christ because it has not yet occurred. Peter defended this prophecy and told how the universe will dissolve and be replaced by a new one. It will be one in which righteousness will dwell. God and Christ will be victorious at last.

Evangelistic Emphasis

There is a universal yearning for security. We desperately want a secure income. We want to know that we will continue to have a roof over our heads and food in the pantry. We want reassurance that our health is sound. We do not want to be threatened by war or natural disaster.

Spiritually, we want to be sure that all is well with our souls. To be able to promise this will win the attention and often the conversion of those in the world.

This passage promises that if we will be faithful to the Lord we will never fall. It adds that we will have an abundant entrance into the everlasting kingdom of our Lord and Savior Jesus Christ. Such an ironclad guarantee is far better than we could ever hope for in the conditions of this life. We could not be assured of such security in the financial or health realms.

If you would be a messenger of the good news, find those who are anxious and afraid and tell them of an abundant entrance into the heavenly kingdom. It is not a meager or scant entrance, but an abundant one. We will not just barely make it, but we will be generously and gladly welcomed home.

Memory Selection

"According as his divine power hath given unto us all things that pertain unto life and godliness, through the knowledge of him that hath called us to glory and virtue."
II Peter 1:3.

Our security is in his divine power. People who experience insecurity and guilt are focused on their own shortcomings and sins. They fear they are not saved because they know they have been negligent and disobedient. They do not usually hear the message of security because they think the promise is invalidated by their lapses. It is vitally important that they learn the lesson that security is in God, not in us. None of us could have enough faith in our own goodness to take us to heaven. Any of us can have enough faith in His divine power to take us there.

In his generosity he has given us "all things that pertain unto life and godliness." There is nothing lacking in his provisions for us. Out of His unlimited bounty, He has supplied everything that we need.

The One by whom we relate to Him is Jesus Christ. Christianity is not an amorphous philosophy of virtuous living. It is faith in a person. God's love is channeled to us in Christ. In Jesus, we see the mercy, forgiveness, goodness, and love of God. If one is wondering how to get a handle on how to relate to God, the answer is by relating to Jesus Christ through faith.

Weekday Problems

Elsie laments the fact that she has not grown as a Christian. Her faith is weak. Her interest in the Scriptures is at a low ebb. She rarely prays. She sees others happy in a growing faith and she feels neglected and deprived.

Over the years she has made a number of resolutions to practice better spiritual discipline but she has never followed through. She has started Bible reading programs, but has let them lapse when she ran into passages that confused her. She has prayed intermittently but has not developed a real prayer relationship with God. She has made scattered attempts to visit shutins or others who are lonely, but has been distracted from continuing.

She thinks it must be easier for others. She has had so many conflicts and discouragements. She thinks things will get better some time in the future.

If you spoke to Elsie she would tell you that she has a true faith in the Lord and that Christianity is important to her. She does not attribute her lack of growth to her level of interest, but rather blames it on outside forces that have interfered.

* Outline a plan for Elsie to change the course of her spiritual life.
* Is Elsie unusual or does everyone have conflicts and discouragements?

Superintendent's Sermonette

Satan will try to destroy or pervert anything which is righteous. First-century leaders in the church were aware of this and warned believers about it. They knew that the best way to combat Satan and heresy was to grow in grace and the knowledge of Jesus Christ. This would prevent them from backsliding and help them maintain a good testimony to the world. We should follow this same procedure today.

Apostates are those who have left the truths of God's Word and allowed themselves to be governed by Satanic and human ideas. It is unfortunate that apostasy has flourished in eastern religions, cults and even in some churches.

As we study II Peter, let us determine to grow spiritually so that we may be strong in the faith and ready to deal with apostates.

We wonder about those who choose to remain in apostate groups and work for renewal from within. We applaud those who choose to come out from among them and be separate. To their own Master they stand or fall (Rom. 14:4).

This Lesson in <u>Your</u> Life

Divine grace does not eliminate the need for human initiative. Our text is a very grace-oriented passage. Our faith and our salvation are the gifts of His divine power. We are the recipients of great and precious promises. Our efforts toward Christian growth are not attempts to deserve the gifts of God but are a response to those gifts.

Therefore, we ought to give all diligence to growth. This suggests first that growth is not an accident. It does not just happen but is a response to our effort and planning. The reason that some people are thirty- or forty-year-old infants as far as the faith is concerned, is that they have made no significant effort to grow. As a child who did not learn to walk, talk, read, or eat solid food would appear strangely retarded at age thirty, so the Christian who has not given attention to growth is retarded spiritually.

How do we give diligence to growth? Any of us could give a good set of answers. A study of the Scriptures helps us to grow in knowledge. A serious and persistent commitment to prayer helps. Exercising ourselves in ministry to others makes us grow. As in physical life, nourishing food and ample exercise will enhance growth.

Faith, of course, is our starting point. All is based on our confidence in Jesus as our Savior. To that we should add virtue. As we well know, Christianity is not mere claim but it is expressed in goodness in life. To that basic goodness we should add solid and perceptive knowledge. It is not enough simply to be good. We must have an informed goodness. We must develop the ability to teach others and to defend the faith against those who would oppose it.

Knowledge and goodness must not be rash and impetuous. They must be disciplined, directed, and controlled. For proper physical growth there must be good food and exercise in proper amounts. Huge meals for a week do not prepare one to go a week without eating. One does not lie on a couch until he is flabby and then benefit by running a marathon. He who is serious about Christian growth will plan a regular and consistent program that is balanced between worship, study, and ministry.

The word "patience" in this passage is closer to our word "endurance" or "perseverance." It is the ability to continue a program under distressing conditions or when progress is not immediately apparent. I suppose that no one experiences the Christian pilgrimage as a steady upward walk, with no interruptions. There are stops and starts, stumblings and risings, discouraging times and joyful ones. If one quits the first time he hits a stumbling block, he will not get far. We need to develop patience.

Then we must add godliness. This, I believe, refers to the ability to return good for evil and to treat all men well regardless of how they treat us. It is the highest level of human behavior. It indicates our kinship with the heavenly Father who makes His sun to shine and His rain to fall on both the good and the evil.

When these qualities are all in our lives, we should grace them with kindness and love. Even the most pious of lives can be stark and rigid if it is not softened by a gentle spirit.

Seed Thoughts

1. Why did Peter call himself a servant and an apostle of Christ?
He considered himself to be a love slave and a sent-one for Christ. He mixed humility with authority.

2. What common bond did Peter have with all true believers?
It was the bond of saving faith that came through the righteousness imparted by God and Christ.

3. How did Peter expect grace and peace to be multiplied?
These would be multiplied in believers by experiential knowledge of God and Christ.

4. What do divine promises produce within true believers?
They produce the divine nature within them, not in the sense of God's essence but in the sense of His holiness.

5. What seven characteristics should Christians develop?
They should develop excellence, knowledge, self-control, patience, piety, brotherly kindness, and Christian love.

(Please Turn Page)

---

1. Why did Peter call himself a servant and an apostle of Christ?

2. What common bond did Peter have with all true believers?

3. How did Peter expect grace and peace to be multiplied?

4. What do divine promises produce within true believers?

5. What seven characteristics should Christians develop?

6. How does II Peter 1:3-9 describe a backslider?

7. How should believers keep from falling back into sin?

8. What kind of entrance will faithful believers make into the everlasting kingdom of Christ?

9. Why did Peter warn believers about spiritual dangers if they were established in the truth?

10. Why did Peter write his two letters to believers?

Seed Thoughts - Continued

He considered himself to be a love slave and a sent-one for Christ. He mixed humility with authority.

It was the bond of saving faith that came through the righteousness imparted by God and Christ.

These would be multiplied in believers by experiential knowledge of God and Christ.

They produce the divine nature within them, not in the sense of God's essence but in the sense of His holiness.

They should develop excellence, knowledge, self-control, patience, piety, brotherly kindness, and Christian love.

He is barren, unfruitful, spiritually blind, and forgetful of salvation.

They should diligently examine their calling and election by God to make sure they are in the faith.

They will receive an abundant welcome to the kingdom when it comes.

He felt he had an apostolic responsibility to do this at all times.

He wanted them to continue warning believers, even after his departure from this life (I Pet. 1:15).

6. How does II Peter 1:3-9 describe a backslider?
He is barren, unfruitful, spiritually blind, and forgetful of salvation.

7. How should believers keep from falling back into sin?
They should diligently examine their calling and election by God to make sure they are in the faith.

8. What kind of entrance will faithful believers make into the everlasting kingdom of Christ?
They will receive an abundant welcome to the kingdom when it comes.

9. Why did Peter warn believers about spiritual dangers if they were established in the truth?
He felt he had an apostolic responsibility to do this at all times.

10. Why did Peter write his two letters to believers?
He wanted them to continue warning believers, even after his departure from this life (I Pet. 1:15).

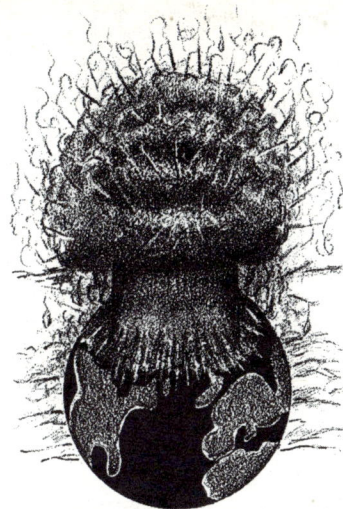

THE CHOICE: REPENT OR JUDGMENT

Focused On The Future

2 Peter 3:3. Knowing this first, that there shall come in the last days scoffers, walking after their own lusts,
4. And saying, Where is the promise of his coming? for since the fathers fell asleep, all things continue as they were from the beginning of the creation.
5. For this they willingly are ignorant of, that by the word of God the heavens were of old, and the earth standing out of the water and in the water:
6. Whereby the world that then was, being overflowed with water, perished:
7. But the heavens and the earth, which are now, by the same word are kept in store, reserved unto fire against the day of judgment and perdition of ungodly men.
8. But, beloved, be not ignorant of this one thing, that one day is with the Lord as a thousand years, and a thousand years as one day.
9. The Lord is not slack concerning his promise, as some men count slackness; but is longsuffering to us-ward, not willing that any should perish, but that all should come to repentance.
10. But the day of the Lord will come as a thief in the night; in the which the heavens shall pass away with a great noise, and the elements shall melt with fervent heat, the earth also and the works that are therein shall be burned up.
11. Seeing then that all these things shall be dissolved, what manner of persons ought ye to be in all holy conversation and godliness,
12. Looking for and hasting unto the coming of the day of God, wherein the heavens being on fire shall be dissolved, and the elements shall melt with fervent heat?
13. Nevertheless we, according to his promise, look for new heavens and a new earth, wherein dwelleth righteousness.
14. Wherefore, beloved, seeing that ye look for such things, be diligent that ye may be found of him in peace, without spot, and blameless.

MEMORY SELECTION
2 Peter 3:13
DEVOTIONAL READING
Isaiah 55:1-13

BACKGROUND SCRIPTURE
2 Peter 3:3-14
PRINTED SCRIPTURE
2 Peter 3:3-14

Teacher's Target

Bible-believers have feelings, and they do not like others to scoff at them . One of their feelings can develop into resentment, and this can lead to ridicule of unbelievers. It can become a vicious circle leading nowhere. What Christians need to do is to know what God's Word says and defend it as the truth, It can give them comfort, hope, and direction. Perhaps it will lead to conversion of the lost.

Help your students to Study what Peter wrote about the second coming of Christ, how to cope with unbelief regarding it, and what to expect when this universe is dissolved by fire and a new one is put in its place. Peter claimed that concentration on these things can motivate believers to be diligent in maintaining their testimony for Christ. They are moving toward an eternity of righteousness and peace never equaled on this earth.

Lesson Introduction

Peter said that he wrote his second epistle to remind believers of the words spoken by Old Testament prophets and of the commandment of Christ given to them through the New Testament apostles. He was referring to the doctrine of the second coming of Christ, as shown by the context. The argument used by the scoffers to discount this prophecy would be that everything continues as it has in the past. This leaves no room for change predicated on divine prediction.

One of the interesting things mentioned by Peter was that time is viewed differently by men from how it is viewed by God. A day with Him is as a thousand years, and vice versa. His promise will surely be fulfilled when His timing is right. Then will come the ultimate dissolution of the heavens and earth and the emergence of new ones featuring righteousness. Scoffers will have eternity to ponder that.

Teaching Outline

I. Coming: II Pet. 3:3-9
   A . Ridicule: 3-4
   B. Reservation: 5-7
   C. Relativity: 8
   D. Repentance: 9

II. Change: II Pet. 3:10-14
   A. Dissolution: 10
   B. Determination: 11-12
   C. Desire: 13
   D. Diligence: 14

Daily Bible Readings

Mon. Beware False Teachers
2 Peter 3:3-4
Tue. God's Timetable
2 Peter 3:5-6
Wed. A Day is as 1000 Years
2 Peter 3:7-8
Thu. The Lord is Not Slack
2 Peter 3:9
Fri. As a Thief in the Night
2 Peter 3:10
Sat. What Manner of Persons?
2 Peter 3:11-12
Sun. New Heavens and a New Earth
2 Peter 3:13-14

Verse By Verse

I. Coming: II Pet. 3:3-9

A. Ridicule: 3-4
3. Knowing this first, that there shall come in the last days scoffers, walking after their own lusts,
4a. And saying, Where is the promise of his coming?

The first thing mentioned by Peter was that scoffers would arise in the last days, behaving according to their own passions (desires) and asking where the fulfillment of the promise of Christ's coming was. According to Hebrews 1:2, the last days began when God spoke to the world through the first coming of His Son, and they have continued to the present time. No one but God knows how much longer this age of grace will continue, but it will end when Christ comes again. Scoffers, walking according to their own lusts, will not be anxious for Christ to come, and they will try to discount it.

4b. ... for since the fathers fell asleep, all things continue as they were from the beginning of the creation

"Fathers fell asleep" is a euphemism for "ancestors died." The scoffers will claim that everything has remained unchanged since the time of creation as succeeding generations came and went. An argument such as this leaves no room for change, and we have all learned that change is inevitable, especially when God says that it is coming. Impatience can lead to unbelief.

B. Reservation: 5-7
5. For this they willingly are ignorant of, that by the word of God the heavens were of old, and the earth standing out of the water and in the water:
6. Whereby the world that then was, being overflowed with water, perished.

Peter said that scoffers deliberately ignore a previous revamping of the earth. At the time of creation, God separated land from water. In those days there was no rain, for God watered the earth by a heavy dew (Gen. 2:6). When men became extremely sinful, God told Noah and his family to build a large ark, store it with food, and gather in samples of animals. He then opened up the fountains of the deep and sent down a massive deluge of rain to flood the earth and slay all not safe in the ark (Gen. 6-7). " [God] spared not the old world, but saved Noah the eighth person [along with seven others in his family], a preacher of righteousness, bringing in the flood upon the world of the ungodly" (II Pet. 2:5).

The covenant God made with Noah, plus all creatures yet to live, was that He would not scourge the earth with a massive flood again. He set His rainbow in the sky as a sign of this promise (Gen. 9:8-17), That meant that any further revamping of the earth would be done by some other means, and we now learn what that will be.

7. But the heavens and the earth, which are now, by the same word are kept in store, reserved unto fire against the day of judgment and perdition of ungodly men,

Peter expanded his thought to include both the heavens and the earth, meaning the whole universe. He said that the current universe, by the same word (words,

401

commandment—vs. 2) of God, has been kept in store and reserved for the day of divine judgment and the perdition (destruction) of ungodly men. This subject receives fuller treatment when we get to verses 10-13. He simply drew a parallel here between the two means of revamping, water and fire.

C. Relativity: 8
8. But, beloved, be not ignorant of this one thing, that one day is with the Lord as a thousand years, and a thousand years as one day.

In contrast to the scoffers who were described as being willingly ignorant of (or who deliberately ignored) the massive flood of Noah's time, Peter said that believers should not be ignorant of an amazing fact. It was that time is relative to the Lord. A day can seem like a thousand years to Him, or a thousand years can seem like a day. He is not bound by time as men are. We are now learning from space scientists that time can be relative indeed. Traveling at the speed of light (186,300 miles per second) in the vacuum of outer space, spacecraft face new concepts of time. Men may someday see time in the same way that God now sees it.

D. Repentance: 9
9. The Lord is not slack concerning his promise, as some men count slackness; but is longsuffering to us-ward, not willing that any should perish, but that all should come to repentance.

Peter said that the Lord does not renege on His promise to send Christ back to the earth again. The promise is as solid as it ever was, despite the passage of time. Scoffers who reject the promise because of a lengthy passage of time overlook an important reason for the delay. The Lord is giving men an extended opportunity to heed His call to repentance given through His servants.

Be very careful how you handle the latter part of this verse. It does not teach universal salvation. It states that God is not willing (desirous) that any should perish, and He would like all to come to the place of repentance and salvation (II Pet. 3:15). However, God does not force anyone to be saved. Repentance must be voluntary in order to be valid. It is unfortunate that "Christianity" has sometimes been spread by the sword rather than by persuasion, and that kind could never be valid.

II. Change: II Pet. 3:10-14

A. Dissolution: 10
10a. But the day of the Lord will come as a thief in the night; . . .

Verses 8-9 appear to have been parenthetical, and verse 10 picks up where verse 7 began. The heavens and the earth are reserved for future action scheduled for the day of the Lord. Time will give way to eternity as the old universe disappears and the new universe emerges. "I saw a new heaven and a new earth: for the first heaven and the first earth were passed away; and there was no more sea" (Rev. 21:1).

The swiftness and surprise associated with the day of the Lord, which is seen as a period of time, evidently refers to the second coming of Christ. After that event, other events are fairly predictable, such as the judgment of believers and marriage of the Lamb and His bride in heaven and the great tribulation, judgment of nations, and final eternal reward of the faithful.

10b. . . . in which the heavens shall pass away with a great noise, and the elements shall melt with fervent heat, the earth also and the works that are therein shall be burned up.

The end of the period of time known as the day of the Lord will feature a gigantic dissolution of the universe. This will be accompanied by great noise and a meltdown of stars and planets, including the earth. All that was accomplished on the earth will be consumed by fire. This will be done by divine action, not by men's efforts.

B. Determination: 11-12
11. Seeing then that all these things shall be dissolved, what manner of persons ought ye to be in all holy conversation and

godliness,

12. Looking for and hasting unto the coming of the day of God, wherein the heavens being on fire shall be dissolved, and the elements shall melt with fervent heat?

These verses seem to be parenthetical. Peter paused to challenge believers to consider the kind of lives they should be living in light of the coming dissolution of the universe. He wanted them to devote themselves to holy conversation (conduct, behavior) and to godliness. Here is an argument against the materialism which afflicts even God's children today. All <u>things</u> will be dissolved. Only the moral and spiritual values they hold will pass through that fire unscathed. The determination of Christians should be to emphasize what is eternally real, and they do that by developing themselves rather than by accumulating things.

C. Desire: 13

13. Nevertheless we, according to his promise, look for new heavens and a new earth, wherein dwelleth righteousness.

The divine promise goes back as far as Isaiah 65:17-19: "For, behold, I create new heavens and a new earth: and the former shall not be remembered, nor come into mind. But be ye glad and rejoice for ever in that which I create for, behold, I create Jerusalem a rejoicing, and her people a joy. And I will rejoice in Jerusalem, and joy in my people: and the voice of weeping shall be no more heard in her, nor the voice of crying." This is very similar to the wording of Revelation 21:1, 4, and 10, where the new Jerusalem is mentioned.

The all-powerful God and His Son, Who created the universe (John 1:3; Col. 1:16; Heb. 1:2), will convert all material into energy and then back again into material things, but with righteousness dwelling in them. Satan and his demonic and human hosts will be consigned to the lake of fire forever. "There shall in no wise enter into it [New Jerusalem] any thing that defileth, neither whatsoever worketh abomination, or maketh a lie: but they which are written in the Lamb's book of life" (Rev. 21:27). This is the desire of Christians, and this desire will be fulfilled.

D. Diligence: 14

14. Wherefore, beloved, seeing that ye look for such things, be diligent that ye may be found of him in peace, without spot, and blameless.

This verse is similar in tone to verse 11. Peter urged believers who looked forward to the new universe to diligently live for the Lord here on this present earth. When Christ comes back again, He should find His followers at peace ("free from fears and agitating passions and moral conflicts"—Amplified Bible), He should also find them living without spot (spotless, pure) and being blameless (faultless). They cannot be sinlessly perfect as Christ was, but they can try to be as Christlike as possible.

Evangelistic Emphasis

The Lord does not threaten, but He does require accountability. There is a great deal of difference between the two. One is a coercive act which punishes those who do not conform. The other lays out expectations and the consequences of not meeting them. There is no vindictiveness in requiring accountability. There is simply the recognition that it makes a difference how we live. Some ways of living produce happier fruits than others.

In God's world, there is accountability built in. For example, there are natural consequences of smoking heavily over a period of many years. That is not because the smoker is unloved by God or God desires to teach him a lesson by giving him lung cancer. It is because the damage from smoking is inherent in the act. The results of smoking are worse than the results of not smoking.

On the other hand, there are benefits to a healthy life style. A good diet, an exercise program, and a positive mental outlook have beneficial results. This is not because of an arbitrary decision made by an authority figure, but this, too, is inherent in these practices.

In a larger sense there is such accountability built into the whole of life. We are responsible for how we live, both spiritually and physically. The fact that one can persevere in bad habits for years with apparent impunity does not mean that he has escaped the necessity of being accountable.

Memory Selection
"Nevertheless we, according to his promise, look for new heavens and a new earth, wherein dwelleth righteousness."
II Peter 3:13.

In the trials and struggles of this life, the Christian lives in hope of a better home. That hope is one of the most sustaining forces we have. Our hearts hunger to hope. We can stand almost anything if we can believe in the possibility that things will get better. We can make it through the darkest tunnel if there is the faintest glimmer of light at the end of it.

People are not normally driven to despair by current pains and pressures but by the loss of hope. Someone who has been involved in painful struggle for years will be able to persevere until he reaches the point of thinking, "Things are never going to get better." Then the wind goes out of his sails and he collapses. Things have gotten no worse. He just lost the sustaining expectation that things would get better.

When we ourselves are sick or have friends or family members who are sick, we need to be able to hope they will improve. If we cannot hope they will improve we need to be able to hope that things will be well with them after death. We need to be able to look for new heavens and a new earth.

Weekday Problems

Don is a happy-go-lucky type of person who does not worry much about what might happen tomorrow. He is not really opposed to Christianity but neither does he have much interest in it. His life is not mean or evil as much as it is simply irresponsible. He does what is easy, comfortable, and fun. He brings some pleasure to people who love him, but he has no real sense of purpose. He has never given serious consideration to the idea that he is accountable for what he accomplishes for God in life.

Dean, in contrast, lives in a state of constant agitation. He worries about the end of the world and about judgment. He wonders whether he is living a good enough life. He is almost frozen with fear that the Lord will return and find him in an unprepared state. People who know him feel that he lives a devout life. Yet he seems to be a bundle of worry and fear rather than a trusting believer in the joy and peace of the Lord's return.

* What do Don and Dean have in common?
* Are each of them being irresponsible in different ways?
* How can the doctrine of accountability speak to both of their problems?

Superintendent's Sermonette

Gunpowder, composed of potassium nitrate, charcoal, and sulfur, was the first explosive known, Some think the Chinese first invented it, while others give credit to Roger Bacon, an English monk in the thirteenth century. It was manufactured in England in 1334 and in Germany in 1340. Since that time we have graduated to the hydrogen bomb with its fantastic destructive power. Some people have feared that madmen are capable of blowing up our whole planet, but the Bible appears to teach otherwise.

Prophecy tells us that God will be the One Who dissolves the universe at the end of time as we know it. All things can be reduced to energy, and God controls that. He used it once to create this universe, and He will use it again to create a new universe.

Let us be thankful that we belong to our Creator-God, Let us live in such a way that we bring honor and glory to Him and His dear Son. Our goal is a worthy one, for we look forward to the coming of new heavens and a new earth in which righteousness will dwell.

This Lesson in <u>Your</u> Life

Few mistakes can have more serious consequences than assuming something will not happen because it has not happened yet. It is true that some occurrences are predictable because they have happened on a regular basis in the past. We can anticipate sunrises, new moons, rising tides, changes of seasons, and a variety of other things.

However, not all things are this way. There are new things under the sun. Some things happen that have never happened before. Creation was one. The flood in the days of Noah was another. Noah's neighbors probably thought he was crazy, but as God had warned, there was a flood. Noah was not crazy but wise to be prepared for what had not happened before.

Jesus was brought into the world without the involvement of a human father. It had not happened before, but that did not prevent it from happening then. He was resurrected as a victor over death. Even the handful of earlier resurrections were not like His. Others were raised only to die again. He was raised to live and reign forever.

The coming of the Holy Spirit on the day of Pentecost was a new phenomenon. It had not happened before but it did then. It ushered in the Christian era and filled the disciples with the message of Christ. It was new but none-the-less real.

With this background of God doing new things when He chooses to do so, we should be soberly aware that He is not limited to what has been done before. Those who scoff at the doctrine of the Second Coming of Christ expose their folly. "For generations things have gone along the same, why should they change now?" they ask. The answer is that God has never been locked into a pattern of repeating Himself. He did that which was new in creation. He did that which was new at the flood. He will do what is new with the coming of the Lord and the final judgment.

When will He do it? It will be when he elects to. As He is not a slave to His past actions, He also is not bound by our timetable. He transcends time. What seems to us to be but a day is as a thousand years to Him. What seems to us to be a thousand years is as a day to Him. He will not be put on a human schedule by His creation. He will do what He will do when He decides to do it.

This does not imply that He is capricious or that He takes His promises lightly. While He is not bound by our expectations or our schedule, He is serious about doing what He has promised to do. What He has said He will do, He will do. His word can be depended upon.

Why has He waited so long? His reasons are redemptive. He has lingered to give added opportunity for repentance and preparation. That should be responded to, not presumed upon.

How will we know when the Day of the Lord is approaching? We will not have any particular knowledge of this. It will be a surprising event. It will be dramatic and highly visible but it will not be preceded by readable signs that give us the opportunity to do a human countdown that will predict the time.

What is the proper response to this doctrine on our part? The answer to that is really quite simple and obvious. We respond by maintaining a continual state of preparation. There will be no advance warning that allows last-minute cramming.

In view of the coming judgment, should we be afraid? There is no point in fear if we are living faithful lives. His coming will be a time of joy and victory. We will dwell with Him in peace.

Seed Thoughts

1. What scoffers are described in II Peter 3:3?
They are unbelievers or apostates who ridicule divine promises, and they will be especially active in the last days.

2. Why might men scoff at the promise of Christ's second coming?
Motivated by their own sinful lusts, they are not ready for Christ to come and want to say it will not happen.

3. Why is the scoffers' argument against the second coming of Christ weak and invalid?
It assumes that change is impossible and that divine prophecy is untrue.

4. What previous biblical example of God's power do scoffers deliberately ignore?
They ignore the destructive flood of Noah's time as a means by which God dealt with sinners of that period.

5. Since God has ruled out another massive flood, what means will He use to revamp the earth?
God will revamp not only the earth, but the universe, with fire.

(Please Turn Page)

---

1. What scoffers are described in II Peter 3:3?

2. Why might men scoff at the promise of Christ's second coming?

3. Why is the scoffers' argument against the second coming of Christ weak and invalid?

4. What previous biblical example of God's power do scoffers deliberately ignore?

5. Since God has ruled out another massive flood, what means will He use to revamp the earth?

6. How does God view time?

7. Why does God delay fulfilling His promise of revamping?

8. What is the day of the Lord?

9. What effect should knowledge of the coming of a new universe have on Christians?

10. How will the new universe be different from this one?

They are unbelievers or apostates who ridicule divine promises, and they will be especially active in the last days.

Motivated by their own sinful lusts, they are not ready for Christ to come and want to say it will not happen.

It assumes that change is impossible and that divine prophecy is untrue.

They ignore the destructive flood of Noah's time as a means by which God dealt with sinners of that period.

God will revamp not only the earth, but the universe, with fire.

Time is relative to God, a day being as a thousand years, and vice versa.

God is longsuffering (patient) with sinful men, giving them opportunity to come to repentance,

The day of the Lord is the time of the Lord's second coming for the judgment of the world and the salvation of believers.

It should motivate them to live holy and godly lives, pleasing Him in Whose hands their destiny lies.

Righteousness will dwell in it, and all that is evil will be subjugated.

Seed Thoughts - Continued

6. How does God view time?
Time is relative to God, a day being as a thousand years, and vice versa.

7. Why does God delay fulfilling His promise of revamping?
God is longsuffering (patient) with sinful men, giving them opportunity to come to repentance,

8. What is the day of the Lord?
The day of the Lord is the time of the Lord's second coming for the judgment of the world and the salvation of believers.

9. What effect should knowledge of the coming of a new universe have on Christians?
It should motivate them to live holy and godly lives, pleasing Him in Whose hands their destiny lies.

10. How will the new universe be different from this one?
Righteousness will dwell in it, and all that is evil will be subjugated.

GOD'S FINAL JUDGMENT FALLS ON EDOM

The Lord Will Restore Judah

Obadiah 1. The vision of Obadiah. Thus saith the Lord God concerning Edom; We have heard a rumor from the Lord, and an ambassador is sent among the heathen. Arise ye, and let us rise up against her in battle.
2. Behold, I have made thee small among the heathen: thou art greatly despised.
3. The pride of thine heart hath deceived thee, thou that dwellest in the clefts of the rock, whose habitation is high; that saith in his heart, Who shall bring me down to the ground?
4. Though thou exalt thyself as the eagle, and though thou set thy nest among the stars, thence will I bring thee down, saith the Lord.
Obadiah 10. For thy violence against thy brother Jacob shame shall cover thee, and thou shalt be cut off for ever.
11. In the day that thou stoodest on the other side, in the day that the strangers carried away captive his forces, and foreigners entered into his gates, and cast lots upon Jerusalem, even thou wast as one of them.
Obadiah 15. For the day of the Lord is near upon all the heathen: as thou hast done, it shall be done unto thee: thy reward shall return upon thine own head.
Obadiah 17. But upon mount Zion shall be deliverance, and there shall be holiness; and the house of Jacob shall possess their possessions.
Obadiah 21. And saviors shall come up on mount Zion to judge the mount of Esau; and the kingdom shall be the Lord's.

MEMORY SELECTION
Obadiah 15
DEVOTIONAL READING
Psalm 96:7-13

BACKGROUND SCRIPTURE
Obadiah
PRINTED SCRIPTURE
Obadiah 1-4, 10-11, 15, 17, 21

Teacher's Target

We begin our quarter with seven lessons based on selected texts from five of the minor prophets. Our first lesson studies Obadiah, the smallest book in the Old Testament.

We know nothing about the background of Obadiah, but his name meant "servant of Jehovah." Similarities exist between Obadiah's book and Jeremiah 49, suggesting that both may have been based on some earlier, well-known prophecy. The book of Obadiah is characterized by a strong sense of justice, with God serving as Edom's divine Judge.

Help your students to see in Obadiah how The Lord worked to humiliate the enemies of the people of Judah and to restore to the Jews that which He had previously given to them. Believers today need the comfort and encouragement which come from realizing that God still cares for those who put their hope and trust in Him.

Lesson Introduction

Edom, meaning "red," was the nation which descended from Esau, twin brother of Jacob, born to Isaac and Rebekah. Edom was also called Seir or Mount Seir, the territory occupied south of Judah between the Dead Sea and the Gulf of Aqaba, totaling some 400 square miles. Esau married a daughter of the Horite chief who originally lived there, and the Edomites probably absorbed the Horites over the years. Headed by eight kings long before the Israelites ever had kings, Edom refused to let Israel pass through its land when coming from Egypt to Canaan.

Edom came under Israel's domination under King David, but Edom gained the ascendency by revolt while Jehoram was king of Judah. Edom joined Babylon in humiliating Jerusalem in 586 B.C. Edom became the province of Idumea in the Persian Empire, and Antipater, the father of Herod the Great, came from there. The Idumeans disappeared after Rome leveled Jerusalem in A.D. 70.

Teaching Outline

I. Edom's humiliation: Obad. 1-4
 A. Report: 1
 B. Reduction: 2
 C. Reason: 3-4
II. Edom's sin: Obad. 10-11
 A. Violence: 10
 B. Victimization: 11
III. Edom's punishment: Obad. 15
 A. Day: 15a
 B. Deed: 15b
IV. Judah's restoration: Obad. 17, 21
 A. Deliverance: 17
 B. Deliverers: 21

Daily Bible Readings

Mon. Despised by the Heathen
Obadiah 1-2
Tue. Pride Hath Deceived
Obadiah 3-4
Wed. Vulnerable
Obadiah 5-7
Thu. Judgment Coming
Obadiah 8-9
Fri. Sins of Judah
Obadiah 10-14
Sat. The Day of the Lord
Obadiah 15-16
Sun. Ultimate Victory
Obadiah 17-21

Verse By Verse

I. Edom's humiliation: Obad. 1-4

A. Report: 1
1a. The vision of Obadiah. Thus saith the Lord God concerning Edom; ...
The only thing Obadiah mentioned about himself was that this vision was given to him by the Lord God regarding Edom's future.
1b. We have heard a rumour from the Lord, and an ambassador is sent among the heathen, Arise ye, and let us rise up against her in battle.
See Jeremiah 49:14. A rumour (report) has been heard. A trial is about to be held, and an ambassador (messenger) has been sent out by the divine Judge to tell the heathen (nations) to gather together and rise up against Edom in battle. It is implied that God will use other nations to punish Edom, even though they may also be evil and eventually have to be dealt with by God. The Assyrians and the Babylonians may have been especially in mind here.

B. Reduction: 2
2. Behold, I have made thee small among the heathen: thou art greatly despised
See Jeremiah 49:15. Edom had considered itself to be great among the nations of the Middle East. The Creator of the earth and sovereign Lord of all nations was not intimidated by this. He declared that He had reduced Edom to the status of being small and despised among the nations. Although this referred to coming humiliation, it was stated as if it were already true.

C. Reason: 3-4
3. The pride of thine heart hath deceived thee, thou that dwellest in the clefts of the rock, whose habitation is high; that saith in his heart, Who shall bring me down to the ground?
See Jeremiah 49:16a. Edom had placed its trust in its unique topography. Edomites felt secure in a stronghold of a granite range of fifteen to twenty miles running north to south and featuring cliffs as high as two thousand feet. Of particular pride was a plateau called Sela in Old Testament times and later called Petra. Reached only through a small ravine, Edomites did not think they could be successfully attacked if they took a stand there. This led to the boast that no one could bring them down.
4. Though thou exalt thyself as the eagle, and though thou set thy nest among the stars, thence will I bring thee down, saith the Lord.
See Jeremiah 49:16b. Hyperbole was used here for emphasis. God invited the Edomites to lift themselves up with eagles and with stars in the sky. It would make no difference to Him, for He had the power and means for bringing them down in a crash. He could work according to principles which would thwart every defensive strategy they devised. He could implement the truth that "pride goeth before destruction, and an haughty spirit before a fall" (Prov. 16sl8).

If you want to note comparisons between Obadiah and Jeremiah 49, see the following:

Obadiah	Jeremiah 49
Vs. 5a	Vs. 9b
Vs. 5	Vs. 9a
Vs. 6	Vs. 10a
Vs. 8	Vs. 7
Vs. 9	Vs. 20

II. Edom's sin: Obad. 10-11

A. Violence: 10
10. For thy violence against thy brother Jacob shame shall cover thee, and thou shalt be cut off for ever.

Not only were Edomites guilty of great pride in themselves but they were guilty of violence against the Jews. Esau and Jacob had been twin brothers. Animosities which had developed between them as young men had been smoothed over later in life. However, the descendants of Esau had mistreated the descendants of Jacob. God said that shame would cover the Edomites for this, and they would be cut off forever. Violence led to national destruction by divine decree.

B. Victimization: 11
11. In the day that thou stoodest on the other side, in the day that the strangers carried away captive his forces, and foreigners entered into his gates, and cast lots upon Jerusalem, even thou wast as one of them.

God, the divine Judge, indicted Edom for standing aside (aloof) at the time that Judah was taken over by her enemies. Strangers, including Philistines, Arabians, Syrians, and Chaldeans captured the forces (hosts) of Jews and carried off their wealth. Foreigners (aliens) entered into Jerusalem and other cities of Judah by breaking down their gates. They cast lots in the division of the spoils of war coming into their possession. Most of this probably referred to the sack of Jerusalem by Babylonia in 586 B.C.

God condemned Edom for acting as an enemy to Judah during her time of trouble. Obadiah 12-14 spells out the details. The Edomites looked on while the Jews were deported. They rejoiced in their destruction. They mocked them. They went in and helped themselves to loot. They stood at the crossroads and captured Jews trying to escape and then turned them over to their enemies. They victimized those who should have been treated as brothers descending from a common father, Isaac.

III. Edom's punishment: Obad. 15

A. Day: 15a
15a. For the day of the Lord is near upon all the heathen: . . .

The day of the Lord is a term used to describe the time when God will judge evil and vindicate righteousness. He has done these things many times in the past and continues to do them in the present. The specific meaning of the term refers to the ultimate judgment of the nations which will take place at the second coming of Christ down onto the earth. On an individual basis, it seems to refer to the great white throne judgment mentioned in Revelation 20:11-15. God was saying through Obadiah that divine judgment was near for sinful nations such as Edom, and in subsequent centuries the nation of Edom disappeared from the world scene.

B. Deed: 15b
15b. . . . **as thou hast done, it shall be done unto thee: thy reward shall return upon thine own head.**

Here is the negative version of the golden rule that we should treat others as we ourselves like to be treated. The Edomites were told that what they had done to others would be done to them. "You will get back what you have given" (Today's English Version). "Your acts will boomerang upon your heads" (Living Bible).

What God predicted eventually came to pass. The Nabateans managed to overcome the Edomites and push them out. They settled on the west side of the Dead Sea, making Hebron the capital of their territory in southern Judah. The Maccabees (Jewish independents) subdued them in the second century before Christ and absorbed them until they shared in the destruction, along with Jews, by the Roman general named Titus in A.D. 70.

Obadiah 16 stated that, not only Edom, but all heathen nations, would drink the bitter dregs of divine judgment and punishment. Some would appear never to have existed.

IV. Judah's restoration: Obad. 17, 21

A. Deliverance: 17
17a. But upon mount Zion shall be deliverance, . . .
In contrast to the judgment scheduled for Edom and all other evil nations, God predicted the restoration of Judah. Mount Zion represented the Jewish nation, and it would experience deliverance by God's power The deliverance would come in the form of deportees in the east being allowed to return to Palestine seventy years after the Babylonian captivity began.

17b; . . .and there shall be holiness; . . .
The basis on which God would bring the Jews back to their homeland was repentance for sin on their part. Once the Jews gave up their sins, they could begin to live holy lives again. This demanded separation from evil and separation unto righteousness. We normally use the term sanctification to describe this today.

17c. . . .and the house of Jacob shall possess their possessions.
This described the recovery of inherited land in Palestine following the end of the Babylonian captivity The Jews had to enter into a massive program of rebuilding of the temple, walls, and dwellings in Jerusalem and other parts of Judah in the face of pagan opposition. Obadiah 18-20 tells us that the Jews (house of Jacob, house of Joseph) would turn against Edom and devour it as fire consumes stubble. Jews would move into the hill country of Edom, the plains of Philistia, the fields of Ephraim and Samaria, and as far north as Tyre and Sidon The tribe of Benjamin would repossess the land of Gilead on the eastern side of the Jordan River.

B. Deliverers: 21
21a. And saviours shall come up on mount Zion to judge the mount of Esau; . . .
The book of Obadiah began with reference to divine judgment against Edom. It ended with reference to human deliverers acting on God's behalf to rule over the mount of Esau (Edom) from the mount of Zion in Jerusalem. This evidently is now historic fact.

21b. . . .and the kingdom shall be the Lord's.
We should not read too much into this. It was probably the nearer fulfillment which was intended here. God would bring His people back from captivity and rule over them as their heavenly King, working through civil and sacred leaders as His representatives on the earth. God's beloved Son, our Savior, will rule the world in righteousness.

The book of Obadiah, along with other portions of scripture, reminds us that God is sovereign over all. He raises up rulers andputs them down. He raises up nations and takes them into oblivion. There is nothing permanent as far as this world is concerned to which we may anchor ourselves, for all is temporary and changing. Our hope must be in God Who changes not.

When human justice fails, as it often does, our comfort and hope is that divine justice will ultimately prevail. The book of Obadiah underscores this truth in its short but intense treatment of the nation of Edom.

Evangelistic Emphasis

We live in a world of shattered dreams and broken promises. Perhaps all of us envisioned the ways our lives would develop. We had plans and goals. We anticipated that we would reach certain vocational levels and accumulate some measure of money and possessions.

In many cases, the circumstances of life have robbed us of the fulfillment of those dreams. Perhaps we wanted to be a professional and could not afford to go to college. Perhaps our heart was set on being a doctor and we could not get into medical school. Perhaps health problems created catastrophic expenses that depleted our savings. Perhaps business failures or poor investment decisions wiped out all our holdings.

We may have been promised advancement or opportunities by someone we trusted. We may have been greatly distressed to find those promises reneged on.

What an exhilarating freshness there is in the knowledge that when the Lord's promise is the foundation of our dreams, we can be confident it will be fulfilled. There is at least one area of life where we do not need to be afraid of disappointments. What the Lord has promised will happen as certainly as the sun will rise in the morning. We can enjoy the prospect of it with as much confidence as if it had already occurred.

Memory Selection

"For the day of the Lord is near upon all the heathen: as thou hast done, it shall be done unto thee: thy reward shall return upon thine own head."
Obadiah 15.

Our memory selection is a reminder that all actions have their consequences. Those who do the Lord's will will be blessed and those who rebel against his will will experience the consequences of that.

This doctrine is not based on the idea that God is vindictive. Rather it is based on the fact that it makes a real difference how we live. It makes a difference whether or not we step into the path of a speeding truck. It makes a difference whether or not we jump out of a window on the tenth story of a building. It makes a difference whether or not we breathe carbon monoxide.

While those are negative differences, there are also positive ones. It makes a difference whether we eat a nutritious diet and get proper exercise. It makes a difference whether we get proper rest and avoid excessive stress. Those who do these things will experience positive results from them.

The same principle is true in regard to spiritual matters. Hate, greed, malice, and lust are corrosives that are damaging to one's happiness and welfare. Love, mercy, forgiveness, and integrity are nutrients that feed a happy and productive life.

Weekday Problems

Tom was reared in a family that lived below the poverty level in a major city. He lived in an area that was densely populated and where apartment projects were not properly maintained. A lot of young people hung out on the streets where drugs and crime were everywhere evident.

Tom's mother had given him an unusual amount of love and approval. His self-esteem was healthy and he dreamed dreams of rising to a higher standard of living. He hoped to get his mother out of the ghetto and did not anticipate rearing his own family, when the time came, in those circumstances.

One day the police picked up Tom. In a case of mistaken identity he was accused of an armed robbery he had nothing to do with. There was no money for bail or for effective legal representation. He was convicted and sentenced to three to five years in the penitentiary.

He was at first heartbroken and then bitter. Those in his neighborhood who had not lived up to his principles were free to roam the streets selling drugs and engaging in other illegal activities. Yet he was in prison for what someone else had done.

* Does Tom have a right to feel as he does?
* Even if he does have such a right, are such feelings good for him and his future?
* What can he do to deal with these feelings?

Superintendent's Sermonette

Socialism is widespread in our modern world. Even bankrupt communism likes to mask itself as being socialistic. There are nations which claim to care for their people from the womb to the tomb, the cradle to the grave, by imposing excessive taxes on them. However, even in these countries there are people facing problems which seem unsolvable. These include alcoholism, illicit drugs, diseases, sexual promiscuity, pessimism, spiritual deprivation, and suicide. There is also always the possiblity of foreign domination.

God raised up the Israelites in the ancient world to be a lighthouse to the nations When they sinned, God chastized them by allowing foreigners to dominate them. When His people repented and turned from their wicked ways, He restored them and punished their oppressors. The little book of Obadiah tells of God's plan to overthrow Edom for its sins and restore Judah. Nations today need to learn that their only hope must be in God and not in their own inventions. Let us do our part in turning our nation toward God and righteousness.

This Lesson in **Your** Life

Obadiah's prophecy came during a period of national despair in Israel. Although they were the people of God, it appeared that other nations were receiving all the blessings and they were experiencing defeat and failure. Obadiah's message to Israel was that current discouragements were temporary episodes on the way to ultimate victory.

This is a lesson that will help us through some of the struggles and difficulties of our own lives. We sometimes feel that we are not making any progress. We may even feel that we are losing ground. At the same time, we may observe others who, without the benefit of faith and prayer, seem to be highly successful.

Like Israel of Obadiah's day, we need to be reminded that there are dark nights before beautiful sunrises, there are often pains before healing, and there is often discouragement before victory.

There is also a lesson here to those who are enjoying temporary successes on the way to ultimate disaster. Edom was swelled with pride and felt that there was no enemy that could defeat them. Obadiah warned that this was not the final outcome and should not be trusted.

This lesson can be meaningful to us when we are trying to understand the success of the profane and corrupt. It can also be a warning to us when we are enjoying a prosperity that is not founded on our faith in God.

A third lesson in this passage is that warnings can be good news. We usually think of good news as being the promise of blessings. The warnings that caution us to avoid disasters can be equally beneficial to us.

Warnings are not the same as threats. They have a caring, protective quality. We warn children about the danger of being injured in traffic or being burned on a stove. This is not to deprive them of anything but to protect them from an unhappy experience. We warn because we love.

God also warns us because he loves us. He never desires to deprive us of anything that would be good for us. He simply points out to us that there are things that might appear pleasant but have unpleasant consequences. He warns us because he loves us.

This passage also teaches that there will be an ultimate judgment and it must be taken seriously. While a person's life is being lived, there will be periods of time when good is not instantly rewarded and evil is not instantly punished. During such periods, some tend to think that it does not make that much difference which they do. Obadiah reminds us that the fact that sin may go temporarily unpunished does not mean that it is not taken seriously by God. He also teaches that righteousness may temporarily appear to be unrewarding, but that it will not ultimately be so.

Finally, Obadiah points out that God's promises can be depended on. Other things in our world may change with the changing tides, but God's promises will always be true and can always be counted on.

Seed Thoughts

1. Why do Obadiah and Jeremiah 49 contain similar materials?
Scholars suggest that they may have based their information on some well known previous prophecy about Edom.

2. How does the book of Obadiah remind us of a court trial?
The nations are called to hear God's indictment of Edom for her sins against Judah and her punishment.

3. What was Edom's sin as shown in Obadiah 3-4?
Edom was guilty of pride in her position and power, thinking herself too high to be brought down.

4. What does God do with proud people?
He warns them that they will fall, and if they refuse to heed Him, He brings them crashing down,

5. What was Edom's sin as shown in Obadiah 10-11?
Edom was guilty of standing with Judah's enemies when they overcame her.

---

1. Why do Obadiah and Jeremiah 49 contain similar materials?

2. How does the book of Obadiah remind us of a court trial?

3. What was Edom's sin as shown in Obadiah 3-4?

4. What does God do with proud people?

5. What was Edom's sin as shown in Obadiah 10-11?

6. What is meant by the term "day of the Lord?"

7. What is the opposite of the golden rule?

8. What is required for people to experience divine deliverance, holiness, and repossession?

9. How did God fulfill His promises of deliverance to the Jews?

(Please Turn Page)

Seed Thoughts - Continued

Scholars suggest that they may have based their information on some well known previous prophecy about Edom.

The nations are called to hear God's indictment of Edom for her sins against Judah and her punishment.

Edom was guilty of pride in her position and power, thinking herself too high to be brought down.

He warns them that they will fall, and if they refuse to heed Him, He brings them crashing down,

Edom was guilty of standing with Judah's enemies when they overcame her.

It refers to a time when God judges evil and vindicates righteousness. The ultimate judgment comes in the end time.

Expect the evil you do to others to be brought back upon your own head.

They must repent of their sins, separate themselves <u>from</u> evil and <u>unto</u> righteousness, and claim God's blessings.

After seventy years of Babylonian captivity, He brought the Jews back to Palestine to rebuild their nation,

6. What is meant by the term "day of the Lord?"
It refers to a time when God judges evil and vindicates righteousness. The ultimate judgment comes in the end time.

7. What is the opposite of the golden rule?
Expect the evil you do to others to be brought back upon your own head.

8. What is required for people to experience divine deliverance, holiness, and repossession?
They must repent of their sins, separate themselves <u>from</u> evil and <u>unto</u> righteousness, and claim God's blessings.

9. How did God fulfill His promises of deliverance to the Jews?
After seventy years of Babylonian captivity, He brought the Jews back to Palestine to rebuild their nation,

Fleeing From God

Jonah 1:1. Now the word of the Lord came unto Jonah the son of Amittai, saying,
2. Arise, go to Nineveh, that great city, and cry against it; for their wickedness is come up before me.
3. But Jonah rose up to flee unto Tarshish from the presence of the Lord, and went down to Joppa; and he found a ship going to Tarshish: so he paid the fare thereof and went down into it, to go with them unto Tarshish from the presence of the Lord.
4. But the Lord sent out a great wind into the sea, and there was a mighty tempest in the sea, so that the ship was like to be broken.
5. Then the mariners were afraid, and cried every man unto his god, and cast forth the wares that were in the ship into the sea, to lighten it of them. But Jonah was gone down into the sides of the ship; and he lay, and was fast asleep.
6. So the shipmaster came to him, and said unto him, What meanest thou, O sleeper? arise, call upon thy God, if so be that God will think upon us, that we perish not.
7. And they said every one to his fellow, Come, and let us cast lots, that we may know for whose cause this evil is upon us. So they cast lots, and the lot fell upon Jonah.
8. Then said they unto him, Tell us, we pray thee, for whose cause this evil is upon us; What is thine occupation? and whence comest thou? what is thy country? and of what people art thou?
9. And he said unto them, I am an Hebrew; and I fear the Lord, the God of heaven, which hath made the sea and the dry land.
Jonah 1:15. So they took up Jonah, and cast him forth into the sea: and the sea ceased from her raging.
16. Then the men feared the Lord exceedingly, and offered a sacrifice unto the Lord, and made vows .
17. Now the Lord had prepared a great fish to swallow up Jonah. And Jonah was in the belly of the fish three days and three nights.

MEMORY SELECTION
Jonah 1:3
DEVOTIONAL READING
Psalm 139:7-12

BACKGROUND SCRIPTURE
Jonah 1-2
PRINTED SCRIPTURE
Jonah 1:1-9,15-17

Teacher's Target

This lesson and the next are based on the book of Jonah. This prophet hated Nineveh and its people. He did not want them to repent and be saved from divine destruction. God used him, anyway. The first time Jonah was told to go to Nineveh on a preaching mission, he headed in the opposite direction. God used the elements of nature and the fear of heathen shipmates to stop Jonah's flight and prepare him for his second call to Nineveh.

~~Help your students to realize that they~~ we can never hide from God nor escape His punitive actions. He will use whatever force is required in order to steer ~~them~~ us in the right direction and accomplish His sovereign will. It is far better to listen to Him, agree with Him, and obey Him right from the start. He seeks such individuals to carry out His redemptive program on the earth.

Lesson Introduction

It may seem amazing, but the negative prophet named Jonah served as a foretype of the Lord Jesus Christ. Jonah was sent by God twice to take the message of repentance to people in need, Jesus was sent by God once to make redemption possible. Jonah spent three days and nights in the great fish (or whale) God had prepared for him. Jesus used this as a sign of His Own death and resurrection (Matt. 12:40). Jonah carried the message of salvation to Gentiles in Nineveh. Jesus died and rose again in order that the whole world might be offered salvation.

What we learn in type from Jonah, and in reality from Jesus, we ought to put into practice in our own lives. God has placed us at a time and place in human history which make us responsible for getting the gospel to the lost. We need to act as partners with the Lord in reaching this goal to the best of our ability.

Teaching Outline

I. Flight: Jonah 1:1-3
   A. Demand: 1-2
   B. Departure: 3

II. Fear: Jonah 1:4-9
   A. Storm: 4-5a
   B. Sleeper: 5b-6
   C. Selection: 7
   D. Search: 8-9

III. Favors: Jonah 1:15-17
   A. Calmness: 15-16
   B. Compartment: 17

Daily Bible Readings

Mon. Go to Nineveh
Jonah 1:1-2
Tue. Jonah Flees
Jonah 1:3
Wed. A Great Storm
Jonah 1:4-10
Thu. Jonah Cast Overboard
Jonah 1:11-17
Fri. Jonah Prays
Jonah 2:1-4
Sat. Prayer Continued
Jonah 2:5-8
Sun. Jonah Saved
Jonah 2:9-10

Verse By Verse

I. Flight: Jonah 1:1-3

A. Demand: 1-2
1. **Now the word of the Lord came unto Jonah the son of Amittai, saying,**
Comparing Jonah 1:1-2 with 3:1-2, we learn that God spoke to the son of Amittai about the Assyrian city of Nineveh. Jonah had predicted during the reign of Jeroboam II that the boundaries of Israel to the north would be restored to where they had been in the time of David and Solomon. Jonah then lived in Gathhepher in the territory of the tribe of Zebulun (II Kings 14:25).
2. **Arise, go to Nineveh, that great city, and cry against it; for their wickedness is come up before me.**
It is likely that Jonah had been told in God's first call that he was to preach a message of repentance to Nineveh (Jonah 3:2). He did not want to do this, for the Assyrians were Israel's mortal enemies and had been oppressing her sorely on the northern borders. Nineveh was a great city because it included the cities of Rehoboth, Calah, and Resen within its territory (Gen. 10:11-12). Some time after Jonah's day, about 700 B.C., Sennacherib would make it his capital. It was located on the east bank of the Tigris River in ancient Mesopotamia (Iraq). It was known for its wickedness in the form of fertility cult worship and cruel treatment of captives gained through warfare.

B. Departure: 3
3. **But Jonah rose up to flee unto Tarshish from the presence of the Lord, and went down to Joppa; and he found a ship going to Tarshish: so he paid the fare thereof, and went down into it, to go with them unto Tarshish from the presence of the Lord.**
Instead of heading in the direction of Nineveh to the northeast, Jonah went down to the seaport of Joppa to book passage on a ship going to Tarshish. We are not sure where Tarshish was located, but some identify it with Tartessus, a city on the Atlantic coast of Spain. Some think it was a Semitic mining colony at the mouth of the Guadalquivir River west of the Rock of Gibraltar (Ezek 27: 12). If this was true, it was certainly in the opposite direction from Nineveh.
Twice we are told in Jonah 1:3 that the prophet sought to flee from the presence of the Lord by heading toward Tarshish. Jonah evidently felt that removing himself far from Nineveh would somehow take him away from the Lord or perhaps nullify His command.

II. Fear: Jonah 1:4-9

A. Storm: 4-5a
4 **But the Lord sent out a great wind into the sea, and there was a mighty tempest in the sea, so that the ship was like to be broken.**
This verse makes it clear that God will use His control of nature to carry out His divine purpose. He cast a raging storm onto the Great (Mediterranean) Sea which threatened to break up the ship. This was definitely an "act of God" and was brought upon many people for the sake of one wretched fugitive from God's will.
5a. **Then the mariners were afraid, and cried every man unto**

his god, and cast forth the wares that were in the ship into the sea, to lighten it of them.

The well-seasoned sailors on the ship were probably Phoenicians used to handling crises such as this, but even they were terrified at the power of this God-sent storm. They were pagans, devoted to a variety of Canaanite gods, and each one cried to his own deity for help. They also took the reasonable precaution of throwing cargo (and perhaps equipment) overboard in order to lighten the ship and help it to ride out the storm. These steps apparently did not have any effect on the tempest, as implied by Jonah 1:15. They became increasingly desperate.

B. Sleeper: 5b-6
5b. But Jonah was gone down into the sides of the ship; and he lay, and was fast asleep.

Jonah had evidently been exhausted by his emotional disobedience of the Lord's command and by his hasty trip down to Joppa. He went down into a remote place on the lower deck of the ship and fell into a sleep so deep that not even the storm awoke him.

6. So the shipmaster came to him, and said unto him, What meanest thou, O sleeper? arise, call upon thy God, if so be that God will think upon us, that we perish not.

The ship's captain was told about Jonah, perhaps by sailors who had taken cargo up out of the hold to cast overboard. The captain came to him, woke him up, and demanded that he pray to his God that everyone on board would not perish by drowning. The captain was typical of pagans who sought help from any god (or God) available in a time of deathly peril. We are not told if Jonah did as the captain commanded.

C. Selection: 7
7a. And they said every one to his fellow, Come, and let us cast lots, that we may know for whose cause this evil is upon us.

The pagan sailors decided that someone on board the ship was guilty of offending deity and bringing this calamity on all of them. This did not seem fair, and they wanted to isolate him and deal with him for the good of all the others. Casting lots as a form of divination was used by most ancients. Even the Hebrews used it under God's control to make decisions, as in the case of Achan (Josh 7:14) and in choosing Saul to be king (I Sam. 10:20-21). The apostles used it to choose Matthias to replace Judas Iscariot (Acts 1:23-26). This probably involved the use of white and black pebbles, rather than the dice used today.

7b. So they cast lots, and the lot fell upon Jonah

We assume that God made use of the casting of lots in this case to show that Jonah was the one guilty on board the ship and that he was responsible for the raging storm. Any other information would have to come from Jonah himself.

D. Search: 3-9
8. Then said they unto him, Tell us, we pray thee, for whose cause this evil is upon us; What is thine occupation? and whence comest thou? what is thy country? and of what people art thou?

It appears that the sailors surrounded Jonah and peppered him with all of these questions. He seems to have answered only the last question (vs. 9). The men were searching for clues to explain the phenomenon of the God-sent storm. They asked:

(1) Who caused this evil to come on us?
(2) What is your occupation?
(3) Where do you come from?
(4) What is your country (nationality)?

9. And he said unto them, I am an Hebrew; and I fear the Lord, the God of heaven, which hath made the sea and the dry land.

Jonah did not tell the sailors what his occupation was nor where his home was. He did admit that he was a Hebrew. His other comment may have helped answer the first question the men had asked, for Jonah said that he feared (reverenced) Jehovah, Creator of the world. He had already told them that he was fleeing from the presence of the Lord, and they became exceedingly afraid because of what Jonah had done to offend his God. They then asked him what they should do in order to calm the sea, and he told them to cast him overboard. The men were unwilling to do this at first, preferring to try to row hard to reach land. When this did no good, they decided that they would have to take Jonah's advice, but they prayed to the Lord that He would not hold them accountable for doing it (Jonah 1:10-14).

III. Favors: Jonah 1:15-17

A. Calmness: 15
15. So they took up Jonah, and cast him forth into the sea: and the sea ceased from her raging.

God bestowed two favors after the sailors cast Jonah into the sea. The first one was to calm the storm. This made the sailors realize that Jonah had given them good advice and that the God of the Hebrews did indeed control nature They were very impressed.

16. Then the men feared the Lord exceedingly, and offered a sacrifice unto the Lord, and made vows.

The sailors were so awed by what had happened that they feared (reverenced) the God of the Hebrews exceedingly. They had sacrificed Jonah to the sea, and now they found something to sacrifice to the Lord. They made vows to serve Jehovah, although we do not know if they meant to serve Him exclusively. The chances were that they meant to add Him to their pantheon of other gods

B. Compartment: 17
17a. Now the Lord had prepared a great fish to swallow up Jonah.

The second favor God bestowed, following the calming of the storm, was to take care of his errant prophet. The Lord had prepared a large fish to swallow Jonah. Some think that the term whale used in Matthew 12:40 was a mistranslation. Whatever the creature was, God had prepared it in such a way that it had a compartment within itself where Jonah could survive for a brief time.

17b. And Jonah was in the belly of the fish three days and three nights.

There is an honest difference of opinion among evangelical scholars regarding the time involved here. Some claim that Jonah was in the sea creature for a full seventy-two hours. Others think the literal hours could have been shorter according to Old Testament reckoning of time. The important thing is that God saved Jonah from death in a most unusual and miraculous way. This miracle is denied by some scholars. Evangelicals would do well to avoid arguing about the literal hours involved and put emphasis on upholding the literal miracle itself.

Chapter 2 of Jonah tells us what happened to the prophet. Verses 2-9 record the prayer he made to God from the belly of the creature. Verse 10 says, "And the Lord spake unto the fish, and it vomited out Jonah upon the dry land." We are not told where this was, but it was probably somewhere along the eastern coast of the Great (Mediterranean) Sea. We can imagine that this traumatic experience left Jonah weary and perhaps especially sensitive to wind and the sun's rays (Jonah 4:6-9). Now God was ready to renew His commission that Jonah go to Nineveh and preach to its people.

Evangelistic Emphasis

Jonah was a reluctant evangelist. The people of Nineveh were a despised group to him. He did not want to go there. Once there, he did not want to preach in such a way that the people might repent. Having done so, he was angry when the people did repent and God showed mercy to them.

There is an enormous amount of good news in this passage. Part of it has to do with the fact that the power is in the message rather than in the messenger. It is nice when people have the opportunity to hear the gospel from one who is eloquent and personable. However, when that is not possible, the gospel does not lose its power.

Further, this passage teaches that God is tenderhearted toward those who repent even when they appear obnoxious to others. We may be guilty of scandalous sins but if we will turn contritely to the Lord, He will look on us with mercy.

Third, this passage has an evangelistic emphasis in that it is not too late to turn to the Lord. We may feel guilty and discouraged because of the length of time we have rejected the Lord and the waste of our lives that has resulted. Indeed it would have been better if we had turned to the Lord sooner. However, that is water under the bridge. The question is, "What should we do now? Is it too late?" The answer is, "No, it is not too late."

The loving Lord will happily relent on matters of judgment when he sees repentance in the hearts of people. He is not eager to condemn but to save. He will do so if we will give him the opportunity.

Memory Selection

"Jonah rose up to flee unto Tarshish from the presence of the Lord."
Jonah 1:3.

How do we react to the call of the Lord? Are we like Jonah? Do we decide whether or not to obey on the basis of whether or not the commandment is agreeable to us or reasonable to us? Do we consider the possibility of alternatives to obedience? Do we think about fleeing as Jonah did?

A better way of responding is to consider how to get started doing what the Lord is asking. Jonah could have used the time, the energy, and the money that he spent trying to escape to accomplish something far more effective.

When we have something disagreeable to do, it is often better to do it at once. The resources that would have been used in avoiding our duty can be invested in doing it. Our period of agitation will be over sooner.

If we can learn from Jonah we may be able to prevent tragedy in our own lives. His experience tells us that it is impossible to flee the presence of the Lord. The Lord was in the sea as well as on the shore. He was in Tarshish as well as at home. From the belly of the great fish, God was able to hear Jonah's prayer. When Jonah got to Nineveh, the Lord was there.

Let us learn that there is nowhere to flee from the Lord. We must deal with Him where we are.

Weekday Problems

Your teenage son, Ken has a friend named Jerry. You have serious concerns that Jerry's influence on Ken is damaging. The two of them seem always to be on the fringe of getting into trouble. Ken is a good-spirited young man but is easily influenced by others, both in good and bad ways.

Late one night you get a call from the police. Ken and Jerry have been arrested in the act of robbing a convenience store. In the course of the robbery the store operator pulled a gun and Ken, frightened and panicky, shot him.

The heartbreak and anxiety are enormous. The legal costs are so high that they place serious strains on the rest of the family. You know that Ken's future has been seriously compromised. There is a certainty of a criminal record and the probability of time in the penitentiary. It seems that your dearest dreams have been shattered. Much that you have given your life for is gone.

Jerry then comes by to express his regret and to ask your forgiveness.

* Would you be able to rejoice at the change of heart in Jerry?
* How do you deal with your anger and bitterness?
* Does the Lord expect you to forgive Jerry and go on as though nothing has happened?

Superintendent's Sermonette

The best kind of discipline is self-discipline. If that is lacking, some other person may supply it for you. In some cases, it may come from God above. It takes discipline to follow the routine schedules of life. It takes even more discipline to make ourselves do things which we do not want to do because they are extraordinary. God wanted Jonah, an ancient prophet, to do something special. He told him to go to Israel's enemies in Nineveh and preach repentance to them. Jonah refused to go, and he got on board a ship going to Tarshish in the opposite direction.

God used the power of a raging sea-storm and the fear of pagan sailors to halt Jonah's trip, Jonah was cast out of the ship in order to get the storm stopped, and it looked as if he were going to drown, but God saved him in a most unusual way. It took this to persuade Jonah to do God's will. We can avoid a lot of trouble if we will submit ourselves to God's discipline and make it our own, Are you ready to put yourself under God's control every day?

This Lesson in <u>Your</u> Life

Jonah is one of the wonderful stories in the Bible that is a favorite to both young and old. Many of us began to learn about Jonah and the whale when we were scarcely more than toddlers. We did not then know all the adult lessons about bigotry, resentment, and rebellion that are in the book. There are a number of ways in which Jonah can be applied directly to our own lives.

One has to do with the way we deal with unpleasant duties. We may not be called on to go to Nineveh, but we inevitably will be required to do some things that are not easy to do. We will sometimes be tempted to try to evade those responsibilities as Jonah did. At other times we will procrastinate, putting off the disagreeable as long as possible. At times we may simply rebel, feeling that we cannot bring ourselves to do something so unpleasant.

One lesson of Jonah is that we ultimately have to face our responsibilities in life, even the difficult and disagreeable ones. The sooner we are able to deal with them in a straightforward way, the better off we will be. Jonah did not succeed in avoiding his duty. He merely postponed doing it. In the postponement there was danger and hardship. When we see our duty, let us be swift to do it, even if it is something we do not want to do.

Another lesson has to do with facing frightening situations that are beyond our control. The frightening storm that could be calmed only by Jonah's being thrown overboard was one such situation. At a time like that we have no alternative other than dependence on God. The book of Jonah reminds us that some problems are beyond our power to fix. We have to entrust them to God.

A third lesson is that it is impossible to run away from our true responsibility in life. Some things are expected of us that we must do or be held accountable for not doing them. Being responsible is a part of being human. We can move, change jobs, plead inability, or try in other ways to avoid being responsible. Nothing works. We were made to be responsible creatures. We cannot run away from that.

A fourth lesson is that we cannot reject people that God accepts. It pleased Jonah for the people of Nineveh to be under the judgment of God. It angered him for God to be forgiving to people he hated.

Sometimes this is a real problem for us. God is able to love people who are very hard for us to love. Yet if we are children of God, we must learn to love those He loves. We must remember that even those who are hard to love are made by God and made in his image. They are objects of His love and the beneficiaries of the death of Christ on the cross. In the light of those facts, we cannot refuse to love them.

Seed Thoughts

1. How do we know that Jonah was a real prophet in Israel?
Second Kings 14:25 refers to Jonah as having made a prophecy regarding Israel during the reign of Jeroboam II

2. Why did God want Jonah to go to the enemy city of Nineveh?
The people of Nineveh were wicked, and God wanted repentance preached to them (Jonah 1:2; 3:2). God was merciful.

3. How did Jonah try to flee from the presence of the Lord?
He went on board a ship bound for Tarshish in the opposite direction from Nineveh, perhaps in Spain.

4. Why is it impossible to escape from God's presence?
God, by His Holy Spirit, is omnipresent (everywhere present) in the universe (Ps. 139:7-8)

5. Was the tempest sent to threaten the ship an "act of God?"
This one was, for God began and ended it when Jonah's identity and guilt were revealed to his shipmates.

(Please Turn Page)

---

1. How do we know that Jonah was a real prophet in Israel?

2. Why did God want Jonah go to the enemy city of Nineveh?

3. How did Jonah try to flee from the presence of the Lord?

4. Why is it impossible to escape from God's presence?

5. Was the tempest sent to threaten the ship an "act of God?"

6. Why did the ship's captain tell Jonah to pray to God?

7. Should Christians today cast lots to decide things?

8. Were the sailors more honorable than Jonah was?

9. How did the pagans react to God who saved them from disaster?

10. How did God save Jonah?

Second Kings 14:25 refers to Jonah as having made a prophecy regarding Israel during the reign of Jeroboam II

The people of Nineveh were wicked, and God wanted repentance preached to them (Jonah 1:2; 3:2). God was merciful.

He went on board a ship bound for Tarshish in the opposite direction from Nineveh, perhaps in Spain.

God, by His Holy Spirit, is omnipresent (everywhere present) in the universe (Ps. 139:7-8)

This one was, for God began and ended it when Jonah's identity and guilt were revealed to his shipmates.

Pagan prayers had accomplished nothing, and the captain thought that prayer to Jonah's God might help,

This custom sometimes was used by God to reveal His will. Christians today claim better ways to know it. Discuss.

They tried to row to land to keep from throwing him overboard, whereas he cared nothing for lost souls in Nineveh.

The sailors reverenced Jehovah and vowed to serve Him, but we don't know if they meant to serve Him exclusively.

God had prepared a great fish to keep Jonah alive until He relanded him. We have to accept this miracle by faith.

Seed Thoughts - Continued

6. Why did the ship's captain tell Jonah to pray to God?
Pagan prayers had accomplished nothing, and the captain thought that prayer to Jonah's God might help,

7. Should Christians today cast lots to decide things?
This custom sometimes was used by God to reveal His will. Christians today claim better ways to know it. Discuss.

8. Were the sailors more honorable than Jonah was?
They tried to row to land to keep from throwing him overboard, whereas he cared nothing for lost souls in Nineveh.

9. How did the pagans react to God who saved them from disaster?
The sailors reverenced Jehovah and vowed to serve Him, but we don't know if they meant to serve Him exclusively.

10. How did God save Jonah?
God had prepared a great fish to keep Jonah alive until He relanded him. We have to accept this miracle by faith.

Jonah Sulks, And God Saves

Jonah 3:1. And the word of the Lord came unto Jonah the second time, saying,
2. Arise, go unto Nineveh, that great city, and preach unto it the preaching that I bid thee.
3. So Jonah arose, and went unto Nineveh, according to the word of the Lord. Now Nineveh was an exceedingly great city of three days' journey.
4. And Jonah began to enter into the city a day's journey, and he cried, and said, Yet forty days, and Nineveh shall be overthrown.
5. So the people of Nineveh believed God, and proclaimed a fast, and put on sackcloth, from the greatest of them even to the least of them.
Jonah 3:10. And God saw their works, that they turned from their evil way; and God repented of the evil, that he had said that he would do unto them: and he did not do it.
Jonah 4:1. But it displeased Jonah exceedingly, and he was very angry.

2. And he prayed unto the Lord, and said, I pray thee, O Lord, was not this my saying, when I was yet in my country? Therefore I fled before unto Tarshish: for I knew that thou art a gracious God, and merciful, slow to anger, and of great kindness, and repentest thee of evil.
3. Therefore now, O Lord, take, I beseech thee, my life from me; for it is better for me to die than to live.
4. Then said the Lord, Doest thou well to be angry?
Jonah 4:10. Then said the Lord, Thou hast had pity on the gourd, for the which thou hast not labored, neither madest it grow; which came up in a night, and perished in a night.
11. And should not I spare Nineveh, that great city, wherein are more than six-score thousand persons that cannot discern between their right hand and their left; and also much cattle?

MEMORY SELECTION
Jonah 4:11
DEVOTIONAL READING
Psalm 146:1-7

BACKGROUND SCRIPTURE
Jonah 3-4
PRINTED SCRIPTURE
Jonah 3:1-5,10, 4:1-4,10-11

Teacher's Target

In our last lesson, we learned that Jonah was cast into the sea, swallowed by a great fish, and deposited on the shoreline three days later. He then proceeded to the city of Nineveh and entered it to proclaim divine judgment was due to come on it in forty days. The people heeded the message and repented. Jonah was displeased at this and still hoped the Lord would destroy Nineveh. God had to teach him a lesson regarding compassion.

Help your students to remember that "the Lord . . . is longsuffering [patient] to us - ward [people], not willing [desiring] that any should perish, but that all should come to repentance" (II Pet. 3:9). It was because of His mercy that ancient Nineveh escaped judgment in Jonah's time. He is compassionate toward sinners today, and He wants us to be compassionate toward them, too. We should be especially considerate of children.

Lesson Introduction

A true prophet of God needs not only a message but also a merciful disposition. Jonah lacked this. He went to Nineveh under divine duress, not because he cared for Israel's enemies, He may have actually enjoyed telling the Ninevites that God was planning to destroy them in forty days. He was most unhappy when they believed him, repented of their sins, and sought God's mercy. Jonah delayed leaving the area, hoping that Nineveh would be overthrown. He probably wanted to go back to Israel to report about it to his fellow countrymen.

The Lord used a simple but effective means for teaching Jonah the need for mercy. The gourd which sprang up in a night and withered in a night distressed Jonah because of his own personal discomfort. God called his attention to the fact that there were over 120,000 children in Nineveh who deserved an opportunity to live.

Teaching Outline

I. Acceptance: Jonah 3:1-5, 10
   A. Demand: 1-2
   B. Departure: 3a
   C. Declaration: 3b-4
   D. Decisions: 5, 10

II. Anger: Jonah 4:1-4
   A. Disappointment: 1-2
   B. Death-wish: 3-4

III. Argument: Jonah 4:10-11
   A. Pity I: 10
   B. Pity II: 11

Daily Bible Readings

Mon. A Second Call
Jonah 3:1-2
Tue. Preaching in Nineveh
Jonah 3:3-4
Wed. Repentance
Jonah 3:5-7
Thu. Saved
Jonah 3:8-10
Fri. Jonah Angry
Jonah 4:1-3
Sat. The Gourd
Jonah 4:4-8
Sun. Jonah Learns a Lesson
Jonah 4:9-11

Verse By Verse

I. Acceptance: Jonah 3:1-5, 10

A. **Demand: 1-2**
1. And the word of the Lord came unto Jonah the second time, saying,
2. Arise, go unto Nineveh, that great city, and preach unto it the preaching that I bid thee.

God's first call to Jonah had come to him at home (probably at Gathhepher, II Kings 14:25). God had told him to go to Nineveh and cry out against it, for the wickedness of its people had come up before Him (Jonah 1:1-2). God's second call came at some unnamed location (probably somewhere along the eastern shoreline of the Great Sea). God told him to go to Nineveh and preach to the people whatever He told him to say.

It would appear that Jonah was not told the content of the message to be given the second time God contacted him. However, he apparently remembered from the first call that he was to cry out against Nineveh. At the same time, he knew that God was merciful, and he expected God to relent, if the Ninevites repented (Jonah 4:2).

There may have been two things which motivated Jonah to accept God's second call. One was his fear of putting his life in jeopardy again by refusing to go. The other was his desire to pronounce doom on Nineveh and then hopefully see it performed. Jonah was obviously a prophet with a very weak character. God may have wanted Jonah to go to Nineveh to strengthen his character, but we have no record of Jonah's ministry following this trip.

B. **Departure: 3a**
3a. So Jonah arose, and went unto Nineveh, according to the word of the Lord.

Feeling that he had no choice but to go, and perhaps relishing the prospect of seeing Nineveh destroyed, Jonah rose up to begin the long trip. He obeyed the word of the Lord, but he did it reluctantly. He thus became a negative biblical example of a person who serves God with a bad attitude. We might wonder why God used Jonah. It helped to show that the message can be more important than the messenger, and God can use any messenger He chooses, even if that individual appears to be unworthy to us.

C. **Declaration: 3b-4**
3b. Now Nineveh was an exceeding great city of three days' journey.

When Jonah finally got to ancient Mesopotamia, drained by the Tigris and Euphrates Rivers, he discovered Nineveh and its surrounding communities to be a vast district. Nineveh itself might be a walled city only eight miles in circumference, but its outlying district could have accommodated over 175,000 people and been thirty to sixty miles across. It was a big mission field.

4. And Jonah began to enter into the city a day's journey, and he cried, and said, Yet forty days, and Nineveh shall be overthrown.

Jonah entered Nineveh and spent a day proclaiming that it was doomed in forty days. There must have been something about his appearance and message which gave authority to what he said, because the people listened. Some individuals seem more effective in open air evangelism than others.

D. Decisions: 5, 10
5. So the people of Nineveh believed God, and proclaimed a fast, and put on sackcloth, from the greatest of them even to the least of them.

The first decision resulting from Jonah's preaching was that the Ninevites accepted him as God's spokesman, believed God's message, proclaimed a fast, and put on sackcloth for mourning. This involved all levels of society. Even the king rose up from his throne, laid his royal robe aside, and put on sackcloth to sit in ashes. He sent out a decree to all of his people that they and their animals should eat nothing, should wear sackcloth, and should cry out to God for forgiveness of sins. His hope was that the Lord would repent (relent) and withhold the announced calamity, allowing the Ninevites to survive (Jonah 3:6-9).

10. And God saw their works, that they turned from their evil way and God repented of the evil, that he had said that he would do unto them; and he did it not

God saw the Ninevites go into mourning for their sins and cry out to Him for pardon. He saw them forsake the violence for which they were known, particularly their cruelty to captives. When it said that He repented of the evil He had planned for them and did not bring it upon them, it did not mean that He was fickle or vacillatory. It meant that He was touched by their petitions and chose to withhold judgment because He was merciful. Perhaps a better word for repent when being used for God is the word relent, meaning to soften, mollify, or even abandon what He announced would be done.

II. Anger: Jonah 4:1-4

A. Disappointment: 1-2
1. But it displeased Jonah exceedingly, and he was very angry.

Repentance by people on the mission field is the goal and greatest blessing of missionaries. This was not the case with Jonah. He was very unhappy and angry with the success of his one-day mission. He did not want the Ninevites to repent and be saved from destruction. Fierce Assyrians had raided across Israel's northern borders to create havoc. They had threatened the very existence of the nation We can understand why Jonah hated them and wanted them dead.

2a. And he prayed unto the Lord, and said, I pray thee, O Lord, was not this my saying, when I was yet in my country?

In spite of his deep anger, Jonah prayed to the Lord. He seemed to be arguing with God by saying that He had done just what Jonah was afraid He would do while he was back in Israel. In other words, Jonah disagreed with God and His action, and that was a dangerous position to take.

2b. Therefore I fled before unto Tarshish: ...

Jonah now sought to justify himself for trying to run away from God and His will by boarding a ship to go to Tarshish in the opposite direction from Nineveh.

2c. ...for I knew that thou art a gracious God, and merciful, slow to anger, and of great kindness, and repentest thee of the evil.

Taken by itself, this part of the verse is a wonderful testimony to the attributes of God—grace, mercy, patience, and kindness. However, Jonah used them in his criticism of God. It was obvious that Jonah wanted God to show these attributes to the Jews but to withhold them from the pagan Ninevites. That could have happened, and it would have happened, except for one important reason. The Ninevites had sincerely repented of their sins and cried out to God for pardon. It was His nature to respond favorably to them, despite Jonah's opinion of them.

B. Death-wish: 3-4
3. Therefore now, O Lord, take, I beseech thee, my life from me; for it is better for me to die than to live.

We can only speculate on what

motivated Jonah to express this death-wish twice (see vss. 8-9). We might think that he did this because of petulance, but there may have been another reason. Jonah may have been afraid to go home to Israel and be accused of serving as God's instrument of deliverance for enemies of his country. That may be why he thought it would be better to die than to live any longer, perhaps as a perpetual fugitive from his home. He did not threaten to commit suicide, but he did want God to take his life from him.

4. Then said the Lord, Doest thou well to be angry?

God probably meant this question to probe for the motivation for Jonah's great anger and expose it for what it was. However, it may be that Jonah thought God implied that there was no cause for that anger.

Jonah went outside the city and set up a booth where he might sit and watch for the destruction of Nineveh in forty days, perhaps thinking that God would remove the cause for his anger. God then began to teach Jonah the meaning of compassion. He first had a gourd grow rapidly up over Jonah's booth to protect him from wind and sunlight. Jonah's skin may have been very sensitive because of being in the fish's stomach for three days and nights, and he appreciated this divine kindness (Jonah 4: 5-6).

The next morning God sent a worm to cut the gourd and cause it to wither and die. When the sun Came up, and a vehement east wind sent by God blew on Jonah, he fainted and wished again that he could die. When God questioned him about this, Jonah said that he was justified in wanting to die due to his suffering over loss of the gourd (Jonah 4:7-9).

III. Argument: Jonah 4:10-11
A. Pity I: 10

10. Then said the Lord, Thou hast had pity on the gourd, for the which thou hast not laboured, neither madest it grow; which came up in a night, and perished in a night.

God said that Jonah had shown pity on the leafy gourd plant which had shaded his booth, even though he had not planted it or made it grow from one night to the next. Jonah's real pity, of course, was directed at himself because he had lost the plant. Now God was ready to make His point about the need for compassion toward people, who were vastly more important than a plant.

B. Pity II: 11

11. And should not I spare Nineveh, that great city, wherein are more than sixscore thousand persons that cannot discern between their right hand and their left hand; and also much cattle?

This rhetorical question might be even better put into declarative form. God claimed His right to spare Nineveh, a great city (or district). In it lived more than 120,000 children too young to know their right hands from their left hands, probably referring to those about four years old and under. There were also many cattle (animals of various kinds) in it.

God wanted Jonah to admit that these children and animals could not be considered enemies of Israel and deserved the right to live. All of the people and animals had humiliated themselves before the Lord and earned the right to receive His pity, mercy, and pardon. We hope that Jonah accepted God's lesson.

Evangelistic Emphasis

Sometimes a message can be either good news or bad news depending on how one responds to it. To coastal residents, the news of an approaching hurricane can be life-saving or devastating. If they respond to the news by moving into an area of safety, they will be spared because they heard the news. If they hear that destruction is coming and do nothing about it, they may suffer tragic loss.

So it is with a message of the judgment of God. If that message is heard as a warning and is heeded by repentance, the message of judgment is a life saver. If, however, the message is heard and ignored, the news is terribly bad.

The story of Jonah illustrates that principle graphically. The city of Nineveh was a center of wickedness. It was an offense to God and He sent Jonah to pronounce a condemnation on it. On the surface it seems to be a message of bad news.

The people of Nineveh took the message as a warning. Somehow they found the ability to hope that God might change his mind about their punishment if they showed sincere repentance. From the king down, the people of Nineveh showed abject sorrow for their sins. In sackcloth and ashes, and with fasting, they prayed earnestly that God would turn His anger from them.

Because of their response, the bad news became good news. The threat of punishment became the pathway to forgiveness. Let us remember, for our sakes and for those we teach, much which appears to be bad news can be the occasion for important change. That change may result in salvation.

Memory Selection

"Should not I spare Nineveh, that great city, wherein are more than sixscore thousand persons that cannot discern between their right hand and their left hand; and also much cattle?"
Jonah 4:11.

The worth of a soul is beyond calculation. If we could imagine that amount and multiply it by one hundred twenty thousand, we would see that the value is enough to challenge our utmost Christian compassion.

Further, we should not devalue the significance of people because they are ignorant or pagan. Those who have had fewer opportunities have an even greater claim on our love and ministry than do those who have been more privileged.

No one should be deprived of a knowledge of Christ because he did not learn to read when he was a child. Neither should a person be penalized because he has never been taken to church and therefore has not heard preaching and participated in Christian worship. Nor should one have to suffer because he has not been exposed to the Scriptures.

Disadvantaged people should attract Christian compassion as a magnet attracts iron.

Weekday Problems

Joseph grew up on a farm where his family barely eked out a living. The soil was not rich and it seemed that the rains rarely came. When they did come, it often was at the wrong time and interfered with rather than helped farming. When Joseph's parents died, he became the owner of the farm. He wondered whether it was a blessing or a curse. He seemed to have few options, so he lived on the land and continued the meager existence of his youth.

On one otherwise ordinary day, Joseph received a visit from a representative of an oil company. Geologists had determined that there could be oil under the farm. A lease was signed. Drilling began and within weeks a new oil well was yielding a generous flow. Joseph was elated at his new wealth. He built a new house, bought a better car, and began living at a more comfortable level. The old anxieties about expenses and crop failures disappeared. It seemed that all of his troubles were over.

A year or so later the flow of oil began to decrease. Soon it was only a trickle and the royalty checks fell to nearly nothing.

* Have you had unusual good fortune come into your life apart from anything you did to earn it?
* Have you had a flow of blessings to stop apart from anything you did to cause it?
* If you were in Joseph's place, how would you feel about the beginning of the flow of oil? the end of the flow?

Superintendent's Sermonette

Retribution involves paying people back for evil they have done. It has been the motivating force behind many actions down through human history. Horrible deeds have gone under the questionable label of sweet revenge. Getting even has unleashed some of the most despicable acts possible and has seldom solved real problems. Jonah resisted taking God's warning to Nineveh because he hated these enemies of Israel and wanted them destroyed. When his preaching produced widespread repentance, he became angry and wanted to die.

Holding onto the hope that God might still overthrow Nineveh, Jonah watched from the sidelines. He was taught a lesson in compassion by the Lord through the growth and death of a special gourd plant.

The book of Jonah teaches us that the ultimate and best solution to evil and the temptation to seek revenge is to show people the steadfast love of God. No one wins through retribution, but everyone wins through repentance and the forgiveness by God which results from it.

This Lesson in **Your** Life

Sometimes God has to repeat Himself. He spoke to Jonah a second time and commanded him to go and preach to the people of Nineveh. This is a comment on the patience and persistence of God. The only reason He would need to give a command twice is for the benefit of the person who received that command. God could have communicated with the people of Nineveh through other people or in other ways. He spoke to Jonah a second time for Jonah's benefit.

The fact that God sometimes gives a command twice is not something that should be presumed on. A divine command should be obeyed when it is first heard. If we are fortunate enough to hear a command a second time, we should thank God for His patience with us, and we should obey instantly.

Jonah was commanded to preach to Nineveh. It was not an option. We, likewise, are commanded to take the gospel to the world. That is not an option. We should not think of it in terms of whether we will respond but rather of "How can we fulfill the mission?"

The power of preaching is such that it changes people even when it is done in the wrong spirit or the wrong way. Jonah's anger and prejudice must have been apparent. This did not prevent the word from being heard.

The effectiveness of preaching depends more on the hearers than on the speaker. Nineveh had the right to respond even though the message was delivered in a poor spirit.

Most of us, at one time or another, experience a period in which the preaching we hear is not pleasing to us. We may dislike the preacher. His mannerisms may be offensive. His attitude may show a lack of caring. We can redeem that preaching by our response to it. We can learn, resolve to change, or we can challenge the preaching. A positive response brings good fruits out of even poor preaching.

Grown people pout too! It is not a mature thing to do but some of us have not fully grown out of it.

Christ teaches us to love our enemies and return good for evil. Yet sometimes we are like Jonah. We want to see our enemies punished. It makes us angry for them to avoid the consequences of their actions. As we grow in the Christian faith we will learn to be pained with others' pain even if they have caused pain to us in the past.

One major message of the book of Jonah is that we should keep our value priorities straight. Jonah allowed himself to become so distorted that he had more regard for a plant than for one hundred twenty thousand people. This seems like such a grotesque distortion that we think we would never be guilty of it. We may do something similar, however, when we put personal indulgence ahead of the missionary and benevolent work of the church. We may enjoy luxuries or electronic gadgets at the cost of the funds that would feed hungry stomachs or evangelize lost souls.

Seed Thoughts

1. Could racial prejudice have moved Jonah to hate Nineveh?
It may have, but nothing alludes to that. It is more likely that Assyrian ferocity against Israel moved him.

2. How does the Bible tell us to deal with our enemies?
Jesus said to love them and pray for them to change (Matt. 5:44). Paul said to overcome evil with good (Rom. 12:21).

3. How did Jonah react to God's warning of doom for Nineveh?
Jonah seemed to relish the thought of Nineveh being overthrown, and he seemed to preach it willingly.

4. How did the Ninevites react to God's warning message?
From the king on down, they went into immediate mourning and cried out to God to withhold judgment.

5. How might believers react today if sinners repent and seek pardon?
They might rejoice. They might become angry, as Jonah did. They might doubt it.

(Please Turn Page)

---

1. Could racial prejudice have moved Jonah to hate Nineveh?

2. How does the Bible tell us to deal with our enemies?

3. How did Jonah react to God's warning of doom for Nineveh?

4. How did the Ninevites react to God's warning message?

5. How might believers react today if sinners repent and seek pardon?

6. How did God react to the Ninevites when they repented?

7. How did Jonah react to God's pardon of the Ninevites?

8. How does God react toward a believer who blames Him for being good toward sinners?

9. What role did the fast-growing gourd plant have in teaching Jonah?

10. Does God have special love for little children and animals?

It may have, but nothing alludes to that. It is more likely that Assyrian ferocity against Israel moved him.

Jesus said to love them and pray for them to change (Matt. 5:44). Paul said to overcome evil with good (Rom. 12:21).

Jonah seemed to relish the thought of Nineveh being overthrown, and he seemed to preach it willingly.

From the king on down, they went into immediate mourning and cried out to God to withhold judgment.

They might rejoice. They might become angry, as Jonah did. They might doubt it.

He showed His attributes of grace, mercy, patience, and great kindness. He relented and withheld judgment.

He was so disappointed and angry that he wanted to die. He may have feared that Israelites would blame him for his part in their enemies' deliverance.

God rebukes that believer and tries to help him see His viewpoint.

God used the plant to teach Jonah the need for pity, first for his own discomfort and then for the lives of others.

Jonah 4:11 implies that God favors them and wants them treated well.

Seed Thoughts - Continued

6. How did God react to the Ninevites when they repented?
He showed His attributes of grace, mercy, patience, and great kindness. He relented and withheld judgment.

7. How did Jonah react to God's pardon of the Ninevites?
He was so disappointed and angry that he wanted to die. He may have feared that Israelites would blame him for his part in their enemies' deliverance.

8. How does God react toward a believer who blames Him for being good toward sinners?
God rebukes that believer and tries to help him see His viewpoint.

9. What role did the fast-growing gourd plant have in teaching Jonah?
God used the plant to teach Jonah the need for pity, first for his own discomfort and then for the lives of others.

10. Does God have special love for little children and animals?
Jonah 4:11 implies that God favors them and wants them treated well.

Judgment And Salvation

Nahum 1:2. God is jealous, and the Lord revengeth; the Lord revengeth, and is furious; the Lord will take vengeance on his adversaries, and he reserveth wrath for his enemies.
3. The Lord is slow to anger, and great in power, and will not at all acquit the wicked: the Lord hath his way in the whirlwind and in the storm, and the clouds are the dust of his feet.
Nahum 1:6. Who can stand before his indignation? and who can abide in the fierceness of his anger? his fury is poured out like fire, and the rocks are thrown down by him.
7. The Lord is good, a strong hold in the day of trouble; and he knoweth them that trust in him.
8. But with an overrunning flood he will make an utter end of the place thereof, and darkness shall pursue his enemies.
9. What do ye imagine against the Lord? he will make an utter end: affliction shall not rise up the second time.
Nahum 1:12. Thus saith the Lord; Though they be quiet, and likewise many, yet thus shall they be cut down, when he shall pass through. Though I have afflicted thee, I will afflict thee no more.
13. For now will I break his yoke from off thee, and will burst thy bonds in sunder.
Nahum 1:15. Behold upon the mountains the feet of him that bringeth good tidings, that publisheth peace! O Judah, keep thy solemn feasts, perform thy vows: for the wicked shall no more pass through thee; he is utterly cut off.

MEMORY SELECTION
Nahum 1:7
DEVOTIONAL READING
Psalm 47:1-9

BACKGROUND SCRIPTURE
Nahum
PRINTED SCRIPTURE
Nahum 1:2-3, 6-9, 12-13, 15

Teacher's Target

Our two lessons from the book of Jonah revealed God's concern for the pagan city of Nineveh. The people there heard the divine warning of judgment, repented, and were spared. Nahum is different, for it tells of the coming destruction of Nineveh which occurred about a century later in 612 B.C. The combined might of the Babylonians and Medes laid it low. It was probably the only Gentile city which could be labeled apostate, and that apostasy led to its downfall.

Help your students to realize that the great love of God is counterbalanced by His great anger with unrepentant sinners. His holiness demands that He bring judgment on the wicked, if they refuse to receive His mercy. They can only blame themselves if they are doomed rather than saved. They share in the responsibility for their own destiny.

Lesson Introduction

Assyria had swept down over the northern kingdom of Israel and subdued it in 722 B.C. The southern kingdom of Judah still survived but would fall to Babylon in 586 B.C. It was between these dates, and not long after the northern kingdom fell, that the book of Nahum was written. The name of the book was the name of its author, Nahum the Elkoshite. We are not sure of the location of Elkosh nor do we know anything about Nahum's life.

The Lord had used Assyria, with its capital at Nineveh, as His rod of anger against Israel. He had allowed the Assyrians to conquer the people there, but He had not approved of their cruelty and greed. Now it was Nineveh's turn to face divine judgment. The prophecy of Nahum helped the Jews in Judah to realize that Jehovah would avenge the destruction of Israel, and this encouraged the Jews who sought His protection against the rising Babylonians.

Teaching Outline

I. God's jealousy: Nah. 1:2-3
  A. Revenge: 2
  B. Retribution: 3
II. God's fury: Nah. 1:6-9
  A. Indignation: 6
  B. Information: 7-8
  C. Imagination: 9
III. God's deliverance: Nah. 1:12-13
  A. Ruler: 12a
  B. Release: 12b-13
IV. God's peace: Nah. 1:15
  A. Tidings: 15a
  B. Thanksgiving: 15b

Daily Bible Readings

Mon. The Sovereignty of God
Nahum 1:1-5
Tue. None can Stand Before Him
Nahum 1:6-11
Wed. I Will Afflict Thee No More
Nahum 1:12-15
Thu. The Fall of Nineveh
Nahum 2:1-13
Fri. Nineveh Will be Shamed
Nahum 3:1-6
Sat. Destruction Will be Complete
Nahum 3:7-12
Sun. No Healing for Nineveh
Nahum 3:13-19

Verse By Verse

I. God's jealousy: Nah. 1:2-3

A. Revenge: 2
2. God is jealous, and the Lord revengeth; the Lord revengeth, and is furious; the Lord will take vengeance on his adversaries, and he reserveth wrath for his enemies.

When the Bible speaks of the Lord being jealous, it is not meant in the petty way in which the term applies to men. It refers to God's determination to uphold His holiness and righteous control over men. This involves Him taking vengeance on pagans or apostates who harm His children. He considers the adversaries of His people to be His adversaries, as well, and He will be furious against them.

B. Retribution: 3
3a. The Lord is slow to anger, and great in power, and will not at all acquit the wicked: ...

The patience of God allows His anger to build up slowly. However, the fact that He may move slowly against sinners should not be misconstrued to think that He is lacking in power to carry out His warnings. He will not acquit (clear) the wicked (guilty). He will come against them in His Own time.

3b. ...the Lord hath his way in the whirlwind and in the storm, and the clouds are the dust of his feet.

Nahum described the power of God as that expressed in the whirlwind and storm. A similar passage showing God's power in thunder, lightning, thick cloud, fire, smoke, and earthquake is Exodus 19:16-18. Pagan poets spoke of their gods riding on clouds, but the Hebrew psalmist said that Jehovah made the clouds His chariot (Ps. 104:3).

Nahum's poem went on to describe God rebuking the sea and rivers, drying them up. Bashan with its rich pastures, Carmel with its vineyards, and Lebanon with its cedars withered at God's word. The mountains were altered by earthquakes, the hills melted, and fires scorched the earth at God's presence, affecting all people (Nah. 1:4-5).

II. God's fury: Nah. 1:6-9

A. Indignation: 6
6a. Who can stand before his indignation? and who can abide in the fierceness of his anger?

Seeing that God can control the elements of nature itself, what puny man could hope to withstand His indignation against him? Who could survive the fierceness (fire, fury) of His anger? These were rhetorical questions, for their answers were obvious. No mere mortal could endure divine judgment.

6b. ...his fury is poured out like fire, and the rocks are thrown down by him.

This is a return to the language of fire and earthquake found in verse 5. God is seen as using these forces of nature to express His anger against sinners.

B. Information: 7-8
7a. The Lord is good, a strong hold in the day of trouble; ...

In order to balance his description of God, Nahum said that He was not only angry with sinners, but He was good with the righteous. He provided a place of safety during a time of trouble. He was a fortress and refuge.

7b. . . .and he knoweth them that trust in him.

"The Lord knoweth the way of the righteous" (Ps. 1:6). God knows where those who trust in Him are and what they need. The implication is clear that He intends to supply their need and honor their trust in Him. Paul later wrote, "My God shall supply all your need according to his riches in glory by Christ Jesus" (Phil. 4:19).

8. But with an overrunning flood he will make an utter end of the place thereof, and darkness shall pursue his enemies.

In contrast to the loving care God promised His children, Nahum said that He would send a flood to destroy the enemy's place. Darkness would pursue His enemies. History reveals that the Tigris River flooded, carrying away the gates of Nineveh and undermining the palace foundations, allowing the Babylonians to enter and burn the city. The latter part of the verse is interpreted various ways. One is that God would pursue His enemies into darkness or all night long.

Another is that He would send them to their deaths. Both could be right.

C. Imagination: 9
9a. What do ye imagine against the Lord?

The prophet seemed to be asking the Assyrians what they could hope to do to contend with Jehovah, the God of the Jews. Nothing they could imagine doing against Him would be successful, for He was all-powerful.

9b. . . .he will make an utter end: affliction shall not rise up the second time.

Nahum was simply saying that one blow by the Lord against Nineveh would be enough. He would not have to do it a second time. One version gives this a slight twist by saying, "Affliction [which My people shall suffer from Assyria] shall not rise up the second time" (Amplified Bible).

Nahum said that the Assyrians would be intertwined as thorns to repel their enemies, but they would not be able to endure the fire which would destroy them. Their drunken carousing would contribute to their downfall. The wicked counselor coming out of Assyria to plot against the Lord probably referred to Sennacherib (705-681 B.C.) (Nah. 1:10-11).

III. God's deliverance: Nah. 1:12-13

A. Ruler: 12a
12a. Thus saith the Lord; Though they be quiet, and likewise many, yet thus shall they be cut down when he shall pass through.

The Lord here appeared to speak to His people and encourage them. He said that the Assyrians might be quiet (secure in their complete strength) and many in number, but they would be cut down, when he passed through. Some think this referred to the Lord or His death-angel passing through the Assyrian host. Others think that it referred to the wicked counselor (Sennacherib) passing away or going back to Nineveh after his army was decimated. Second Kings 19:35-37 tells of the angel of the Lord slaying 185,000 soldiers as they camped outside of Jerusalem one night and of Sennacherib returning to Nineveh, where his own sons murdered him in the temple of his god named Nisroch.

B. Release: 12b-13
12b. Though I have afflicted thee, I will afflict thee no more.

Whether this was meant in the latter part of verse 9 or not, it seems clear that here it meant that Jehovah would not allow the Jews to be afflicted by Assyria again. He had used the pagan nation to chastise His wayward people, but that would not happen a second time. Assyria was headed for divine judgment and destruction.

13. For now will I break his yoke from off thee, and will burst thy bonds in sunder.

The Assyrians had not only conquered the northern kingdom of Israel, but they had reduced the southern kingdom of Judah to a vassal status, paying tribute. God said that He would break the Assyrian yoke from off the neck of Judah and cut her bonds in two. See a similar reference in Isaiah 14:25—"I [God] will break the Assyrian in my land, and upon my mountains tread him under foot: then shall his yoke depart from off them [Jews], and his burden depart from off their shoulders." This gave Jews hope in the midst of their oppression.

Nahum said that the Lord had a prediction for Sennacherib. His name would no longer be sown, meaning that his royal dynasty would become extinct. His great-grandson, Saracus, committed suicide as the Assyrian Empire declined. The images in Sennacherib's temple would be destroyed. The conquering Medes and Babylonians were against idolatry. Sennacherib's death would come by the hands of two of his sons, Adrammelech and Sharezer, who then fled to Armenia (II Kings 19:37; Isa. 37:38) (Nah. 1:15).

IV. God's peace: Nah. 1:15

A. Tidings: 15a
15a. Behold upon the mountains the feet of him that bringeth good tidings, that publisheth peace!

Nahum 1 contains a poem regarding the greatness of God. Nahum 2 and 3 contain a poem regarding the overthrow of Nineveh. Nahum 1:15 seems to be a transition verse connecting the two. It could go at the end of chapter 1 or at the beginning of chapter 2.

In the first part of Nahum 1:15, the prophet called Judah's attention to a messenger running down the mountains to bring the good news of the enemy's destruction and the coming of peace again. What began with the deaths of 185,000 in one night due to the death-angel in Sennacherib's time would continue until Assyria fell to the Medes and Babylonians in 612 B.C., thus bringing at least temporary peace to Judah.

B. Thanksgiving: 15b
15b. O Judah, keep thy solemn feasts, perform thy vows: for the wicked shall no more pass through thee; he is utterly cut off.

It had been very difficult, or even impossible, for the Jews to follow their regular schedule of religious festivals while under pressure by the Assyrians. Now that peace was coming, they were reminded to go back to that schedule again. They were also told to perform whatever religious vows they had taken, perhaps when they were pleading with God for deliverance from foreign oppression.

Nahum declared that the wicked Assyrians would no more pass through Judah, spreading persecution and hardship Assyria was to be utterly cut off.

The battle in the streets of Nineveh is described in chapter 2. Some people have foolishly seen in Nahum 2:4 what they think to be a reference to our modern automobiles —"Chariots shall rage in the streets, they shall justle [jostle] one against another in the broad ways: they shall seem like torches, they shall run like the lightnings." Such an interpretation is not worthy of serious Bible students. This verse describes ancient chariots in graphic ways.

Chapter 3 continued the narration of the overthrow of Nineveh, showing that what she had sown was now to be reaped. The last verse of Nahum said, "There is no healing of thy bruise; thy wound is grievous: all that hear the bruit [news, fate, report] of thee shall clap the hands over thee: for upon whom hath not thy wickedness passed continually?" (Nah. 3:19).

The city which once knew repentance and pardon experienced destruction and death.

Evangelistic Emphasis

There can be no doubt that the wages of sin is death. We see evidence of that fact all about us. The result of malice, greed, lust, and pride is death to relationships. It is death to one's own sense of well being and happiness. It is sometimes physical death and is always death to one's relationship to God.

Some people seem to be hoping for the "good news" that this fact is not true in their case. They would like to continue in sin without experiencing the inevitable result of it. That will never be the case. Sin is contrary to the holiness of God. It cannot, by definition, be productive of life rather than death.

What then is the good news to sinners? It is that God is slow to anger and great in power. Although sin will never produce life, God can overcome sin. He can break the power that sin has over us. He has more redemptive power than sin has destructive power.

We have no option about whether sin is good or bad or about whether it produces life or death. We do, however, have the option of placing our trust in God who loves us, is patient with us, and who is more powerful than sin.

Note that we cannot evade His justice or escape His anger. Neither can we minimize the sin in our lives enough to persuade Him to ignore it. There is no way that sin, even what we would consider minor or rare sin, will ever be condoned by a Holy God. Our only hope is to depend on God's patience and His mercy.

Memory Selection

"The Lord is good, a strong hold in the day of trouble; and he knoweth them that trust in him."
Nahum 1:7.

The fact that the Lord is so fierce in His anger against evil is a comfort to those who want to be safe in His arms. We are protected by His passionate rejection of that which would harm us. If He felt less strongly about our enemies we would be in danger.

Suppose, for example, your beloved child were diagnosed as having a dreadful disease that threatened his life. Would you want a physician who was apathetic about that disease? Or, on the other hand, would you want a doctor who was intensely dedicated to the eradication of that disease and the protection of those who are victims of it?

Fury against the disease and love for the patient go hand in hand. Neither can be compromised without also compromising the other. God's anger against sin should not frighten us. He is angry against that which threatens us. To feel less strongly about sin would mean that He also feels less strongly about our care and protection.

Weekday Problems

Paul and Tom graduated from college together and both took entry level jobs with a large company. Paul was extremely conscientious and believed that if he did his work thoroughly and well, it would be noticed and he would advance in the company. Tom had a somewhat different plan for getting ahead. He stressed the cultivation of friendships and counted on those to assure his advancement. He believed it is "who you know, not what you know" that matters.

During the first several years the two young men rose in the company at a similar pace. Both became department heads and the next promotion would have made either a vice president. Such a move would be the first decisive difference in their career paths. They could not make it together and the chosen one would permanently outrank the other in money, status, and power.

As they neared the day when the coveted position would open, there was open tension between the two. Paul felt that he was better qualified than Tom because of his growing knowledge and competence in his work. Tom felt that his superior relationships with company officials made him a natural for the promotion.

* Which do you suppose will get the job?
* How will Paul feel if Tom is promoted over him?
* Will these feelings destroy his confidence in the value of hard and dedicated work?

Superintendent's Sermonette

We like to think that we live in civilized society governed by the rule of law and order. However, we realize that there is much that is savage and depraved in people. When the thin veneer of respectability is peeled away, some horrible facts stand out. We are faced with an epidemic of immorality, venereal diseases, dishonesty, lying, cheating, greed, selfishness, prejudice, discrimination, and a general breakdown of authority by God or man. We never know when we shall become the focus of any or all of these things by others.

Ancient Israel had been the object of concentrated ferocity by the Assyrians and fell to them in 722 B.C. Judah was threatened and mistreated, God sent prophets to give His people hope, and Nahum was one of them. In his little book is the record of what happened. Nineveh, the Assyrian capital saved by Jonah's preaching, had apostasized. God now predicted its doom, and it came to pass about a century later, When we fear for our future, let us remember what God has done for His people in the past, and let us trust Him today.

This Lesson in <u>Your</u> Life

This lesson deals with two facts about God. Both are true, and we get into trouble when we see one without also seeing the other. The first is that God is a holy God. He makes no compromises with evil. Evil is absolutely contrary to his nature. He cannot relate to it. He does not excuse it. He does not ignore it. He is not apathetic in his feelings toward it.

Evil does not ever get a toehold, much less a beachhead, in its opposition to God. Those people who continue to live in deliberate sin are subject to the judgment of the God who is furious with evil and who reserves wrath for his adversaries. They will fall before his indignation and be crushed by the fierceness of his anger.

The second fact about God in this lesson is that He is slow to anger and a protector of His people. He is great in power and He allows no quarter to those who would harm His children. He who controls the whirlwind and the storm is able to avenge His adversaries and shelter His people.

Some people err on the side of not giving adequate emphasis to the first of these facts. They fail to appreciate the enormity of God's anger against sin. They suppose that occasional sin can be overlooked or that "petty" sin is not of serious consequence.

One of the primary purposes of this passage is to dispel any such notions we might have. The patience and love of God do not diminish the fact that He is adamant against sin. None of it is inconsequential. Our attitude toward evil needs to be soberly examined. Though we will, on occasion, have lapses, we must not make any treaty with sin, regardless of how minor. We, like God, must hate evil with a passionate hatred.

On the other hand, some people err on the side of not trusting enough in the redemptive and protective power of God. They live in a continual sense of guilt and fear. They are so conscious of the sin in their lives that they cannot fully trust the power and love of God to overcome it.

The ideal balance is to give full weight to the judgment of God against sin and to have full trust in God's willingness and ability to protect us from its effects. To weaken either side of this equation results in either a death-dealing compromise or a life-denying insecurity. Unfortunately, some people weaken both sides, losing both the battle with evil and the quest for peace.

In addition to dealing with these questions about our own lives, this passage helps with a vexing question about others. We may sometimes wonder whether wrongdoers truly will be punished for their sins. In the strongest possible terms we are assured that they will. If we have any lingering doubt whether there will be ultimate equity in the battle against evil, this passage should resolve it.

Seed Thoughts

1. In what way is God jealous?
It is not in our petty, human way. It refers to His upholding His holiness and righteous control over men.

2. How can God be a God of love and a God of fury, too?
They are complementary aspects of His personality, His sense of justice demands that the righteous be honored and that the wicked be condemned.

3. Does God's slowness to anger imply that He is weak in any way?
No, God's patience with sinners shows that He is strong and desires to show mercy toward them if they will repent.

4. Does God use elements of nature to display His anger with men?
The Bible refers to God using such things as wind, fire, storm, and earthquake to deal with men.

5. How does God treat those who put their trust in Him?
He is good to them, blessing them in many ways. He serves as a stronghold for them in times of trouble.

(Please Turn Page)

---

1. In what way is God jealous?

2. How can God be a God of love and a God of fury, too?

3. Does God's slowness to anger imply that He is weak in any way?

4. Does God use elements of nature to display His anger with men?

5. How does God treat those who put their trust in Him?

6. How could a man imagine that he could defy the Lord?

7. How does God overcome men who seem to be unassailable?

8. Does God afflict His people?

9. How should God's people act after they receive good tidings of peace and deliverance?

10. What happened to Assyria?

Seed Thoughts - Continued

It is not in our petty, human way. It refers to His upholding His holiness and righteous control over men.

They are complementary aspects of His personality, His sense of justice demands that the righteous be honored and that the wicked be condemned.

No, God's patience with sinners shows that He is strong and desires to show mercy toward them if they will repent.

The Bible refers to God using such things as wind, fire, storm, and earthquake to deal with men.

He is good to them, blessing them in many ways. He serves as a stronghold for them in times of trouble.

He would have to have an imperfect concept of God and His perfect attributes.

With His infinitely superior wisdom, He finds a way to break through their defenses and subdue them.

He chastises them if they turn from Him and devote themselves to other objects of affection. Discuss examples.

They should restore their schedule of spiritual observances which have lapsed. They should fulfill promises made to God when they were pleading for deliverance.

Assyria, and its capital of Nineveh, were conquered and ruled over by the Medes and the Babylonians (612 B.C.).

6. How could a man imagine that he could defy the Lord?
He would have to have an imperfect concept of God and His perfect attributes.

7. How does God overcome men who seem to be unassailable?
With His infinitely superior wisdom, He finds a way to break through their defenses and subdue them.

8. Does God afflict His people?
He chastises them if they turn from Him and devote themselves to other objects of affection. Discuss examples.

9. How should God's people act after they receive good tidings of peace and deliverance?
They should restore their schedule of spiritual observances which have lapsed. They should fulfill promises made to God when they were pleading for deliverance.

10. What happened to Assyria?
Assyria, and its capital of Nineveh, were conquered and ruled over by the Medes and the Babylonians (612 B.C.).

A Question And An Answer

Habakkuk 1:1. The burden which Habakkuk the prophet did see.
2. O Lord, how long shall I cry, and thou wilt not hear? even cry out unto thee of violence, and thou wilt not save!
3. Why dost thou show me iniquity, and cause me to behold grievance? for spoiling and violence are before me: and there are that raise up strife and contention.
4. Therefore the law is slacked, and judgment doth never go forth: for the wicked doth compass about the righteous; therefore wrong judgment proceedeth.
5. Behold ye among the heathen, and regard, and wonder marvelously: for I will work a work in your days, which ye will not believe, though it be told you.
6. For, lo, I raise up the Chaldeans, that bitter and hasty nation, which shall march through the breadth of the land, to possess the dwelling places that are not theirs.
7. They are terrible and dreadful: their judgment and their dignity shall proceed of themselves.
Habakkuk 2:1. I will stand upon my watch, and set me upon the tower, and will watch to see what he will say unto me, and what I shall answer when I am reproved.
2. And the Lord answered me, and said, Write the vision, and make it plain upon tables, that he may run that readeth it.
3. For the vision is yet for an appointed time, but at the end it shall speak, and not lie: though it tarry, wait for it; because it will surely come, it will not tarry.
4. Behold, his soul which is lifted up is not upright in him: but the just shall live by his faith.

MEMORY SELECTION
Habakkuk 2:4
DEVOTIONAL READING
Psalm 68:1-3

BACKGROUND SCRIPTURE
Habakkuk
PRINTED SCRIPTURE
Habakkuk 1:1-7; 2:1-4

Teacher's Target

The northern kingdom of Israel had fallen to the Assyrians in 722 B.C. God had used these pagans to chastise His Own wayward people.

Judah had also been wayward, but God had been patient with her. When Habakkuk questioned this, God told him that Judah's chastisement was also coming. It would be by the pagan Chaldeans (Babylonians). God's faithful children would have to suffer along with the wicked, but the just (righteous) individual would live by his faith.

Help your students to understand and appreciate the germinal importance of Habakkuk 2:4—"The just shall live by his faith"—and its appearance in Romans 1:17, Galatians 3:11, and Hebrews 10:38. Help them to realize its importance to the Protestant Reformation and its doctrines of justification by faith and the universal priesthood of believers. During the age of grace, believers can go directly to God through Christ, their High Priest (Heb. 10:19-21).

Lesson Introduction

No nation has ever been wholly devoted to the Lord. This was true of Israel, God's chosen people, throughout its long history. It has also been true of every Gentile nation, even those which professed to belong to God and to Christ. Therefore, those who have walked with God have been individuals and groups which took a stand in the midst of unbelievers or apostates.

We know nothing about the life of Habakkuk but what can be inferred from his book. It is clear, however, that he was a true prophet of God in the midst of a corrupt generation of Jews. He had a high view of Jehovah and could not at first understand how He would use a pagan people to chastise His Own chosen people, Habakkuk had to learn that God took care of His Own as individuals, even while He dealt with nations as a whole.

Teaching Outline

I. Perplexity: Hab . 1:1-4
 A. Questions: 1-3a
 B. Quandry: 3b-4

II . Prediction: Hab, 1: 5-7
 A. Work: 5
 B. Wrath: 6-7

III. Principle: Hab . 2: 1-4
 A. Intention: 1
 B. Instruction: 2-3
 C. Inspiration: 4

Daily Bible Readings

Mon. How Long, O Lord?
Habakkuk 1:1-11
Tue. Can You Not Help?
Habakkuk 1:12-17
Wed. Judgment Will Come
Habakkuk 2:1-8
Thu. All Will See
Habakkuk 2:9-14
Fri. Sin Will Not Bring Profit
Habakkuk 2:15-20
Sat. Will the Innocent Suffer?
Habakkuk 3:1-16
Sun. I will Rejoice in the Lord
Habakkuk 3:17-19

Verse By Verse

I. Perplexity: Hab. 1

A. Questions: 1-3a
1. **The burden which Habakkuk the prophet did see.**
It was toward the end of the seventh century before Christ that the prophet Habakkuk was deeply concerned for Judah, He called his concern a burden (heavy weight). It appears that he had a vision which prompted him to write his little book.

2a. **O Lord, how long shall I cry, and thou wilt not hear!**
Habakkuk cried out to the Lord because of the anguish in his heart. He wanted to know how long he should pray without receiving a response from the Lord, He surely did not doubt God's ability to hear him, but he was anxious for His response.

2b. **. . .even cry out unto thee of violence, and thou wilt not save!**
It seems that Habakkuk was talking to God about violence perpetrated by the Jews against one another and perhaps by them against any foreigners among them. The prophet wanted the Lord to deal with the wicked, delivering all righteous victims from their grasp.

3a. **Why dost thou shew me iniquity, and cause me to behold grievance?**
Habakkuk's righteous soul was vexed by what he observed in Judah. He wondered why God allowed him to see the general sin, evil, and trouble abroad in the land. He felt that God must know how grieved and saddened he was because of the arguing, quarreling, bribery, and assaulting taking place in his homeland. Here, again, the idea was that Habakkuk was anxious for God to <u>do</u> something about this.

B. Quandry: 3b-4
3b. **. . .for spoiling and violence are before me: and there are that raise up strife and contention.**
Habakkuk switched from questions here to descriptions of the situation in Judah. He must have known that God knew all about these things, but the prophet felt like expressing his own revulsion. He was appalled by the spoiling and violence (destruction and oppression) and by the strife and contention (arguing and fighting) going on around him. He must have felt much the same as Lot when he lived in ancient Sodom (II Pet. 2:7-8).

4a. **Therefore the law is slacked, and judgment doth never go forth: . . .**
Assyrian control over Judah was waning, and Babylonian power was rising. The king of Judah should have governed his people according to the law of God given through Moses at Mount Sinai. This could have been possible, because the foreign power sought tribute primarily and did not want to be involved in day-to-day government. However, the Jewish king ignored the law of God, and judgment (justice) was absent.

4b. **. . .for the wicked doth compass about the righteous therefore wrong judgment proceedeth.**
In the absence of true justice, perversion took place in the court system. Wicked men bribed greedy judges to decide in their favor. The innocent became victims of wrong

judicial rulings. The impact of this on the moral and spiritual fabric of the nation of Judah can be imagined.

II. Prediction: Hab. 1:5-7

A. Work: 5

5. Behold ye among the heathen, and regard, and wonder marvelously: for I will work a work in your days, which ye will not believe, though it be told you.

God spoke in the plural here to Habakkuk and all others who would listen. He said that He would do something among the heathen (nations) which the Jews would observe and be amazed to see. During their lifetime, He would perform a deed which they would find hard to believe even though it had been predicted. If Habakkuk and the righteous remnant in Judah had been amazed at the patience of God with sinners, they would be even more amazed at what He was going to do to Judah by means of a pagan nation. The apostle Paul later quoted from this verse when warning unbelieving Jews in the synagogue at Antioch of Pisidia (Acts 13:40-41).

B. Wrath: 6-7

6. For, lo, I raise up the Chaldeans, that bitter and hasty nation, which shall march through the breadth of the land, to possess the dwelling places that are not their's.

God said that He was raising up the Chaldeans (Babylonians) to be a world power. He described them as bitter (fierce) and hasty (impetuous, restless). He said that they would march out across the world (actually the Middle East) and take over the dwellings which belonged to others. Daniel 7:4 described Babylon as being "like a lion, and had eagle's wings," thus confirming the ferocity and swiftness of this new power.

7. They are terrible and dreadful: their judgment and their dignity shall proceed of themselves.

The description of Babylon continued down through verse 11. God said that the Babylonians would be terrible (causing terror to others) and dreadful (bringing fear to others). Their form of judgment (justice) and their dignity (authority) would come from their own strength. In other words, they would do as they pleased and be a law unto themselves. We must keep in mind, however, that this would be true only within the divine limits placed upon them by God.

Habakkuk 1:12-13 is not in our printed text for this lesson, but you would do well to look at it, because it prepares the way for the next part of the lesson based on Habakkuk 2:1-4. In this section, the prophet questioned God regarding His decision to use the pagan Babylonians to chastise the Jews. He obviously considered the Babylonians to be even worse than the sinful Jews, and he could not understand why God would make them His instruments of chastisement.

III. Principle: Hab. 2:1-4

A. Intention: 1

1. I will stand upon my watch, and set me upon the tower and will watch to see what he will say unto me, and what I shall answer when I am reproved.

Habakkuk felt that he had been forward in his complaint to the Lord. He said that he would take up a watching position in a watchtower to wait for a divine answer of rebuke. Some scholars would argue for the prophet ascending a literal watchtower here, while others would say that Habakkuk meant to convey the concept of prayerful meditation. This would appear to have been in mind when the following paraphrase was made: "I will [in my thinking] stand upon my post of observation, and station myself on the tower or fortress, and will watch to see what He will say within me, and what answer I will make [as His mouthpiece] to the perplexities of my complaint against Him" (Amplified Bible).

It is wise for believers to spend time waiting on the Lord rather than plunging ahead without clear direction, but we tend to be impatient many times. Faith and hope operate during the waiting periods as we trust the One Who knows the beginning and the end to do what is right, even if we know that we may be reproved for what we asked.

B. Instruction: 2-3
2. And the Lord answered me, and said, Write the vision, and make it plain upon tables, that he may run that readeth it.

We are not told how long it took for the Lord to answer Habakkuk. When He spoke, God told the prophet to write down the vision plainly on tables (tablets), probably made of clay. The contents of the message were to be so striking that anyone who read them would run to tell others about them.

3. For the vision is yet for an appointed time, but at the end it shall speak, and not lie: though it tarry, wait for it; because it will surely come, it will not tarry.

God told Habakkuk that the vision He was giving looked ahead to a future time. It might seem long in coming, but it would surely come as predicted. Skipping over verse 4 for now, see in verse 5 a description of the invading Chaldeans (mentioned here collectively as "a proud man"). Note next the five taunting songs in which their fall would be shown in five woes (vss 6, 9, 12, 15, 19). The God who chastised His Own people for their sins would surely punish the Babylonians for their sins, too.

C. Inspiration: 4
4a. Behold, his soul which is lifted up is not upright in him: . . .

We are not told who is described here, but it seems safe to assume that it referred to either a proud Jew or Babylonian. A person who is proud and depending on his own wisdom and strength cannot be upright (righteous) before God In spite of whatever intelligence or resources he may have, he cannot succeed by arraying himself against God and His people. The woes described in the latter part of chapter 2 apply to those who steal, covet, are violent, get drunk, and worship idols There is nothing ahead but destruction and death, unless God's mercy interposes itself because of repentance.

4b. . . .but the just shall live by his faith.

There is tremendous power in these few words. Ezekiel 18:5 and 9 say the same thing. Both Habakkuk and Ezekiel seem to refer to the preservation of physical life, even when death strikes all around. Individuals in the righteous remnant in ancient Judah could depend on God to take care of them as the Babylonians came to wreak havoc on their nation.

Having said that, however, other references to this principle of righteousness bringing life through faith in God make it clear that more than physical existence is involved. Romans 1:17, Galatians 3:11, and Hebrews 10:38 indicate that eternal life is promised to those who put their faith in God and in His beloved Son, Jesus Christ. Because Christ had died by the time those books were written, the doctrines of justification by faith and the universal priesthood of believers had taken hold.

The law of God with its penalties for sin was superseded by the grace of God and its provision for imparted righteousness. Thus it was that Paul could write, "He [God] hath made him [Christ] to be sin [a sin-offering] for us, who knew no [personal] sin that we might be made the righteousness of God in him" (II Cor, 5:21). The germinal truth planted in Habakkuk 2:4 grew into the marvelous teaching of justification by faith.

Evangelistic Emphasis

This passage deals in good news for those who are already servants of God. They sometimes get discouraged, as Habakkuk did. They need to have dilemmas resolved and find a way to believe in spite of obstacles.

One problem that is dealt with is the matter of the timetable of working out the will of God. Sometimes when we do not see anything happening, we conclude that promises are not going to be kept. Habakkuk is here assured that God's promises will be kept, but it will be on God's schedule. The fact that a promise is delayed beyond our expectations is not cause for concern. It may be that God had never intended to settle the matter at the time we wanted it to be settled. It may be that He is not late, but we are early in our expectations.

A second problem that is dealt with is that God can use unexpected partners in the carrying out of His will. Habakkuk looked around and saw no one that could bring about the judgement that was needed. The problem was that he saw the Chaldeans but did not see them as a resource. God saw a way to use a bitter and rash nation to accomplish something for good.

Habakkuk's worries, like some of ours were unnecessary. God was moving decisively toward the fulfillment of His will. It was not on Habakkuk's timetable and was not in a way that Habakkuk could anticipate. Nevertheless God was able to handle it and His promise was secure. He likewise is able to handle the problems that discourage us and His promise to us is secure.

Memory Selection

"The just shall live by his faith."
Habakkuk 2:4.

The vital principle of the Christian life is not what we are experiencing, but who we trust. There are a lot of factors in life that we cannot control. We may have sickness, sorrows, and pains. They may be entirely unrelated to anything we may have done to cause them. There may be nothing we can do to find relief from them.

While we sometimes can do nothing to change our circumstances, we are always free to decide how we will live in them. We can decide what our values are and what we believe in. Regardless of the problem that we have, we will be better off if we face it with a trust in God.

The just do not live right because it is easy, because it pays well, because it is a way to avoid problems, or because they always get instant answers to prayers. They live by faith, faith in a loving and just God who always keeps His promises.

When we observe the world we live in by sight, we see a great deal of injustice. When we observe it by faith we can see God resolving some problems now and working toward a day when all will be resolved.

Weekday Problems

"It made me question my calling," the minister said. He was talking about the marriage breakup of two of his closest friends. The couple were parents of three small children. They had been active and involved in church. They had been personal friends of the minister and his wife.

The minister felt that if he had really been sensitive to their needs and had been fully in touch with God's powers, the marriage could have been saved. Now the man and woman were living in separate towns. The children were divided between two homes. There was heartbreak and tragedy.

Beyond that there was a discouragement that approached despair in the minister's heart. "How is the will of God being worked out in this situation? When can I expect to see redemptive things begin to happen? Where did I go wrong? Did I fail them? Did I fail God? Should I really be a minister when I cannot even help my best friends?"

* Was the minister at fault and did he need to feel responsibility for the marriage failure?
* Even if he were not at fault, how can he deal with his feelings of responsibility and inadequacy?

Superintendent's Sermonette

We are indebted to such Old Testament references as Ezekiel 18:5 and 9 and Habakkuk 2:4 for the germinal truth which eventually led to New Testament teaching on justification by faith in Christ alone. The concept of preserving physical life through faith in God led to the concept of receiving eternal life through faith in Christ.

This wonderful truth was obscured during the medieval period because church leaders sought power and iron-clad control over believers. Doctrines from the Bible were adulterated by man-made traditions. Priestly rituals were considered necessary for obtaining salvation. Threat of excommunication was used to control independent thinkers.

Yearning for deliverance, laymen turned to righteous clergymen and discovered the truth that "the just shall live by faith." Let us be thankful for the freedom brought by the Protestant Reformation led by such men as Luther, Calvin, and Zwingli as they taught this truth. Let us fully support those who faithfully teach it today.

This Lesson in <u>Your</u> Life

Deep within us there is a need to feel that we live in a reasonable world. We need to feel that there is some justice, some relationship between what we do and what happens to us. It is deeply disturbing to see someone who is innocent and good be stricken with major traumas. It is also disturbing to see those who are clearly corrupt enjoying prosperity and success. It makes us wonder, "What is the use of trying to live right?" "What difference does it make?" When we begin asking those questions we are near the point of despair.

From our point of view a later answer sometimes seems like no answer at all. If our problem is why the innocent suffer and why the wicked prosper, a later answer does not seem relevant. By the time the answer comes the innocent will have done more suffering and the wicked will have enjoyed more prosperity. We want an immediate answer.

In fact, we may want more than that. We may want to know why the inequity ever existed in the first place. It is not enough to fix a problem that we believe never should have existed in the first place.

These were some of the problems that afflicted Habakkuk. He felt that he was in an intolerable situation that never should have existed in the first place. Further, he had cried to God about the burden of his heart and did not feel that he had been heard.

Not only did he feel that God had not yet answered his prayer. He was beginning to feel that God might never answer his prayer. If he had prayed this long with no results, why should he believe that an additional time of prayer would yield anything different?

One of the wonderful things about the Bible is that it takes us bravely into the heart of our most difficult problems. There are not easy answers to these questions. There is no facile solution to life's most serious struggles. There is not a glib slogan that can deal with human despair.

We will sometimes feel burdened and helpless in the face of life's assaults. We will pray and will not see any instant response. We will look around for sources of help and will not be able to recognize any. We, like Habakkuk, will want to say,"O Lord, how long shall I cry, and thou wilt not hear!"

From Habakkuk we learn three things. One is that the resolution to our most serious problems is sometimes in the struggle with them. In Gethsemane, Jesus did not find a way to avoid the cross but He did find the strength to face it. Habakkuk did not find immediate relief for his frustration but he found a faith and hope that would see him through it.

A second thing is that we can be sure that justice will be done. However unlikely that at some times may seem, God will find a way to work it out. His people will be blessed and the wicked will be held accountable for their wickedness.

A third lesson is that the world is full of resources that can be used to work out God's will. We are surrounded by potential blessings. Those forces which seem most unlikely may be marshalled to bring peace and justice to us and to the world.

Seed Thoughts

1. In what way was the burden seen by Habakkuk a double one?
He saw not only the destruction of Judah but of Babylon, as well.

2. Did Habakkuk really think that God did not hear his cry?
This is unlikely. What Habakkuk wanted was for God not only to hear his cry but to respond to it with action against sin.

3. What happens when the law of God becomes slack?
In both religious and civil matters, justice is withheld or perverted by wicked judges open to bribery or intimidation in various forms.

4. Why is some information given by God difficult to believe?
It comes from outside of the usual human thought-patterns and seems to be incredible.

5. What amazing news did God give to Habakkuk about Judah?
God said He would raise up Chaldea (Babylon) to chastise Judah for her sins.

(Please Turn Page)

---

1. In what way was the burden seen by Habakkuk a double one?

2. Did Habakkuk really think that God did not hear his cry?

3. What happens when the law of God becomes slack?

4. Why is some information given by God difficult to believe?

5. What amazing news did God give to Habakkuk about Judah?

6. What bothered Habakkuk as far as Babylon was concerned?

7. How should Christians today think about discipline by unbelieving government officials?

8. Is there ever an exception to obeying civil authorities?

9. What prospect does the proud and unrighteous man have?

10. What prospect does the humble and righteous man have?

Seed Thoughts - Continued

He saw not only the destruction of Judah but of Babylon, as well.

This is unlikely. What Habakkuk wanted was for God not only to hear his cry but to respond to it with action against sin.

In both religious and civil matters, justice is withheld or perverted by wicked judges open to bribery or intimidation in various forms.

It comes from outside of the usual human thought-patterns and seems to be incredible.

God said He would raise up Chaldea (Babylon) to chastise Judah for her sins.

He could not understand how God could use a pagan nation to chastise His Own people, whom he considered more righteous.

If Christians break the law, they need to submit to civil authority and pay the penalty imposed (Rom. 13:1-7).

If unscriptural demands are made, we should follow Acts 5:29—"We ought to obey God rather than men."

He can look forward only to divine condemnation and eternal punishment.

He can experience an abundant life here on earth and expect eternal life with God and Christ in heaven.

6. What bothered Habakkuk as far as Babylon was concerned?
He could not understand how God could use a pagan nation to chastise His Own people, whom he considered more righteous.

7. How should Christians today think about discipline by unbelieving government officials?
If Christians break the law, they need to submit to civil authority and pay the penalty imposed (Rom. 13:1-7).

8. Is there ever an exception to obeying civil authorities?
If unscriptural demands are made, we should follow Acts 5:29—"We ought to obey God rather than men."

9. What prospect does the proud and unrighteous man have?
He can look forward only to divine condemnation and eternal punishment.

10. What prospect does the humble and righteous man have?
He can experience an abundant life here on earth and expect eternal life with God and Christ in heaven.

Threatened Destruction Of Humankind

Zephaniah 1. The word of the Lord which came unto Zephaniah the son of Cushi, the son of Gedaliah, the son of Amariah, the son of Hizkiah, in the days of Josiah the son of Amon king of Judah.
2. I will utterly consume all things from off the land, saith the Lord.
3. I will consume man and beast; I will consume the fowls of the heaven, and the fishes of the sea, and the stumbling blocks with the wicked; and I will cut off man from off the land, saith the Lord.
Zephaniah 1:7. Hold thy peace at the presence of the Lord God: for the day of the Lord is at hand: for the Lord hath prepared a sacrifice, he hath bid his guests.
Zephaniah 1:12. And it shall come to pass at that time, that I will search Jerusalem with candles, and punish the men that are settled on their lees: that say in their heart, The Lord will not do good, neither will he do evil.
Zephaniah 2:1. Gather yourselves together, yea, gather together, O nation not desired;
2. Before the decree bring forth, before the day pass as the chaff, before the fierce anger of the Lord come upon you, before the day of the Lord's anger come upon you.
3. Seek ye the Lord, all ye meek of the earth, which have wrought his judgment; ye shall be hid in the day of the Lord's anger.

MEMORY SELECTION
Zephaniah 2:3
DEVOTIONAL READING
Proverbs 14:26-35

BACKGROUND SCRIPTURE
Zephaniah 1-2
PRINTED SCRIPTURE
Zephaniah 1:1-3,7,12; 2;1-3

Teacher's Target

The reigns of evil Manasseh (692-638 B.C.) and Amon (638-637 B.C.) had ended, and the reign of good Josiah (637-607 B.C.) had begun. Zephaniah had been born during the reign of Manasseh but did not serve as a prophet until the early part of Josiah's reign, probably around 627-626 B.C. It is assumed that he wrote his prophecy soon afterward. Despite Josiah's spiritual reforms, Judah was headed toward apostasy and judgment by God under Babylon.

Help your students to see that God's servants must continue to warn against sin in good times and bad times. The natural tendency of men is to follow their sinful natures. They must be shown God's high standards and urged to rise up to them with His help. The Lord may be sought and found, and divine judgment may be avoided. Let us be models whom others may imitate.

Lesson Introduction

Zephaniah, a contemporary of Jeremiah, pursued his prophetic role during the period between the fall of Samaria (722 B.C.) and the fall of Jerusalem (586 B.C.). God was being patient with Judah and sending prophets to call the Jews to repentance. There was a revival of the law of God and the worship of Jehovah under Josiah's administration, but the people still practiced idolatry in secret.

Zephaniah predicted the coming of the Babylonians in judgment upon Judah, prefiguring the divine judgment scheduled for sinners in the end times. He foretold judgment on the nations of Philistia, Moab, Ethiopia, and Assyria. He complained of the immoral state of Jerusalem. He told of the final judgment of the nations and of the Messianic Kingdom which was to come.

Teaching Outline

I. Sweeps Zeph. 1:1-3
   A. Contacting: 1
   B. Consuming: 2-3
II. Sacrifice: Zeph. 1:7
   A. Presence: 7a
   B. Preparation: 7b
III. Search I: Zeph. 1:12
   A. Action: 12a
   B. Attitude: 12b
IV. Search II: Zeph. 2:1-3
   A. Prayer: 1-2
   B. Pursuit: 3a
   C. Prospect: 3b

Daily Bible Readings

Mon. Judgment is Coming
Zephaniah 1:1-6
Tue. Even Princes to be Punished
Zephaniah 1:7-11
Wed. A Day of Wrath
Zephaniah 1:12-15
Thu. Riches Will Not Protect
Zephaniah 1:16-18
Fri. Seek the Lord
Zephaniah 2:1-3
Sat. Heathens a Desolation
Zephaniah 2:4-11
Sun. Heathens to be Ridiculed
Zephaniah 2:12-15

Verse By Verse

I. Sweep: Zeph. 1:1-3

A. Contacting:
1. The word of the Lord which came unto Zephaniah the son of Cushi, the son of Gedaliah, the son of Amariah, the son of Hizkiah, in the days of Josiah, the son of Amon, king of Judah.

The word of the Lord came to Zephaniah and thus made him a prophet. Positions in the priesthood were passed from father to son, but God might call anyone to be a prophet. Zephaniah descended from Hizkiah (whom some think was righteous Hezekiah), Amariah, Gedaliah, and Cushi. He ministered during the reign of the righteous Josiah, son of wicked Amon. Josiah reigned from 637-607 B.C.

B. Consuming: 2-3
2. I will utterly consume all things from off the land, saith the Lord. With these harsh words, God made His message of impending doom known to the Jews.

The word consume derives from a term meaning to utterly sweep away. When the Lord said that, He may have referred to a large part of the Middle East He could have used the barbaric Scythians from North of the Black Sea who were overrunning western Asia and the Babylonians who were gaining power fast.

3. I will consume man and beast: I will consume the fowls of the heaven, and the fishes of the sea, and the stumblingblocks with the wicked; and I will cut off man from off the land, saith the Lord.

The Authorized Version uses the term land in verses 2 and 3, while other versions use the term earth. We know that God destroyed the earth by flood in Noah's time (Gen. 7:17-24) and that He will ultimately destroy it by fire at the end times (II Pet. 3:10-13). Meanwhile, He brings judgment on various parts of the earth when sin operates. He said through Zephaniah that He would bring destruction to men and animals, including birds and fish, and to stumblingblocks (idols) and those who worship them. This probably pertained specifically to Palestine and to any pagan areas in the Middle East where God's people had been persecuted.

Note that in verses 4-6 specific reference is made to Judah and Jerusalem. God said that He would stretch out His hand of judgment against them, cutting off the remnants of Baal and the names of the Chemarims (long robed priests representing idols). He would cut off those who went to their rooftops to worship the sun, moon, and stars. He would cut off those who claimed to serve Jehovah but who served Malcham (Molech, Milcom) instead. He would cut off those who had abandoned Him and those who had not sought after Him Divine patience would yield to divine judgment on all who ignored the Lord.

II. Sacrifice: Zeph. 1:7

A. Presence: 7a
7a. Hold thy peace at the presence of the Lord God: . . .

This reminds us of Habakkuk 2:20—"The Lord is in his holy temple: let all the earth keep silence before him." The time when men could brazenly parade their sins would come to an end. They would have to appear before the Judge of all the earth. No one could escape when the time came to appear in God's presence to give account of oneself

B. Preparation: 7b
7b. . . .for the day of the Lord is at hand: for the Lord hath prepared a sacrifice, he hath bid his guests.

Preparation for the day of the Lord, meaning the day of judgment, had been made before it actually came. The fact that it had seemed to be delayed was due to the longsuffering (patience) of the Lord toward sinners. Since the Jews, as a whole, refused to give themselves to the Lord in worship and service, He had prepared them to be a sacrifice, and He had invited foreigners to be His guests as executioners of His wayward people. This was a most awesome statement of doom. Verses 8-11 continue the description of divine judgment on the Jews. God said that He would punish members of the royal family in Judah. He would punish those who wore foreign clothing, showing their love of foreign gods and customs. He would punish those who leap on the threshold (gain entrance to people's houses to rob them) and then fill up their masters' houses with the fruits of their violence and deceit. One paraphrase of Zephaniah 1:10 reads, "A cry of alarm will begin at the farthest gate of Jerusalem [the fish gate], coming closer and closer until the noise of the advancing army reaches the very top of the hill where the city is built" (Living Bible). Those who lived in Maktesh (a depression where business people operated) would be cut down. Moneychangers would share their doom

III. Search I: Zeph. 1:12

A. Actions: 12a
12a. And it shall come to pass at that time, that I will search Jerusalem with candles, and punish the men that are settled on their lees: . . .

The thoroughness of the divine search for sinners was to be indicated by the use of candles (lamps, lanterns) as the Lord looked into every dark corner of Jerusalem. The sinners discovered would be compared to the dregs deposited from wine or liquor (Isa. 25:6). They would be "men who [like old wine] are thickening and settling on their lees" (Amplified Bible). The terms means to be complacent and self-satisfied, perhaps even in a drunken stupor.

B. Attitude: 12b
12b. . . .that say in their heart, The Lord will not do good, neither will he do evil.

The attitude of these sinners would be that God would be indifferent to them. They would not accept the concept that God does good to the righteous and brings punishment to the evil. They seemed to feel that things happened in a haphazard fashion. They may have felt this way because they thought He lacked interest or power for doing anything to them.

Verses 13-18 continue the description of God's judgment on sinners. Their goods would become spoils for the enemy. Their houses would be left desolate, The new houses they built would not be inhabited. The vineyards they had planted would not yield wine for them. The great day of the Lord was fast approaching. Strong men would weep bitterly.

Wrath, trouble, distress, wastefulness, desolation, darkness, gloom, clouds, and thick darkness were terms used to describe the day. Trumpet blasts and battle cries would be heard. Men would stagger as though blinded. Blood would be shed. Neither silver nor gold would be able to deliver them as the whole land was devoured by the fire of God's anger and desire to get rid of them.

IV. Search II: Zeph. 2:1-3

A. Prayer: 1-2
1. Gather yourselves together, yea, gather together, O nation not desired;

Here was an invitation for the Jews to come to God in prayer.

They were told to gather themselves together. They were collectively called a nation not desired, meaning that they were shameless in their apostasy.

2a. Before the decree bring forth,...

Time was very important. If the sinful Jews were going to seek God's help, they would have to move quickly. They would have to act before the judgment decree was implemented They could not be sure when it would come. "Boast not thyself of to morrow; for thou knowest not what a day may bring forth" (Prov. 27:1).

2b. ...before the day pass as the chaff, ...

The Jews were challenged to repent of their sins before their opportunity to be saved from destruction was blown away as chaff in a strong wind

2c. ...before the fierce anger of the Lord come upon you, ...

The only hope that the Jews had was to placate the Lord Jehovah and turn aside His fierce anger before it consumed them in the form of foreign invasion. It has been suggested that this could have begun with the Scythians and been finished by the Babylonians God used such people who, although they were pagans, were rods (instruments) of anger under His control.

2d. ... before the day of the Lord's anger come upon you.

This evidently referred to the day when God's judgment was scheduled to begin against His people in Judah. When that came, there was to be no opportunity for repentance, and only the righteous remnant could expect God to care for them during the holocaust which would take place. All others would have to take their deserved punishment.

B. Pursuit: 3a

3a. Seek ye the Lord, all ye meek of the earth, which have wrought his judgment seek righteousness, seek meekness: ...

This appears to have been directed toward the righteous remnant in Judah and perhaps to any others who would repent of their sins and join them. They were urged to search for the Lord, meaning to search for His help. They were described as meek (humble) and as those who wrought his judgment (tried to do His will, tried to keep His ordinance or commands). They were urged to search for righteousness and meekness, meaning that they were to do what was right and remain humble before the Lord.

C. Prospect: 3b

3b. ... it may be ye shall be hid in the day of the Lord's anger.

Hope was held out to the righteous that they could survive the fire-storm about to break upon Judah. Everything was in God's sovereign power, and He could bring them through this horrible experience as testimonies to His keeping ability. We do know that there were survivors of the overthrow of Judah and Jerusalem. We do know that many were deported eastward to Babylon to live in exile. We do know that some were left in the land to look after it, although they fled to Egypt after staging a hopeless revolt. We do know that about 50,000 returned from the Babylonian captivity to rebuild after being away for seventy years.

We live in a far more dangerous world today than ancient Judah did, because the weapons of war are much greater. We could be engulfed in a holocaust more terrible than any which has gone before. What hope do we have in light of these circumstances? Our hope is the same as the righteous remnant in Judah had, for God is our refuge in time of trouble (Ps. 9:9). He can deliver us from death, or He can deliver us through it into His Own glorious presence.

Evangelistic Emphasis

Evangelism in the Christian sense is not only good news. It is also undeserved good news. As Zephaniah preached, Israel and the surrounding nations were in sad shape. Idolatry was rampant. The situation was so bad that the Lord had determined that he would utterly consume the land. All were deserving of judgment. None were deserving of reward.

It was in that dire situation that Zephaniah called for repentance. In spite of the fact that the people did not deserve the gracious gifts of God, the prophet felt that if their penitence was sincere, they might receive those gifts anyway.

Our evangelistic efforts need to be geared to this type of appeal. The gospel is undeserved good news. It will not make much sense to the self righteous. To those, however, who feel a sense of guilt, separation, and hopelessness, it will be marvellous good news indeed.

As a doctor goes not to the healthy but to the sick, let us go not to the "righteous" but to the sinful. Into the chasm of hopelessness and despair that they feel, let us urge, "Turn to the Lord that His gracious and generous love may forgive your sins and hide his anger from you."

Memory Selection

"Seek ye the Lord, all ye meek of the earth, which have wrought his judgment; seek righteousness, seek meekness."
Zephaniah 2:3.

While no one has any right to presume on the grace of God, there are some qualities that will improve the basis of our hope for it. Two of those qualities are mentioned here: righteousness and meekness.

It is true that we can never be righteous enough to merit salvation. Nevertheless it is also true that the Lord loves righteousness and loves to see us being righteous. By our righteousness we avoid expanding our estrangement from God and incline His heart to hear our prayers and respond to us.

It is further true that humility commends us to God. because of our sin, we have nothing to be conceited about. It would be utter folly for those of us who are sinners to stand before a holy God with any degree of pride. The most incongruous thing I can think of is arrogant worship. The two terms are mutually exclusive.

One of the tragic perceptions that is abroad in the world today is that the church is smug and that Christians think they are better than other people. I think that is usually a misconception. Most Christians that I know are not arrogant people. However, we should remember that the appearance of pride is as alienating to God as it is to man.

Weekday Problems

Tim lives in a constant state of fear. He reads newspapers and books that talk about all the dangers that exist in the world. His mind is full of data about weapon systems, international tensions, and conspiracies. He is fully informed about the spread of terminal illnesses, the dangers of insecticides on our food, the depletion of the ozone layer, and the pollution of our air and water. He knows in detail about the huge sections of the globe where there is oppressive hunger and life-threatening poverty. He knows all about crime, drugs, overcrowded prisons, and a variety of other problems that threaten the human race.

Tim has convinced himself that the human race is on the verge of destroying itself. He thinks that problems are irreversibly escalating and that there is no possible future other than mass destruction.

* Are there indications that the world we live in is headed for destruction in the foreseeable future?
* If so, will the destruction occur as a result of man's flaws or will it be by direct divine intervention?
* In the light of many negative factors in the world, how should we live and what attitude should we have?

Superintendent's Sermonette

Many people, perhaps the majority, seem to have a perverted concept of God. They describe Him blitheLy as "the man upstairs," "the good Lord," and a sort of glorified Santa Claus. They profane His name in everyday conversation, but they want His help when things go wrong. They accept Him as a God of love, but they reject Him as a God of wrath, They want His bLessings but not His justice for themselves. Paul described them as "having a form of godliness, but denying the power thereof" (II Tim. 3:5).

The Bible presents God in much different terms, He is a God of love, but He is also a God of wrath. He blesses those who obey and serve Him, but He judges those who disobey and ignore Him. He is patient with sinners, but His cup of wrath spills over on them when it is full. In our lesson today, we are going to study the warnings of Zephaniah to the sinful people of Judah. They were scheduled for judgment, but the righteous could expect God's protection. The world today is in the same situation.

This Lesson in <u>Your</u> Life

A prophet is one who brings the message of God to bear on a contemporary situation. Zephaniah expressed the judgment of God on the people of his day. However, there are many parallels that make his message relevant to the people of our day. Notice some of the lessons we can learn from this prophet.

First, we can learn the seriousness of disobeying God. People have often disobeyed God. When there was no immediate effect, they sometimes have assumed that God can be disobeyed with impunity. Not every one's experience is like that of Ananias and Sapphira in the book of Acts. They disobeyed God and were instantly stricken dead. However, many others have disobeyed God and been allowed to continue on their way as though nothing had happened.

Not all sins carry with them the weight of instant judgment. God, in His mercy and patience, sometimes allows things to continue until a later accounting. Never, however, should this be presumed on to conclude that one can live in disobedience and avoid accountability.

In the days of Zephaniah there was a nonchalance about idolatry. The thundering words of the prophet reminded the people that there was no such nonchalance in the mind of God. He was at the point of contemplating the destruction of all humankind. Though men may take disobedience lightly, God does not.

A second lesson of Zephaniah is the importance of reverence. He urged the people to remain reverently silent as they contemplated the judgment of God. Our day has been lacking in this dimension of reverence. Some have denied God. Some have rejected Him. Still others have accepted Him in a familiar way as though He were less than God.

In Christ we have learned a great deal about the closeness of God, but that does not detract from His greatness. He loves us and is a Father to us. That does not mean that we should assume that it is not urgent that we obey Him with reverence and awe.

A third lesson of Zephaniah is the certainty of judgment. Though it may appear that people get along fine when they are living in a state of disobedience, the reality is that sooner or later there will be a day of reckoning. All of us will be held accountable for our sins. Our hope is in the forgiveness and mercy of God. If we are thinking that He does not take sin seriously and might not hold us accountable, we are grievously mistaken.

A key lesson of this prophet is the danger of cynicism. He speaks of those who say, "The Lord will not do good, neither will he do evil." These are the people who have lost confidence of the Lord's active involvement in the world. They think it does not matter much one way or the other how we live. Do they have a surprise in store? Such cynicism accomplishes nothing and holds grave danger.

A final lesson of the book is that there is always hope when there is repentance. "It may be that ye shall be hid in the day of the Lord's anger," Zephaniah says. Apart from God's mercy our situation is hopeless. If we repent, He may shelter us.

Seed Thoughts

1. Who could be a prophet of God?
Since it was not inherited, as that of a priest was, the role of prophet went to whomever God chose and gifted for it.

2. What was the word of the Lord which came to Zephaniah?
It was that Judah had sinned, and judgment was coming unless she sought repentance from the Lord.

3. What does it mean for God to utterly consume all things from off the land?
It means that He makes a complete sweep of men and animals within a given area as a divine judgment.

4. What stumbling blocks did God promise to sweep away in Judah?
This apparently referred to idols. Our "idols" today may be other types of objects of affection. Discuss.

5. How should one act in the presence of the Lord?
He should be silent and seek to know what God says and plans to do.

(Please Turn Page)

---

1. Who could be a prophet of God?

2. What was the word of the Lord which came to Zephaniah?

3. What does it mean for God to utterly consume all things from off the land?

4. What stumbling blocks did God promise to sweep away in Judah?

5. How should one act in the presence of the Lord?

6. What was the day of the Lord mentioned by Zephaniah?

7. Name the sacrifice and the guests in Zephaniah 1:7.

8. What do Jonah 1:3-4 and Zephaniah 1:12 teach about God?

9. Why is timing important in repentance for sin?

10. What hope does a righteous remnant have in time of trouble?

Seed Thoughts - Continued

6. What was the day of the Lord mentioned by Zephaniah?
It referred to coming judgement, evidently by Babylon. It ultimately refers to final judgment following the age of grace in the end times.

7. Name the sacrifice and the guests in Zephaniah 1:7.
Sinful Judah was to be the sacrifice, and foreigners were to be the guests invited to consume the Jews.

8. What do Jonah 1:3-4 and Zephaniah 1:12 teach about God?
They show us that no one can hide from the presence of God and not be discovered by Him,

9. Why is timing important in repentance for sin?
Waiting too long to repent can cause people to move beyond their opportunity (Zeph. 2:2 -II Cor. 6:2).

10. What hope does a righteous remnant have in time of trouble?
It can trust the Lord to deliver it, either <u>from</u> death or <u>through</u> it.

Since it was not inherited, as that of a priest was, the role of prophet went to whomever God chose and gifted for it.

It was that Judah had sinned, and judgment was coming unless she sought repentance from the Lord.

It means that He makes a complete sweep of men and animals within a given area as a divine judgment.

This apparently referred to idols. Our "idols" today may be other types of objects of affection. Discuss.

He should be silent and seek to know what God says and plans to do.

It referred to coming judgement, evidently by Babylon. It ultimately refers to final judgment following the age of grace in the end times.

Sinful Judah was to be the sacrifice, and foreigners were to be the guests invited to consume the Jews.

They show us that no one can hide from the presence of God and not be discovered by Him,

---

Waiting too long to repent can cause people to move beyond their opportunity (Zeph. 2:2 -II Cor. 6:2).

It can trust the Lord to deliver it, either <u>from</u> death or <u>through</u> it.

God Will Restore Israel

Zephaniah 3:12. I will also leave in the midst of thee an afflicted and poor people, and they shall trust in the name of the Lord.

Zephaniah 3:14. Sing, O daughter of Zion; shout, O Israel; be glad and rejoice with all the heart, O daughter of Jerusalem.

15. The Lord hath taken away thy judgments, he hath cast out thine enemy: the king of Israel, even the Lord, is in the midst of thee: thou shalt not see evil any more.

16. In that day it shall be said to Jerusalem, Fear thou not: and to Zion, let not thine hands be slack.

17. The Lord thy God in the midst of thee is mighty; he will save, he will rejoice over thee with joy; he will rest in his love, he will joy over thee with singing.

18. I will gather them that are sorrowful for the solemn assembly, who are of thee, to whom the reproach of it was a burden.

19. Behold, at that time I will undo all that afflict thee: and I will save her that halteth, and gather her that was driven out; and I will get them praise and fame in every land where they have been put to shame.

20. At that time will I bring you again, even in the time that I gather you: for I will make you a name and a praise among all people of the earth, when I turn back your captivity before your eyes, saith the Lord.

MEMORY SELECTION
Zephaniah 3:17
DEVOTIONAL READING
Psalm 51:10-19

BACKGROUND SCRIPTURE
Zephaniah 3
PRINTED SCRIPTURE
Zephaniah 3:12,14-20

Teacher's Target

God never used pagan nations as instruments by which to chastise His Own people without also punishing these nations. Certain nations scheduled for judgment were named in Zephaniah 2:4-15 (Philistia, Moab, Ethiopia, and Assyria). The prophet reviewed the immoral state of Jerusalem in his time, referring to it as being filthy, polluted, and oppressive. The princes (officials), prophets, and priests were guilty (Zeph. 3:1-7). They would repent, and then God would gather the heathen nations for judgment (Zeph. 3:8).

Help your students to realize that Divine chastisement is designed to move God's people back to fellowship with Him and the righteousness which follows. The times when the Jews repented of their sins and were restored to fellowship with God were forerunners of the time coming when they will turn as a whole to Him and be welcomed into the kingdom led by their Messiah and Savior, Jesus Christ.

Lesson Introduction

God told His repentant people to wait upon Him while He dealt with the pagan nations which had oppressed them (Zeph. 3:8). He said that He would then turn to the people (His special people, the Jews) and give them a pure language that they might worship and serve Him. Those dispersed afar would return and offer themselves to Him again. The shame which had characterized them when they were spiritual rebels would fall away. Those who were proud among them would be taken out (Zeph. 3:9-11).

We now come to our printed text of Zephania 3:12 and 14-20, and we will include consideration of verse 13, as well. This little prophetic book ends on a high note of optimism regarding God's people. No doubt it had a nearer fulfillment in view, but it may also have had an additional, fulfillment in view of the Messianic Kingdom.

Teaching Outline

I. Poverty: Zeph. 3:12
   A. Remainders 12a
   B. Reliance: 12b

II. Presence: Zeph. 3:14-15
   A. Celebrations 14
   B. Considerations: 15

III. Predictions: Zeph. 3:16-20
   A. Encouragement: 16
   B. Enjoyment: 17
   C. Enhancement: 18-20

Daily Bible Readings

Mon. Jerusalem Reproved
Zephaniah 3:1-3
Tue. Prophets and Priests Have Failed
Zephaniah 3:4-7
Wed. I will Call My People Back
Zephaniah 3:8-9
Thu. My People to be Restored
Zephaniah 3:10-13
Fri. Time to Sing
Zephaniah 3:14-15
Sat. The Lord Accepts Repentance
Zephaniah 3:16-18
Sun. Restoration
Zephaniah 3:19-20

Verse By Verse

I. Poverty: Zeph. 3:12

A. Remainder: 12a
12a. I will also leave in the midst of thee an afflicted and poor people, . . .

The holy mountain mentioned in Zephaniah 3:11 apparently referred to Mount Zion, the sacred spot in Jerusalem. Note references to this in verses 14 and 16. Verse 12 seems to describe the righteous remnant left among God's people after the proud and haughty rebels were removed. It was during the humiliating experience of the Babylonian captivity that the Jews abandoned their love of idols. The wealthy ones stayed for the most part in the east, while the poor ones volunteered to return to Palestine and rebuilt what had been destroyed seventy years earlier. It was in and through such people as this that the Lord was pleased to carry on His work.

B. Reliance: 12b
12b. . . . and they shall trust in the name of the Lord.

Jews who had stopped trusting in their own strength and wisdom had to rely on the name of Jehovah. This involved drawing on all of the divine attributes which that name represented. Were they weak? They could draw on His almighty power. Were they baffled? They could draw on His infinite wisdom.

Zephaniah predicted that the righteous remnant of Jews would not commit sin, speak lies, nor practice deceit. As sheep belonging to their divine Shepherd, they would feed and lie down in His pastures, and no adversaries would make them afraid (Zeph. 3:13). In this description we see the <u>ideal</u> people of God living righteously and resting in the protection their loving Father provides. We have to admit that, in reality, the Jews did not live up to this ideal description, but that should not detract from the positive picture presented here of what can happen when God's people are in fellowship with Him. The remainder of Zephaniah 3 dwells on this theme. It gives a goal for which all believers, Jewish and Gentile, might strive.

II. Presence: Zeph. 3:14-15

A. Celebration: 14
14. Sing, O daughter of Zion shout, O Israel; be glad and rejoice with all the heart, O daughter of Jerusalem.

Zephaniah said that repentance would lead to restoration, and restoration would lead to rejoicing. Jewish women were leaders in celebrating a good relationship with the Lord, For example, when God led the Israelites through the Red Sea and drowned the pursuing Egyptians, we read, "Miriam the prophetess, the sister of Aaron [and Moses], took a timbrel in her hand and all the women went out after her with timbrels and with dances. And Miriam answered them, Sing ye to the Lord, for he hath triumphed gloriously; the horse and the rider [from Egypt] hath he thrown into the sea" (Exod, 1:20-21).

Therefore, it was appropriate for Zephaniah to urge the women from sacred Mount Zion and from all of Jerusalem to sing, be glad, and rejoice with all their heart when the Jews were restored to their beloved land. What was to happen following the return from captivity in Babylon would prefigure what is going to happen when God gathers the Jews from all over the world to Palestine in the end times. Note use of the term gather in verses 18, 19, and 20.

B. Considerations: 15
15a. The Lord hath taken away thy judgments, he hath cast out thine enemy:
Speaking as if it had already taken place, Zephaniah described the time when the Lord would take away the judgments (punishments) used with the Jews. He would cast out their enemy, meaning the pagans who would be God's instruments for chastising His Own people. After repentance had taken place, the need for such divine rods of anger would disperse.

15b. ... the king of Israel, even the Lord, is in the midst of thee: thou shalt not see evil any more.
Zephaniah said that, in the ideal time to come, God's people would have their King in their midst, and they would not have to experience evil (adversity) anymore. We know that the Jews did not have kings after the Babylonian captivity, except foreign kings who ruled over them. They did not have kings during the time of independence under the Maccabees during the second century before Christ nor within their current state of Israel since independence came again in 1945. Therefore, Zephaniah 3:15 must refer to Jehovah being their King in a spiritual sense while they served Him after the Babylonian captivity and Christ being their literal King when He came to set up His kingdom. In either case, the protection of God and Christ cause His people to be unafraid of evil brought against them by the world.

The element of trust by God's people would be essential in both types of situations. We know that the Jews had enemies surrounding them as they sought to rebuild their homeland after the Babylonian captivity ended. We know that Satan is on hand to threaten people in Christ's kingdom. The believers' resource in every age is faith in God.

III. Predictions: Zeph. 3:16-20

A. Encouragement: 16
16. In that day it shall be said to Jerusalem, Fear thou not: and to Zion, Let not thine hands be slack.
The word of encouragement in the day of restoration would be for Jerusalem (the Jews) to not be afraid. It would be for Zion (the Jews) to refrain from letting their hands (or heads) hang down in despair, as if weak from fear. These terms refer to any demonstration of despair which people might use.

B. Enjoyment: 17
17a. The Lord thy God in the midst of thee is mighty; he will save, ...
Restoration to fellowship with God means that His presence returns to dwell in the midst of His people. He is an all-powerful God, and He will save those who trust in Him. He will protect them against disasters in nature and disasters caused by men.

17b. ... he will rejoice over thee with joy; he will rest in his love, he will joy over thee with singing.
Having saved His people from all that would harm them, God will rejoice over them, making them His objects of joy. The next thought is obscure. One concept is that God will "rest [in silent satisfaction] and in His love He will be silent and make no mention [of past sins, or even recall them]" (Amplified Bible). Another paraphrase is, "He will love you and not accuse you" (Living Bible). Still another is, "In his love he will give you new life" (Today's English Version). Finally, "He will rest you in His love" (Berkeley). The last thought in the verse is that God will rejoice over His people with singing. We cannot help but wonder what it would sound like to hear God Himself sing.

C. Enhancement: 18-20
18. I will gather them that are sorrowful for the solemn assembly, who are of thee, to whom the reproach of it was a burden.
The Lord said that He would gather Jews who had sorrowfully yearned for the solemn assembly.

Jeremiah later complained, "The ways of [or roads to] Zion do mourn, because none come to the solemn [Jewish religious] feasts" (Lam. 1:4). The fact that the Jews had no temple anymore, and that they were not free to attend their religious convocations, had caused pagan people to heap reproach (derision, mockery) upon them, and this had naturally been a burden to bear. Rather than the reputation of the Jews and Jehovah being further denigrated, it would now be enhanced.

19a. Behold, at that time I will undo all that afflict thee: . . .

God said that, at the time of deliverance, He would deal with the pagans who had afflicted His people. History shows that He allowed them to be overwhelmed by enemies.

19b. . . . and I will save her that halteth, and gather her that was driven out; . . .

God said that He would rescue those who were helpless and gather together those who had been deported from their homeland.

19c. . . . and I will get them praise and fame in every land where they have been put to shame.

Where the Jews had been objects of reproach, God said that He would make them objects of praise and fame (good name, reputation) in every land where they had been shamed. Many who were deported to the east remained where they were and became respectable members of the societies in which they had been settled as humiliated captives.

20a. At that time will I bring you again, even in the time that I gather you: . . .

It seems obvious that this is a summary verse designed to conclude the book It contains little that is new, and it may have been written for the sake of emphasis to underscore God's promise to bring the Jews back home to Palestine following dispersal.

20b. . . . for I will make you a name and a praise among all people of the earth, when I turn back your captivity before your eyes, saith the Lord.

Note here that God said He would enhance the reputation of the Jews "among all people of the earth." This suggests that their fame would be universal, rather than being limited to their places of captivity.

It is interesting to see again the promise made to Abraham, father of the Hebrew race, stating that "in thee shall all families of the earth be blessed" (Gen. 12:3). Many think that this refers not only to the remarkable contributions made by Jews around the world but specifically to the fact that it was through them that God gave the Messiah, Jesus Christ, Who would bless the whole world.

Evangelistic Emphasis

Regardless of how bad a situation is, God can bring hope to it. During the time of Zephaniah, Israel was in a very corrupt state. Disobedience was rampant. Idolatry was common. Rulers were cruel. Judges were dishonest. Even prophets were treacherous. To look at the spiritual state of the nation, one would think there was no hope. It appeared that the only way to get rid of the mess was to destroy the nation.

Out of that rubble God promised to raise up a devout remnant. They would be His people, represent His will, and be protected from the destruction that was about to come on the wicked. They would be a humble and believing people.

Where was God going to find these people? He was going to gather them up out of the corrupt nation. In spite of the general spiritual decline, there were still a number of faithful believers in the nation. God was capable of identifying them and gathering them up so that His purpose for Israel could be preserved.

When you are discouraged about evangelism and it seems that no one is interested, remember that there are humble and devout people who are ready to be gathered up to be the people of God. God knows who they are and will not allow them to be destroyed.

Memory Selection

"The Lord thy God in the midst of thee is mighty; he will save, he will rejoice over thee with joy; he will rest in his love."
Zephaniah 3:17.

A prophet does not decide what his message will be. He delivers the message God gives him to deliver. He may be a believer in positive thinking, but God may ask him to deliver a message of condemnation.

Zephaniah was primarily a prophet of judgment. The bulk of his message is condemnation of corruption and warning of impending destruction. Zephaniah did not have any choice about this. He simply did what God commanded him to do.

Yet even in this context there is a ray of hope. It rests on three things:

First, it rests on the Lord's power. He is mighty and is not at the mercy of the evil conditions in the land.

Second, it rests on the Lord's nature. He will save. He has that kind of heart and spirit.

Third, it rests on the Lord's love. He is not a God who abandons His people because they get in trouble. He looks for ways to help and for remnants to save.

Weekday Problems

"The church is so corrupt, I cannot tolerate it any longer," Pearl said. "I have seen problems before but it has gotten so bad now that I can no longer consider it the church of God."

Then she listed some of the problems she saw in the church. She believed that she had observed insincerity in the pulpit. Those who preached unselfishness seemed to display greed. Those who preached purity sometimes demonstrated crudeness or even open corruption. Ministers sometimes seemed to exploit rather than to serve people.

Among the members of the church she saw a widespread attitude of indifference. People did not seem to take their responsibilities seriously. They were careless about church attendance and listless in worship when they did attend. They seemed to be more concerned about their own comfort and pleasure than about fulfilling the mission of the Lord. There was more worry about a broken air conditioner than about the lost being reached in a mission program.

* Is Pearl correct about the state of the church?
* Does God always have a remnant of humble and devout Christians in the church?
* When the church seems corrupt should we leave it or seek to be part of a remnant that will be gathered together by God to restore the church?

Superintendent's Sermonette

A paradox is a belief which seems opposed to common sense and yet in fact is true. If we belong to the Lord and are guided by divine principles, we will appear paradoxical to worldly-minded people. For example, if we are persecuted and poor, the world will think that we are weak, and yet we may be our strongest because we trust in the Lord (Zeph. 3:12). If we sing and rejoice, even though we are alienated and threatened, we will appear to be foolish, and yet we are wise to believe in God's promise of deliverance from our enemies (Zeph. 3:14-15).

The repentant Jews of Zephaniah's time could look at their detractors and feel confident that Jehovah would work on their behalf. If we are walking in fellowship with the Lord today, we can have that same kind of confidence. Let us be ready and willing to look at harsh circumstances and not be intimidated or depressed by them. God expects us to be living paradoxes who seem to be contrary to common sense but who know the reality of trusting God for everything.

This Lesson in <u>Your</u> Life

One lesson we should learn from Zephaniah is the importance of a remnant in the church. This has always been considered vital. When God was planning to destroy the wicked city of Sodom, Abraham begged Him to relent on the basis of a remnant of righteous people in the cities. God agreed to withhold destruction if fifty righteous people could be found. Then the number was lowered and lowered again. Finally God agreed that if only ten righteous people could be found the city would be saved. Unfortunately Sodom did not have a remnant even that large. Only ten good people could have saved a city.

A handful of good people can be a great force in the preservation of a nation as well. The writer of Proverbs tells us, "Righteousness exalteth a nation: but sin is a reproach to any people." (Proverbs 14:34). When we are humbly faithful to the will of God, we not only receive blessings ourselves but we also project a saving influence into the society we are a part of.

History seems to warn us that both churches and nations seem to go through periods of increased corruption. In some ways it may be more important to be righteous during a time of prevailing corruption than at any other time.

Zephaniah points out that the presence of a remnant is a cause for rejoicing. Sensitive Christians have many discouragements in life. They have a great need for things that will improve their morale during bad times. Therefore, when they find even small numbers of faithful people they should be encouraged and inspired. Though the sky is generally black, a small ray of light is a cause to sing and be glad.

Another lesson that Zephaniah teaches is that bad situations can be redeemed. Rather than give up we should remember that we worship a God who can take away judgments. He is a God of mercy. We may have had experience with people who held grudges and maintained a vindictive spirit, but God is not like that.

Sometimes people have trouble trusting in the forgiveness of God because they have not been forgiven by other people. We should remember that God's capacity for loving and forgiving is greater than ours. It is far better to be in His hands than in the hands of a mean-spirited person.

Zephaniah also points out that God does not overlook pockets of goodness. A simple and quiet Christian will not be overlooked even if he is in the midst of a sea of evildoers. God will find him, gather him with His other servants, and protect them all from their enemies.

Further, Zephaniah promises that God will restore respect to Israel. He will make them a name. Sometimes we hesitate to say so, but all of us deeply desire approval. We want to be respected by others. God will see to it that we have this need met, just as He sees to it that all our needs are met.

Seed Thoughts

1. What happens as backsliders wait upon the Lord (Zeph. 3:8)?
Humbled before Him, they may expect Him to oppose their enemies and deliver them from the shame of defeat.

2. How may affliction and poverty be positive influences?
They can cause us to stop trusting in ourselves and cause us to trust in the unlimited power and wisdom of God.

3. What results if a righteous remnant stop sinning, lying, and deceiving (Zeph. 3:13)?
God, as their divine Shepherd, will feed, rest, and protect them

4. What allows God's people to sing and shout with joy while faced with harsh circumstances?
Their faith helps them to look beyond present difficulties and believe that God will deliver them in His Own time.

5. What effect does despair in believers have on unbelievers?
It undermines the believer's testimony and discourages sinners from believing.

(Please Turn Page)

---

1. What happens as backsliders wait upon the Lord (Zeph. 3:8)?

2. How may affliction and poverty be positive influences?

3. What results if a righteous remnant stop sinning, lying, and deceiving (Zeph. 3:13)?

4. What allows God's people to sing and shout with joy while faced with harsh circumstances?

5. What effect does despair in believers have on unbelievers?

6. How can Christians have God in their midst?

7. How does God's presence in us help us face the world?

8. Does God ever sing?

9. What will be the ultimate enhancement of God's people?

10. How can we confound our enemies?

Seed Thoughts - Continued

6. How can Christians have God in their midst?
God and Christ dwell within believers by means of the Holy Spirit.

7. How does God's presence in us help us face the world?
"Greater is he that is in you, than he that is in the world" (I John 4:4). We gain confidence by experiencing this.

8. Does God ever sing?
Zephaniah 3:17 says that God saves His people and then rejoices over them with singing. Meditate on this truth.

9. What will be the ultimate enhancement of God's people?
The entrance of redeemed Jews and Gentiles into the Messianic Kingdom.

10. How can we confound our enemies?
By trusting in God and triumphing over every obstacle through faith.

Humbled before Him, they may expect Him to oppose their enemies and deliver them from the shame of defeat.

They can cause us to stop trusting in ourselves and cause us to trust in the unlimited power and wisdom of God.

God, as their divine Shepherd, will feed, rest, and protect them

Their faith helps them to look beyond present difficulties and believe that God will deliver them in His Own time.

It undermines the believer's testimony and discourages sinners from believing.

God and Christ dwell within believers by means of the Holy Spirit.

"Greater is he that is in you, than he that is in the world" (I John 4:4). We gain confidence by experiencing this.

Zephaniah 3:17 says that God saves His people and then rejoices over them with singing. Meditate on this truth.

The entrance of redeemed Jews and Gentiles into the Messianic Kingdom.

By trusting in God and triumphing over every obstacle through faith.

Understand What You Teach

I Timothy 1:3. As I besought thee to abide still at Ephesus, when I went into Macedonia, that thou mightest charge some that they teach no other doctrine.
4. Neither give heed to fables and endless genealogies, which minister questions, rather than godly edifying which is in faith: so do.
5. Now the end of the commandment is charity out of a pure heart, and of a good conscience, and of faith unfeigned:
6. From which some having swerved have turned aside unto vain jangling;
7. Desiring to be teachers of the law; understand neither what they say, nor whereof they affirm.
8. But we know that the law is good, if a man use it lawfully;
9. Knowing this, that the law is not made for a righteous man, but for the lawless and disobedient, for the ungodly and for sinners, for unholy and profane, for murderers of fathers and murderers of mothers, for manslayers,
10. For whoremongers, for them that defile themselves with mankind, for menstealers, for liars, for perjured persons, and if there be any other thing that is contrary to sound doctrine;
11. According to the glorious gospel of the blessed God, which was committed to my trust.
I Timothy 1:18. This charge I commit unto thee, son Timothy, according to the prophecies which went before on thee, that thou by them mightest war a good warfare;
19. Holding faith, and a good conscience; which some having put away concerning faith have made shipwreck:
20. Of whom is Hymenaeus and Alexander; whom I have delivered unto Satan, that they may learn not to blaspheme.

MEMORY SELECTION
I Timothy 1:5
DEVOTIONAL READING
James 3:1-5

BACKGROUND SCRIPTURE
I Timothy 1
PRINTED SCRIPTURE
I Timothy 1:3-11,18-20

Teacher's Target

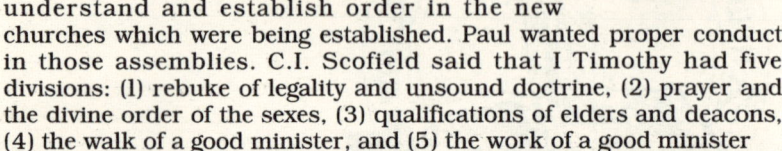

Paul's two epistles to Timothy and one to Titus were written to help these younger men better understand and establish order in the new churches which were being established. Paul wanted proper conduct in those assemblies. C.I. Scofield said that I Timothy had five divisions: (1) rebuke of legality and unsound doctrine, (2) prayer and the divine order of the sexes, (3) qualifications of elders and deacons, (4) the walk of a good minister, and (5) the work of a good minister.

Help your students to see what Paul had to state regarding legality and unsound doctrine in the first division (I Tim. 1:1-20). Impress upon them the vital importance of knowing, loving, and acting upon divine truth. The revealed Word of God is the source book for the development of sound doctrine and its application in everyday life.

Lesson Introduction

Various influences were arrayed against the revealed truth of God in the first century. These included pagan fables (myths, legends) and long genealogies promoted by the Gnostics seeking to tie people to angels and on upward to God Himself. They also included legalisms (man-made regulations) promoted by Judaizers to bind people to the law of Moses, even the parts already fulfilled in Christ. The moral parts of the law were still applicable to sinners, and Christians could join Jews in supporting them.

Paul gave a stirring testimony to show the great change which had taken place in his own life after he was converted to Christ. He then challenged Timothy to hold true to the faith and a good conscience. Paul was grieved over the loss of believers, such as Hymenaeus and Alexander, from the true faith. He turned them over to Satan so that they would learn not to blaspheme God.

Teaching Outline

I. Charge I: I Tim. 1:3-5
   A. Reminder: 3-4
   B. Result: 5

II. Controversy: I Tim. 1:6-11
   A. Apostates: 6-7
   B. Approval: 8
   C. Application: 9-11

III. Charge II: I Tim. 1:18-20
   A. Adherence: 18-19a
   B. Abandonment: 19b-20

Daily Bible Readings

Mon. To Timothy, My Son
I Timothy 1:1-2
Tue. Avoid Idle Speculation
I Timothy 1:3-5
Wed. Wrong Motivation
I Timothy 1:6-7
Thu. The Law is Good
I Timothy 1:8-10
Fri. The Gospel of Grace
I Timothy 1:11-14
Sat. To Save Sinners
I Timothy 1:15-17
Sun. War a Good Warfare
I Timothy 1:18-20

Verse By Verse

I. Charge I: I Tim. 1:3-5

A. Reminder: 3-4
**3. As I besought thee to abide still at Ephesus, when I went into Macedonia, that thou mightest charge some that they teach no other doctrine,
4. Neither give heed to fables and endless genealogies, which minister questions, rather than godly edifying which is in faith: so do.**

This was obviously all one sentence as it came from the mind of Paul. The last two words of "so do" are supplied by the translators, Let us back up to the beginning and see what Paul wanted Timothy to do.

Paul had asked Timothy to remain behind in Ephesus while he himself went over to Macedonia (northern Greece). After visiting Greece, Paul had come back to Macedonia and met Timothy and others, and they had accompanied him as he headed for Jerusalem (Acts 20:1-3).

While Timothy was in Ephesus, he was given the task of teaching others to refrain from teaching false doctrine. Paul was very intense about this matter. "Though we, or an angel from heaven, preach any other gospel unto you than that which we have preached unto you, let him be accursed" (Gal. 1:8). John had also been adamant about it. "If there come any unto you, and bring not this doctrine [of Christ] , receive him not into your house, neither bid him God speed: for he that biddeth him God speed is partaker of his evil deeds" (II John 10-11).

Paul told Timothy to avoid giving heed to fables and endless genealogies. We know that the ancient world was filled with pagan myths and legends. We know that the Gnostics of the first century taught that people could be connected to spirits (angels) and aeons and thus trace their descent back to God Himself. These were hurtful teachings, raising many questions rather than building people up in the true faith. Paul wanted Timothy to charge young pastors to avoid these heretical teachings.

B. Result: 5
5. Now the end of the commandment is charity out of a pure heart, and of a good conscience, and of faith unfeigned:

Paul said that the objective or goal of true Christian doctrine was to produce love which comes from a pure heart, a good conscience, and sincere faith. Faith, defined as sound doctrine, purifies the heart and cleanses the conscience of guilt (Acts 15:9; Titus 1:15). The end of the gospel and of the law of God is love, Both have to be understood and put into their proper sequence. The law came first to lead men to Christ, and then the gospel operated through Christ.

II. Controversy: I Tim. 1:6-11

A. Apostates: 6-7
6. From which some having swerved have turned aside unto vain jangling;

Paul told Timothy that some individuals had swerved (wandered away, missed the mark) and ended up in vain jangling (meaningless talk, foolish discussions). In order to prevent this from happening, sincere believers would have to be guided by pure hearts, clear consciences, and sound doctrine (that is basic to sincere faith).

7. Desiring to be teachers of the law; understanding neither what they say, nor whereof they affirm.

The term "teachers of the law" is all one word in the Greek (<u>nomodidaskaloi</u>) and it appears as doctors of the law in Luke 5:17 and in its singular form when describing Gamaliel in Acts 5:34. The men Paul described here seemed to be false teachers who went beyond even the Judaizers mentioned in Romans and Galatians, for they added to the law of Moses by using fables and heresies (vs. 4), Paul said that they were ignorant, teaching things in a confident manner which they did not understand.

B. Approval: 8
8. But we know that the law is good, if a man use it lawfully;

Look ahead to verse 11. Paul said that the law of Moses was good if it was used properly and in accordance with the glorious gospel. In other words, it gives a knowledge of sin and points to the good news that Christ can save from sin.

C. Application: 9-11
9a. Knowing this, that the law is not made for a righteous man, but for the lawless and disobedient, for the ungodly and for sinners, for unholy and profane, . . .

It was typical of Paul to make a general statement and then follow it with a long list of examples. He seemed to do it here. He said that the law of God was not created to reprove righteous men but those who were lawless (lawbreakers), disobedient (criminals, rebels, unruly), ungodly (God-haters), sinners, unholy (irreverent, impious), and profane (irreligious, unspiritual). Note how Paul became more and more specific as his list continued.

9b. . . . for murderers of fathers and murderers of mothers, for manslayers,

10. For whoremongers, for them that defile themselves with mankind, for menstealers, for liars, for perjured persons, and if there be any other thing that is contrary to sound doctrine;

Paul's list of specific sinners included murderers of fathers and mothers, manslayers (murder in general—homicide), whoremongers, them that defile themselves with mankind, menstealers, liars, perjured persons, and any others doing anything contrary to the sound doctrine of Christ.

11. According to the glorious gospel of the blessed God, which was committed to my trust.

Paul seemed to come full circle here. He had said that the goal of the charge (command) to avoid false doctrine was to produce love (vss. 3-5). He saw the law of God as helpful in guiding people away from sin and toward love. Sound doctrine was based on the glorious gospel of God, and that had been given to Paul to propagate.

Verses 12-17 are not in our printed text for this lesson, but they contain Paul's personal testimony, perhaps as an encouragement for young Timothy. Paul said that God had counted him faithful and put him into the ministry, even though he had once been blasphemous and had persecuted and injured Christ's followers. He said that he had obtained mercy from God, because he had done these things in ignorance. God's grace had come to him, "along with the faith and love that are in Christ Jesus" (I Tim. 1:14, New International Version).

Paul went on to say that Christ came into the world to save sinners, of whom he was chief. Since Christ had been patient with him, Paul could serve as an example for other sinners seeking eternal life. He concluded his testimony with a doxology—"Now unto the King eternal, immortal, invisible, the only wise God, be honour and glory for ever and ever. Amen." (I Tim. 1:17). Now we return to Paul's charge to Timothy.

III. Charge II: I Tim. 1:18-20

A. Adherence 18-19a
18. This charge I commit unto thee, son Timothy, according to

**the prophecies which went before on thee, that thou by them mightest war a good warfare;
19a. Holding faith, and a good conscience; ...**

Whether we call this a new charge or a repetition of the original charge given in verse 3, Paul wanted Timothy to wage continued warfare against false teachers, One way that he could do this was to teach others sound doctrine and hold them to it. Reference to "the prophecies which went before on thee" probably went back to what men had said about Timothy when he joined Paul's missionary team in the Derbe-Lystra-Iconium region of central Asia Minor (Turkey). Timothy had been "well reported of by the brethren," and "him would Paul have to go forth with him" (Acts 16:2-3). Another possibility is that Paul was referring to things said about Timothy by New Testament prophets, perhaps at his ordination by laying on of the hands of the presbytery (I Tim. 4:14). Paul wanted Timothy to hold onto sound faith (set of doctrines) and to keep a clear conscience (see vs, 5). Adherence to the truth was absolutely necessary to the work of the ministry.

**B. Abandonment: 19b-20
19b. ... which some having put away concerning faith have made shipwreck: ...**

Here again, Paul moved from the general to the specific. He first mentioned that there were individuals in the first century who had rejected sound doctrine and a clear conscience, and, as a result, had made shipwreck of their ministry, Some feel that the "which" here refers to the conscience, and that some had gone against their knowledge of right and wrong and had thus lost their faith. The first interpretation seems preferable. The loss of sound doctrine and/or conscience can lead to spiritual shipwreck.

20a. Of whom is Hymenaeus and Alexander ...

Hymenaus is mentioned in II Timothy as a heretic, along with a man named Philetus. "Shun profane and vain babblings: for they will increase unto more ungodliness. And their word [teaching] will eat [spread] as doth a canker [gangrene]: of whom is Hymanaeus and Philetus; who concerning the truth have erred, saying that the resurrection is past already; and overthrow the faith of some" (II Tim. 2:16-18). Alexander may have been the coppersmith who opposed apostolic teaching (II Tim, 4:14).

20b. ... whom I have delivered unto Satan, that they may learn not to blaspheme.

Some interpret this to mean that Paul had excommunicated Hymanaeus and Alexander. However, others think that Paul turned the two over to affliction by Satan in order that they might learn to stop their blasphemy and perhaps be restored to fellowship at a later time. We hear no more about them.

In this first lesson from I Timothy we have learned the importance of having a pure heart, clear conscience, and sound faith. Our second one will show us how to train ourselves in godliness (I Tim. 4:1-16). Our third one will help us set our priorities, favoring spiritual concerns (I Tim, 6:6-14, 17-21).

Evangelistic Emphasis

Christianity is a religion of love, acceptance, forgiveness, and tolerance. It is because of these compassionate aspects of it that we can be secure. However, it would be a mistake to conclude that it is an indiscriminate religion in regard to truth and righteousness. Although Christianity teaches that we should love, accept, and forgive the sinner, it does not teach that we should be indifferent toward sin. While we should be tolerant of those who have differing views, we must not be unaware of the difference between truth and falseness.

Paul, more than any other New Testament writer, wrote of the grace of God. He did so with great power, giving his readers a strong sense of security. He himself relied heavily on the grace of God. He once described himself as the chief of sinners who had been saved by the grace of God. He believed strongly in forgiveness and mercy.

Paul is the perfect example of the fact that strong faith in the grace of God is not cause for doctrinal tangents or error. It is not necessary to be mushy-headed about doctrine in order to be patient with the sinner.

The human body needs both the structure of the skeleton and the softness of flesh. So also the Christian needs the sturdiness of sound doctrine and the softness of an understanding attitude. Doctrinal correctness without compassion results in a rigid and abrasive caricature of Christianity. Compassion without a strong commitment to truth results in an ineffectual glob of warm feelings.

As an evangelist, you will love people, understand them, forgive them, be patient with them, and be tolerant of their mistakes. You also, and this is Paul's point in our lesson today, must clearly teach them the facts of the gospel.

Memory Selection

"Now the end of the commandment is charity out of a pure heart, and a good conscience, and of faith unfeigned."

The greatest protector of our secure relationship to Christ is our own personal integrity. He will never let us go, so the danger is that we might leave Him. This danger can be avoided by having a pure heart, a good conscience, and a sincere faith.

This is a matter of enormous importance in the New Testament. There are many examples of sincere mistakes being easily forgiven. The warnings, however, against hypocrisy are solemn and severe. If we will stay honest with the Lord He can deal readily with whatever other problems we might have. If we try to deceive Him we block the processes by which forgiveness can come.

There are many things that are important in Christianity. It is important to be prayerful, kind, studious, merciful, etc. Nothing is more important than being real. It is basic to all else that we do. As you contemplate your responsibility to God, begin by examining your heart for purity, your conscience to be sure you are inwardly devoted, and your faith to see that it is unpretentious.

Weekday Problems

Danny and Freddie attend different churches but work for the same company. Both have a strong commitment to evangelism. Danny's commitment is expressed in a very structured and methodical way. He makes appointments to sit down with people to teach them the doctrinal truths of Christianity. He has a prepared set of lessons which he goes over with each person. At the conclusion he asks for a decision.

Danny's approach is so rational that many respond to it. They are well-informed but often insecure Christians. Somehow the warm assurance of Christ's love has not grown in their hearts.

Freddie has no set approach but simply tries to be loving and encouraging to people. He talks freely about his faith and assures others that the Lord loves them and will receive them. Many are attracted by his kindness. They tend to be gentle and affectionate people who know little about Christian doctrine.

* Does your church have a good balance between these two aspects of evangelism?
* If not, which way does it lean? What can be done to improve the balance?

Superintendent's Sermonette

We live in a society which is largely dedicated to change. We associate change with progress. It is true that science and technology have brought us many wonderful inventions which have revolutionized our lives in medicine, communication, transportation, and other fields. However, human nature has remained the same, and problems faced by the ancients are still faced by us today. That is why the Bible, an old book, is relevant in modern times. It is still a reliable guide for our faith and practice.

The advice which the veteran apostle Paul gave to the young preacher Timothy is still applicable in our lives. We need to avoid involvement with fables derived from pagan sources. We need to avoid legalisms which detract from the truth about Christ. We need to dedicate ourselves to the love which is developed by a pure heart, a clear conscience, and sincere faith (sound doctrine). If we follow this path, we can avoid the shipwreck which comes to those who drift onto the shoals of legalism and heresy.

This Lesson in <u>Your</u> Life

This challenge to responsible teaching contains a series of warnings about potential problems. The first is a warning against tangents. One of the purposes of Christian teaching is to keep us centered. Our objective is not innovation. It is not our responsibility to come up with new things all the time. It is rather our charge to keep calling people back to the fundamentals of faith.

Fanciful speculations on moot points can be seductive. Sometimes we would find it easier to play games with them than to practice turning the other cheek and going the second mile. It may be more titillating to speculate on the unknown than to meditate on what it means to "do justice, love kindness, and walk humbly" with God.

The test of whether a doctrinal dispute is worth spending time and energy on is whether the solution to it is edifying. Will the correct solution make us more loving? More honest? More pure in heart? More dedicated to Christ? If so, it is a vital matter worthy of much thought and study. If, however, it is a question which will do nothing more than occupy our time and satisfy our curiosity we should avoid it.

Another warning is that teaching should be from the proper motivation. To desire the prestige of a teacher without being willing to accept the discipline of careful preparation is a danger to the church. Such a person will not only have little to teach, but will also be tempted to idle speculations in an attempt to make an impression. The motivation for teaching should be the desire to serve others, not the desire to elevate oneself.

Even something as good as the law can do harm if it is used in the wrong way or with the wrong motive. This is in harmony with our experience in many areas of our lives. A sharp knife can be a helpful tool or a dangerous weapon depending on how it is used. A fire can be a servant of man's needs or a destroyer of life and property.

So the law will be our guide and help if we use it in the way it was intended. It tells us clearly what the Lord's will is and warns us of the consequences of not obeying His will. If the law is misused it becomes a burden to the righteous and is scoffed at by offenders.

Another warning is that we are in a serious battle, a war. The forces of both good and evil in the world are strong. Nothing should be taken for granted. It is not easy to be a devout Christian in a corrupt world. Deviations from truth are everywhere and many of them are very enticing. We should see our work as a war against evil. We often will be involved, not in consultation, but in confrontation. We must be soldiers as well as teachers.

Seed Thoughts

1. Why did Paul leave Timothy behind in Ephesus when he went to Macedonia (northern Greece)?
He wanted Timothy to charge others to teach no false doctrine.

2. Why did Paul write I Timothy?
He wanted to urge Timothy to continue doing what he had done in Ephesus.

3. What other scripture references support I Timothy 1:3?
Paul's remarks in Galatians 1:8 and John's remarks in II John 10-11 warn against teaching of a false gospel.

4. What might compare to "fables and endless genealogies" today?
Their modern counterparts might be found in the teachings of the new age movement, cults, and eastern religions.

5. What did Paul say was the goal of true Christian doctrine?
He said that it was to produce love which comes from a pure heart, a good conscience, and sincere faith. This faith is defined as sound doctrine.

(Please Turn Page)

---

1. Why did Paul leave Timothy behind in Ephesus when he went to Macedonia (northern Greece)?

2. Why did Paul write I Timothy?

3. What other scripture references support I Timothy 1:3?

4. What might compare to "fables and endless genealogies" today?

5. What did Paul say was the goal of true Christian doctrine?

6. How did Judaistic legalism originate in the first century?

7. Why did God give the law?

8. How important is it for us to teach sound doctrine and challenge others to do the same?

9. What two things must believers have to avoid spiritual shipwreck?

10. What did Paul do with Hymanaeus and Alexander?

Seed Thoughts - Continued

He wanted Timothy to charge others to teach no false doctrine.

He wanted to urge Timothy to continue doing what he had done in Ephesus.

Paul's remarks in Galatians 1:8 and John's remarks in II John 10-11 warn against teaching of a false gospel.

Their modern counterparts might be found in the teachings of the new age movement, cults, and eastern religions.

He said that it was to produce love which comes from a pure heart, a good conscience, and sincere faith. This faith is defined as sound doctrine.

It developed when supposed teachers of the law of Moses did not know what they were talking about but confidently taught it, anyway.

It showed men their sin and their desperate need for a Savior from heaven. It prepared the way for the gospel.

Paul counted it so important that he referred to it as spiritual warfare, and he urged Timothy to be a warrior.

They must have sincere faith (based on sound doctrine) and a good (clear) conscience.

He delivered them over to Satan to teach them not to blaspheme.

6. How did Judaistic legalism originate in the first century?
It developed when supposed teachers of the law of Moses did not know what they were talking about but confidently taught it, anyway.

7. Why did God give the law?
It showed men their sin and their desperate need for a Savior from heaven. It prepared the way for the gospel.

8. How important is it for us to teach sound doctrine and challenge others to do the same?
Paul counted it so important that he referred to it as spiritual warfare, and he urged Timothy to be a warrior.

9. What two things must believers have to avoid spiritual shipwreck?
They must have sincere faith (based on sound doctrine) and a good (clear) conscience.

10. What did Paul do with Hymanaeus and Alexander?
He delivered them over to Satan to teach them not to blaspheme.

GREEK ATHLETE—65 A.D.

Train Yourself In Godliness

I Timothy 4:1. Now the Spirit speaketh expressly, that in the latter times some shall depart from the faith, giving heed to seducing spirits, and doctrines of devils;
2. Speaking lies in hypocrisy; having their conscience seared with a hot iron;
3. Forbidding to marry, and commanding to abstain from meats, which God hath created to be received with thanksgiving of them which believe and know the truth.
4. For every creature of God is good, and nothing to be refused, if it be received with thanksgiving:
5. For it is sanctified by the word of God and prayer.
6. If thou put the brethren in remembrance of these things, thou shalt be a good minister of Jesus Christ, nourished up in the words of faith and of good doctrine, whereunto thou hast attained.
7. But refuse profane and old wives' fables, and exercise thyself rather unto godliness.
8. For bodily exercise profiteth little: but godliness is profitable unto all things, having promise of the life that now is, and of that which is to come.
9. This is a faithful saying and worthy of all acceptation.
10. For therefore we both labor and suffer reproach, because we trust in the living God, who is the Savior of all men, specially of those that believe.
11. These things command and teach.
12. Let no man despise thy youth; but be thou an example of the believers, in word, in conversation, in charity, in spirit, in faith, in purity.
13. Till I come, give attendance to reading, to exhortation, to doctrine.
14. Neglect not the gift that is in thee, which was given thee by prophecy, with the laying on of the hands of the presbytery.
15. Meditate upon these things; give thyself wholly to them; that thy profiting may appear to all.
16. Take heed unto thyself, and unto the doctrine; continue in them: for in doing this thou shalt both save thyself, and them that hear thee.

MEMORY SELECTION
I Timothy 4:7,8
DEVOTIONAL READING
2 Peter 1:3-11

BACKGROUND SCRIPTURE
I Timothy 4
PRINTED SCRIPTURE
I Timothy 4

Teacher's Target

This is the fourth division of I Timothy and deals with the walk of a good minister of Jesus Christ (I Tim. 4:1-16). Paul was concerned that his son in the gospel protect himself against false teachers motivated "by seducing spirits, and doctrines of devils" (I Tim. 4:1), He again warned Timothy about legalism, mentioning prohibitions against marrying and abstaining from certain meats. He again warned him against fables. He urged him to grow in godliness. Despite his youth, he told Timothy to set a good example for others to follow.

Help your students to beware of false teachers both inside and outside the church and learn what to do about them. Encourage them to grow in grace, exercising themselves unto godliness. This is the best way to avoid the pitfalls of false teachings. This growth is based on study of God's Word and application of it in real-life situations.

Lesson Introduction

Some aspects of our society may be based on values derived from our Judeo-Christian heritage, but in many ways we have veered off into secular humanism. We may think that we are too sophisticated to be governed by old superstitions, but these are still around and affect many people. Esoteric cults with their teaching about avatars (divine incarnations) who deserve men's praise and service are proliferating. Judaistic legalists have been replaced by so-called Christian legalists. Theological liberalism has led many people into apostasy.

Against this background of humanism, superstition, cultism, legalism, and apostasy we have the unadulterated revelation of God in His Holy Word. If we want to develop godliness, we must study its truth, love it, and use it. That was true in the first century of the Christian era, and it is true now.

Teaching Outline

I. Exhortation: I Tim. 4:1-6
   A. Apostasy: 1a
   B. Aberrations: 1b-5
   C. Accountability: 6

II. Exercise: I Tim. 4:7-10
   A. Desire: 7-8
   B. Deposit: 9-10

III. Example: I Tim. 4:11-16
   A. Reputation: 11-12
   B. Resources: 13-14
   C. Results: 15-16

Daily Bible Readings

Mon. Some Shall Depart
I Timothy 4:1-2
Tue. False Doctrine
I Timothy 4:3-5
Wed. Exercise Godliness
I Timothy 4:6-7
Thu. A Faithful Saying
I Timothy 4:8-9
Fri. Our Trust is in God
I Timothy 4:10-11
Sat. Be An Example
I Timothy 4:12-13
Sun. Be Diligent
I Timothy 4:14-16

Verse By Verse

I. Exhortation: I Tim. 4:1-6

A. Apostacy: 1a
1a. Now the Spirit speaketh expressly, that in the latter times some shall depart from the faith, . . .

There is one good Spirit, and that is the Holy Spirit. Christians are led by Him, although they are sometimes aided by good angels who are also ministering spirits (Heb. 1:14). It was the Holy Spirit Who told Paul that in the latter times, beginning with the first century of the Christian era, there would be some believers who would depart from (abandon) the faith (set of beliefs) given to them by Christ and the apostles. These would be known as apostates. They existed then, and they exist now.

B. Aberrations: 1b-5
1b. . . . giving heed to seducing spirits, and doctrines of devils;

Paul said that apostates accepted the seductive teachings of devils (fallen angels). Satan and his hosts, cast out of heaven, have sought to mislead people on the earth throughout human history, beginning with the first couple, Adam and Eve This evidently was due to accelerate during the age of grace. Paul wrote that pagans who sacrificed to idols were actually sacrificing to devils (I Cor. 10:19-20). We have their modern counterparts in Satanists and spiritualists. Many of their beliefs are printed in what is called the <u>Satanic Bible</u> and <u>Satanic Rituals</u>. Christians (and some non-Christians) who read these are horrified and feel threatened by them. Police officials are beginning to admit that some crimes against animals and people are traceable to these teachings.

2. Speaking lies in hypocrisy; having their conscience seared with a hot iron;

Apostates motivated by demonic forces will tell lies with straight faces, their consciences having been seared as with a hot iron. Having abused their God-given ability to know right from wrong, they may begin to believe their erroneous teachings themselves.

3a. Forbidding to marry, . . .

This prohibition by some apostates may have derived from the Gnostic teaching that the flesh was evil and that normal sexual drives should be repressed in order to be more spiritual. Contrast this with Paul's advice that young women should marry, bear children, and guide their households (I Tim. 5:14). The writer of Hebrews stated, "Marriage is honourable in all, and the bed undefiled" (Heb, 13:4).

3b. . . . and commanding to abstain from meats, which God hath created to be received with thanksgiving of them which believe and know the truth.

4. For every creature of God is good, and nothing to be refused, if it be received with thanksgiving . . .

5. For it is sanctified by the word of God and prayer.

This sounds as if it might have come from Judaizers who wanted to force believers in Christ to live under Mosaic dietary laws. Paul dealt with this matter more at length in I Corinthians 8, He also wrote, "Let no man therefore judge you in meat, or in drink, or in respect of an holyday, or of the new moon, or of the sabbath days: which are a shadow [type, figure] of things to come; but the body [reality, fulfillment] is of Christ" (Col. 2:16-17).

Therefore, Paul could state that it was all right to eat the various creatures which God had given to be received with thanksgiving by believers not under Jewish law. They were sanctified (qualified) for use by God's Word and by prayer. You might want to look briefly at Peter's vision as described in Acts 10:9-16 and 11:5-10, even though the vision was designed primarily to make Peter willing to minister to Gentiles at the home of Cornelius in Caesarea (Acts 10:28; 11:17).

C. Accountability: 6
6a. If thou put the brethren in remembrance of these things, thou shalt be a good minister of Jesus Christ, . . .

Note the condition that if Timothy would remind other believers of the pitfalls of apostasy and legalism, he would qualify as a good minister of Christ. He had a responsibility to make believers aware of their liberties in Christ,

6b. . . . nourished up in the words of faith and of good doctrine, whereunto thou hast attained.

If Timothy did as Paul suggested, both he and his people would be nourished (spiritually fed) in the words of faith (set of beliefs based on divine truth) and in good doctrine (sound teaching), a process which had already been developing.

II. Exercise: I Tim. 4:7-10

A. Desire: 7-8
7. But refuse profane and old wives' fables, and exercise thyself rather unto godliness.

It was common for old women to pass along tales and superstitions from one generation to another, but Paul considered them useless and even harmful. He urged Timothy to put his efforts toward developing godliness instead. Fables, no matter how whimsical or interesting, could not be compared with God's truth. Spiritual fitness demanded spiritual exercise.

8. For bodily exercise profiteth little: but godliness is profitable unto all things, having promise of life that now is, and of that which is to come.

Paul was not belittling physical exercise here, but he was saying that it profits a person only for a short time. On the other hand, godliness profits a person during this life and prepares him for the life to come. Living a righteous life protects believers from many debilitating things on this earth. It also has promise (sure hope) of glorious blessings in heaven for eternity.

B. Deposits: 9-10
9. This is a faithful saying and worthy of all acceptation.

We are not sure if this verse belongs with verse 8 or verse 10. However, the statement in verse 8 about the promise of life to come receives elaboration in verse 10.

10. For therefore we both labour and suffer reproach, because we trust in the living God, who is the Saviour of all men, specially of those that believe.

The hard work and the suffering of reproach are endured by Christians because they trust in the living God and know they will ultimately be vindicated. Be careful that you do not give an implication that God, being called the Savior of all men, causes anyone to think you are teaching universal salvation. The final part of the verse qualifies what precedes it. God had Christ die so that He might offer salvation to all men, but only those who believe and accept it are truly saved from their sins. It has been said that God is Potentially the Savior of all men, but He is effectually the Savior only of those who trust in Him. They must deposit their faith in Him.

III. Example: I Tim. 4:11-16

A. Reputation: 11-12
11. These things command and teach.

Paul wanted Timothy to teach divine truths with authority. They had behind them the reputation of God Himself and could be spoken with great confidence.

12. Let no man despise thy youth: but be thou an example of the believers in word, in conversation, in charity, in spirit, in faith, in purity.

Although Paul thought of Timothy as being young, Timothy may have been in his thirties. That was the time, of course, when men began their Life work. Jesus was thirty when He began His ministry. Paul told Timothy not to let anyone make light (think against) his youth. If he lacked maturity, he could make up for it by exemplary living before all men. He was to set an example in (l) <u>word</u>, meaning clear and pure expression, (2) <u>conversation</u>, meaning conduct or behavior (now an archaic term), (3) <u>charity</u>, meaning love toward others, (4) <u>spirit</u>, meaning spiritual development (omitted in oldest and best manuscripts),(5) <u>faith</u>, meaning faithfulness and dependability to God and men, and (6) <u>Purity</u>, meaning clean thoughts and actions (or careful attention to religious duties).

B. Resources: 13-14
13. Till I come, give attendance to reading, to exhortation, to doctrine.

Timothy could expect to learn much from the veteran Paul after he rejoined him. In the meantime, Timothy was to be diligent in his reading of the Word of God (Old Testament, oral teaching concerning Christ, and any New Testament books in existence). He was urged to exhort others to follow divine truths found in these sources. He was to preach and teach sound doctrine. The revealed truths of God were his main resource.

14. Neglect not the gift that is in thee, which was given thee by prophecy, with the laying on of the hands of the presbytery.

Timothy evidently received a special gift for preaching, teaching, and counseling at the time the men of the presbytery laid their hands on him and prayed over him as they ordained him to the Christian ministry. Support for this is also found in various references (Acts 17:14; 19:22; I Cor. 4:17; Phil. 2:19; I Thess. 3:2, and II Tim. 2:2; 4:5). The proof that he had it was shown in the many ways that he used it. It was a resource Paul valued highly.

C. Results: 15-16
15. Meditate upon these things; give thyself wholly to them; that thy profiting may appear to all.

Paul wanted Timothy to make meditation on spiritual things his top priority, for, as we shall see next week, "godliness with contentment is great gain" (I Tim. 6:6). By giving himself wholly to these pursuits, Timothy could be of profit (benefit, help) to all those under his care. A person cannot lead others where he has not gone first himself in spiritual experience.

16. Take heed unto thyself, and unto the doctrine; continue in them: for in doing this thou shalt both save thyself, and them that hear thee.

Paul felt that a minister and his people needed to work together to understand and apply divine truths in their lives. When they did this, they confirmed their position in Christ and were free to grow to maturity in Him. They could save themselves from being snared by the pitfalls laid in their path by apostate teachers.

Evangelistic Emphasis

There are some basic questions that seem to have been common to all men. They include, Who am I? Where did I come from? What am I doing here? Where am I going? Our lesson today deals with "What am I doing here?" We have a deep need for a sense of purpose for our lives.

Most people will experience a sense of depression if they do not believe that there is something they are supposed to do and that it makes a difference whether they do it or not. John Gardner was on target when he wrote, "The best kept secret in America today is that people would rather work hard for something they believe in than enjoy a pampered idleness." (Excellence, p. 148).

An important part of evangelism is calling people to the fulfillment of their purpose in life. Evangelism does not sell people on the "easy payment" plan. It reminds them that they are created by God and that there is a purpose for their lives. It calls on them to fulfill that purpose even if they must do so at great cost or risk.

Calling people to a devoted life is not imposing a burden on them. It is rather giving them a gift. It is a recognition of their worth and an identification of their purpose. It will bring them happiness and fulfillment. It will combat the problem of feeling insignificant and purposeless.

As you teach others the good news of God's forgiveness, don't forget to give them the gift of a high call to meaningful Christian service.

Memory Selection

"**Exercise thyself rather unto godliness. . . . Godliness is profitable unto all things, having promise of the life that now is, and of that which is to come.**"
I Timothy 4:7,8.

We currently seem to be in the midst of a fitness craze. By the thousands, people are walking, jogging, biking, swimming, playing all sorts of sports, and doing all kinds of exercises. We are more diet conscious than we have ever been before. We are exercising ourselves toward better health.

Paul would have approved that emphasis. He considered bodily exercise profitable. Yet, he said, there is a kind of exercise that is even more profitable. "Exercise thyself ... unto godliness," he challenged. It makes us ask the questions "How?" and "Why?"

The answer to the "How?" is the development of spiritual disciplines. As with physical fitness, diet and exercise are important — there can be no spiritual growth without nutrition and activity. We must read, hear, and otherwise ingest the spiritual nourishment of the gospel. Our exercise program must involve prayer, loving ministry, the practice of Christian mercy, and the active pursuit of the spread of the kingdom.

The "Why?" is answered by Paul in our text. Physical exercise has a value of limited duration. Godliness is profitable forever. It has the promise, not only of benefits in this life, but also of blessings in the life to come.

Weekday Problems

Carl was highly motivated but not well focused in his life. No one wanted to do better than he did. He was willing to help with everything that needed to be done. His highest aspiration was to be an exemplary Christian who accomplished a great deal for Christ in life.

He wanted to be a minister but before he got started with his schooling he became involved working with a youth camp. The work was worthwhile and satisfying, but the pay was low and school had to be delayed.

When the church needed money for various programs, Carl always gave everything he had. His generosity was admirable but it kept him so spread out that he was never able to pursue any goal with any real depth.

Now Carl is approaching middle age and looks back wistfully on his desire to be a minister. He has let a great portion of life pass him by. He has done good things, but has made little progress on his major goal. He has never denied his primary purpose in life, but has delayed it bit by bit until it has become increasingly unfeasible.

* Explain the statement, "One cannot say 'Yes' to anything unless he says 'No' to enough things to make his 'Yes' meaningful."
* Explain why one's central purpose in life must be planned rather than just allowed to happen.

Superintendent's Sermonette

It is Christ in us by His HoLy Spirit that makes it possible for us to walk as good and faithful servants of the Lord. It has been said that "the best defense is a good offense," and that is true in spiritual warfare. Paul urged young Timothy to be ready to deal with all kinds of diversions in his ministry. He had to look out for apostates who had departed from the faith. He had to beware of seductive demons and their influence on hypocrites and men with seared consciences. He had to resist religious legalists with their man-made regulations. He had to refuse old wives' fables then in vogue.

Instead, he was to exercise his spiritual muscles by developing godliness which was valuable in this life and the next. He was to become a good example for others to follow. He was to study God's Word and stir up the gift of communication he had received when he was ordained. We need young men such as Timothy to fill our pulpits and lead our congregations today, and we need veteran leaders such as Paul to encourage their development.

This Lesson in <u>Your</u> Life

This passage sounds almost like orders that would be given to a soldier going into battle. It calls for discipline, direction, integrity, determination, and concentration. These are all qualities that we need to have as we seek to live a fruitful Christian life.

First, there is a warning of the dangers that will be encountered. There will be false doctrine and deliberate deception. One cannot always appeal to the best in others because some have consciences that have been seared with a hot iron.

Second, we must teach as we go. When we are in a battle with the forces of evil, we are in a battle for the minds and hearts as well as for a physical following.

We must be prepared for discouragement and betrayal as well as for overt attacks. As Christ was denied and betrayed, so also will we be. As He suffered hurt from those who were close to Him, so also will we. When we have those experiences they will tend to demoralize us when we are most vulnerable.

People will be critical of us without just cause. Timothy was likely to be the object of age-discrimination because of his youth. We may be discriminated against either because of our youth or our age. In our case it may be that we experience rejection because people feel we are out-dated or irrelevant.

Some accusations, Paul reminded Timothy, are best answered by a good example. Paul urged Timothy to rise above unjust criticism by demonstrating his faithfulness by his life.

Still another lesson is that we must continue to care for the inner life even in the heat of controversy. In our busy lives we tend to neglect reading and meditation. These are a part of the fuel that can keep us going. It is important to find a place for them.

Neither should we lose confidence in ourselves or our gifts when we are attacked. As a little girl is reported to have said, "God made me. I am wonderful because God doesn't make junk!" We need to remember that we were made by God and we were given a charge. We belong in this battle. Let us wage it with vigor.

Paul urges Timothy to give himself wholly to his task. Being an evangelist is too large a responsibility and involves too many different factors to do it well with a half effort.

Paul's final charge is that Timothy be careful of his own life as well as of his teaching. Teachers are involved in their own salvation as well as the salvation of others. What a tragedy it is when one leads others to a saving relationship with Christ and, while doing so, neglects his own spirituality so that he loses such a relationship. All of us need to heed this warning, "Live and teach in such a way that you will save yourself as well as those who hear you."

Seed Thoughts

1. When have apostates to Christianity operated in the world?
The "latter times" mentioned in I Timothy 4:1 refer to the age of grace between Christ's first and second comings.

2. Who motivates apostates?
Paul said that they are led astray by seducing devils and their doctrines.

3. What allows hypocrites to tell lies?
They have consciences which have been seared as with a hot iron, and they may even begin to believe their own lies.

4. What power do legalists seek?
History has shown that they try to gain control over every aspect of their devotees' lives, including whether or not to marry and what they may or may not eat.

5. Where does a person begin in becoming a good minister of God?
He learns God's Word, is nourished by it himself, and uses it to build up others in their faith.

(Please Turn Page)

---

1. When have apostates to Christianity operated in the world?

2. Who motivates apostates?

3. What allows hypocrites to tell lies?

4. What power do legalists seek?

5. Where does a person begin in becoming a good minister of God?

6. Why should a Christian leader avoid old wives' fables?

7. Did Paul say that physical exercise was of little value?

8. Does I Timothy 4:10 teach universal salvation of all men?

9. What did Paul mean when he told Timothy not to let anyone despise his youth?

10. What resources did Timothy have?

Seed Thoughts - Continued

The "latter times" mentioned in I Timothy 4:1 refer to the age of grace between Christ's first and second comings.

Paul said that they are led astray by seducing devils and their doctrines.

They have consciences which have been seared as with a hot iron, and they may even begin to believe their own lies.

History has shown that they try to gain control over every aspect of their devotees' lives, including whether or not to marry and what they may or may not eat.

He learns God's Word, is nourished by it himself, and uses it to build up others in their faith.

They may be interesting as folklore, but they have no value in developing godliness within believers.

No, he often referred to athletes, but he counted spiritual exercise as valuable for both this life and the next

No, it teaches that God is potentially the Savior of all men because He sent Christ to die for all, but He is effectually the Savior of believers.

He meant that young Timothy could set an example of godliness which no one could despise.

He had the resource of the Word of God and the resource of a gift of communication received at his ordination.

6. Why should a Christian leader avoid old wives' fables?
They may be interesting as folklore, but they have no value in developing godliness within believers.

7. Did Paul say that physical exercise was of little value?
No, he often referred to athletes, but he counted spiritual exercise as valuable for both this life and the next

8. Does I Timothy 4:10 teach universal salvation of all men?
No, it teaches that God is potentially the Savior of all men because He sent Christ to die for all, but He is effectually the Savior of believers.

9. What did Paul mean when he told Timothy not to let anyone despise his youth?
He meant that young Timothy could set an example of godliness which no one could despise.

10. What resources did Timothy have?
He had the resource of the Word of God and the resource of a gift of communication received at his ordination.

Set Your Priorities

I Timothy 6:6. But godliness with contentment is great gain.
7. For we brought nothing into this world, and it is certain we can carry nothing out.
8. And having food and raiment let us be therewith content.
9. But they that will be rich fall into temptation and a snare, and into many foolish and hurtful lusts, which drown men in destruction and perdition.
10. For the love of money is the root of all evil: which while some coveted after, they have erred from the faith, and pierce themselves through with many sorrows.
11. But thou, O man of God, flee these things; and follow after righteousness, godliness, faith, love, patience, meekness.
12. Fight the good fight of faith, lay hold on eternal life, whereunto thou art also called and hast professed a good profession before many witnesses.
13. I give thee charge in the sight of God, who quickeneth all things, and before Christ Jesus, who before Pontius Pilate witnessed a good confession:
14. That thou keep this commandment without spot, rebukeable, until the appearing of our Lord Jesus Christ:
I Timothy 6:17. Charge them that are rich in the world, that they be not highminded, nor trust in uncertain riches, but in the living God, who giveth us richly all things to enjoy;
18. That they do good, that they be rich in good works, ready to distribute, willing to communicate;
19. Laying up in store for themselves a good foundation against the time to come that they may lay hold on eternal life.
20. O Timothy, keep that which is committed to thy trust, avoiding profane and vain babblings, and opposition of science falsely so called:
21. Which some professing have erred concerning the faith. Grace be with thee. Amen.

MEMORY SELECTION
I Timothy 6:11
DEVOTIONAL READING
I John 3:7-12
BACKGROUND SCRIPTURE
I Timothy 6:2c-21
PRINTED SCRIPTURE
I Timothy 6:6-14,17-21

Teacher's Target

If you listen to what the world is saying, you will hear that "the good life" centers on such things as money, prestige, and power. Many people focus on these things and devote their lives to them, whether they are successful or not in obtaining them. Those who aspire to be teachers or preach may also be driven by them and find that their original desire to benefit humanity through knowledge becomes secondary to personal advancement.

Help your students to appreciate what Paul wrote to Timothy about Christian teachers being content with godliness rather than material gain. The craving to be rich leads to spiritual temptation and dangers. If effort is expended, let it be in "the good fight of faith" (I Tim. 6:12), If riches are to be gained, let them be "good works" (I Tim. 6: 18). They can be sent on ahead to heaven (Matt. 6:19-21).

Lesson Introduction

Chapter 4 of I Timothy deals with the walk of a good minister of Jesus Christ. Chapters 5 and 6 deal with the work of a good minister. Our lesson text includes most of chapter 6. It bears a close resemblance to chapter 4 of II Timothy. Whereas Paul had told Timothy to "fight the good fight of faith" (I Tim. 6:12), he later wrote, "I have fought a good fight, I have finished my course, I have kept the faith" (II Tim. 4:7).

It was obvious that Paul felt he had not much longer to live, and he was concerned that younger men, such as Timothy, would carry on after he passed away. If we believers have a heritage to leave to those who follow us, let it be that they will see godliness in us and find it so rewarding that they will devote their lives to it, as well. Let us teach this by precept and example.

Teaching Outline

I. Contentment: I Tim. 6:6-11a
   A. Statement: 6
   B. Situation: 7
   C. Satisfaction: 8
   D. Snare: 9-10
   E. Suggestions 11a
II. Consistency: I Tim. 6:11b-14
   A. Development: 11b-12
   B. Determination: 13-14
III. Contribution: I Tim. 6:17-19
   A. Warning: 17
   B. Works: 18-19
IV. Commitment: I Tim. 6:20-21
   A. Babblings: 20-21a
   B. Benediction: 21b

Daily Bible Readings

Mon. Avoid False Teachers
I Timothy 6:2c-4
Tue. Godliness
With Contentment
I Timothy 6:5-8
Wed. The Love of Money
I Timothy 6:9-10
Thu. Fight the Good Fight
I Timothy 6:11-12
Fri. Keep the Commandment
I Timothy 6:13-16
Sat. Charge to the Rich
I Timothy 6:17-19
Sun. Keep Your Trust
I Timothy 6:20-21

Verse By Verse

I. Contentment: I Tim. 6:6-11a

A. Statement: 6
6. But godliness with contentment is great gain.

Go back to verses 3-5 to see Paul's negative description of the typical false teacher of that time. He supposed that godliness was a way to gain riches. Paul wanted Timothy to realize that contentment with godliness is a great gain in itself, not as the means for reaching a material goal. This is the basic statement on which subsequent verses depend. Material things cannot be substituted for spiritual blessings.

B. Situation: 7
7. For we brought nothing into this world, and it is certain we can carry nothing out.

Job 1:21 had said it long before—"Naked came I out of my mother's womb, and naked shall I return thither [into the womb of the earth]," During a person's lifetime, God determines how many material things he will have. When life is over, that person will depart and leave all material acquisitions behind. However, a believer can send the treasure of good works on ahead and be rewarded for them later on (Matt 6:19-21; I Cor. 3:14). This is the human situation, and it cannot be changed.

C. Satisfaction: 8
8. And having food and raiment let us be therewith content.

As a prisoner, Paul had learned to be content, whether he was destitute or abounding in material things (Phil. 4:11-12). He was concerned that Timothy see value in spiritual things rather than in material things. Paul was convinced that God would supply a believe's needs (Phil. 4:19). He urged Timothy to be content with sustaining food and basic clothing.

D. Snare: 9-10
9. But they that will be rich fall into temptation and a snare, and into many foolish and hurtful lusts, which drown men in destruction and perdition.

Those who devote themselves to fulfilling a deep craving for wealth become vulnerable to temptation and a snare. Who sets the trap? Look at I Timothy 3:7, and you will see that the devil (Satan) sets the snare. He knows that greed leads to many foolish and hurtful lusts (passions, cravings). He will use it to drown men in destruction of their souls and ultimate consignment to perdition (the lake of fire). This is the destiny waiting for all unrepentant sinners.

10a. For the love of money is the root of all evil: . . .

Handle this thought with great care. Money in and of itself is not evil nor does it necessarily produce evil. What is dangerous is a driving compulsion for money and what it can buy. Whenever desire is turned away from God and directed toward earthly things, the human heart is headed for trouble. The love of money is a root of many evils, leading to such sins as jealousy, greed, robbery, and even murder.

10b. . . . which while some coveted after, they have erred from the faith, and pierced themselves through with many sorrows.

Those who give top priority to chasing after money and what it can buy will naturally veer away from the faith based on divine truth. "The care of [concern for] this world, and the deceitfulness of riches, choke the word [of faith]" (Matt. 13:22). There are thorns which will pierce these individuals through with many sorrows. Being rich is no guarantee against having problems, and those who gain riches unlawfully are most at risk. They must eventually realize that nothing good arising out of their riches was worth the evil produced by greed.

E. Suggestion: 11a
11a. But thou, O man of God, flee these things; . . .

Paul knew that greed could even affect a man of God. He warned Timothy to flee from it as if it were a pursuing beast The use of the plural here shows that Paul realized greed could produce many evil influences to pursue the unwary child of God. We now come to a sudden switch to the positive things Paul wanted Timothy to find.

II. Consistency: I Tim 6:11b-14

A. Development: 11b-12
11b. . . .and follow after righteousness, godliness, faith, love, patience, meekness

Note how similar this list of six virtues is to the nine fruits of the Spirit listed by Paul in Galatians 5:22-23. God sends His Holy Spirit to develop these things in believers. Righteousness is a general term for good living. Godliness refers to imitation of God's qualities. Faith may mean trust in God, faithfulness to Him, or both. Love is that given by God and shown to others in acts of kindness. Patience can mean endurance. Meekness is humility such as Christ showed in coming to die for sinners. Paul wanted Timothy to follow after (pursue) these in a deliberate and consistent way.

12. Fight the good fight of faith, lay hold on eternal life, whereunto thou art also called, and hast professed a good profession before many witnesses.

Note the similarity of this to Jude 3 and its challenge for believers to "earnestly contend for the faith which was once delivered unto the saints." This referred to the gospel truth. Paul urged Timothy to do his part in the spiritual warfare required to hold up the gospel to men. He was to persevere until the time came for him to lay hold of eternal life. God had called him to this, and he had made a good profession of his hope before many witnesses, perhaps when he was ordained by the presbytery as described in I Timothy 4:14.

B. Determination: 13-14
13. I give thee charge in the sight of God, who quickeneth all things, and before Christ Jesus, who before Pontius Pilate witnessed a good confession; . . .

Paul wanted to give a charge (challenge) to Timothy, and he called on God, Who gives life to all, and on Christ, Who gave a good testimony to Pontius Pilate, to be witnesses to this event. It was a solemn event as indicated by Paul's references to the first and second persons in the triune Godhead.

14. That thou keep this commandment without spot, unrebukeable, until the appearing of our Lord Jesus Christ:

The term "commandment," as it is used here, evidently referred to all that God required of believers after revealing the gospel to them. Paul wanted Timothy to be determined that he would fulfill all that God demanded of him and do it without blemish or rebuke. This was to be done until the second coming of Jesus Christ to the earth. He was asking this young man to be as perfect as possible in fulfillment of his ministerial commission.

III. Contribution: I Tim. 6:17-19

A. Warning: 17
17. Charge them that are rich in this world, that they be not highminded, nor trust in uncertain riches, but in the living God, who giveth us richly all things to enjoy;

Paul did not condemn riches nor the people who were rich in this world's goods, but he did want Timothy to warn them about becoming highminded (proud, arrogant). What they had come from God. They were merely temporary stewards of it. They would have to give an account of it some day. They were not to put their trust in riches, which are uncertain (can be given or taken away). Their trust was to be in the living God, the Source of all things given to men to enjoy.

B. Works: 18-19
18 That they do good, that they be rich in good works, ready to distribute, willing to communicate;

It is worth considering the possibility that God allows some individuals to be rich because He knows they can handle it well. He also knows who cannot handle it. Those who are rich should be urged to do good works. They should be more concerned about being rich in good works than being rich in material things. Rather than hoarding what they have, they should be ready to distribute their resources as God directs. The term "communicate" also refers to sharing of resources.

Paul realized that giving to others was a means of joy. In talking to the Ephesian elders he said, "Remember the words of the Lord Jesus, how he said, It is more blessed to give than to receive" (Acts 20:35). In writing to the Galatians, he said, "As we have therefore opportunity, let us do good unto all men, especially unto them who are of the household of faith" (Gal. 6:10).

19. Laying up in store for themselves a good foundation against the time to come, that they may lay hold on eternal life.

As mentioned before in this lesson, Matthew 6:19-21 comments on what Paul had to say here. Believers who do good works are laying up treasure in heaven, and they will be rewarded for that in the end time (I Cor. 3:14). Reference to laying hold on eternal life is found in I Timothy 6:12 and 19. In both cases, it does not imply earning eternal life. It simply refers to moving consistently toward the time when believers will come into their eternal inheritance.

IV. Commitment: I Tim. 6:20-21

A. Babblings: 20-21a
20. O Timothy, keep that which is committed to thy trust, avoiding profane and vain babblings, and oppositions of science falsely so called:
21a. Which some professing have erred concerning the faith.

In these summary verses we see Paul urging Timothy to do two things. First, he wanted Timothy to keep that which had been committed to his trust, This meant that he was to guard the deposit of truth which he had been given. This could be done by sound teaching and by worthy example. Second, he wanted Timothy to avoid doctrinal errors. These came from profane desecrations of holy things and from vain babblings (foolish speculations). Paul referred to opposition to the gospel from false knowledge. Some careless believers had become apostate by following false teachings, thus drifting away from the true faith.

B. Benediction: 21b
21b Grace be with thee. Amen.
Paul ended his epistle with this brief benediction on young Timothy.

Evangelistic Emphasis

Most people in the world are concerned, in one way or another, with the accumulation of some assets. Some may want financial assets such as bank accounts, investments, or equity in real estate. Others may be more concerned with those assets they can use and enjoy such as houses, cars, boats, club memberships, etc. Some want assets that make them feel secure such as insurance and pension plans. Almost all want something as a product of their labor and effort.

This nearly universal desire can be appealed to in effective evangelism. Paul does not criticize the desire but rather attempts to guide it. How can we accumulate something of lasting value? "We brought nothing into this world, and it is certain that we can carry nothing out." Therefore, it does not make sense to devote too much attention to the gathering of peripheral assets. If we are able to take care of our basic needs, that is sufficient in that category.

Where should our major efforts lie? Paul says they should be in the areas that transcend physical life. Let us invest in godliness. That is productive of great gain, both now and eternally.

In your evangelistic efforts, look for the opportunity to take an existing desire (the desire to accumulate assets) and direct it toward a Christian decision (do that which brings eternal dividends).

Memory Selection

"Follow after righteousness, godliness, faith, love, patience, meekness."
Timothy 6:11.

Much of the teaching of the Bible is so simple that it seems that it ought to be obvious to us. It would appear that everyone would know to follow the list of virtues that are in our memory selection for today. As a matter of fact probably everyone does know. Still we need to be reminded and called back from the tangents we sometimes get on.

There is a great power in simply trying to be as good as we can. Reflecting on and giving attention to being more patient will make our lives better. Deciding that we are going to act in a consistently loving way will help us to do so. Resolving that we will live a righteous life will elevate our behavior toward the example that Christ set for us.

To a great extent, we are what we have set out to become. If we have set out to be righteous, patient, and meek, we will grow into those virtues as time passes. It is vital that we set out to flee what is evil and to embrace that which is good.

Weekday Problems

Bob is an intelligent and energetic individual who is particularly gifted in understanding hydraulics. He has developed industrial pumps and other equipment that have revolutionized some areas of the field. His company has grown rapidly and is now a highly profitable supplier.

Bob wrote a manual explaining in simple language some principles of hydraulics. It captured widespread attention and hundreds of thousands were sold. Bob cleared enough on the manual alone to make a good living.

He began to lecture in the field and soon attracted large numbers who were willing to pay generous fees to attend his classes. This teaching provided enough income to make him a wealthy man.

Wise investments have provided him with still another income. Bob has done so well that he could easily live on one tenth of his income from various sources.

* What special problems and responsibilities does Bob have because of his wealth?
* What special opportunities does he have?
* Discuss the difference between the spiritual problems of those who are very rich and those who are very poor.

Superintendent's Sermonette

If God allows a believer to inherit or accumulate riches, a great responsibility goes along with the privilege. As a faithful steward of these resources, the believer should live modestly on some of them and use the rest in service to God. There are times and situations in which God's work requires large sums of money, property, or material things. The rich believer has them available for use, and he can bless others by donating them. If he makes a will before he dies, he can designate how his resources will be used to bless others after he has moved on to his heavenly reward.

Historically speaking, most converts to Christ have come from the lower and middle classes of society rather than from the upper class. God may not allow them to have many of this world's resources, but they can contribute their share to advance His work. He may make them partners in stewardship of the resources given by rich believers to His work. Whether we have a little or a lot, let us devote ourselves to that which has eternal value —God's program for redeeming the world.

This Lesson in Your Life

The first epistle to Timothy is a gold mine of practical advice. Paul begins today's lesson with some guidance on where we can best invest our life's energies. Many investments have great risk. What we invest in godliness and contentment is guaranteed to produce great gain. It is not at risk to thieves, business reverses, stock market slumps, economic depressions, or any of the other forces that wipe out many investments.

It is significant that he says "godliness with contentment." Living a virtuous life can be a sterile and frustrating experience if one is constantly lamenting the absence of financial prosperity and luxury. For godliness to bring happiness, we must see its value and be gratified with the blessings of the godly life.

When we think about it, it is reasonable to be happy that we are in a secure relationship with the Lord. Other types of riches will be taken from us at death if not before. Those who are rich have special problems and dangers. Those who are godly have the lasting benefits and the current peace. It is the best of both worlds.

Paul deals with some special temptations that are especially dangerous to the rich. Although we may not consider ourselves rich, it would be wise to listen to the counsel that Paul gives. Many are rich and have not realized it because they compare themselves to others who are richer. If we have assets and income beyond those we need for food and clothing, we would do well to heed this warning.

The warning is that the desire for riches and the love of money get people in trouble. Money itself is morally and spiritually neutral. A controlling desire for money will steer our lives down wrong paths. Not only does God not approve of our being controlled by a lust for money, but we bring pain and sorrow on ourselves.

One important thing to notice in I Timothy is the emphasis placed on one's own effort to do the will of God. "Fight the good fight of faith, lay hold on eternal life . . . Keep this commandment without spot." Some religious teachers have put so much stress on God's work in salvation that they have de-emphasized human effort.

It goes without saying that we are saved entirely by the grace of God. Without that grace there could be no salvation. However, under the umbrella of that grace there is room and need for human effort. Such effort is not to be an attempt to earn salvation. It is rather an attempt to cooperate with the grace of God in the realizing of our own salvation.

Timothy, though young, is charged to challenge the vested interest of the world. He is to face those forces which oppose Christianity with courage. He is not to back down when contrary forces seek to intimidate him.

Paul closes our lesson today with a prayer for Timothy. After challenging the young man to be strong, faithful, courageous, and energetic, he closed softly with the prayer, "Grace be with thee."

Seed Thoughts

1. How should Christian teachers view godliness?
They should not see it as a way to gain riches but as a spiritual gain which outweighs material blessings.

2. How do we enter the world and leave it as far as material things are concerned?
We came naked and with nothing into the world and we will leave it the same way. Materials are not transferable.

3. Is there anything we can send on ahead of us?
Yes, for our good works go before us and will be rewarded (Matt. 6:19-21; I Tim, 6:18-19).

4. Where may true contentment in life be found?
It is found in trusting God, believing that He will supply all our needs.

5. What is a root of many evils?
Satan uses their greed to ensnare them, draw them into hurtful passions, and drag them down to eternal perdition.

(Please Turn Page)

---

1. How should Christian teachers view godliness?

2. How do we enter the world and leave it as far as material things are concerned?

3. Is there anything we can send on ahead of us?

4. Where may true contentment in life be found?

5. What danger do greedy people face?

5. What is a root of many evils?

7. Rather than riches, what should the man of God pursue?

8. How does a believer lay hold of eternal life?

9. How can rich believers make good use of their money?

10. What did Paul tell Timothy to avoid?

Seed Thoughts - Continued

They should not see it as a way to gain riches but as a spiritual gain which outweighs material blessings.

We came naked and with nothing into the world and we will leave it the same way. Materials are not transferable.

Yes, for our good works go before us and will be rewarded (Matt. 6:19-21; I Tim, 6:18-19).

It is found in trusting God, believing that He will supply all our needs.

Satan uses their greed to ensnare them, draw them into hurtful passions, and drag them down to eternal perdition.

The love of money spawns many evils. Money itself is neither good nor bad.

He should seek for the Christian virtues of righteousness, godliness, faith, love, patience, and meekness.

He fights the good fight of faith until the time comes for him to claim his eternal inheritance.

They can devote their resources to performing good works for the Lord, realizing that they are only stewards of what He allows them to have.

He said to avoid profane (blasphemous) and vain (foolish) babblings of false science (knowledge).

6. What is a root of many evils?
The love of money spawns many evils. Money itself is neither good nor bad.

7. Rather than riches, what should the man of God pursue?
He should seek for the Christian virtues of righteousness, godliness, faith, love, patience, and meekness.

8. How does a believer lay hold of eternal life?
He fights the good fight of faith until the time comes for him to claim his eternal inheritance.

9. How can rich believers make good use of their money?
They can devote their resources to performing good works for the Lord, realizing that they are only stewards of what He allows them to have.

10. What did Paul tell Timothy to avoid?
He said to avoid profane (blasphemous) and vain (foolish) babblings of false science (knowledge).

"I TEACH MY CLASS THE TRUTH"

Handle God's Word Rightly

2 Timothy 2:1. Thou therefore, my son, be strong in the grace that is in Christ Jesus.

2. And the things that thou hast heard of me among many witnesses, the same commit thou to faithful men, who shall be able to teach others also.

3. Thou therefore endure hardness, as a good soldier of Jesus Christ.

4. No man that warreth entangleth himself with the affairs of this life; that he may please him who hath chosen him to be a soldier.

5. And if a man also strive for masteries, yet is he not crowned, except he strive lawfully.

6. The husbandman that laboreth must be first partaker of the fruits.

7. Consider what I say; and the Lord give thee understanding in all things.

8. Remember that Jesus Christ of the seed of David was raised from the dead according to my gospel:

9. Wherein I suffer trouble, as an evil doer, even unto bonds; but the word of God is not bound.

10. Therefore I endure all things for the elect's sakes, that they may also obtain the salvation which is in Christ Jesus with eternal glory.

11. It is a faithful saying: For if we be dead with, him, we shall also live with him:

12. If we suffer, we shall also reign with him: if we deny him, he also will deny us:

13. If we believe not, yet he abideth faithful: he cannot deny himself.

14. Of these things put them in remembrance, charging them before the Lord that they strive not about words to no profit, but to the subverting of the hearers.

15. Study to show thyself approved unto God, a workman that needeth not to be ashamed, rightly dividing the word of truth.

MEMORY SELECTION
2 Timothy 2:15
DEVOTIONAL READING
Philippians 1:12-18

BACKGROUND SCRIPTURE
2 Timothy 2:1-19
PRINTED SCRIPTURE
2 Timothy 2:1-15

Teacher's Target

In his effort to get Timothy to live up to his spiritual potential, Paul referred to him as a soldier, racer, farmer, and workman (II Tim. 2:3, 5, 6, 15). Paul knew the pressures which came upon Timothy in a time of apostasy, and he wanted to urge the younger man to endure whatever was brought against him. Paul mentioned that he himself endured trouble, even unto bonds, in order to make the risen Christ known to others. He challenged Timothy to be an approved servant of God, rightly dividing the Word of truth (II Tim. 2:15).

Help your students [WE NEED] to identify themselves with Timothy. All Christians need to see themselves as ministering the gospel to others. Satan will make this difficult as he and his hosts seek to spread apostasy. It is good to remember that "he [Christ] that is in you [is greater] than he that is in the world" (I John 4:4).

Lesson Introduction

Paul had told Timothy to "hold fast the form [pattern] of sound words" which he had heard from him. That good thing (deposit of truth) was to be kept by the power of the Holy Spirit. Many in Asia (Turkey) had turned away from Paul, including Phygellus and Hermogenes, but Onesiphorus had remained faithful to him in Rome and Ephesus (II Tim. 1:13-18). Paul naturally wanted Timothy to follow the example laid down by Onesiphorus.

Paul mentioned four things Timothy could do: (1) He could be strong in the grace that is in Christ, (2) He could commit the things he had learned to faithful men, who could teach them to others, (3) He could suffer persecution for Christ's sake, and (4) He could study to show himself approved unto God as one correctly handling the Word of truth. These are good goals for us today, as well.

Teaching Outline

I. Strength: II Tim. 2:1-2
 A. Resolution: 1
 B. Reproduction: 2
II. Soldier: II Tim. 2:3-7
 A. Endurance: 3
 B. Examples: 4-6
 C. Encouragement: 7
III. Suffering: II Tim. 2:8-13
 A. Contribution: 8-10
 B. Conditions: 11-13
IV. Study: II Tim. 2:14-15
 A. Worthlessness: 14
 B. Workman: 15

Daily Bible Readings

Mon. Be Strong
2 Timothy 2:1-2
Tue. Endure Hardship
2 Timothy 2:3-6
Wed. Remember Jesus Christ
2 Timothy 2:7-8
Thu. The Word is Not Bound
2 Timothy 2:9-10
Fri. A Faithful Saying
2 Timothy 2:11-14
Sat. Rightly Dividing the Word
2 Timothy 2:15-16
Sun. The Foundation of God is Sure
2 Timothy 2:17-19

Verse By Verse

I. Strength: II Tim. 2:1-2

A. Resolution: 1
1. **Thou therefore, my son, be strong in the grace that is in Christ Jesus.**

Hoping that Timothy would develop spiritually and be like Onesiphorus (II Tim. 1:16-18), Paul urged him, as his son in the gospel, to be strong in the grace which characterized Jesus Christ. This strengthening was not automatic or self-generated. It had to be sought from the Lord, and it had to be imparted by His Holy Spirit. It required resolution on the part of young Timothy.

B. Reproduction: 2
2. **And the things that thou hast heard of me among many witnesses, the same commit thou to faithful men, who shall be able to teach others also.**

Paul said that Timothy had heard truths taught by him in the presence of many witnesses. If he had any doubt about what Paul had taught, he could check with those witnesses to get his facts straight. He was then to pass on the information to faithful men, who would be able to teach others. By this means, divine truths could be propagated by multiplication rather than by mere addition. Believers would reproduce themselves spiritually in others.

II. Soldier: II Tim. 2:3-7

A. Endurance: 3
3. **Thou therefore endure hardness, as a good soldier of Jesus Christ.**

Paul apparently believed that Christ had suffered His alloted quota in order to make redemption of sinners possible. After He ascended to heaven, it was His followers who were called upon to fill up their quota of suffering to make the message of redemption known to the world. Paul wrote," [I] now rejoice in my sufferings for you, and fill up that [quota] which is behind of the afflictions of Christ in my flesh for his body's sake, which is the church" (Col. 1:24). He wanted Timothy to do the same thing, and that would require the ability to endure hardness (hardship) such as that faced by a veteran soldier. Paul saw Timothy as one striving for victory, and he next mentioned various examples of this.

B. Examples: 4-6
4. **No man that warreth entangleth himself with the affairs of this life; that he may please him who hath chosen him to be a soldier.**

Paul said that a good soldier did not allow himself to become entangled with the ordinary affairs of life. He pulled away from those things and devoted himself to pleasing his commander, the one who chose him to fight. God had chosen Timothy to be fully committed to spiritual warfare.

5. **And if a man also strive for mastery, yet is he not crowned, except he strive lawfully.**

Greek athletes in the ancient world were known for their hard training and discipline, Paul said that Timothy should be like the racer, following the rules, and winning the laurel "crown" for coming in first.

6. **The husbandman that**

laboureth must be first partaker of the fruits.

A husbandman (farmer) had to work hard to produce a crop, but he was the first to eat of it when it was harvested. Paul wanted Timothy to taste of the truths of God before attempting to share them with others.

C. Encouragement: 7
7. Consider what I say; and the Lord give thee understanding in all things.

Paul invited Timothy to consider (ponder, meditate, reflect, think on) the metaphors he had just used—soldier, racer, farmer. He was confident that the Lord would give Timothy insight into the meaning of these illustrations and help him to adapt them to his spiritual life and his ministry. The wording here reminds us of I Timothy 4:15-16.

III. Suffering: II Tim. 2:8-13

A. Contribution: 8-10
8. Remember that Jesus Christ of the seed of David was raised from the dead according to my gospel:

Paul told Timothy to keep remembering that Jesus Christ, a descendant of King David, as the Messiah was supposed to be, had been raised from the dead according to the gospel. This was the central truth of the apostolic message preached in the first century of the Christian era. It was because the God-Man died to atone for sin and rose again for justification of sinners that Paul and all believers could profit from the gospel. Since Jesus did that for them, they were obligated to suffer for His sake. He had made His contribution to them, and now it was their turn to make their contribution to Him.

9. Wherein I suffer trouble, as an evil doer, even unto bonds; but the word of God is not bound.

Paul said that he was in trouble, a prisoner of Rome, as though he were a criminal and deserved his bonds (chains, shackles). However, he rejoiced in the fact that the Word of God could not be bound (chained, shackled). It was having its desired effect, even while he was under house arrest (cf. Acts 28:30-31). Converts to Christ had been made within the household of Caesar himself (Phil. 4:22).

10. Therefore I endure all things for the elect's sakes, that they may also obtain the salvation which is in Christ Jesus with eternal glory.

Paul said that he endured all the hard persecutions involved in preaching the gospel for the sake of the elect. He referred to those chosen of God and called to Himself through faith in Christ. God, by His foreknowledge, knew who the elect (chosen, appointed, predestined) would be, and He called them to Himself and justified them. He will also glorify them at the right time (Rom. 8: 29-30).

B. Conditions: 11-13
11. It is a faithful saying: For if we be dead with him, we shall also live with him:

The balanced structure of verses 11-13 suggests that the faithful or trustworthy saying came from an early church hymn or formula spoken by New Testament prophets in Christian assemblies (I Cor. 14:26).

The first condition is this: If we died with Christ, then we shall also live with Him. It is in dying to self and sin that we are raised to newness of life in Him (Rom, 6:4). If we should physically die before He returns, He will raise us up to be with Him (I Thess. 4:13-18).

12a. If we suffer, we shall also reign with him: . . .

The second condition is this: If we suffer for Christ's sake, then we shall reign with Him. John wrote of believers when he said, "They shall be priests of God and of Christ, and shall reign with him a thousand years" (Rev. 20:6),

12b. . . . if we deny him, he also will deny us:

The third condition is this: If we deny (disown, reject) Christ, He will deny us.

Jesus Himself said, "Whosoever shall deny me before men, him will I also deny before my Father which is in heaven" (Matt. 10:33). The word "ashamed" is used in place of "deny" in Mark 8:38 and Luke 9:26, but the idea is the same. Those references refer to what will happen when Christ comes again.

13. If we believe not, yet he abideth faithful: he cannot deny himself

The fourth condition is this: If we believe not', Christ will remain faithful, for He cannot deny Himself. Consider this paraphrase—"Even when we are too weak to have any faith left, he remains faithful to us and will help us, for he cannot disown us who are part of himself, and he will always carry out his promises to us" (Living Bible).

IV. Study: II Tim. 2:14-15

A. Worthlessness: 14

14. Of these things put them in remembrance, charging them before the Lord that they strive not about words to no profit, but to the subverting of the hearers.

Paul had warned about useless words before (I Tim. 6:4-5), He returned to this theme here, telling Timothy to challenge teachers to avoid strife over words (concepts, ideas, teachings) which amount to nothing, All this does is get listeners riled up and confused. It could cause them to lose their faith. In contrast to that, Paul wanted Timothy to concentrate on the truths of God's Holy Word.

B. Workman: 15

15a. Study to shew thyself approved unto God, . . .

Paul wanted Timothy to make a deliberate and conscious effort to be diligent in his study of divine truths. His goal was not to be so much approved by men as to be approved by God Himself. The proof of his success would be in how well he handled himself when going through various trials where the principles of God's Word had to be applied.

15b. . . . a workman that needeth not to be ashamed, . . .

Day-laborers or those in the various trades may not have had much, but they were proud of their skills and of their ability to put in a good day's work for a day's pay. Paul wanted Timothy to feel satisfied when he did his best to serve the Lord. He did not want him to be ashamed of himself.

15c. . . . rightly dividing the word of truth.

Paul had written that Christian soldiers were to take "the sword of the Spirit', which is the word of God" and use it in spiritual warfare (Eph. 6:17), He used this same concept with Timothy here, urging him to rightly divide (correctly handle) the word of truth. He was to march straight forward, "teach no other doctrine" (I Tim. 1:3), and let God's Word do its mighty work.

In order to properly use the Word of God, we need to know its facts, extract its principles, and learn how to make applications of them in real Life. We must appeal to the head (intellect), heart (emotions), and hands (wills) of those who listen to us. If we will depend on the Holy Spirit at each step in the process, He will cause us to be effective in winning souls to Christ and building up saints in their most holy faith.

Evangelistic Emphasis

Perhaps the best news in this passage is the possibility of knowing the nature and will of God. God so transcends man that we could not possibly know Him without His revealing Himself to us. He is infinite and we are finite. The finite cannot deduce the infinite. He is creator and we are creature. The creature cannot deduce the creator. He is holy and we are sinful. The sinful cannot deduce the holy. He is perfect truth while we still have pockets of ignorance and error. The false cannot deduce perfect truth.

God, in His graciousness, has revealed Himself to us in the Scriptures. This revelation is a gift we could have in no other way. Through that gift we can have huge insights, not only into the nature of God, but also into the nature of all reality including ourselves.

In gratitude for this wonderful gift, we should study the Bible hungrily and diligently. It is an absolutely unique resource that is essential to our spiritual and eternal well-being.

As we seek to be evangelistic in our lives, we need to point out to others how wonderful it is to be able to know God. It seems that every thoughtful person would be eager to have responsible information about the person and nature of God. When the Bible is presented as a resource toward this end, it will be viewed in a new light. Many will come to it gladly because they will see that it responds to the hungers of thei

Memory Selection

"Study to show thyself approved unto God, a workman that needeth not to be ashamed, rightly dividing the word of truth."
II Timothy 2 : 15 .

The word "study" in this passage means to concentrate on or to give diligent attention to. In the Revised Standard Version it is translated, "Do your best." It is a call to recognize how important a knowledge of the Scriptures is and how earnestly we ought to pursue such knowledge.

One thing this text emphasizes is that significant knowledge is the result of significant effort. It does not come easily or accidentally. Sometimes when we see others with good biblical knowledge we assume that they have a special gift. It is more likely that they have expended the time and energy to dig out that knowledge. They have studied (made an energetic effort) to learn the Word.

Such effort is admired and approved by God. He takes note of those who take the acquiring of Bible knowledge seriously. There is divine approval of workmen, not of idlers.

This passage asks a confrontational question, "Are you doing the hard work necessary to gain a respectable knowledge of the Word of God?" People who do not read the Scriptures, who do not meditate on them, who do not attend classes, and who do not expose themselves to the stimulation of other minds need to give careful heed to this admonition.

Weekday Problems

Barry has spent a lot of time studying the Bible but has somehow failed to grasp the central message of it. He sees it as a collection of isolated texts. He does not see them as being interconnected or as contributing to a main theme. As a result he excerpts texts from here and there to construct a rationale which supports any idea he might currently have.

No one can question his sincerity, but his understanding of the Bible is so strange and individualistic that it does not communicate with others. He, on the other hand, not realizing the subjectiveness of his approach, cannot see why everybody does not see things like he does.

He thinks that because he can refer to a text to support his beliefs that those beliefs are biblical. He does not realize that he is taking texts out of context to try to prove things they were never intended to teach.

* How can you encourage Barry to develop a better understanding of the Bible as a coordinated whole?
* Would it help to quote proof texts back to him to demonstrate how he is misusing the Bible? Why or why not?

Superintendent's Sermonette

Treatment of clergymen in our broadcast media has been deplorable. They are presented as hypocrites, wimps, and misfits. Scandals centering on certain televangelists in recent years have caused the news media to downgrade clergymen in general. In a generation dedicated to non-stop "partying," serious Christians who refuse to participate are ridiculed and made to look abnormal. Pressures to conform can become almost unbearable. Discouragement can lead to cessation of effort for God.

That is why we need a lesson such as the one we have today. Paul had learned how to swim upstream against the strong flow of worldly pressures, and he wanted to help Timothy do the same. He challenged him to be a hardened soldier ready for spiritual battle. He compared him to a runner racing to win the prize of God's approval. He reminded him that the industrious farmer tastes the first of the harvested crops. He urged him to be a workman who could properly handle God's truth. Let us resist the world's pressures, and let us encourage one another to serve God well.

This Lesson in **Your** Life

"You can prove anything by the Bible," is a statement often made. People come to this conclusion because of the misuse of Scriptures. There are those who have gone to the Scriptures to find support for their own views and prejudices. They inevitably find something that, to their satisfaction, supports them.

This is a grotesque abuse of the Scriptures. It perverts God's revelation of Himself into an instrument for reinforcing human error. When this is done the Scriptures do not teach, they are used. Those who would exploit the Scriptures in this way can use them to teach almost anything they wish.

Those, however, who come to the Bible to hear its message do not find it teaching a variety of conflicting messages. They find it teaching that God is creator and sovereign. They find it teaching that Jesus is loving and redemptive. They find it teaching that the Holy Spirit is assuring and interceding. They find it teaching that we should love all men, be forgiving in our attitude, and return good for evil.

Those who handle the Word rightly find it sitting in judgment on their sinfulness. The Word does not approve wrong and it never ceases to affirm truth and right. It is not true that anything can be proved by the Bible.

What is the right way to handle the Bible? It begins with the attitude with which we come to the Scriptures. We must come seeking to know the will of God. We must be willing to be enlightened and willing to be changed by what we learn.

As we study the Scriptures we must do so in a responsible way. The Bible did not descend from heaven by parachute. It was written by specific people, to specific audiences, and in specific settings. These things have to be taken into consideration if we are to glean from the Bible its message. The book of Genesis did not come out of the same context as the book of Romans. Both have a vital message for us, but each has to be studied in the light of the setting in which it came to be.

Further, there are many different types of writing in the Bible. The Psalms are poetic lyrics written to be sung. Proverbs is largely a collection of epigrams. Ezekiel, Daniel, and Revelation are apocalyptic literature. The prophets wrote in one way and the gospel writers in another. Many of Paul's writings were in the form of personal letters. Handling the Word rightly means being sensitive to all these communication clues.

The Bible was written over a period of many centuries. It is vital that the stories of primitive cultures be seen in their context and that the loving and spiritual message of the Sermon on the Mount be seen in its proper setting. Tensions in the first century church need to be understood to come to a meaningful knowledge of the Corinthian epistles. A knowledge of the historical record of the book of Acts is essential to an understanding of many of the epistles.

It all boils down to coming to the Scriptures with a reverent desire to understand the truth that God is revealed to us. When we read, as on bended knee, to hear the Word of the Lord, we will be enlightened, instructed and sometimes judged.

Seed Thoughts

1. How may a Christian be strong?
Although weak in himself, he can grow strong in the grace that is in Christ. Growth in grace is essential.

2. What is the best way to propagate the gospel?
We should teach it to others, who, in turn, are able to teach it to others. Multiplication is better than addition.

3. What is one way a Christian soldier hardens himself for battle?
He refuses to become entangled in the affairs of this world so that he may be at the disposal of his commander.

4. How should a believer run the Christian race?
He must follow the rules (principles) laid down for him in God's Holy Word.

5. Why should a farmer be first partaker of his crops?
He should try his food before giving it to others. The same is true of the believer who seeks to give spiritual nourishment to others.

(Please Turn Page)

---

1. How may a Christian be strong?

2. What is the best way to propagate the gospel?

3. What is one way a Christian soldier hardens himself for battle?

4. How should a believer run the Christian race?

5. Why should a farmer be first partaker of his crops?

6. What is the central truth of the gospel which we should defend?

7. Why should believers endure persecution for Christ's sake?

8. What sure prospects do believers have to counter balance the suffering they endure for Christ?

9 What does arguing about words produce?

10. How can a Bible student be approved by God?

Seed Thoughts - Continued

Although weak in himself, he can grow strong in the grace that is in Christ. Growth in grace is essential.

We should teach it to others, who, in turn, are able to teach it to others. Multiplication is better than addition.

He refuses to become entangled in the affairs of this world so that he may be at the disposal of his commander.

He must follow the rules (principles) laid down for him in God's Holy Word.

He should try his food before giving it to others. The same is true of the believer who seeks to give spiritual nourishment to others.

It is that Christ died and rose again for our justification.

They should do it so that the Word of God can go forth, contact the elect, and call them to repentance and salvation.

They know that if they die for Him, they will live again. They know that if they suffer for Him, they will reign with Him, He gives them sustaining grace.

It often leads to strife and confusion, if it diverges from God's Holy Word.

He can handle God's Word properly, learning its facts, extracting its principles, and applying them in real life.

6. What is the central truth of the gospel which we should defend?
It is that Christ died and rose again for our justification.

7. Why should believers endure persecution for Christ's sake?
They should do it so that the Word of God can go forth, contact the elect, and call them to repentance and salvation.

8. What sure prospects do believers have to counter balance the suffering they endure for Christ?
They know that if they die for Him, they will live again. They know that if they suffer for Him, they will reign with Him, He gives them sustaining grace.

9 What does arguing about words produce?
It often leads to strife and confusion, if it diverges from God's Holy Word.

10. How can a Bible student be approved by God?
He can handle God's Word properly, learning its facts, extracting its principles, and applying them in real life.

Fulfill Your Ministry Faithfully

2 Timothy 3:10. But thou hast fully known my doctrine, manner of life, purpose, faith, longsuffering, charity, patience.

11. Persecutions, afflictions, which came unto me at Antioch, at Iconium, at Lystra; what persecutions I endured: but out of them all the Lord delivered me.

12. Yea, and all that will live godly in Christ Jesus shall suffer persecution.

13. But evil men and seducers shall wax worse and worse, deceiving, and being deceived.

14. But continue thou in the things which thou hast learned and hast been assured of, knowing of whom thou hast learned them;

15. And that from a child thou hast known the holy scriptures, which are able to make thee wise unto salvation through faith which is in Christ Jesus.

16. All scripture is given by inspiration of God, and is profitable for doctrine, for reproof, for correction, for instruction in righteousness:

17. That the man of God may be perfect, thoroughly furnished unto all good works.

2 Timothy 4:1. I charge thee therefore before God, and the Lord Jesus Christ who shall judge the quick and the dead at his appearing and his kingdom;

2. Preach the word, be instant in season, out of season; reprove, rebuke, exhort with all longsuffering and doctrine.

3. For the time will come when they will not endure sound doctrine; but after their own lusts shall they heap to themselves teachers, having itching ears;

4. And they shall turn away their ears from the truth, and shall be turned unto fables.

5. But watch thou in all things, endure afflictions, do the work of an evangelist, make full proof of thy ministry.

MEMORY SELECTION
2 Timothy 4:2
DEVOTIONAL READING
2 Corinthians 5:3-10

BACKGROUND SCRIPTURE
2 Timothy 3:10-4:8
PRINTED SCRIPTURE
2 Timothy 3:10-4:5

Teacher's Target

It is one thing to be called to and equipped for a ministry, and it is another thing to actually fulfill that ministry. Reading between the lines, it would appear that Timothy had eased back on what God told him to do. Paul, the mature veteran, sought to persuade the younger man to live up to his potential. He and others would be needed to do God's work when Paul passed from the scene (II Tim. 4:6).

Help your students to identify themselves not only as believers but also as servants called by God to do His work, whether it is in a full-time vocation or in conjunction with another vocation. God has chosen and honored all His children to serve Him, and we all need to be encouraged to do it. "For we are his workmanship, created in Christ Jesus unto good works" (Eph. 2:10).

Lesson Introduction

It is disappointing for knowledge and talent to go unused. Timothy was the son of a Jewess and of a Greek (Acts 16:1). His grandmother, Lois, and his mother, Eunice, had brought him up in the Jewish faith and prepared him to become a Christian (II Tim. 1:5; 3:14-15). He had been ordained to the ministry by the laying on of hands by the presbytery and Paul himself (I Tim. 4:14; II Tim. 1:6). Paul was anxious for Timothy to stir up the gift of prophecy which he had received.

As you study about Timothy, help students to realize that each has an ability that can be used in the Lord's work.. It is sad if that ability is not used. Using such scriptures as I Corinthians 12:4-11, 28 and Ephesians 4:11-13, encourage your students to determine what their gift or gifts might be and to make use of what God has bestowed.

Teaching Outline

I. Persecutions II Tim. 3:10-13
   A. Experience: 10-11
   B. Expectation: 12-13

II. Perseverance: II Tim. 3:14-17
   A. Inducement: 14-15
   B. Inspiration: 16-17

III. Proof: II Tim. 4:1-5
   A. Demand: 1-2
   B. Danger: 3-4
   C. Deportment: 5

Daily Bible Readings

Mon. The Lord Delivered Me
2 Timothy 3:10-11
Tue. Worse Will Come
2 Timothy 3:12-13
Wed. Be True
2 Timothy 3:14-15
Thu. The Scriptures are Reliable
2 Timothy 3:16-17
Fri. Preach the Word
2 Timothy 4:1-2
Sat. Some Will Reject
2 Timothy 4:3-5
Sun. My Life Nears the End
2 Timothy 4:6-8

Verse By Verse

I. Persecutions: II Tim. 3:10-13

A. Experience: 10-11
10. But thou hast fully known my doctrine, manner of life, purpose, faith, longsuffering, charity, patience,

Having warned Timothy previously in this chapter about apostate teachers, Paul wanted to remind him that his own Christian character was quite the opposite. His doctrine (teaching), manner of life (behavior), purpose (objective), faith in God, longsuffering (patience under pressure), charity (love), and patience (defined here as endurance) were there for all to see.

11. Persecutions, afflictions, which came unto me at Antioch, at Iconium, at Lystra; what persecutions I endured: but out of them all the Lord delivered me.

Paul recalled the mistreatment he had received at Antioch, Iconium, and Lystra. It was at Antioch in Pisidia (south central Turkey) that unbelieving Jews had criticized, contradicted, and blasphemed when Paul spoke to them (Acts 13:45). When the Word of God went forth throughout the region, the Jews stirred up the people and had Paul and Barnabas expelled from their coasts (boundaries) (Acts 13:49-50). It was at Iconium that the missionaries were assaulted by Gentiles and Jews who wanted to stone them (Acts 14:5). It was at Lystra that hateful Jews from Antioch and Iconium came and persuaded the people to stone Paul. Dragged outside of the city and left for dead, Paul revived and went back into the city (Acts 14:19-20). By his own testimony, he said that the Lord delivered him from all of these life-threatening situations.

B. Expectation: 12-13
12. Yea, and all that will live godly in Christ Jesus shall suffer persecution.

This is a general statement applicable to Christians in all generations. If we have had to suffer only ridicule and harassment for our faith, we are fortunate. However, others have suffered physical assaults, loss of personal freedoms, loss of properties, loss of material goods, banishment, and even martyrdom. If circumstances change for us, we might suffer these things, too. We need to spiritually fortify ourselves now if we would be ready for these trials.

13. But evil men and seducers shall wax worse and worse, deceiving, and being deceived.

Paul foresaw that the age of grace would produce ungodly men and spiritual seducers who would become increasingly troublesome. They would deceive others, and they themselves would be deceived. This may mean that they would come to believe their own lies, or it may mean that they would come to believe the lies of other deceivers. We now live in an age in which cultic teachings are widespread and are leading many people astray. Our best defense and offense is loyalty to the unadulterated Word of God as revealed in the Old and New Testaments of our Holy Bible.

II. Perseverance: II Tim. 3:14-17

A. Inducement: 14-15
14. But continue thou in the things which thou hast learned and hast been assured of, knowing

of whom thou hast learned them

Paul wanted to induce Timothy to consider his background and be thankful for the solid Christian teaching he had received from himself and others. It was because Timothy trusted these individuals that he was assured that their teachings were right. There is the implication here that Timothy had learned these things not only from precept but by example. He had also learned them by putting them into use in his own life.

15. And that from a child thou hast known the holy scriptures, which are able to make thee wise unto salvation through faith which is in Christ Jesus.

Due to the influence of his Jewish grandmother, Lois, and his Jewish mother, Eunice, Timothy had been taught from the holy scriptures, meaning the Old Testament. These were able to prepare him for the coming of the Messiah, and he believed on Christ as the Messiah when he heard the gospel brought to his area by missionaries. Oral truth had been added to written truth in this way. As the years moved along, the three synoptic Gospels of Matthew, Mark, and Luke were written, along with the book of Acts (also by Luke) and various letters by such men as Paul, James, Peter, and Jude. John's Gospel, the letters, and the book of Revelation would be written toward the end of the first century of the Christian era. All would later be tested for authenticity and genuineness by early church fathers before being added to the New Testament canon as we have it today.

B. Inspiration: 16-17
16a. All scripture is given by inspiration of God, . . .

This is a powerful and crucial statement. It declares that all true revelation from God was breathed into existence by Him. There are many other scriptures in the world which came from human or demonic sources, and they form the bases for false religions and cults. God's Word, as contained in our Old and New Testaments, is an extension of Himself and cannot be altered or destroyed.

16b. . . . and is profitable for doctrine, for reproof, for correction, for instruction in righteousness:

Paul said that the truth of God is valuable for doctrine (teaching), for reproving sinners, for correcting the disobedient, and for training people in holy living.

17. That the man of God may be perfect, thoroughly furnished unto all good works.

The end result of interaction between the believer and the Word of God is a process whereby the believer is thoroughly equipped and made perfect (mature) enough to do the good works God has ordained for him or her to do (Eph. 2:10).

III. Proof: II Tim. 4:1-5

A. Demand: 1-2
1. I charge thee therefore before God, and the Lord Jesus Christ, who shall judge the quick and the dead at his appearing and his kingdom; . . .

Realizing that he must soon die (II Tim. 4:6), Paul charged Timothy to be a good minister of Jesus Christ. This charge was made with God the Father and the Lord Jesus Christ as Witnesses, a most solemn thing to do. He described Christ as the One Who will return to judge both the quick (living) and the dead. Now came Paul's demand upon Timothy.

2a. Preach the word . . .

There were many topics which could be presented in the ancient world. Paul was well educated, knowing the various philosophies current in his time. This was shown in his remarks to the Greek scholars on Mars' hill in Athens. However, only a few were ready to accept the gospel there (Acts 17:22-34). When Paul arrived in Corinth he said, "I determined not to know any thing among you, save Jesus Christ, and him crucified" (I Cor. 2:2). A strong church was founded there. Paul wanted Timothy to put his emphasis on preaching God's Holy Word.

2b. . . . be instant in season, out of season . . .

Paul wanted Timothy to be ready to present the truth to others whether or not it was convenient and whether or not it would receive a good welcome and response. Personal feeling was not to determine whether God's truth was given out or withheld. A good minister was willing to preach the truth in both favorable and unfavorable circumstances.

2c. . . . reprove, rebuke, exhort with all longsuffering and doctrine.

To reprove or rebuke someone meant much the same. This was to be done in order to draw a person under conviction by the Holy Spirit. To exhort a person was to show him how to correct his errors by adhering to divine truth. All of these things were to be done with great patience and by use of pure doctrine from the Word of God.

B. Danger: 3-4
3a. For the time will come when they will not endure sound doctrine; . . .

Paul knew by reason, revelation, or both that the time was coming when apostate teachers would become popular with weak believers. These people would not be willing to listen to sound teaching, no doubt because it demanded too much from them in holy living. They would seek substitutes.

3b. . . . but after their own lusts shall they heap to themselves teachers, having itching ears;
4. And they shall turn away their ears from the truth, and shall be turned unto fables.

The ancient pagan world had many false teachers to offer their services to weak believers. These were rooted in human philosophies, mystery cults, and barbarism. After rejecting the truth of God, apostates would be driven by their lusts (passions) and gather around themselves the kind of teachers who would tickle their ears and turn them away from what truth they had. In its place they would offer fables (myths, legends). These human and demonic teachings would drag them down to perdition, and they would take many along with them.

It is worth noting that myths are making a come back in the world today. The New Age, occult, and Satanic groups are using them in propagating their ideas. Even liberal or neo-orthodox theologians have suggested that there can be "truth in myth" and in this condescending way say that even biblical "legends" may be useful. We do not need that kind of patronizing attitude for Bible truths.

C. Deportment: 5
5a. But watch thou in all things, endure afflictions, . . .

Paul was using military terms here. He saw Timothy as a good soldier of Jesus Christ and had already challenged him to endure hardness (II Tim. 2:3). He now told him to be on guard, calmly facing possible conflicts with the hosts of spiritual darkness. When afflictions came for the cause of Christ, he was to endure them by God's sustaining grace.

5b. . . . do the work of an evangelist, make full proof of thy ministry.

Paul used spiritual terms here, He saw Timothy as a soul winner. He urged him to prove this by being responsible for all of the tasks God gave him to do.

Evangelistic Emphasis

When we look at our text today we have a great sense of identity with today's world. Every day's news tells us of crime, cruelty, betrayal, deception, corruption, and perversion. It is not the kind of climate that we would expect the gospel to thrive in.

Paul was urging Timothy to be a faithful evangelist in a similar kind of world. There were persecutions, afflictions, evil men, and slanderers. Hearers tended to prefer a message which asked little of them and flattered their prejudices.

It would not seem that such a world was a good field for evangelism. Yet Paul charged Timothy to preach the word both in and out of season.

For three reasons the gospel needs to be preached in this kind of world. The first is that there is a need for it. The more sin there is in the world, the greater the need for a redemptive message. The second reason is that people are hurting. They need the solace and hope that is given by the good news of the gospel. The third reason is that it is our job to preach the gospel. We are responsible to be true to that charge regardless of how hospitable our audience is. As Paul said in another place, it is our place to sow the seed, but it is God who gives the increase. We are not responsible for the response of those to whom we preach. We are responsible to do the preaching and the encouraging. We will rejoice over a positive response and regret a negative one. Howevch does not change on the basis of what kind of resp

Memory Selection

"Preach the word; be instant in season, out of season; reprove, rebuke, exhort with all longsuffering and doctrine."
II Timothy 4:2.

Paul challenges Timothy with a staccato directive, "Preach the word." There are only three words, all of them one syllable. There can be no confusion, misunderstanding, or evasion. The charge is direct and simple.

Having given the clear command, Paul adds some more specific directions. The word should be preached both in season and out of season. There are times when it seems there is a great interest in the gospel and these times should be taken advantage of. At other times the climate seems adverse for preaching. Even then a soul might be found who is interested.

Preaching good news does not mean preaching total approval of a person's behavior. Sometimes it is important to reprove and rebuke. The only way we can honor the good is by clearly distinguishing it from the bad. If a person is to be helped, the negative aspects of his life must be confronted and corrected.

Then we must exhort, or urge a proper response. It matters to us whether people accept Christ or not. We beg and plead when we think it will help. We do so patiently while continuing to teach.

Weekday Problems

Sarah is a woman of average intelligence and nominal skills. Throughout her life she has been around people who learned faster than she did and who were able to excel her in nearly every activity she participated in. The one thing that no one ever bested her in is persistence. Since she was a girl she always steadily pursued her objective until her task was completed.

In school she was not an honor student but every assignment was completed on time, her attendance record was excellent, and with hard work she was able to make above-average grades. At work she is respected for her consistency and dependability. She has made steady, though not rapid, progress. She will never be president of her company but she is esteemed for her craftsmanship.

As a wife and mother she is dearly loved for her faithfulness and unselfishness. Others may be able to cook better, but no one is more loyal and trustworthy.

* Discuss the fact that Sarah's good qualities are often taken for granted and not highly appreciated by employers, church, and family.
* In the Christian value system, compare the importance of faithfulness with talent, intelligence, and creativity.

Superintendent's Sermonette

Too often we view the world as a passive place. We see it offering us many options, but we feel in control and able to take or leave them without feeling harassed or forced. The fact is, however, that there are dark forces at work in our contacts with the world every day. We are bombarded by evil and ungodly concepts and practices. In moments of deception or weakness, we can be swept up with the tide and thrown upon the rocks.

Paul did not see the world as a passive, friendly, accommodating place. He battled his way through the Mediterranean world, and he had the scars to prove it. When he found Timothy being rather timid about Christian warfare, he advised him to stir up the gift of prophecy (proclamation) and get the gospel out to as many people as possible. Veteran soldiers of Christ such as Paul had to be replaced by developing soldiers such as Timothy. The same is true for us today. We must be spiritually active, if we hope to fulfill the commission given to us by Christ to evangelize and educate the people of our generation.

This Lesson in <u>Your</u> Life

We have some sayings that are in harmony with today's lesson. They include, "Talk is cheap," "Put your money where your mouth is," "Put up or shut up," and "Actions speak louder than words." The point is that our Christian faith needs to be lived instead of just talked about. That requires a much greater effort and involves more complexities.

If we are to live our faith, Paul says we will have to endure hardship. Conscientious Christians learn that it is often easier not to fulfill Christian responsibilities. Decisions, however, must be made on the basis of what is right, not what is easy. Sacrifices must be made. Difficult tasks must be completed.

Further, if we are faithful to the Lord, we must avoid distracting entanglements with other interests in life. This is referring not only to sinful activities. It also refers to innocent interests that divert us from our major purpose. As a soldier cannot maintain his other activities while serving as a soldier, so the Christian must eliminate conflicting interests so he can concentrate on his duty to the Lord.

Still further, living our faith means that we must be careful to have an informed faith. Being busy is not a guarantee of being on track. The effective Christian will constantly be evaluating his direction to see that he is doing what the Lord wants him to do.

Those who are serious about their calling have some resources that will help them in the fulfillment of it. One is the memory of Jesus Christ. Although He was the Son of God, the seed of David, and the giver of salvation, He still had to suffer. If He were not spared, we need not expect that we will be spared. If He faced His suffering with faithfulness, we need to follow His example and face our suffering with faithfulness.

One problem that occurs when people go through hard times is the feeling of being isolated. We tend to feel that our suffering is rare or unique. The realization that others suffer also helps us keep from feeling alone or different. We are in noble company when we suffer in our attempts to be Christian.

In Timothy's case, Paul could encourage him by reminding him of his background in the faith. He was well-grounded in the faith, having been taught the Scriptures since he was a child. Those deep roots which had been established by those he loved would serve him well when his faith was tested.

The final motivation that Paul gave was a reminder of how important faithfulness is. Before God and Christ and in the light of coming judgment, Paul urged Timothy to be true to his mission in spite of all opposition and hardship.

Seed Thoughts

1. How important is one's Christian testimony to others?
How we believe, act, fulfill our purpose, and show patience, love, and endurance may affect others' destinies.

2. Is there anything good about persecutions and afflictions?
They strengthen the faith and character of a believer who trusts God to deliver him out of them all.

3. Can any believers hope to avoid persecution for Christ?
Paul thought that all would experience some persecution. We are fortunate if all we have is harassment or ridicule.

4. What is the antidote for spiritual deception?
It is the knowledge and practice of spiritual principles set forth in the unadulterated Word of God.

5. How should the inspired Scriptures be used?
They can teach truth, reprove evil, correct disobedience, and give training in holy living.

(Please Turn Page)

---

1. How important is one's Christian testimony to others?

2. Is there anything good about persecutions and afflictions?

3. Can any believers hope to avoid persecution for Christ?

4. What is the antidote for spiritual deception?

5. How should the inspired Scriptures be used?

6. What is the end-result of using God's Word properly?

7. Who stand as witnesses to a serious spiritual challenge?

8. How should God's Word be preached?

9. What do people do when they become tired of hearing the truth?

10. How are military terms used for spiritual reasons in II Tim. 4:5?

Seed Thoughts - Continued

How we believe, act, fulfill our purpose, and show patience, love, and endurance may affect others' destinies.

They strengthen the faith and character of a believer who trusts God to deliver him out of them all.

Paul thought that all would experience some persecution. We are fortunate if all we have is harassment or ridicule.

It is the knowledge and practice of spiritual principles set forth in the unadulterated Word of God.

They can teach truth, reprove evil, correct disobedience, and give training in holy living.

The process produces individuals who are thoroughly equipped to do good works.

Paul called on God and Christ to do this. Angels and other believers may also serve in this capacity.

It should be preached consistently despite circumstances and should be done with great patience.

They seek for substitutes from human and Satanic sources who will tell them only what they want to hear.

By being on guard and being ready to endure afflictions, Christ's soldiers propagate the gospel and prove their worth.

6. What is the end-result of using God's Word properly?
The process produces individuals who are thoroughly equipped to do good works.

7. Who stand as witnesses to a serious spiritual challenge?
Paul called on God and Christ to do this. Angels and other believers may also serve in this capacity.

8. How should God's Word be preached?
It should be preached consistently despite circumstances and should be done with great patience.

9. What do people do when they become tired of hearing the truth?
They seek for substitutes from human and Satanic sources who will tell them only what they want to hear.

10. How are military terms used for spiritual reasons in II Tim. 4:5?
By being on guard and being ready to endure afflictions, Christ's soldiers propagate the gospel and prove their worth.

CHRISTIAN DOES YOUR LIFE MIRROR JESUS?

Be A Model In Deeds And Word

Titus 2:7. In all things showing thyself a pattern of good works: in doctrine showing uncorruptness, gravity, sincerity,
8. Sound speech, that cannot be condemned; that he that is of the contrary part may be ashamed, having no evil thing to say of you.
Titus 2:11. For the grace of God that bringeth salvation hath appeared to all men,
12. Teaching us that, denying ungodliness and worldly lusts, we should live soberly, righteously, and godly, in this present world;
13. Looking for that blessed hope, and the glorious appearing of the great God and our Savior Jesus Christ;
14. Who gave himself for us, that he might redeem us from all iniquity, and purify unto himself a peculiar people, zealous of good works.
Titus 3:1. Put them in mind to be subject to principalities and powers, to obey magistrates, to be ready to every good work,
2. To speak evil of no man, to be no brawlers, but gentle, showing all meekness unto all men.
3. For we ourselves also were sometimes foolish, disobedient, deceived, serving divers lusts and pleasures, living in malice and envy, hateful, and hating one another.
4. But after that the kindness and love of God our Savior toward man appeared,
5. Not by works of righteousness which we have done, but according to his mercy he saved us, by the washing of regeneration, and renewing of the Holy Ghost;
6. Which he shed on us abundantly through Jesus Christ our Savior;
7. That being justified by his grace, we should be made heirs according to the hope of eternal life.
8. This is a faithful saying, and these things I will that thou affirm constantly, that they which have believed in God might be careful to maintain good works. These things are good and profitable unto men.

MEMORY SELECTION
Titus 2:7
DEVOTIONAL READING
James 2:22-26

BACKGROUND SCRIPTURE
Titus
PRINTED SCRIPTURE
Titus 2:7-8,11-14;3:1-8

Teacher's Target

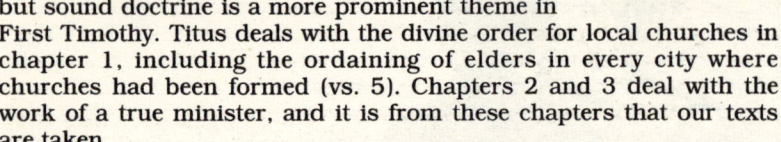

First Timothy and Titus are quite similar. Both emphasize the divine order for local churches, but sound doctrine is a more prominent theme in First Timothy. Titus deals with the divine order for local churches in chapter 1, including the ordaining of elders in every city where churches had been formed (vs. 5). Chapters 2 and 3 deal with the work of a true minister, and it is from these chapters that our texts are taken.

Help your students to see what God expects from leaders in local churches. They are to be spiritual models in deed and word for others to follow. Sober, righteous, godly living is to be the norm, especially in light of the coming appearance of our Savior Jesus Christ. It is only by God's grace that we are delivered from sin, and it is by grace that we will inherit eternal life.

Lesson Introduction

Paul expected church members to maintain good testimonies both inside and outside the church. Titus 2 contains suggestions for aged men, aged women, young women, young men, and servants. Proper relationships between individuals were to be governed by the grace of God. Believers were to live righteously and look forward to the coming of Christ and the final results of salvation. Titus 3 contains suggestions for believers getting along with secular officials. By living good lives they could enhance their reputations. By doing good works they could soften attitudes toward them. Heretics who could harm their testimony were to be warned and then rejected if unrepentant.

Church leaders should take these suggestions seriously today. Local churches can be strengthened internally and externally by applying these principles.

Teaching Outline

I. Example: Titus 2:7-8
   A. Showing: 7-8a
   B. Shaming: 8b
II. Expectation: Titus 2:11-14
   A. Help: 11-12
   B. Hope: 13-14
III. Exhortation: Titus 3:1-2
   A. Regulations: 1
   B. Relationships: 2
IV. Exchanges Titus 3:3-8
   A. Review: 3
   B. Regeneration: 4-7
   C. Reaffirmation: 8

Daily Bible Readings

Mon. My Son in the Faith
Titus 1:1-4
Tue. Ordaining Church Leaders
Titus 1:5-16
Wed. Sound Doctrine
Titus 2:1-8
Thu. Live Righteously
Titus 2:9-15
Fri. Saved by Mercy
Titus 3:1-5
Sat. Justified by Grace
Titus 3:6-11
Sun. Maintain Good Works
Titus 3:12-15

Verse By Verse

I. **Example: Titus 2:7-3**

A. **Showing: 7-8a**
**7. In all things shewing thyself a pattern of good works: in doctrine shewing uncorruptness, gravity, sincerity,
8a. Sound speech, that cannot be condemned; ...**

Paul wanted young men, such as Titus, to be examples (models) of good works in the church. When teaching divine doctrine, they were to show uncorruptness (unadulterated truth), gravity (seriousness), sincerity (missing in the oldest Greek manuscripts but certainly important), and soundness of speech which could not be condemned. In other words, they were to rightly divide (handle) the Word of truth (II Tim. 2:15).

B. **Shaming: 8b**
8b. ... that he that is of the contrary part may be ashamed, having no evil thing to say of you.

Paul wanted Titus to teach and live divine truth in such a way that enemies of the gospel, such as pagan Cretans and troublesome Judaizers mentioned in Titus 1:10-14, could not criticize him. His testimony would then cause them to be ashamed.

Paul believed that sound doctrine would help aged men and women, young men and women, and servants to maintain good Christian testimonies (Titus 2:1-10). Now we come to the basis upon which such teaching should be done.

II. **Expectation: Titus 2:11-14**

A. **Help: 11-12**
11. For the grace of God that bringeth salvation hath appeared to all men, ...

The grace of God is that unmerited favor or blessing which He pours out on those who love and serve Him, It was personified in Jesus Christ, His beloved Son, Who came to the earth that all men might be saved through faith. Christ's followers were commissioned to take the gospel of grace to the whole world (Matt. 28:19-20). Note that the things taught by Christ coincided with what are mentioned in Titus 2:12.

12. Teaching us that, denying ungodliness and worldly lusts, we should live soberly, righteously, and godly, in this present world;

Note the negative and positive aspects in this verse. Christ taught that believers should deny ungodliness and worldly lusts (passions). More will be said on this subject when we get to Titus 3:2-3. Christ also taught that believers should live soberly (in a disciplined manner), righteously (in an upright manner), and godly (in a pious manner) in the midst of their sinful generation. Paul urged believers to "shine as lights in the world, holding forth the word of life" (Phil. 2:15-16). Help received by means of divine grace was to be repaid in part by faithful service for the Lord

B. **Hope: 13-14**
13. Looking for that blessed hope, and the glorious appearing of the great God and our Saviour Jesus Christ;

As divine grace operated in believers to keep them from sin and move them toward righteousness, Paul wanted them to look forward with anticipation to the appearance of their great God and Savior, Jesus

Christ. There is nothing wrong in calling Jesus God, for He is divine, and this did not detract in any way from God the Father. Paul called this anticipation or expectation "that blessed hope," for hope was personified in Christ.

14. Who gave himself for us, that he might redeem us from all iniquity, and purify unto himself a peculiar people, zealous of good works.

The reason that believers have a sure hope in Christ for the future is that He gave them hope in the past. He came down from heaven to die on the cross at Calvary and atone for their sins. By this act, He redeemed them from all iniquity, and they needed only to accept this by faith in order to be saved. He also, by this act, purified them and made them His peculiar (special, precious) people. He expected them to be devoted to good works as a way of expressing their gratitude for what He had done for them. Saving faith produces working believers (Eph. 2:8-10).

Paul urged young Titus to speak (teach, tell, mention), to exhort (encourage, advise, warn), and to rebuke (correct, reprove) the wayward from a position of full authority (Titus 2:15). We are reminded of Paul's admonition to young Timothy to let no one make light of his youth but to be an example to follow in word, behavior, love, spirit, faith, and purity (I Tim. 4:12).

III. Exhortation: Titus 3:1-2

A. Regulations: 1
1. Put them in mind to be subject to principalities and powers, to obey magistrates, to be ready to every good work,

Paul urged Titus to remind believers that they should obey principalities and powers (government officials) and magistrates (probably judges). This no doubt referred to authorities seeking to do their work well. Romans 13:1-6 refers to them in this role as "God's ministers" to uphold what is good and punish what is bad. In cases where officials demanded that Christians do evil, the principle of Acts 5:29 was to prevail—"We ought to obey God rather than men," Paul told Titus to urge believers to be ready to do every good work as a way to maintain their Christian testimony.

B. Relationships: 2
2a. To speak evil of no man, to be no brawlers, . . .

Whether dealing with fellow believers, government officials, or men in general, Paul wanted believers to avoid slander, gossip, and severe criticism. He wanted them to avoid involvement in brawling (boisterous quarreling). Some of the new converts may have been sorely tempted to slip back into their old lifestyle.

2b. . . . but gentle, shewing all meekness unto all men.

One of the nine fruits of the Spirit in believers is gentleness (Gal. 5:22-23). It was given through the ministry of the Holy Spirit in order to help develop good relationships. Meekness is also one of the nine fruits and is bestowed in the same way and for the same purpose. To be gentle and meek is not meant to describe cowardice or vacillation. It means to be strong but sensitive and self-effacing.

IV. Exchange: Titus 3:3-8

A. Review: 3
3. For we ourselves also were sometimes foolish, disobedient, deceived, serving divers lusts and pleasures, living in malice and envy, hateful, and hating one another.

Paul reviewed what believers used to be when they were yet in sin. They had been foolish (irrational), disobedient to God, deceived (led astray) by Satan, servants to various passions and sinful pleasures, motivated by malice (resentment) and envy, hating others, and hating themselves.

B. Regeneration: 4-7
4. But after that the kindness and love of God our Saviour toward men appeared,
5a. Not by works of righteousness which we have done, but according to his mercy he saved us, . . .

It was the coming to the earth by Christ, here given the title of "God our Saviour," which revealed divine kindness and love to men. He was the just One dying for the unjust. Nothing that sinful men could do of their own wisdom or strength could rescue them from the penalty of sin. The prophet wrote, "Our [self-]righteousnesses are as filthy rags [in God's sight]" (Isa. 64:6). Sinners were not saved by works (acts) meriting righteousness, something taught by non-Christian religions, They were saved by the mercy of God shown to them in Christ. He took on Him the penalty sinners deserved.

5b. . . . by the washing of regeneration, and renewing of the Holy Ghost;
6. Which he shed on us abundantly through Jesus Christ our Saviour; . . .

The cleansing of sin which takes place at the moment of salvation results in the impartation of new life. The renewal which goes on is under the direction of the Holy Spirit. He is the Agent of God's redeeming love. "The love of God is shed abroad in our hearts by the Holy Ghost which is given unto us" (Rom. 5:5)

7. That being justified by his grace, we should be made heirs according to the hope of eternal life.

Saving grace mediated to believers by the Holy Spirit brings cleansing, regeneration, and justification. To be justified is to be accounted as righteous before God, as if we had never sinned. God sees us as we are hidden in Christ and covered by His atoning blood. In that unique position, we become heirs with Christ of all that God has and can look forward to enjoying it for eternity.

In another place, Paul wrote, "The Spirit itself [Himself] beareth witness with our spirit, that we are the [redeemed and adopted] children of God: and if children, then heirs; heirs of God, and joint-heirs with Christ; if so be that we suffer with him, that we may be also glorified together" (Rom. 8:16-17).

C. Reaffirmation: 8
8a This is a faithful saying, and these things I will that thou affirm constantly, that they which have believed in God might be careful to maintain good works.

Verses 8-11 contain Paul's concluding remarks regarding godly living, while the remaining verses feature personal remarks. Paul wanted Titus to be persuaded that there was a definite connection between doctrine and service. Saving faith came first, and good works followed. Faith was the root, and works were the fruit.

8b. These things are good and profitable unto men.

Paul believed that good works were not only valuable in themselves, but they produced good results for those who became involved in them.

Thus we come to the end of six lessons based on selected texts from I and II Timothy and Titus. It is hoped that the guidelines for ministry presented in these lessons will be retained and put to good use in the lives of your students, for we are all the servants (ministers) of God and Christ.

Evangelistic Emphasis

Most people want to live better lives than they do. Most people intend to live better at some future date. Most people would be better satisfied with themselves and would have more self-esteem if they did live better lives.

If you believe that the above things are true, as I do, you will be doing a real favor to people when you provide them with motivation to live better. You will not be adding to their burdens but to their satisfactions. The gospel call to righteousness is a gift, not merely an expectation. It is a help to people to be what they want to be. It is an aid to the fulfillment of their own dreams.

Our text today has the warm assurance of God's grace and also an encouraging coaxing into a proper response to that grace. It is a positive motivation. It does not threaten. It calls. It does not generate fear. It rather generates gratitude.

If we are secure in His mercy, confident of our salvation, and thankful for His goodness, we will want to respond with loving commitment. It is only natural that we should do so.

When we do so, a host of blessings come into our lives. We have a peace that comes from the absence of guilt and fear. We have positive feelings of satisfaction as a result of doing what we know we should do. We have an inner happiness that comes from our relationship with G͏od and improve͏d relationships with our fellow men.

It is importan͏t to teach the call of Christ as well as the

Memory Selection

"In all things showing thyself a pattern of good works."
Titus 2:7.

There is no higher call to Christian behavior than this one. The inclusive statement, "in all things," makes it clear that every area of life is being considered. The Christian is not merely responsible for his behavior at church or in religious activities. He also has a Christian responsibility to have integrity and conscientiousness at his job, with his family, in his community, and in his leisure activities.

It is the Christian's task to demonstrate Christian behavior. We are not merely to point the way, explain how it ought to be done, or coach others to do right. We are to model Christian behavior for them. They should be able to watch our lives and learn from them how a Christian should behave. We are to be patterns for them to follow.

This modeling is to be in good works. We are not porcelain saints to be admired for our pious appearance. We are to be respected for what we do. Let others be able to observe what we do and know, without the interpretation of verbal commentary, how Christians should live.

Weekday Problems

Joseph knows more about the Bible than anyone else you know. In terms of being informative, there is no one that can be of more help to you. He has a magnificent grasp of the grace of God and with words can decimate anyone who would undermine it with a doctrine of works-righteousness.

Regrettably, his life does not measure up to the impressiveness of his knowledge. He is spoiled and selfish. He shows little consideration of others or patience with them. He is the master of sarcasm and is constantly saying biting things about others.

Joseph also is careless about fulfilling his responsibilities. His bills are paid late and sometimes not at all. He misses appointments without bothering to call. He does not do his share of work either at home or on the job. He seems to think he is smarter than others and that he should not be judged by their standards.

* Explain the relationship between the grace of God and good works.
* How can people be motivated to do good works if they are not saved by them?
* Do you believe that most people really want to live better lives?

Superintendent's Sermonette

Since God is perfect and complete, He must have a sense of humor and approve of His children enjoying humor, as well. However, there seems to be a trend in recent years to foster fun among believers in situations which ought to be devoted to sober and serious thoughts and actions. There is always the danger that local churches will try to gain and retain people, especially the young, by offering superfluous and unworthy programs. We need to remind ourselves periodically of the gravity of spiritual things and their importance.

Paul's letter to Titus emphasizes the need for church leaders to be grave, sincere, and sound in speech and to follow this up with good works which are valuable to all. Christians do not have to duplicate the world in order to get people's interest and hold it. The teachings of Christ have a power and attractiveness all their own. The deep joy and satisfaction which comes from learning them and living them before a pagan world is far superior to any manufactured fun. Let us strive to be more serious about our faith.

This Lesson in Your Life

There is an ancient story about a king who needed a driver for his chariot. It was a prestigious job and those who took the most pride in their driving skills clamored for the opportunity. The applicants were narrowed down to three finalists. As a test of their skills they were taken to a narrow mountain road with a deep chasm on one side. They were told to demonstrate their driving ability by driving on that road.

The first drove fast and perilously close to the edge to show that he was so much in control that he did not fear making a mistake. The second drove even faster and nearer the edge. He seemed to have so much ability and confidence that he could drive anywhere without making a mistake.

When it was time for the third driver to show his ability he drove a moderate speed and as far from the edge as he could get. The king selected the third driver because, he said, "Wisdom is as important as skill. I want a driver who will stay as far away from trouble as possible."

This is what Paul is saying to Titus. He warns that Titus should not skirt the edge of scandalous behavior. He is to avoid all marginal behavior and to live in such an exemplary way that his critics will be embarrassed.

To us, this lesson is saying, "Don't try to see how much you can get away with." "Don't get as close to sin as you can without committing it.." Rather, "Live in a way that is indisputably right."

"Always choose the high road." "Always make the safest and best choice, not the marginal one."

Paul admonishes that we should let our speech be such that no one would question it. Let it be so obviously good and pure that anyone who criticized it would look ridiculous. We should so live that any evil spoken of us would be incredible to those who heard it.

Paul further says that such living is the appropriate response to grace. We do not respond to the goodness and generosity of God with ingratitude and disobedience. We are so touched by his kindness to us that we want to do everything we can to please him.

The primary motivation for Christian living is being attracted by the love of God. It is not the fear of hell, but the goodness of God, that makes men want to be truly good. The threat of punishment can exercise some control over behavior. It cannot melt the heart and make people have a great desire to be inwardly good.

To right-thinking people the appeal of grace is irresistible. How could we be anything but loving toward one who has loved us so totally and vulnerably? We would not slap the face of one who laid down his life for us. We would exert every effort to do that which would please him and show our appreciation. So we should deny ungodliness and live righteously.

This loving relationship with God should spill over into the rest of our lives and make us considerate and conscientious in all other relationships as well. We should be good citizens of our nation, constructive participants in our society, and a positive influence on all with whom we come in contact.

We should never forget that in living good lives we are not attempting to earn our salvation by our works. We are merely responding to the mercy of God.

Seed Thoughts

1. How can we enhance Christian doctrine by our attitude?
We can treat it in an unadulterated, grave, sincere, solid way to show that we consider it to be most important.

2. How can we make people opposed to us feel ashamed?
We can practice what we preach and teach, depriving them of the validity of criticisms they make against us.

3. What did the grace of God teach us when it appeared?
Jesus, grace personified, taught us to deny ungodliness and worldly lusts and to live soberly, righteously, and godly in this present world.

4. Why did Jesus give Himself for us on the cross at Calvary?
He wanted to redeem us from sin, purify us unto himself, and make us zealous of good works.

5. What do we owe officials?
We should obey them whenever possible and be ready to do good works for them.

(Please Turn Page)

---

1. How can we enhance Christian doctrine by our attitude?

2. How can we make people opposed to us feel ashamed?

3. What did the grace of God teach us when it appeared?

4. Why did Jesus give Himself for us on the cross at Calvary?

5. What do we owe officials?

6. What traits should replace slander and brawling in Christians?

7. What was the divine antidote for foolishness, disobedience, deception, lusts, malice, envy, and hatred displayed by sinners?

8. What do non-Christian religions demand for "salvation"?

9. How does God save us?

10. Who are God's heirs?

We can treat it in an unadulterated, grave, sincere, solid way to show that we consider it to be most important.

We can practice what we preach and teach, depriving them of the validity of criticisms they make against us.

Jesus, grace personified, taught us to deny ungodliness and worldly lusts and to live soberly, righteously, and godly in this present world.

He wanted to redeem us from sin, purify us unto himself, and make us zealous of good works.

We should obey them whenever possible and be ready to do good works for them.

Christians should be known for their gentleness and meekness, two of the nine fruits of the Spirit (Gal. 5:22-23).

The kindness and love of God our Savior toward men appeared in Christ.

They demand works of self-righteousness as defined by them. They call for "salvation" by human efforts.

According to His mercy, He saves us by the washing of regeneration and renewal by the Holy Spirit.

Those who have been justified by grace through faith in Christ are heirs according to their hope of eternal life.

Seed Thoughts - Continued

6. What traits should replace slander and brawling in Christians?
Christians should be known for their gentleness and meekness, two of the nine fruits of the Spirit (Gal. 5:22-23).

7. What was the divine antidote for foolishness, disobedience, deception, lusts, malice, envy, and hatred displayed by sinners?
The kindness and love of God our Savior toward men appeared in Christ.

8. What do non-Christian religions demand for "salvation"?
They demand works of self-righteousness as defined by them. They call for "salvation" by human efforts.

9. How does God save us?
According to His mercy, He saves us by the washing of regeneration and renewal by the Holy Spirit.

10. Who are God's heirs?
Those who have been justified by grace through faith in Christ are heirs according to their hope of eternal life.

LESSON PLAN

(This outline may serve as a check list to help teachers avoid overlooking items that will strengthen their preparation for each lesson.)

1. GREETING AND WELCOME — Each class should begin in a warm and friendly spirit that will immediately reinforce the students.

2. PRAYER CONCERNS — Soliciting the concerns of each class member's heart and praying about those concerns helps to bond the class into a more personal group.

3. INTRODUCTION — Early in the class there should be a clear statement of the objective of the lesson and a focusing of attention on that lesson. Teacher's Target, Lesson Introduction, and Teaching Outline will help.

4. PRESENTATION AND INFORMATION- A Bible class should be generous in the presentation of factual knowledge. Verse by Verse and Memory Selection will be useful.

5. DISCUSSION AND OBSERVATIONS - In most cases it is helpful to allow class members to participate actively in the class. Weekday Problems and Seed Thoughts are designed to stimulate this.

6. APPLICATION AND MOTIVATION — Every lesson should have a clear application to daily life and incentive for improvement. This Lesson in Your Life and Evangelistic Emphasis have been planned to help this.

7. BENEDICTION — It has been demonstrated that people are hungry to be blessed. Close each class with some appropriate blessing on those in the group.

IDEAS AND INSIGHTS
(Use these pages to make brief notes on things you want to remember for future use.)

IDEAS AND INSIGHTS

FAVORITE SCRIPTURES

(Make a note of Scripture passages which have special meaning and which you will want to reread periodically.)

SUPPLEMENTARY MATERIALS
(Note books, tapes, periodicals, or other references which you have found helpful or others have referred to and you wish to check.)

PRAYER CONCERNS
(Often prayer concerns mentioned in class need to be remembered, checked on, and prayed for over a period or time. Note them here.)